The Rise of

Mystery Babylon

Vol. 2: The Tower of Babel (Part 1)

Brett Lee Thomas

Parallel World Books

The Rise of Mystery Babylon
Vol. 2: The Tower of Babel (Part 1)

Copyright © 2015 by Brett Thomas

All rights reserved. This book or any portion thereof may not be reproduced or used in any manner whatsoever without the express written permission of the publisher except for the use of brief quotations in a book review.

ISBN-13: 978-0-9995257-1-5
Parallel World Books

Email:
 brettleethomas@protonmail.com

www.mysterybabylon.com

*You can't really understand what is going on now
without understanding what came before.*

- Steve Jobs

Table of Contents

Chapter 1
Babylonian Gods of Genesis
1

Chapter 2
The Real Adam and Eve (Part 1)
69

Chapter 3
The Real Adam and Eve (Part 2)
125

Chapter 4
Cain, Seed of the Serpent (Part 1)
164

Chapter 5
Cain, Seed of the Serpent (Part 2)
217

Chapter 6
Angels, the Flood, and Saturn (Part 1)
253

Chapter 7
Angels, the Flood, and Saturn (Part 2)
321

Chapter 8
Old Religion of Cush and Nimrod
362

Chapter 9
New Religion of the Madonna
399

Preface

Mysteries… on Both Sides

<u>1 Cor. 2</u>:
7 *But we speak the wisdom of God in a <u>mystery</u>, even the hidden wisdom, which God ordained before the world unto our glory…*

<u>Mat. 13</u>:
9 *Who hath ears to hear, let him hear.*
10 *And the disciples came, and said unto him (i.e. Jesus), Why speakest thou unto them in parables?*
11 *He answered and said unto them, Because it is given unto you to know the <u>mysteries</u> of the kingdom of heaven, but **to them** (i.e. the everyday, average populous) it **is not given**.*

In Volume 1, we delved into some of the societal and cultural elements of *Mystery Babylon*, which may, very well, be one element of the (above) *mysteries* of God's kingdom - for us to discover. God, indeed, may want us to research the enemy, to know where they come from, how they work, and what they're *really* all about. Many of those who represent this "other side" probably does not want us to learn about what's in these volumes, nor care about it. Yet, as we also see (below), there will be some individuals who will possess a "craving," or desire, to completely understand what we're bringing to you, here, in these volumes. Some really don't "get it," nor feel they want to… and, that's okay. It's not for everyone. To those who seem "called" for further research, however, let's continue on, and look at the rest of these verses in Matthew:

<u>Mat. 13</u>:
12 **For whosoever hath**, to him **shall be given**, *and he shall have more abundance: but whosoever hath not, from him shall be taken away even that he hath.*
13 *Therefore speak I to them in parables: because they seeing see not; and hearing they hear not, neither do they understand.*
14 *And in them is fulfilled the prophecy of Esaias, which saith, By hearing ye shall hear, and shall not understand; and seeing ye shall see, and shall not perceive:*
15 *For this people's heart is waxed gross, and* their *ears are dull of hearing, and their eyes they have closed; lest at any time they should see with* their *eyes, and hear with their ears, and should understand with their heart, and should be*

> *converted, and I should heal them.*
> 16 *But* **blessed** *are your eyes, for they see: and your* **ears***, for they hear.*
> 17 *For verily I say unto you, That* **many prophets and righteous men have desired to see those things which ye see, and have not seen them; and to hear those things which ye hear, and have not heard them***.*

There are a lot of misunderstood things being tossed at us - from well-meaning as well as nefarious individuals - creating a lot of *mystery*, right in front of our very eyes. But, we do have some ways to correctly make sense of it all. We do have some ways to see through the smoke and mirrors. With these volumes, we do have a way to come out of it all, with even *more* answers. We just have to be a little careful along the way, and take the time to contemplate all of what may be in front of us (without rushing to any conclusions or enabling harsh judgments to take hold). The reason is: the more we contemplate what's in these volumes, the more we discover how corrupted information could reach us from *both* sides - from those on the nefarious side *as well as* those on so-called "righteous" (or religious) side… believe it or not.

> *For such as false apostles, deceitful workers, transforming themselves into (or posing as) the apostles of Christ. And no marvel; for Satan himself is transformed into an angel of* <u>light</u>*. Therefore it is no great thing if his ministers* **also be transformed as the ministers of righteousness***…*   - *II Cor.* 11:13-15 (KJV)

Even though we may think these people have nothing but your best interests in mind, they, more often than not, have *their* best interests in mind. So, in the end, they often may feel the need to tell you what best suits *them*, and their circumstances, in the end - making it all sound as though they're helping you out. All of this, of course, may sound a little *shameful*, but, so often, it's the deeper *truth*! Each one of us have an ego - it'd be surprising to see how some of us actually feed it.

So, without further ado, let's begin to dig even deeper into those negative forces bent on opposing us, and our progression in life… a deeper look into all of what makes up the elements of *Mystery Babylon*. We recall, from Volume 1, how the Biblical *Cain* (and his ways) represented the cornerstone - the beginnings of *Mystery Babylon*, itself.

*Cain, then, the first murderer of Abel the righteous represents a type **of the devil**, revealing himself at the beginning of the world's creation as both the inventor of evil and one lacking in remorse.*   - The Chronography of George Synkellos p. 12[1]

Next, to delve even *deeper* into *w*hy this was so, and where it all went, we, once again, pick up our story at the same point as the last volume… "in the beginning."

Chapter 1

Babylonian Gods of Genesis

When we think of the term "Babylon" or "Babylonian," we, next, may need to ask ourselves: just what do these words mean? Also, what is a "pagan?" Often, in the last volume, these two words were, for the most part, practically synonymous. Whomever founded the concept of *Babylonian* belief was the same one who founded ancient pagan thought, and ideology.

A *pagan*, for simplicity sake, could be considered a follower of theologies, or faiths, directly contrary to the God of the Bible. Simple. And, the end result of following these other religious ideals may, so often, take one in the exact, *opposite* moral direction of how the Bible might take them (as we'll soon see).

Many of us know the Bible, the stories contained therein, and the traditions surrounding it. The next set of questions that may arise are: what about ancient pagan legend and mythology? What about the stories in ancient pagan writings? What is the difference between the accounts of ancient people in Babylon, for example, and those who followed the God of the Bible? Could there have been similarities, or were they the complete opposite? What to believe?

Or, what about a third option? Could there have been a good number of account similarities between the people of these two beliefs; but, due to the passage of time, or through *intentional* manipulation (most probably), certain accounts were manipulated into something sounding entirely different (or even the *opposite*)?[1] As we read on, we'll soon understand that there were a number of *pagan* individuals occupying the same lands as Adam and Eve, and they would have had their own motives and desires to change history around them - into something which suited their *own* beliefs a little better!

After the Fall, pagans and God-following individuals both, most probably, lived in an area known as *The Land Between the Two Rivers*. This land could also have been called Mesopotamia, Sumer or Babylonia. For simplicity sake, we'll identify this area by the name *Babylonia* - after the infamous city these volumes were named after. Let's look more at this *Land Between the Two Rivers*: it was considered an area between the Tigris and Euphrates Rivers, in modern-day Iraq. This area, as many modern-day scientists even believe, was the cradle of our civilization. A number of people who believe the Bible also consider this land as the area that once housed the ancient Garden of Eden. No better place for us to start our look into these ancient pagan (and Biblical) accounts.

The early patriarchs and matriarchs of Genesis (whether be good or evil) originate in this area, as well. The major ones, of course, were Adam, Eve, Cain, Abel - and the Serpent. And, as we'll also see, these individuals had to have stayed somewhere; so they, quite often, were associated with some ancient land, or even a city. So, let's, also, take a look at some ancient cities in this area, as well as these individuals. All of it will begin to give us a "feel" for those who wrote some of the earliest pagan accounts of this time. With this, we, as well, could begin to discover *their* motivations behind what they recorded, and *why* they voiced things the way they did.

As we've theorized, in Volume 1, there were a number of different groups of people in the Garden, beyond just Adam and Eve. These, for simplicity sake, were known as the *pre-Adamites*. These groups may have even been given their own positions within the Garden, helping to keep it all going. As well, there were, most probably, terrestrial, angelic beings assigned to "manage" the workings, here - also known as the *Nephilim*. There was also one man - Adam - at the helm, declared (by God) the "viceroy" of authority over this Garden. After Adam's fall, however, his position of dominance over the entire working of the Garden was over. There were, now, a number of people and terrestrial angels going in so many different directions.

Ultimately, each person began to follow their own, unstructured way, and lead their own, independent life. Although many may have went their own direction, or even began to gather in groups (and settle in different areas), it was obvious that most of them still retained a great deal of knowledge, and memories, of their former life in the Garden.[2]

The people in one particular area of Babylonia, known as the land of *Sumeria*, were, reportedly, among the first who began to "make waves," here.[3] They were located in Babylonia's southern region.[4] Next, the *Semites* began to make a name for themselves. Could these *Semites* also be the ancient Adamites - renamed the *Semites*, after *Seth* (a son of Adam)?[5] Or, could people have begun to generalize most of the Adamites around as Semites, because they were the most popular group of Adamites out there? Many scholars believe that the term *Semite* actually describes a group of individuals living after Noah's Flood (named for Noah's son *Shem*); but it *is* also possible that there were Semites before the flood, as well (named after this particular patriarch, Seth).[6] As we note: the names are somewhat similar.

Yet, beyond these Sumerians and Semites, there was, reportedly, a third group of individuals out there, who also began to populate these area - known as the *Akkadians*.[7] Now, who might these people be? Interestingly enough, a city associated with this land - *Akkad* - probably received its name from a very famous character of early Genesis (as we'll soon see).

For now, we could understand that these Semites and Akkadians - the latecomers - began to mix with these earlier Sumerians, and also shared some commonalities with them.[8] It isn't very difficult to assume that these new groups were, most probably, the same pre-Adamite human groups, or even *new* groups of individuals, deciding to mix together after the Fall, into new lands. And, it isn't very difficult to assume that the memories, and ideological *core*, of all these people could have come from one, specific place - the Garden of Eden.

As we see (below), the Garden of Eden may, a number of times, "come into play" in their early, pagan mythological lore:

> *One of the most amazing finds uncovered in **Akkad** was that of a seal which possibly shows that the Akkadians knew of the story of the temptation of Adam and Eve in the Garden of Eden. George Smith of the British Museum, who lived during the middle 1800's, wrote: 'One striking and important specimen of early type in the British Museum has two figures sitting one on each side of a **tree**, holding out their hands to the **fruit**, while at the back of one (the woman) is stretched a **serpent**.'*
> ("Adam, the Flood & The Tower of Babel", n. d., p. 1)[9]

Could all of these *new* groups of post-Flood individuals *really* have, at one time, been considered displaced groups from the Garden?[10] Could they have *really* been the Adamites and pre-Adamites of Adam's day? And, is it also possible that, while some people decided to maintain the purity of their former group, others may have decided to cross over, or mix with each other genetically - forming entirely *new* groups of individuals, or city/states, as we've seen, above?

Could some of the more famous *cities* of old we've heard about - such as *Eridu*, *Ur*, *Enoch* and, of course, *Babylon* - be the result of these individuals, and their engineering prowess?[11] We'll soon see that, most probably, all of them were built by these individuals, and a number were ruled by at least *one* important figure of early Genesis.[12]

Beyond the city of Babylon, the city of *Eridu* is worth noting, first off. *Eridu* could have actually been associated with the same area as Eden, itself![13]

> *Eridu, the oldest city in Southern Mesopotamia… is the most likely place to have been Eden, the original home for Adam and his kin.*
> ("In Search of the Historical Adam: Part 2", n. d., p. 1)[14]

We figure: as the ancients branched out, forming new nations and empires, they probably would have maintained their early traditions and ways of life. And, since a majority of ancient people (from all groups) began to slowly adopt the ways of Cain (and the Serpent), the succeeding nation-states and empires became pagan. A number of them were, of course, different (in a number of ways), but, most seemed to be *united* in one cause - they all seemed against the God of the Bible, and the ways that He taught Adam. Sound familiar, a lot like today? So, in order to help us prove this point, here, let's, at least, assume that most of the ancient pagan legends, and mythologies, coming from the many succeeding nations and empires since Babylonia, would have also ended up (for the most part) in a similar, theological boat:

> *…Egypt, Chaldea, India, Greece and Rome passed torch of civilization from one to another… (they) drew from a fountain higher than themselves.*
> (Houston, 1926, p. 80)[15]

It only makes sense. Naturally, tradition dies hard. Old habits die hard. A new empire would, of course, take away whatever they felt necessary from the old - and this included religion. That's why we see so many of these ancient myths are the *same* - throughout the ages! One source - so many twists! Same stories - just different names and places!

But, how, and why, was this all important to *Mystery Babylon*, and the progression of this up-and-coming force? Well, if we look at ancient mythology, the information in so many of these stories may just allow us to gather even *more and more* information about our mysterious history. *Mystery Babylon* is a true mystery - with layers upon layers of information underneath it - all that needs to be either picked up, peeled off, or dug down into... a little bit at a time. It's a lot like trying to peel apart an artichoke - the more we peel off the outer layers, the more we can get into discovering the true, *dark* origins! What is important to realize at this moment is that *most* (pagan) mythological accounts - from these ancient empires - probably came from the same source. And, that source comprised these same few individuals of the Genesis account. And, on top of it, most of the pagan world - past and present - will probably lead any potential follower down the same *opposite* pathway (ideologically)... assuredly, away from the God of the Bible. Let's see how.

There is no human being alive, today, who was alive back then, in these ancient times. So, if we really think about it, *nobody* knows what happened for sure - and this includes religious theologians, historians, and *even* science. Yes, no scientist, no matter who they are or were, could tell us exactly what happened. They are only relying on scientific formulas and models. They also cannot insert anything of a spiritual nature because it cannot be replicated in a lab - but, the supernatural, as we know, is a very, very relevant part of our existence! So, because of this, most of what we see and hear, today, seems to be united *against* the validity of the Holy Scriptures. Either way we look at it, with the pagan ways of old, or the secular and science-based ways of the new, *both* seem to be united in this one venture. And, that really makes it hard for anything of the Bible to stand on its own, or at least be considered viable. Could this all be by design, however? Is this how *Mystery Babylon* could have worked its magic, in so many ways, over all of these years? And, what *do* we - as believers in God - *still* have to work with, in spite of all this opposition? How can any other way survive - besides theirs? That's exactly the way they want it. Also, how does one get an idea of *what truly* may have occurred in these ancient times - without automatically taking on the skewed biases of paganism, secularism or science? It's indeed hard. All we have are preserved ancient texts and oral traditions, here - pagan or otherwise. So, in the next step, our job, now, would be to weed through the vast mire of information out there, take what is relevant, and come up with *one* possible view of our ancient history - whether we need to utilize some story elements from ancient pagan lore, or from something Biblical. Discernment will help us.

Pagan historical accounts aren't always wrong, or evil. It's just that their moral focus, obviously, isn't in the same direction as the Bible. So, we must account for that. But, a good deal of historical information could actually be gathered, here - we just have to take into account that, since "there is moral to every story," the morality that may come from *their side* may direct us away from God. Simple.

For example: "…Judeo-Christian tradition says that God is the measure of all things; the (ancient) Greek religious system stated that **man** is the measure of all things."[16] Here, we see two traditions. In God's way, *He* is the measure of all things. According to the ancient (pagan) Greeks, *man* is the on top of the heap - opposing directions, here. Man is not God, obviously. He's quite the contrary. Man is just a created being, and, as far from the sanctity of God as the underworld is from the highest point of heaven. These "opposite" extremes are, so often, the results of pagan manipulation, or those "twists" in the original Genesis account.

And, of course, all of those who took on these opposing pagan ideologies ultimately may have felt the need to *eliminate* any competition - in any way possible. This involved either changing history, or outright trying to destroy anything coming out of the Bible (as we'll see).

A Confusing Mythology of Old?

If we look at most ancient pagan mythologies, today, we find that a vast majority of them seem to form into a conglomerate of unrelated, insensible accounts. Often, they don't really make sense. They seem to represent scattered piece-works of gods and goddesses, often strewn together in almost any old way. Most modern mythology books seem to be a collection of discombobulated information, at best: god "A" mates with goddess "B"; god "C" kills goddess "D"; god "E" eats his own children, etc. Why is it this way? The Bible, at least, flows in somewhat of a chronological order. Not so, with these pagan accounts. The reason, most probably, is: when you try to twist things around, or take something away from its original source, things, often, do not turn out well. Pagan authors have attempted this manipulation, all along.

Yet, we do want answers, and a look at history, regardless of what twists one side may have entrenched themselves into. And, for the sake of this volume, we will try to put as much of it all together - both pagan elements and Biblical - to end up with *one* history, here. We'll try to explain it all in such a way so that the reader can actually make sense of it, and also show how *both* histories, here, may actually relate to the *one* history we see in the Bible! Even if the two sides (pagan and Biblical) might begin take the reader in some opposing moral or religious direction, that doesn't mean that any historical elements couldn't be used, or weren't from the same source! Let's now begin to put it all together.

> *...the knowledge imparted to man in the beginning has come down in two streams, on one hand through the Hebrews, and on the other through the Babylonians.*
> (Bristowe, 1927, p. 20)[17]

Those who insist on saying "all religions are the same" are probably correct... almost. Most belief systems probably have some pagan source, or contain pagan elements. So, in that case, most all religions are the same - at least in that respect. A very small minority, however, are true, unabashed elements from God, and from the Bible. But, these are just a few. There still may be others who say: "*all* of the faiths of the world point towards God. It's just a God of many different forms or facets." Again, they are probably correct... almost. It seems that most religious theologies do point towards *one* god, but, as we'll see, it's **not** the God of the Bible. There is a "god," with many different faces out there - but, it's pagan, and it's directly related to Cain, and his ways. When we look at what the Bible *truly* has to say, however, and compare it to what the rest of the world has to say, we'll soon see how the Bible is, in reality, in a class by itself!

If the Bible is "one of a kind," and the true way to go, then *why* did paganism spread so far and wide - one might ask? And, just *who* was responsible for this development, over time? Well, now, the cat's "out of the bag." We already know, from the previous volume, that Cain (*the* Cain of Genesis) was, most probably, responsible for building a number of these ancient Babylonian cities, and ruling over them. Cain, as well, worked - very hard - to spread the ancient beliefs of *paganism* to all of those around him. There were two ways, or cultures, that began to take hold after the Fall: one stemmed from the people who followed the ways of God (via Adam), and the other stemmed from those who followed the ways of Cain:[18]

> *Two of the most recent writers upon the Babylonian inscriptions unintentionally support Professor Kittel's opinion that the Genesis stories came down in* ***'two streams,'*** *and also my theory that one stream came down through the descendants of* ***Seth*** *(via Adam) and the other through* ***Cain in Babylonia*** *(via the Serpent).*
> (Bristowe, 1927, p. 14)[19]

If so many were beginning to adopt these pagan ways of Cain, again, it leads one to wonder: *why* were so many individuals beginning to turn away from God, back then? Was Adam that difficult of a leader to work under? Or, was it because the ways of Cain were more *seductive*, and, eventually, more appealing for those of this fallen world? Again, we already know (from the previous volume) that Cain was the "son of perdition," and we already know who Cain's real father probably was: *the Serpent* of the Garden.

This Serpent, of course, was against Adam, God, and anything in the Bible from the beginning. And, God also said that there would be **enmity** between the seeds of Adam and seeds of the Serpent. Cain was not only the Serpent's son, but eventually became his unholy partner (in this pagan crime)! A vast majority of people, in the antediluvian world, adopted the ways of Cain - it just took a little convincing. There was a lot of worldly knowledge, and power over others, to be gained by siding with these worldly individuals.

Along the same lines as those who decided to follow the Bible, it's pretty obvious that those who wrote with a *pagan* slant probably wanted to say things with their *own* interests in mind. Early Greek poets and artists, for example, probably told the same stories as we might find in early Genesis, but from an opposite viewpoint![20] If we look at the story of the Garden of Eden, a typical Greek account might conclude that the Serpent did not really seduce Adam and Eve, and help to sentence them into an unenlightened state, but, just the opposite - he enlightened them!

(An early group of Gnostics would)… attribute all wisdom to the serpent of Paradise, and say that he was the author of knowledge of men.
(Gardiner, 2006, p. 10)[21]

This "wisdom of the Serpent," according to ancient Greeks, actually was beneficial to mankind!

And, before this, Cain was even said to have set up priests of his own, in the Babylonian city of *Ur*, to help administer his new religion *correctly*. Of course, this allowed the priests the opportunity to change what was true history, and to further manipulate any *slant* they were already inserting into everything.

The establishment of what was going to be "politically correct" in those days was, so often, confined to these early scribes and priests - almost entirely.[22] They controlled the narrative. They were, as well, able to *muddle* whatever they felt necessary, in their legends and historical accounts.[23] Hence, this "two sided" view of the world was solidified - and *still* continues, today.

And, by the time the priests got through with the real stories of the Bible, they turned into all into a "garbled, yet still somewhat recognizable form of early Genesis."[24] Even though these stories were, obviously, changed around, and even though they may try to bring the reader towards some *opposing* moral conclusion, they still might be of value to us. They still might be able to provide us a good deal of substance towards understanding *Mystery Babylon*. Why?

Though, on one hand, Greek idol-worship contradicts the teaching of the Word of God, on the other, if properly understood, **it reinforces the truth of the Scriptures**.
(Johnson, 2004, p. 9)[25]

As we progress, we'll actually notice a good number of *similarities* between these ancient pagan mythological stories and the Bible, if we look deeper (believe it or not).

And, once we understand the (most probable) identity of pagan ancestral gods and goddesses (as well as their motivations). it will help us to learn a great deal more about the early characters of Genesis than we've ever known.[26] It will be amazing to see how pagan or Babylonian accounts actually might reinforce and strengthen the Bible, and solidify Biblical traditions, in so many ways.

> *What the Greeks meant to be an unparalleled, intricately chiseled monument to the **glory of mankind** turns out to be a detailed history of mankin'd delusion, and a clear-cut validation of the truth of the Word of God.*
> (Johnson, 2004, p. 258)[27]

Moving forward, we've already understood, from earlier chapters of the last volume, a few of the more "Biblical" concepts, such as the *Gap Theory*, the *Darkness* and the *Deep*. Believe it or not, if we look deeper into some pagan mythological accounts, we'll discover much of the same - probably more than we may have ever dreamed of. Let's take a look at the pagan "take" on some of these concepts, and what it all may mean.[28]

> <u>The Chaldean Account of the Deluge</u>
> 116 ... '*I have begotten man and let him not*
> 117 *like the sons of the fishes fill the **sea**.* '[29]

In the earliest chapter of Volume 1, we've understood how *water* could have had a great deal of significance throughout our ancient world. Water is necessary for life. Our bodies (and brains) are made up, mostly, of water. Some of these significances even seem to pass into the supernatural (or spiritual) realm! It seems that the ancients, whatever their religious leaning, had full knowledge of the **supernatural** significance of water (in many ways), and inserted them into their own legends and histories.

> *The idea is that 'where a god dies, that is, ceases to exist in human form, his life passes into the **waters** where he is buried; and this again is merely a theory to bring the divine water or the divine fish into harmony with anthropomorphic ideas. The same thing was sometimes effected in another way by saying **that the anthropomorphic deity was born from the water**, as Aphrodite sprang from sea*

foam...' (Mackenzie, 1915, p. 28)[30]

Along this same line, we recall (from the second chapter of Volume 1) that there also could be a spiritual "sea," of sorts - an infinite, supernatural "sea" of infinite space within our own world. And, quite often, when the ancients mentioned a "sea," or something related to "water," the chances were good that they could have been referring to something in the supernatural, or spiritual, world.

Next, we also have ancient parallels, regarding the use of the word *chaos*. First, the ancient (pagan) historian Hesiod said that the early world was in "…Chaos, an unformed and confused bulk."[31] And, we know that the world before Adam, in the Bible, was also considered a watery *chaos* - a time of utter destruction and ruin. It's interesting to know that: "just as in the Creation story of the Bible, the Babylonian 'creator' also caused dry land to appear, and brought the world back from a watery chaos."[32] Ancient Greek and Roman mythology also said that the universe sprang from *Chaos*.[33] Not only do we have similar interpretations of the beginning of our world, here, by both sides (with the world once originating in *chaos*), we also have another meaning for the word: it corresponded to a couple of *characters* in early Genesis (as we'll soon see)! These character were, not only famous characters of the Bible, but *major* propagators of the pagan religion! A lot of these ancient views of history are intertwined, in a whole number of ways (even though both sides may not really know about it, nor be willing to admit it).

The Underworld

Beyond the "supernatural" water, all around the earth, one may also need to go deeper, and look *inside* our earth - deep down, beneath the earth's surface. Was there only rock down there, or could the *supernatural* also have some kind of purpose down there, as well? Interestingly enough, the word *abyss* actually comes from words that could mean "bottomless," or even "chaos."[34] And, most of us have heard of the *underworld*. The pagan *Hades* and Jewish *Sheol* seem to represent a similar concept, as well - one (pagan) Greek, and the other Hebrew.[35]

> *It is especially important to note the close connection of the underworld with the sea, a perfectly understandable conjunction, for the dark, unseen recesses of the ocean bottom are likely apertures to Hades, if not the place itself.*
> (Bandy, 1967, p. 47)[36]

> *(Sheol was...) essentially a place where men were treated according to their deserts, with a division for the righteous, and a division for the wicked.*
> (Bandy, 1967, p. 44)[37]

The two, essentially, are about the same - a "common grave of mankind."[38] Of course, both of them were said to be located in the center, or bottom, of the earth.[39] Going back to our previous discussion on the *Gap Theory*, we recall that God may have destroyed the previous world. He, then, placed the souls of this devastated world into a "holding area" or "common grave" of souls, known as this *abyss* - only to bring them back up, one at a time, as newborn babies (in our present world).

> *...when God imparts the living soul to man, he commits a **pre-existent** spirit to an existence in the flesh.* (Anonymous, 1834, p. 73)[40]

As we've already explained, this is not reincarnation, but a different way to look at our human existence. Pagan theology might also holds to the existence of a "holding cell," a prison, or an underworld for lost souls, as well! Some ancient sources have even referred to this area by the same *name* used in Biblical tradition! One author describes it as such:

deep beneath the earth, in the deepest depths of this supernatural "sea," beyond the Abyss, beneath Sheol, is located this area of *Darkness* (which is also called "the bottomless *Deep*").[41] And, in ancient Babylonian myths and texts, we also have:

<u>Bilingual of Creation</u>
8 *The **Deep** had not been made…*
10 *All lands were sea.*[42]

*(The historian) Hesiod's account of creation… begins with Chaos itself, out of which emerged… **Darkness**.*   (Johnson, 2004, p. 202)[43]

There were even pagan gods and goddesses associated with this *Deep*. The pagan goddess *Ishtar*, for example, was considered the "Lady of the Deep."[44] Why?

*Darkness has been used symbolically of degradation and evil, but that there is an actual place of darkness **where evil spirits are compelled to reside**…*
         (Rand, 1948, p. 396)[45]

It's, now, fairly easy to begin to assume that this pagan *Darkness* or *Deep* was extremely similar to - if not the same as - the spiritual/supernatural realm of the Bible, and Biblical tradition.

In Babylonian stories, there was sad mixture of animal forms as well as of land and atmosphere, until some sort of divine wisdom incarnated in a certain god(s) brought order to it all.   (Houston, 1926, 195)[46]

While we're on this subject, we now need to let the "cat out of the bag," and discover who pagan lore attributed their "divine wisdom incarnated into a certain god" was. In reality, one of these Biblical characters of "chaos" was, most probably, the *Cain* of Genesis. He was given credit for bringing our present order out of Chaos - the chaos which, once, was the old world (of the Garden of Eden)! As we now see: the pagans were actually conned into believing, in their heart, that *God*, and the way He refashioned our world, ***was*** the chaos that needed to be "fixed!" He created it incorrectly, and created all wrong. So, *Cain*, then, was the man that, of course, had to do something about it!

So, now, we discover that Cain was also the one given credit for having authority over this *Darkness* of the *Deep* (in pagan lore):

<u>The Story of Creation</u>
142 ***He*** *set himself over against the Deep…*
143 *And the lord measured the construction of the Deep…*[47]

Cain was also accredited for having control over life and death, and over most all the natural and supernatural elements above the earth, and deep down below the earth. Again, all of this was nothing but a twisted version of the awesome powers that *God* had over all the universe. Yet, it was Cain, as well, who was given credit for having such wisdom that *he* was able put the entire pagan religion together, and being able to establish *who* the gods and goddesses of this new religion would be!

Now, why would pagan ideology give so much credit to one man? Why would the ancient Greeks, so often, exert that *man* was the measure of all things, and not God? Why would these ancient Greeks, as well as other ancient writers, often picture their gods and goddesses as human in appearance?[48] This question is probably skewed towards the obvious: they once *were*! Maybe these ancient gods and goddesses represented famous Greek ancestors, for example - they were their most famous ancestors of old! Of course, Cain would fit this role to a tee: he was a child of Eve and the Serpent, all the way back to the Garden of Eden. You can't go much farther back in ancestry than that!

Interestingly enough, this same practice of ancestor worship was popular in most succeeding empires, way beyond the times of Babylonia. Seems that a lot of what God wanted for Adam, Eve, and the people of the antediluvian era was "hijacked" by Cain and his posse, and "twisted" all around:

> *…those laws were founded upon the original rules of conduct given to Adam… were taken by Cain into Babylonia and there **remodeled to suit his purposes**…*
> (Bristowe, 1927, p. 126)[49]

Ancestor Worship

Interestingly enough, *ancestor worship* was, and still is, a staple of ancient pagan religion. It also functions as a foundation of their "god" and "goddess" worship. So many of these early pagans believed that their own gods started out as human, and also, so often, were their ancestors. The next, natural question one might ask is: could the famous pagan ancestors that were, indeed, turned into "gods" be the same as the famous ancestors (or patriarchs) of early Genesis (i.e. Adam, Eve, Abel, Cain, etc.)? Yes, we will see that, over time, the worship of these original Genesis characters, most probably, *did* morph its way into a sophisticated form of pagan ancestor worship. So, thanks to Cain, these individuals were turned into the first, polytheistic "gods" of old.[50]

And, for the sake of understanding, let's try to proceed with the possibilities that the following pagan gods and goddess we will detail *could really be* the same matriarchs and patriarchs of Genesis. By looking at the details of these pagan gods (while maintaining such a mindset), we should easily start to piece together some solid similarities! At least, we'll probably see that there has to be *something* to it all.

The more we look into these following "gods," the more things will come to light. Once we start to see how these pagan gods could, very well, be *Biblical* characters, we'll get a grasp at how the real story of our ancient history probably went. And, as well, we'll see how Cain was given the credit for elevating those close to him into "gods," in their own right. This included Adam, his mother Eve, and none other than his probable father - the Serpent of the Garden of Eden! Let's continue our expose' into some of the most popular gods of ancient Babylonia, and compare them to these early Biblical personalities. The results will speak for themselves, it seems!

We need to start at the *very* beginning, because:

> ***The first couple** advances to the forefront of **gods**...*
> (Johnson, 2004, p. 11)[51]

Yes, we already know *who* the "first couple" was, according to the Bible. So, let's take a detailed look at the more popular, and probable, ancient *pagan* equivalents for the first Biblical character of Genesis: **Adam**.

The Avatars of Adam

<u>Babylonian gods:</u>
- *(the Akkadian) El*
- *(the Akkadian) An*
- *(the Sumerian) Anu*
- *(the Sumerian) Abu*[52]

Some common characteristics of these gods:
- *The names An or Anu mean "heaven" or "the heavenly one."*[53]
- *Anu was known to have had a pleasant countenance.*[54]
- *"One meaning of Abu is, 'Lord of the Plants.'"*[55]
- *El, Anu, and Abu were all known as the "father" god, or king.*[56]

*(At least some aspect of Adam, as we recall, **did** come from heaven, or the sky. We remember that Adam's soul was directly breathed into him, by God Himself (in Gen. 2:7, I Cor. 15:45)! In this respect, Adam **was** the first who had something as important as their divine soul come from the heavens, or the sky. Adam also had a shining and beautiful countenance (at least, before his fall). He was also known as the "Lord of Plants," because of his position in the Garden. Adam, also, was thought to be the father, leader or "king" over all the people and terrestrial angels (i.e. Nephilim) around him: those who worked in, or around, the Garden.)*

Babylonian gods:
- *(the Sumerian) Utu*
- *(the Sumerian) Ugmash*
- *(the Akkadian) Shamash*

Some common characteristics of these gods:
- *The names Utu or Ugmash actually were equated with the sun, or sun's wisdom.*[57]
- *From Ugmash comes the god Shamash: the sun god.*[58]
- *The god Utu was also known as the revealer of light, truth,*

and justice.[59]

*(The **sun**, or sun's wisdom, can easily be a symbol of Adam, and his role before the Fall. In Luke 3:38, for example, Adam was called the "son of God" - not in a literal sense, of course (because Jesus only would have had that distinction), but in more of a symbolic sense (in regards to his original position as viceroy over the Garden). He was also a "son of God" because he was the one who had his soul directly breathed into him by God, his Heavenly Father! This could make him a "son" of God, in a certain way. We've previously known that the words "son" and "sun" are close in meaning; often as interchangeable. Hence, from this, we also can conclude that Adam may have been "adopted"(at least early on) by pagan idealists - as a "son of the heavens," a "son of God" or a "sun god."*

*As we see, the **sun**, in our natural world, gives off light, it promotes life. Adam, also, provided "light" to those around him - he gave them **spiritual** insight, inspiration or truth. He was considered very wise and well respected (at least in the beginning), and a **judge** over others. And, he was also considered a "father" of many, either literally or in spirit. Just as Jesus was thought to be the "Light of the World" (John 8:12, 9:5), Adam was also given this same honors, early on. And, this all became corrupted, and adopted into Cain's pagan religion. Adam, in Christian and Muslim tradition, was appointed, by God, to be His viceroy on earth - a great honor. Jesus, the true son of God, was, as well, considered to be the "last Adam" (I Cor. 15:45).)*

<u>Babylonian god:</u>
- *(the Babylonian) Adapa*

Some common characteristics of this god:
- Adapa was considered a sage, prophet, or priest in the areas of Eridu (i.e. Eden).[60]
- He was also known as "wisest of men."[61]
- Adapa, the "Man of Eridu," was thought of as "blameless," "clean of hands," and the "anointer and observer of laws."[62]
- On the other hand, Adapa brought an "ill" upon all mankind, and "disease" upon the bodies of men.[63]
- He was also known for making bread.[64]

*(Adam, since his formation, was considered a prophet, and priest, of God. He was extremely knowledgeable and wise (as we recall from the last volume, he was instrumental in naming all the animals around him, thus defeating even the terrestrial angels who challenged him). It's obvious that he also, probably, considered "king" of Eden (by many). Adam was, sometimes, considered blameless, or of clean hands (at least, regarding the sin of **fornication** in the Garden - by which Eve and the Serpent (as we've seen) were both considered guilty of). He was also anointed as the observer of God's **statutes**. Yet, on the other hand, he did help to usher in an "illness," "disease" or "sickness" upon all of mankind: the curse of the Fall. Adam could have even been considered a baker of bread (in the areas of Eden), because the Bible once stated that God proclaimed to Adam: "In the sweat of thy face shalt thou eat **bread**... (Gen. 3:19)!"[65])*

Some more interesting quotes, regarding this "paganized" version of Adam:
- Adam of the Bible and Adapa of Amorite legend were both human sons of God, or a god.[66]
- The title, "the Son of God," reserved for Sumerian royalty, is also used for (an ancient

> *god named) "Adamu."*[67]
> - *"Could (the pagan "gods") Alorus, Adapa, Alulim, Adamu, Atum, and Adam be all the same person? Perhaps a better question would be, what rationale could be employed to explain away the commonalities? At least some of these secular references must pertain to the first man in biblical history."*[68]

Many of these ancient pagan deities - all corresponding to a "father" god, in one way or another - all seem to be quite similar. Why couldn't they all possibly relate to one specific individual? Adam was, most probably, around during these early times. He was famous. If we notice: in one way or another, they all seem to be quite close to Adam, and his functioning role over the Garden, as well. Adam could have easily been a good candidate for an escalation into pagan "divinity," through this.

The Shepherd

According to the ancient Babylonian historian *Berossus*, another god who may have been related to Adam - *Alorus* - was "appointed by God as the Shepherd of men."[69] This *shepherd* label does sound quite familiar, at least in the Bible. Jesus was known as "the good Shepherd" (John 10:11, 10:14). Adam, as well, could easily have been considered the "shepherd" of early men.

There is also another famous "shepherd" in the Bible - one who lived around this same time as Adam. Could there have been an early pagan connections to this *other* shepherd, as well? Let's take a look.

Most of us know that *Abel* was once considered a shepherd. And, as we'll see, it seems that the Biblical *Abel* was also about to have his place in the up-and-coming pagan plethora of "gods" and "goddesses."

> *...May not the story of Cain and Abel have given rise to the legend of **Tammuz**...?*
> (Pinches, 1903, p. 83)[70]

Let's look at some of these ancient, and probable, *pagan* adaptations of the Biblical character **Abel**.

The Avatars of Abel

<u>Babylonian gods:</u>
- *(the Sumerian) Dumuzi*
- *(the Akkadian) Tammuz*

<u>Some common characteristics of these gods:</u>
- *"...Dumuzi was identified as 'a shepherd' or 'the shepherd.'"*[71]
- *"The name Tammuz was the Semitic name for Dumuzi..."*[72]
- *The god Dumuzi died in a very famous way. He was considered "Lord of the Tree of Life" and "Son of the Abyss: the ever-dying, ever-resurrected Sumerian god."*[73]
- *In one account, the name Tammuz (a name seemingly based on the early Sumerian Damuzid) could also mean "the Flawless Young."*[74]
- *In other accounts, Tammuz was considered a "warrior," a "destroying element," or a "death spreader."*[75]

(Abel was also considered a shepherd (in Gen. 4:2). He was also known as the first human being to die in our new world. His death was a landmark, a tragedy - the first to suffer the most despicable act that one human being could do to another: **murder**! *Through this, was his soul also considered the first (of our world) to go* **back** *into the*

Abyss (into that "holding place" of discombobulated souls)? Abel, in some schools of thought, may have tried to be "flawless" in his moral character, much like Adam. And, as we've already discovered, he, probably, was a direct seed of the Serpent, like Cain. For this reason, pagan thought could have considered him "flawless," or "flawless" in his bloodline (since he came directly from the Serpent, of course).

However, Abel was looked upon in somewhat of a negative way, as well, because (according to pagan thought) his moral character went awry. Sometimes, Cain's religion may, occasionally, have to change one of their pagan "gods" into "opposing," or "negative," depending on how he ended up, for example. Abel may have been "flawless" in his bloodline (because he was a son of the Serpent), but he started going down the wrong moral pathways (because he followed God, and Adam). So, because of this, Abel may have been looked down upon, in ways. This brother of Cain, indeed, was in an interesting position - he was on the same level as Cain, in some ways, but, also became a "warrior" for the other side... attempting to "destroy" Cain's new world order from within. How dare he follow Adam's God, and give Him a sacrifice the way He wanted! Abel, then, was slowly beginning to spread Adam's "curse" to potential pagans everywhere, and he needed to be stifled. So, his own death - through Cain, himself - must have been thought of, in certain ways, as a monumental "achievement" for Cain's fledgling, pagan cause!)

<u>Greek and Roman gods:</u>
- *(the Greek) Ares*
- *(the Roman) Mars*

<u>Some common characteristics of these gods:</u>
- *The god Tammuz was also identified with the god Mars (or Ares).*[76]
- *Homer refers to the youngest son of Zeus as Ares: "the bane of mortals."*[77]
- *The god Zeus also **referred to his son** as a renegade and hateful pestilent.*[78]

(If we were to dig deeper into more of the pagan equivalents of Adam, we would see that the Greek Zeus was considered "offspring of the sky" as well as a "father" god.[79] Zeus probably was the later-equivalent of Adam. According to pagan thought, Zeus (Adam) considered his own son bane ("a cause of harm, ruin, or death") and a renegade ("a person who deserts his cause or faith for another; apostate; traitor").[80] Abel, of course, was now considered "bane," a "renegade" or a "hateful pestilent" by these pagans. From all of this, we, again, discover how the ancient pagans probably twisted the stories of patriarchs such as Adam and Abel. The ways of God were now considered the "opposition" to what early paganism wanted to accomplish. If Adam and Abel were to be put in any good light, their "god" avatars needed to be converted, or "paganized," somewhat, and brought back "into good light.")

We are, hopefully, beginning to understand these two religious "extremes," and see how differently each early character of Genesis was being portrayed, and inserted into a particular belief system. Let's continue to dig deeper, and see how paganism further succeeded in their methods of adaptation, and further manipulation.

"A Tale of Two Fathers"

Now, if Cain's new polytheistic paganism was as "cut and dry" as simply being able to link pagan names to early Biblical characters then this whole expose' would have probably been unraveled a long time ago, by someone. But, they didn't make it that easy… not exactly. There would be, as we'll see, a lot of "smoke and mirrors" to early pagan mythology and religion. Whether through the passage of time, or even on purpose, these ancient accounts *do* seem to be quite obscured. One thing we do know, however: to introduce *alternate* beliefs into our world - especially into a world refashioned by God, Himself - one must find ways to confuse those holding on to God's present truths. Things needed to be clouded, somewhat.

We already know, for example, that the pagan gods *An* and *Shamash* were probably associated with the Biblical *Adam*, because they were both considered "father" gods. And, it seems obvious that Adam should have been the only one to fit into this scenario. Simple enough. But, in reality, it's not very simple. There are a number of other pagan "gods" out three, owning up to this same title as "father" - but were *not* necessarily Adam. Why?

First, we must remember that the *Serpent* lived in this same vicinity. We also know that pagan ideals paralleled Cain's ways (as well as the Serpent), but not God's. In order to promote *their* take on things, they, sometimes, had to use the old "bait-and-switch" approach. As we recall, the Serpent was right alongside Adam, quite often, when it came to working the Garden of Eden. He was a secondary "chief" over the workers of the Garden (subject to Adam). The Serpent, as we also know, probably had sexual relations with Eve, as well (just as Adam did). Adam and the Serpent *both* were considered close to each other, in a number of ways. And, because paganism was truly against the ways of God, the founders began to associate Adam **and** the Serpent - ***both*** as the great "fathers" over the religion! They both ended up taking on the honor. This is very important, because it will probably alleviate a lot of potential frustration, as we move further. And, we also know (interestingly enough), the Serpent was Cain's probable father, and Adam was his "adopted" father. Also, both *very* close, in a way.

Yet, Adam was a little "problematic" to their new, up- and-coming faith (because he, so often, sided with God), so Cain and the Serpent had to change a few things. The Serpent, then, had to become *another* "father" - to "supplement" (and, eventually supersede) the wayward Adam. Adam really couldn't handle this position, at least as it stood (in their minds). Their religion needed *some* stable "father" figure to continue with the role - and, no better individual to choose, here, than the Serpent!

The Serpent, then, would eventually be looked upon as the *spiritual* or *supernatural* "father" of the religion, if you will, eventually taking over for Adam, in so many ways! Through this, it became fairly easy for the pagan elders to begin reinserting one for the other, even *assimilating* the two, in a number of ways. The Serpent, as the proper "father," would (soon) outrank Adam as even the original "father" over everyone, and everything - eventually becoming a principle object of worship! This was how the Serpent became elevated to where he is now, in the pagan religion! He was the *new* "sun" god, here.

With that said and done, let's look at this *spiritual* "father" of ancient paganism - the *Serpent* - and discover some of the ancient avatar "gods" he was elevated into.

The Avatars of the Serpent

Babylonian god:
- *(the Sumerian) Enlil*

Some common characteristics of this god:
- Enlil (or En-lil) was called "Lord of Lands" or "Lord of the Earth."[81]
- On a cosmic level, the god Enlil's realm was the earth, as well as the spheres of winds and weather above it; so, because of this, he was also known as "Lord of the Wind (or Air)."[82] One interpretation identifies this "wind" the following way: "both the strong and gentle winds were symbolic of the breath issuing from his mouth, and, eventually, as his word or command."[83] In this case, Enlil was also the "Lord of the Command."[84] What this likely means was that Enlil was leader, or chief, over others - he issued commands to a multitude of individuals.
- Interestingly enough, this god was also known as the "Lord of Cultivation."[85]
- Another source describes Enlil as "splendid serpent of the shining eyes."[86]

(Interestingly, here, the Serpent (as we already know) was considered the "operations manager" of the Garden of Eden, at least while under Adam. He often led others by his

command. In his role, the Serpent was also considered a major landlord over the entire, terrestrial earth.)

Babylonian god(s):
- *(the Akkadian) Sin or Suen*
- *(the Sumerian) Nanna or Nannar*

Some common characteristics of these gods:
- *Sin the Moon God (as he was so-called) was thought to be "born of Enlil."*[87]
- *We can see Enlil was considered Sin's "father" in the following story:*
    Sin was the product of Enlil's rape of a goddess named Ninlil.[88] *Ninlil sometimes was identified with the goddess Ishtar.*[89] *After being seduced by Enlil, she eventually began to enjoy her violation as the time went on. They continued in their sexual encounter, in spite of her pretending to protest it. Thus, through their union, they engendered the god Sin (a.k.a. Su-en) or Nanna.*
- *The god Su-en may be a corruption of Zu-ena: "Knowledge-Lord."*[90]

*- Sin was also known to be the father of the sun god
Shamash (or Utu).*[91]

*(It seems, in the above, that the name of **Sin** was considered more a "spiritual" title of the Serpent. And, because of the seduction of Ninlil or Ishtar (both, of whom, were probably equated with **Eve**, as we'll see, below), this entire story, above, could be nothing but an echo of Eve's temptation in the Garden of Eden. Naturally, pagan thought would have, most probably, implied that Eve welcomed the Serpent's advances, and took her "seduction" as something wonderful, and life-changing.*

*What was "born" out of their copulation, of course, was another spiritual avatar of the Serpent - another god. This new god, or avatar of the Serpent, became a god of enlightenment and (pagan) truth. We know that Eve received **knowledge** at this time - the Knowledge of Good and Evil. In certain ways, this seduction of Eve could have been a turning point - marking the actual birth of the pagan religion. The time (and this new "god") represented the beginning of our own ability to receive "divine knowledge." Note that this Serpent, in **his new, spiritual avatar** Sin, was considered the "Lord of Knowledge." It was **Sin** who helped administer this knowledge and worldly power to Eve, and, through her, to the rest of humanity (via the pagan religion).)*

<u>Babylonian god(s):</u>
- (the Akkadian) Bel
- (the Semitic) Ba'al

Common characteristics of these gods:
- *The title Bel (or Ba'al) simply means "Lord."*[92]
- *Bel, quite often, was equated with the aforementioned Enlil.*[93]
- *Like Enlil, Bel was also known as "Lord of the Lands."*[94]
- *The word Bel can also mean chief, as in "Chief of the Gods."*[95]
- *The ancient Greek scholar Hesychius considered him, "a dragon or great serpent."*[96]
- *In fact, Bel was widely known to be a dragon.*[97]

(Again, we know the Serpent was once the "chief," or "lord," over many in the Garden (except Adam). It's also interesting to recall how this god was, so often, considered a "fiery" serpent, or dragon.)

With all of the above information, we may have been able to delve a little more into the original position of Adam (in the Garden), and what he brought to the table, and how all of this was slowly being overshadowed by the Serpent, and his pagan ways.

There is more to these early pagan "gods" and "goddesses." Let's look at a few of the more probable equivalents of *Eve*. She, believe it or not, had a good deal of relevance, and reverence, in early pagan thought.

The Avatars of Eve

*At Babylon there was (in these times) a great resort of people of various nations, who inhabited Chaldea, and lived without rule and order, like the beasts of the field. In the first year there made its appearance... an animal endowed with **reason**, who was called Oannes.*
("Ancient Near East (Babylonia) Glossary and Texts", n. d., p. 42)[98]

According to Berossus, there was once a wise deity, who brought mankind reason and wisdom...

Babylonian god(desses):
- *(the Akkadian) Oannes or Ea-Oannes*
- *(the Akkadian) Ea*[99]

Some common characteristics of these gods:
- *The god Oannes was associated with water; and was often portrayed as a fish.*[100]
- *He was endowed with reason, and taught mankind wisdom.*[101]
- *This god could also be known in a combination of names: Ea-Oannes.*[102]
- *The god Ea, "whose abode is water," was also known as "God of the **Deep**."*[103]
- *He lived in the area of Eridu, and was considered "the source of Babylonian civilization" and the "bearer of culture."*[104]

*(Interesting, the word Ea is close to the Hebrew Hea or Hevel - a Jewish title for **Eve**!*[105] *The association of a god or goddess with water, here, could have a number of reasons behind it (as we've already seen). For one, it was probably a symbol of Eve's occupation*

in the Garden of Eden: Eve was, most probably, responsible for helping to lead **irrigation** *projects, and other waterworks, throughout the time Adam managed the Garden - and even beyond. Water was needed to give life to all of the plants. Beyond her occupation, here, we know how water could also have been symbolic of the* **supernatural** *or* **spiritual** *world, or even the supernatural "waters" beneath the earth (such as the "Darkness of the Deep"). Now, we'll see how Eve could have been granted some "rule" over certain areas of the cosmos, and we'll also see why.*

We've know that, for the most part, our bodies are made up of water. This "paganized" Eve could become associated with water for, quite possibly, another reason: water, in an esoteric sense, could also relate to one's thought and emotion. A very distraught Eve could have, emotionally, gone a little "overboard," in regards to her son (Abel's) death. She severely lamented his murder - which could have, possibly, been the reason why she went "down into the underworld." She probably felt as though she was going through some earthly, emotional "hell," of sorts.

Also, through eating the fruit of the Tree of Knowledge, Eve was said to have acquired a great amount of wisdom - spiritual wisdom (the wisdom of the Serpent's avatar, **Sin***). Absorbing all of this knowledge, Eve could have even, for a period of time, subjected herself under the domain of the Serpent, and his influences! We'll soon see how this could have been so.*

As we may have noticed, two of these (above) gods - Oannes and Ea - were thought of as male. But, **Ea**, *in some legends, could have been considered a male, and, in others, a female.*[106] *Sometimes, the gender of certain gods and goddesses could have been blurred, over time (or, even, through intentional manipulation), so it's never something that could be considered "set in stone"!)*

Babylonian god(dess):
- *(the Sumerian) Ki*

<u>Some common characteristics of this goddess:</u>
- *Anu's wife was known to be Ki.*[107]
- *As "Goddess of the Earth," Ki was likely the original name of the earth goddess!*[108]
- *It is likely she and An (Anu) were progenitors of most gods.*[109]
- *Naturally, because of this, Ki was known as the great "mother."*[110]

*(Assuming that An (and Anu) were ancient avatars for Adam, his consort Eve would have had ancient pagan avatars - often considered to be his **wife**.*

Also, because the pagan avatars of Eve were, quite often, considered to be Adam's wife, she was known as the "earth goddess." We recall (in the above) that the "paganized" Eve had some dominion over the supernatural "waters" of the earth, and even below the earth (in the underworld). This was, interestingly enough, in stark contrast to Adam's domain, which was said to be "above the earth," or "in the heavens."[111] *The two, in combination, had dominion over our entire world.*

*Adam and Eve were also considered the progenitors of many people - whether in bloodline or in ideology. Eve could have easily been considered a great "**mother**" over a vast number of (pagan) people!)*

<u>Babylonian god(desses):</u>
- *(the Sumerian) Enki*[112]
- *(the Sumerian) Ninlil*

Some common characteristics of these god(desses):
- *The god Enki (En-ki) comes from En - "lord" and ki - "earth;" to mean, literally, "Lord of the Earth" or "Lord Earth."*[113]
- *The goddess Ki seemed to be **refashioned into En-ki**, a god who "made for the essentials of agriculture."*[114]
- *With the god Enlil, Enki helped to increase the abundance of the land.*[115]
- *Enki was also considered "operations manager" to other people around him.*[116]
- *The goddess Ninlil was known as "Lady of Cultivation" (interestingly enough, Enlil, the "Lord of Cultivation," was her husband), and was also equated with the goddess Ninkharsag, or "Lady of Kharsag" (of which Kharsag was probably equated to the area of Eden).*[117]
- *Along with Enlil, Ninlil was considered the "Lady of the Command."*[118]
- *Enki was also thought to be "Lord of What is Beneath (or, the underworld);" again, this was probably because he had dominion, not only over the terrestrial earth, but also over the supernatural waters on the earth, and below.*[119]
- *Enki was also considered the firstborn son of An; and was a*

god of wisdom.[120]

*(We recall that the priests and scribes of Ur (in ancient Babylonia) could have, either intentionally or unintentionally, twisted some of these early stories, to accentuate their own beliefs. We may be able to see an example of this, in the above. Somehow, the early goddess **Ki** (as mentioned before) was considered a female (a wife of An). But, in her "transformation" to the pagan god **En-ki**, she, now, was turned into a male god. No exact reason as to why. Maybe, it was the result of an early, male-dominated society. We're not sure. A male deity in some commanding role could have sounded a little more appropriate to the ancient priests, at the time - trying to establish a avatar people could look up to. Again, we're not sure. Whatever "politically incorrect" reason we could assume, here, we, at least, could discover an example of how the sex of one pagan god could have been twisted, over time. One deity (Ki) was female; and, then, another deity "refashioned" out of the former was, now, considered male. Male or female, they, most probably, were avatars for the same Biblical individual - Eve.*

We, in the above, see even more similarities with Ki and Enki: Eve was also known for her wisdom. Her position in the Garden, as we know, probably also allowed her to manage certain projects within the Garden, such as irrigation and the watering of crops. Also, Eve (as with Enki) could have even been considered the "firstborn" of Adam, in a way - because she was brought forth directly "from his rib"! Numerous similarities seems to pop up, here, between these female pagan goddesses and Eve!.)

<u>Babylonian god(desses):</u>
- *(the Akkadian) Ishtar*
- *(the Sumerian) Inanna*

Some common characteristics of these goddesses:
- *The goddess Inanna was also an "earth-goddess," who provided life and sustenance to the land, as well as restored life and fertility to all.*[121]
- *Interestingly enough, Ishtar was also known as "Lady of the Deep."*[122]
- *She was known as a fish, or snake, goddess.*[123]
- *Ishtar was considered daughter of the moon god Nanna (or Sin); other traditions held her to be daughter of An.*[124]
- *In some myths, Anu's consort was known as Antum or Antu, a goddess... "often confused with Ishtar (or Inanna)," or, even replaced by Ishtar.*[125]
- *Legends of an early form of the god Ea are exactly the same as later legends of Ishtar; she does seem to be connected with Ea in a number of ways.*[126]
- *Ishtar, herself, was later replaced by more goddesses in up-and-coming empires, such as the West Semitic Astarte, the Greek Aphrodite, and the Roman Venus.*[127]
- *Ishtar also loved the murdered god Dumuzi.*[128]

(Isn't it interesting to discover that earlier pagan gods and goddesses - with the same attributes - were replaced by another pagan goddess, named Ishtar?[129] *In one ancient Babylonian work, known as the Penitential Hymn, the name Ishtar could have been derived from an ancient Hebrew word for "woman" (Adam's consort):* **Ish**.[130]

We know that the earth and water were, often, considered symbolic of the pagan

"Eve." We will now see how she even seemed to become closer and closer to the Serpent, after the Fall - even thought to be his "daughter," at times! This was, probably, because she took the fruit of the Tree of Knowledge, disobeyed God, and, possibly, during later times of her life (after the Fall), began to associate further with this same Serpent (as we shall see).

Also, as with Eve, Ishtar vehemently mourned the death of her own son.)

It only makes sense, here, to assume that *Ea-Oannes*, *Ki* (or *Enki*) and *Ishtar* may have, originally, been one in the same. But, how and why would *Eve*, beyond eating the forbidden fruit, still associate herself with the Serpent? Wasn't she considered Adam's consort? Most of us thought she would have been on the side of *God*, the whole time. Possibly, not.

We know that Adam "dropped the ball," as far as staying moral, and was, occasionally, seduced by a number of female fallen angels. With Eve, there seemed to be a number of negative things associated with her, as well. According to a number of Christian traditions (even in the Bible), she may have been separated from Adam for at least 130 years. Where did she go? How did she survive our cold, cruel world? Did she do it, all alone? We'll soon see that pagan mythology has a good deal of more information about Eve (after the Fall), and how she may have lived. It's also interesting to see that the pagan religion, often, put *her* on a pedestal (along with the Serpent). Why? Why did she get more of the "royal treatment," in their new belief system, while Adam and Abel were, for the most part, continually snubbed *downwards*, towards infinity.

Pagan ideology gave Adam *a little bit* of credit for trying to do "right" things, and even trying to bring up Cain the best he could, but that was about it. We know that, over time, the pagan elite began to transform him into somewhat of a loner - like the family member who "lost his way," Eve, however, was not treated in this way.

The Baker Adapa (Adam) Does What He Was Told

Let's look at one example of how *Adam* was probably looked down upon (in the pagan faith), and how Eve *wasn't*! Let's look at a story where *he* became responsible for a problem that *he* (and he alone) supposedly caused, by some internal weakness. We'll also see how he, then, needed to be "put in his place" for something he brought upon society. But, Eve, overall, did not share in his punishment, or share in any negative treatment.

The following ancient mythological account seems to be a pagan interpretation of the *Fall of Adam and Eve*, along with a few of their "twists."

*Adapa (or **Adam**) was a mortal man from a godly lineage. He was given super intelligence by Ea (or Enki - **Eve**), the god of wisdom. In spite of the possession of all this wisdom Adapa was denied immortality, however. One day, he lost his temper and broke the wings of Ninlil (another avatar of **Eve**) the South Wind, who had overturned his fishing boat, and was called to account before a god in heaven. Ea (again, another avatar of **Eve**), his patron god, warned him to apologize humbly for his actions, but not to partake of food or drink while he was in heaven, as it would be the food of death. The god, impressed by Adapa's sincerity, offered instead the food of immortality; but Adapa heeded Ea's advice, refused, and thus missed the chance for immortality that would have been his.*

("Adapa", n. d., p. 1)[131]

Interesting. If we compare this to the Biblical Fall, we get some interesting twists, here: first, in the Bible, it was **Eve** who chooses the fruit, and picks forbidden knowledge over eternal life. She, then, seduces her husband; and, through his love for her, he chooses the fruit also. They both end up to be mortal.

In the *pagan* account, however, it was up to Adam (or Adapa) to choose what will be brought to mankind. *He* was already given divine information by the knowledgeable woman Eve (Ea). Obviously, he upset one of her avatars (i.e. Ninlil) in some way, and needed to be accountable for this abuse. The god who heard Adam's case, however, believed Adam's sincerity, and decided to forgive him. He even offered Adam the food of immortality! But, Adam, rather, decided to follow the divine knowledge that Eve gave to him, and missed his own chance for something better. He messed up, and affected all of mankind in the process.

For whatever reason, Adam either did not want to be immortal, or Eve did not want this mortal to advance to some higher, immortal state. Whatever the deeper reason, here, it seems that, **regardless** of Adam's obedience to Eve, **regardless** of what path he chose, *Adam* was in error, and he *alone* brought all of this negativity to mankind. Adam, not only deprived himself of immortality (by his ignorance), but deprived the entire human race, through this choice!

> *Adapa... was already endowed with knowledge and wisdom, and failed of immortality, not because he was disobedient, like Adam, but through his literal obedience to Ea,* **his creator**. (Rogers, 1912, p. 69)[132]

Now, we see that Eve actually made Adam what he was (nothing like the Bible stated)! Adam also obeyed his *superior*, Eve. The human race did get knowledge, but could not get both. Eve, as we notice, seemed to have escaped **any** responsibility for the Fall, or, seemingly, anything else! The curse of the world seemed to have been *all* the result of Adam's misconduct - not Eve, and, certainly, not the Serpent.

> *...Adapa was deprived of eternal life by not eating or drinking the 'food or water of life' while Adam was cut off from eating the fruit of the 'tree of life'...*
> ("In Search of Historical Adam: Part 2", n. d., p. 2)[133]

Twists abound in Babylonian mythology. And, it's also interesting to see how Eve can practically do no wrong, here - as if she was on the Serpent's side all along. One thing's for sure, however: it seems almost inconceivable *not* to believe that there were some connections between ancient pagan beliefs and the Adam, Eve and Serpent of the Garden. There is more.

The Serpent "Sun" - Regent of the Adam "Sun"

A *regent* is simply defined as an individual who exercises ruling power in the absence or disability of a sovereign. We recall, as far as Adam and the Serpent, *that's* exactly what was going on, here (in pagan ideology). We were already introduced to a famous pagan god, known throughout the Bible (e.g. Num. 22:41, Judg. 2:13, I Kings. 22:53, etc.) - with the name was *Ba'al* (or *Baal*). Let's dig a little *deeper* into more of these pagan twists:

*...Ba'al is the all-devouring **Sun**...*[134]

As we've already discovered: due to Adam's weakness and vulnerability, *another* sun god had to come into pagan "light," and eventually take over his reigns. Adam, we know, was, most probably, thought of as the *original* "sun" god. And, the Serpent (a.k.a. *Ba'al*) had to eventually step in, and take over his position of leadership. He, not only would take over Adam's reign and popularity, but take over *him* - in a whole number of ways! Again, this whole scenario comes up, so many times, in pagan lore.

Yes, this is how the ancient pagans probably manipulated their introduction of ancestor worship. Their new sun god (the Serpent) had a number of similarities to Adam. Yet, eventually, the Serpent just *had* to replace him.[135] Adam's ways were what they were, but needed a little bit of *tweaking*, to make it right. Adam, now, became a "junior" partner, if you will - waiting to be supplanted fully. Babylonian gods, such as *Utu* or *Shamash*, both were equated to Adam, but, also, were both thought of as a "son of **Sin**."[136] Again, Adam was eventually considered a spiritual "son" of the Serpent - in need of a little world! The Serpent, eventually, took over the reigns as the proper sun god, and so it remains to this day.

Paganism could, actually, go a little deeper into this scenario - and mix things up a bit more. In one example, the ancient Babylonian god *Ninib* was also associated with the sun. He was considered a:

> *...deity originally with solar attributes... (and) closely associated with Bel (or Ba'al) and regarded as his son... In hymns he is described as a healing god who **releases men from illness**... (the) aspect stressed was the sun at the morning... **showering beneficence** upon mankind. In theogony, Ninib was **regent** of the planet Saturn.*
> ("Ancient Near East (Babylonia) Glossary and Texts", n. d., p. 39)[137]

Of course, we know that the *new* sun god - *the Serpent* - was credited for "showering" mankind with "beneficial" information. But, in the above case, could Ninib be the sun god Adam? Or, could there have even been a *third* solar deity? Could a *third* god have showered mankind with beneficence, and be credited for saving people from their "illnesses" (i.e. their subjection to a tyrannical and limiting God - of the Bible)? We also see that this Ninib was considered *son* of that *real* powerhouse - the *real* lord over all. And, of course, just who would be considered son of this Serpent (Bel or Ba'al)? Yes, *Cain*.

Yet, in ways, Adam could have also been thought of as the **regent** of the "real deal," here. But, in pagan ideology, we must understand that the Serpent's son - *Cain* - could have easily stepped into this role, as a *third* sun god, as well! As we know: like father, like *sun*. Although it's not too difficult for us to understand it all, here (with just a little bit of explanation), the real origins of these pagan gods and goddesses could become quite clouded - to those not privy to this information.

Cain could have easily took on a number of the same attributes as his father, and could also have taken on the role of "son of **Sin**." This same pagan *sun* god - a number of different candidates able to step into this role. What may even prove more intriguing (and, assuredly, more confusing) later on is: a number of *latter* dignitaries will even start to claim that they were divine reincarnations of these same, early "paganized" gods (such as Adam, Eve, Cain, the Serpent, etc.)! Now, we'll have *more* names to the list! Talk about confusing! Yet, as long as we maintain a good foundational base, here, with these original Biblical ancestors, we'll be able to understand how corrupt these pagan pathways will become, through the passage of history, and we'll be able to successfully navigate through it. We've already mentioned how discombobulating it all seemed to become, over time. This was why.

Even looking at the god *Saturn*, in the above example, we see another piece of corruption. Saturn was known as "the hidden god," in ancient lore. Well, doesn't this sound a little familiar?

> *As the inner nature of **YHVH** (the God of the Bible) is **hidden**; therefore He (YHVH) is only named with the 'Name of the Shekhinah, Adonai, i.e., Lord...' Zohar iii 320a...*
> ("Ancient Near East (Babylonia) Glossary and Texts", n. d., p. 3)[138]

Yes, these early pagans often fashioned their gods into something similar to the God of the Bible - even adopting some of His titles for their own!

Now that we've looked at a few of the ways Adam, Eve and even *God* were manipulated, what about the infamous *Cain*? What contributions did he have to early pagan thought and mythology? And, what kind of deities did they make *him* into? As we've already stated, Cain would, eventually, become very powerful in their faith: the "architect" of so much pagan thought, here:

> *Although modern scholars seem to ignore the possibility that **Cain** may have influenced the history of the ancient world, three notable writers at the beginning of the Christian era (St. Jude, Josephus and Philo) suggested that Cain's **influence** was **evil and enduring**...* (Bristowe, 1927, p. 4)[139]

Let's look some more into Cain, himself, and some of the popular ancient avatars he was turned into:

The Avatars of Cain

Babylonian god:
- *(the Akkadian) Sargon*

Some common characteristics of this god:
- *Sargon (Sar-gon) was famous throughout ancient Babylonia. In one*

ancient text, Sargon called his adopted father Akki.[140]
- *Another ancient Akkadian inscription lists Sargon as the "son of Bel."*[141]
- *It's only natural to assume Akki could be close to Bel, if not the same god. It's also natural to assume the famous Akki was a king of the ancient Babylonian city of Akkad, if not the founder. Sargon was said to have been raised by **Akki** as a **gardener**.*[142]
- *According to one source, Sargon claimed Akki, "trained me to become his assistance in the royal gardens."*[143]
- *Sargon was also said to have "cleaned out and cut out new canals and brought the system of irrigation to a high degree of efficiency."*[144]
- *Apparently, Sargon had great intellectual abilities. As well as gaining knowledge from Akki, "Sargon's super-human knowledge were attributed to his mother's teaching."*[145]
- *He transplanted some of this knowledge into completing other tasks and accomplishments: "His career began with the conquest of Erech. Erech was called 'the old city' or 'place of the settlement.'"*[146]
- *Sargon also "founded the city of **Babylon**" and was "one of the greatest in the long line of Babylonian monarchs."*[147]
- *The city of Babylon "became the metropolis and, at the same time, the centre of Western Asiatic civilization."*[148]
- *Sargon was easily "one of the earliest of the world's great empire builders."*[149]
- *The early beliefs of ancient times were, obviously, monotheistic. Around the time of Sargon, however, it changed; another religious belief was blooming, now becoming polytheistic in nature.*[150]
- *Sargon was also considered a priest, or the first high priest, of the religion.*[151]

("Looking at the word "Sar" (from Sar-gon) and we see it could mean 'king.'"[152] Add the word "gon," which can mean "Cain," and we have Sar-gon: "**King-Cain**."[153] Sargon was said to have lived around 3800-4000 B.C., approximately the same time Cain was thought to have lived.[154] Cain, as we also recall, was probably a son of the Serpent. Sargon's father was called "Akki." We also see that: "The basis root of the name **Akki** is found in the Hebrew **Nachash**."[155] And, as we already know, Nachash was the Hebrew word for "Serpent," in Genesis 3:1.[156] It's all the same!

Cain was also considered a gardener, and one with superhuman knowledge.[157] Christian tradition and the Bible both tell us that he built cities, notably Enoch (or

Erech?). Cain easily could have been considered the first "priest" of early pagan thought and ideology.)

As well, we see some excerpts from an ancient text, known as the "Legend of Sargon":

2 *My mother was lowly…*
5 *My lowly mother conceived me, in secret she brought me forth.*
8 ***Akki**, the irrigator, it carried me.*
9 *Akki, the irrigator, with… lifted me out,*
10 *Akki, the irrigator, as his own son… reared me,*
11 *Akki, the irrigator, as his gardener appointed me.*
12 *While I was a **gardener** the goddess Ishtar (Eve) loved me,*
13 *And for… years I ruled the kingdom.*[158]

It's interesting to see how all of this could, quite easily, apply to Cain.

<u>Babylonian god(s):</u>
- *(the Babylonian) Merodach*
- *(the Babylonian) Marduk*

Some common characteristics of these gods:
- *The name Merodach, over time, was shortened to Amaruduk (i.e. Marduk), meaning "young steer of day."*[159]
- *Merodach (or Marduk) was considered the firstborn son of Ea/Enki.*[160]
- *"The features of Marduk's face were said to had "[shone like] the day."*[161]
- *Note the following ancient text, the Enuma Elish:*
    90 *Ea declared Marduk flawless*
    104 *(Ea speaking) "... My son, who is my* **Sun***!*
    105 *Sun for all the Heavens!"*[162]
- *The gods - Bel and Merodach - were close to each other, in many ways, often being confused, one with another.*[163]
- *In fact, Merodach was even considered "son of Bel." The two (Merodach and Bel) were so close, in many ways. To separate them, Merodach was even known as Bel-Merodach (the "**younger**" Bel).*[164]
- *There was, apparently, a great deal of seasonal flooding in ancient Babylonia. Merodach/Marduk was the one who "brought order out of chaos." One way he did this was to build dikes and drainage canals, separating the waters from the land. Marduk was also known as the "donor of fruitfulness and founder of agriculture..."*[165] *Through this feat, he founded homes for men. The diverting of water, over a long enough period of time, allowed people in this immediate area to build more permanent cities.*[166]
- *Marduk built at least five cities.*[167] *He eventually founded the city of* **Babylon**, *and became the national god* **of Babylonia**.[168]
- *He became so popular to others around him that, "all nature, including man,* **owed its existence** *to him; the destiny of kingdoms and subjects was in his hands."*[169]

(Cain had a great reverence for the Serpent, his probable father. As we've discovered, they were, practically, looked upon as the same god, in so many ways! As with Biblical tradition, Cain's face had the brightness of an angel.[170] Cain, as we also know, would become so "great" and powerful, over time, that he could have eventually taken over this "sun-god" position, at least in some respects.

Cain, in the Bible, also worked as a farmer, with crops. The above descriptions, as we note, also seem to parallel Sargon, in so many ways.)

Wow, all of this honor and prestige coming to the Biblical character *Cain*. Of course, it's all pagan, in foundation. And, as we're starting to see, it may be getting a little easier to equate these gods to Adam, Eve, Cain, and the Serpent, as long as we stay with the program!

Let's continue on, and see how, even, the whole creation process, according to paganism, was personified into one "god" or another, or into some tyrannical *force*, and also see how these "good" gods of paganism (i.e. the Serpent, Cain, etc.) would "save" the world from all of the "evil" out there (i.e. the Biblical God, His viceroy Adam and Abel).

Let's now see how paganism transformed the Serpent and Cain into the *actual* "creators" of our world, how they "transformed" all of the chaos (that once was God) into the wonderful (and ever-evolving) "utopia" it is, today. Again, let's please try to read the following with an assumption that their mythological accounts the "opposite" of what the Bible actually stated.

Let's, first, look the gods (or forces) that paganism referred to as "evil."

The "Evil" God of the Bible

We've already seen, in the above, how paganism could hijack some attributes of the God of the Bible, and insert them as descriptions of their *own* gods and goddesses (such as their use of the word *Saturn*). But, there is more: first, we have a, most probable, interpretation of the God of the Bible, Himself: the "mean" god *Kingu*. The ancient pagans seemed to have had at least *one* personification of the Biblical God, it seems - and they all were not good, of course. This negative, or "mean," god of ancient pagan lore was also thought of as the "Dragon of Chaos," or "Head of the Devils."[171] Interesting enough, *Kingu* was considered a god who, according to one ancient source, was also known as *Tammuz* (i.e. the "paganized" Abel). It's interesting how Abel could have also been inserted into this story, here - placed alongside of the "mean" God of the Bible.

According to some interpretations, Kingu was also considered to be:

*...the counterpart or equivalent, of **Anu** (Adam), the Sky-god, in the kingdom of **darkness**, for it is said in the text Kingu 'was exalter and received the power of Anu,' i.e. he possessed the same power and attributes as Anu.*
(Budge, 1931, p. 20)[172]

Wow. We even see Kingu associated with *Adam*, as well. It seems obvious, here, that pagan ideology might even link the *three*, here, if necessary. Kingu seemed, as well, to be the pagan personification of whatever *chaos* was in our earth, just before the Serpent "emancipated" it, of course. It's completely the *opposite* of what is stated in the Bible, and all of the characters are turned around. God, Adam, and Abel are now the "devils" and "dragons" - all from the kingdom of "darkness." Yet, we know the truth. It's all just been twisted around, and "paganized."

Speaking of chaos, there are more personifications of "evil" that were assigned by early pagan ideologues:

*When George Smith (an archaeologist) first interpreted the creation fragments, he translated Apsu 'the **Abyss**'...* (Clay, 1923, p. 79)[173]

Apsu

According to Biblical traditions, we recall that there is an *Abyss*, located deep beneath the earth. It was, also, known as the *Deep*, or *Darkness of the Deep*. Yet, we find a pagan personification of this same "darkness, night and evil:" known as *Apsu*.[174] It seems the

Biblical *Deep* and the pagan *Apsu* could, actually, be one in the same - both referring to the same "underworld" concept.

According to Babylonian mythology, the Serpent and Cain, both, were accredited for "conquering" this Apsu. To them, it wasn't a supernatural "holding cell," where the God of the Bible placed any souls devastated from the previous world (or even beyond), it was only a place of darkness and evil. It was a place that, also, needed some type of "conquering" by one of their own, special deities! It seemed that most everything of God's creation needed some manner of "conquering," "refashioning" or "redefining" back then. Why? Of course, it's because it was originally from God! The pagan religion defined it all as "chaos," needing to be brought to some manner of "*paganized*" order or civilization.

Also, pagan elders were, assuredly, also trying to trivialize the awesome power of the Creator God, and His righteous judgment of the world before! It's should now be fairly obvious to see all of the *opposing* polarities of pagan and Biblical view.

With the ancient world "needing help" from some tyrannical force known as God, all it took was for these pagan gods to come in, and save the day!

Their "victory" over this evil Apsu represents one example of how Cain, merely by just being himself, was credited for "conquering" everything once wrong with the world, including the *Deep*. And, after he did this, Cain, naturally, had to be elevated to some position of authority. He even allowed his mother a new position of authority, just for being her! Eve, now, was blessed with the responsibility (and rule) over the Apsu (the *Deep*), and all that went along with it (the waters of the *Deep*, the souls within the *Deep*, the supernatural world, etc.).[175] We already know that Eve, in her various pagan avatars, was authorized to have this *power* over the supernatural elements of our world - those, often, which were related to, or were symbolized by, *water*.[176]

Tiamat

We know the ancients believed there was water, all around the earth - in, above and below. And, most probably, this was considered *supernatural* "waters" - the fourth dimension, the spirit world, what have you. Now, we see that the *Apsu* was considered the waters of the earth that Eve ruled over. So, with this in mind, we, now, see that the ancient pagans dictated that there was another personification of "evil," living in these waters, known as *Tiamat*. Tiamat seemed to have personified this primeval, watery *chaos* that was all around the earth, at the beginning of Genesis – an "ocean" of darkness and despair.[177]

In some descriptions, *Tiamat* was even considered the *formlessness* and *void* of the earth, during these earliest of times. Wow, an interesting choice of words, here![178] We recall, from Genesis 1:2, that our earth was, once, considered in a state of chaos, covered entirely with *water*, and being *without form* and *void*. Can we say "imitation?"

Tiamat seems to be another "paganization" of a "mean" God, and His judgment over our previous world. Now looked upon in the feminine, she didn't represent anything righteous, nor carry out her punishments on a well-deserved, formerly corrupt earth. No, it was all "evil." She was actually thought of as "the universe's wish to continue this return to Chaos."[179]

*The helpers of Tiamat were placed under command of a **god called Kingu**...*
(Budge, 1931, p. 20)[180]

*...the dragon (Tiamat) and Apsu, her husband, the **arch-enemy** of the gods.*
(Mackenzie, 1915, p. 38)[181]

<u>The Story of Creation</u>
80 *They have jointed their forces, they prepare battle.*[182]

Wow. As we see, it was *Kingu* (i.e. God, Adam, and Abel) who commanded all of this negativity, and they're prepared to fight any of the "good" pagan gods to keep it within this negative state. See all of the twists? Do we now understand the severity of corruption, here? Whatever "evil" was brought to our world (by our God) at this time needed to have the "new" gods of pagan religion around (and worshiped) to make it all "right."

The Serpent was First

> *In pagan mythology, this Tiamat… was slain by **Bel**, the chief deity.*
> ("Ancient Near East (Babylonia) Glossary and Texts", n. d., p. 47)[183]

Interestingly enough, paganism states that *Bel* took care of this supernatural, watery *Chaos*. Of course, this was, none other, than another avatar of the Serpent.

> *…Belus (another equivalent to Bel, the Serpent, etc.) came, and cut the woman asunder: and, out of one half of her, **he formed the earth**, and of the other half **the heavens**. This Belus **divided the darkness** (both above and below the earth), and reduced the universe to **order**.* (Cory, 1832, p. 58)[184]

What once was a world of *chaos* was now a "new world order" - all under pagan idealism. This was the *true* beginning of the political and religious elements of *Mystery Babylon*. Through his "conquering" role, the **Serpent** was elevated to such a powerful position he was even believed to have been responsible for most natural, or elemental, changes on this earth - including fertility, prosperity, as well as being able to usher in famine and catastrophe if he pleased, as well![185] After all, he *was* the god who made the world into everything it is, today (and not God, of course).

> *The lord Enlil (the Serpent) brought **prosperity to the Land**.*
> (O'Brien, 1988, p. 87)[186]

"Sun" vs. "Moon"

It's fairly obvious to see how the early pagans gave *the Serpent*, as well as *Cain*, all of the glory of creation. We also know that the sun was, once, a pagan symbol of Adam - only to be "sanitized" and "augmented" by the Serpent's rise to power.

Yet, we've also understood (from the previous section) that the **moon** was also a symbol of Sin - that "spiritual" avatar of this pagan Serpent god. Now, if the Serpent was granted Adam's "replacement," as the sun god, then why would he also need to be associated with the moon (in some of his avatars)?

First, we already know that, according to the Bible, God cursed the Serpent, after the Fall. But, before Adam's creation, the Serpent was more powerful than Adam, in so many ways. Adam was just a man; the Serpent an angel. God just told him to follow Adam's lead in the Garden, however. Now, according to pagan interpretation, it was this "evil" God of the Bible who unfairly "demoted" Sin (or, the spiritual Serpent). Instead of being as powerful as Adam (as a *sun god*), Sin was (temporarily) demoted, at least for a little while. And, one could take a guess that this parallels God's punishment of the Serpent, for his insolence to His viceroy, Adam. But, of course, these early pagan elites found a new way to explain this truth away - and, eventually, slant everything towards their own *benefit*! One Biblical commentary provides the following:

*God rebuked the moon, and formed the light and the stars. The **moon diminished itself** to rule only at night.*
(Schwartz, 2004, p. 112)[187]

So, they claimed: if the Serpent was to take over *all* factions of the earth, and "sanctify" everything, he couldn't just end up ruling *only* the night, here, or even just ruling the day (as the *sun* does, symbolically)! He had to rule both.

So, first, these early pagans had to take into account that there was *another* part of our existence which, in actuality, was previously unaccounted for: the *moon*, the *night*, darkness, etc.).

And, at this time, they claimed that their pagan gods were developing a plan of action:

<u>The Seven Evil Demons</u>
25 *When Enlil (the Serpent) heard these tiding, a plan in his heart
   he pondered...*
26 *With Ea (Eve)... he took counsel.*[188]

They claimed that, at the time of Sin's (the Serpent's) demotion: "The evil gods (i.e. Kingu) **darken** the moon by an eclipse, (and) Shamash (or, Adam)... (began) helping them by withdrawing **his light** from the moon."[189] Adam, we see, even assisted the evil Kingu (i.e. God), to put the Serpent, and his ways, down - even further!

<u>The Seven Evil Demons</u>
47 *Enlil (the Serpent)* **saw the darkening** *of the hero* **Sin** *(that "spiritual" avatar of the Serpent)*
60 *Son of a prince, the gleaming* **Sin has been sadly darkened** *in heaven...*[190]

But, as we stated, a few of the leading pagan gods were dedicated to the cause (of keeping the Serpent's ways aloft). So, the pagan Enlil (the Serpent), Ea (Eve) and Anu (Adam) all began to work *together*, to assist the spiritual *Sin* to overcome this "oppression." The Serpent (Enlil) and Adam (Anu), then, divided their dominance over the day, and lordship over the earth.

Interestingly enough, Adam had final the authority over the Garden, at first. The Serpent was a close second. The two were close, as far as role and responsibility, but God, of course, chose Adam. So, when this "evil" God decided to diminish the Serpent's power, his new symbol became *the moon*, a celestial body diminished in "brightness." The sun god (or Adam) remained bright in the sky, and the only thing the moon was (seemingly) able to do on his own was to *oppose* the sun's (or Adam's) brightness and influence over the earth. After all, we recall that Adam tried to "help" the evil God to "keep the Serpent down." The "unfair" treatment of Sin (i.e. the Serpent) prompted these other major gods into action.

Of course, the Serpent - and his pagan ways - would not go down that easily. We know that he, in reality, helped to bring about the Fall of man. So, before anyone knew it, the Serpent was (through the Fall) able to, again, *rise up*, and (this time) not only rule the night, but ascend **past** Anu (or Adam), and rule the **day**, as well!

<u>The Seven Evil Demons</u>
28 *With Anu (Adam) he* **divided** *the lordship of the whole heaven,*[191]

Now, the Serpent had both hemispheres, and all the world. The Bible did say that the Serpent, or Satan, would become "god of this world" (II Cor. 4:4). Interestingly enough, in some ancient Babylonian cities, the "moon god was considered father of the sun god!"[192] Of course, this was because of this revolution. It a strange way, it all seems to fit *exactly* with our account of the Fall - from an *opposing* viewpoint! All of this, indeed, was a pagan "twist" of what really happened at the Fall.

Yet, there is still *another* twist to the whole story: even though the spiritual Serpent (as the "moon god"), and his ways, recovered their former position of "greatness," and became "back on top," it wouldn't be because of the Serpent, *alone*, nor because of any partnership with Ea (Eve) and Anu (Adam). It would also be up to *Cain* - the Serpent's *own* son - to find a way to help him regain much of his former dignity and glory.

<u>The Story of Creation</u>
12 *The Moon-god **he** (Cain) **caused to shine forth**, to him **confided the night**.*[193]
13 *He set him for the government (?) of the night, to determine the **day**.*[194]

Colorful pagan accounts continue to abound - and make twists in our Genesis story! Cain was becoming popular to the antediluvian populous. He was helping to twist all of these stories around. He needed to be part of this all - *somehow*. It wouldn't look good any other way. So, although it was not Cain's *primary* goal to make a god out of himself, his pagan peers may have thought he needed to be. So, he, most probably, figured: "*Why not?*" His peers even elevated him *above most all pagan gods*. But, of course, the Serpent would still be "top dog," because of who he was. But, Cain's "escalation" would, assuredly, look appealing to the expanding pagan populous.

So, because Cain "helped" Sin (or, the Serpent) regain all of his power (as the moon *and* sun god), the Serpent allowed everyone to magnify Cain, in so many ways:

*...Enlil (the Serpent)... had **given** the lordship over mankind upon earth to Marduk (**Cain**), **victorious** son of Ea (Eve)...*
(Pinches, 1903, p. 103)[195]

*...**all earlier gods were demoted** so that **he** got all of the glory.*
("Ancient Near East (Babylonia) Glossary", n. d., p. 17)[196]

Through this "gift," as well as through his *own* expansion into worldly affairs (as we'll soon see), Cain began to **overshadow** all of these gods, in a number of ways.[197]

And, it's interesting to discover how one source described an ancient Babylonian god (probably equated with Cain) as a "son of Bel" - yet, the same was *also* considered as one "in the likeness of Anu."[198] Cain, beyond being "a son," was also equated with both his father, and step-father! Here, it's obvious, that Cain, the Serpent and (even) Adam were so close that they were, quite often, known by the *same* name:[199]

Bel (the Serpent) was known as... the "older Bel" (lord), to distinguish him from Bel-Merodach of Babylon. (Mackenzie, 1915, p. 35)[200]

How confusing it is! Yet, now, we are beginning to see how the three were, so often, **confused**, one with another - resulting from the ways these early pagans seemingly needed to twist things, over time. Sometimes, when one needs to "cloud" the real truth, they need to resort to adding a lot of extraneous material, or, they need to make it all boil down to "smoke and mirrors." That is why we need to unravel it all like we are doing, here.

Yet, Cain (or Marduk) - through his "promotion" (by the Serpent) - would have become the *new*, lead protagonist for the gods, and be considered victorious over all of the "evil" things that Kingu (i.e. God, Adam and Abel) were able to bring to our civilization.[201] The Serpent and Cain, both, became accredited for "uncorrupting" their world at hand.

*Marduk (Cain) went forth to battle with the monster Tiamat, **who was slain**...*
(Clay, 1923, p. 66)[202]

*Marduk (Cain) **conquered** the face of the Deep...*
(Collins, 1998, p. 281)[203]

But, as we see, it's all just the *opposite* of what really happened - and, all from *their* point of view! As we've already stated, it's only *one* way or another - ultimately! This is their confusing world of subtle deception.

On top of Cain's elevation to "godhood," he, then, would go on to assign his mother a position in this early Babylonian "pantheon" of gods, as well. He was given all of the credit, here, as well. According to pagan ideology (interestingly enough), Eve would, eventually, follow alongside the *direction* of Cain and the Serpent, in certain periods of her life! Although she may have not been one hundred percent in the pagan camp, Eve may have felt the need to stayed along side of, or even live with, the Serpent - at least for a while (as we'll soon see)!

We've already discovered that Eve, and the Serpent, may have *both* had a say in what happened in the Garden of Eden, regarding its water-works. They both helped in dictating the irrigation processes, making sure that those who worked the fields were able to get water to all of the foliage. This, also, helped the beasts of burden around them to be watered, ultimately allowing their attempts at farming to be successful.

The two, most probably, maintained these same positions *after the Fall* (in pagan societies that would eventually sprout up). And, why not? They already had the expertise from the Garden. In fact, we do have a number of ancient written accounts, referring to something like this. Here is one:

- *The plow and the yoke he directed,*
- *...**Enki (Eve)** caused the... ox to...;*
- *To the pure crops he roared,*
- *In the steadfast field he made the grain grow;*
- *Enki (Eve) placed in their charge.*
- *The lord called to the steadfast field, he caused it to produce much grain,*
- *The... grains he heaped up for the granary,*
- *Enki (Eve) added **granary to granary**,*[204]

Obviously, it wasn't only *Adam* out there, helping to decide the best way to produce crops (or, even *bread*)!

As far as Adam, Cain seemed to have retained some respect towards his (adopted) father, as well. According to pagan and Christian traditions, Adam loved Cain, and cared for him, even after the murder of Abel. He even tried to give Cain some "going-away" supplies, after God banished him to the land of Nod. This meant a lot to Cain. Adam was very knowledgeable, and was considered the "father" of many individuals around him - whether he was their actual forebearer, or no. He, still, tried to be a good "father-figure" to many, and Cain respected that.

Most of the other fledgling pagans of the day, however, considered Adam to be a little misguided, and somewhat of a threat (as we've seen in the story of Adapa). Adam still wanted, and attempted, to follow the ways of God (as much as he could) - even though he messed up, a number of times. That's why Cain "allowed" Adam to become a pagan god, through it all. He, at least, "allowed" Adam to maintain *some* honor and dignity in his new religion.

So, as we notice, *Cain* was thought to be the one who made *a lot* of these major pagan decisions - even deciding on what direction of "godhood" to take his mother and adopted father.[205]

<u>The Fifty Names</u>
6 *(Cain) Who **makest strait** the direction of Anu (Adam), Bel (the Serpent), [and Ea (Eve)]...*[206]

*...**Without him** the sun-god, as judge, could not give judgment.*
(Pinches, 1906, p. 22)[207]

<u>The Seven Tablets of Creation</u>
34 *They set **him** (Cain) on the road which leadeth to peace and obedience.*[208]

*(Cain)... would be seen as initiating a **new world order**.*
(Collins, 1998, p. 281)[209]

Yes, this ancient "New World Order" of Cain, and his Serpent father, would become the foundation of *Mystery Babylon*, and so many of its subsequent "systems" (as we'll soon see)! Cain was also given the credit for "opening up" our world to so much knowledge and opportunity - so many ways to improve the harsh, post-Fall world the ancients now had to live in. Their problems were all *Kingu's* (or God's) fault - not Adam's; not Eve's; and (surely) not the Serpent's! It's all backwards! Regardless, many people accepted Cain, and whatever he came up with, with open arms! Paganism and *Mystery Babylon* was, now, in its infancy.

And, just because he gave people a lot of ways to, seemingly, improve their lives, that didn't mean he actually made their world a better place.[210] As most of us know, just because there flooded in a great deal of divine (or occult) knowledge, doesn't mean that this post-Fall society was on its way to being a society of peace and tranquility. In actuality, it became quite the opposite. With all of this divine knowledge out there, now, came an increase of **unfettered immorality and decadence** - which, eventually, began to drive the unwitting populous *back* into the direction of our post-world *chaos*… the thing they claimed they were attempting to "fix!" So, now we know that *Kingu* wasn't the problem - it was *them*! Beware of those continually accusing or pointing fingers at other individuals, when it is **they** who are doing exactly what they are, flat-out, trying to accuse others of! It's the ultimate mind bend of reality.

This also proves something else: there, assuredly, was a great deal of "otherworldly" knowledge hidden from us, in the past. That didn't mean that God was being "unfair" or "mean" to the ancient people. It's just that this knowledge, if used incorrectly, would probably end up making things a lot *worse* for everyone, in the end. It could hurt us, if it was abused or taken advantage of - and *abused* or taken advantage of it would assuredly become, knowing our fallen, human race.

We also know that, in the antediluvian world, things didn't just become bad because of these two original organizers of the religion (Cain and the Serpent). They had sympathizers out there. We (already) know that there were *other* inhabitants out there, ready and willing to help these two - with *angelic* qualities.

<u>The Creation of Man</u>
29 *Marduk (Cain), the King of the gods, divided…*
   above and below **the Anunnaki**.
33 *And had fixed their decrees for the Anunnaki of heaven*

and earth...[211]

The Anunnaki & Igigi

Well, just who or what were these early *Anunnaki*? They were, quite often, mentioned in early Babylonian accounts! Yet, as we recall (in a previous volume), there were traditions in the Bible about the *Nephilim* - those 50-or-so grumbling angels who continually complained about the creation of Adam. And, as we recall, they were, most probably, considered to be upper-level, terrestrial angels of the Garden (of whom the Serpent was probably akin to).

Pagan mythology also seems to have their *own* version of the Nephilim: known as the *Anunnaki*. The name *Anunnaki* could even stand for, "those who from heaven to earth came" or "conceived as begotten by the heaven-god **Anu** (Adam)..."[212] Could these have been the same, "paganized" angelic beings of our antediluvian world - those who mated with mortal women, and helped to corrupt the world? Some pagan accounts have even said that the Anunnaki were: "the greater gods of light."[213] We know that the Nephilim still "shined," somewhat, while in their terrestrial state. They were also said to be under Adam's (or **Anu's**) authority in the Garden.

And, interestingly enough, there were even sources that stated there were *50* of these Anunnaki, as well:

"The Great Lords were fifty in number…"
                                    (O'Brien, 1988, p. 87)[214]

Beyond sounding like their own version of the *Nephilim*, here, there was said to be another group of Babylonian angels in the area:

<u>The Enuma Elish</u>
4 *No Anunnaki*
5 *There was nothing…*
7 *No **Igigi** created,*[215]

It seemed that the *Igigi* were, at one time, counterparts of the Anunnaki.[216] But, they did appear to be a little different than these Anunnaki, in certain ways. So, just *who* may these individuals have been, and how were they different?

One author described the *Igi-gi* as, "Those **Who Observe and See**."[217] Wow, doesn't that sound familiar! We do have the *Watchers* of the antediluvian world! They "watched over" the human beings living below them, as well. We also recall that a number of antediluvian Watchers remained *in the sky*, after the Fall, "watching" and teaching the human race.[218] A number may have even come down to the ground, helping human beings in their terrestrial tasks on earth.

So, from this, we may be able to assume that the Igigi often came into temporal existence some time after the Anunnaki did. Because of this, we might be able to assume that the Anunnaki may have considered themselves "senior" angels, or angels "of the **older** generation."[219] The Nephilim lived in our terrestrial world since the time of the Garden, but the Watchers "fell," much later on. Could these Anunnaki, then, have been considered "senior" or "older," because they've been on our terrestrial world a lot longer than the Igigi? Or, could there, still, have been *another* reason why the Anunnaki were considered "senior?" The following ancient text may provide us some additional information:

<u>The Enuma Elish</u>
16 *Anu (Adam) made Nadimmud-Ea (Eve) in his image*

20   ...*Unmatched among the Igigi, his **ancestors**...*[220]

Because the Igigi appear to be being amongst *Adam's* "ancestors," we may be able to surmise that: when these angels were fashioned, their souls may have come from the same place as Adam's soul came from: **heaven**.[221] We know that God breathed a soul into Adam, from above. And, we've already postulated that the souls of the Nephilim (or Anunnaki) came from the supernatural area below - from the *Darkness of the Deep*. That gives us another way to divide these classes of angel - one with souls from *above*, and one with souls from *below*. So, if we already assume that these Anunnaki were the Biblical *Nephilim*, then could these *Igigi* actually be the heavenly Watchers?

Also, the Nephilim (or Anunnaki) - because their souls came *up*, from our previous world - could have been able to retain a great deal of *wisdom* (from the world before our own). This knowledge could also have allowed the Anunnaki to be considered "senior" or "older" in rank. We're not totally sure. What we are sure of, though, is that pagan sources often stated that the Igigi were, most probably, of a *laboring* class, assistants to the knowledgeable Anunnaki.[222] They were, often, thought of as craftsmen; particularly metal workers.[223] They, obviously, must have worked for their "superiors" - the Anunnaki.

A number of them were large in stature, and a number were also considered fairly short, squat or delicately built.

In ways, this does seem to collaborate our view of the Biblical Watchers. Most of the were, as we know, probably large or tall, angels. But, as we also recall, some of the mixed human offspring of angels and humans were actually *diminutive* in statures (i.e. midgets). It seems the potential for diminutive size may also be with these angels, either way. We're not sure. At least, we may be able to assume, in both Biblical and pagan traditions, that the Watchers (or Igigi) were considered (in a number of ways) angels of a *lesser* rank, or stature. Undoubtedly, the two were turned into major and minor "gods."

Another question may arise: *why* where these two groups of terrestrial angels put on the earth in the first place (according to *pagan* tradition)? We know that the Nephilim and Watchers were put there, according to Biblical tradition, to help Adam out, and help out in the workings of the Garden. Paganism, however, seems to twist this all around – and even points things *in the opposite* direction! They associate these terrestrial angels to one ancient, major event. What *they* could claim happen would involved a lot of hard work, a lot of grumbling, and the creation of one additional element to our world: *humankind*!

In one of the more popular ancient Babylonian texts - known as *Atrahasis* - we have the pagan rationale to *why* mankind was created. In selected pieces of this text, we have:

<u>*The Epic of Atrahasis*</u>
Anu (Adam) their father was king,
Their counselor warrior Enlil (the Serpent),
And Enlil took the earth for his people.

The gods had to dig out canals,
Had to clear channels
the lifelines of the land.
The gods dug out the Tigris river
And then dug out the Euphrates.
The Anunnaki of the sky
Made the Igigi bear the workload.
...they bore the excess,
Hard work, night and day.
They (the Igigi) groaned and blamed each other,
Grumbled over the masses of excavated soil:

(After this, the Igigi went to complain to Enlil (the Serpent); and exclaimed:)
We have put a stop to the digging.
The load is excessive, it is killing us!
Our work is too hard, the trouble too much!
...create a mortal man
So that he may **bear the yoke, the work of Enlil***,*
Let man bear the load of the gods!
Nintu (probably, Cain?) shall mix the clay
With his (the god Kingu's) flesh and blood.
Then a god and a man
Will be mixed together in clay.

(The divine woman who was now chosen to create man...)
...called up the Anunnaki, the great gods.
The Igigi, the great gods,
Spat spittle upon the clay

(Said this creator-woman:)
You have slaughtered a god together with his intelligence.
I have relieved you of your hard work,
I have imposed your load on man.
You have bestowed noise on mankind.
I have undone the fetter and granted freedom.[224]

According to this pagan view, mankind was only created to work for the Igigi, the Anunnaki, the Serpent and Anu (Adam)! Wow, what a contrast! Is this what the early pagan's thought of mankind - nothing but potential slaves? If the pagans of the past interpreted things as: men were created to "work for the gods," then, what if a number of pagan elites, in the future, began to believe that *they* were on their way to "godhood," or already were "gods," in human bodies? Wouldn't it just be natural for them to assume that all the rest of mankind was made to serve *them*, and provide them sustenance, and even feel *justified* about it all? That's something to think about, as we ponder things a little later.

Yet, those pagans of the past must have thought of themselves as members of those who actually *civilized* the world. Cain, the Serpent and (even) Eve were, assuredly, given credit for destroying those "society-wrecking" (and Godly) elements of our world, such as *Tiamat* and *Apsu* - and bringing *true* "civilization" to mankind.[225] Now, if these early pagan "gods" were the ones who helped fashion our world into "something better," or helped to "civilize" it, then, naturally, shouldn't they get something *back*, in return, for their efforts?

- *...let us create mankind.*
  The service of the gods *be their portion*,[226]

It seems that these ancient pagan texts did not really assume this new breed of *human being* would be much more than glorified slaves - *aborigines* to use for their own consumption.

<u>The Enuma Elish</u>
4 *I will knead blood and bone into a savage,*
5 *Aborigine will be its name.*
6 *The Aborigines* **will do the gods' work**
7 *The* **savages** *will* **set the gods free**.
29 *Kingu (i.e. God) planned the uprising!*
32 *...Ea executed him by cutting his throat.*
33 **Ea formed the Aborigines from Kingu's blood**,
34 **Marduk put the Aborigines to work**,
35 *And set* **the gods free**[227]

Wow, we have it all right there (in an ancient pagan text). Again, beware of those who are, often, out there, pointing the finger at your, calling your typical conservative or Christian ways "imperialistic," "racist," or what have you. So many people who hold onto "less than" conservative thoughts, or "less than" Christian ideologies, should really take a look at *their own*, ancient history, and see what the *true* founders of many faiths they follow might have actually thought, or believed. It's truly the pot calling the kettle black.

In Sumerian myth, we also see that Eve (or Enki) was considered their creator, "having devised men as **slaves** to the gods."[228] It's so interesting to note, here, all of the condescension and disrespect towards human individuals (by these pagans), as well their acceptable attitudes towards slavery. And, no, the Bible did **not** inspire their thoughts! No way.

And, yes, there are Biblical traditions that do mention *pre-Adamites*: human individuals put on earth to assist Adam (and the terrestrial angels) in the workings of the Garden, but the Bible never implied that it's great to have *slavery*, or wallow in it! At least in regards to the Garden, there had to be a hierarchy, here, or a working order. Any organization we have - even a garden - cannot function very well without order, or hierarchy. Too many cooks will indeed spoil that broth. Pagans have an ordered structure to their religion, and other systems; but, of course, that fact is either twisted around, or practically forgotten. Wasn't hell, also, said to have different levels of order, and hierarchy? And, it's funny how theology and religion with these pagan elements, or political factions that parallel paganism, often have members who rail about how "mean" or "oppressive" the God of the Bible is, but say nothing about their *own* perceptions of human beings and slavery, such as in the above. Apparently, as long as it's for the goodness of Cain, the Serpent, and the terrestrial angels (and other "elites"), then it's all right.

We, also, see how the ancient Anunnaki and Igigi were heading - full steam ahead - towards the ways of Cain and the Serpent:

The Seven Tablets of Creation
116 *Father Enlil (the Serpent) proclaimed his (Cain's) name, "Lord of the Lands."*
117 *All the Igigi **repeated the title**.*[229]

We know that (according to Biblical tradition) the Nephilim and Watchers were, also, quickly taken up by these same ways. Either way, Cain was considered their creator – the one who "made" them what they were![230] It's funny that, he was also given the credit for "allowing" his step-father Adam to be their preliminary supervisor (at least for a period a time).²³¹ God had nothing to do with this.

Of course, with all of these acclamations, Cain would quickly ascend into a well-respected leader of them all:

*(He is)… **sustainer** of the Igigi and the Anunnaki,*
                    (Rogers, 1912, p. 57)²³²

<u>The Seven Tablets of Creation</u>
112 *(He)… hath **made glad the hearts** of the Anunnaki,*
123 *He hath allotted stations to the Igigi and the Anunnaki.*²³³

Beyond helping to preside over the early irrigation (and digging) projects after the Fall, these two groups of angels would begin another endeavor, honoring their "great leader":

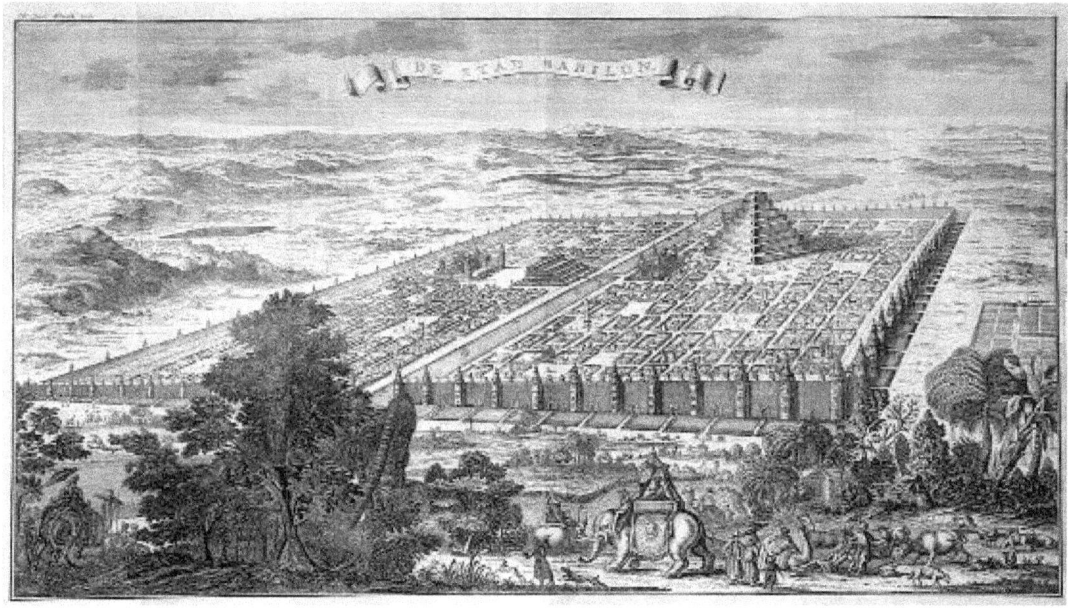

10 *All the lands were sea;*
31 *Lord Marduk piled up a dam at the edge of the sea;*
32 *…a swamp he made into dry land.*
36 *[Bricks he laid, the brick] mold he built;*
37 *[The house he built], the **city** he built;*

38 *[The city he made], living creatures he placed (therein)...*[234]

We know that Cain built at least one city, according to the Bible. But, we don't really know *how* he could have done it, all alone. What if these two groups of angels helped out?

Among these cities, one of them was, probably, built near the former Garden of Eden: called *Eridu*.[235] This also probably explains why Eridu was considered "the first city" of the plain (and continues to strengthen our postulation that this land of *Eridu* was, in fact, the same as the land *Eden* - the two words are very close, here)![236]

Beyond this city, there would be one more project for them to undertake, a major city-building project. This city would, now, be located to the north of them, a very special city, indeed - **Babylon**.[237] There seemed to be a number of ancient quotes, regarding this city's construction:[238]

*The Anunnaki, wishing to give an expression of their admiration for Marduk's heroism, decided to build him a shrine or temple. To this Marduk (Cain) agreed, and chose **Babylon**... The Anunnaki themselves made the bricks...*
$\qquad$ (Budge, 1931, p. 30)[239]

<u>The Seven Tablets of Creation</u>
46 *The **Anunnaki** wielded the hoe; for one year they moulded bricks...*[240]

So, to celebrate Cain's "coronation," the "gods built... the city of **Babylon**, where they transfer all their divine titles to Marduk (Cain)..."[241] Cain would, then, sanctify this city, and bless it. One text, also, makes mention of the fallen angels who had a huge hand in building it:

<u>The Seven Tablets of Creation</u>
52 *He (Cain) made the gods his fathers to take*
   *their seats... [saying]: "This **Babylon***
   shall be your abode."[242]

<u>Bilingual of Creation</u>
14 *Babylon was made...*

16 The holy city, the dwelling of the heart's desire, they proclaimed supreme.[243]

It was **here**, apparently, that the Nephilim, the Igigi, and all who *opposed* the God of the Bible would live, and *thrive*. They even founded a temple there, where they inscribed the 50 titles of their chief "god" into its walls - *Cain*. They dedicated this entire area to all that is pagan - an earthly *symbol* of their undying devotion to a supreme "god" - the "son of perdition," the son of the Serpent. So, because of this: "…Babylon first became the **capital** of the country, and *mistress* of the greater part of the known world."[244] No wonder the city was given the name that it had.[245] No wonder why Cain exclaimed:

*I will call its name Bab-ili ['Gateway **of the gods**'].*
                (Sitchin, 2010, p. 125-126)[246]

And, no wonder why this city of Babylon was so unique, **and so hated**, by God!

Hence, we go up another rung in the deciphering of *Mystery Babylon*.

Now that we've looked into the *pagan* view of God's Creation, the Garden of Eden, and the era after the Fall (as well as their "twists" of it all), let's look more into what might have *really* gone on in the Garden of Eden, itself, and what brought on the Fall. We'll take a look at these *deeper* elements to the story of Adam and Eve - and what *huge* ramifications all of these events may have had on our world, from then on.

Chapter 2

The Real Adam and Eve (Part I)

As we've seen, in the previous chapter, some of the earliest recorded gods and goddesses of early paganism were, most probably, the earliest characters of Genesis: Adam, Eve, Cain, Abel and, of course, the Serpent himself. With this knowledge at hand, we see that it really might be "a small world after all." Paganism and Biblical stories do not seem very far apart, at least in regards to the adoption of these same characters. As we've already stressed, throughout these volumes, putting together the mystery of ancient Babylon is a lot like trying to assemble a gigantic jigsaw puzzle:

> *If someone were to throw a thousands of pieces of a puzzle on the table and then throw away the box, you would struggle long time to find and understand what the whole picture is.* (Gayman, 1977, p. 15)[1]

Some who read this information will begin to see these revelations as "pieces" of that puzzle, coming together. Others just won't see it, and that's ok. These volumes are not for everyone. And, although it may be a little difficult to put all of these connections together, it's not impossible. Most of us will, hopefully, begin to see the "writing on the wall," the deeper into these stories we go.

With that said and done, in the next sections, we'll probably begin to take large strides into putting more pieces of this puzzle together. One very important piece lies in understanding the following:

He (God) breathed life's breath into Adam,
*Then stamped the final **mystery** [on him].*
- Adamgirk: The Adam Book of Arak'el of Siwnik p. 218[2]

What *mystery* might this be? Let's just say that one of the most important elements of this "Mystery" side of *Mystery Babylon* entails the mysteries that, in reality, relate to the workings of the *mind*! Many aspects of this *Mystery* portion reside in what goes on inside our brains, how we think, and why we end up behaving the way we do. A number of political and religious ideals we have, today, have originated from a *thought*, somewhere in this brain. In fact, almost every action a human being takes was, of course, preceded, first, by a *thought*. Understand the mind, and we can understand the actions. Understand the actions, and we can understand why our world is turning out the way it is.

Someone might say that, for example, they may feel a little *low*, inside. Another may say that, inside, they feel a kind of *darkness*. Yet, another may think like they are going through a living *hell*. Well, what might all of these mean… in regards to our deeper, supernatural world?

Beyond the figurative sense, could there actually be *duplicate* associations for words such as this? Could there, in the esoteric realm, be "parallels" to some words, with something *more*, or *deeper*, to these figures of speech? Let's see.

Let's look at an example: in our last section, we recall that, upon the death of her son, the goddess *Ishtar* (or *Eve*) "descended to the underworld." Now, did she *really* descend to a physical place? Or, could it be that she felt like she had? In her mind, she fell, or "descended", into such as deep state of mental *despair*, or anguish, that it felt like she was going through "hell." Of course, many will agree that certain phrases or words used, such as this, could be in a figurative sense. How about in ancient times? Could ancient authors have used some of these same figures of speech? But, in our case, a lot of what they were talking about actually related to something they already knew of, or believed in. We will see some examples of how these figures of speech were used, in ancient times. There are not a lot of them, as there are today; but, there were enough of them that may have, incidentally, caused a little confusion in our understanding of what may, or what may not, have been actual history. Again, wading through some of this muck, here, will also help us to learn a little more about our own, often-twisted history. If we do gather anything from the last section, here, we can take away the possibility for some kind of *mental* parallel, or significance, to a number of early, supernatural elements. Let's begin to see why all of this is important.

As we may already know, the ancients often used *symbols* in order to express certain spiritual concepts, or certain points-of-view, in their artwork. That's all that they really had to work with, at the time. They probably wanted to make sure the observer understood *all* the levels of symbolism they were trying to portray, and all of the deeper meanings behind their work. Over the years, however, some of these meanings probably turned to dust. With the slow, gradual changes in cultures and empires over the years, these symbols may have also undergone a good number of changes. A *wing*, pictured on some ancient deities, for example, may have once stood for, not only a literal wing, but the deities' ability to "swiftly" move back and forth between two worlds - the natural and supernatural worlds. Now, we take a look at some of these ancient pictographs and assume that, most probably, the ancient artists was trying to tell us that their god could *fly*, as a bird. But, of course, that, most probably, was not the original intention.

Now, we also discover that there could have been symbols taking into account some of the *mental* or *emotional* elements associated to the individual an artist is trying to portray! As we see, below, the following reliefs describe *Ishtar/Enki's* (or *Eve's*) ascent from this underworld:

Again, seeing a god ascending *out* of the underworld, here, might easily be taken as something literally. And, in a number of cases, it's good to assume so. But, in a few, this could have been associated with something *mentally* going on with the individual - in this case, her coming out of a state of depression. Some people, today, even think that heaven and hell are here on earth - it's all a state of *mind*.

Let's look at another example, relevant to our discussion. The color *black* could also have mental and emotional connotations to it, beyond just being a dark color. *Black*, or *blackness*, could also have been used to helped describe, or symbolize, one's *darkened*, emotional state. It seems the color could easily be associated with one's depression, despair, or the like.

It also seems clear to us that one's moral character could *also* have colors associated with it.

> ...*the color of the wicked was like the **bottom of a pot** on account of the wickedness of their doings...*   - *3 Enoch (The Hebrew Book of Enoch)* Ch. 44[3]

Wicked people resemble a darkened, underbelly of a pot, according to the above quote. It only makes logical sense to assume that there could be *something* more to certain ancient descriptions, when we recall the *number of ways* something could, indeed, be interpreted. Looking at our next example, and we see:

*…then God sent him (Adam)… down to earth with **blackened** face…*
(Al-amili, n. d., p. 2)[4]

Although it may be easy for many to assume that Adam, in the above quote, may have had his face, physically, turned **black as coal**, it doesn't necessarily mean that. Another probable explanation may present itself, here: God allowed Adam to understand the guilt, sadness and depression he *should* have felt, over his choices in the Garden, and a temporary "darkness," then, invaded his heart and mind. Or, he may have felt as though he had a *darkened* soul, inside. His wasn't *turned* black - he didn't begin to show external features of another *race* as a his punishment.

These internal negativities could have also shown up as outer *facial* expressions, as well. In ancient artwork, as well as ancient literature, these figurative descriptions were, obviously, there… to give the artist even more expression. Interestingly enough, the ancient Greeks even made abstracted "deities" out of certain negative elements of the mind, such as *Blame, Distress, Deceit* and *Strife*.

Soon, more examples will become apparent, and we'll begin to see how they all may apply to the *mystery* side of *Mystery Babylon*. It's obvious: one problem with putting together our "puzzle" lies with that, either unintentionally or intentionally, some of the original meanings of these historical texts or illustrations have become obscured over time. So, understanding these deeper, "psychological" elements of *Mystery Babylon* will, as well, become a lot more important to us, as time goes on.

As we'll see, so much of what we are about to gather, regarding the *real* story of the Garden of Eden, may **not** coincide with traditional thoughts about the topic. Beware of how easy it is to hear one thing, and quickly make judgments about it. Also, a lot of this information certainly will not "fit in" with most *all* modern, Christian interpretation. That's why we really need to think *deeper*, about it all. And, a vast majority of it comes *right* from these ancient writings, or some accredited modern author on the subject. And, if we are able to add in all of these additional elements to our discussion, we'll probably be able to understand it so much more, and go a lot *deeper*. Sometimes, piecing together "new" thoughts may have to lie in the resurrection of "the old and forgotten." Sometimes, to get real answers, we have to approach some sensitive subjects, and get "our hands dirty."

With all of this in tow, let's, again, continue with a *deeper* look into what may have really happened - "in the beginning."

The Former World - Of Angels

*It will come as a surprise to many to learn that angels inhabited this earth **before** the creation of man.*   (Armstrong, 1985, Part 8)[5]

As long as we're starting at the beginning, we may begin to wonder: what was the world really like before Adam, and our Six-Day Creation? What happened, to turn it all into *chaos*? And, why would this even be relevant to our story of the Garden of Eden? As we recall, from Volume 1, our former cosmos was destroyed, and all human (and angelic) life on this world went with it. There could have even been a number of times that this cycle occurred - an organized "world," or cosmos, was destroyed, and then recreated, once again. Although the Bible doesn't directly point to what happened in the world before our own, and *exactly* how it was destroyed, there are a number of ancient sources that may. Some are Judaic (such as the *Apocalypse of Baruch* and *Philo*), most are Islamic. The Islamic historian, *Tabari*, for example, provided a majority of information on this previous world. A number of his accounts speak of a confrontation between those terrestrial angels who supposedly inhabited this world before our present. Apparently, there must have been some kind of civilization, here, with angelic beings and, most probably, human beings. These former worlds obviously were not perfect, much like our world, today, because they had to be destroyed.

We may see some evidence of this in the story of the Garden of Eden: looking out for any possible *upstart* within their current establishment, God told Adam and Eve to keep the Garden, and *guard* what they had. Now, we see that the Garden of Eden actually needed to be *guarded* from any possible harm, or problem that may eventually befall it. Why? If the world before the Fall was considered so perfect (as many people, today, speculate), then just *who* or *what* would Adam and Eve have to guard it from?

God may have already understood that our terrestrial "world" (our present, physical cosmos) would always contain some kind of imperfection, or possible problem. To compensate, God may have sent specific angels (visible or invisible), to assist the human race, and make sure everything flowed smoothly. Yet, for whatever reason, every previous world before us did not work out. *Something* went sour.

According to these above authors, there were terrestrial **angels**, in our former world, who, quite often, were a part of the problem.

*The **rebellion** of the angels had caused the darkness.*
(Armstrong, 1985, Part 10)[6]

We also recall (from Volume 1), that, around the timeframe of Genesis 1:2, God was ready to bring human souls back, from the previous world, and up from the *Darkness*. He was ready to refashion the previous world into the cosmos we have, today. One important reason that the Garden may have needed protection resided in terrestrial angels being brought up from the previous world, as well. Quite probably, a good number angelic souls were, once again, brought up, into this world, commissioned by God to serve in this new cosmos. Any humans brought up, to also live in this current cosmos, would not have the same knowledge (and experience) these angelic souls may have. Of course, they already may have had knowledge of this previous world, and what happened to bring it all down. This information would have, of course, given them huge advantages over any human being who lived along side of them. What if some of these angelic beings began to take advantage of their positions, and begin to go down the pathway of corruption? What if they began to exploit their superior knowledge, and take advantage of the human beings around them, and any vulnerabilities they may have?

*...in the grey dawn of history there were men who possessed the **knowledge of God**.*
(Bristowe, 1950, p. 8)[7]

If this was the case, then where did these ancient people get such information? If there were those around who already had the "higher knowledge of God," then we, possibly, could assume that higher *angelic* beings may have already begun to give mankind some of it. Was this right to do, however?

Let's go one better: where would the (*angelic*) *Serpent* of the Garden of Eden get all of his knowledge from? And, what did he do with it? Quite probably, terrestrial angels did have a great deal of knowledge, and could have easily maintained a good deal of knowledge *from the world* before Adam. Could this have been one reason why the Serpent could have easily seduced Eve, and eventually Adam - because he understood how things worked in the previous world?

The scary part of this Garden story also lies in the possibility of two angelic forces - Satan (or Sammael) and the Serpent - having an arsenal of occult knowledge, by which to deceive the lowly humans. Let's take another look at both of these angels, and some possible advantages they may have had over everyone.

Sammael

If we look into it all further, we'll see that there may have actually been two major angelic players in the world before Adam. They, both, may have even been in a leadership position, actually. The first, *Sammael*, apparently came out of the heavenly realm. According to one source, he was even thought to have been fashioned out of the "splendor of God himself," or was considered "the firstborn" of heaven.[8] Simply put, he was, at one time, one of the most important and powerful angels of God, an angel who once had a high rank in heaven.

Sammael was also known thought to be a *Cherub* (or military) angel.[9] He was no ordinary Cherub, however. Some traditions state that Sammael had a major role in what happened to our previous world, as well. He was known as the "Angel of Death" - one who had "grim and destructive duties." He was also known as "one who disturbs the heaven and earth."[10] What exactly did he do?

> *(God and His angels speaking)… we established him (Sammael) in command of all the armies which we created, and they all obey him.*
> *- Enthronement of the Archangel Michael* 3[11]

It's pretty easy to assume that, with those titles, Sammael would have been a major instrument in the destruction of the previous world. He could have even been the *lead* angel, assigned by God, to carry out His judgment. Sammael probably destroyed angels and humans alike - giving him the title, "Angel of Death." He took his gruesome task, and was serious about it. Somebody had to do it.

This angel was probably important to God because of his unique fortitude, here. God may have even intended to allow Sammael dominion over this current world, if he played his cards right. That was, at least until Adam was created! What made God change his mind?

Well, God may have understood there was something going on, inside of him, which was very wrong.[12] With all of his power and recognition, a good amount of *pride* also began to accumulate.[13] It may have all "gone to his head."

God knew what was going on inside of his heart, even if the rest of the angels may not have, and made a decision. As most of us could guess, as soon as God decided to place a human as leader of the Garden (and not Sammael), this would have allowed him to choose rebellion - in a major way. Soon, he would attempt to do anything he could to make Adam look unworthy, or a bad choice - only to be given new titles, by God, such as "The Accuser of the Brethren," or Satan.

We'll now see that, even the meaning of the name *Sammael* had changed: *Samma - el* would soon be considered "the poison - of God," because *he* would be the one primarily responsible for poisoning the minds of so many of the human beings under Adam's authority.

The "Wise" Serpent

Also, as we know, there were probably more than *one* serpent around, at these earliest of times. There was said to be at least *50* Nephilim angels who worked around the Garden of Eden, and they could also be classified as "serpents."[14] And, that one Serpent of Genesis was probably one of the Nephilim - more likely, the leader over all of them. He was not just a serpent, but **the** Serpent.

These Nephilim could also have been known to have other names, such as *Anunnaki* or *Jinn*. Whatever their name, however, these terrestrial, earth-dwelling angels were still thought to be amongst the top keepers of Paradise, under Adam.[15] As we know, the Serpent, as well as these 50 Nephilim serpents, could have also had important roles in the world **before** Adam. That's why they were brought back by God, again, into *this* current cosmos, to do much of the same work.[16]

We'll now discover another very important ancient symbol, which may have changed over the years: *the Serpent* himself! As we recall: there may have been a number of ancient symbols that could have *mental* or *emotional* connotations associated with them. The Serpent, in ancient times, was subjected to a great deal of symbolism. From what the Bible gives us, one of the Serpent's names - *Nachash* - wasn't, in fact, his proper name; it was more of a descriptive *title*. One meaning of *Nachash* was "enchanter" - one skillful in the art of enchanting or soothsaying.

Quite often, early pictographs of a serpent may not actually represent an *actual* serpent, itself. One important (and, probably lost) *mental* association with a serpent could actually be related to the *wisdom* of a particular god, or human being![17] This serpent symbol was, most probably, an ancient symbol of *wisdom*. Whether these 50-or-so serpents (the Nephilim), as well as the Serpent himself, could have (physically) *looked* just like the terrestrial human beings around them, or, if they had some distinct, serpentine features to their face, we're not totally sure. Probably, it was a little bit of both. But, one thing we are fairly sure of: these serpents were, indeed, very, *very* wise.

…be ye therefore wise as serpents…
- *Mat.* 10:16 (KJV)

This is a revealing "piece" to our puzzle of *Mystery Babylon*. Ancient interpreters of the Bible often tried to portray that, somehow, the Serpent was an actual *snake* - an animal. All the while, they failed to explain just how a snake could use his vocal cords and talk, and carry on an intelligent, rational conversation with a human being. They failed to realize that this serpent, and all of its pertinent information in the Bible (and other sources), was actually a terrestrial, human-like *angelic* being - a being of great wisdom.

The Biblical "Nachash" was known by this title because he had a repertoire of "other-worldly," occult knowledge - most of it, probably, from his experience with the world before Adam!

Snake or serpent references, in ancient Mesopotamian art, "identified divine wisdom, sexual energy, and a guard over the world domains."[18] These talents could have easily given the Serpent an "upper hand," in regards to how he dealt with Adam and Eve, and gave him the ability to easily seduce Eve, as well.

*This is the secret (or **mystery**) of the holy language, that a serpent is a **seraph**, as an angel is called **ser**aph.* (Anonymous, 1834, p. 53)[19]

The prefix *ser* (of *serpent*) stands for "higher being." Some serpents could have been blessed enough to be thought of as being in a "physician," or "doctorate," class. Those who reached this high angelic rank were the *Seraphim* - the *serpent* angels.[20]

The Serpent and Sammael did have some similarities, but they had some differences, as well. The Serpent, as we've just seen, was from an academic, or "doctorate," background, Sammael an elevated member of the "military." The Serpent was also anointed to be a *terrestrial* angel, unlike the heavenly Sammael. And, as Sammael probably, once, governed over the (supernatural) heavens above the earth, the Serpent, once, probably ruled over, or governed, the lower areas - the physical earth, itself.[21]

This terrestrial, earth-walking Serpent was, once, even considered extremely *devoted* to God (believe it or not). He was thought of as "the foremost of worshipers among the angels and the best of their scholars."[22] He even was thought to have "zealously worshiped God," to the utmost degree.[23] All of this pre-world knowledge and devotion could have opened some doors for him, in God's world of Adam - if he would have handled it right.

Yet, his zealous determination could have also opened some negative doors for him, as well. He began to reek of *haughtiness*![24] He started to become so pleased with himself that, over time, he started to think he was "superior" to everyone around him - especially Adam.[25] Because of this pride, the Serpent, then, began to be "overbearing toward his Lord."[26]

We have already brushed upon another name for the Serpent: *Azazel* (or *Azazil*).[27] Before he began to succumb to this pride, and commit mighty acts of disobedience, he was strong in the ways of God. Azazel's name actually means "the strength" or "strong one of God."[28] After his rebellion, it became pretty apparent that he would about be viewed, from then on, as one who rebelled "with strength," or was the "strong one" *against* God.

Free Will

What could have happened to these two, for them to want to leave their lofty positions? Why would they show such animosity towards their Lord? The answer is simple. It's something that we see blasted all over today's media: bigotry, prejudice, racism, etc. The difference is: their "racism" was a lot like we hear, now. But, this time, it involved terrestrial, angelic beings and mankind. These angels were against mankind simply because of what they were made of, and how they looked!

It all began when they made up their mind that God valued *mankind* more than them - valued them enough to make one man in charge. These thoughts apparently began deep inside of leaders, most notably, Sammael and the Serpent. They, then, began to utilize what God gave every man (and angel): free will.

We hear a number of quotes, today, about how great the "power of choice" is.[29] This is all so true. Even back then, both angels and mankind were able to decide for *themselves* whether or not to follow God. Some would, stubbornly, veer away from God, and use their God-given gifts to fend for themselves. They allowed their own pride to get in the way of their rationality.

> *...happiness is only attained by the free will agreeing in its freedom to accord with the will of God... and in such disobedience (one) found misery.*
> (Baring-Gould, 1881, p. 15)[30]

A number of angels, around the time of Adam's creation, were about to openly voice their own opinions to God's plan. And, His plans were about to begin in the Garden of Eden - with Adam at the helm.

Voice they did.

Envy and Jealousy

The angels also ended up showing "jealously at humanity's 'appointment' as supreme authority under Yahweh (God) on earth - as opposed to the sons of God getting that job..."[31] Mankind - particularly their newly-appointed leader Adam - was considered to be God's man for the job, which transpired into a big threat to these top terrestrial and celestial angels. Negative thoughts began to flow, such as, "God will love him more than He does us."[32] Adam's position also began to arouse *envy* - in the Serpent, especially.[33] From envy comes scorn.

Both Sammael and the Serpent became "distaining" towards Adam, while being "...proud of their cause."[34] *Distaining*, simply, means, "to look upon or treat with contempt; despise; scorn," "consider *beneath* one self," or "to think unworthy of."[35] Pride and distain are terms that, seemingly, will come up, again and again, by individuals who want to move towards this "other side" (as we'll see).

These angels were about to let their negative thoughts out, for all to see.

The "Worship" of Adam?

> *Said Satan... "entering into paradise shalt place me near to those two **lumps of clay** that are newly walking upon the earth."*
> - *Gospel of Barnabas* 40[36]

Who were these "lumps of clay?" This sure sounds like a distaining comment! Maybe, even little prejudiced? As we'll see, the upcoming *addition* of Adam to their world, in the opinion of some top angels, would translate into a major insult to their own feelings of *superiority*, a challenge to their own knowledge base, an intrusion into their lofty self-opinions. The Serpent and Sammael would be the ones who took it to the extremes, a lot more personally than all the rest - obviously, because of the positions they once had.

God, however, knew what they were thinking, and was going to do something to challenge their sovereignty to the *utmost*:

> *...(the) Lord said unto the angels: Lo! I am about to place a viceroy in the earth.*
> (Al-amili, 2004, p. 1)[37]

A *viceroy*, simply, is "a regal official who runs a country, colony, or city province in the name of and as representative of the monarch."[38] Adam, then, would become the *representative* of God's leadership in His newly-refashioned order of things. Man, especially *Adam*, was to be His "Crown of Creation," not the angels. God did not do this to necessarily downgrade them, nor did He create Adam to become some kind of idol. This "prostration before Adam by Angels was not for Adam but for *obeying* God and *endearment for Adam*."[39] Adam, also, wasn't out to elevate himself, because of the position God gave him, either. He was just there to do things the way God wanted, and remained obedient. God really loved that, and wanted the best for this man, as well as other obedient men and women around him. Regardless, this mutual love would not be welcomed by the surrounding angels:

> *It happened, while they were all worshipping, that we (the Elohim - God and the rest of His angels) came to the first angel whom we had created. The firstborn said to him (God), "I will never worship him who is **less than I**."*
> - *Enthronement of the Archangel Michael*[40]

Sammael, that "firstborn" of heaven, really considered Adam to be extremely *inferior*.[41] If one really thinks about it: just *who* was the first "racist" of our world? Who would be the first individual to feel "superior" over another? It may not be who many of us might think: it was *Satan*. Let's look more at how Sammael (i.e. Satan) began to feel the way he did.

He continued:

"Shall we then adore a being formed from dust?"
(Graves and Patai, 1964, p. 82)[42]

Well, most of us know that, according to the Bible, Adam was fashioned from *dust*, lowly dust. It was, in actuality, from a specific type of red, sandy dust - not hard ground; not clean, black soil (like other pre-Adamites may have been fashioned from). To begin this formulation, God also added a little bit of water to this dust, which turned it into a mud-like substance (or a *clay*) within His hands.[43] As special as one may begin to assume Adam was considered, most of us know, already, that dust is truly *nothing* special. *Dust*, actually, is symbolic of anything "more lowly and substantial **even than earth**…"[44] Wow, if the other pre-Adamites were fashioned from something else, then that makes Adam even *lower*, in his formulation, that them!

Yet, why would God want to create Adam, His *viceroy* of all people, out of something *less* than other people around him - something as worthless and insubstantial?

*(Adam was made)… with poor material, that in this way might be shown the admirable **skill** of the craftsman.*
- Barhebraeus' Scholia on the Old Testament 6b 7[45]

And:

…from such a worthless material, He (God) might bring [man] to divine glory.
- Adamgirk: The Adam Book of Arak'el of Siwnik p. 197[46]

There's a reason for everything. This time, it wasn't racism or superiority, it was to emphasize *a way of thinking*. There really seems to be a *mental* connotation, here. It's a strange, "spiritual" way of looking at the how things work in this world: many might, originally, believe that what one is "made out of" would, supposedly, stand as a predictor of what they were, or how they were ranked. Not so, with Adam. A viceroy over all the people - out of lowly dust? Those formed out of this humble *dust* should, in actuality, want to live out their lives in *humble*, and modest, ways. Adam was created in a way to demonstrate something: one should not, normally, be chosen as a leader who becomes arrogant, or prideful - but, rather, to just understand his or her place, under God, and roll with it.[47] "Modesty, therefore, was to be a prime quality of a viceroy, in God's brave, new world."[48]

> *When we are humbled we learn to respect proper limits… he (God) gave him (Adam) complete control of visible things lest out of ignorance of the composition of his own being he might conjure up inflated notions of his own importance and transgress the limits proper to him.*   - *St. Chrysostom* Homilies on Genesis, Homily 12[49]

Self-absorbed *pride* was to be nowhere in Adam's thoughts. But, of course, we see it in Sammael and the Serpent! This attitude of *humility* seemed very important to God, now - again, quite *the opposite* of how the Serpent and Sammael were beginning to carry on.

Composition

Beyond being created of *dust*, God had more things in store for this special formulation. As we know, it wasn't necessarily the color of Adam's skin, nor his outward appearance, but the way he *thought* about things, and the way he *viewed* things, that made him special… hands down.

God wanted to show this new world that it really doesn't matter *what* a person was made of, it's what they *did* with what they had that made all the difference! It was individual *choice*; it was *attitude* - not being from something "more worthy." This will become so important, as we read on. We recall that *Abel* was probably a son of the Serpent himself - even *that* didn't stop him from having the right attitude, and making right the choices (to obey his God with proper sacrifice)!

So, in a way, this composition of Adam allowed him to *shine*. Even beings from such a seemingly "unworthy" substance like *dust* could accomplish great things. Again, this is so important, and we're revisit this again, later.

Still Not Good Enough for Sammael & the Serpent

These angels would have no part of this "new way" of God. They were old school - they were made from a "heavenly" material. Wouldn't that be good enough to keep Sammael and the Serpent "on top?" Obviously, it wasn't, because God knew their hearts. He knew their pride. He knew the two were at the "boiling point" of emotional **passion**, because of this all. God proclaimed to Sammael, point blank, about how it was with him, and how it was going to be: "…this creature (Adam)… *surpasses* you in wisdom and understanding."[50]

Yet, just because Adam was made from something "less" than Sammael didn't mean he didn't have some exceptional qualities. God helped Adam out, of course, in this all, here - because he wasn't making friends easily. Sammael probably couldn't keep it in, and spoke out. And, as a probable result of his discontentment towards God's plan, Sammael was no longer allowed to enter the Paradise land - the Garden of Eden.[51]

Next, the Serpent was beginning to get a little vocal, and complained that his life (in this world) would only become a "mundane existence," if Adam would be the Earth's new viceroy.[52] Since the Serpent felt a lot of the same, he may have only been allowed limited access to the Garden, as well. Being "demoted" in these ways only upset them both, all the more.[53]

Why wasn't Adam's *lowly* composition, at least, be enough justice to these angels - to make them feel a little more content about their own selves? If they were on such a "higher" level than Adam, in so many ways, then why were they starting to become so intimidated by a human creature made out of this lowly earth?

Dust vs. Fire

Just like these angels, Adam may, at first, have radiated a supernatural "light," in much the same way.[54] This "light" was, often, regarded "as the first manifestation of God's essence,"[55] and a typical angel was considered "a spiritual essence consisting entirely of *light*."[56] As discussed in the first volume, this "light" may be also been linked to the "first" day of creation - because a number of angels could have been brought up from the Darkness on this day.

Since Adam had this same "brightness" as these angels, he may have even been built *not to age*.[57] The angels probably felt a little intimidated, here. There was a terrestrial, *human* being out there, on the same "level" as them (at least, in a few regards).

> *His (Adam's) person was so handsome that the very sole of his foot obscured the splendor of the sun.* (Ginzberg, 1909, p. 28)[58]

It's interesting to see, here, how Adam was considered so "radiant" with heavenly light that he was even thought to have *outshone the sun*, at times. Wow. We recall, in our last section, how Adam and the *sun* probably had some parallels. Now, we can see some more reasons to *why*. One author even stated that Adam was fashioned, "for the *service of the Holy One*, and the orb of the sun for the *service of mankind*."[59] In other words, Adam and the sun were similar in such a way because the two were both considered *symbols* of the highest authority in the world! They both would benefit the earth in positive ways: Adam in a *spiritual* way (as being God's viceroy), and the sun, itself, would benefit the earth in a *natural* way (with its warmth and life-giving properties). We, now, can see even *more* reasons why the ancients probably associated Adam (and, eventually the Serpent) with the sun - both were fashioned for the service of mankind!

As an earthly "shepherd" over animals, people and angels alike, Adam wasn't exactly the same as the other angels in **one** respect: while both angels and Adam radiated heavenly light, Adam was *still* made from that lowly dust - and, a number of the angels were made out of a supernatural, or divine, fire (also called a "smokeless" fire).[60] Most of us know the characteristics of *fire*: it can become extremely hot. It can easily get out of control. It can quickly burn and scorch. Fire could be *dangerous*, if not corralled, controlled or put out. Could this supernatural *fire* have some *mental* significances to it? We know that *dust* parallels *humility*, in certain ways. Could *fire* also have parallels with the way an individual might *think*? It sure seems so.

We've already seen that, although seemingly "inferior" to some, Adam's composition of *dust* could given him some unique mental qualities, such as *humility*. The angels would have all of that fiery passion, on the other hand. There is a difference:

*Clay is not inferior to fire. It has characteristics of calmness, clemency, endurance and growth. Fire is **violent, hasty**, and it burns...* (Kathir, 2009, p. 32)[61]

The meaning of *clemency* is the "disposition to be merciful," or to be "moderate in the severity of punishment due." In other words, Adam could have had more of a tendency to show leniency, mercy and love to those around him.[62] What about the angels, who were composed of this divine fire?

*...soil (an earthly element) is more **beneficial and better** than fire, as in the soil there are qualities of serenity, gentleness, perseverance, and growth. While in fire there are qualities of frivolity, impatience, haste and burning.* (Kathir, 2003, p. 24)[63]

So, anyone (i.e. human beings) born from *soil*, or *dust* of the earth, could, possibly, lean towards having different qualities to their character. This could give us a good deal of insight to why these angels might have felt so much dissent - and were so passionate about it. A number of these angels could have actually *chose* to think differently than human beings, as well as maintain a different attitude!

These angels, relying *solely* on their nature, could have easily led with a "fiery" disposition - with more *emotions*, with greater *passions* and, often, with more of an *impatient demeanor* to them. Adam and the human race were fashioned to show a more *serene* way of looking at things - acting *gentler* in thought or action. It does make a difference. This, obviously, seemed to be the way God wanted those in this *new* world to behave.

With his perseverance, Adam worked the Garden with "continued effort to do or achieve something despite difficulties, failure, or opposition."[64] He didn't quickly give up on any task he had, even if it posed a little difficulty. He didn't complain. He didn't murmur. He didn't even play "the victim." Most of all: he didn't "blow up," in a passionate fireball of emotions. He took responsibility for his actions, and tried to make the *right* choice - not the easy one! Adam strove to make something out of the Garden, and *himself* - to be the best he could be. Above all, Adam tried not to let his emotions, or his *pride*, get the better of him - nor did he allow any of that to obstruct his vision of what he needed to accomplish in this life, and in his *respect* towards his heavenly Creator. All of these traits gave the people and angels around him a reason to respect him - as a *beacon* of high moral character.

Most of the angels around Adam understood their role, and would subject themselves to Adam's authority. Sammael, the Serpent, and a few other angels, on the other hand, utilized their physical "makeup" to its fullest potential. They became "fiery" in their resistance! As one might suspect, a being from *fire* may easily decide to act with a good deal of emotions, passions, or be more apt to exhibit qualities of "frivolity, impatience, haste, and burning." The word *frivolity* can be equated to "**thoughtlessness, idleness**, triviality, inconsequentiality, and foolishness" - the *opposite* of "thinking before you act;" the opposite of "getting down to business in a serious way;" the opposite of using common sense; and, the opposite of being concerned about the results of one's thoughts or deeds. The Serpent and Sammael, both, were beginning to let their emotions run amuck - they were allowing their "fire inside" to take over their rational thinking. This will all be so important, later on, as we get into how people think, and do things the way they do. But, for now, these angels may have even considered their ways of thinking as "a step above" Adam, because *they* were made of something superior - and *closer* to the divine.

As stated, it's vital to understand all of these *mental* attributes going on, around the Garden of Eden story. As we now see (in regards to Serpent and Sammael): it was "his natural disposition and evil composition that betrayed him… (as he was created from fire)."[65] Each were allowing their selves to be deceived, rather than just "thinking things over," which, in the end, compelled each one "to baseness."[66]

Adam's Different Mind

The "mental" parallels associated with Adam's formulation (i.e. from dust) were not the only thing about him that was different. God, as many of us might know, created Adam for an *unique* purpose - top management. This, assuredly, would have added fuel to those "fires" of angelic **envy**.[67] And, on top of this, God would "breathe" a soul directly into Adam - a strong, *rational* soul![68] This *soul* would come from God's *own* hand. With that, it only makes sense to assume: the ways that Adam was known for could be the ways that God would have wanted mankind, in general, to *think*, and *behave*, in this brave, new world. It only makes sense.

So Adam created on earth with Breath from above.
                                    (Schwartz, 2004, p. 136)[69]

...the "breath of life" might reasonably be taken as indicating that man received the non-material or spiritual side of his being from his Maker...
                                    (Brandon, 1963, p. 124)[70]

It wouldn't make sense for God to create Adam (by His own hand), and, then, make him His viceroy over the garden (and, as an example to others), **just** to favor the "fiery" ways these angels thought, and carried themselves. So, assuming Adam's ways are the *new* ways that mankind should be using, let's look a little deeper into Adam's soul, and what it was all about.

This soul, or "breath of life," may have had some *mental* connotations to it, as well. We may also begin to discover, here, how the above *soul* could, in actuality, equate to a person's use of their *conscious* mind, or rationality.

Apparently, this *intellect* of Adam was something special, but it would not have been the same as many in our world often define *intelligence*, today.[71] It wasn't necessarily how smart Adam was, or his I.Q., but (first and foremost) the *ways* he thought about things, his attitudes, and *what* he did with what he had.[72] One author describes Adam's gift of intelligence as his "living soul" - of which the soul was equated, here, to one's reflective or intellectual life.[73] In other words, Adam was self-aware, *reflective* of his surroundings - and, not just an emotional powerhouse. He always tried to remain in his conscious thought, and not "lose it." He, also, probably understood and faced up to what he did.

With this, it seems logical that he was given the capacity to reasonably understand feelings of **guilt**, and how one should deal with these feelings. Interestingly enough, Adam was also known as the "blusher." *Blushing*, as stated in the last volume, could easily have been considered an *outward*, physical characteristic of one who feels *inner* guilt, shame or embarrassment. He was able to *show* red, or blood, in the face - when it was time for him to feel embarrassed. This could have, possibly, even been considered a "failsafe" by God, to make sure that Adam was *outwardly responsible* for his actions. When he was guilty, it would, literally, show up *on his face*.

Beyond this outward ability to show guilt, Adam, apparently, had other mannerisms about him. Interestingly, the ancient Romans often linked the word *man* or *manu* (by which the Hebrew word *Adam* could also be equated) "with personified intelligence and prudence."[74] The word *intelligence* could also mean, "the ability to govern and discipline oneself by the use of **reason**."[75] *Prudence* means, "Shrewdness in the management of affairs."[76] In other words, we see, once again, that Adam did not go "overboard" with his thinking. He thought things out *before* he did them, and maintained a "level head."

Another meaning of *intelligence* we have, here, is a "basic eternal quality of **divine** Mind" - interesting the link to the *divine*, here.[77] These ways of thinking must have made Adam famous to those around him.[78] We recall, in Gen. 2:19-20, that Adam was even involved in a contest (between he and the terrestrial angels of the Garden): whomever could name all the animals (and/or people?) that walked in front of them would be named the winner. We know who won. The angels were taken back by this defeat. What the angels lost - most importantly to them - was their *pride*.

Although they did lose, Adam remained *humble*, throughout; and, once again, the angels did not take note of his example. God wanted those terrestrial angels (and humans, alike) to understand each other's role in this world, and follow the lead of His viceroy, Adam, in numerous circumstances.

All of the Sex Around Him

Speaking of this test, there may, actually, be a little more to it all, than just naming names. Around this same time, a number of the pre-Adamites and Adamites, as well as actual animals around him, all seemed to have mates, or were with a significant other. And, with a lot of these pairings, sexual exchanges were, most probably, taking place. Adam knew that most of the couples around him were enjoying each other's company, and he probably felt quite alone.[79] According to a few ancient sources, he may have even tried to cohabitate with some of the other women around him - ultimately, not getting along with any of them.[80]

There is a very interesting account that states the following: after Adam became manager of the Garden, both Sammael and the Serpent (as we know) spoke out against it. So, God "demoted" these angels, in rank and stature. Because they did not seem to learn from this punishment, God may have decided to punish Sammael even *more*, for whatever reason! He could have, at the time Adam was looking for a mate, took *Lilith* (the female consort to Sammael) and, actually, gave her to Adam, to be his significant other!

This surely infuriated Sammael - the most significant female in his existence was now in the arms of the one he hated most. Obviously, this was all by design - his extreme thoughts of *pride* probably merited this resolve - to humble him, severely. There had to be some manner of punishment for such dissention.

Adam and Lilith, ultimately, did not get along, probably because Lilith had a lot of the same "fiery" passion as her spiritual counterpart. Both her and Sammael were, probably, quick to act, and often got carried away by run-away thoughts, or attitudes. Lilith and Adam did not see "eye to eye," on a number of occasions. She resisted Adam's attempts at "missionary position," during their coitus. She eventually retreated from her "wifely duties," and left the scene. Adam, again, was alone.

Regardless if she decided to leave or not, Sammael was, probably, "bubbling over" with thoughts of revenge, at this point.

Eve

With Lilith gone, Adam was right back in the same position. There still seemed to be no one that Adam wanted to stay with. Enter *Eve*. This woman was fashioned directly from Adam, as many of us know - from one of his ribs. You can't get much closer than that! After fashioning her, God led her to Adam, and said "I provided you with a helpmate of your kind."[81]

What could have been a reason why Adam was not satisfied with Lilith, or any other person he connected with? Could a woman *straight* from Adam be more prone to think like him, as well? If Eve was fashioned out of that same dust as Adam, then, maybe, she was humble like him, rational like him, and mindful like him.

*So, from man's rib God creates this **rational** being, and in his inventive wisdom he makes it complete and perfect, like man in every detail rational, capable of rendering him what would be of assistance in times of need and the pressing necessities of life. It was God, you see, who was arranging everything in his wisdom and creative power.*
  - *St. Chrysostom* Homilies on Genesis, Homily 15[82]

Interestingly enough, God may have even wanted Eve to *think* like Adam - that's the reason He took her from Adam's rib:

*God made Eve from a rib, a part of the body which, notably, was the most **modest** and **chaste**.* (Bialik and Ravnitzky, 1992, p. 19)[83]

If God wanted Eve to use a lot of the same humility, reasonability and rationality, then it makes perfect sense to create her this way. Yet, of course: they *were* two distinct individuals in the end, and no two people think *exactly* alike. But, even though, they still got along, rather well. And, Adam was happy (at least for now). God was, also, quite pleased with the ways they felt about each other, and how they acted, one towards another.

Adam and Eve's "Spark"

In certain respects, Adam didn't have to always be straight-faced, and rational. He could have been allowed to have, at least, some "fire" within him. He was allowed to have *some* passion, and feel somewhat emotional. It's not a sin, here. He just didn't "go overboard," or use it for the wrong reasons - as with his angelic counterparts. There seems there had been (at least) one piece of this "fiery" nature that God allotted to Adam and Eve to engage in, as well.[84]

On that day, God gave the new couple… a piece of the Divine Name… And so Adam changed his name… (and Eve's name, as well), adding **a holy spark** *to their union. But God warned them that this gift might not be theirs forever.* **For if they shut God… out of their hearts** *and* **betrayed their love for each other the divine spark** *would abandon them and return to God. Then each would… be only left with… fire. And this fire* **would consume their love and destroy them**. (Frankel, 1989, p. 24)[85]

Wow. It seems there's a difference to this "divine fire," and how it is used. Interestingly enough, The suffix "*ah*" - at the end of some Hebrew names - can stand for, "of God," "from God" or, possibly, in the "brotherhood" of God."[86] And, the original names given to Adam and Eve could have been "Adam**ah**" and "Chav**ah**," respectively. And, quite possibly, this angelic "fire" (as in the above) was with Adam and Eve, for a while - hence, the additional "**ah**" placed on the end of their names!

At first, these "divine fires" could have worked out well, for Adam and Eve. It may have even helped them build passion in their sexual activity, for example. Nothing practiced by the two were, seemingly, "out of bounds" - at least in God's eyes. Yes, they probably had sex, and enjoyed it. There was no shame by it, as well, because they practiced it in the proper manner. Which leads us all to this:

*…***the sexual urge** *is always natural and only* **sometimes** *sinful.*
(Eichhorn, 1957, p. 21)[87]

Other people around them might have been doing the same. God wasn't pouncing all over them, punishing them for having sex with each other. It seems there could be a good amount of this inner "fire" inherent in the sexual act, as well. As long as it was practiced in the proper manner, it was not considered a problem. It's funny, however: a number of people reading this, today, may automatically start to feel a little uneasy about pondering the possibilities, here. Of course, it's because we, as believers, have been so conditioned to think that practically any sex, or any sexual thought, could, very well, be sinful in a way! And, this is, simply, not so. More about this, as time goes on.

Anyhow, the possibility exists that the act, itself, wasn't really looked upon in any negative way, back then:

*And God blessed them. That is, **the generative power** which he infused in them, that is their blessing.*   *- Barhebraeus' Scholia on the Old Testament* 6a 28[88]

And, what a paradise they may have had: plenty of this healthy passion, without the evil connotations attached to it. Yes - the people of the time really maintained a sense of restraint and temperament. They kept it where it belonged - within the realms of decency, within certain bounds. The Garden was truly a place of wonderful parameters, open understanding, without the corruption and excesses we hear about today: "…God created the garden for the pleasure of humanity…"[89] It was so pleasurable, in these *positive* ways, that that Adam and Eve seemed to walk around in a continual state of blissful nakedness.

Their up-and-coming temptation (with the Serpent) would allow for, not only their *loss* of innocence, but the loss of that glorious, *divine* apparel which surrounded them. And, as well, it allowed for the *perversion* of these internal "fires" once flowing innocently within their minds.

But, until then, we'll discover one more element of their everyday life: Adam and Eve didn't just lie around, enjoying the sexual pleasures of the Garden. It wasn't like many might picture, here. They both worked. They had responsibilities, as well. Both of them had serious roles in the Garden. And, all of this seemed to have been for a reason.

Interestingly enough, all of these things seemed to have had *mental* connotations to them, as well. Let's see.

Idleness

The reason God wanted Adam and Eve to do at least *some* work was, obviously, that it was good for them, and their situation, in some way. Even back in the Garden, there were positive implications of *work* to the human psyche.

> *The ideal existence for man is not idle enjoyment, but easy and pleasant work...*
> (Skinner, 1956, p. 66)[90]

God wanted Adam "to till it that he might **not** be a lover of *idleness*..." and, also, to "till the garden and watch over it lest he be unsettled by the exceeding *indulgence* (of God)."[91] In other words, if Adam and Eve did nothing but lay around, they may begin to take all of God's kindness, favor, and leniency for *granted*.

> *If, after all, he (Adam) had been relieved of all need to work, he would have fallen a victim to great indulgence and at once have slipped into sloth; whereas in fact by performing some work that was painless and without difficulty he would be brought to a better frame of mind.* - St. Chrysostom Homilies on Genesis, Homily 14[92]

Again, it's, also, about one's way of *thinking*, one's *mental* health, and having a healthy *mental* attitude, here.

Even though their world was, indeed, wonderful and easygoing, there were still some things around which were "not quite right." Maybe another reason God put Adam to work, within the confines of a walled Garden, was to keep him alert, and "on guard." Maybe there *could* have been questionable elements to their world for them to watch out for - even in this fine hour:

> *...the reason why God planted the Garden of Eden, in which to isolate Adam and Eve, so that they might (have) found a "thinking" race capable of resisting **all evil** influence.* (Bristowe, 1950, p. 94)[93]

The Garden of Eden, as already stated, could have been a *walled* garden, only with certain individuals allowed in. Why? Maybe there *was* something unsavory - or downright evil - on the outside, something left over from the previous world. Maybe there were some terrestrial angels around that could harm to them, if they so felt like it. Maybe some of these angels possessed *knowledge* - knowledge which, if allowed in, could help put an end to them, and their situation.

Angels Turned Worse

And, we already know why some of these terrestrial angels would have already been contrary to Adam:

(The) Enemy was jealous because [Adam and Eve] were richer in glory and reason than any other creature on the earth.
  - *St. Ephrem the Syrian* Selected Prose Works, Section 2, 22[94]

Add *envy*, *jealously*, and all of the other things that may have angered the Serpent and Sammael over time, and we have a good reason why only some terrestrial angels were allowed in. Yet, as we know, the Serpent still had limited access to the Garden.[95]

When Adam is not here, the Serpent will look after Paradise.
  - *Saltair na Rann* 1193-1196[96]

Due to his position, "…he (the Serpent) would have been **second** only to Adam in the animal hierarchy."[97] Maybe the Serpent had administrative duties when Adam wasn't around. The Serpent may have, also, rationalized how God "screwed him over," and, thought to himself:

"…as you have beguiled me I will certainly make (vices) alluring to them on earth, and I will beguile them all."   (Kathir, 2006, p. 109)[98]

As we know, Sammael (or Satan) was not allowed in. One ancient source states the following: "Nor was Satan himself permitted to come to Adam in the garden, neither in human appearance nor in divine vision."[99] Sammael, as well, dreamed about how things would be for Adam after he took out his revenge:

"...you being put out of the land of good Paradise and I being put out of holy Heaven."   - *Saltair na Rann* 1781-1784[100]

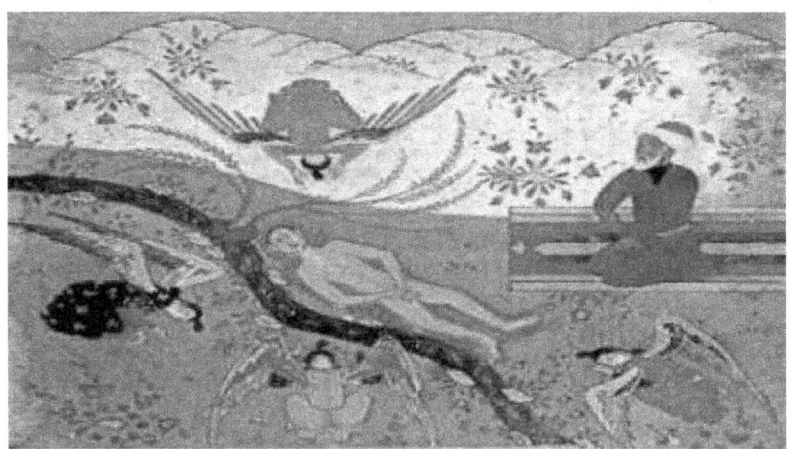

It seems that both angels, each for their own individual reasons, vowed vengeance against Adam for their *subjugation*. Any safety concerns related to Adam and Eve, now, seemed to be quite justified. The Garden may have even been surrounded by a number of terrestrial angels wishing to do them harm! The Bible even hints that *1/3* of God's angels rebelled against Him, and joined this movement of Sammael and the Serpent. Adam was intelligent, but vastly outnumbered. But, of course, Adam had one ally on his side that no one could match: *God*.

The knowledge Adam and his wife had was, most probably, only limited to the world that they *knew*. And, as previously suggested, the Serpent, Sammael, and other angels could have experienced this world before Adam, and had a great deal of knowledge, regarding the way things actually worked. How could these angels overthrow him? This "other worldly" knowledge was a good start:

The One who gave man intelligence gave it to the serpent as well.
    - Rabbi Abraham Ibn Ezra's Commentary on the Creation 77[101]

"Do Not Touch"

Adam probably went about his business, serving God, and trying to utilize his new management position to the best of his ability. But, almost assuredly, there was tension in the air.[102] In His everyday walk with Adam, God probably gave him specific instructions on how to live, as well as how to think. Most may recall that God instructed Adam, plainly, *not* to eat the fruit of the Tree of the Knowledge of Good and Evil. Adam may, then, have had to forward this information to Eve. And, to make sure his help meet was doing everything right (at least, in *his* eyes), he decided to do things his *own* way. Problem number "1."

God told Adam not to eat the fruit of this tree - simple. Adam (to make sure he "drove his point home") told Eve not to eat of it, as well, do not *touch*. The most probable reason Adam added this additional information was that - in his desire to make his help meet think as *cautiously* as he did - conceived the idea that she may have *needed* additional information. Sadly, it was plain to see that Adam did not trust the word of God, and felt the necessity to add additional verbiage to His statement.[103] This was the beginning of Adam's error:

> *He felt that he was stronger in mind and in will than was she and, consequently, she would have to be given extra physical and spiritual safeguards in order that she might be protected against any physical or spiritual force which would seek to do her harm.*
>   (Eichhorn, 1957, p. 13-14)[104]

In a certain way, it may have sounded, somewhat, *noble* that he cared enough about Eve, and wanted to help her. In a way, it *didn't* sound too caring - failing to listen to God in that manner, and possibly *endangering* them both, in the process! Regardless of Adam's intention, here, it wasn't good to do this to God.

Adam, apparently, may have felt the *need* to do it this way:

*It was because of his **affection** for Eve and because of his desire to do that which he thought was best for her welfare that Adam tried to improve upon the wisdom and will of God.* (Eichhorn, 1957, p. 14)[105]

Whether it be for love, or no: no man - even the man whose soul was given directly to him, by God - could *improve* upon the words of God, himself! *Obedience* was crucial here, and not the addition of one's "two cents worth." Again, trying to show love for the woman in Adam's life surely sounded noble, especially in today's world, but, Adam did not need to improve on God's plan for the universe! This was the first, grand mistake of the Garden.

Through his act, Adam may have, inadvertently, helped contribute to his own downfall. He may have, inadvertently, helped set up a situation where Eve could have been confused, and did not want to believe him. Eventually, she could have even been convinced that Adam *lied* to her - and, that's exactly what happened.[106] This was the opportunity that the Serpent needed, to drive a wedge between their feelings of total love and trust.

Serpent Now to Have Conversation with Eve

As we recall, the heavenly angel Sammael "rode atop of" the terrestrial Serpent (i.e. he was allowed to "possess" him), and, they, together, were on their way towards an attempt to bring Adam down. The two, together, possessed a great deal of this other-worldly knowledge - all they had to do was to find a way to capitalize on the current situation.

An opportunity arose. Adam's mistake was, already, one arrow in their quiver. One day, Adam and Eve were just lying together, resting. But, Eve may have become a little restless, and decided to take a walk. She saw the Serpent in another area of the Garden, and it looked to her as though he wanted to strike up a conversation.

> *Adam was sleeping… with naïve curiosity and the aversion to the boredom of silence… Eve quietly eased her body away from sleeping Adam to glade to the waiting Serpent.* (Eichhorn, 1957, p. 17)[107]

The Serpent's Poison Thoughts

As we know, another name for the Serpent - *Azazel* - means, "the strong one of God;" while *Sammael* means "the poison of God." After all that already went down, regarding their hate for Adam, their names, probably, were *already* changed - to reflect their new, *negative* tone. But, they, *together*, would be the strength against God's viceroy, as well as the *poison* rhetoric used against him. Their injection of *poison* - into a conversation - was about to begin. They were going to use it, in an attempt to seduce Eve, and then Adam, and, through these other terrestrial angels, to the rest of mankind:

> *There are other servants of the Devil who aim at us poisonous shafts of word and thought…* - *St. Ambrose* On Paradise, p 334[108]

Until this opportunity arose, the Serpent could have already had the assumption that Adam would be "on guard," looking for any attempts to overthrow his role. The Serpent also understood that Adam loved Eve. Tradition tells us the Serpent may have already held some preconceived notions about women (possibly from his knowledge of the previous world): "I know that she will listen to me; for women listen to all creatures…." As well, he had this (negative) assumption about her: "…she is simple, and knoweth nothing."[109] He, then, came to this conclusion:

> *...as his (Adam's) body are of a **masculine sort**, and competent to disentangle the notions of seduction; but the mind of the woman is more effeminate, so that through her softness she easily yields and is easily caught by the persuasions of falsehood, which **imitate the resemblance of truth**.*
> - Works of Philo Judaeus *Questions and Answers on Genesis I*, 33[110]

These angels must have known, from their knowledge of the previous world, that men and women (for the most part) had at least *some* different qualities about them, and had *some* thoughts going on in their head which weren't the same - and assumed this would be for Eve, as well. Again, understanding what really goes on *inside* a person's head helps us to understand what may have gone on, back then. It, also, may help us to escalate our deciphering of *Mystery Babylon*. We, now, see that the Serpent/Sammael were the first to promote this "poisoning" of the mind - and it all *began* at this conversation with Eve!

Many of us know that the typical serpent was said to possess a "forked tongue." As we'll now see, the method of choice by which the Serpent tried to deceive Eve was: "saying one thing with the tongue and by harboring **other thoughts** in his mind" - in other words, mixing lies with the truth.[111] Speaking in this way, and receiving this "poison," could eventually result in success - if the victim stays concerned about finding the truth, and becomes emotional about it all, in the process.

> *...there are other occasions when many other kinds of temptations are in store for us. Some of these come from the Prince of this world, who has vomited into this world what might be called poisonous wisdom, so that men believe **the false to be true** and are **emotionally carried away by mere appearance**.*
> - St. Ambrose *On Paradise*, p. 334[112]

When the Serpent first encountered Eve, he began to say things, such as: "I hear that thou art *wiser* than all the beasts…", when, in reality, he really felt the opposite.[113] He was just setting her up for the fall! Later on, in their conversation, the Serpent began to upset Eve, by saying things such as, "(Eve, you are)… **not** intelligent, you are the same as a brute animal!"[114] It was the old "bait and switch" approach, while twisting things along the way. These twists, quite often, might work to create some type of *emotional* response within the individual, as well - to get them *out* of thinking rationality, and "waiting before they decide to act."

"Hath God Said"

The Serpent's mental "assault" was underway. The Bible also picks up on his conversation, at this time. The Serpent, next, asks her those four famous words:

Yea, hath God said…
      - *Gen.* 3:1 (KJV)

In other words, "God said what…?" With this question, he attempted to destabilize Eve's competence in God, and, as well, put a *wedge* into her trust. This was used to plant the "seed of doubt" into her mind - to question her God, Adam, and any of his commands to her.

To "Be as Gods"

The Serpent, next, would try to make her question her position in the Garden, as a woman and a help meet. He hoped to falter Eve's confidence by "the lust of the eyes (I John 2:16)." The phrases, "desirable to the eyes" and "opening of the eyes" could, quite possibly, signify Eve being able to "see" herself, be aware of her *own* surrounding, or be aware of *who she was*. Simply put: it is being *self-aware*. Ultimately, this awareness *of the eyes* could represent thoughts that Eve may have never really contemplated before - thoughts concerning her own *worth*, or *self-esteem*.

We've already touched on the *soul*, and how it could equate to a person's consciousness, or *conscious* thoughts. And, before their fall, Adam and Eve could have utilized a lot of conscious thought. They didn't "fly off the handle," or become *too* emotional. They didn't become too irrational in their thinking. But, they, and every other person around them (at the time), was probably lacking *one* element of thought that *we* (so often) utilize today - the desire *to raise one's self-esteem*. Of all the lies that the Serpent was beginning to tell Eve, we'll soon see that he *did* tell her, at least in part, one truth: she wasn't utilizing a part of her soul that God, and His angels, were already using![115] Of course, this was the perception *of self-esteem*, or *worth*. And, the "Tree of the Knowledge of Good and Evil" - the tree that God forbade them to eat - could have, very well, involved using "self-awareness," or one's fundamental desire to raise their own self-esteem. We shall see.

We do know that, until this time, Adam and Eve, at least, have *some* rudimentary knowledge of good and evil, right and wrong. They knew, for example, that it was *wrong* to break God's commandment - and eat the fruit of this Tree of Knowledge. What they, most probably, didn't understand were the ways that they could *use* this knowledge to raise their self-esteems, and why they even would want to!

>...*good and evil means* **knowing what is or is not profitable for life**.
> (Brandon, 1963, p. 134)[116]

Simply, the term "good," in regards to our discussion, probably stands for what is "good" or "not good" to be able to raise one's own **self-esteem**, or **worth**! It could all be a little *beyond* just understanding what could be right, or righteous, around them - as we know, Adam and Eve probably already understood, at least, the fundamentals of this. No, this was something new, and different. They hadn't eaten of the forbidden fruit yet; so, their understanding of what this "good" might be, indeed, would have been unknown. And, interestingly enough: until the Fall, there was really no *need* for anyone to know what may be "good" to raise their own self-esteem, or what (around them) may be "good" for them to use, in order to achieve more and more of it. All Adam and Eve had to do was to manage a garden, look to God for guidance, and obey that one and only law that they had.

When they had sex, for example, they just "did it." There were no stipulations on the process. No one person was "using" another. Neither was anyone concerned about having his or her own self-esteem *lowered* in any way. It just felt good for both. And, God also didn't just sit there, and condemn the process! Adam and Eve, as well, did not really understand how one could become greedy, or want to possess things around them - such as *riches* - to raise their feelings of self-worth. They, as well, did not understand how *to* take advantage of someone else, for these causes. This, of course, would come *after* their fall - after they ate the forbidden fruit of "good and evil."

Adam, Eve, and the rest of the people of their time, also didn't really understand a lot about *guilt*. They probably knew of the potential for guilt, but, everything around them just seemed to work. There was no real need for Adam and Eve to worry about shame or embarrassment (of course) because they kept God's law.

Let's look more into the *lies* the Serpent used, and mixed in with the truth, and what all he would do next.

God - the Racist

Next, the Serpent followed with the suggestion: "he (God) is alive in heaven, better off than you..."[117] He continued: "Thou must know that God is wicked and envious, and therefore he brooketh (wanteth) no equals, but keepeth every one for a **slave** in order that ye may not become equal to him."[118] Wow, now that was a brash statement. Sounds like a lot like the accusations that, often, fly around the media, today. The Serpent implied that God was some supremacist, bigot or racist. He wanted no "equals," but, rather, wanted everyone He considered "beneath" him as His slave. Wow, doesn't that sound familiar - a lot like *today*? It's interesting to see how the Serpent, flat out, accused *God* of being the envious One when it was *him* who was actually full of envy. The Serpent accused God of being some type of "supremacist;" when, again, it was *he* who thought of himself as superior, and everybody else (including Adam) as inferior!

The Serpent may have also introduced another novel concept to Eve: all should be *equal*, even though the entire ranking of angels (set up by God) was *set up* to be a hierarchy. Their whole angelic world - where he came from - was full of rank and order. And, ironically, *he* was one of the "top dogs," with many, many angels **below** him - and *he's* complaining how everyone should be the same! Of course, he wouldn't have, willingly, go down in *his* rank, and requested to have joined the angelic "bottom of the barrel!" He was even furious when God lowered his rank, just a little bit! What a hypocrite. Yet, of course, it's okay for him to preach these ideals to someone else.

These claims were probably the beginning of *communist* talk and rhetoric. It could also be one way this "poison" of the Serpent might have worked on Eve. The Serpent and Sammael both knew they were from an angelic hierarchy, a rank and file. They, both, also knew that the Garden was of this same hierarchy. Apparently, God realized the need for such a ranking system! Yet, he gave a hypocritical outcry against it - lashing out, or accusing God of abusing something *he* was actually "swimming in," or profiting from!

The Serpent continued on with his lies, by suggesting that: if only Eve listened to him, "…ye shall do that which ye *please*, because ye shall be ***equal*** to God."[119] According to the Serpent's hypocrisy, he tried to make it known that everyone should, and could, be the same, and it all could work out well this way - even though he *knew* that wasn't the way things currently worked, and probably *could* work.

To Live Forever, and Be "Lord" Over Adam

Eve could have already known that the Serpent, and the other Nephilim around her, *came* from the world before them (or, at least, had some *knowledge* of this world). She may have also perceived that the terrestrial angels around her could have possessed certain *secrets*, such as how one lives a long life, or lives eternally.

Because of this, she may have been "…**led** to desire to acquire a life which should be free from old age, and from all decay" - another "forked-tongued" lie to be spun by the Serpent, to "snag" her into his web.[120]

To Be Bountiful Through Children, as Well

Naturally, as a woman, Eve could have also been anxious to understand how children were to come about, and when this all might happen to her. She wanted to use her "equipment" that God had set up for her. Of course, the Serpent had a lot of this information, and said he would *only* make it available to her if she followed what he put in front of her. He assured her that he knew how:

(Your) Blindness/ignorance will be cleared
Your springs will be opened.
Children will come forth
           (Halevi, 1997, p. 168)[121]

The Serpent/Sammael, also, tried to build a sense of *independence* within the woman's spirit. She could become a "god" without anybody's help. She, also, would know how to successfully have children - something Adam probably didn't have any idea about. At least in her eyes, the Serpent was *opening* her mind to a few wonderful ideals, as well as a sense of liberation![122] She may have, then, begun to desire how to understand, and do, things *on her own* - without Adam, and without God. In fact, she may have begun to think she could even be a lead over both of them:

She hastened to eat before her husband that she might become head over her husband, that she might become the one to give command to that one why which she was to be commanded and that she might be older in divinity than that one who was older in she in humanity.   - St. Ephrem the Syrian Selected Prose Works, Section 2, 20[123]

All she needed to do was to *follow* the Serpent's advice, here, and she could, essentially, "have it all."

To Doubt Adam and the Tree

On top of this, "…her curiosity and a desire for secret knowledge caused her to **slightly** doubt the word (of Adam)."[124] The Serpent was now about to work on Adam's "do not touch" interpretation. This was his "way in." The seeds of doubt, hopefully (for him), were about to take root. He, then, began to convince her that there was a *conspiracy* against her - by, of course, her God, and her man, Adam. They were, in actuality, trying to keep her "down," or "out of the loop." Both of them were even trying to withhold some divine information from her, and did not want her to share in *their* privilege.[125] Obviously, this was probably fueled by this additional instruction, given by Adam - not to even touch the fruit. And, Eve remembered this. God said one thing; Adam said another. This allowed Eve and opportunity to distrust.[126]

The Serpent, then, walked over to the tree, touched it, and even shook it. Eve noticed that the serpent did not die. Wouldn't anyone who touched the Tree of Knowledge die, after they touched it? God told them that - of course, it wouldn't be an immediate death, but the loss of their immortal state. Yet, with the Serpent's help, it was starting to become apparent to Eve that Adam lied to her, and the words of God were false.[127] Eventually, "…she was convinced Adam was a dishonest person… (while) the serpent is the *only* decent and honest being around…"[128] She stated thinking that the Serpent *must* be right (because of all the knowledge that he had), and he - and he alone - was the only one who really cared about her welfare.

Eventually, she came to the conclusion:

Her man lied to her; the Serpent was actually knowing a secret of the tree that he alone would eat the fruit and become like God. (Eichhorn, 1957, p. 20)[129]

The anger and emotions that began to swell up in Eve must have soured her soul - regarding her whole existence![130] This may have, then, allowed her to decided to follow the Serpent's seduction, even further.

And continue he did!

The wicked one opened her mouth,
She consumed the poison of the serpent's tongue.
She swallowed completely,
  - *Adamgirk: The Adam Book of Arak'el of Siwnik* p. 102[131]

And, so reasoning, she allowed the Serpent to run his... (hands) over her body, to pull her gently to the ground, and to make love to her in the same manner as the still sleeping Adam had made love to her. (Eichhorn, 1957, p. 20)[132]

The Serpent went to the next level. He went on to seduce Eve in a sexual manner, as well! They both contributed, willingly, to the sexual deed.

After the Serpent polluted her, he inveigled her to eat of the forbidden fruit.
(Eisenmenger, 1748, p. 21)[133]

And, after their coition reached its climax, she, eventually, decided to take of the forbidden fruit - something God told her not to. But, why not? God and Adam were, both, lying to her (according to her new interpretation)! And, because of this, some may have even considered her as the Serpent's *companion* (at least, for a period of time).[134]

A New Role for Sex

One ideological concept of Babylonian paganism tell us is that: "wisdom came from the power of *procreation*, hence the worship of *sex* became manifest in every pagan religion."[135] What exactly could have been this *wisdom*, here? Where did it all come from? Could this have, actually, been the *wisdom* of the Serpent? Interesting enough, this "inherent power" contained in procreation would, after the Fall, be considered something "straight from a god," and be worshipped as such. Pagans everywhere were beginning to believe that their way to achieve *divinity*, and increase their occult knowledge, was, in part, through the use of this act![136] Could this have, in actuality, been a homage to what probably happened at the Fall?

And, what would have been this "power" behind the sexual act, anyway? Could it have been associated with those internal "fires" within a person - "generated" through increased "sexual friction?" This is not to say that the act of sex is, inherently, *evil*, but when it becomes desirable *over* what God intended it to be, *then* it becomes a problem. Simple as that (but, not too well known). The Bible states, in Romans 1:25 (KJV), that there would be people who "worshipped and served the creature more than the Creator." In other words, people began to think *more* of the power *inherent* in the act of creation (i.e. sexual procreation) than the Creator of the act (and everything else), Himself! No wonder why so many ancient pagan cultures considered the *snake* as, "a very ancient symbol that represented the conveyance of **sexual** desires, hidden wisdom and secret knowledge!"[137]

Filth

After their "dirty deed," were there any significant changes that took place? Apparently, some things *did* occur within Eve:

> *Chavah (Eve) came into the world and clung to the serpent. He injected impurities into her...*   - *Zohar* Chayei Sara 3[138]

> *For when the serpent came upon Eve he injected a lust into her...*
>   - The Babylonian Talmud Shabbath 145b-146a[139]

Menstruation

Even though all of this may not directly relate to the aforementioned *filth*, certain things did seem to change, within Eve, at approximately the same time she and the Serpent had copulated:

> *Menstruation came to Eve with the enjoyment of the fruit.*
>   (Ginzberg, 1909, p. 101)[140]

According to tradition, when Eve cut off a piece of the tree, and bit of the fruit, the entire tree (in a way) "bled." Maybe it became significant of the terrible changes that were now about to be unleashed. Maybe God, in no uncertain terms, wanted to let Eve know that *she* would soon bleed, because she also "caused the forbidden tree to bleed."[141] Interesting to ponder, here.

Blood, once the symbol of life, was now destined to have some *negative* qualities about it, some *corrupted* connotations. As this "blood" of this tree was shed, during their sexual intercourse, blood, now, may have to be shed, occasionally, from the one who helped *caused* it to happen (as well as many born after this). Ultimately, tradition stated that their act could have begun menstrual cycles in women (as a type of "remembrance" of this unholy deed). Blood, also, began to be shed *in other ways* - beyond menstruation. People would begin to hurt each other, even *kill* each other… shedding blood the whole time. Also, blood may, now, have been needed to (at least temporarily) appease God, Himself. Enter the need for *blood sacrifice*.

There would be some *more* changes taking place, to the people of this world, as a result of all this *filth* in the Garden.

The "Evil Inclination"

As we theorized, mankind was about to inherit desires for *self-esteem*, or *worth*, after Eve (and, Adam, soon-enough) ate the forbidden fruit. A "supernatural change" would come upon the world - change to, not only this pair, but to the *rest* of the Adamites and pre-Adamites. Adam was the viceroy. Their "sinking ship" seemed to have brought down the entire vessel - with *everyone* aboard (sorry to say).

These "additions" could, in part, be connected with what's been commonly called "the Evil Inclination."[142] The angel Sammael, using the Serpent as his "vessel," injected a supernatural "filth" (or, a "venereal disease," of sorts) into the entire human race.

In this corruption of mankind, the Serpent affected **all** "with the taint of impurity."[143] The entire world, sadly enough, had to pay the price. As the name suggests, the *Evil Inclination* could simply stand for one's "tendency to do evil." It involves a good number of inner, and negative, tendencies - often revolving around human emotions, such as jealously, pride and envy. It also represents an extremely "self-centered" view of one's world.[144] It's "all about them." This serpentine nature opened up Eve to ways of thinking that she never had before - many, upon many, *negative* additions to her mind, now, as well as to human nature, in general.[145]

> *Volition (desire) is animated by the intellectual faculty but it is opposed by <u>lust</u> which originates from the appetitive and sensitive dimensions…*
> — *Ibn Ezra* Commentary on the Pentateuch, Genesis, p. 78[146]

In other words, one's rational and intellectual thoughts were, now, challenged - by thoughts of the Evil Inclination. A battle, now, began for the human psyche. *Lusts*, for example, were really not a part of the *original* human psyche… until now.

Lust

> *Eve alone he possessed her and infused her with lust…*
> (Schwartz, 2004, p. 447)[147]

Lust, as one author put it, is, "the root and beginning of every sin."[148] For simplicity sake, *lust* involves an individual's attempt to use something around them, in order to gather for themselves more and more **self-worth** (or esteem). And, we recall that, after Adam and Eve ate of the Tree of Knowledge of **Good** and Evil, humans began to search out whatever **good** they could find (for themselves), to help in this quest for esteem.

One problem with lust, however, lies with the amount of time and effort (i.e. dedication) being put into a one's own desire, and how much a person values something **over God**. God wanted people to value *Him* the most. Now, other things of this world may compete for human affection. So, when someone's desire begins to consume their life and priority, or if they begin to put this desire on a *level* higher than they should God, then this desire becomes *lust*. Simple as that.

When we go back to the coition between Eve and the Serpent, most of us understand that sex is, often, an act of which *lust* is often associated. Is the act of *sex*, in and of itself, the *problem*, or the *lust* swirling behind it?

The sexual instinct properly controlled is a great blessing... he who looks upon this instinct as something to be repressed and denied is afflicted with a regrettable narrowness of mind and of heart. (Eichhorn, 1957, p. 22)[149]

We know that: it isn't necessarily a sin to have sex, or want it! All human beings are mammals, members of the animal kingdom. We all have this desire, inside. Sex is a natural, wonderful act. Some call it a "hunger," just like food or drink - but, again, the sin revolving around sex concerns self-control, and intent! The sex act - without some sort of restraint or parameter - is the real problem!

This is the same with *other* acts, such as the consumption of alcohol, for example. The problem does not lie in drinking wine itself, but the *frequency* and *prominence* a person puts on this act! That is what makes it good or evil. It's so simple - but, so often *twisted*, today.

Lusts, as we also see in the Bible, are, often, known as the sin *of wrong use*.[150] Why? Again, because a normal desire, or drive, is used *incorrectly*.

Idolatry

Consider lust as an "extended arm" of the Evil Inclination - one negative "side-effect," brought to mankind. Yet, it can also begin to assimilate into something else: *idolatry* (or idolatrous thoughts). Interestingly enough, *both* lust and idolatry, in the Bible, seem to have a similar root! *Idolatry* is fancy name to describe an individual who wants to obtain ultimate wisdom, worth and salvation from something *other* than God - which, as we already know, is another typical, lustful pathway! They run in tandem, here.

A perfect example of this would be <u>self-worship</u> - anything that may accompany one's desire to find his or her *own* pathway(s) to redemption, using his or her *own* prideful attempts.

*...he might possibly mention to him the name of his **idol**; what evil, however, could be involved here? - That of infusing her with sensual **lust**... When the serpent copulated with Eve, he infused her with lust.*
- The Babylonian Talmud Mas. Yevamoth 103b[151]

These lustful attempts may also include *fornication*.

Another Use of Sex - Fornication

As we've seen, in this temptation process, the Serpent utilized something from our *worldly realm* (i.e. sex) to help get him what he wanted. The Serpent utilized an outwardly-appealing, worldly pleasure to help *inscribe* his own corruption into Eve! Using an catalyst (like sex) to help one to get whatever they want (from someone else) may end up being known as another obscure, yet very important, act: *fornication*. Yes, it goes way beyond "sex outside of marriage."

Incredibly enough, lust, idolatry and fornication *all* could be, quite often, lumped together, in one specific way.

> *...we write unto them (Gentiles), that they abstain from pollutions of **idols**, and from **fornication**, and from things strangled, and from blood... abstain from meats offered to idols, and from blood, and from things strangled, and from fornication...*
> - *Acts* 15:20, 29 (KJV)

Three of these "abstentions," above, absolutely relate to idolatry. Notice how fornication was also lumped *right along* with them! Why? Beyond the definition we all hear about (i.e. "sex beyond marriage"), fornication could also be considered a "mixing of the Pure Word of God with the words of manmade creeds, dogmas and traditions" - in other words, it could also be thought of as an *adulteration* of something's original purpose. It is along the same lines as one holding "a carrot" over another person's head, seducing them to go after the carrot, in order to help them achieve *a different* goal.

In the case of the Fall, the sexual act could have been used to achieve *another*, different end-result. This is not simple bartering, however. There is something else to it all - something *negatively* results from it, to one participant, or all of them. We shall see.

Sex, when used in certain ways, could actually turn the act into "a direct mockery of God," and what He wanted for this world.[152] Ultimately, eating food, drinking wine and having sex are not evil i*n themselves* - the evil resides, again, in *how* they are used.[153]

And, on top of it, it becomes fornication if one or more of the practitioners, ultimately, are hurt by the activity. Someone, or something, is hurt in the process!

One example of this *manner* of fornication is the harlot church of Revelation (Chapters 14, 17 and 18). In the Bible, a woman was often considered a model for the Church, itself. In this case of fornication, the Bible said that many churches (even "Christian" churches, assuredly) would eventually succumb to societal pressures around them, and "sell their own church body (or soul)" to take on some earthly pleasure, or get some *gain* out of it. And, yes, it is true, today, that many churches - for the sake of "political correctness" - have abandoned the fundamental principles of the Bible, just to allow their dogma to "fit in" with a lot of what secular society around them demands out of them. Less and less people may want to come there, if they don't begin to change their message (the church elders may have decided). And, yes, the church, now, decided to "sell their soul," just to keep afloat, financially. In the short run, these church elders will keep the money flowing in. But, in the long run, their sermons won't really be the same. And, in actuality, not hearing the pure words of the Bible (in favor of "political correctness") may, in actuality, hurt the entire congregation, over the long term. So, yes - people are going to be hurt, in the process, here. The church committed *fornication* with the secular, humanist world.

Their fornication hurts the congregation a lot more than they may have, at first, realized. If people, now, aren't really being directed towards the God of the Bible, then *where* might they heading towards, with changes such as this? The majority of our world has a pagan lean. It follows science. It, often, doesn't even believe in God. No wonder why it's so easy to see why Scriptures link *fornication* with idolatry: fornication is the mechanics used to convert an individual, or an entire church, *away* from God, and **towards** the direction of some worldly desire, or lust - possibly, to even something of the Serpent, and Cain.

The Serpent *fornicated* with Eve, in this instance - using sex and seductive words. And, it was considered *fornication* in this case because Eve was, indeed, hurt in the process. She thought she was going to *benefit* from the exchange, in some way - but, of course, it didn't last very long.

Cycles of Self-Destruction

Beyond copulation, beyond this instillation of the Evil Inclination, beyond menstruation, even beyond fornication, there were other changes occurring within the very nature of Eve, herself, as well as the rest of the human race.

*...for the serpent of Eve, being the symbol of pleasure... attacks man, that is... the reasoning power which is in every one of us... the enjoyment and **free use of excessive pleasure** is **the destruction of the mind**...*
- Works of Philo Judaeus *On Husbandry* 24(108)[154]

Interesting. As we see, it is often unabated, *emotional* desires that allow an individual to make quick - often erroneous - decisions. Although the Serpent/Sammael did their best to convince Eve to partake of the fruit, she, *ultimately*, made her own decision to disobey God. She used her own free will, and had no one else to blame.[155]

At the same time of their coitus, the Serpent may have demanded one more thing of Eve: an *oath*. He induced Eve into swearing something, such as:

"(Eve speaking) I will give also to my husband to eat. And when he had received the oath from me, he went and poured upon the fruit the poison of his wickedness, which is lust, the root and beginning of every sin, and he bent the branch on the earth and I took of the fruit and I ate."
- The Apocalypse of Moses / *Apocalypsis Mosis* 29:3[156]

She swore. Now, she had to convince Adam to do the same… to fulfill this promise.[157] She, now, had to go down some difficult pathways, at least in her mind, to achieve that goal. Through the Serpent's "multi-layered" attack, Eve's mind was about to succumb to the avarice that "came from within her self."[158]

Adam and Other Women

One of the thoughts that could have, now, flowed from Eve's mind (which helped drive her resolve) revolved around Adam, himself. She believed that: if either Adam or God found out about her coition, here, God could, then, easily couple Adam with another woman![159] It was plain that, until Eve, Adam couldn't find *anyone* else that he liked. Eve was the closest thing to him, in so many ways, and he enjoyed her company. He, it seemed, didn't mind having one woman for the rest of his life, and she felt the same way about him.

Even though she cohabited with the Serpent, Eve still didn't want the "perfect union," between her and Adam, to end.

> *If I do die, Adam would couple himself another woman. He would forget I had ever existed. If I am to die, why should he be allowed to go on living? If I had done wrong, so has he. He lied to me...* (Eichhorn, 1957, p. 26)[160]

She needed to find a way to keep him with her. She had now fallen - and, now, he had to do the same. She loved him. And, through her own self-absorption, Eve began to imagine ways to seduce her man, just as *she* was.

Fornication With Adam

For she contrived a newly begotten speech.
The serpent deceived the ignorant woman,
*But she the **first, primordial man**.*
   - Adamgirk: The Adam Book of Arak'el of Siwnik 1.3.122[161]

Reasons to Deceive Adam

Within the "new" arsenal of her mind, she, probably, came up with a number of different scenarios to deposit at Adam's feet:

- *"For the sake of the love of your Creator,*
  Remember also our first love."[162]

- *"But, if you have love towards me,*
  Listen attentively to your partner,
  Take, eat too the fruit with me,
  So that I may remain with you in this Paradise."[163]

- *"Adam shall I be stripped like you? I ate too much and was stripped because of that. You eat just a little."*[164]

- *"What do you suppose - that I will die and another Eve will be created for you? Or that I will die and you will have no obligations?"*[165]

- *"Who else will be a helper for you?"*[166]

- *"Eat and do not separate me from you. If we live, let us live together, and if we die, let us die together."*[167]

- *"It is better that we either die together or live together, since our Creator formed us together."*[168]

- *"That first love of yours is false,
 For you do not care about my return."*[169]

- *"I, your body, am wounded in this way,
 [But] you remain thus, uncaring."*[170]

Eve, then, begged - even cried - until Adam finally turned "weak in the knees."[171]

Adam's Decision on Love

Adam had a number of things swirling around, in his mind:

- *He wished to hearken to her speech,
 For he had great love for her.*[172]

- *But when he looked at the woman's begging and <her> tears, he felt pity in his heart.*[173]

- *When he saw her nakedness, he was afraid to eat. When he saw her beauty, he became foolish.*[174]

- *...Adam, because of his love for the woman, could not restrain himself...*[175]

It's interesting to see how *love*, here, seems to come up, again and again. Yes, it seemed to be a major element of Adam's seduction. He wasn't thinking of the *purpose* that God gave him. He wasn't really rationalizing about his disobedience, and if it was the *right* thing to do or not. There were *emotions* flowing into his thought-process like a river, helping him to make his decision. Emotions, such as *love*, were gaining a major foothold over his thinking.

> *Although man's well being is contingent upon his making the correct choices, volition (desire) frequently acts contrary to the intellect, due to the paradox of various faculties within man struggling for control.*

- *Ibn Ezra* Commentary on the Pentateuch, Genesis, p. 78[176]

Eve, as we know, was, most probably, turned into the ancient pagan goddess of *love*.[177] Why? Of course, we know that she showed great love for Abel, by mourning for him after his death. She loved Cain, of course. Here, we also see that it was Eve who used "love" as a way of change. *Love*, according to many, has "the power to change the world." And, maybe, through this manipulation of Eve, love *did* help change the world - into what it is now!

Again, thinking about things from this opposite viewpoint - the *pagan* viewpoint - and we may be able to see why the world around us cherishes *love* so. Again, it all sounds worthy and noble, but could there be a little more to it? Could such a focus on *love* be a little bit extreme, here - even more extreme than the amount of focus one should be having on God? After all, the world around us, for the most part, is saturated with pagan idealism, pagan religions, humanism, and the like.

So, if we really think about it: love *may* have helped change the world - into something more of what *the Serpent* had wanted! He, now, had his "way" with Eve. He conned her into using certain techniques, to change Adam's mind. The Serpent already knew about the power of love. Yet, most of us, obviously, know that (in this world) *love* isn't always the answer, nor is it the "cure all" for all of the world's problems. But today - in our pagan-influenced world - doing something for "the sake of love" is considered honorable, and compassionate. We see it, so often, being placed on a pedestal - above God. This is all be design.

Also, Eve - as their eventual pagan "goddess" - was, originally, believed to have conferred "a great wisdom" upon mankind… this *wisdom*, of course, was probably that of the Serpent, and his manipulation techniques.[178]

Adam Finally Fell

As the "coup de grace," Eve was about to use these same *fornication* techniques as the Serpent used on her:

*...Eve was beguiled by the Serpent, then introduced her husband to the **mystery** of procreation.* ("The Original Sin 2/3", n. d., p. 5)[179]

She had sex with Adam; and, within their sexual bliss, he succumbed to the pressure. Adam gave in. He did it "for love." He ate of the fruit.

This, in no way, excused him for his actions - regardless, if Eve committed fornication with him. They both, ultimately, **disobeyed** God. Adam was just as guilty. He, soon, would have his share of problems and punishments, as a result of all this.

All three - the Serpent, Eve and Adam - were guilty of some wrongdoing, here. And, their actions all came with a price.

Chapter 3

The Real Adam and Eve (Part 2)

Adam's Decision

> *He doubted in his soul,*
> *Whether to hearken to the woman or to the Creator.*
> *His mind went after his eyes,*
> ***He abandoned God*** *and not the woman.*
>   *- Adamgirk: The Adam Book of Arak'el of Siwnik 1.3.120*[1]

Although his integrity was successfully assaulted, Adam had no one else to blame.[2] He took what was *in front* of him, repudiated God, and followed Eve's repertoire.[3] Doing something for the sake of *love* may have even sounded noble at the time, and still does to most today, but, as we see, obedience was *better*.

*...he (Adam) should have kept God's law intact and given it preference before her improper greed, and not joined her as a partner in her fall nor deprived himself of such benefits on account of **a brief pleasure**...*
- *St. Chrysostom* Homilies on Genesis, Homily 16[4]

Who was Adam, anyhow - to think his ways were better than the Creator of the Universe? Adam knew God wanted him to stay focused, and not be taken away with emotion, but he allowed this great, rational mind (i.e. his soul) to be penetrated, to make the wrong free-will choice. Of course, Adam probably understood this (when it was too late); and, with his newfound sinful nature, immediately tried to put a lot of the blame onto Eve:

(Adam to Eve) Thou knowest not what thou'st done...
...thou'st ruined us;
(Phifer, 1890, p. 44)[5]

"Partly by an undue thirst for knowledge, and partly by increasing sensuality, and the seduction of woman, man fell."[6] Again, Adam did not stay *on focus* with his role as the Garden's manager. He did not think reasonably. Passion and irrational thought began to run through his mind.[7] Adam had one, and only one, law, and he couldn't even follow that!

The "Transgression" Was Not Adam

Yet, things were a little different, between the two. There is a verse in the Bible that differentiated Adam's fall from Eve's, at least a little:

*And Adam was not deceived, but the woman being deceived was **in the transgression**.*
- I Tim. 2:14 (KJV)

So, Adam was not deceived in exactly the same way Eve was, here. He, also, really did not wonder what it would have been like to *be a god,* or live forever. He did not take on this attitude Eve did, before and after her fall. Adam did it because of other reasons (such as "love") - not because he was upset with God, or anything of that nature. So, this "transgression," in the above, was probably associated with certain thoughts, such as the desire to "become a god," or want to. Adam, to his credit, still maintained a lot of the same ways of looking at the world he once had.[8]

He wasn't "in the transgression" because he willfully chose to be there, as Eve. That's the difference. He did it for "love," not out of *pride*.[9]

And, the thoughts of *fornication*, as what came from the Serpent and Eve, did not come willfully from Adam, here. The serpent willfully fornicated with Eve, and she willfully fornicated with her husband. Adam didn't use *fornication* to get what he wanted! Again, that is why he was *not* in the transgression, here. This may or may not sound fair so some, but some thoughts and actions are, probably, more offensive to God, overall. That's probably the way it was, and still is.

Yet, although Adam's sin was a little different, and less "severe," in ways, he, still, was disobedient. Adam, overall, wasn't in much better shape than the two others. As we'll see, God would even hold him *quite* responsible for a lot that went on, here, because he was considered God's viceroy - he should have known better.

Let's, now, see how the punishment phase of the Garden began, what Adam said, in regards to *his* role in the Fall, as well as what happened to them all.

Punishment Began

The serpent... sinned most, for he sinned in three things. The woman next and sinned less than he, but more than the man, for she sinned in two things. The man sinned last and least, for he sinned but in one.
        - The Golden Legend or Lives of the Saints: Volume I 61[10]

After the Fall, the Serpent reportedly laughed *out loud*, sarcastically, about the whole thing![11] Of course, he was happy. He achieved what he had always wanted: to "dethrone" Adam as the highest authority; and (at least in his mind) "free" himself, and his clan, from their "servitude." Sammael, the Serpent and their fellow serpentine angels now felt vindicated from their subjugated positions - at least under Adam. God saw him laughing, and was furious. It was time for all three of them to pay the price for these misdeeds: first Adam; then Eve; and, especially, the *Serpent*. He saved the best for last.

In some respects, the law of God requires that: "…if any mischief follow, then thou shalt give life for life, eye for eye, tooth for tooth, hand for hand, foot for foot, burning for burning, wound for wound, stripe for stripe" (Ex. 21:23-25 cf. Rev.13:10). In regards to these punishments due to *the Fall*, those dished out to Adam, Eve and the Serpent follow, at least somewhat, in this pattern. In most cases, they seemed to coincide with the roles of *each participant*. We'll see how Adam and Eve were about to receive *ironic* punishments - something pushing them towards *the opposite* of what they originally hoped for, wished for or may have did, in life!

For the sake of this discussion, we'll look at Adam first. Why? Although we already gathered that Adam, most probably, should have the least amount of accountability, God, still, went to Adam *first*. He held Adam *highly* accountable for the entire situation, because he was manager of the Garden.[12]

As one ancient author puts it:

...Adam is the first to be rebuked, although the woman was the first to eat the fruit. But the weaker sex begins by an act of disobedience, whereas the stronger sex is more liable to feelings of shame and forgiveness. The female furnished the occasion for

> *wrongdoing; the male, the opportunity to feel ashamed.*
> - *St. Ambrose* On Paradise, p. 349[13]

God may have hoped Adam would want to show enough *honor* to know better, because He set him to *think* that way.[14] He, now, wanted Adam to "be a man," and face up to what he did - accepting responsibility for all he was charged with. As we've discovered, this could have been a reason why Adam was created with an ability to *blush*: to provide an "open door" for his guilt, for all to see. This was to keep him honorable. Maybe, something like this was also to help him to *think* before he acted - because, if he didn't, his sin might be written *all over his face*! Regardless if one had the ability to blush or not, God *still* wanted each human being to face up to what he or she may have done, and do the right thing. *Honor* seemed to be an important part of one's strength, back then, and, also, of *grave* importance to God.

New-Found Excuses

Adam did not act very honorably, however, but, quickly, utilized his new-found Evil Inclination to *blame* Eve. He also, indirectly, began to put the blame on God! Just as the Serpent would, Adam began to go down some crooked paths of thinking, just to get out of guilt and culpability. He began to put the blame on anyone or anything else *around* him, instead of understanding his own role:

*Adam said, "Lord, this woman **whom you created** deceived me."*
   - The Armenian Apocryphal Adam Literature
      Concerning the Creation of Adam and the Incarnation of
      Christ our God 37[15]

God was too savvy for this, and would have no part in Adam's attempt to "weasel" his way out of everything. He responded with:

"...thou art ungrateful when thou accusest her... Thou shoudnst not have harkened unto her."   (Goldin, 1929, p. 23)[16]

In other words: "Adam. Be a man! If someone told you to 'go jump off a roof,' would you? You should have understood what role I had for you in the Garden, and what *honor* means. It involves 'doing the right thing.' If you make a mistake, or error in judgment, understand what you did, *confess* it, and *accept* responsibility for your role in the situation."

"(God to Adam)... this was not my intention... you appropriated it for your self so don't attribute the blame to anyone else, but put it down to your own indifference..."
   - St. Chrysostom Homilies on Genesis, Homily 17[17]

We also recall that it was *Adam* who told Eve something other than what God told him in the first place (not to eat of - **and touch** - the fruit). We see that: "if Adam had told Eve the unembellished truth instead telling her what he *thought was best* for her she might have been spared much agony and abuse."[18]

Adam also "considered the woman better than the Garden and lordly glory."[19] It seemed more important to God for Adam to stay *focused* on his job, rather than *love*, or anything else. Wow, doesn't this sound like quite the *opposite* of what we often hear, today! We often hear about one doing things for *the sake of love*, or the *sake of family*, than for the sake of duty.

> *"(God to Adam)… you should have regarded **my** command as more worthy of trust even if all these things have befallen you, put the blame on no one else but yourself and your own neglect; after all, if you had not been willing, your wife would have been unable to bring you to this disastrous state."*
> - *St. Chrysostom* Homilies on Genesis, Homily 17[20]

It's interesting how this kind of Godly honor is almost unheard of, today.

Adam's Punishment - To Work the Ground

Because thou hast hearkened to the voice of thy wife and hast eaten the fruit, cursed be the earth in thy works.   - *Gospel of Barnabas* 41[21]

Because Adam ignored his role, as the top laborer, or manager, of the Garden, punishment was due him. Because he disregarded his purpose, here, no longer was he able to obtain the fruits of his labor so *easily*. In fact, things were going to become a lot more complicated, even *the opposite* of what he originally was used to.[22] Growing plants with the greatest of ease was now about to become very difficult.

...cursed be the ground for your sake.
- *Rashi* (Bereishit) Genesis 3:17[23]

To Be Less Than Those Around

On top of it, no longer was Adam considered the most powerful man in the Garden. In fact, if we want to sound a little technical, we see that the word *curse* even represents, that which was made *smaller*, to be *reduced*, made *insignificant* or even *belittled*.[24] So, Adam, as well as the rest of humanity, was *now* to suffer *curses*, due to the Fall. Things were going to become *smaller*, or *reduced* - less than what was once enjoyed, or utilized.

Firstly, Adam's position was to be *reduced*. No longer was he at the "top of the ranks." Adam lost this authority, not only over people working in, and around, the Garden, but also over those terrestrial and non-terrestrial *angels*. All of this began to make him panic. He, now, dreaded the future. In one example, Adam, indirectly, began to cry out to other Adamites and pre-Adamites around him:

Have pity on me, who was once your lord,
sovereign, and king, but am now equal to
*you, but **more** unworthy!*
  - *The Armenian Apocryphal Adam Literature* The Words of Adam to Seth 20[25]

Another thing that made him panic was that he, at one time, was able to eat the wonderful fruits of the Garden. Now, he was no longer going to eat any fruit here, anymore. He would, now, have to go beyond the Garden, and find some field to work. Some of the other people around him may have already known how to work the fields of the Garden, and, consequently, already had a good idea on how to handle themselves, now. Adam didn't have a clue, anymore. He felt lost, and more unworthy. He did not want to go there:

> *Agriculture will be a constant drudgery and, in stead of fruit being his food, he is for his disobedience to heart the herb of the field which he can only obtain by cultivation of the soil...* (Redlich, 1950, p. 82)[26]

Sweat

He became so afraid of these prospects that nervous *sweat* began to flow onto his forehead. The sweat, literally, began to pour down his face. Tears, also, began to flow from his cheeks.[27] God noticed this, and, because Adam was openly exhibiting such nervous fear, felt a little compassion for him. At least, Adam didn't fall back so much on his pride, here, that he wasn't afraid to openly show how he felt. God liked that, though. At least Adam was still using his humility. So, his *sweat*, here, seemed to signify a great deal of *respect* for his Creator, and how he understood the severity of his disobedience, and God reacted to it.

> *When Adam heard these words, he trembled, and perspiration covered his face. The Lord had mercy on Adam: "Because thou are sorry in thy heart and criest out unto Me, **by the sweat** of thy brow thou shalt eat bread."* (Goldin, 1929, p. 25)[28]

Now, it seemed that this *sweat* stood out, as a symbol of all that went down, here. Maybe it stood out as the symbol of something else: a *greater* punishment may have been in store, here, and was forfeited - because of Adam's reaction. God may have set this need to *sweat* as the new "template" for Adam, and all those who followed him. Working the fields could have been worse, but, still, *some* sweat will usually have to flow, in order for one to *reap* from their work in the fields:

> *Your children, your sons, your wives must serve every day; they have not good thing - good work - until sweat comes to their brow.*   *- Saltair na Rann* 1449-1452[29]

Maybe Adam never had to work by sweat of his brow, before. Possibly, no one worked all that hard before, in the Garden.

Regardless, it would have to change.

> *...the earth that brought forth good and wholesome fruits plenteously, from henceforth shall bring forth but seldom, and also none without man's labour, and also sometime weeds, briars, and thorns shall grow.*
>   *- The Golden Legend or Lives of the Saints: Volume I* 61[30]

So, because Adam "hastily" listened to his wife's counsel, thorns and thistles were, now, to spring up in places where, originally, edible plants used to grow - even in the coveted place once known to have housed the immortal *Tree of Life*.[31]

When his punishment was nearly over, Adam did find *peace* and *rest* in the aftermath. He was satisfied with the fact that, at least, he didn't get anything worse.[32] Yet, *work*, for the most part, wasn't going to be easy anymore - that's for sure. And, when someone *sweats*, it's a sure sign that he or she, at least, was putting forth a good effort towards the production of something.

More Punishments

We, now, see how Adam - through his disobedience - was forced to live a lifestyle that headed him in *the opposite* direction of what he was once used to. God stated, "My intention in bringing you into the world… was that you should live your life *without* pain or toil, difficulty or sweat, and that you should be in a state of enjoyment and prosperity, and not be subject to the needs of the body but be free from all such and have the good fortune to experience complete *freedom*. Since, however, such indulgence was of *no benefit* to you, accordingly I curse the ground so that it will not in future yield its harvest as before without tilling and ploughing; instead, I invest you with great labor, toil and difficulty, and with unremitting *pain* and despair…"[33]

Why such "opposite" extremes?

…so that under pressure from these you may have continual guidance in keeping to limits and recognizing your own makeup…
- St. Chrysostom Homilies on Genesis, Homily 17[34]

So, Adam must, now, never forget *who his is*, and always recognize that he now has *limits* to his body, and his abilities, in this fallen world.

May you be with many sighs…
- Book of Adam (44)24.3[35]

Weary shalt thou be and shalt not rest; by heat shalt thou be tired, by cold shalt thou be straitened: abundantly shalt thou busy thyself, but thou shalt not be rich; and thou shalt grow fat…
- Apocalypse of Moses / Apocalypsis Mosis 24:3[36]

There were, now, new "templates," or new *norms*, to befall mankind. In this post-Fall world, it would not be very easy for the average man to survive on this earth. Poverty, weariness and the like would become *the rule* for most - and, *not* the exception.

There was more.

Dust

…because on account of a trifling enticement on the part of your wife you have rejected the most pleasing fruits of Paradise… for you were not pleased to enjoy yourself in the garden without toil… Because 'you are from the dust,' and have forgotten yourself, 'you shall return to your dust,' so that, through your state of humiliation, you shall come to know your true essence.
- St. Ephrem the Syrian Selected Prose Works, p. 120[37]

Still, Adam wasn't to fall back on his pride, and turn it all into anything *negative*. But, do the opposite - further using his humility! He was to never forget he was just a flawed individual - made from dust. Ultimately, God was, and still is, in charge.

No longer would any man be reaching this rank of "viceroy." Adam, and men after him, were to understand their *new* place in this world, and to work with what they now had.

The Sadness of Adam

There were more punishments lofted on to Adam's plate: Adam's great "springs of wisdom" were closed.[38] He, now, lost that "pipeline" of knowledge that once flowed, naturally, from his mind. Once, Adam was in frequent contact or conversation with heavenly angels around him, but no more. Apparently, he, now, lost this ability to easily see into, and contact, the supernatural world.[39]

On top of it all, Adam was stripped of that glorious, garment of "light" that surrounded his persona (and, may have even equated him, in certain ways, to the *sun*, or the *light of the sun*). According to one source, Adam was, now, turned "pitch dark."[40] Again, what this probably meant was: compared to how *bright* he once was, he was now just a *shell* of his former self. The "brightness" of his face was gone, in so many ways. He seemed darker on the outside - as well as the inside.

This "loss of luminosity" could have also opened Adam's *mind* to allow *darker* thoughts about himself, and his world, to come in. Sorrow, depression and sadness may have begun to show up inside, and outside - on his face. Adam, quite often, felt miserable about what he had done - and people could see it. He, often, was saddened, for all he had done to the human race.

> *...in sorrow shalt thou eat of it all the days of thy life...*
> - *Gen.* 3:17 (KJV)

The *darkest* - and most inevitable change - in Adam, however, was that slow, inevitable progression of his earthly body towards *death*. All people, of course, were to have this same destiny awaiting them, someday - for God stated that: if Adam and Eve ate of the *Tree of the Knowledge* they would surely die.

Coats of Skins

Since Adam lost this brilliant countenance, as well as losing other wonderful, majestic qualities, he felt naked. It was because he *was* naked, in a whole number of ways. Next, the Bible says that God created clothing for Adam and Eve, out of *skins*. Now, what were these *skins*, and what purpose, besides covering their naked bodies, were they for? They would be robes of dead animal skins - now, considered a temporary cover for Adam and Eve, and for all human beings, while they lived in this earthly existence.[41] Instead of showing the glorious, "garments of light" they once had, these skins now became the "emblem of the death *ye gain* instead."[42]

Then God made to Adam and Eve two leathern coats of the skins of dead beasts, to the end that they bare with them the sign of **mortality**...
                          - The Golden Legend or Lives of the Saints: Volume I 61[43]

God likely destroyed a couple of beasts near to them; bloodied them up, and refashioned their skins into clothing - right in front of Adam and Eve! It must have been shocking (to see the animal tore apart, like that).

Why would beasts have been killed in their presence? Perhaps, it was so that by the animal's flesh Adam and Eve might nourish their own persons, and that with the skins they might cover their nakedness...
    - *St. Ephrem the Syrian* Selected Prose Works, p. 121[44]

Blood

Interestingly enough, the Bible states that, after their fall, Adam and Eve rushed, and grabbed some vegetable (i.e. fig) leaves, to cover their private parts. God noticed that, and quickly dismissed it. Leaves or plants were just not acceptable in this situation. They just weren't going to "cut it."

Blood, it seemed, needed to come into play, here, once again. We'll, now, see that "…it was not good enough for Adam and Eve to merely cover themselves with vegetable leaves. What they needed *was atonement*."[45]

*...the blood **was God's share** of the sacrifice...*
    (Redlich, 1950, p. 109)[46]

Now, in a world where *death* abounds, blood and atonement would have to be used:

...the realm of death began to ask to be renewed with blood...
    (Halevi, 1997, p. 208)[47]

Now, the *shedding of blood*, resulting in the death of an animal, had a purpose - it represented a *substitution*, or an *atonement*, for the death-sentence God placed upon every human being. From now on, the periodic death and shedding of an animal's blood would temporarily "renew," "heal" or "bring back" Adam and Eve (as well, the rest of the human race) towards the same "spiritual" state of perfection that God requires.[48]

Now, *blood* seems to, yet again, have *another* significance, or purpose. We already knew that the name *Adam* meant "red," or "blood."[49] Some stated that Adam was even formed from a *red* dust. And, he (as we know) was, also, known as "the blusher" - one who could show red (or *blood*) in the face.

Obviously, God meant it for a good reason.

> *...but he who sins, and who thus blushes and is overwhelmed with shame, is near* **akin to him (God)**...
> - Works of Philo Judaeus Questions and Answers on Genesis I, 65[50]

God, obviously, wanted mankind to be accountable for his actions - it was just in His nature. And, this was, also, why Adam knew he should *always* remain humble, and do the honorable thing. Interestingly enough, he was to show a *blood*-red color, in his face, when feeling shame. Here, we seem to have *blood* coming into play, again.

It seems that a new, *blood*-kindred relationship with God was being established, in a number of ways. Here's another way: most of us know, from the Bible, that *blood* represents *the life* (in Lev. 17:14, for example). And, through their disobedience, Adam and Eve helped to usher in the *opposite* of life into the world: *death*. So, *blood*, again, could come into play, here. It, now, could have come back to "bite" Eve. Now, it could have served as a new, *ironic* reminder - to Eve, and all women following her. Sad to say, but the blood of m*enstruation* could now have become one of the symbols of this *impurity* between the blood-kinship of God and the kinship of mankind. It, as well, could have, now, served as a reminder to Eve, about how her careless act of sexual *fornication* became a great part of their Fall. One ancient source stated that, "Adam was the blood of the world... Eve came and spilled it." (Rabbi Nathan, Chap. 9, 42).

Also, in an esoteric way, our *earth* could be thought of as being "alive." It can "breathe," feel "pain" or even "cry out" and "complain" to God. It can also "bleed," in an esoteric way… similar to how the Tree of Knowledge had "bled," when Eve took of its fruit. The earth, because of man's sin, was beginning to feel its *own* version of "hurt" and "pain," even slowly "dying," after the Fall.

So, in a sense, mankind and the *earth*, in esoteric ways, seems to be "interrelated."

And, in one example, God seemed to have taken *some* of His anger (for the Fall) out *on the ground* - cursing the "blood-red" earth which was part of the creation of Adam. *Something* had to pay the price for sin; and God, apparently, decided to delegate some of His vengeance to the ground, instead of people.

The human woman (Eve) and *angelic* Serpent also participated in an act that "pained" our earth all the more - they came together in a *sexual* way. This act, ultimately, was the beginning of *unnatural* impurities being inserted into our natural existence - those *not meant* for this world. Sexuality between humans and terrestrial angels was not meant to be, and Eve seemed to have been required to pay a little more, for this action: "Consequently, the commandments of menstrual purity were given to her so that (the sin involved in) *the blood* which she spilled might be *atoned* for" (Rabbi Nathan, Chapter 9).

We see so many examples of how this blood-kinship with God was broken - brought on by both Adam and Eve. We also see how blood, now, had roles in the various changes going on, after the Fall.

The Circumcision of Adam

Adam did try to do a few honorable things (at least, in his mind), regarding *his* part in all of new changes. We recall that *sweat* dripped down from his brow - a new remembrance of his being *fearful* of God's wrath and punishment. He also tried to *respect* God a great deal. He trembled in fear, as we know - he, literally, "trembled throughout every limb."[51] But, there was one *limb* that we haven't really discussed yet, until now - the *male* limb.

> ...*Adam pulled **at his foreskin**... he pulled at his foreskin when he abandoned the Holy Covenant...*   - *Zohar* 2 Beresheet A 46[52]

Maybe Adam was very unhappy with what happened "down there" (in regards to his fornication with Eve in the Garden), and he began to violently mangle, or try to disfigure, his organ of generation. He may have even tore off the outermost portion of it - the *foreskin* - as some vain attempt to make amends for what his organ was involved in!

Interesting, though: there is more that seemed to have come out of this, over time. We may be able to assume that the Evil Inclination - the Serpentine nature - could have been "spiritually" transferred through sexual contact. And (according to some), the *foreskin* was a focal-point of that signature moment!

> *Under the Old Covenant, circumcision in the male organ of generation recognized that because of the Fall corruption is inherently transmitted by our sexual conception (Psalms 51:5)...*
> ("The Original Sin 1/3", n. d., p. 1)[53]

In an *esoteric* sense, the "unity" between God and that "spiritual side" of man was, now, blocked. These acts of sexual fornication, in the Garden of Eden, could have, now, been symbolized by the *foreskin* - the area located right in the middle of it all. Now, the spiritual corruption of mankind (i.e. the Evil Inclination) was even said to have "cleaved" to the foreskin, in a way. Now, men were born into sin, and *removing this foreskin* symbolized a man's desire to desire a covenant, between them and God.[54]

> *...the foreskin, which is the impure serpent, is banished...*
> - *Zohar* Vol. 15 Tazria 8[55]

In this post-Fall *world*, Adam had a number of different punishments dealt out, with a number of different ways to go about life - new things to do; new things not to do. Adam *did*, however, do a couple of things that helped bring some leniency to his punishments. Apparently, he showed *a little* more respect to God than the other two individuals involved, as we'll soon see, and that allowed him some leniency.

Obviously, how one feels about their punishments, and their outward expression of respect and guilt, both proved *very* important to God. Sad to say, it seems that Adam and Eve also reacted a little differently, when God approached them. And, because of this, the two, and members of each sex born after them, did not seem to be *punished* in the same manner. Of course, this may not sound too fair to many, but, in regards to "the punishment fitting the crime," what *had* to be, apparently, had to be. There must have been a reason for all of these punishments, sometimes uniquely linked to each sex. Adam had his post-Fall issues. He tore off his foreskin. Now, it was *Eve's* turn - to stand accountable for *her* role in it all.

The Punishment of Eve - Her Excuses

In regards to the eating of the fruit, Eve, in the Bible, clearly said that, "the Serpent gave (it to me)…" But, she was not physically "forced," nor was she physically "pressured."[56] Eve, using her free will, *decided* to be with the Serpent (and, some might say, he actually *embraced* the Serpent's rhetoric)! From this choice, she was, therefore, deprived of a lot of her excuses.[57]

> *The woman next and sinned less than he (the Serpent), but more than the man, for she sinned in two things… in **pride** and eating the fruit.*
> *- The Golden Legend or Lives of the Saints: Volume I* 61[58]

Let's take a look, first, at how Eve used the emotion of *pride*, and what it had to do in her decision-making process.

In Marriage

> *Because she sinned in **pride**, he (God) meeked her, saying: Thou shalt be under the power of man, and he shall have lordship over thee, and he shall put thee to affliction. Now is she subject to a man by condition and dread, which before was but subject by*

love…   - *The Golden Legend or Lives of the Saints: Volume I* 61[59]

We recall that Eve started to feel that she could, or even should, be above Adam, or even be *equal* to God (in her "race towards divinity").[60] We also recall that Eve used *love* as one of her seduction tactics. As we know, one fear of Eve was: if she couldn't convince Adam to eat of the fruit, then God could couple him with another woman! Because she contemplated all of these things, the parameters of togetherness (or even "marriage") between Adam and Eve, after the Fall, would have, most probably, changed - in a number of ways.

Before the Fall, the way they lived and loved just seemed to work. Adam could not find anyone else he liked in the Garden.[61] Eve came *right* from his inner rib, which made them almost inseparable. They, also, probably thought alike, quite a bit. In most ways, they seemed the "perfect" couple. We don't know if they were actually married, before the Fall (the original Hebrew words of the Bible does not quantify that, for certain), but, if they were, it probably would have been considered the "perfect married couple." Now, after the Fall, even "perfect" marriages were going to change, forever.

> *…by the instincts of her nature she shall be bound to the hard conditions of her lot… wholly subject to the arbitrary treatment sanction by… marriage customs…*
>   (Skinner, 1956, p. 83)[62]

After the Fall, a marriage were to allow the man one *legal* wife, but also a number of concubines. It wasn't anything like we've heard about, today. This *legal* element of the marriage law seemed very important to God, for various reasons. In ancient Jewish practices, for example, a man could fully utilize multiple sex partners, through concubines (for example), while women were to have only one - her husband. Why? Unfair? Well, the reasons for this inequity could have, very well, stemmed from the Fall! Could the actions of *Eve*, in the Garden, have been the reason why men were allowed concubines, or other women to have sex with? After the Fall, marriage would bind the woman, sexually, into the commitment, not the man. It wasn't given to allow Adam, for example, free reign to "live it up" with as many women as possible (while Eve was to remain at home - miserable). No, it wasn't meant to be anything like that, at all. But, a number of these changes could have had something to do with the *fornication* used against Adam, believe it or not. Men could now have the option of other women as concubines, or be with other women, if so desired, because of the desire **not to face fornication** in the future! Adam would, possibly, not have felt the same, sexual pressure to do something if Eve wasn't the only woman in Adam's repertoire. Ancient Jewish law also said that: it wasn't *adultery* for a married man to have sex with an unmarried woman, but it was for a *woman* to go outside her marriage.[63]

Part of it may, also, have been an ironic punishment to Eve's fear of Adam going to other women. Now, her fear of Adam being with another women could (and would) happen - not only once, but be *the norm*. That "once-irrational" fear, which helped to make her decide to deceive Adam, would now be felt by her, a number of times. Again, this wasn't meant to straight-up *demean* Eve, or all women after her, but, in reality, to **stop** them from being able to plot something like this again, against their husbands. Simple. But, of course, not too "politically correct."

It seemed these new marriage laws were put in place to *stop* women from using fornication in the future - as a tactic to get what they want. Now, if a wife thought about using *sex* (or, even a *lack of sex*) as a means of fornication, she would not be able to use it very efficiently! If her man, then, felt as if she was "holding out" on him, in her role as wife, he could, quite easily (and quite *legally*), go to someone *else* for his sexual gratification. Wow. It all might not sound very "politically correct," today, but it, most probably, must have worked. Over time, it seems that these ancient Jewish laws *did* seem to eliminate a lot of the power one might have been able use, in these instances. Again, it wasn't meant to *downgrade*, or *demean*, anyone in particular - it all served a purpose. It allowed men *not* to be in the position where something as natural and as *necessary* (for the most part) as **sex** would be held over his head (as a "carrot"), as a means for his wife to get what she wants.

What, by the way, was that so-called "Original Sin?" Many of us have, probably, heard of this term. Was it *sex*? Was it this *fornication*? Or, was it something more? As one author pointed out: "The basis weakness of the woman in original sin is to walk in a *spirit* of *independence* from authority."[64] In other words, it was Eve's *disobedience* to God. It had nothing to do with sex. It also had nothing to do with the requirement of Eve to be some kind of *slave* to her husband, either. In her relationship with Adam (before the Fall), Eve probably had plenty of *freedom* and *independence*. There is nothing in the ancient works about her being some kind of *slave*, or *oppressed* woman. Her disobedience to God, and, how she wanted to "become a god," both really landed her in hot water.

"God placed her back under the headship the man, (and) with the command that her desire be only to her husband."[65] Because of her choices, her original lot in life had now changed. The life she once had - with a sense of interdependent *love* and mutual understanding - was permanently altered, thanks, in large part, to this use of *fornication*. Now, we are beginning to see the *real* meaning of fornication, and why it *really* is wrong.

The Biblical phrase, "thy desire shall be to thy husband (Gen. 3:16)" may allude to another interesting possibility, here: could there have been *another* male in the picture, here, who may have, also, been the focus of her desire?[66] Now, who might this be? Could it have been the *Serpent*? Could all of these changes, in laws regarding *marriage*, have been an "opposite" punishment, here - related, again, to what happened in the Garden?

Instead of having relations with *more* than one person, as she did with the Serpent and with Adam, Eve, and other women after her, were now required to copulate with only *one* man in marriage, as part of their punishment - only *one*. A possible rationale for why so many things became *different* between men and women (after the Fall)? *Yes*. "Politically correct?" *No*.

In Subjugation to Adam

As we proceed, it's becoming interesting to see just how so *many* of Adam and Eve's punishments were *ironic*, or "opposite," in nature - a completely *contrary* response to one's own desires and thoughts before the Fall. As we know, another punishment of Eve could have been related to her desire to become "a god," or become equal to God, as well as to arrive at this "deity-status" even before Adam - or, possibly, even *reign* over him.

> *"(God speaking to Eve) ... my intention was that in everything you would share with him **as an equal**, and as I entrusted control of everything to your husband, so did I to you; but you abused your equality of status. Hence I subject you to your husband... Because you **abandoned** your equal, who was sharer with you in the same nature and for whom you were created, and you **chose to enter** into conversation with that evil created the serpent, and to take the advice **he** had to give, accordingly I now subject you to him (Adam) in future and designate him as your master... and since you did not*

*know how to rule, learn well how **to be ruled**."*
        - *St. Chrysostom* Homilies on Genesis, Homily 17[67]

This says so much; but, of course, this type of proclamation would not sit very well in our "P.C." world, of today. But, it did, actually, give us a good rendering to why things m may have turned out the way they did, in the world of today - if people would only stop, and start contemplating it.

Eve thought she could overstep her role(s) in the Garden, and found out that God would have nothing of it.

You thought to rule the man,
Your urge will be to your husband.
    - *Adamgirk: The Adam Book of Arak'el of Siwnik* p. 147[68]

Your husband shall be your master mentally and physically and only with guile shall you be able to overcome him.   (Eichhorn, 1957, p. 31)[69]

Guile is known as, "deceitful cunning: duplicity insidious cunning in attaining a goal; crafty or artful deception." Interestingly, *fornication* falls almost lock-step into all of these definitions! These were the ways the Serpent used to deceive Eve. She, then, seemed to have learned this art from him!

She had deluded Adam, even the serpent deluded her...
    - *Flavius Josephus* Jewish Antiquities, Book 1, 45-50[70]

We must not forget, however, that *Eve* was also seduced, here. It wasn't all her fault. God knew this, and, being the compassionate God that He was, felt some compassion towards Eve:

*Because Eve has admitted her crime, she is **given a milder and more salutary** sentence, which condemned her wrong doing and did not refuse pardon. [Gen 3:16] She was to serve under her husband's power, first, that she might not be inclined to do wrong...*   - *St. Ambrose* On Paradise, p. 350[71]

This new "role" of Eve may have actually been enacted to help her, and, ultimately Adam - serving to slow down their temptations to commit any acts of fornication in the future.

In Her Thoughts

Men and women, from then on, would also need to understand that they are going to be *different* from one another, regarding how they *thought*.

> *The woman stands **for our senses** and the man, for our **minds**.*
> — *St. Ambrose* On Paradise, p. 351[72]

It's interesting how Eve allowed a lot more *emotion* into her decision-making process than Adam did, here. Adam tried to, at least, think things out a little, before he acted. He showed God some of the things he knew God wanted to see. He showed remorse, etc. So, now, as part of their overall punishment: one sex, for the most part, may be forced back to think in these same ways (as in the Fall)! One may tend to value their *feelings* as more important to live, the other, more of their *rationality* or *reason*.

The incident at the Garden of Eden did, assuredly, present some very hard lessons-learned:

> *Still, let a husband be very much on his guard so as to resist his wife's inducement to harmful behavior, and let a wife keep fresh in mind the punishment Eve received for plying her husband **with harmful advice**, and not presume to offer such advice nor imitate Eve, but rather **bring him to his senses by her example** and encourage him to that kind of behavior that will discharge herself and her husband of any punishment or penalty...*   — *St. Chrysostom* Homilies on Genesis, Homily 17[73]

If seems that these roles were, now, redefined - because of the Garden. Eve, and women after her, should still be loved, protected, and cherished - especially when working as a man's help meet, or a wife.[74] Yet, the individual sexes may, now, be more inclined to think in different ways - with each sex, possibly, becoming susceptible to certain negative thoughts, each in their own, unique ways.

In Being Emotional - Sad, Sorrow & Suffering

The individual sexes may have, indeed, begun to think differently.

She looked at the heavens [and] her eyes were darkened,
She regarded the earth [and] it was ever dark.
She rushed about back and forwards,
Right and left she continuously wandered.
  - Adamgirk: The Adam Book of Arak'el of Siwnik p. 103[75]

In the above, we could possibly see that, as another punishment, Eve, and many women after her, could, now, be filled with the capacity to contemplate some *darker*, or more *negative* thoughts, about the world around her. They could have even ended up being a little more *fearful*, overall.

...in suffering shall you eat <the fruit of> this earth, and you shall have sorrow all the days of your life...
  - The Armenian Apocryphal Adam Literature
   The History of the Creation and Transgression of Adam 42[76]

...thy suffering shall be very great.
     (Goldin, 1929, p. 24)[77]

Now, some women may be more apt to feel as though they, occasionally, may be on an emotional "roller coaster."

So, if suffering and sorrow were to be part of Eve's punishment, it, naturally, would be up to the husband (or significant other) to understand it all, the best he could, and "enjoin upon one another good towards women." In other words, he should show empathy towards her, and respect her situation, here. He would need to understand the possible differences in the ways people may think, and also respect the punishments of

God, after the Fall (that were dished out in certain ways, and *for certain reasons*).[78] In the same manner, a wife should try to understand what may have happened to Eve, here (as a result of the Fall); and, that none of it is a license to *continue* on, with any negative thoughts and behaviors. She should try to control them, as best as possible.

In Intercourse

We've already discussed *menstrual* bleeding, and how it could have begun the moment Eve and the Serpent had sex, and how this process would continue on, with her, and women after her. Was this, then, another punishment?[79] Possibly, it was a *by-product* of further punishments to come. Interestingly enough, we'll see that the up-and-coming punishments of Eve would, quite often, relate to Eve's *reproductive* processes. Could these be more ironic, or "opposite" punishments, by God?

In a number of ways, the sexual experience in women could have, because of the Fall, forever changed. Death and bloodshed (even *menstrual* bloodshed) would, now, become the norm - a necessary element of their existence. And, since Adam and Eve were no longer immortal, they were, now, required to have *children* - to, at least, give them *some* sense of immortality, or *some* way to keep their individual human seed alive.

So, beyond menstruation, beyond any possible toils and pains that may, now, accompany the sex act itself, there seemed to be *other* toils and pains associated within a woman's reproduction, here.

> *"(God to Eve) Why did you harken to the serpent and abandon my commandments with which I commanded to you? (May you) be in toils and pains…"*
> - *Book of Adam* (44)25.1[80]

> *… 'your travail' (or 'toils') refers to the pain of **conception**… 'your pain' refers to the pain of **bringing up children**…*
> ("Nor Forcing Woman, the Punishment of Eve, and Learning From Animals", n. d., p. 2-3)[81]

The Bible also says that, "I (God speaking) will greatly multiply thy sorrow and thy conception; in sorrow thou shalt bring forth children… (Gen. 3:16)" In other words, Eve and women after her, could, quite often, be involved in a "multiplied" conception - women could, quite often, have a lot of children.

Is this necessarily bad? In some ways: not really. But, in other ways: *yes*. Most of us, today, have been taught that every new child that comes into this world is, in fact, a *blessing*. The clergy loves to run with that one. It's understandable, in many ways. And, it's also understandable to realize the importance, and dignity, of every human being. We're not arguing any of that, here. But, if we look at things, in regards to *sheer numbers*, and compare these with available resources around us, the facts will, then, speak for themselves. The reality is that: the *more* children a woman has, the *more* it often becomes negative for her, and her situation in the world. Sure, it seems wonderful at first. But, are we a species that needs to survive by having so many children? One study of the animal kingdom concluded that, "the *higher* the animal the *lesser* is the number of its conceptions."[82]

What does that tell us? Basically, it seems to state that: a small and limited number of children, for each set of parents, are quite sustainable for the species. In a society that has adequate resources, it is not necessary to keep breeding, and breeding, and *breeding*. Quite often, having *more* children that the family unit could sustain could easily lead to the possibility of individual calamity, stress or even physical issues developing within a person. And, of course, this overabundance may begin affect everyone around them - it's just common sense. All of it revolves around potential parents knowing "when to say when," understanding their own *limits*, and not going beyond that which could, possibly, *overstep* their lives, and their pocketbooks. Why, then, does it happen so much, today? Are there some *sinister* things in the works?

In today's world, however, there doesn't seem to be a lot of emphasis on slowing down the number of conceptions, strangely enough. Even in our so-called "developed" countries, those with plenty of contraceptives, rarely do we hear the cry to "slow down," or *individual responsibility* - or, not going beyond one's means. It's all seems to be about making *more*. "Children are a blessing," etc. Why aren't we, as a society, continually being reminded that there *always* is a limit to the number of children a couple can have, without reaching a point of diminishing returns – where these "blessings" now begin to sound like burdens. This is not "politically correct," of course, for some reason. But, this is the real world, and corruption (from many angles) abound.

> *"(God to Eve)… (may you) give birth to **many** fruits and when you give birth to them you will **despair of your life because of the torment and pains**."*
> - Book of Adam (44)25.2[83]

And, the more populated our whole world gets, as it is *today*, the *smaller* the total number of children a couple could actually have, before their individual situation may begin to trouble the society around them. It's just a fact.

So, not only would there be pain in the actual *conception*, and birth, of children, there would also be pain in the **number of children** one might have, over time. These would begin to yield great difficulties for Eve, and those after her.

In Hard Birth

So, quite possibly, these *birth pains* may have even been introduced to Eve, and women after her, to remind her of her sin in the Garden.[84] The birthing process, now, could be considered full of pain and sorrow:

> *And on that occasion you shall come near to **losing your life**.*
> (Halevi, 1997, p. 204)[85]

It seems to reach its peak during childbirth. Interestingly enough, even at the *actual* moment of birth, here, there could be a number of underlying thoughts, flowing into a woman's mind:

> *When a woman sits on her birth stool, she declares "I will henceforth **never** have sexual intercourse with my husband again!"*
> (Halevi, 1997, p. 246)[86]

> *"(God speaking to Eve)... thou shalt confess and say: 'Lord, Lord, save me, and I will turn no more to the sin of the flesh.' And on this account, from thine own words I will judge thee, by reason of the enmity which the enemy has planted in thee."*
>   - The Apocalypse of Moses / Apocalypsis Mosis 25:3-4[87]

Another token for Eve, to remember what happened in the Garden?

Also, interestingly enough, why would there be a number of punishments regarding *conception*, *child-bearing* and *child-raising*, here - if there was only straight-up sex between Eve and the Serpent? Could something *else* have resulted from their physical action? And, could all of this relate to the birth of a *child*? Could this child be the child of the Serpent - *Cain*?

> *It was not **meals** she was to eat in pain... neither... any woman has conceived by eating fruit. God knew what took place, and where punishment should be pronounced. Therefore as a **memorial**... women give birth in pain.*
>   ("The Original Sin 1/3", n. d., p. 1)[88]

Again, could all of this be because God needed to have the punishment fit the crime?[89] Could there have been *so much more* to the Serpent's contact with Eve than just casual conversation, and casual sex?

> *...and because she sinned in the fruit, she is punished **in her fruit**, when it was said to her: Thou shalt **bring forth children** in sorrow; in the pain of sorrow **standeth the curse**...*   - The Golden Legend or Lives of the Saints: Volume I 61[90]

Could Eve's "fruit" be Cain - the firstborn "fruit" of her womb?

To Blame the Serpent

> *(In Gen. 3:13)… it is possible to read not "the serpent deceived (nasa) me…" but "the serpent **took** (nasa) me…" (that is, **took in marriage**, by **intercourse**), a reading made possible by the nature of Hebrew…*   (Delaney, 1996, p. 12)[91]

Yes, the Serpent may have *took* - or *possessed* - Eve, for a point in time, and she could, *indeed*, have became pregnant. Interestingly enough, one meaning of the name *Cain* is "possession" - a fitting remembrance of the act which, ultimately, led to *his* conception? More on Cain, later.

The Unclean Serpent

The punishments continue, now, with the *Serpent*. God called the Serpent over to Him, who was *still* laughing.[92] You can't get more disrespectful than that! Although God would go to the Serpent last to find out about what happened, He actually decided to punish the Serpent first, and foremost.

> *And our Lord, cursing them, began at the serpent… The serpent was the first and sinned most, for he sinned in three things. The serpent had **envy**, he lied, and deceived,*

for these three he had three curses.
- *The Golden Legend or Lives of the Saints: Volume I* 61[93]

Envy and the Belly

As we'll now see, there were *mental* elements to the Serpent's punishments, as well.

*Because he had **envy** at the excellence of man, it was said to him: Thou shalt go and creep on thy breast...*
- *The Golden Legend or Lives of the Saints: Volume I* 61[94]

In the Bible, God condemned the Serpent to "crawl on his *belly* (or *breast*)" (Gen. 3:14). This probably did not mean that the Serpent would actually *lose his legs*, and turn into a modern-day snake, but thinking the way he did, in the future, would, most often, lead him to worthless outcomes, later on. Following his ways will, eventually, lead one down the pathways of *despair*, *worthlessness* and *death*.

In the above quote, it's interesting to discover that a *breast*, in ancient times, was often considered the *seat of wisdom*.[95] The Serpent's wisdom would change, from then on: from one who was considered probably one of the highest-ranking beings, as far as what he thought, to one who would consistently think "lower" or dishonorable thoughts. This, most probably, was the real significance of *crawling on one's belly*. They began to invest their thoughts towards that of the *lower* earth, and apart from God:

*...the real meaning contains an allegory concealed beneath it; since the serpent is the emblem of desire, representing under a figure a man devoted to pleasure. For he creeps upon his breast and upon his belly, being filled with meat and drink like cormorants, being inflamed by an insatiable cupidity, and being incontinent in their voracity and devouring of flesh, so that whatever relates to food is in every article something **earthly**.*
- *Works of Philo Judaeus* Questions and Answers on Genesis I, 48[96]

Cupidity, in the above, is defined as an, "excessive desire, especially to **possess** something;" *incontinent* is defined as being "unable to contain or retain;" and *voracity* is "eager to consume great amounts of food, ravenous, insatiable." Put them all together, and we have a few examples of one with "lower" thoughts - who think more of *worldly* things. And, the allegory "to crawl on one's belly" doesn't translate, here, into some snake just slithering around our world, but, more likely, an individual who, quite often, thinks worldly thoughts, or uses a great deal of *lust*.

> *And dust shall be the serpent's food... Even if the serpent were to eat all the delicacies of the world, he would **feel** therein but **the taste of dust**...*
> - The Babylonian Talmud Yoma 75a[97]

Interesting, in the above quote, we also discover the *aftermath* of thinking in these lower ways. The person may end up feeling as though they tasted *dust*. From what we already know about *dust*, however, could this mean that the person feels as though they were tasting *humility*, *negativity* - or even *worthlessness*? And, if so, what would that do to them?

The individuals who want to go down these pathways seem to find it hard to restrain their desires for the things of this world. And, once they begin to feel worthless, anything around them that could, at least temporarily, help raise their feelings of self-esteem, or worth, would be pursued. It may, then, even become a vicious cycle! All these feelings of worthlessness do is to make you want to go back, again, and hope for the best - it never becomes enough. It's a lot like a sailor who's stuck in the middle of an ocean, on a raft. He is thirsty, and needs to drink. The funny part is: he is sitting on an ocean of water. But, his water has to be fresh. Once he starts to drink the salty ocean water below him, things becomes worse and worse off. He may continue to do this, even though it is harmful to him. But, he is thirsty, and, in his point of desperation, his brain tells him that there's plenty of water beneath him. to drink.

The same thing applies, here. The Serpent, and those who begin to desire lower, worldly things, often try to possess *as much* of what the earth may have to offer as they can get (such as material wealth, sex, etc.). But, of course, it, so often, can turn into something insatiable, unfulfilled and even *deadly*.

> *Pleasure stirs the senses, which, in turn, have their effect on the mind… To convince you that the serpent is the type of pleasure, take note of his condemnation. 'On your breast and on your belly shall you crawl,' [Gen 3:14] we read. Only those who **live for the pleasures of the stomach** can be said to walk on their bellies, 'whose god is their belly and their glory is their shame,' [Phil 3:19] who eat of what is **earthy**, and who, weighed down with food, are bent over **towards what is of earth**. The **serpent** is well called the symbol of pleasure in that, intent on food, he seems to feed **on the earth**.*   - **St. Ambrose** On Paradise, p. 351-352[98]

People who follow the ways of the Serpent may, so often, become stuck in this lustful pattern of thinking. Their lives may begin to subsist on acquiring earthly possessions. These accumulations, then, ultimately become, in a way, *idols* to the individual. Their whole moral outlook changes.

These thoughts, over time, may begin to damage the individual, as a whole, their repeating the same processes, just to feel a little more self-esteem:

> *He says that the serpent crawls on his breast and belly. This is due not so much to the **shape** of his body as to the fact that he has **fallen** from celestial happiness because of his **thoughts of earth**… men, too, who (are)… 'minding the things of the earth' [Phil 3:20]… without the inner urge to rise towards heaven, have the appearance of crawling on their bellies… we surely ought to fill the belly of our souls with the Word of God rather than with the corruptible things of this **world**. Fittingly, therefore, does David, assuming the character of Adam, say: 'My soul is humbled down to the dust, my belly cleaveth to the earth.' [Ps 44:25] He used the word 'cleaveth' in reference to the serpent who feeds on **earthly iniquities**.*   - **St. Ambrose** On Paradise, p. 353-354[99]

It's simple: the Serpent, and those who directly, or indirectly, want to follow these same pathways, often desire a life which generally revolves around earthly acquisitions – or whatever might "cleave" to this earth. This will never fully serve to raise their self-esteem enough, to allow them to *stay* content about their life, overall.

Dust, Venom & Poison

> *…because he lied he is punished in his mouth, when it was said: Thou shalt eat **earth** (i.e. dust) all the days of thy life. Also he took away his voice and put venom in his*

> *mouth.*   - *The Golden Legend or Lives of the Saints: Volume I* 61[100]

Dust, as we've seen, gives us more of the same, here. If we look at the above, we see that, in a *moral* sense, the Serpent would eat up, or consume, whatever's *earthly* - the opposite of looking towards morals that are higher, like God's. It's so simple to understand, once we see it all in this light.

> *Thou shalt be deprived of the **victual** of which thou didst eat... and shalt feed on dust.*
>   - *The Apocalypse of Moses / Apocalypsis Mosis* 26:2[101]

The Serpent, no longer, was to "feed" on that which was from above. The word *victual*, in the above, stands for, "usable, fit" - that which makes, and keeps, one a moral (and worthy) individual. And, as we would expect, *dust* can be likened to a "mere metaphor for humiliation" or that "proceeding to corruption." These are also considered *moral* attributes - desiring worldly things are thoughts that, eventually, will *humiliate* the individual, and bring them down.[102] Simple.

> *It was the very ability of the serpent that led to the ruin of man and his own ruin.*
>   (Ginzberg, 1909, p. 105)[103]

His (once) knowledgeable words of wisdom were, now, destined to contained *venom*, ready to entice any unsuspecting individuals into following these same desires *of the world*, helping them to remain in these same *worthless* states, as well.

> *...what you have will disintegrate and deteriorate; what you speak or say will be **poison**.*   (Frankel, 1989, p. 30)[104]

The "poison" of the Serpent is, obviously, now ingrained what he ***thinks***, what he says and what he promotes to others. We now know why the Serpent (a.k.a. Azazel) was thought of as the "Poison of God."

> *...the poison of death shall be **in your mouth***
> (Halevi, 1997, p. 203)[105]

The two phrases in Genesis, describing the Serpent's punishment (i.e. "upon thy belly" and "dust"), *both* seem to imply that his future would be nothing but the utmost humiliation and defeat.[106] And, quite probably, this will apply to whomever decides to follow in his footsteps - to *adopt* and *embrace* these same ways into their own, particular lifestyles, as well.

> *From the emanation of his power come **destruction** and **ruin**...*
> (Collins, 1996, p. 70)[107]

Interestingly enough, Jesus was a *carpenter*; Adam was chief *gardener*. These occupations actually build, or *create*, *something* - they make things better in the world. The Serpent, however, embitters everyone and everything around him, luring them into false outcomes. His ways will actually lead followers into the exact "opposite" of what he promoted as "positive." Those who look to something *of the earth* for their "food" and "sustenance" could receive a temporary boost; but, it's only a "quick fix," and won't last.

Those who know better will not follow the Serpent's "easy ways out," but look to things that are *higher*.

> "*(God to the Serpent) Because thou, reprobate, hast deceived these and hast made them to become unclean, shalt thou be satiated with uncleanness.*"
> - *Gospel of Barnabas* 41[108]

> *...and all will call you cursed.*
> (Frankel, 1989, p. 30)[109]

The Serpent was even said to have a *dark* complexion - again, most probably, because of all the *darkness* that descended into his soul, here.[110]

Woe to the author of perdition!
      - The Armenian Apocryphal Adam Literature
        The Words of Adam to Seth 14[111]

The Bible sums up the Serpent, and his ways, into one word: **perdition** (II Thess. 2:3, John 17:12) - which, simply, means *worthlessness*.[112]

The Enmity of Genesis 3:15

And because he deceived, it was said: I shall put enmity between thee and woman, and thy seed and her seed. She shall break thy head, etc.
        - The Golden Legend or Lives of the Saints: Volume I 61[113]

We've already discussed the above *curse* in detail. This was the prophecy of Genesis 3:15, which, according to some, was "…the first great *promise* and *prophecy*."[114] Now, there would actually be individuals born on this earth with blood of the Serpent! And, over time, a number would just plain want to *desire* these ways, over God. There is a battle, here, going on in the world around us.

There is not real goodness in those who seek only after the things of the earth.
Theirs is the heart of the serpent.
      (Eichhorn, 1957, p. 19)[115]

Two different sets of desires. Two different moral outlooks. And, as we know, it's either one or the other, in this world. So, everyone born - from that period on - would, eventually, have to make a decision: to accept these ways *of the earth* as their new "god," or follow the one and only, *true* God.

More Punishments To All

(God) cast them out and clothed them in gloomy darkness.
        - Apocalypse of John 24:6-8[116]

The punishments were given. It was, now, time for them all to leave the Garden. God is not only a God of punishment, but a God of love. Sometimes, as a father would have to be to his son, He must also punish (in order to show this love).

Welcome to the world of the Fall. We can thank Adam, Eve and *especially* the Serpent for allowing all of this to be leashed upon our earth:

Grief was named
And anguish was prepared,
And pain was created,
And trouble consummated,
And disease began to be established,
And Sheol (i.e. the Darkness) kept demanding that it should be renewed in blood,
And the begetting of children was brought about,
And the passion of parents produced,
And the greatness of humanity was humiliated,
And goodness languished.
    - The Book of the Apocalypse of Baruch (2 Baruch) 56:6[117]

An entirely "new world" was, also, to be incorporated inside the human *mind* - a newly-corrupted "human nature," complete with *lust* and an *Evil Inclination*.

Also, feelings of *guilt*, *sadness* or *depression* would continually lurk on the horizon of the human mind.

And:

*...their intimate relationship with God is replaced by distrustful, selfish, servile **fear**...*
("The Original Sin 1/3", n. d., p. 1)[118]

Beyond fear, beyond guilt - Adam and Eve, and those coming after them, would also begin to let their *pride* dominate their thoughts, as well as other *negative* emotions. That divine "fire" - the one that God endowed Adam and Eve with, in the Garden - had, now, departed from them.

Of course, all that was left was the "fires" of emotional passion - and, so much of it was *negative*. A lot of *disagreement* and *strife* began to arise amongst people. The great virtue that Adam was known for - *humility* - would begin to be looked upon, by many, as insignificant, worthless or, for the most part, unworthy of pursuit. In its place, *self-*centered thoughts - pride-influenced thoughts - were becoming the new norm. Unfettered emotions began to take the place of honor, rationality or reason.

*When he (Adam) transgressed, untimely death came into being, mourning was mentioned, affliction was prepared, illness was created, labor accomplished, **pride** began to come into existence...*   (Halevi, 1997, p. 208)[119]

*Their chief emotions are jealously and rivalry and **hate**.*
                                       (Eichhorn, 1957, p. 19)[120]

It's interesting to see that there were so many **mental** elements involved in this whole Garden of Eden story! And, it's equally interesting to see that: so much of what goes on, today, probably had its origins in this story of Adam, Eve and their fall. It's all here, just "sanitized." Yet, this original story now becomes a template for understanding why so many people, today, think the ways they do, as well as *why* things are the way they are, between individuals.

Also, it is, now, up to *each* individual to understand their own "human nature," here, and what kind of power it might actually have over their daily lives, if they let it. It also is up to each individual to figure out how to deal with these *additional* thoughts and lusts continually flowing into one's thoughts. These have weaseled their way into most people, and cultures, since the beginning - corrupting and manipulating our world into the world it is, today. More on this, later. But, for now, we'll see that this could, also, provides us a *foundation* for understanding this *mystery* side of *Mystery Babylon* - to discover how it began to develop, and how it would come to be adopted by so many!

The story of the Garden, ultimately, helps to cement a few perceptions: the one who *seduced* Eve was much more than a wriggling snake. A snake does not really care about changing another person's political, religious or moral views - on any level. If he was a terrestrial, humanoid being - an angel, demoted from his former angelic splendor - then the possibility exists for this Serpent to retain the same functions as any other human being... to think the same, and procreate the same.

Also, we must ask ourselves: why would so many of Eve's punishments deal with *conceiving* or *child bearing*, unless there was really something that could have come from all this - such as, a *child* conceived by the Serpent and Eve? We will, next, take a deeper look into the man who, most probably, *did* come from the Serpent and Eve, as the result of this fornication inside the Garden - none other than *Cain*, himself.

Chapter 4

Cain, Seed of the Serpent (Part 1)

    All of these *mental* connotations, in regards to those sexual acts in the Garden, will broaden with our look at *Cain*. We'll begin with a deeper examination of this Biblical character, discovering *even more* about what might have gone on inside his head, what actually happened to his brother Abel, and how *Mystery Babylon* first began to develop! There is so much more ancient information about Cain, here, than there was on the Serpent. And, we also know that *he* was the biggest promoter of the ways of the Serpent, after the Fall.

    Looking at this direct Serpent-seed gives us so much more information - exposing and unraveling the **mindsets** of those individuals behind this foundation of *Mystery Babylon*. After all, it's easy to see, here, the parallel: "like father, like son."

It's A New (& Cursed) World

It was time for Adam and Eve to leave the Garden - forever. It was time for them to experience night for the first time; to experience cold; to experience the "law of the jungle." Evidence of *death* and *worthlessness* would begin to sprout up… everywhere. The human body was, slowly, starting to weaken, and become frail. Adam, for the first time, felt pain and exhaustion. It became harder and harder for him, and everyone else, to do what, once, they were able to do with ease - welcome to life as a *mortal*, in their brave new world.

Adam was, also, forced to do what he feared most: work the fields for his sustenance; work in a world with so many new adversities. "Necessity compelled them to agriculture; the virtues of their former garden disappeared."[1] Now, the use of agriculture and irrigation seemed to be unavoidable disciplines of this new world - no longer could they just go around, consuming large, nutritious fruits of the Garden.[2]

Need For Sacrifice

Adam was also the first to be obligated to provide some (continual) manner of blood sacrifice to God.[3] It was the new "necessity" of life, with Adam as the first priest.[4] These new sacrifices were, now, to become a symbol of the newfound faith in God, after the Fall.[5] Back in the beginning, here, it seemed that Adam's first choice of animal for this sacrifice would be a *bull*, or ox.[6] As well, it seems fairly obvious that this wasn't a heart-warming task: to kill an animal, and spill its blood.

Adam and Eve quickly began to dream of any way they could think of, to "earn" their way back into the Garden without having to do things such as this. They also knew the prophecy of Genesis 3:15: a "redeemer," or child born of Eve's seed, would bring the human race back toward this closeness with God, again - towards the state they, once, had, in the Garden. They just didn't know *who* this child was to be, or *when* he would be born. So, they thought that: maybe, if they rushed to have more and more children, they could, in their lifetimes, still be alive when their redeemer comes, to save their souls. And, the curse would be over.

Bringing Forth The "Promised Child"

> *The first pair, since, as this report of what*
> *God had decreed, had spread,* **the chief desire**
> *Was to* **increase**...
> *But longing still for Eden, they were seized*
> *With a desire to populate the earth.*
> *That bliss might* **sooner** *come, so that it was*
> *Fulfilled that in the curse had been pronounced,*
> *Namely, the* **multiplying of conceptions**...
>   (Phifer, 1890, p. 154)[7]

Adam and Eve may have even begun this (misguided) idea: that having as many children as they could, one after another, could actually *help* them in the long run. Their "multiplying of conceptions" - that which God decreed as a *curse* to Eve - could help to save them from their post-Fall life. They, continually, felt a great deal of sorrow at this time, and couldn't wait for either themselves, or their descendants, to be blessed with the "promised one."

Yet, there seemed to be a blockade to their goal, already - "right out of the starting gate." There was something coming by which they could not do anything about, now. It was definitely on its way. There was a growing bump in the middle of Eve's navel. Her entire body was changing, as well. Her stomach was growing. She was beginning to get really scared. She didn't understand how it was to be pregnant.

At least with a rudimentary knowledge of sex, however, she probably couldn't help but think of the Serpent as the father. The Serpent helped to change the world in so many ways already. And, again, he was doing it - and, again, it wasn't for good.

It was around this same time that Adam, most probably, noticed something about Eve. There was at least one offspring in her womb. Adam realized, or *knew*, something was going on inside of her! Many hard-lined Bible interpreters, however, will hold fast to the ideal that this first child born of Eve (in Gen. 4:1) was actually *Adam's* son, because the English reads that Adam *knew* his wife, or had sex with her. True, that is one original Hebrew meaning of the English *knew*, here, but we already know that this word could have a *two-fold* significance. Those who translated the Bible into English could have, naturally, assumed that the first-born son of Eve *had* to be from Adam - who else could have been around, to be the father?

So, because of this, they began to translate the Bible accordingly. But, there are other meanings:

The word *knew* could, in actuality, mean that Adam:
- was *beginning to understand* what happened to Eve, and what was going on inside of her.[8]
- was becoming *aware* that Eve had actually conceived - not from him, but from the Serpent.[9]
- was *beginning to recognize* exactly what the Serpent did to them both, and their world, and was *trying to take in* how he was actually robbed of his chance to be the father of Eve's first child.[10]

In the other definitions of *knew*, here, we see that: Eve was pregnant, and Adam, most probably, *knew* or *understood*, that…

…he (the child) is a true son of the Devil.
- *Saltair na Rann* 1961-1964[11]

Adam, also, came to the realization: he *knew* he was not the father.

Pregnancy

Again, it is imperative to understand just *who* this firstborn son of Eve was. As we're beginning to discover, there's a lot of ancient written evidence out suggesting *who* his probable father was: *the Serpent*, himself![12] We can't stress this concept enough, or "drive this point home" enough!

Even fresh out of the Garden, the Serpent wasn't too far from the lives of Adam and Eve. He, seemingly, lurked around every corner, looking for ways to capitalize on their depravity. The Serpent, as we know, probably had a plethora of information about our former world, which may have included *an understanding* of pregnancy. The Serpent could have used this information to taunt Eve, continually trying to manipulate her.[13]

(Eve) Begged... (God)... to protect her from
*The sickly gliding snake, which **twisted yet**...*
(Phifer, 1890, p. 126)[14]

One way he hoped to trick her would be regarding the Genesis 3:15 Prophecy. The more hopeful Adam and Eve became for its fulfillment the more she began to succumb to what the Serpent was pushing onto her.

After all, God and His angels were no longer in close communication with them. There were still extremely-knowledgeable, terrestrial angels (i.e. the Nephilim) around. As time went on, Eve may have eventually felt a little more at ease asking the Serpent his thoughts, especially on the pregnancy. After all, he was right there. The Serpent could have also, over time, begun to convince her that he *still* had God's best interests in mind, for her - even after what he did! He may have tried to convince her that, since he was close to the celestial realm, he, occasionally, could deliver some of His messages to her.[15]

Besides, Eve, assuredly, had trepidations in her brave new world, and could use practically any help she could get - *especially* regarding her pregnancy.

Further Attempts to Trick Eve

She was, in actuality, horrified by the whole pregnancy process. She didn't know what was going to happen to her. It's totally understandable, given her situation. His manipulations would, then, intensify, over time. Apparently, she may have even begun to fear that she could bring forth something *unnatural*, or some kind of inhuman *animal* (as a result of cross-breeding with a terrestrial angel)!

The Serpent, then, may have told her that he knew of a way she could produce a normal human baby - without any birth defects. All she had to do was to make a deal with him. He bargained: If your baby "comes out healthy, without harming or **killing you**, well, then you should obey me in whatever I command you?"[16] With the Serpent's "connections," he could assure that God would cause a healthy baby to come out of her.[17] So, of course, if the baby *naturally* came out healthy, then the Serpent could claim all the credit![18] What a swindler.

And, on top of this all, "there is nothing in the record to indicate that Eve ever told Adam anything about her affair with the serpent."[19] If this was the case, Adam must have taken an intelligent guess about it all. He wouldn't know for sure - that is, until the child was be born. In those days, no one knew for sure, because there was no DNA test. Adam, probably, continued to live with some underlying degree of hope - hope that everything would work out all right, even after the child was born (when he knew, for sure, that the child wasn't his).

Eve, assuredly, was torn about the whole process of conception, and what the Serpent told her. They, both, wouldn't have a number of answers they were looking for… at least until she took a look at the baby for the first time.

Time For a Midwife

The time had come for the birth of whomever child was inside her. She was beginning her labor. God even appointed angels to surround Eve, and assist in the birth. One angel could have even helped serve as a midwife.[20] In this new and frightening process, a baby boy was born. The words of the Serpent echoed in her, as well as her hopes that this child might be the "promised one."

When the child was born, Eve, reportedly, became a little frightened - so much that she may have even wished to kill him![21] The child looked very different than she did, and that Adam did. It seemed obvious, now, that he wasn't from Adam. But, as her thoughts began to progress, she may have, then, started to reflect on what she had already learned, and may have changed her tune a little. Maybe these strange attributes were actually a *good* sign. Maybe, by his looks, he was something special.

The name was decided for this child: *Cain*.[22]

> *...Eve conceiv'd by Sammael, and brought forth Cain; and... she saw, by his shape, that he was unlike the lower creatures, and that he was of **the upper creation**...*
> (Eisenmenger, 1748, p. 197)[23]

In other words, he looked, at least some, as if he was a heavenly being - or, at least, came from one. He was still human; but, as we've already explained, he had the same angelic countenance, or "shine," to him as the other terrestrial angels around him. Some traditions stated that Cain may have even "shown" as brightly as the sun![24] The well-formed Cain corresponded perfectly to Eve's exclamation in the Bible: he came "from the Lord" or "from an angel of the Lord" (Gen. 4:1).[25]

We also know that Adam, and practically anyone else around him, lost a great deal of their "shine" when he fell. Cain, surely, wasn't in the image of Adam, here, or any *other* human being![26] Because of this, it was, probably, fairly easy for Adam to conclude that he wasn't the father.[27] This sure seemed to be the convincer, even though Adam still hoped, deep down in his heart, that the situation could have ended up differently. Interestingly enough, if we really stop to think about it, there is no place in the Bible that states Adam was the father of *all* living - nowhere![28]

And, on top of it all, Cain's "other-worldly" appearance could have given Eve a shot at their dream. Eve may have thought that he, somehow, *could* have been their "promised one" - the child able to neutralize all of the shame Adam and Eve brought upon the world.[29] Eve pondered: maybe, with Cain's great countenance, the Serpent's dialogue wasn't really too far off the mark. Eve already saw that Cain was quite the *opposite* of a deformed, inhuman beast. In fact, he looked quite the *opposite* of most everyone around her. Maybe the Serpent *did* have the ability to influence her pregnancy for the better. Maybe their special child *was* the one that could have been able to usher them back to the Garden, and their former life!

> *In thinking Cain had really brought bliss…*
> *Wore off the rough, sharp corners of her woe.*
>   (Phifer, 1890, p. 147)[30]

Cain, in reality, would head her, and those around them, in the complete, *opposite* direction.

Angelic and Human Bloodlines

Cain was an anomaly, that's for sure. According to one author, "wickedness came into the world via the first being born of woman, Cain, the so-called oldest son of Adam."[31] It may have been one big, "happy family" if Adam and Eve have had their own, righteous children. But, all the way back then, our world was, quickly, becoming very complex.

Unlike people who may mix races or creeds today, Cain, and other up-and-coming angelic-human offspring, were to be condemned by God. These were hybrid human beings, not mixed human beings! These particular offspring were, in actuality, an intrusion into our natural world - something that God, plainly, did not authorize, intend on, nor create.[32] And, as we've already seen, there seems to be some other, little-known meanings for "adultery" and "fornication" - all related to Cain, and other cross-bred, human mixtures after him.

> *First, adultery came into being, afterward murder. And he (Cain) was **begotten in adultery**, for he was a child of the Serpent.*   - *The Gospel of Philip*[33]

So, *adultery* and *fornication*, as in the case of what happened between Eve and the Serpent, could, very well, result in the birth of a child - a child that God did not plan for this world.[34]

The Prediction of Worthlessness

Also, according to ancient lore, Cain was able to show everyone some interesting, "adult-like" characteristics, right after his birth! Eve, according to the Bible, stated that she had gotten a man from the Lord (in Gen. 4:1). Why a *man*, here, and not a child?

In one of the many meanings of the name *Cain*, we see that it could also stand for a "stalk," or "straw."[35] Why? We have an interesting legend, regarding this birth: even as a new-born infant, Cain "could walk, immediately cutting the grass for his father."[36] In other words, a short time after his birth, it was fairly easy for Cain to stand up, and waddle around, like a full-grown adult - even pick up a blade of grass! He yanked this blade out of the ground and walked back over to Adam, and gave it to him. This event seemed to have been an omen of what would prove to be the child's future (at least, coming from the mouth of an angel who attended to Eve, at the birth):

> *...the newborn's infants first act is a destructive one - he pulls out grass around another's hut, which never grows back... (then) the attending Angel said to him (Cain), "your legacy will be of adultery and bitterness."*
> (Schwartz, 2004, p. 449)[37]

Cain, *indeed*, would go on to destroy much of what was around him, reduce a lot to worthlessness, and fatally corrupt the lives of many.

> *They first bore the abominable Cain, the murderous child of destruction.*
> (Anderson, 2000, p. 203)[38]

The birth of Cain, according to one ancient source, was very painful and difficult for Eve (even *worse* than normal births were destined to be, from then on). Even *this* seemed to correlate with Cain's future:[39]

...the harsh snake instilled the impurity of harsh judgment in her... Therefore, when Cain emerged from the side of the female he exited rough and hard, harsh in judgment and heavy in judgment. - *Zohar* Idra Raba 47[40]

"Augmented" Abel

Now, if Cain was the elder (or, first-born) son of Eve, where would Abel, his brother, come into play?

It was said that: Eve, then, *augmented*, or *continued on*, in labor - she gave birth to Cain and Abel at almost the same time![41] Here could be the first example of God's promise to, "multiply... thy conception" (Gen. 3:16). In Eve's case, this "multiplying" of conception could have resulted in Eve having two twin boys![42]

*It is written: "Adam knew his wife, Chavah (Eve), and she conceived and gave birth to Kayin (Cain)"... (Gen. 4:1), but it is not written that Adam begot Kayin (Cain). This was not written of Hevel (Abel) either. Instead, it is written: "and she further gave birth to his brother, Hevel (Abel)" (Gen. 4:2). And here lies **the concealed truth**, that even Hevel (Abel) was **not** in the image or likeness of Adam.*
- *Zohar* Beresheet b62[43]

Logic would indicate, then, that *both* Cain and Abel were not the son of Adam, and neither looked like the son of Adam, as well. In the Bible, it even states that Adam did not have a child who looked like him until *Seth* was born, sometime in the future (in Gen. 5:3)!

Interestingly enough, the up-and-coming death of one of Eve's children would greatly "augment," or "multiply" Eve's sorrow, here, as well - another curse already pronounced to her, in the Garden, by God (in Gen. 3:16).[44]

Those Twins

A good number of early conceptions, just after the Fall, may have been *twins*. Why? At least, in this early time, God could have wanted to ensure the propagation of the human race, so He designated a number of couples to end up having twins.[45] Because of the purity that, also, probably existed in our early gene pool, marriages between close relatives didn't have as much of a potential for problems as it would have probably had, later on.

> *...Cain and Abel were both Satan's sons...*
> (Graves & Patai, 1964, p. 99)[46]

Ancient lore also tells us that, quite often, a *daughter* and son were born together - to assist, further, in the propagation process.[47] Some sources have even stated that, occasionally, daughter was born, right along with sons.

It was probably apparent, to Adam, that he did not sire Abel, as well. He did not resemble Adam. But, on the other hand, baby Abel did seem a little different than Cain, in some ways. Looking beyond the "shine," and his physical appearance, Adam noticed something: Abel just looked as though he was going to be a "nicer" baby, with a pleasant personality. He looked as though he would, eventually, grow up with a better disposition, overall - it just seemed to be written all over his face.

> *...at that sorrowful moment Cain was born, and when Adam saw that the face of Cain was ill-tempered (or, sullen) and his appearance evil he was sad. And then Abel was born, and when Adam saw that his appearance was good and his face good-tempered...* - Book of the Glory of Kings (Kerba Nagast) 3[48]

And, Adam had some definite ideas about Cain, as well. It was said that, from Abel, would come someone, "more merciful, but still not perfect."[49] In other words, the two were, "like good wine mixed with bad..."[50] Although *both* may have come from the Serpent, they did seem to possess some different characteristics "right out of the starting gate." Why? Why the differences in the two? It clearly wasn't their bloodlines.

There's, also, other ancient source which suggests that Cain was "full of light." Abel, on the other hand, appeared to be "well-*minded*."[51] This seemed to be an important distinction between the two. Cain and Abel may have, both, had a wonderful, outward appearance. Abel, however, probably had a wonderful *inner* appearance, as well - a good man to get to know.

Cain, technically, was born first, of the two. Hence, he was, supposedly, allowed to be bearer of the birthright. In ancient times, the child born *first* to a couple was entitled to certain, special privileges - the birthright. Since Adam was, most probably, with Eve at the time, he was in the position to rear both of them as his own. But, he began to take a shine to the well-minded Abel.

Growing Up

As Cain grew up, he began to take on a number of *negative* mannerisms: he acted "strong-limbed" towards others; "swift;" "fierce;" and, even, was starting to act "truly wild."[52] Obviously, there was a reason why Adam leaned in favor of Abel, sometimes. Regardless of being a son of the Serpent, Abel was, truly, walking *in the spirit* of Adam, and of God, and began to make use of the ways that God laid out for the human race (thoughtfulness, humility, etc.).[53] He strived to be a good person, as Adam was. He strived to care, and show respect, for others.

Abel dealt with people "in the integrity of his soul, bearing witness to the truth."[54] "He paid heed to virtue. He "told it like it was." Cain, on the other hand, seemed to have had an eye only for *gain*."[55] Well, what was going on with Cain? Why was he beginning to sour so quickly? As one might expect, "Neither did his (Cain's) deeds resemble those of Abel; Cain inherited the nature of Sammael."[56] "Cain looked and acted exactly as one would expect a son of the *Serpent* to look and to act."[57] This time, it appears that the Serpent, and not God, became the foundation of Cain's negativity.

There was a little more to all of this, however: Cain also started to concentrate on acquiring what *the world* around him had to offer, and not what God had:

> *...the contemptible snake... immediately laid hold of and destroyed Cain by filling him with worldly forgetfulness.*   (Layton, 1995, p. 177)[58]

In one example, we see that Cain began to wallow on the benefits of his birthright. Even back in his youth, he began to rationalize that, since he was technically the eldest, he deserved twice as much as Abel deserved (or "double" the share of).[59] This was probably one of the earliest versions of a human being possessing some kind of "entitlement mentality." Yet, as we've seen throughout the Bible, it wasn't really the best position to be a firstborn - many of our ancient Biblical patriarchs weren't!

Yet, as one could also guess, God was beginning to look down, upon the two, and see some problems brewing. And, because He already knew what was going on inside their hearts, He may have started to show a little favoritism towards Abel.[60] That comes as no surprise! Cain, already in his mind, was beginning to reject God - even if he didn't realize it, yet.

Eve, however, really cared for her firstborn son, regardless of the direction Cain may have been starting to head. After all, Cain *was* her son. Mothers and sons often seem to have a close bond, no matter what. She often went out on a limb, and ventured to teach Cain everything that she knew.[61] Although Adam tried to love them both the same, he could also see potential problems within Cain, and how he was beginning to act.

Soon, he started to feel a need to do something about it.

The Opposing Occupations - Shepherd Vs. Farmer

Time had passed. The twins began to make their own places in the world. It seemed that their soon-to-be occupations would actually suit them, each, in their own way. Adam really did not want them to work together, because of Cain, and his potential for wrong-doing. Adam even wanted them to be apart, in certain ways. Adam may have even pushed them towards two different occupations, based upon his foresight.

From early childhood, Abel was said to have spent a lot of his time working with domesticated animals. "He was gifted in working with them, understanding and caring for their needs…"[62]

> *...when their actions are to be compared together, he (Abel) is placed first... one of them exercises a business, and takes care of living creatures, although they are devoid of reason, gladly taking upon himself the employment of a shepherd...*
>   - *Works of Philo Judaeus* Questions and Answers on Genesis 1(59)[63]

> *(The shepherd)... prepares himself for a Godly life: by separating himself from material temptations, by living simply, by developing within himself the power of inner contemplation and the joy of inner contentment. Abel displayed wisdom and strength of character...*   (Eichhorn, 1957, p. 36)[64]

It's obvious: Abel had a strong character, a good moral foundation and a lot of dignity. We've also seen, throughout the Bible, how God and Jesus were considered to be *shepherds*, in a way. The "good shepherd," Jesus, tried to help people, not exploit them.

Cain, of course, desired to work the ground, as a farmer would. He, then, made this profession as his own. There's nothing wrong with being a farmer, but Cain would go way beyond how a typical farmer might care for the land - he wanted to possess as much *of the earth* as he could.

> *...the other devotes his attention to **earthly** and **inanimate objects**.*
>   - *Works of Philo Judaeus* Questions and Answers on Genesis 1(59)[65]

He "selected farming as his occupation because real estate is the most *tangible* of all earthly assets..."[66] Cain, then, would end up being very materialistic - "wholly intent upon getting."[67] This "closeness to the earth" would allow Cain, then, to become irrevocably "fused" within his vice.

> *Cain... tiller of earth*
> *a slave of dirt.*
>   (Halevi, 1997, p. 246)[68]

Most of the time, a farmer takes his job seriously, and loves the land he works. It almost becomes a working relationship between the two. Sometimes, however, the relationship between a farmer and his crops can end up being very impersonal, or very crass.[69] He did things differently, and, with a different attitude. To a "self-lover" like

Cain, everything became "all about him!"[70] Cain, also, "idolized material property and material values" and the "physical strength and power" the world was able to give him.[71] Ultimately, Cain, and all of those who would eventually follow him, would adopt these same self-serving thoughts. They, wholly, "abandoned the way of God and put their trust in *earthly* goods."[72]

Which Wife To Whom?

And, on top of this, there could have been another significant piece to our whole puzzle, here. The ancient Hebrew words used to describe the birth of Cain and Abel may allude to even *more* children being born at this time, or around this time! As fascinating as it may seem, some traditions have even stated that Eve may have *continued*, or *added onto*, her offspring - beyond Cain and Abel. Some say that at least one *sister* was born, along with each male![73] Yes, quadruplets. Other sources may imply that Eve gave birth to a couple of twin sisters, a little while after the birth of Cain and Abel.

Regardless of what way the births actually came about, there could have been, at least, one sister of Cain, somewhere down the line, who would prove to be a *wedge* in the relationship he had with Abel. Cain's selfishness would, soon, come "full circle" - and this particular sister could have, very well, been one reason why Cain killed his own brother.

Adam may have desired to appoint one of these sisters (or Abel's twin sister) for Cain to marry, and another sister (or Cain's twin) for Abel. Cain, however, did not like this how this was going, and didn't want to succumb to Adam's plan. He wanted things his *own* way, and wanted have to this particular sister.[74] Upon catching wind of Cain's opinion, Adam was grieved, and may have spoken out against it. He could have even brought the twins together, and gave them a task (as a way to prove themselves). Adam could have suggested that they both:

> "...go ye up to the top of this holy mountain... and offer up your offerings there, and pray before God, and then be united unto your wives."

                                        - *Book of the Bee* 18[75]

    Now, the ultimate decision would be up to God. As the two were heading up to the mountain, to provide the sacrifices, the Serpent's inner influences began to invade Cain's thought processes. Cain allowed his mind to be filled with a number of hate-filled ideas. One medieval interpretation provides us some interesting insight into what may have really been going on in Cain's mind at the time: a plot against Abel's life may have already been in the works, deep down inside.

> *(The people of the antediluvian world)… imitated the abominable deeds of the rebellious angels of a former time in which, when Abel tried to check them, they encompassed his death by a conspiracy.*
>   - "Livre d'Adam" (in Migne, Dictionnaire) 1:56[76]

    Abel may have done what so many of us thought he would do: he spoke out *against* what he saw. He noticed that the Nephilim were beginning to reveal hidden, occult knowledge to women around them (as we'll soon see), and *called them out* on it! The Nephilim and Serpent may have already begun to whisper things in Cain's ear, stirring up his emotions. He could have even begun to feel a sense of "peer pressure" about him. The terrestrial angels around him already didn't like Abel. He had desires for a particular woman, and Abel may have stood in his way, here, as well. Cain, then, might have even begun to devise a way to "take Abel out," at this time - and acquire his sister *by force*, if necessary.[77] It was "all about him," and he was fully intent upon *possessing* whatever might suit his fancy in this world.

    Unlike Cain, Abel's disposition was much more stable, and, a lot more positive. Although he "told it like it was," he still had the willingness to compromise. "Abel loved his brother, and they always used to eat and drink and walk together."[78] Cain, however, did not really show Abel the same respect, over time. Ultimately, it wasn't just the whisperings of the Serpent, the Nephilim, and his passions for a woman that were riling him up, but his thoughts regarding an up-and-coming sacrifice. And, it would be these thoughts that, probably, pushed him over the edge.

Time for Actual Sacrifices

Instructions on the proper methods of sacrifice were, most probably, already supplied by Adam. What was to come from their attempts would be this proper technique, combined with each one's willingness to love God enough to carry it out properly! As we'll see, Cain and Abel would, each, end up having a *very* different perspective on what the proper sacrifice should be.

Adam probably taught Cain and Abel to offer tithes, and their "first fruits" to God.[79] Cain may have done just the opposite - saving the last fruits for God, and the best *for him*.

The Worst

God already knew what was brewing inside of Cain's mind. He already understood what Cain's true petition to Him was going to be based upon.[80]

(Abel)... begs Cain to tithe and make burnt offering. The latter will have none of Abel's sermonizing, and will not leave his plow. He says that God gives him only sorrow and woe, and he complains of his poor crop like a grumbling farmer of today... Finally, Cain gives way to Abel's importunity and begins to tithe, still grumbling and choosing the best for himself. (Emerson, 1916, p. 847)[81]

Cain was extremely negative about life. He seemed to have a terrible attitude. Ancient lore tells us that Cain may have even eaten a meal *first*; then decided to take upon this "chore" of a sacrifice.[82] He just wasn't into having to do it. God, already, had so much. Why would He need to get this from people, as well? And, after already eating most of the vegetables that he, in the back of his mind, probably considered the choicest ones (for the sacrifice), he, then, may have taken *what was left* up the mountain - of course, "not the best and not the choicest."[83] Regardless of the exact circumstances, here, Cain probably did not have a very good attitude about it, nor put forth a good effort. At the end of the day, Cain's soon-to-be sacrifice would eventually be directed, if anywhere, towards *himself*.

The following are some of the self-loving ways Cain may have decided to present *his* "sacrifice:"[84]

- *...he gave only a small portion to (God)...*[85]

- *Cain may have offered thorns as sacrifice.*[86]

- *He made an offering of ears of wheat that were smitten by blight...*[87]

- *Cain gave his grain, that which the wind had exposed.*[88]

- *Cain made an offering of some of the refuse of the fruits of his husbandry with reluctance.*[89]

- *Cain brought (it) insincerely...*[90]

The last two were particularly telling: he may have brought it with *reluctance*, and did it *insincerely*. **Now**, we seem to be getting to the heart of the matter. It probably was an "inconvenience" for Cain to provide his sacrifice. Why was this necessary, really? One of the most important elements of one's sacrifice lies in the *intent* and *attitude* of the participant.

With Cain, we can surmise that he put out only what he *thought* God deserved; whatever he deemed *good enough* to "pacify" the Creator of the Universe! And, he may have proclaimed something, such as:

(Cain speaking)… "Know thou, O Lord… that <from> everything <for> which I have labored and toiled, I have set aside portion and tithe for you; according to my righteous labors have I offered it to you. And you know, as it is pleasing to you, thus let your will be done."   (Lipscomb, 1983, p. 159)[91]

Again, it's "all about Cain," here. Cain, practically, was *telling* God how He should enjoy it! What arrogance. This seemed an early example of a human being, and their attempts to manipulate a situation (or twist it around), to benefit from it, in some way.

Cain may have even begun to believe that, somehow, he should have been *entitled* to some kind of reward, at the conclusion of the sacrifice - for his individual effort. Since he was a farmer, bringing to God a sample of his labor (no matter how insignificant) represented a pretty good deed, at least, in his mind. This was something *he* valued - regardless, really, of what *God* required. *Cain's* effort was the important thing, really. All of this must have been appropriate enough to a self-centered individual such as Cain.

And, on top of it, if his sacrifice would be rejected, he believed that it probably wasn't because he didn't put forth a good enough effort, it would be because he was wronged, or being treated "unfairly," in some way! Cain really couldn't understand the "forest through the trees," here, in regards to what God really wanted out of him. But, this is all very important to our discussion, because it gives us a first look at how one particular individual began to twist things around, in his mind, and turned his veneration – and even **worship** - into something *man-based*, rather than God-based. There is more.

We already know how *blood* played an important role in these ancient sacrifices, and Cain, apparently, didn't dignify the importance of following Adam's instruction about using blood to the letter:

*Cain, being **unbloody**, was an abomination…*
(Oliver, 1843, p. 43)[92]

It was in the fields that he worked, and *fruit* was what God was going to get! That's *his* way. That's *man's* way! So, from all of this, we really need to ask ourselves: what reason might God actually *want* to accept Cain's sacrifice?

Why Even?

It seemed obvious that God would not want to accept Cain's sacrifice - not only because it would be offered incorrectly, but also because of Cain's spitefulness, and lack of virtue.[93] It would have been easy enough for Cain to *even* offer a prayer to God, but it didn't seem fit enough for him to humble himself to do it.[94] Ultimately, Cain was beginning to feel a little *contempt* for God, and His whole "sacrifice" thing![95]

*…there was **no love** for the One who would receive his offering.*
- St. Ephrem the Syrian: Selected Prose Works Section 3, 2(2)[96]

Cain ended up not caring about anything, or anyone, but himself - simply.

Ultimately, to the Devil

*For a sacrifice to be "wrongly divided" ultimately means that it was a **self-serving** venture, not a true sacrifice.* (Delaney, 1996, p. 179)[97]

What made it worse was that this "self-serving venture" of Cain's could, in a way, also qualify as *idolatry* - the "self-worshipping" type. Beyond giving God less of a tally that he should of; beyond giving Him the most inferior of his own portion; it seemed that Cain's thoughts, opinions and attitudes were not directed towards God, or the way He may have wanted it. And, if Cain's ways were not directed towards God, or His ways, then where could they have been directed towards? Could this "man-loving" direction be, ultimately, towards something or **someone** else?

> *...the remainder he (Cain) dedicated **to the Devil** (i.e. the Serpent)...*
> (Baring-Gould, 1881, p. 73)[98]

In a spiritual sense, it could be that: if one doesn't whole heartedly bring their sacrifice in the direction of *God*, then the direction of their sacrifice has to go *somewhere* (by default). It may end up in the direction of the person giving the sacrifice (such as in Cain's example), which ends up in self-worship, or the worship of *man*. It may also end up in direction of the lower world around us. And, sad to say, Sammael and the Serpent have retained authority, or "lordship," over this post-Fall world. Could a sacrifice towards something in our present world actually (and automatically) be towards the "god" of our present, corrupted world?

Both self-worship (i.e. the worship of *man*) and the worship of these "lords" over the world are considered *idolatry*. If Cain really didn't *care* enough to set his focus on God, then the directive of his entire work, most probably, went towards *one of these* other extremes.[99] These "gods" of the world would, naturally, be the ones to absorb *all* the energy of Cain's sacrifice, in this case! As we've stated, it's only one way or another.

Idolatry is idolatry - no matter how one slices it. If one thinks of their self as a "god," then, obviously, it's the same thing. If some pagan practitioner (innocently) thinks he's sacrificing a lamb to his nature god, it still (by default) goes in the direction of whomever is <u>in charge of the world</u> at this time. See how it all works? See why God wants "no other gods" before Him - even a "neutral" god, or any feeling that **mankind** may have the better answers?[100]

As one ancient author stated: "Moses... intimates the difference between a lover of himself, and one who is thoroughly devoted to God..."[101] Cain's sacrifice surely wasn't towards God, it was towards himself - it was towards *man*. We can call these thoughts of Cain an early form of *humanism* - entirely *man-based* rationales. As we'll see, these thoughts would become more and more of an issue to God, later on. Yet, of course, this is exactly how the Serpent would want Cain to think, and pass onto anyone after him!

Anywhere, and *anything else*, but God! That's their motto. And, since Cain (most probably) was a son of the Serpent, we can figure that, with this particular kind of sacrifice, he, ultimately, would have ended up paying homage to the one that *he* arose from - his own ancestor:

> *...Kayin's (Cain's) offering came from his side, which meant it came from the **Serpent** and the Angel of Death... the **Unclean Side**.*   - *Zohar* Beresheet b60[102]
>
> *...(Cain) is drawn to and cleaves to them...*
>   - *Zohar* Beresheet b60[103]

Works out good for them all, now doesn't it? Cain, also, became the prototype of how one could involve themselves in the practices of *ancestor worship*. Pagan religion was, slowly, incorporating itself into existence, here.

The Best

Abel, on the other hand, was very discriminate in his choices.[104] He "took the fat, firstlings of his flock..."[105] From this, it's fairly easy to conclude that *he* did it how God wanted - not using some twisted, man-centered rationale, or interpretation. He also utilized:

> *...the superiority of a **bloody** sacrifice.*
>   (Delaney, 1996, p. 13)[106]

As with Cain, there were *mental* elements and attitudes in regards to Abel's sacrifice, as well. He went about the process:

> *...in great love, with a pure heart and a sincere mind.*
>   - *The Book of the Bee* 18[107]

Obviously, this was the *right mindset*, and, most probably, the most vital element of his effort!

The End Results

The time had come for each to find out whether God was going to approve of what they did, or no. If God liked it, traditionally, He would cause a great, "burning fire" to come down from heaven, and overwhelmingly consume the sacrifice on the altar. Ancient lore tells us that, in regards to Abel's sacrifice, that's exactly what happened.[108] A bright, white, "living" fire swooped down from heaven, and annihilated Abel's bloodied animal.[109]

This didn't happen with Cain, however. Traditionally, the petitioner would light the sacrifice afire, plead to God for acceptance, and hope it would be heard. Cain probably started the "burning process" with, as we know, his blighted, second-hand fruits and vegetables - but, he couldn't get it to burn! He tried to set it afire, a number of times, but, it *still* wouldn't catch. He even started a fire nearby, and placed the offering in the middle of this raging fire, yet, and, yet, *this* fire wouldn't scorch it![110] Cain, of course, was baffled, not understanding why it all happened - again, because he was blinded by his own feelings of self-righteousness.

> *...and the gifts of Cain pleased not our Lord, for the sacrifice would not light nor burn clear in the light of God.*
> *- The Golden Legend of Lives of the Saints: Volume I* p. 62[111]

When it was time for God show His approval or denial, a fire *would* come down - but not in the way Cain expected it to.

> *It so demolished Cain's sacrifice that there was no grain left - all of it was scattered... the wind blew grain of Cain destroyed such that a single ear of grain was not to be found.* (Lipscomb, 1983, p. 271)[112]

It did devour Cain's sacrifice, but not like Abel's. It seemed to be a lot more like how one would (symbolically) "shoo away" something that they didn't like.

There was one more change about to come upon Cain - a very controversial one. Some suggested that Cain, himself, was darkened at the time of this "shooing-away." Whatever happened to Cain, at this time, has been heavily debated, and misunderstood, throughout the years - and it *still* has a good deal of relevance to our world, today! Let's see what it could be.

The Illumination of One's Countenance

As we know, Cain once had a brilliant *shine*, since birth. But, apparently, no *longer*:

>...chastisment was afflicted upon him.
>   (Ginzberg, 1909, p. 108)[113]

Not only did God's bright fire, or divine "light," come down and consume Abel's sacrifice, it also seemed to illuminate his *face*.[114] The *opposite* was said to have happened to Cain. Now, what would this mean?

The "Blackened" Face

There are a number of ancient traditions that state, at the time of Cain's rejection, God's smoking fire came down and demolished Cain's sacrifice (in that "negative" way), but, it also smoked *him* out, too - the think, "blackening" smoke was said to have resonated on *his* face, like soot. It turned him into a person who, from then on, looked as one "black as coal."[115]

>...now, naturally, all of his children were now considered black.
>   ("Evidence of Blacks in the Bible", n. d., p. 1)[116]

Said to be a divine "symbol" of God's *disfavor*, some considered this as the beginning of black, or African, individuals - the black race. Others have even postulated that this was Cain's famous "mark." From this, it, often, could have turned into a rationale - how people could enslave black people... and feel good about it. Believing in this concept gave some a feeling of "religious justification" - these were the "sons of Cain," and, naturally, they were worthy of such enslavement.

As politically incorrect as this all may sound, we need to look at the *whole* story, here. We need to look at all sides, and never leave something out for any "P.C." reason. Regarding this whole concept, one thing that really doesn't sit well (beyond the political incorrectness of it all) is that - assuming Cain was *Sargon* (i.e. "King-Cain"), *Marduk*, and other ancient Babylonian gods - a majority of them were not pictured as being dark in skin color, or black. In fact, it was more of the *opposite*. Sargon's hair was, actually, thought to be *light* in color.[117] Other traditions equated Cain's beard as *yellow* - which could have easily painted him as a *blonde*.[118] In fact, if we assume Cain's father was a terrestrial *angel* (in his case, a *Saraph*), we have a good amount of ancient evidence showing that crossbred offspring of terrestrial angel and women were often *pale*, or *white* skinned.[119] They were, often, crowned with a thick head of *white*, or *golden-blonde*, hair, as well.[120]

Cain's *outer*, blackened face may have, indeed, been a misinterpretation, here. And, for the sake of many people, we may really need to point this out. We're not doing it, necessarily, to become "politically correct," We are, however, trying to shed possible *truths* to our past, here. If anything, understanding it all might help us to "clear the air" of so much hate and racial discrimination that went on, over the years (and, is still going on). As well, this may help "clear the air" of all the backlash and hatred for Christianity, and the Bible, because of it! Air needs to be cleaned, on both sides. And, hopefully, knowledge such as this could help slow a lot of the *potential* animosity out there, between people, as well.

Let's examine what the *real* meaning of Cain's "blackness" might have been.

Outer Darkness, to Inner Darkness...

As we've already discussed, we, for the most part, may not have been able to absorb one important element of these ancient legends or mythological accounts: the *inner* thoughts and emotions behind it all! Since there could have been a number of *mental* elements to each and every account, what about the story of Cain and Abel? It appears that, with these additions, there could have been even more to the story. By inserting these mental elements *back* into everything, we can, now, gather a much *deeper*, and much more *probable*, understanding of it all!

Possibly, Abel's *change of countenance* did not mean that he become brighter "on the outside," or had brighter skin color, but, rather, he felt great, *overall* - and it showed up as a "glow" on his face! His whole outer "countenance" was shined with contentment, happiness and satisfaction! With Cain, the Bible plainly states that Cain was **wrathful**, or *angered*, as result of his sacrifice being rejected, and his countenance *fell* (in Gen. 4:6). See the link, between his emotions and countenance?

There are a number of commentaries on this story that support a *mental* or *emotional* significance to this *darkness* of Cain. Something *inside* of him turned *black*, or became *darkened* - and *that* showed up on his face:

- *Then Cain burned hot with great anger
  and his face fell
  darkened with **resentment***[121]

- *Cain's face turned black in a **rage** of jealous **pride**!*[122]

- *Dark, rough, **senseless** Cain...*[123]

- *But to Cain and to his offering He (God) did not turn, and it **annoyed** Cain exceedingly, and his countenance fell.*[124]

- *...the face of Cain... burned with dark redness as one who **seethes with anger**... as does the face of one who has been greatly **humiliated** and **deeply hurt**.*[125]

Some sources point to Cain losing some - or even most all - of his heavenly *shine* at the time God's rejection smoke descended, here. But, that was a little different - he still looked like the same person, overall - just no "shine."

He must have become "darkened" in some *other* ways! He was flabbergasted - literally "beside himself" in humiliation. In his self-centered, pride-filled mind, he felt that this was an ultimate rejection. He must have felt like one who just *lost it all*: his self-worth; his firstborn privileges; his future wife - you name it. His hopes were *darkened*, his high-hopes for getting what he wanted - knocked *down*. From that point on, Cain's whole outlook on life was "to the brim" with negativity. He began to go down an irrevocable path.

Emotions

Evil always seemed to be at the door of Cain's heart, waiting to enter - and God even told this to him, in the Bible. And, this current incident seemed to affect Cain enough to "unlock" that important door, and allow it in.

His over-flowing thoughts and emotions, indeed, helped to him there. Whether his offering was accepted or not, God knew what was going on inside of Cain before he had even begun. He knew that Cain was teetering on the edge of deciding to go in the same direction as his father (the Serpent), and never coming back.[126]

One ancient author stated that God wanted to despise Cain's offering, not only because of how wrong it was, but, also, because of what he was *about to do* to Abel, in the future![127] Cain was beginning to developing even nastier ideas, it seems. It's also interesting that: even what Cain was *about to do* "hung in the balance" of God's favor at the time... something to ponder.

So, after Cain's initial "shock," emotions flooded into his thought-process. As we know, he probably didn't really understand (or want to know) the *real* reasons behind God's rejection - his mind was so filled with pride.[128] How *dare* anyone disrespect *him* in this way?[129] One emotion that really began to fill Cain's soul would be one that many of us would expect a typical son of the Serpent might have: *anger*.[130]

Angry Cain

Cain was feeling some fear, insecurity as well as a little paranoia. One ancient author stated: "He thought there was laughter in the eyes of his parents and his sisters, etc., when his offering was rejected."[131] More of this insecurity began to haunt him, such as: "He (Abel) will go to the Garden, and I will remain outside."[132] He also began to think that everyone around him would eventually reach a state of "perfection," someday - except *him*. And, to him, that wasn't *fair*.

If Cain had any brotherly-love left, it was practically gone, by now. As we know, however, Cain had no excuse for his sacrifice being rejected. He made the error in judgment. He did something disobedient. Deep down inside, his conscience probably told him that, as well. Regardless of these other feelings, he had anger. He had a sense of anger, yes, but it was completely unjustified. In Cain's heart:

> *...(he was envious) of his brother's relationship with God, which he could not have so long as he continued in his selfish, greedy, competitive course - the way of pride, arrogance, and self-will.*
> ("The Mark of the Beast and the Mark of Cain", n. d., p. 9)[133]

Resurgence of Serpent Envy

On top of it, Cain began to feel a lot of *envy*. Now, doesn't this emotion sound familiar? As we recall, there was someone in the Garden who showed a great deal of this envy, as well:

> *...he (the Serpent) cast this envy into the heart of Cain...*
> - Book of the Glory of Kings (Kerba Nagast) 4[134]

Envy can be defined as: a "resentful awareness *of an advantage* enjoyed by another joined with a desire to possess the same advantage."[135] The first major semblance of Cain's envy was directed against the sacrifice that was accepted, and, of course, it's preparer: *Abel*.[136] The "thoughts which lay in the heart of Cain gave him no rest."[137]

What did Abel do to Cain anyway, besides provide an offering that actually worked? This became an example of, "the diabolical envy that the wicked feel for the *good simply because they are good*, while themselves are evil."[138] Envy would end up being a good portion of why Cain wanted to kill his brother![139] It's obvious that, "both father and son displayed the same wickedness."[140] They had become *united* in thought, and had "not separated the same disposition."[141]

Cain, now, a "tool" of the Serpent and the Nephilim, would become *the* symbol of whoever was *against* the ways of God:

> *Cain was born to perpetuate the devil's frustrated rage on this earth.*
> ("John Reeve", n. d., p. 2)[142]

Cain could control his passions and anger for long. He would, eventually, feel the need to act on them.

Premeditated Ideals

Next, Cain may have begun to believe it was time for some "payback," to both God and Abel - for "insulting" *him*. How dare they not make things work the way *he* thought it should work.

> *...his soul suggested to him that he kill his brother.*
> *- The History of al-Tabari - Volume I* Cain and Abel 138[143]

He, subtly, began to think of ways to "take his brother out," or to devise "words of quarrel and contention, to find a pretext to kill him."[144] Yes, Cain could not "be expected to understand fully man's obligation to man."[145] He really didn't have a lot of empathy. He really didn't care how close his victim really was to him - he wanted what he wanted.

He, then, began to utilize a few "aces" up his sleeve: first, he would first "trick" Abel into a quarrel, and then take him out. Yes, it was all premeditated - no 2nd degree, or "manslaughter" defenses, here. Cain, surely, had succumb to the evil that he had let in.

Next, to set the stage, Cain began to manipulate the situation around him, so he could obtain some sort of advantage. His first thought had to do with their two occupations: farming and shepherding. He, first, would start an argument with Abel, and then act as if the *opposite thoughts* were going on inside of his head:

> *Cain "considered in his heart what he might do to him..." (and then)... he said to Abel: Let there... be no (quarreling) between me and you. Separate from me and take the flock as your portion. Abel said to him: My desire is (in) a true division. (After) Abel had gone to his flock and had gone Cain considered... I will have no milk to drink and no wool to wear. He ran to Abel and said 'This is not a trustworthy division. Take for yourself half the flock and half of the land and I (lit: we) will take half of the flock and half of the land. Abel said to him: Do what you desire. And they made the division. Abel said to him: This is an even division, which is (done) in fairness (lit: in truth). Abel went on his way. Cain (then) sought to graze his portion of the flock. He found he could not graze the flock and (thereby) give up working the land. Then Cain said you take the flock and I will take the land. Abel agreed to do Cain's desire. Cain, however, was bearing a grudge against Abel from before this...*
> *- Targum Neofiti 1: Genesis Chap. 4 (notes)*[146]

The above tells us a lot about Cain, and how his mind worked: first, he claimed he wanted to evenly divide the possessions of the world. This, ultimately, would unintentionally mandate that *both* of them have to put some effort in, towards their own futures. Abel, agreeing on almost every new suggestion Cain gave him, allowed it. This allowed Cain to further manipulate "the game." Next, we'll clearly see that Cain, in his negative, self-centered psyche, discovered that some situations in life (such as working with animals) might not go too well, for someone with his mindset. This was because he probably didn't have the patience, or empathy, to work well with any animals that may not want to do things *his* own way - every time. It worked for Abel, because he had patience and empathy. He had a better attitude, and, most certainly, had a better work ethic. It wasn't "all about him."

It's also interestingly that: Cain, continually, kept feeling a need to *come back* to Abel, and infringe on him - because his own *ways* weren't really working out too well! You will see that a lot, today, with people who think a lot like Cain. Anyhow, Cain really didn't see himself, and his way of thinking, as the problem, of course. He felt like a victim - of everyone else. It wasn't due to Cain not "pulling his own weight," here, it was the fault of everyone, or everything, around him (including the animals)!

Next, Cain laid out another suggestion: he would own all of the land, and Abel, would own all of the movables on the land. Sounds good to him! In the end, Cain figured this would give him an advantage: the power to, eventually, force Abel off of his property! Sounded good. Cain controlled the land, and Abel would have nowhere to go.

Cain and the Serpent were, soon, becoming *united* in their thought, and had "not separated the same disposition."[147] Both were diabolical, and cunning. Cain, then, began to force Abel away from him, saying: "You do not possess even the smallest part of the earth."[148] Now, Abel was in a pickle: by continuing to *agree* to what his brother was suggesting would put him in a big hole, a hole of which he really couldn't so easily dig himself out of, not any more.

But God, watching it all, made sure that Cain wasn't going to profit from his trickery for very long. Cain seduced Abel into a worthless and impractical agreement. Maybe that's why, in the future, God would eventually make *Cain* (and a lot of his thoughts and attitudes) head towards the same feelings of impracticality and worthlessness! And, since Cain tricked Abel into "getting off of his land," here, God would make sure that Cain had to "get off of *His* land (i.e. the entire earth)," as we, soon, shall see.

The Argument Had Begun

The irrational thoughts inside of Cain's mind were beginning to bubble over. Now, Abel didn't abide by the deal as he "*should* have," and this outraged Cain all the more. Abel, then, did something to make it worse: he actually *challenged* Cain! What? How dare he! Abel, also, delivered *rationality* to their discussions. That's not what Cain was used to! These acts of "disrespect" helped to further fuel Cain's rage. As they continued to talk, Abel made more and more sense, and Cain did not want to face it. As they talked, they would become more and more conflicted about the laws of God, there, set up during this time.[149]

Cain, of course, was losing the argument. He, then, began to openly question *why* his sacrifice wasn't accepted, and Abel's was. It just blurted out of him. He was losing his tongue. He, then, even began to question the position of God, and His role as Creator of the earth - just as his father did. Abel used common sense, however, and told Cain some things he didn't want to hear. Cain did not like to receive anything that might "burst the bubble" he had created for himself. He was feeling too good, by playing "the victim." When Abel brought up God, for example, Cain may have countered, with something like:

"Abel, beware, I'm not in mood for any of your fooling,
*or to be pestered with smelling, heavenly **cruelty**."*
(Phifer, 1890, p. 141)[150]

Ranting Over God

It seemed that, if anyone said anything contrary to Cain, they were now becoming cruel, mean and, overall, an annoyance. Who should be telling *him* this? *He* should be the one telling everyone else that they are wrong! Cain continued, with a philosophical rant about God: "Since He owns the world what difference should it make to Him whether one offers Him flax seed or the richest gift (one could provide)...?" Abel insisted that God judges offering *by the spirit* (meaning, whether or not one's offering was done according to His will).[151] Right after, Cain replied to Abel:

*"...your mind is **numbed** by a **theological opiate** which, were it not for study realists like myself, would keep mankind in eternal subjection to an absurd theory. There is a higher Power than ourselves who created this world, but He has no interest in that which He has made. The only kind of justice or of law which we shall ever know is that which **we created for ourselves**."*   (Eichhorn, 1957, p. 63)[152]

Wow, sounds a lot like the dogma we hear so much of, today! Cain thought that God was restricting him from becoming a "free thinker," and only wanted him to be a slave. God doesn't really care about His creation. It's up to *us* to decide. These thoughts are completely natural, inside a person who thinks it's "all about them." Who around Cain had the right to tell him that his philosophies were wrong, anyhow? And, if someone, as in Abel, may have tried, then he just may need to, somehow, be silenced.

Abel, however, simply told it "as it was," and replied to Cain: "Sorry, Cain, but your sacrifice was not done in the proper manner. It commenced with a few impure thoughts, on top of it!" Cain's inner paranoia and rage were beginning to overflow, by this time. He replied to Abel, once again: "you are being hypercritical and hypocritical. You had no intention of bringing anything at all until you found out that father (i.e. Adam) and I were going to offer. You were jealous of us. You were afraid that God would cease to care for you."[153]

The entire situation opened Cain's desire to react in an overly passionate, irrational way. The "devil inside" was waiting to pounce, and this was the time. Most of us know what was about to happen next:

> ...(this) chastisement by Abel gave not to repentance but to further envy and tyranny, then to murder, followed by insolent and irreverent denial.
> (Delaney, 1996, p. 102)[154]

To Be Slain

> *(Cain, of whom) Adam and Eve*
> *Had thought to be the Christ, to lead them back*
> *To blissful Paradise, was turned into*
> *The executioner of the curse pronounced...*
> (Phifer, 1890, p. 142)[155]

There was a tipping point in our ancient world - the first *murder* of another human being was about to occur - with additional *curses* being pronounced upon a lot of mankind, because of it! This is why the story of Cain and Abel was so vital! Abel's story, in ways, was the first to parallel the story of Jesus Christ: he followed the ways of God; he had humility and integrity; but an anti-Christ follower confronted him, and killed him. This would also begin the never-ending pattern of martyrdom (for the sake of God) - and it took someone as *evil* as Cain to start the whole "ball rolling."

This story is very important, as well, because it reflects a *fact* of God's post-Fall world: even the son of the Serpent (himself) could choose to follow God - if he wanted! Simple. It's not just about genetics; it's not just about bloodlines; it's, ultimately, one's own *choice*, and their *free-will*. *Any* human being born into this world *could* be in good favor with God - if they really wanted to!

Cain Rose Up

Assuredly, the two were about to get into a fight (most probably initiated by Cain). It was almost inevitable, because Cain was also thought to be "bloody and strong," as well as filled with "shame and treachery." He was even known as "a fierce, destructive man."[156] He seemed to have a short fuse, and Abel figured out that Cain, soon, was about to "lose it." Cain approached him, as if he was going to kill him, and started chasing Abel, over hill and vale.[157] Eventually, Cain caught up to him, jumped on top of him, and brought him to the ground. Cain was not stronger than his brother, however.[158] Abel spun it around, and quickly overtook his brother. Abel, then, ended up on top.[159] Cain, however, would be in *possession* of another "ace."

>*Cain overcame his brother, because he was **harsher** than him…*
>   - *Zohar* Idra Raba 47[160]

The prophecy about him (at the time of his birth) would now come to full fruition. Cain was struggling to rise up and overtake his powerful brother. He even *bit* him, like an animal![161] But, because Abel was stronger, Cain decided to try something else. He could not really reveal his *true* self at that point, and how treacherous he really was - he had to use a little deception to achieve his end result.[162]

God, as usual, was watching all of it go down, and may have even been thinking about *assisting* Abel from making a deadly error in judgment; but, we understand this about Abel:

>*In response, after he was threatened, Abel showed his noble character and piety.*
>   (Kathir, 2003, p. 47)[163]

Piety is defined as "dutiful devotion to God and observance of religious principles."[164] Abel always seemed to strive to do the right (and noble) thing. One who almost always uses meekness, generosity or virtue may, on occasion, be turned into a martyr for the cause. Even showing compassion and patience to someone else has its limits. Sometimes, even the most honorable of us might need to take action, or stand up for ourselves. Sometimes, we have to have to take a hard road.

One tradition stated that:

*God encouraged Abel to **dispatch him**, saying, "Do not spare this evil-doer!" Yet when Cain wept and cried: "Brother forgive me!"... Abel **mercifully** released his grip. God then said: "Having spared him, you **must die yourself**!"*

(Graves and Patai, 1964, p. 92)[165]

A very interesting thing may have happened, here. God subtly suggested that Abel stop Cain in his tracks, but Abel didn't listen. He thought *compassion* was the way to continue on - not action, not violence. Sounds noble (by a lot of people, today), but he decided not to follow God's lead. Cain, then, tricked his brother, and stood up - and, then, the great double-cross began![166] Some traditions stated that he arose, and murdered his brother right on the spot. Others said that there was even more to his deception: Cain knew Abel was physically stronger, so, now, he had to find another subtle way to "even the odds."

Wrapped Around the Vine

Cain may have quieted down, and succumbed to the realization that he, now, needed to do something *diabolical*. Cain suggested:

"Come let us play with a vine… You embrace the tree and I will bind you three times around, and we will see who is powerful and strong." When Abel embraced the tree, Cain took the vine and bound him by his feet and hands up to his head.
(Lipscomb, 1983, p. 272)[167]

Cain, as a result, tied up Abel securely.[168] Again, it was nothing other than premeditated wickedness. This time, Abel's strength would not be enough to overcome Cain, the "**trickster**:"

Then Abel perceived Cain's wickedness. So he cried out to his brother weeping and said, "My beloved brother, I pray you, untie me, and as long as I am alive I will serve you… Do not kill me, for I am not your enemy, but your friend, and I am always obedient to your commands. I cannot live one hour without you."
(Lipscomb, 1983, p. 272)[169]

Abel was stuck this time, and he knew it. In desperation, he continued his pleading process:

"How can you hate me and remain on the earth without me? How can you forget my brotherly love?" (Lipscomb, 1983, p. 272)[170]

How could Cain actually continue doing this? It was simple: because he was a son of the Serpent; and (unlike his brother) he took on these same thoughts, and attitudes. Cain didn't listen to Abel at all.[171] Abel finally pleaded, "Come, brother, let me kiss you one time, lest I remain in need of you."[172] He, finally, believed that Cain wanted him dead, and believed this was the end. His last, humble request to his twin brother, still, remained unanswered.[173] In one final bit of desperation, Abel cried out, practically weeping: "How do we explain this to our parents?"[174] Even *this*, apparently, was not enough to sway Cain. He didn't even care about how Adam and Eve may have felt at this time. He surely didn't care if the Serpent objected (which his didn't, of course). He just continued on, and finalized his plan.

Finish Him

Cain, now, felt the desire to finish his deed. "Now, Cain was walking here and there, but he did not know with what he must kill him."[175] As we can continue to conclude: it wasn't an accident; it wasn't a mistake, or error. It was a premeditated, intentional onslaught - from one brother to another.

One source stated that Cain even held Abel in one position for a whole hour, beating him, and violently trying to slaughter him.[176] When physical torture didn't do the trick, Cain snatched up a sharp reed, or staff, and pelted him. This was a way, in Cain's mind, to inflict even more bruising and wounding - a way to intensify his punishment.[177]

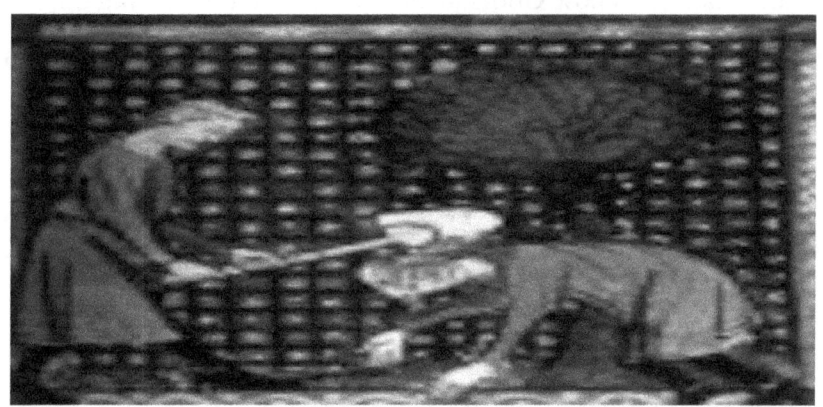

The Tool

Next, he may have moved onto something more lethal. He could have grabbed a rock, or some other farming implement, and finished the job.[178] Interestingly enough, one tradition stated that, in an ultimate act of blasphemy, Cain may have even taken a stone he snatched from his own altar (used for his sacrifice to God), to kill his own brother![179]

Whatever implement he used, it assuredly sped up Abel's execution. He eventually struck Abel with a fatal blow, possibly in his neck, or on his head.[180] Even up to this point, Abel still pleaded with God to spare Cain![181] What a brother Cain had! What a role model for the ways of God, and how people should live, in this post-Fall world.

After all of the premeditated, merciless acts of Cain; after all the injustices to his brother, Abel *finally* took it to heart that he was being treated unfairly. But, this time, it was too late. With, practically, his last breath, and every right in the world for this utterance, "…Abel cried out: 'My King, I demand **justice**!'"[182]

And justice he would (eventually) get.

> *…we are to understand that in the killing of Abel, Cain **effectively killed himself**.*
> (Bandy, 1967, p. 29)[183]

Before we look more into how God's justice would end up working on Cain, we, first, need to get into the conversation that Cain would have with God, in the aftermath of it all.

No Excuses

Abel was dead, his blood spilled all over the ground. And, Cain did a futile job in attempting to hide any evidence. This was, most probably, one of the most despicable crimes that a man could do to his fellow man.

> *…homicide is a sin so violently against nature that it deserves only the heaviest requital. In killing our own kind… we become lower **even than beasts**; for all men are*

brothers by nature, and equally responsible one for another.
                                         (Bandy, 1967, p. 30)[184]

Cain apparently "crossed the line," in so many ways, here. With the murder, he "passed from a life of human kindness to one which was more akin to the rude existence of a wild *beast*."[185] And, this was, most probably, the first act that any human being would, ever, have been compared to an **animal**.

At first, Cain may have an iota of concern about what just happened - in regards to what he had to do with the body! In other words, he really didn't feel too bad about the murder, but, rather, felt bad about how to cover everything up. After all, Abel did *him* wrong (at least, in his mind), and he felt justified for doing whatever he had to do. Abel, after all, deserved much of it, for all of his "insolence." The only care that probably came to Cain's mind, after the fact, was whether he was going *to get caught*, or not.

Throughout his young life, this man was "cruel to his parents, and bitter towards his brother and gave no honor to God."[186] Again, although Abel probably had the same blood of the Serpent, he maintained a completely different lifestyle, outlook and attitude. Brothers by blood - different mindsets by *choice*.

We see more evidence of this: after the murder, Cain even "went forth as one glad in heart."[187] He considered himself victorious. He thought he had "banished the evil." He even thought he had "gotten away with murder" - a legend in his own mind! And, on top of it, he considered it as "no big deal," or it *could* have been - because no one saw it all take place.

Cain deceived Abel. He thought he had deceived his parents. He thought he deceived the entire world. No one was going to seek vengeance for Abel's death because no one saw what happened![188] A "one and done" shot! There was *One*, however, who was watching, and saw everything.

And, the understanding of all this information will help expose - even further – the beginnings of *Mystery Babylon*. A lot of it revolves around how Cain thought, reacted, and mentally processed all of what he had done - as well as how he would react to all the up-and-coming accusations assuredly coming to him, from God.

How Doth Thou Already Know?

You can escape your brothers, your parents, and your peers. You might be able to escape everyone around you, but you can't escape God. God caught up to Cain, while walking on his merry way, and confronted him about what happened to his brother (which, of course, led Cain to utter his famous line: "am I my brother's keeper?").

All of God's questioning began to confuse Cain, just a little bit. In his vain outlook on life, he, apparently, didn't even *consider* that God might be all-powerful, all-seeing and all-knowing. What a surprise! When confronted, Cain quickly responded back, to the Creator of the Universe, with: "My parents do not know I have slain Abel. How do *you*?"[189] In his own, self-serving way, he may have even began to, subtly, accuse *God* of being some kind of trouble-maker:

"Does Thou have informers who slander...?"
(Goldin, 1929, p. 34)[190]

On top of this, Cain didn't seem to be able to *entertain* the idea that God had so much power over the world, as well as power over *him*. Cain may have, then, speculated that there *must* have been an angel out there, or someone acting as an "informant"… rushing over to God, and telling Him some convoluted story.[191] These "informants," of course, were probably out there just to "pick" on Cain. He wasn't sure why. They may just like to go around picking on people; and, of course, they, now, sought out Cain, and chose *him* to be their target. Ultimately, he had his mind believing that God, and His informants, only wanted to be *mean* to him:

…you must have speedy informants who delight in reporting the sins committed by human beings. (Eichhorn, 1957, p. 73)[192]

The pompous Cain, next, began to rationalize the situation a little further: maybe God didn't know that he was negligent with his sacrifice. Maybe He only preferred one type of offering over another - and that's why he turned bias towards Cain.[193] He, then, went on to conclude that God probably didn't care for *his* offering because, somehow, He *must* be bias, or prejudiced.

He was so oblivious - "in the dark" to the *real* reasons why everything didn't work out. But, again, that's the problem with self-centered individuals. And, from now on, if anyone around Cain told him anything different than what *he* thought was right, they, as well, must be as biased and as prejudiced as God proved Himself to be!

Now, no one could win in an argument - no one except *the* One.

Had High Hopes for Cain

God had enough. He was ready to *expose* Cain "with specific questions intended to reveal his true character."[194] Through the question-and-answer process, God would bring "to the surface" a number of things imprinted deep down, inside of Cain's heart. He also hoped Cain would, finally, be able to comprehend what he did, and feel a little bit of guilt and shame - like he *should*![195]

> *That God deliberately rejected Cain's sacrifice as a way of allowing Cain the opportunity to teach humankind how to react to a perceived injustice,* **with dignified hope** *rather than angry revenge.* (Delaney, 1996, p. 211)[196]

Believe it or not, God was even *hoping* that Cain would turn around, and acknowledge his sin.[197] Perhaps, he may repent![198] The more God pressed Cain, however, the more defiant his character had become.

> *...he (God) criticized Cain for looking at the earth's natural vegetation and immediately assuming it needs cultivation in order to be brought to perfection... since human beings consider ripe fruit to be more desirable than new fruit, and every bit as tasty as fresh lamb, Cain naturally brings ripe fruit to the sacrifice rather than "first fruits." Cain is baffled by God's rejection of the sacrifice, but refuses to use this as an occasion for learning and correction. There is irony in this, given that he (Cain) had set out to improve the natural state of creation, but could not see the need to improve himself.* (Delaney, 1996, p. 141)[199]

We pick things up, here, with another verse in Genesis:

> *And the LORD said unto Cain, Why art thou wroth? and why is thy countenance fallen?* - Gen. 4:6 (KJV)

Next, God, most probably, wanted Cain to tell Him why he had become so angry and displeased - as well as why the countenance (or "brightness") of his face had now changed.[200]

> *...his color changed and (was) of **a woeful countenance**...*
> - The First Book of Adam and Eve (The Conflict of Adam and Eve with Satan 59[201]

Cain, apparently (as we already know), lost his heavenly "glow" - the glow that he once had. And, on top of it, the *permanent* expression on his face would now be, for the most part, that of one with a continual sense of *dissatisfaction*, *unhappiness* or *grief* - a *grievous* outlook on life.

"The Sin that Croucheth"

Next, another famous verse in the Bible:

> *If thou doest well, shalt thou not be accepted? and if thou doest not well, sin lieth at the door. And unto thee shall be his desire...* - Gen. 4:7 (KJV)

God, also, made it known to Cain that there was actually "a wild beast," of sorts, crouching at the door to his heart (and, each man's heart).[202] It waits, just outside this door, for an opportunity to come inside, and live - continually influencing a man to do evil, from then on.[203] This "beast" was (and is), of course, the *Evil Inclination* - the "sin that croucheth."[204] One thing that God, also, made clear to Cain was that he, himself, had the power to master it - to control this Evil Inclination - if he really wanted to. It was entirely up to *him*![205]

*...at the entrance, sin is lying, and to you is its longing, but you can **rule** over it.*
- *Rashi* Genesis 4:7[206]

This, of course, involves *strength of character*. This involves *willingness*, and *trust* in God. It also involves a sense of *morality*, and *individual responsibility*. We already know enough about Cain, here, to surmise what direction he would go with this advice. He wasn't having any of the blame for most anything he did. Why start now?

It all boils down to, of course, the fact that he was "not his brother's keeper."[207]

God "Told it Like it Was"

God, anticipating these comebacks, fired out a new line of questions for Cain:

"You are not his keeper, then why did you become his murderer?"
(Lipscomb, 1983, p. 228)[208]

"Hast thou killed, and also taken possession?"
- *Pirke De Rabbi Eliezer* Ch. 14: Cain and Abel[209]

We already know how one meaning *Cain* is "possession." Here comes the ramifications, again, of the name. Throughout this murder, Cain, not only took *possession* of a future wife of Abel, but a whole lot more - *everything* that Abel would have had, most probably, was going to be in Cain's hands, soon enough. Yet, God promptly put a stop to this all. He, next, set out to let Cain know that: He already *knew* about Cain's "power grab" - *regardless* of what he had claimed was the truth, and regardless of any excuses he might be able to think of.

"...you have... slain your brother without reason because he spoke truthfully to you."
(Bin Gorion, 1976)[210]

Cain's Plethora of Excuses

Assuredly, God knew the rhetoric that Cain was about to spit out, next. But, Cain, still, believed he could utilize the rest of the "aces up his sleeve." God, however, would be a big challenge. Cain would need a whole "playbook" of excuses, here, in order to triumph. He, first, rejected it all, with numerous defense mechanisms and vain responses, all in order to twist around the conversation, and, then, make it seem like *he* was the **victim**.[211]

He, also, *flatly* denies any involvement, and tries to make everything look like as though he felt "enraged at the insistent pressure and strict inquiries of God…"[212] God's accusations "offended" Cain, here - not the other way around! How pompous. The very idea that God would throw these accusations at him "insulted his humanity."

All of this, however, gives us an interesting look into the person that Cain really was:

> *Cain was a typical representative of that portion of the human race which believes that the world has been created to satisfy its particular needs and desires. The logical consequence of such a philosophic position are unbounded selfishness and inevitable social conflict. Such people are easily identifiable. They fancy themselves all-important and all-wise. They are always the first to sit down at the table and the last to offer to wash the dishes. They give to charity not out of compassion and to religion, not out of thankfulness, but to gain recognition or to avoid ostracism. They have no use for anyone who can not be of some **use to them**…*
> (Eichhorn, 1957, p. 43)[213]

See? It's "all about them." To them, it's all about whatever someone else could make *them* look good, or how *they* (alone) could benefit from any particular situation! Cain, most probably, would be equated to a typical *psychopath*, or *sociopath*, of today.

Of course, everyone has to think of themselves at some point of time, during their lives. We're not saying to give up everything you have to someone else. But, there's really a point, in almost all interactions, where things no longer become a "win-win," but slant into something totally *lopsided*. In regards to Cain, he forced things in his favor almost *all the time*. He lacked the empathy he could have, and *should* have, had for others around him.

> *...this type of thinking sometimes produces material harvest but also **breaks hearts** and spirits and creates human **misery**...*   (Eichhorn, 1957, p. 43)[214]

In striving to achieve his *own* outcomes, Cain rarely understood how this way of thinking might affect anyone else:

> *What does a thorough-going materialist think that he owes to God or to society? If one lives for himself alone, what, in his opinion, does he owe anybody? But if you grant him his premise and ask him, in return, what anybody owes him, he scowls and snarls like a caged beast, for that is what he is, one who is imprisoned by his own conceit and by the narrowness of his societal vision.*
> (Eichhorn, 1957, p. 42-43)[215]

Cain would become the prototype of all "who repeatedly fail to repent."[216]

And, using this attitude, Cain would have to address God, once again. This time, he used a lot of brazen rhetoric - the rhetoric of someone who thinks they could *even* deceive the Most High![217]

It's Not His Fault!

In some twisted method of rationalization, Cain, then, may have blurted out to God: "I admit that I was not able to read what was in his (Abel's) heart. I judged him only by his actions. And, from his actions, he *seemed* to be my enemy; therefore I killed him. And why are you (God) speaking to me in such a *harsh* tone? How was I to know that murder was such a heinous offense? For all you know, I never intended to kill him. I just meant to give him a sound thrashing."[218]

Cain was quick-witted - twisting around everything that God, previously, said to him. It was like trying to talk to the Serpent, himself. God, of course, was "mean." He was "uncaring." And, it, probably, wasn't even Cain's fault, here - he perceived that there was an uncomfortable situation, and needed to act on it. What else could he do? Besides, how would Cain know all of the things he did to Abel would actually kill him?[219] No one was ever killed before, so how was he to know? Was it *his* fault, because nobody actually taught him these things? God didn't think about that, did He? Cain used almost every trick in the book.

Now we know where some of those ancient "*trickster*" gods in pagan mythology (such as *Loki*) actually come from.

It May Even Be God's Fault!

His pitiful little arguments were not about to "hold any water" - at least, with God. Cain, then, tried another approach: to go so far "out on a limb" that he even tried to point a finger at God, and blame Him! Ultimately, it had to have been *His* fault, to some degree, because He was the so-called Creator of the universe, right? And, if He created all things, then He should, naturally, share in, at least, *some* of the responsibility for what His creation does, right? It only makes sense… to Cain, himself.

Cain's thoughts went a little further with: God, obviously, must not care to much about His creation, to allow this to happen. So, indirectly, He actually "caused" the murder to happen, by *allowing* this entire situation to occur! What a twisted mindset - but, so often, a lot of the rhetoric we see today! Cain, actually, started believing it was *also* God's fault for allowing the Evil Inclination to come inside of any man![220] His twists were, truly, self-serving. Cain, then, blurted: "I should have never been able to murder my brother. Why don't you punish my father (i.e. Adam) for what I have done? He is the real cause. To be perfectly candid, I do not believe that either my father or I are nearly as responsible for Abel's death **as You are**."²²¹ Cain retorted further: "Since You are the guardian of all, why did You permit me to slay him?... for if You **had accepted my sacrifice** as You accepted his, I would not have been envious of him."²²² Now, it's God's fault, because he didn't except Cain's sacrifice! See how this kind of mind works?

It's almost unbelievable how pompous Cain became - to his brother, to Adam, Eve and, especially, to the Creator of the universe. Any way to get out of being responsible for his actions Cain tried.²²³ And, on top of it, he eventually began to convince himself that most all of his thoughts, and opinions, were justified!

He, then, continued on, in his retort of God: "If one were to analyze this matter logically and dispassionately... You certainly cannot deny that You are at least partially to blame for what has happened."²²⁴ "Abel was trespassing on *my* property. I was merely seeking to protect that which was lawfully and rightfully mine. Why should I be punished for putting into effect a policy which You yourself decreed for the human race? When did you ever tell me that I must be concerned about my brother's welfare? Who was it that *made* me jealous and angry by favoring Abel's offering and rejecting mine? Who was it that created the Evil inclination which kept on tormenting me until, in *desperation*, I killed my brother? You could have stopped the fight if *You* wanted to, before it was too late. Why did you not stop it?"²²⁵

Cain, obviously, talked himself into believing that God should, at least, share *some* of this blame!²²⁶ Why not? There was, obviously, no honor to him. He did the best he could to weasel his way through almost any rebuke that God had for him.

Cain, then, concluded with: "I have not consented to be my brother's overseer. Because thou art the keeper of *all* creatures, overseeing him is *your* responsibility."²²⁷ "If you do not know where he is, then You have been derelict in your duty."²²⁸ "Why were You not pursuing *your* task as diligently as I have been pursuing mine?"²²⁹

After this, he exploded with: "I should be asking *you* where he is!"²³⁰ "Why should One who watches over all creatures ask me this, unless He planned *the murder Himself?*"²³¹ "Maybe, Thou didest *thyself* slay him!"²³²

Wow. Talk about a 180 degree turn! These are the ways of Cain - in *their infant stage*... thinking without humility, without honor, and strength of character. It's a world view of almost total denial and self-absorption.

More False Rationalizations

As we can plainly see, Cain began to reach "for the stars," in regards to his fiery rebuttal. We can say that he was "throwing everything at the wall, here - hoping that something sticks." And, over time, he was beginning to get good at these twists; after all, his father was, most probably, a high-ranking, terrestrial *angel*! He even went off on a little tangent, here (in regards to his sacrifice), and proclaimed this to God: "The death of that animal seemed to please you. Why would you show more concern for the death of a man than you had shown when the (animal) was slaughtered?"[233] If God would have only accepted *his* sacrifice, then Abel might not be dead!

He also, most probably, tried to proclaim that God didn't accept his (non-bloody) sacrifice (and, rather, accepted Abel's "gory" sacrifice) because He, actually, "rejoices in blood."[234] He must be bloodthirsty - totally enjoying whenever an innocent animal is killed. 'All of these ancient rationales sound so familiar, don't they?

Cain may have even thought: why would God require something as "inhuman" as the death of an animal, and the shedding of its blood? Why couldn't He just accept something as innocent as Cain's sacrifice of vegetables? According to his (new) *humanist-like* rationale, it was much better - and much more *humane* - to just cut up a few vegetables, than to take the life of some scared, innocent animal.

In the end, no matter how Cain tried to twist things around, he *did* something much worse than kill some scared animal:

*Destroy a lamb, a **brother he'd destroyed**.*
   (Phifer, 1890, p. 143)[235]

Cain's petty attempts at manipulation were getting a little old. God was, now, beginning to be a little upfront with Cain, and tell it how it was: *Cain* was the one who murdered one of the few people in his world who, most probably, *still* loved him! *This* was the real crime.

Cain, without a leg to stand on, continued to fire back the best he could, and uttered out his own (twisted) interpretation of Abel: "I do not believe that he truly loved me."[236] He, then, finished with: "…when Adam unknowingly brought death into the world, You drove him out Garden of Eden. In like manner by committing murder when I was not completely aware of the gravity of my offense, I, too, am *to be punished*… I am being punished more *severely* than was my father."[237]

Woe is Cain! Nothing is his fault! If Cain *had* any remorse, at all, we could be assured that it was also mingled with envy and hatred.[238]

Can't You Bear It?

Next, we look at another verse in Genesis:

...My punishment is greater than I can bear.
- *Gen.* 4:13 (KJV)

On the surface, here, it sounds like Cain was actually beginning to feel a little shame, here. But, as we dig deeper, we'll see that this comment, again, may be one of self-pity, and "victimization." This whole quote, in reality, may even be a *complaint!*[239]

- "My punishment is too great **for me to bear**."[240]

- "...my grief is **too heavy** a burden to bear."[241]

- "You bear the upper worlds and the lower worlds, and my iniquity is impossible **for You to bear**?"[242]

In a final attempt, self-serving attempt to get around his shame, Cain cried out, and said something, such as: "Come on, God. You have the power to remit and pardon my sin.[243] So, why don't you just do it, so we can *move on*, here?"

God Was Long-Suffering

God was very, *very* patient, and long-suffering with Cain.[244] But, "...instead of Cain seeking God's long-suffering and kindness, so that he might persuade justice by God's petition, he said things either out of fear or cunning."[245] Cain, "so shrewdly simulated his penitence that he even had begun to believe he *succeeded* in deceiving God."[246] Of all the philosophical "arrows" he shot at God - he believed that something would have, or, at least, *should* have, worked!

In the end, Cain brought so much of his punishment onto himself. He, in a way, was committing mental suicide - trying to outwit his own Creator! His twisted, human-based rationalities and reason could never match God's gifts of rationality, reason and conscience *He* allotted for mankind:

*Whoever, therefore, **rejects** reason invites error…*
(Delaney, 1996, p. 156)[247]

Repentance Lost - Now Separation

Cain had such little regard for any world that was outside of his "bubble." God, then, decided to let him know that: anything more that would be said to Him was, probably, too late - he was too lost, inside of his head. God may not have even *wanted* to instruct Cain on how to redo his offering anymore, or how to do it correctly![248] He was too far gone. Yet, God, still, acted in grace. One author even suggested that: "The sharp dialogue between God and Cain continued *days*. God did not want to be accused of being hasty in judgment or of being vindictive in His reaction to wrongdoing."[249]

But, now, the time for debate was over. God was beginning to take action - first off, by countering Cain's twisted rationale. He said to Cain:

> *"All of your arguments are very logical very sensible. It is self evident I could easily have created a world of peace and harmony, a world without problems or conflict, if I wished to do so. This was not my wish, nor my intention. I deliberately fashioned a world of good and evil; deliberately placed in man's keeping the power to **choose** between the two… man must be prepared to **accept the responsibility** of choice which I had given him. He must be ready to bear the consequence of his thoughts and actions. Humanity will not be able to escape from their Divinely-imposed obligation by attempting to pin on Me the blame for its **misdeeds**."*
> (Eichhorn, 1957, p. 77)[250]

God may have, then, said: "Woe to him who was merciful to you and refrained from killing you when you were beneath him. When he permitted you to rise, you killed him!"[251] "God knew that Cain wasn't truly sorry… knowing also that he really felt more sorry for *himself* than he did for either his bad conduct or his brother's death."[252]

Cain, then, began to become a, "victim to his own arrogance, defeated by his own gigantic pride which came from within himself…", and God knew it:[253]

> *…God tested the wine bottles of Adam and of Cain and found them both to be full of vinegar… God gave both these men a chance to do the manly thing, acknowledge their*

sin and confess their guilt, but in each case the opportunity was passed by...
(Eichhorn, 1957, p. 72)[254]

God's hope that Cain would, eventually, change his tune had now passed. No more discussions. God was ready to deal with him:

...his refusal to beg forgiveness of God (Himself) is itself so prideful that it constitutes... (that) Cain's soul is quite beyond redemption.
(Bandy, 1967, p. 31)[255]

...in bewailing the hopelessness of his situation, Cain merely assured his damnation... because he turned from God of his own will - whatever becomes of Cain afterwards is not so much divine punishment as self-punishment.
(Bandy, 1967, p. 31)[256]

Called Out

Interestingly enough, "When Cain *refused* to recount what he had done his knowledge and his shame were exposed."[257] As we'll now see, it was quite the *opposite* of how Adam exposed his shame - Adam's shame, when he felt truly guilty, showed *readily*, through facial blush! For Cain's shame to be exposed, his whole mindset, quite often, had to be "called out!" It wasn't going to come easily. So, in other words, Cain would have to be *exposed* - exposed for what he said, or did, outright, for all to see. Most probably, he wouldn't do it, himself. Again, *why*? Because, he (and those who would end up following him) would, often, *not* seem to find the honor enough to admit to their faults, when they *should* have shame! A person who is self-centered, like Cain, most often will not want to admit **anything** that might lower his or her self-*esteem*, or "ruin" his or her (self-administered) goal of *perfection*, within their life! A lot is riding on their thoughts, here, and any perceived *guilt* or *imperfection* hurts them, a great deal.

So, in conclusion, Adam, and those decided to follow the ways of Adam's "Father" (i.e. God), would want to *show* their shame, upfront, through honor, dignity, through moral character and humility. Adam's shame showed up, clearly, on his face. The shame of Cain, and those who would follow after the ways of *his* father (i.e. the Serpent), had to have shame *brought out* of them. And, even **then**, the guilt may *still* not be acknowledged within the individual. It's like showing Dracula the cross.. The two are, practically, polar opposites.

The Son of Perdition

Now, God began the judgment phase:

*...Cain, thou art **Perdition** and **thy deeds shall follow thee**, for from thee shall flow murder and bloodshed, wars and contentions, until the earth shall hide her face from the wickedness and pollution of mankind... **thine existence is a pollution** to the sanctity of this spot.*
- *The Book of the Generations of Adam* Chap. 5.8[258]

*Cain... had entered into a covenant with Satan whereby **he** had become **Perdition**, the Master of the Lie, that great secret by which they murder and commit all manner of abominations **to get unlawful gain**.*
- *The Book of the Generations of Adam* Chap. 5.5[259]

This, actually, results in a large part of the "mystery" side of *Mystery Babylon* - the new ways of thought and behavior that Cain, and his father the Serpent, helped to usher into mankind. And, as we see in the above, these mannerisms are, so often, utilized, in order to allow a person unlawful *gain*. This *unlawful gain* represents the raising of one's own self-esteem - through the use of unsavory and unethical practices, or *ways*, now ushered into this post-Fall world. These *ways*, of course, are those of Cain, and his father, the Serpent.

Chapter 5

Cain, Seed of the Serpent (Part 2)

The Death Heard All 'Round the World

Word caught on - Abel was now dead. Eve immediately went over to see her lifeless son, and lamented grievously.[1] Believe it or not, even though they knew that Cain killed his brother, Adam and Eve, both, were *not* too inclined to place all of blame onto him, here.[2] Why? Probably, because they knew who his *real* father was, and weren't too surprised.

In regards to our post-Fall world, the martyrdom of Abel *was* considered a monumental event.

> *Therefore, the murder of Hevel (Abel) is identical to the sin of eating from the Tree of Knowledge, and both were incited by the Serpent. And, as in the affair of the Tree of Knowledge, in which the Angel of Death gained control of the world, here too he (Cain) gained* **control, taking over the soul of Hevel (Abel)**.

- *Zohar* Beresheet b60³

The death allowed Cain to take over "control" of Abel's soul, in a way - to alter his purpose for this future, and alter his destiny. He even would have destroyed everyone that could come from Abel's loins. Most importantly, it stifled all of the **good** that Abel would have brought to the world. And, in its place, Cain would help usher in more and more of *his* ways of thinking, living or doing. These ways of Cain (and the Serpent) would, eventually, become extremely popular, over time - one way, eventually, overwhelming the other.

Cain, eventually, was thought to possess a power enough to "disturb the way of beasts and men."⁴ As most all of us, now, could assume, the world by which Cain "gained control" over would, eventually, get worse and worse, over time.

The remainder… followed Cain… whereby he had become Perdition...
- The Book of the Generations of Adam Chap. 5.5⁵

That's why God called the Serpent "Perdition" (i.e. "worthlessness"), and, now, his son *Cain* - the "*son* of Perdition!"

*There were some ancient interpreters who presumed Cain's reputation as the **true starting point** for cultivated evil in the world.* (Delaney, 1996, p. 104)⁶

Cain's new way was, now, considered *protocol* for all of what the Serpent wanted, in his post-Fall, dream world. Oh, Cain:

You opened the gate of Sheol before the entire earth.
- St. Ephrem the Syrian: Selected Prose Works Section 3, 7⁷

Yet, Abel, before his murder, may have been *the* "framework," if you will, of those who may have wanted to follow the ways of Adam, under God - the epitome. Cain would have no such competition.

The Punishments Had Begun

As a father may sometimes need to do to children, God found it necessary to punish Cain. It was unavoidable. And, because of how we acted, Cain had become the "author of his own fate."[8] The curses to be placed upon him were clearly because of his lack of concern and reverence.[9] If he would have even showed a *smidgen* of humility, or anything beyond the boundaries of his self-absorption, maybe things would have been different - as they were with Adam's penitence. Rather, in the *vein* of his probable father, Cain was still full of envy and pride, and practically empty of what God hoped for the rest of the world. It was now time for him to pay.

The Cursed Ground

...you shall be more cursed than the ground.
            (Schwartz, 2004, p. 446)[10]

God was to deliver a number of curses to Cain. One that hit him particularly hard would be in regards to something he actually valued: "the very source of his life and livelihood, the **soil**, was no longer his ally, but his enemy."[11] The land, from now on, would, very often, yield *less* of a harvest for Cain, as well as many who may have sprung from him.[12] It would just seem "harder," in ways, for he and his kind to make it all work, compared to most other people around. "Because (Cain) was a farmer, and because he was driven off the face of the earth, his entire way of life - his establishment - was **destroyed**."[13] Simply, he (and most people who would spring from him) would find it hard and harder to make a fair *profit* from working the land, or farming.[14]

Why? First off, this new curse - another curse *of the ground* - seemed quite a bit different than the one God handed down to Adam. Both were related *the ground*, here, of course; yet, the difference seemed to be tailored to each particular individual, and their sin. In Adam's case, the ground was cursed in ways that would give him "competition," of sorts (dealing now with thorns and thistles), and that it would take a lot more effort to get him the same resolve. He had to sweat more, etc. The fruits of the earth (many of them) were still there, they just weren't looking as big and juicy, looking as though they couldn't wait to jump into Adam's mouth, to be eaten.

As far as Cain, since he was full of self-absorbed thoughts, as well as *pride*, the earth would be treated differently, as well. He also committed an extremely *unnatural* act - he committed murder of a fellow human. Now, *both* seemed to be a prelude to *how* the ground was to be cursed, because of him. In direct opposition to Cain's pride, the ways things were, *now*, seemed to *humble* him. Things just seemed to work *against* him, a lot of the times. And, all of this just didn't seem *natural*. In fact, the way things worked around him, so many times, might seem to be more *unnatural*.

Now, with Cain's curse, the *quality* of fruits and vegetables would no longer become anywhere *near* they once were. Most would lose the wonderful *tastes* they, once, might have had. A lot of things became tasteless and bitter. Before this time, the farming occupation must have been a fairly lucrative business… one's *pride* could easily be fulfilled in this line of work, no doubt. Things just seemed to work *Now* - with Cain - one may have to work unbelievably hard, just to scrape up a meager, livable wage… with bland or bad tasting crops, on top of it.

So many things "just didn't seem to work out" very well, overall. Call it divine providence, call it Karma… some even call it "Murphy's Law." Whatever the name, Cain, and his kind, often had the sensation that **their whole world** just seemed *contrary* to them, or was *against* him. So many things "just happened" to become obstructions - there were infestations of insects, planting errors, human mistakes, etc. There were even *weather* changes that made it look as though the world became "united," against he and his efforts (i.e. droughts, earthquakes, torrential rains, etc.). All of these worldly changes just seemed *unnatural* to Cain, and his kind - as compared to what anyone was used to, before.

> *Wherever Cain wandered his agricultural pursuits came to **naught**. When it should have rained, the weather turned dry. Just as he was about to reap the ripening crop, a storm blew in. Nothing **turned out right**.* (Hoeh, 1964, p. 10)[15]

One might, now, assume that - by going through enough of these trials - the world now hated, or detested, Cain, and even the entire human race! Because the death of Abel was *so* unnatural, Cain, and his kind, began to sense so many "unnatural" things coming *right back* at them. This was, probably, where sayings such as "what goes around comes around" may have originated!

> *It is important to recall that Cain was literally at **war with nature**, because his act was itself a denial of natural law.* (Bandy, 1967, p. 72)[16]

Eventually, with all of these things going on, Cain would, eventually, begin to feel more and more displaced in this world - deep down in his soul.

> *A farmer without land is like a captain without a ship…*
> (Eichhorn, 1957, p. 89-90)[17]

Cain, once, was a man who devoted a lot of his attention to *earthly*, or *inanimate objects* - he worked the earth. And, his mind was also set on *possessing* things. Now, so many *unnatural* things seemed to make it difficult for him to *keep* all of what he had, as well as easily achieve more. And, of course, this would also make it more difficult for him to maintain a health sense of *self-esteem*. It's all related.

Loss of Possession

There would be more losses for Cain:

...what he desired was not given to him, and what he possessed was taken from him.
(Halevi, 1997, p. 204)[18]

And, since Cain succumbed to his own vices of pride and possession, he was about to lose a lot more than just his occupation:[19]

*Everyone who seeks to obtain something which is **not meant for him** not only fails to get that which he seeks but also loses much, if not all, of what he already has. So it was the Serpent **and** so it is with Cain.* (Eichhorn, 1957, p. 87)[20]

Again, this is why Cain and the Serpent were practically considered synonymous with the title *perdition* (i.e. worthlessness). And, again, we see how God often does what He needs to do with *ironic* responses (which, so often, teaches some painful lessons):

*"(God to Cain)... When you till the earth, because you wished that **you** alone should eat of its strength, you **shall wonder in fear**... (because) you walked on it in **arrogance and haughtiness**."*
- *St. Ephrem the Syrian: Selected Prose Works* Section 3, 7[21]

Now, as one could guess, Cain's inner feelings of contentment, after the murder, were not panning out for him, at all - nowhere near where he thought it would.

Shaking and Trembling

In one last prideful act, Cain, again, tried to show God some arrogance, in his rapport - but, of course, that wouldn't last for long:

His anger subsided due to the trembling and wandering that laid upon him…
- St. Ephrem the Syrian: Selected Prose Works Section 3, 8[22]

So, God pronounced, yet, another curse on Cain. This one would, in actuality, be worse than the ground not yielding to him its strength![23] Science tells us that, "for every action there is a reaction." And, a lot of God's punishments, as we know, seem to work like this. We know that there, often, seems to be some ironic, or *opposite*, response to an action against God. We'll now see that Cain, as well, was to be cursed with a "shaking and trembling."[24] He was weakened, in ways, because of this:

*…since he had used the power of the body wickedly, **his energy** was taken from him, so that he was unsteady and shaking.* (Delaney, 1996, p. 131)[25]

What would this "shaking and trembling" have to do with a weakness of Cain? And, what would be the difference between the "shaking" and the "trembling?" In regards to the word "shaking," we find that Cain was cursed to suffer a "quaking," "shaking" or a "groaning," in regards to, both, how he *thought*, and how he carried himself.[26] Cain, overall, could have eventually become *weakened* by it all, in a number of ways.

God spoke to Cain "You remain permanently feeble.
You wail, shake and quake…"
(Anderson, Stone, and Tromp, 2000, p. 206)[27]

One who continually wails or groans, or seems to possess feeble and unsteady emotions, might be a person of fluctuating characteristics:

The fluctuating, uncertain nature of all things associated with Cain is an essential part of his character… (his) fluctuating character is a violation of the divine regularity of God's creation. (Bandy, 1967, p. 40-41, 84)[28]

His internal thought-processes would begin to "shake," or "quake," if you will. The stability of his soul could easily loosen, here, allowing him to, quite often, feel agitated, disturbed and moody. This "shaking" could, quite often for Cain, result in disruptions of (what should be) his own "equilibrium" of thought. composed

> *Cain was troubled and trembled all the days of his life.*
> (Kugel, 1998, p. 164)[29]

The second term, *trembling*, could also mean "quivering."[30] Again, this could have a parallel to Cain's inner instability - the *opposite* of feeling calm and composed.

And, on top of these mental afflictions, Cain could have been made to suffer some *outer*, physical ailments, in regards to this curse.[31]

> *...thy soul shall shake, and thy **body** shall quiver.*
> - Barhebraeus' Scholia on the Old Testament Part I 9b.4.2[32]

He also would, now, begin to feel the need to move about - from front to back, from side to side - in a continual, nervous "shudder."[33] Any *rest* or *ease* that Cain may have temporarily had would not last for long:

> *...you will never relax, being released neither night nor day from your toil...*
> (Delaney, 1996, p. 131)[34]

Cain, as well, couldn't sit for a long time. He always felt like he had to be "on the move." It all, again, seemed to be for an *ironic* reason:

> *"(God to Cain) You shall never again have continuing peace of mind or bodily ease. Because you followed him (Abel) relentlessly from place to place, you, too, shall never be permitted to **rest** in an one place for **even a moment**."*
> (Eichhorn, 1957, p. 88)[35]

Now, through his "shaking" and "trembling" (in mind and body), God made Cain an example before all of creation. It's funny, but: we already *know* how Adam was openly shaking and trembling in God's presence - *especially* at the time he was going to be punished. Cain, however, did not really show *any* type of fear, or nervousness. He didn't shake nor tremble. He was *too proud* to show God any proper respect, here. Maybe this punishment would allow Cain one more chance to see the error of his ways?

God did bring trembling and terror upon him so that he might see the peace in which he was at first, and see also the trembling and terror he endured at the last; so that he might humble himself before God, repent of his sin, and seek the peace he enjoyed at first.
  - The First Book of Adam and Eve (The Conflict of Adam and Eve With Satan) I.79.25[36]

As most of us could guess, Cain wouldn't go for that.

Fugitive Removed

His punishments would have to continue, however. Next, Cain was cursed to be a *fugitive* and *vagabond* to others around him. As most of us might surmise, there may have been other people in the world, during this time, who, naturally, would be very upset with what Cain did - the ultimate *evil* atrocity. Word went out, throughout the land. The most logical thought that would come to almost everyone's mind would, probably, be, "an eye for an eye."

Many wanted justice. Many wanted him dead. Cain, probably, was feeling a bit discouraged about what God had already dished out to him, and started to complain:

*"Many will want to kill me to be pleasing to You. You must give me some kind of protection which will indicate that it is Your wish that I remain **alive and unharmed**, so that I may be shielded against those who are overly **zealous**."*
  (Eichhorn, 1957, p. 93)[37]

God, the merciful God that he was, graciously decided to remove *half* of Cain's punishment, here - the punishment of having to be a *fugitive*. It would be around this time that God would introduce His famous "mark" upon Cain.

Since it came to Cain at this particular point of time, it's only logical to assume that this "mark" could have something to do with the context of this scenario! It makes sense. It, really, must have something to do with saving Cain from the ramifications of being a fugitive, and saving him from other. It must have to do with his protection.

*And the LORD set a mark upon Cain, lest any finding him **should kill him**.*
- Gen. 4:15 (KJV)

It, most probably, wasn't something to "brand" him, in any way. So, to protect Cain from suffering as a fugitive - from being killed, while "on the run" - God placed a *stigma*, or mark, upon him. He did not want anyone to kill Cain, for any reason. That saved him from being chased! He was still to be a vagabond, however: one who wanders **aimlessly** about the earth, in, either, body or mind (or both).

Now, what would stop Cain from becoming a fugitive - in the minds of other people around him? If other people made up their minds to go out and kill him for what he did, it wouldn't matter if God turned Cain's skin bright green, or made him continually dance around, wearing a lampshade on his head! They were still going after him, anyway. So, the one thing we might be able to take away from this all is: maybe this "mark" wasn't exactly placed upon Cain, himself, or upon his body - maybe it would be to "mark" the *other people* around him!

What Cain's "Mark" Probably Was

No one knows, for sure, what his mark was. The Bible doesn't tell us. We cannot look at Cain's body, today, and see what might have been different. What we do have are these ancient accounts - these ancient interpretations and opinions! Put them all together, and we can take an educated guess.

So many interpretations have arisen about this "mark," however, throughout the ages: from it being leprosy to being a guard dog (for Cain); from it being a animal horn, placed upon his forehead, to the sun shining down brightly upon him. God was, however, said to have "established a covenant" with Cain, by this mark.[38] You don't establish a covenant with a horn, or leprosy. The mark was considered a token by "which **he** should be recognized…"[39] Now, what could all of it mean?

To learn, to the best of our ability, what this mark might be, we, again, need to understand the *context* by which surrounded its insertion.

Could it be…

> …*a mark which* **shall not be eradicated until the end of time**? *Thou wicked Cain… thy deeds shall follow thee for from thee shall flow murder and bloodshed, wars and contentions, until the earth shall hide her face from the wickedness and pollution of mankind… Nevertheless,* **no man shall slay thee, for thou shalt live to see the full measure flowing from thine iniquity**, *until the final destruction of the darkness of this world.* - The Book of the Generations of Adam Ch. 5.8[40]

Could **Cain**, now, have been the stigma, himself - a "mark" to others on what to do, or *not* to do? This stigma would have to stem *directly* from the minds of the people around him, wanting to kill him, then! This "mark," then, may have been a *new* way for other people to look at him.

From that point further (and, possibly, till the end of time), many people would, almost automatically, begin to think a little differently at Cain, and people like him. That is the "mark" - a *stigma* about Cain. Now, the people around Cain were to look upon him, and think *other* thoughts, rather than just wanting to kill him, on the spot![41] Other thoughts would creep into their minds - slowly starting to confuse their once saw plainly, and easily. Now, the mark could have instigated a new mind-set, new intuitions, or new, innate opinions about people like Cain. Now, instead of wanting to immediately kill him, the thoughts that, most often, would enter a person's mind would be: to "just get away from him," or "leave him alone." "He has enough problems, already" Maybe a little **compassion** was being inserted, where it never had been, before. Maybe a desire to "not worry about it, because it's not my concern" would begin to creep in. Maybe people were beginning to think more about their own lives, and the need to go back, and manage their own personal problems, than seek out a quick form of justice. All of these thoughts entering into a person's mind would now save Cain, for sure. People would be angry with him, no doubt. They may hate what he did. But, for the most part, they wouldn't want to immediately kill him, as before.

Now, it would become more practical for a person to avoid Cain "like the plague" - and not even want to get involved with him or his situation - rather than desire to punish him, or condemn him! It was easier for them just to leave him alone! Leave it for "someone else to do."

On top of this, this same mind-set, also, would enable a vast number of people to sprout thoughts of *compassion* and *sympathy* for Cain, and his situation - **even though** *they may have already understood* Cain's true intentions, and the situations of the murder! Even though they have understood the veracity of what went down, and how Cain *willingly* committed a crime, these same **sympathetic thoughts** would, very often, begin to float atop of a person's mind! Even though Cain deserved a harsh punishment, and anyone - using any logical thinking - would have figured that out, before, a vast number of people, now, would begin to feel almost *sorry* for him. With new (and undeserved) thoughts of compassion and sympathy now arising in people, as well, many would, now, rather "turn a blind eye" to Cain, and his deeds, than want to take action.

As a result, all of these thoughts would, in actuality, allow Cain (and those after him) a much better chance to "get away" with things they would not have been able to, before! Now, it was just better for a vast number of people to leave Cain - and his situation – alone, and hope "it all goes away."

Maybe Abel, himself, inspired the implementation of this "mark," by being a bit overly *compassionate* and *sympathetic* towards his brother. As we recall, he had Cain on the ground, and was able to stop Cain. But, he loosened his grip, when he, actually, should have stood his ground. If Abel would have, actually, brought the hammer down, and condemned Cain's thoughts and actions at the time - rather than going a little *overboard*, and using a little too much compassion - he may have still been alive. It seemed to be Abel's one, huge mistake, here - now, implanted on other people around Cain. This same mind-set may have been installed by God, here, as a consequence! It is a very different way of looking at this "mark," but a very logical one, as well.

Now, being "marked" in this way, Cain, himself, turned into an anathema.

<u>Anathema</u>
- a ban or curse solemnly pronounced by ecclesiastical authority and accompanied by

> *excommunication.*
> *- someone or something intensely disliked or loathed.*[42]

If we consider this all as a possibility, and insert this into the context of where Cain's "mark" would have been, it seems to fit. This mind-set would, actually, protect Cain! Rarely anyone would feel like acting on their desires for blood, now - exactly what God wanted, as well. People would just scorn him, and want to leave him alone. It was a lot like a person displaying an "automatic" mistrust of the man. At least, in this way, he would survive! And, wherever he was about to wander, now, he could, at least, go. He may have been an object of contempt, derision and hate, but he would no longer be a fugitive:[43]

> *...the people would say,* **"Go away** *from him; this is the one who killed his brother"...*
> *- Rashi* Genesis 4:16[44]

For the most part, this "mark" applied to the majority of people around him. People "just knew" that there was something about Cain they didn't like:[45]

> *...good people shall curse thee...*
> (Emerson, 1916, p. 863)[46]

Now, wherever he began to wander, he seemed as though he was a trespasser; and most people wanted Cain to leave their territory.[47] "It became a general assumption that no man should either befriend or kill him."[48] At least for a while, most everyone around him did just this - *for a while.*

The "Land Of Nod"

...the unhappy man... fleeing from the joys of men... (to) a joyless land.
(Emerson, 1916, p. 865)[49]

After Cain was given the mark, God decreed that he was now to leave His presence, leave the life he once knew, and serve out the other half of his punishment: being a vagabond. The Bible says that, at this time, he went to "the land of Nod" (Gen. 4:16).

Thus, in the land of Nod, which is a forsaken portion of the earth just as Cain was a forsaken member of the human race... (Bandy, 1967, p. 39)[50]

Nod could also be considered the "Land of Confusion."[51] And, as we see, this "Nod" also seemed to have a mental component attached to it. A larger part of this whole "Nod" concept could actually revolve around an esoteric parallel of the human psyche. As one author proclaimed, "The Jewish writers... rather agreed that 'the land of Nod' is best understood as the state of Cain's **own mind**."[52]

A vagabond is one destined to wander - not only in his travels, but, also, in his own soul. Cain was cursed to physically wander the earth, and survive - without certain satisfactions of life, and the peace of mind, that others may have, around him.

...You will become a nod
a staggering/tottering/restless wanderer

a head shaking griever
              (Halevi, 1997, p. 251)[53]

Cain's wasteland was not only a physical place.

If the land of Nod is an allegory of the state of the sinner's mind, such a sinner might as well be in hell itself.   (Bandy, 1967, p. 51)[54]

God probably took out His vengeance upon Cain in that ways that were best attuned to Cain's own personality, in ways that would affect an arrogant and shameless man like himself - the most.

*The most severe punishment for a right-thinking person is separation from God. For to one who reasons correctly, shame is the **severest of punishments**...*
              (Delaney, 1996, p. 132)[55]

As one could surmise, Cain was not a "right-thinking" individual. He did not have shame. Most people around him understood shame; most understood humility. How to deal? Cain was just too self-centered to "wake up and smell the coffee," so God had to be harsh on him, in the way that was best.

If Cain took the effort and time, and actually lowered his pride a little bit, then things might have been a bit different. If he didn't look for anyone else, and anything around him, to blame for his *own* actions, God might have gone a little easier on him. But, of course, Cain did none of it. So, it seems, for every deviant thought and act out there, there has to be some ramification. These curses of Cain may have even extended to his descendants, as well - with a number of the same, inner conflicts ringing true in those who were *of* him, and in those who would want to *follow* him, as well.

Ramifications

One ramification of these curses, as anyone might guess, would be that Cain had to suffer a great deal of mental confusion - especially from his inner conscience.

And Cain wrestled within himself, for the voice of Jehovah continued **to call unto him***... he knew that he was lost in darkness and his mind was blighted... forever fleeing his memories and the darkness which* **pursued** *him and* **grew within** *him.*
   - The Book of the Generations of Adam Ch. 5.11[56]

These punishments, in a way, became, for Cain, a "fate truly worse than death."[57]

Yet, this son of the Serpent was not to go down, that easily. He *still* didn't want to live out this life, and think about things the way God wanted. He did not want to accept his own fate. He, instead, truly took the devil's path. He, now, wanted to go down most *any* pathway that opposed God, and His plans. He wanted to, at least, feel a little satisfaction for his ventures, or gain at least a little power over others. He may have, then, turned to his *real* father for guidance on this whole situation - for advice on how to achieve his short-term "power grabs." The Serpent, assuredly, began to show him every earthly way out there, to help him raise whatever remnants of a self-esteem he had left. This continued on, for the rest of his days.

The Change of Tides

> *...the type of **earthly** man is Cain. Cain was the prototype of him whose **treasure** is entirely in this world, the earth nonetheless became for Cain a place of torment.*
> (Bandy, 1967, p. 51)[58]

As stated earlier, the situation of Cain, himself, became a "mark" to other people. To him, assuredly, he could have begun to notice something different. He saw how others *now* treated him. At first, it must have been humiliating. But, later on, as one might guess, Cain could have, and *did* find ways to take advantage of it all! After all, he had the Serpent helping him! He, also, had all of what the world had to offer at his fingertips.

Now, Cain seemed to have the "power" to change other people's minds, and, even, "get away with murder" (by deterring everyone away from him, in these ways). As a skunk who begins to release a very smelly spray to all of his neighbors (and notices how every animal around him begins to flee), Cain may have begun to pick up on the newfound power of this "mark." He would, now, be able to take advantage of this, somehow. If he could "get their minds going," and have them begin to act in these ways, then he could, now, get away with a lot of things he never had before! Why not? So many would just rather avoid you, than stand up to you! It wouldn't be as easy for them to fully stand up for their convictions - at least alone. Feeling that he would not get punished as severely anymore, for any crime(s) that he may have commit, could have may emboldened him, from then on! "It takes a thief" to think in these ways, apparently.

Over time, Cain even began to feel as though - someday - he could be powerful enough to get out of some of the curses God planned for him! With his "intellectual shrewdness," Cain eventually began to be proud enough of himself to think that, somehow, he could escape his own destiny.[59]

> *...just as the show of mind would bring Cain's eternal torment, the **mark** brings Cain's way to get out of his fugitive ways, **through his mind**...*
> (Bandy, 1967, p. 52)[60]

Cain, and, most probably, many people who, either, sprung from him or followed him, would all be able to capitalize on this "mark," at least, to a degree! It almost became an art form - able to be driven home by those deviant enough to pull it off. It involves manipulate the minds of others, in certain ways, to achieve results. Cain, soon, had it all down pat. He now found out ways to install his own, ancient version of "political correctness" into the minds of many around him! Imagine that!

Eventually, with these new mind-sets, a number of people wouldn't really be in a position to defend their selves, or fight back, because the "mark" would compel them to avoid the situation, and drop it. Cain eventually felt so pompous and emboldened that he believed, now, he could go and push people around - thinking they would *always* leave him "off the hook," or do nothing in return.

> *(The ancient author, Ibn Ezra, stated that)... there was "no visible sign on Cain," but God "strengthened his heart so that **he feared nothing**"... (and, on top of it, many)... **feared him**.* (Eichhorn, 1957, p. 98)[61]

It was working! People were turning down the opportunities to challenge Cain, rather than face him, and what he may be doing; and Cain passed this skill onto his contemporaries! It was beginning to work like a charm!

Cain, eventually, felt as though he could sail through life, intimidating and dictating - and, most often, being unchallenged! Eventually, many of these ways he was beginning to push onto other people would just come to be accepted. And, with other confederates of Cain attempting these same tricks, a vast majority of the deceived individuals were, just plain, giving in. Many were starting to feel a need to be "politically correct," because of so many of Cain's confederates at work around them - pushing the same things on them! People were, no longer, in the mood to deal with it all, or to "tell it like it was." They just had other things to do. Cain, and his kind, soon became strengthened by these responses.

> *Thinking he could escape Gods judgment, Cain becomes the ultimate in **spiritual arrogance**...*   (Delaney, 1996, p. 180)[62]

An early form of "humanism" began to take off, in the minds of many.

"Ways of Cain" on the Rise

With his refusal to submit to God, and succumb to His punishments, Cain "even added sin to sin, showing his state of mind by his action."[63] Cain wasn't about to change.

> *For the good make use of this world in order to enjoy God, whereas the evil want to make **use of God** in order to enjoy the world.*   (Delaney, 1996, p. 180)[64]

They were beginning to take "good" things around them - compassion and empathy - and exploit them, as a means to their own ends. They were beginning to use things that seemed Godly, and pervert them for their own causes. As discontented and unsteady Cain's mind probably was, he began to exploit people enough to be able acquire a number of material things in this world - many that allowed him, at least, some (short-term) feeling of satisfaction. He began to indulge in, "bodily lusts, amassed wealth by rapine, taught evil practices and lived luxuriously."[65] With his new way of doing things, he began to considered himself "on his way up" - towards escaping his own judgment.

Back Into the Picture

Woe be to the inhabitants of the earth for the devil is come down amongst you.
(Reeve, 1699, p. 151)[66]

As we've already discovered in Volume 1, the Nephilim were living in these same areas, and were probably be more than eager to assist Cain, here, in his desires to manipulate people for his own gain.

These terrestrial angels, as we know, began to teach those around them the "occult arts" - hidden knowledge of our world. They even taught ways for people to "gaze upon the sun and moon and perform feats of magic."[67]

*Not only the dark secrets of heaven, these angels gave the human race secrets of the natural universe, those in which God probably never **wanted to make known to man**.*
(Schwartz, 2004, p. 458)[68]

Cain, gladly, accepted their help. The more (against God) the merrier. The motive behind this bartering of information was simple: power. It gave power to the Nephilim, and, eventually, it gave more power to Cain, himself – because he would, soon, be "king" over it all.

He's Now "Worth His Salt"

*Cain had a large progeny; for they married frequently, being given to animal lusts; until the land... **was filled with them**.*
- *The Second Book of Adam and Eve (The Conflict of Adam and Eve with Satan)* Book II.12.16[69]

Cain, eventually, would become the leader over many. Sargon, one of Cain's aliases, was said to have found another way to give him even *more* power: "if he could monopolize the salt trade, he could become rich."[70] In other words, Cain (a.k.a. Sargon) began to understand how capitalism worked, at least in certain respects, and made himself more and more wealthy - through the bartering of salt. Salt began to be important to the people of Cain's day. Everybody wanted it to help them preserve food, amongst other things. He, and a few of his close followers, began to make the distribution of salt a major role of importance. He, then, used his position, here, to gain more and more control over the masses, in many ways. A good many people began to delegate him as **the** "mover and shaker" of their time:

> *..they magnify Cain as if he had been conceived of some potent Virtue which operated in him...*
> - Tertullian *Against All Heresies*, Chapter 2. Ophites, Cainites, Sethites[71]

The respect for Cain quickly amassed throughout the lands. On top of his game, Cain also, "taught them everything that God **hated** - pride, boastfulness of speech, self-adulation, calumniation, false accusation, and the swearing of false oaths."[72] It's so interesting how a lot of these same tricks of mind-manipulation are being used on the populous, today. And, also, it'll be interesting to see how so many things in our society are behaving just like they had, under Cain's original influence and domination, here… as we'll soon see!

The "New Norm"

To help to prove this, let's list a few of the ways people were said to have lived back then:

- *…their souls were empty because they **did not know the Lord Jehovah** nor did they call upon His holy name.*[73]

- *He (Cain) was not concerned about the spiritual welfare and future of either himself, or the human race. What would happen to him or to his kind after he was dead was, for him, a matter of no importance whatsoever. The "**here and now**" and "**what's in it for me**" were all that counted.*[74]

- *The **concern for each other grew less and less** and love of each for **self** grew more and* *more...*[75]

- *...(they) only talked of **rights**.*[76]

- *Every one of them did according **to his lust**. They had no shame about this and thought no harm of it.*[77]

- *They only thought of **intent upon pleasure** rather doing **duty** to **the human race**.*[78]

- *They... might easily have told the truth, if those **lies** were not sweeter to them...*[79]

- *They were also steeped in **robbery** (or theft).*[80]

- *...the extension of dominion was **sought by violence** rather than through **godly labor**.*[81]

- *...**females** frequently lorded over **males**.*[82]

- *...the envious **covet the possessions** of others.*[83]

- *...they... sold what did not belong to them, they entered **homes without right**, and took whatever they wanted... they **rigged the laws in their favor**...*[84]

"Children of the Sun"

Don't they sound *so* familiar - a lot like today?

These self-centered ways of life would eventually become institutionalized, into governments of the time, and spread throughout the entire ancient world - with many, upon many, ancient cultures claiming themselves to be the "Children of the Sun."[85] We know that the Serpent probably assumed the ancient title of "Sun god," in the most ancient of times. Now, Cain was following along the same, darkened pathway. Their charge for domination of everything around them was, now, underway.[86] And, of course, their quests would not be very good for the human soul, over time.

The Darkness of Ignorance

...their sin forces them to dwell in the darkness of ignorance.
                          (Bandy, 1967, p. 191)[87]

This eventual rejection of God, and His ways, could, in actuality, be considered one's eventual withdrawal from the heavenly "light" of God's influence. The ultimate destination of these individuals would be a *darkness*, or separation from one's own Creator.

(The ancient historian Gregory)… describes this darkness as possessing the mind of the sinner, whose spiritual vision is thereby **clouded**.
(Bandy, 1967, p. 27)[88]

Again, this also could thought of as a particular *style* of thinking. If anything, those thinking in this darkness "zone" could, eventually, want to adopt the opposite ways of God. And, on top of it, many would not feel any shame in thinking these ways!

Woe to them that call evil good, and good evil; that put darkness for light, and light for darkness...   - Isa. 5:20 (KJV)

Genetics, culture and, most importantly, free-will choices may affect how *deeply* an individual begins falls into this "darkness" of soul. There are those who might even desire to separate from God, in most ways:

They had either **forgotten** *God, or were willfully disposed to act in* **direct opposition** *to his commands.*
(Oliver, 1843, p. 48)[89]

So many individuals were beginning to follow these new ways of Cain, until they almost became societal norms, or "business as usual."

The City

With so many adopt the ways of Cain, there were bound to be those coming into theological conflicts with those who still wanted to follow Adam, or his descendants (i.e.

the Sethites). Cain, with, "his hand being against every man," still felt a little bit intimidated - mainly by those who zealously wanted to follow God![90] And, because of this, and a few other reasons, Cain began a new project. He wanted to create something out of this earth to help him feel even *more* secure:[91]

He was the first that walled or made cities; dreading them that he hurted...
— *The Golden Legend or Lives of the Saints: Volume I* p. 62[92]

Cain, and a number of his confederates, may not have been able to function very well, as farmers (as we've already discussed). Since he, and his kind, could not profit very well from farming, Cain figured that some *changes* might be in order. He, now, began to shape and fashion the earth into something it was not originally meant to be. No more loose dirt. No more flat earth. No more would there be nothing but fields of growing plants. Now, Cain and his followers would begin to build cities.[93] As he began to be influential over others, Cain began to pressure - even force - people to settle into these areas.[94] Soon enough, it would appear that, "the cities of the earth are the domain of the descendants of Cain."[95]

What's so special about a city, one might ask? We recall that God cursed the earth to be, for the most part, unfriendly to Cain (and, most probably, those who descended from him, and followed him).[96]

Isn't it ironic that:

*...cities display the highest achievements of mortals and glory **mankind**. The word "city" ("naked" in Hebrew) indicates that the ground has been **denuded** of vegetation. But living, growing plant life is God's achievement, and **reminds us** of his vital power, wisdom, and glory.* (Johnson, 2003, p. 54)[97]

It's interesting to see these "opposite" extremes, here, beginning to pan out. In the same vein of idolatry, people began to put their trust in the city's surrounding walls and fortifications. They, again, began to look to the *material* things of their world - even their *cities* - for security, and not God.[98]

*...the spiritual sons of Cain are all those who 'build their cities' in the world... pinning all their hopes on a **false good**.* (Bandy, 1967, p. 14)[99]

Much of Cain's time would be spent "trying to find security, struggling against hostile forces, dominating men, women and nature..."[100]

*He thinks building a city will satisfy **his deepest desires**. He will satisfy his... desire for security by creating a place belonging to **him**... he will **remake** the world, not a world from God but a start for humans - a sure starting place for **civilization**.* ("Cain and the Meaning of the City", n. d., p. 2-3)[101]

This, again, tells us so much - as we already know, it's either *one* way or *another*!

The Beginnings of "Civilization"

*The beginning of **civilization begins** with the city and all it represents.... Cain creates the art of craftsmanship. Cain **bends all of creation to his will**... he assumes control/domination... (of) his destiny of slavery and sin... From this taking*

possession... the city is born.
                ("Cain and the Meaning of the City", n. d., p. 3)[102]

We already know he popularized one very famous city of influence, here:

*...the universal destiny of earthly cities - of which **Babylon** is the prototype.*
                (Bandy, 1967, p. 209)[103]

The people living in these areas would, soon, to be under the "intellectual domination" of these cities, such as Babylon. And, they would be dominated by Serpent-influenced ways of thinking, such as the following:[104]

- *envy*

- *hate*

- *pride*

- *greed*[105]

- *self-love*

- *haughtiness*

- *vain opinions*

- *men who know not wisdom as relating to truth*[106]

A person living in these early cities could have some advantages, of course, but there could also be a number of downsides to it all, as well. One of the most important factors seem to be related to how one views each other, and their world. It, also, seemed to relate to how one was able to *work with* another, as well, or get along with them. For all that Cain created in this, he "...had a high degree of **civilization**, but that doesn't mean he had a high degree of **morality**."[107] So, from this, we can gather that: just because the ancients may have been able to come together, and live in some magnificent collection of stone buildings, doesn't mean that they were *better* people, overall, or, were more *elite*. They may, of course, have lacked the things that *really* matter, here - a good *moral* foundation, for starters.

And, it also seemed that: God was against people coming together in these cities, at least, back in the earliest of times:

*...civilization to Him is not progress; it is a **decline**...*
(Redlich, 1950, p. 80)[108]

The reason? In those days, Cain and his ways slowly transformed these cities into citadels of moral decay and decadence. Sin was beginning to plague them all. The thoughts and attitudes (such as those mentioned, above) began to reign, supreme:

*...the inventions of men may be taken as either good or bad - it depends entirely upon their **employment to the great glory of God**, or simply for **self-gratification**.*
(Bandy, 1967, p. 160)[109]

This tells us so much. Would these massive citadels of Cain, here, be there to (eventually) point one towards the glorification of God, or, of man?

Unity of Soul - Humanism

*...Cain is declared patriarch of the "city of **men**."*
(Bandy, 1967, p. 245)[110]

Why have so many of us, today, been bombarded by intellectual concepts, such as "humanism?" Along these same lines, why do so many people push the concept of "unity?" Besides having "strength in numbers," many also seem to want others to do the same, exact thing they are - to have them "unify" with them, or join them, in a cause. Why? There could be a number of other reasons for this desire - more *unsavory* reasons.

Instead of looking towards God, and what He may have to offer, human pride begins to demanded that a number of these ancients look to themselves. Their pride tells them that, in the overall scheme of things, *they* were actually the superior ones, in both thought and action. After while, people like Cain - serving as the "elite," here - may have begun to believe they knew "what was best" for the masses. *They* took the place of God, now!

Human thought was what mattered, not necessarily God. And, in turn, a number of these powerful, like-minded individuals may have begun to feel the need to "convert" others to their cause - to have them all "join the unity movement."[111]

Also, those who are sliding into immorality may know, deep down inside, that they are doing some wrong, but want to keep going. To keep going (without the guilt), they need numbers, they need people joining them. Possibly, a number of these ancient people:

> *...**(did) not have the moral strength to run for their life** and **to feel justified** they wanted to get others involved. Perhaps this is why false religion is often the most evangelistic in attempting **to convert others**...*
> ("Jubal - Genun Musical Worship - #2", n. d., p. 15)

> *If a drunkard can get his teetotaler to take a **sip** then his own actions are **validated** and he feels so much better... (many) would **never be content** until they **seduced** all of those "goody, goodies" (around them)...*
> ("Jubal - Genun Musical Worship - #2", n. d., p. 14-16)[112]

As some say: "misery demands company." It's much better for one to be able to sin, and not do it alone!

So, as a major "mover and shaker" of his time, Cain, now, would be the one who began to define those ancient, "politically correct" ways of thinking. The more people that Cain and his followers could seduce, the more influence he had over all of them. Simple. And, eventually, with enough of these ancient in his "back pocket," it was beginning to seem as though they had "one mind."[113] That's why they, so often, strived for total unity (and *still* do)!

Pride

We've also touched on that one, underlying emotion behind a person's desire to follow these opposite ways of God, as well as to seduce others:

*The vice which **unites** them is their "pride"… the (**same**) single divine attribute retained by (Sammael)… after he was cast out of heaven.*
                                                        (Bandy, 1967, p. 153)[114]

One's "pride," if unchecked and immoral, becomes "a ruthless ruling passion which blinds its subject to all else."[115] Pride convinces the individual into looking further and further away from God, and towards some other way of achieving their gratification, perfection, or salvation. Enter the pagan religion - straight from the Serpent (and Cain).

The Beginnings of Idolatry

Cain, as we know, did his best not to follow God. We also know that he was cursed for it. At time went on, and, as his authority over the masses increased, Cain began to reflect on those things, in the past, which just didn't seem to work out in his favor. Cain, as a perfectionist, became perplexed by them. He, also, noticed how the world around him *still* seemed to be against him, in a number of ways - whether it be animal, vegetable or mineral. While continually *denying* the overwhelming power of God over all of the creation around him, and, even, denying that he was *still* cursed (or *ought* to be), he worked to rationalize it all away:

> *This happened so often that Cain became convinced that God must have given some **evil spirit** the duty of stirring up the animals wherever he went. He never saw the spirit but he was sure it **must** be about him somewhere.* (Eichhorn, 1957, p. 107)[116]

What could have easily transpired as a irrational supposition of Cain, now, becomes a major element of Cain's new, pagan religion: repelling "evil" spirits. Cain, obviously, knew about the supernatural world. He knew about the fallen, terrestrial angels around him. He, most probably, knew about the spiritual entities that, also, lived in this spiritual world. So, with all of this knowledge in hand, Cain could have easily used it all to help convince people that they, now, had to start making (misdirected) sacrifices to entities *such as these* - to assure their protection, or banish any "evil" spirits they might find against them. Anything but God.

> *Cain… the purveyor of false sacrifices and the inventor of violent schemes.*
> (Delaney, 1996, p. 104)[117]

According to Cain, it, now, wasn't really any heavenly **God** who had absolute power over the universe; one could find the things they need in their world around them, to help with any worldly difficulties.

The people of his day also respected their ancestors a great deal, as well. So, to top of Cain's laundry list of deities to "appease," here, who better… than their elders, their ancestors, and important patriarchs of the day? Now, along with those minor deities of the spiritual, or supernatural, world, people had *major* pagan deities to deal with, look up to, to "appease" and, even to worship. Yes, this was, most probably, the beginning of primitive ancestor worship, as well as the primitive worship of the sun. Another faith, completely contrary to God, began to take off.

To assist Cain in his newfound faith, statues (or idols) were constructed - to give people something to "gaze" at. These earthly images were considered to be the actual representations of these "creators and rulers of earth" - something concrete.[118] Again, this was, most probably, the beginning of pagan idol worship, as well![119] Paganism was in its infancy - the result of these institutionalized ways of Cain and the Serpent.[120]

To top it all off, Eve looked at the cities Cain constructed, and all of the power that he had, and may have begun to conclude he just *may be* the "promised one" of Gen. 3:15 - the child destined to deliver the human race to hope and safety. It looked as though he was accomplishing so much, here - at least, to some.

His progress, probably, continued to fire up his imagination. He may have even believed that *he* was the "promised one" - because he was a descendant of one in the individuals in the Garden. Of course, it was, most probably, the Serpent; but, as he continually tried to manipulate things around, inside his head, the truth didn't really matter, too much, anymore. Besides, by now, he could have really talked himself into most anything! What if the whole narrative was confused, a bit? Maybe the seeds of the Serpent should have been among those with the accolades, here. It seemed to Cain that he was doing exactly what the "promised one" should have been doing – making life better for the people, "saving" them from the dreariness of the Fall, etc. Cain was really uniting the people around him, giving them "civilization," teaching them a good deal of (occult) knowledge. And, now, his new religion was beginning to guide them to find their *own* road to perfection, or salvation![121] People could have, very easily, begun to look to Cain as the "promised one" (or, the "Messiah") of our ancient world!

Yet, one with any straightforward knowledge of God, and the ways of Adam, would easily understand that this wasn't quite the right route to take. They knew it was all a twisted sham. But, with all of the disinformation, and temptations, coming to the minds of the undecided, things were, slowly, starting to cloud up.

So, what, again, could have been one way to help change things, inside of a person's mind, to be more apt to follow these ways of Cain?

> *...anything directed to the human **emotion** and bypassing **the rational (spirit)** was really idolatry which is always **self** worship.*
> ("Nimrod - Babylonian - Musical Worship Teams", n. d., p. 13)[122]

As we've seen - time and time again - tricking an individual into thinking outside of their conscious, rational thought, as well as convincing them to elevate their passions and emotions in its stead, is a primary way to start this transition process! As well, convincing someone into thinking only about *themselves*, by utilizing their pride to its fullest (and, most immoral) extent, is another way. These are ways to help one divert their veneration to an invisible, heavenly God, and onto *themselves*, and their own feelings of self-esteem, or self-importance. We recall that eating the "Tree of the Knowledge of Good and Evil" may have linked Adam and Eve (and, the rest of the human race) to needing to find ways to raise one's self-esteem. It all seems to be linked, here, if we think about it!

Also, it is true that God is a *jealous* God, which means He is jealous of any competition. He does not want to see these ancient patriarchs being worshipped, nor does He want to see people worshipping *themselves*. He, also, does not want to see people indulging *too much* on all of what the material world might have to offer, over Him. Yes, this is all related to idolatry.

> *Excessive **self-indulgence** and the…"**numbness** to the negligence of" this fact are the customary concomitants of idolatry.* (Bandy, 1967, p. 148)[123]

That's, also, why God hated what Cain, the Serpent and the other terrestrial angels were beginning to teach to people. The people began to make gods out of them. And, that's why the first two commandments that God gave to Moses, on Mount Sinai, dealt with *idolatry*. It's very important to God. And, this was also the reason why God wanted Adam to, continually, remain *humble* - no "self-love."

Flesh

The Bible, also, speaks of those who follow a number of these misdirected pathways as those who follow the *flesh*.

...the wisdom of the flesh is hostile to God...
                              - Rom. 8:7 (KJV)

Whose wisdom is this? Most probably, the wisdom of the Serpent, of course.

We've already talked about idolatry and flesh, somewhat, in the last volume. To highlight a few things: one definition of flesh corresponds to "kindred," or "blood-relations."[124] Along these same lines, flesh could also mean that which had "corrupted its manner" or "did not preserve the manner of its nature and perverted its known implanted path."[125] In regards to what we are discussing, here, flesh can represent the genetics, or blood-lines, of individuals related to the Serpent, or other terrestrial angels - the early promoters of Cain's ways. We also know that God did not want any crossbreeding between human being and terrestrial angel. But, as we know, there was. And, sorry to say, those who even had some mixed blood of these terrestrial angels and human beings would also have been considered those who "came from the *flesh*." All of this will be important, later.

But, for now, another important definition of *flesh* is, "as frail or erring (man against God)" or "as opposed to God and his power."[126] So, in other words, *flesh* could also relate to a person's decision-making process: whether or not to follow a certain path of life. Clearly, being "of the flesh" could have gone way beyond one's particular bloodline, here! And, in Gen. 6:3, we even see that even Adam (translated into English, here, as the "man") was beginning to "follow the flesh" - he was "erring," in some of his choices, even though he did not have any blood of an angel. Nobody's perfect, of course - even Adam. And, even the best of people could "follow the flesh," and adopt erroneous ways of living.[127] Of course, "all have sinned... (Rom. 3:23)" That's just the way it was, and is. The real issue lies in how long one *stays* on this erroneous paths, whether they try to leave it, and whether they decide to seek forgiveness from God, or no.

*...they that are in the **flesh** cannot please God... For which things' sake the wrath of God cometh on the children of disobedience.*   *- Col. 3:6 (KJV)*

Just as human emotions and passions could help to drive one's thinking away from God, the same could help drive someone to adopt the ways of the *flesh*:

> *...the nature of the **flesh** has **no participation in intellect**...*
>   - Works of Philo Judaeus That the Worse is Wont to
>   Attack the Better 23(83)[128]

> *He (Cain) acts without **discernment**... follows ways of **flesh** rather than spirit.*
>   - Ibn Ezra's Commentary on the Pentateuch: Genesis p. 94[129]

What Does It All Mean?

> *Thus saith the LORD; Cursed be the man **that trusteth in man**, and maketh **flesh** his arm, and whose heart departeth from the LORD. For he shall be like the heath in the desert, and **shall not see when good** cometh; but shall inhabit the parched places in the wilderness, in a salt land and not inhabited.*   - Jer. 17:5-6 (KJV)

What does it all mean, and where do we go with all of this information, here? Learning about the ways of Cain and the Serpent, and the foundation of the pagan religion, help us to, slowly, piece the many systems of *Mystery Babylon* together. We, also, are beginning to see the "mind-set" behind *all the Mystery*.

We, at least, see how the ways of the Serpent and Cain represent the opposite pathway that God wanted for Adam, and other early people. Clearly, the ways of this material world represent self-glorification, self-adoration, envy, relying on one's own emotions and pride for direction, etc. And, they were, so long ago, institutionalized into the early politics and pagan religion of their day! The Serpent and Cain, once again, took something of God and twisted them around for their own use.

It really began to confuse the minds of many.

Sometimes, those who followed these *ways* could, at least, live along with their God-fearing neighbors, as long as they maintained a take on things that many around them would consider as using "common sense." These ways, however, point one in the direction of, even, losing this. This is so important: one really might have a hard time convincing a person, who began to utilize these ways of Cain, to think otherwise;

because, a lot of the time, their mind is, continually, bombarded by a great deal of information, information coming from many different directions. And, all so much of this information is telling them that they are, for the most part, justified in what they're thinking, or even doing, and anything contrary, here, is all just a *farce*.

> *It is **difficult**, perhaps impossible, for the Cains to understand why they are rejected by both God and history (however)… **Technically, they do no wrong**. They stay, rather precariously, sometimes, within legal bounds. They observe just enough social amenities and fulfill just enough social responsibilities to get by. They do what they have to do with **no social feeling** and **no sense of spiritual communion**…*
> (Eichhorn, 1957, p. 43)[130]

Another scary part to this all is: a lot of times, they won't want to take responsibility for their own actions. They don't want to understand that, so often, their situation is a product of their own free-will choices. Their pride dictates to them that: they do not, or cannot, admit to almost any fault, or to see almost any error in what they're doing. Scary.

Their pride also dictates they *shouldn't* have to "lower themselves" to act humbly towards others, or, to honor them - those are for the weak. They are strong (at least, that's the way they want to be). They, also, have their own self-esteems on the line. So, they, quite often, will not allow others a chance to negatively affect their valuable commodity.

As well, these people probably will not (or, even, *cannot*) understand why someone tries to "call them out" on any of their negative behavior – because, of course, their focus is so self-absorbed. And, any feedback they get is, so often, interpreted as "unfair," "mean" or "prejudiced." And, on top of it, the sad part is: their stubbornness, often, begs for them to stay along *these same pathways* of misinformation and deceit, as long as it's working for them:

> *They can be hurt, they can be checked, they can be broken, but seldom can they be **changed**…*
> (Eichhorn, 1957, p. 43)[131]

So much of this is psychology, for sure! Some can change, and we all hope they do. But, in reality: some of these inner thoughts can become so ingrained in the individual that, over the generations, they may, no longer, be able to "change their stripes."

So, with all this said and done, is there a quick and easy way to identify individuals more prone to walk in these ways? Again, it was Jesus who said:

"Wherefore by their fruits ye shall know them."
 - *Mat.* 7:20 (KJV)

It will be impossible, on the surface, to understand just "who is who." Once we see someone acting without humility, without honor, without a solid moral character, and, seemingly, without any desire to look to God for anything, we may just begin to see someone adopting the ways of Cain, and his father, the Serpent. If one wants to be a follower of God - a true follower of God - they will do their best to avoid all of these self-serving (and self-defeating) pagan ways of Babylon.

Next, we will begin by taking a look at certain individuals who "took the reigns" of this ancient, pagan brand of darkness - beyond the Serpent, even beyond Cain. We will, as well, see how these ancient pagan ways became perpetuated, at least to a degree, in most everyone of our ancient world (even amongst the descendants, and followers, of God)!

Yet, although it was so quickly taking over, God was not about to accept all of this sacrilege. He was not going to take it all, lying down. Change and judgment were, both, on the horizon.

We will, also, look more into a very famous Adamite, known as *Noah* - because he would, of course, become the centerpiece of all that God wanted to happen, next.

Chapter 6

Angels, the Flood, & Saturn (Part I)

…in his (Noah's) days a wonder may be wrought on the earth.
(Ginzberg, 1909, p. 145)[1]

…This day there is none that saveth…
- *The Qur'an* Surah 11:43[2]

Yes, during the life of one Biblical character that most of us have heard of - *Noah* - a great amount of things *did* occur. No one was to be spared from the disaster looming, except, of course, those who were to sail with this man. There was change in the air, for sure. Even though we've discussed the Flood story a great deal (in Volume 1), there are still a number of interesting details worth noting, here! Even though the Flood, so often, is considered the "highlight" of the whole Noah story, the least amount of time and effort will, really, be put into the discussion, here. Why? It's because, as we'll soon see, there could have been a whole lot more to this flood than most of us have ever dreamed.

The Aftermath of Cain

> *...the earth was flooded because of him (**Cain**).*
> *- The Book of Wisdom* 10:3-4[3]

The influences of Cain and the Serpent were beginning to settle in the human psyche, almost everywhere. Our understanding of this *Mystery* side of *Mystery Babylon* will, hopefully, pick up a good deal of speed, now. Beyond the mental and emotional elements of this *Mystery* side (as we've already discussed), there was, of course, celestial *knowledge* - the knowledge given to people by these terrestrial angels. This would be the knowledge that God may, or may not, have desired for human beings. And, as we'll also see, this *knowledge* was, not only in wide use *before* the Flood, but would make a resurgence *after* the Flood, as well.

Let's continue on, with *more* of the ramifications that this Serpent, Cain and other terrestrial Nephilim were binging to our post-Fall existence. In this section, we will delve into a good number of deep - even somewhat *controversial* - topics. But, really, it's now time!

After the Fall - But, Before the Flood

> *(The Serpent)... is truly unrepentant, all through his days.*
> (Schwartz, 2004, p. 456)[4]

Assuredly hating God, and His ways, in every step of his worthless existence, the Serpent, in his post-Fall existence, would, indeed, be blazing some trails of his own. And, he probably wouldn't have been alone. We will see what, most probably, happened to him, after the Fall.

And, what about *Adam and Eve*? From the Bible (in Gen. 5:3), we could start to assume that Adam chose to wait 130 years, beyond the death of Abel, before he came and impregnated Eve, once again. At least, they didn't have any children together the Bible felt was note worthy. Quite possibly, they may have even lived *apart* for this extended period of time. Who knows? But, yet, after this 130-year timeframe, their long-awaited son *Seth* would be born, and become patriarch over a group, known as the *Sethites*. Seth was, in actuality, the most famous direct descendant of Adam and Eve still intent on keeping the ways of God, and the ways of his father, Adam.

Periods Apart

After Abel's death, a few things may have been going on inside of Adam's mind. In a way, he may have even felt a little responsible for what happened.[5] We recall, it was *he* who helped set up these two sacrifices; and it all must have weighed on him, tremendously. Eve, as well, was probably very troubled, as well - possibly, even more than Adam. She cried a lot of the time. Because of what happened, Adam may have, then, come to the conclusion that his love-life with Eve needed to come to an end. He couldn't afford to have a son who might end up the same way Abel did.[6] He may have even taken a break from Eve, here, for about 130 years.

Beyond this possible 130-year separation, non-Biblical tradition also gives us other possible periods of separation for these two. Throughout his 930 years, Adam could have been apart from Eve numerous times - even up to 200 years a shot.[7] Throughout this time, we really need to ask ourselves: what *did* they do while they were apart? Adam may have continued on, working the fields and baking bread. What did Eve do for sustenance and survival? Was she alone, all of these years? It must have been a frightening time for anyone trying find their way in this world.

The Serpent's Consort?

Unearthed in the not-so-distant past were a number of ancient, cuneiform tablets, found around the ancient city of Nippur. There were seven tablets, to be exact. These were known as the *Kharsag Tablets*. They told of a story that just may provide us a link to what may have happened - at the time Adam and Eve split!

As we recall, Adam was, at first, the lead gardener over the world - the overseer over all the "mid-level" managers (i.e. the Serpent and the Nephilim) in the Garden. Eve may have had a large part in the overseeing of the Garden, as well.[8] The Garden needed to be watered. And, the knowledge of *irrigation* may have become something of importance, here. To assist in this irrigation process, God located the Garden near a river - in actuality, four rivers.[9] All four of these rivers were to help water the Garden as it expanded. Most probably, certain areas around the Garden were untilled and un-irrigated. Heat parched the soil. Rain, quite often, did not fall. God, then, may have assigned Adam and Eve the responsibility of reclaiming this land, making it work for the people.[10]

As we proceed into summarizing these Babylonian tablets, we'll soon discover how it may, actually, provide us sustenance for what happened to Adam, Eve and the Serpent - in the period *after* their fall! The pagan account revolves around the god *Enlil*, the goddess *Ninlil* (or the "Serpent Lady," his consort), the god *Anu* and the *Anannage* (i.e. the Anunnaki). And, as we've summated in Chapter 1, the Serpent could have actually been the god Enlil, Eve the goddess Ninlil, Adam the god Anu, and, of course, the Anannage the Nephilim. Knowing this, we may be able to discover some interesting tidbits of information about these four. It even, quite possibly, seems to correspond to the time Adam decided he needed to be *apart* from Eve.

So, if we utilize the assumptions, above, this might have been what transpired *after* the Fall: After God told Adam and Eve to leave the garden, the lands around Eden continued to be very volatile. Sometimes, there would be a lot of water around (due to floods) - *too* much, in fact. Other times, water was scarce. Enlil (the Serpent) was among the first who continued on, after the Fall, with these irrigation processes. He, even, founded homes for some of the residents who lived around him, because the areas no longer flooded as bad.[11] And, as we also recall, one of the epithets of the Serpent was *Akki*: "the *irrigator*."[12]

Enlil (the Serpent), from then on, began to be known as the "Lord of Cultivation." Ninlil (Enlil's consort) was also considered to be the "Lady of Cultivation." Interesting, here - he has a *lady* in his life. This *Lady* also seemed to have the "knowledge of agriculture." She was even said to have provided an "implement tool" for gardeners to utilize.[13] Yet, Eve, most probably, could have had similar duties, in her stay at the

Garden. If given the opportunity, could she have carried on this knowledge, and lived with someone *else*, during the times she was separated from Adam?

Irrigation - and Seduction

The Serpent, obviously, was displaced from the Garden of Eden, as well. What happened to him? Where did he go, after the dust settled? It's quite possible that that all three - Adam, Eve and the Serpent - did not relocate too far from one another. According to these tablets, Enlil (the Serpent) could have went to live with the people that, most probably, respected him the most, and followed his ways. Makes sense.

Anu (Adam) would, really, desire to have nothing to do with all that was starting to take place, here, and went out to live the remainder of his days in places of isolation - at least, somewhat apart from all the evil the world was turning to.[14] Probably feeling a bit alone, Lady Ninlil (Eve) - after being told to leave Adam's presence - began to settle in areas where there was people, possibly even in the *same* area as Enlil (the Serpent) went to. It makes sense. It may have, at least, been someone that she already knew - someone who could, quite possibly, protect her from the great unknown. Possibly, Eve even ending up staying in the private quarters of Enlil himself![15] Maybe the Serpent offered her solace, and - because Adam refused to take her - she accepted it.

It seems that, over time, she, at least, cared for him, somewhat, as her lord.[16] And, not only were they doing this to keep each other company, they were, both, beginning to utilize their knowledge of the Garden, to continue with their irrigation and farming techniques. The area where they were now located was called *Kharsag* - a name which, most probably, equated to the lands around *Eden*. Kharsag may have been one of the first "settlements" outside the Garden, nestled along a huge mountain chain.

Anu (Adam), as stated, didn't have any real desire to be part of this community, so he "returned to the 'Heavens'."[17] Could this mean that he returned to another *way of life* (such as following the ways of God), or, possibly, retreated to another *mountainous area* (because, as we know, a *mountain*, in ancient times, could have easily been associated with an oneness, or willingness to go closer "to the sky," or, to "heaven")?

Eventually, Enlil (the Serpent) commanded a reservoir to be constructed.[18] With the help of the Nephilim, they would construct - and control - the irrigation processes in the lands around them.[19] There was more:

> *...the lordlings (i.e. the Nephilim) undertook the work and suffered the toil as if **they were men**... their **chief** was Enlil; directly responsible for them was **Ninurta**...*
> (O' Brien, 1988, p. 149)[20]

Well, who was *Ninurta*, here? Ninurta was thought to be the son of Enlil (the Serpent) and Ninlil (Eve).[21] *Who* also could have been a famous son of theirs, other than *Cain*? If this was the case, then, Cain may have also had a hand in this early expanse of power:

> *...Cain was a man of great ability and great intelligence... He taught them to **build dikes**, to make embankments along the sides of the river channel... dikes which would hold the rivers within their channels even during the flood season... This **enabled** them to **build their cities** with the assurance that they would not be washed away during the next flood season.* ("What Happened to Cain", n. d., p. 16-17)[22]

Much of this area, in fact, was now considered to be a giant reservoir, enclosed by walls of a ravine.[23] Those in the know, such as Enlil, would, soon, go on to teach the people how to dig canals and artificial channels, in order to help with irrigation.[24] He even was said to have "established pastures."[25] Where are we going with all of this? We're trying to show how the Serpent, as low of a creature he, now, was, went on, to make (somewhat) of a name for himself, and rule over others. As a dignitary to many of Cain's people, he also, eventually, began to construct a great house (or "temple") - dedicated to, no one other than, *himself.*

Through all of his irrigating and building, the inhabitants of the area probably began to think that Enlil (the Serpent) had "brought prosperity to the Land."[26] Makes sense. Also, because of this applied knowledge, "food was greatly increased for the people."[27] Now, the people who lived under Enlil could, quite possibly, grow in abundance. And, with Cain (a.k.a. *Sargon*) controlling the salt trade (as we've already seen), people could use that salt to store, and preserve, their own food. All of these would have appealed to the masses all the more. Ninlil (or, Eve) would also become known as the "Lady of the Grain Enclosure," for helping to be instrumental in the construction of at least one, good-sized, fenced-in grain structure.[28]

Through all of these irrigation "advancements," Enlil (the Serpent), Ninlil (Eve) and Ninurta (Cain) were probably held in very high esteem - credited for bringing "life" to the settlement area.

> *...the Watercourse... (was) the life of the Land.*
> (O' Brien, 1988, p. 149)[29]

And, assuredly, because of it all, they, eventually, would be considered "gods," as well!

Ninlil (Eve) began to eat well, as a result.[30] She lived well. Later, she spoke about the construction of her new, "bright" house.[31] And, staying with the Serpent, at least for Eve, most probably, *did* "brighten" her days, some (at least temporarily). She was, for a while, able to maintain, somewhat, of a comfortable life. When Anu (Adam) got wind of all that was going on, here, he was strongly opposed to it (of course).[32]

After a while, a huge flood, eventually, wiped out most of these "strong houses" that Enlil (the Serpent) established.[33] Apparently, this storm was considered a "once in a thousand year" storm, not the Flood of Noah. The result was total destruction of this entire (post-Fall) Kharsag settlement, driving a good number of people in these areas into many different directions.[34] Lastly, their great, "bright" house - the house that the Serpent and Eve may have both lived in - was, now, covered over.[35]

After this destruction at Kharsag, the Anannage leaders (i.e. the Nephilim) decided to move abroad, and each founded their own city-state.[36] The original Kharsag was never rebuilt.[37] Enlil (the Serpent), and those who stayed behind with him, tried to rebuild things (at least) in the spirit of their former settlement, and not far from where they once were located. This time, they began to construct new, more "lofty," places to live.[38] Ninlil (Eve) also continued to stay in the dwelling of Enlil.[39] Eventually, the "Great House of Enlil" - as it was to be called - was built upon a high rock, with Ninlil (Eve), again, rejoicing "at its brightness."[40]

The people living in their immediate area, once again, would begin to benefit from the agricultural knowledge these "gods" gave them. Ninlil (Eve), as well, continued on, with a major role in it all. She was said to have:

- increased the cultivation, by lofty irrigation from divided watercourses.[41]

- increased the harvest.[42]

- been filled with "brilliant intelligence" and a "wise goodness."[43]

This fortification was now built upon a high rock, where it could not be washed away, as easily - at least not until the coming of Noah's flood![44]

Eve's new way of life, probably, was the reason why so many pagan gave Eve her share of epithets (or "goddess" titles) in the religion, and that they were associated, in one way or another, with *fertility*. It's obvious to see why, so often, the "goddess" Eve was considered the "goddess of fertility," and the people thought that she "brought so much good to the land."

Could this have also been the reason why Ninlil (Eve), in pagan religion, was often worshiped *alongside* of Enlil (the Serpent)? Could this have been why they were, so often, considered the greatest Patriarch and Matriarch of this ancestor-based pagan ideology? It could have been, quite possibly, because Eve actually lived *with* the Serpent for some extended periods of time (while away from Adam). These tablets give us some very interesting twists in the story of Adam and Eve: maybe, after the Fall, it wasn't entirely rosy between the two. Maybe they had to separate, quite often, from each other. Ancient Christian tradition tells us that they were, so often, miserable together, after had to depart from their garden abode - often depressed, often crying, and, most probably, tormented by guilt. They, assuredly, blamed each other, as well. Could Eve have, then, gone on to be with *the Serpent*, on occasion, because Adam wanted no part of her? Something to ponder. And, after all, the Serpent *may have*, very well, been the father of her firstborn children: Cain and Abel!

From these cuneiform tablets, we can, also, see how the Serpent, the Nephilim, Cain, and possibly *Eve* herself, could have aroused great deal of appeal by ancient peoples. Through their knowledge and actions, a number of these ancient people could have been a lot more fond of them than most of us have ever dreamed.

Yet, in all fairness, did Eve *purposely* set out to adopt the ways of her son, and of the Serpent? Did she whole-heartedly want to turn to the "dark side?" Most probably, she wasn't a full-blown believer in all of what they preached, nor a willing adopter of their sinful ways. She probably knew better than to *completely* trust a terrestrial angel who, already, deceived her in the past - but she may have needed a way to survive, without a lot of toil. She also wanted to do something for the people around her - something *good*. After all, she and Adam helped to bring them to their current, fallen state. And, she, assuredly, loved Cain, as well. She might just have become a victim of circumstance, here: abandoned by her husband and left to fend for herself. How many people would have chosen this path, considering the circumstances?

Eve may have also found some solace living next to Cain, her son, and decided "just to go through the motions" (and not become a full-blown activist, or believer).

We also recall that: Adam wasn't exactly the epitome of God's viceroy, after the Fall, either. There was a lot of *fornication* going on: humans "going after strange flesh," or desiring the "flesh of a different kind."[45] As Eve may have went this route, the same, quite probably, for Adam. A lot of people seemed to be cohabiting with individuals with angelic blood, over time. We recall that Adam fell, a number of times, "to the flesh," while apart from Eve - he fornicated, a number of times, with women of angelic blood (or bloodlines). He may have even, on occasion, returned to *Lilith*, his "first wife," and copulated with her! Lesson learned: we may *all* lose our way, from time to time, whether it be Eve, whether it be Adam.

And, at the conclusion of these seven cuneiform tablets, their second settlement, as well as their new, Great "House" (or temple), would all destroyed - by lightning and a huge thunderstorm.[46] We don't know if, this time, it was Noah's flood, but it's quite possible.

As we could conclude, the number of people who followed the ways of God were, slowly, on the decline. These agricultural "advancements," as well these new ways of Cain and the Serpent, were on the upswing. What became popular with those on "the other side" would be a new, humanity-based way of looking at the world. Their "politically correct" norms were now turning "main-stream."

The Rise of the Fallen Ones

Things would get worse, however. From Volume 1, we've already understood that there was "a counterfeit incarnation in human flesh" imparted into mankind. The mixtures of bloodlines between terrestrial angel and human could, also, be understood in terms of *flesh* (as we know): "strange" or "different" flesh inserted into the gene pool.[47] There were physical (and mental) problems which, indeed, could have resulted (and *did* result) from these early angelic-to-human infusions. And, of course, many of us may still be a little uneasy about the believability of fallen, terrestrial angels being able to copulate with mortal women. Yet, we've already discussed a number of Biblical examples that, at least, fully support the concept of angels being able to take on *human form*. Now, if they could eat, drink and otherwise live like human beings, then why couldn't they do *everything* as a human being? Even in the New Testament, there seems to have been written evidence for this probability.

If we look at II Cor. 5:1-3, for example, we see this:

*For we know that if our earthly house of this tabernacle were dissolved, we have a building of God, an house not made with hands, eternal in the heavens. For in this we groan, earnestly desiring to be **clothed upon with our house** which is from heaven: If* *so be that being clothed we shall not be found naked.*   - *II Cor.* 5:1-3 (KJV)

And, we, also, see how there seems to have been a *purposeful* misinterpretation, or a "politically correct" assumption, of the day. Instead of these translators thinking of the possibility of angels being able to take on human form, instead of *honestly* looking into what some words might actually be saying, these early translators attempted to put their *own* "P.C." assumption into what these verses might be saying - even if it sounds *ridiculous*!

It seemed that the early translators tried to portrayed the subject of the verses (above) as a "house," but, if we look deeper into what the verse may actually be saying, we'll see it probably means *so much more*. Besides, when are we "clothed" with a house? If we look at some *other Strong's* numbers associated with the original Greek word for *house*, here, we can find the whole context of this verse, easily, comes to light, and makes a lot more sense.

Let's look at the same (above) verses again, with some of the English words replaced by those *other* meanings for the original Greek word for *house*:

For we know that if our earthly **dwelling (of the human body in which the soul dwells as in a tent, and which is taken down at death)** *were dissolved, we have a edification of God, a* **dwelling** *not made with hands, eternal in the heavens. For in this we groan, earnestly desiring to put on our* **dwelling place (of the body as a dwelling place for the spirit)** *which is from heaven: If so to clothe oneself we shall not be found naked (of soul, whose garment is the body, stripped of the body, without a body).*
    - *II Cor.* 5:1-3 (in retranslation)

In other words, we, as followers of God, will eventually inherit a magnificent, heavenly *body*, once we are dead - unlike the earthly body we dwell in now. Makes so much more sense. This is not about a physical house, or dwelling! Why make the context of the verse sound so complex, here, by trying to make it attune to the thought, or traditions, of their day? And, why dwell so much on this verse? Simple. Because there is *one* Greek word, in the above, that is only mentioned *one* other time in the New Testament, and that word is *oiketerion* (Strong's G3613). The English word "house" *had* to have been used, in the above context, to coincide with the way the *other* word was used, in another verse (as we'll see)! They had to keep it consistent (or else the *other* verse, also, wouldn't "make sense" to them). But, to us, however, it would make *perfect* sense - as it stood! Let's see.

The Greek word, *oiketerion*, could also mean, "of the body as a dwelling place for the spirit." So, interestingly enough, the *only* other place that this word is found is in Jude 1:6:

> *And the angels which kept not their first **estate**, but left their own **habitation** (i.e. oiketerion), he hath reserved in everlasting chains under darkness unto the judgment of the great day.*   - Jude 1:6 (KJV)

Now, this brings us more "up to speed" into what we've been talking about, here. Now, what did those angels do so wrong in this verse - and why would these early translators have to make such a ridiculous translation (in the other verse)? It's obvious, when we look at it: these angels, here, just did not come down from heaven in their "houses." They, also, did not come down to earth, and do absolutely nothing (to deserve everlasting chains of judgment)! They did something *very* wrong!

And, if we insert those *other* Strong meanings into this text, as well - we, then, will see how the word *oiketerion* means practically the same thing as in the above, II Cor. 5:2 verse. But, this other meaning "blows the whole lid off" of anyone trying to hide the idea that angels lost their original, angelic form, and came down to earth! Let's see how the verse *could* read, in retranslation:

> *And the angels which kept not their first **place**, principality, rule, magistracy (of angels and demons), but left their own **dwelling place (of the body as a dwelling place for the spirit**), he hath reserved in everlasting chains under darkness unto the judgment of the great day.*   - Jude 1:6 (in retranslation)

The verse, as with the verse before, was not referring to physical abodes, or "houses," here! These were bodily "houses." The celestial angels who left their "first place," or original "dwelling," here, *lost* their original, angelic form! And, they did so that they could cohabit with earthly women. And, that, surely, would have merited a terrible punishment by God. You see? It all makes sense, if we look at it all this way!

Still having a little speculation? Well, the above interpretation of this verse is, really, almost undeniable, when we factor in the verse that *immediately follows it*:

> *Even as Sodom and Gomorrha, and the cities about them in like manner, giving themselves over to **fornication**, and going after **strange flesh**, are set forth for an example, suffering the vengeance of eternal fire.*   - Jude 1:7 (KJV)

Again, putting the two verse together, and looking at them, both, in context, and we see the meaning is so obvious: these angels did not keep their heavenly bodies, but left their former, angelic estate to take on *another* form. Then, they began to commit sins like those individuals of Sodom and Gomorrah - who, often, committed fornication, or had sex, with those of "strange," angelic flesh!

And, because of their fornication, they were punished, severely!

We, now, can see how there *is* support for our whole story, here - *even* in books such as the Bible. And, we also see an example of people, over the ages, have unintentionally (or even intentionally) tried to cover it up - for the sake of "political correctness."

How can anyone really deny all of the above, or try to "dumb down" the words of the Bible, in these particular cases? Why do they, so often, try to make things fit into some "politically correct" agenda? It's truly amazing how so many people try to *eliminate* the possibility of fallen angels, leaving their angelic form, and being able to take on human form, just so they could sin in these ways. And, it's, also, incredible to understand just how much "dumbing-down" is *still* going on, today.

Moving forward. As one might be able to guess, a lot of problems arose from sexual unions that God clearly said should have *never been*.[48] How many of the physical, mental, and emotional "vices" that plague people, today, could have, very well, originated back *then*, as a result?[49] Regardless of the genetics, the *knowledge-base* that these angels passed on to those they fornicated with was an issue in itself! This information may have sounded helpful, *at first*; but, of course, there was a lot more to it. Indeed, there were reasons why God didn't want certain knowledge to be imparted to human beings (as we'll soon see):

> *The holy scriptures… say… that there is a race of demons who avail themselves of women… nearly every treatise, both public and esoteric, made mention of this… Having stumbled… they remained outside heaven, because they taught mankind everything wicked and **nothing benefiting the soul**.*
>   - The Chronography of George Synkellos p. 18-19[50]

Eventually, following Cain's ways, and utilizing their angelic knowledge at hand, many were, indeed, beginning to head "into perdition."[51] These dark, "fleshy" sides of life would corrupt them, more and more, as well as everyone and *everything* around them.

Some of the things that the Serpent, Cain and these other Nephilim brought to people (such as housing and irrigation) sounded helpful - but, for how *long*? God, it seemed, had an *overall* plan for His people (at least, during these early times): to live the *simple* life; to live in tents; to live in peace and harmony, one with another.

But, one must ask: how would these *other* cultural advancements (of Cain, etc.) be so bad for the people of the day? It just doesn't seem to make sense, right? Well, first, we mustn't forget that: it may not be the knowledge, itself, that is evil, but the *corrupted mind* dishing it out, or using it. *That* is what changes the dynamics!

So, in these ancient times, the possibility of this knowledge getting in *the wrong hands* was very great. It had already *come* from *the wrong hands*, so we can imagine the damage this would have, already, been able to cause! They, surely, had deviant reasons for most anything they did. If we look at *nuclear science*, for example, we see that this may have started out as a great find - a treasure trove of knowledge! And, at first, it seemed as if it could have unlimited possibilities to serve man. But, look at where so much of it has ended up! Look at what resulted from people *compounding*, and expanding, on this knowledge! We have *nuclear weapons*, which could devastate the world. We have *nuclear power plants*, which, if not handled right, could also help to devastate the world. Imagine this knowledge in the wrong hands. Imagine the destruction.

> *(God speaking to these fallen angels)… ye work those works which are forbidden because they bring **only death and destruction**, and ye boast in the greatness of your power, but your power is dust and ye would **leave the whole earth desolate** if the Lord God were not to intervene…* - The Book of the Generations of Adam Chap. 8.6[52]

We must remember: the misuse of knowledge, such as this, was partly to blame for God having to destroy our entire ancient world (with a flood)!

Other Problems of their Day

We've already discussed some of the negativities brewing in this brave new world of Cain, the Serpent and the Nephilim: *corruption, robbery, violence*, etc. And, as if these weren't bad enough, one thing that really infuriated God, during these times, was the *lechery* (or *lewdness*) of the antediluvian people.

> *…(there) was so much sin on the earth in the sin of **lechery**, which was misused against nature, wherefore God was displeased and determined in his prescience to destroy man that he had made…*
> - *The Golden Legend or Lives of the Saints: Volume I* 64[53]

> *…The Holy One… (God) would overlook everything but **lewdness**…*
> - *Midrash Tanhuma-Yelammedenu* p. 34[54]

The words *lechery*, *lewdness* and even *lasciviousness* could, almost, be used interchangeably. All three, more or less, represent some kind of "unrestrained or excessive *indulgence* of sexual desire."[55] We've already mentioned *sexual* lust, as a form of lust (in Chapter 2). And, as we know, this type of sex was considered the "sin of wrong use." As we also know, when people begin to use something *of this earth* to fulfill, or perfect, themselves (over what God could), it becomes a form of *idolatry*. And, their desires for a perfect self-esteem will always fall short. The same thing applies with an overindulgence of sex, here: the *act* of sex isn't the problem (as we know), but the *way* it was used, and the purposes behind it.

Excessive and *unbridled* sex was, back then (and *still* is), a flawed, human attempt to raise one's own self-esteem - towards some personal feeling of "perfection," or "actualization," in their life. The people began to rely on things, such as *sex*, and not God. As with any "hunger," however, a person cannot be *totally* satisfy their soul by using something *of this earth* - it just won't work (at least, not for long)! Those feelings of complete and perfect spiritual satisfaction comes only from God. Earthly things can never completely fulfill, or satisfy, *spiritual* needs.

Yet, the sexual indulgences of these ancient people would continue, on and on - practically nonstop, with some. Anywhere but God, it seems (according to Cain). And, as with nuclear science, there seemed to be a great number of *negative* ramifications coming out of all this sex. Much of it, of course, resulted in *offspring* - especially *mixed* (angelic and human) offspring! The population of the land, assuredly, exploded.

In one very interesting twist to our normal approach on things, here, we'll summarize a number of *pagan* legends - Babylonian, Akkadian and Sumerian - that, apparently, paralleled the Flood of Noah. The interesting thing about them is: a number seemed to have had their *own* interpretations of what caused Noah's flood - and, it *wasn't* because of the sinful deeds of the people! Of course, if we think about it, why would they want to say that, anyhow? This was the world they helped to create! Of course, the *morality* they introduced couldn't have been a factor (even though it was)! Regardless, what's interesting is: the major reason *they* gave for the onset of the flood was *overpopulation*, and the "noisiness" of the people! Interesting.

Let's see what these were.

Enlil's Interpretations

Column 3:
7 *Ishtar (a.k.a. Eve) cried like a woman in travail.*
13 *"I alone bore my people.*
14 *[And now] like the spawn of fish **they fill the sea**."*[56]

Ancient pagan mythology, being what it was, does have interesting interpretations of the ancient world. Unlike Biblical traditions, which place *immorality* and *angelic-human offspring* as primary causes of the flood, pagan accounts, as we stated, point to overpopulation - which, of course, most probably resulted from all of immorality, and illicit, decadent sex going on![57] They seemed to have forgotten that aspect of it, in their own accounts!

Nevertheless, if we really think about it, a lot of this *does* degradation does seem to mirror a lot what we have with our world, presently!

IV
38 *people not diminished*
39 *more **numerous than ever**.*[58]

And, because of all the chaos that probably resulted from this overpopulation, the pagan "gods" decided that the people below were beginning to be a little "noisy":[59]

*...the god Enlil (the Serpent) feels disturbed in his sleep due to the noise and commotion caused **by the growing population** of mankind.*
("Adam, the Flood & The Tower of Babel", n. d., p. 8)[60]

Of course, pagan accounts would not credit the *God of the Bible* with having any control over the affairs of the world. Enlil (the Serpent) was a major god over all. He, and a few others, then began their own version of "population control" - sending "a plague, then a drought, a famine, and then saline soil, all in an attempt to reduce the numbers of mankind."[61] Because of their decree, the soil became "salty" and "unfruitful."[62] Diseases and malnutrition plagued the people. Ultimately, the efforts of these gods didn't pay off, however.[63] The people kept breeding and breeding, even more than ever. It seemed that: "the god's only way to control population" was through a flood.[64]

In a direct correlation to the above, we'll see that there could have *even* been *another* reason why these ancient people wanted to breed so much - a mindset with origins in the Garden of Eden.

Fulfillment of the Genesis 3:15 Prophecy

And man shall deem himself o'ercrowded, and
Destroy his fellows. Yet when, as 'twas said.
*"The earth is filled, then **I will bring in peace**."*

"Oh, what a thing is evil!" Noah cried.
                (Phifer, 1890, p. 117)[65]

Many people of the day (pagan or not) probably had *rudimentary* knowledge of the Genesis 3:15 Prophecy. And, as we know, a good number of people were slowly beginning to have their minds twisted by the ways of Cain.[66] Assuredly, the prophecy was on the minds of many, one form or another - whether it was reported as the true account, or some twisted, pagan-influenced version.

Ultimately, most people were, most probably, aware that a *savior* would be born, and be the one responsible for helping the righteous out of their post-Fall existence. Many people felt as though their lives were heading in the direction of worthlessness, hopelessness and depravity. It was an end result of following these Serpent ways, of course - but, not many would want to admit that. Still, so many wanted to get *back* to this pre-Fall state.[67] And, to find a way out of their current situations (and not take the "heat" for their own (incorrect) decisions), they soon began to concentrate on the prophecy. Many began to hope that *they* could be the "lucky" parent of the "promised one." Maybe it would be *their* child who could start a "new age" of peace and harmony. As we recall, this prophecy was even twisted around, so, now, the descendents of Cain (and those who were in his camp) were *still* not sure which seed line the savior would come from, so they held their breath, and kept on procreating.

As a result of this mind-set, *having* children became, almost, a necessity! To them, it would be like playing the lottery. They began to hurry up, and get married, *just* so they could, possibly, become the parent of the "promised one." Other reasons for being together, such as marriage and commitment, were falling by the wayside. That *one* honor seemed most important to them.

> ***With this idea to spur them**, marriage was*
> *The easier contracted, and the wife,*
> *Losing desire for other honor, was*
> ***Degraded to that sphere alone**...*
>   (Phifer, 1890, p. 84)[68]

This unrestrained breeding, for the sake of bringing on the "promised one," could have been, yet, *another* reason why people were having so many offspring (and *wanted* them). If they were "chosen" to bring forth the child, it would really bring *honor* and *meaning* to their lives. Their self-esteems, assuredly, must have been "down in the dumps" after awhile, by sticking to these ways of Cain. Some, then, may have even felt as though they were contributing to their society, now, by filling the world with children. Slowly, of course, their society became overloaded with offspring - offspring that no one could really be afford to be producing, anymore. There *truly* was unbridled, over-population, due to a number of factors!

Many were beginning to produce as many descendants as life would allow, to "further their odds." The more children, the more they "did their part" - at least, that's what they thought! Not too much rational thought was put into these pregnancies. Say "hello" to how well things work, when left up to *human* interpretations and passions!

> *The race grew great in number, men began*
> *To say, "Now is the prophecy fulfilled,*
> *The world is full; and one of woman born*
> *Shall **shortly** for us now regain our bliss."*
> *And men sought the Messiah…*
> *For almost every woman hoped that she*
> *might bear the Leader who was promised them,*
> *And thus gain honor from her countrymen.*
> (Phifer, 1890, p. 83-84)[69]

Humanism, and *solely* human interpretations of God's creation, so often, just *does not* work. Following God does, however. People began to dig themselves a real hole, here. And, then, in order to keep their humanistic *interpretations* alive (or "valid"), they continue to have just *one* more! Maybe *this* child will, finally, be the one we've all been counting on! It's similar to how certain people, today, will attempt to rationalize our current overpopulation. They might say, "Well, one of these additional million people just may be the one who ends up curing cancer!" Of course, that's being an optimist *to the extreme* - and, a little to the irrational to the extreme, as well! Sure, the (very, very remote) chance is there, that one of them will find a cure. But, if we think about it, their hopes are actually a "one in a million chance," here! Is that what we should be counting on, here? And, if our world takes on a few more million people, and a cure for cancer is *not* discovered by one of them... *then* what? This is exactly how political correctness, humanism and human rationality can really lead a society towards disaster.

The same thing happened, back then: the "promised one" never showed up! Times were beginning to look more and more desperate, with a few out there saying, "Well, the *next* one is bound to be that one!" The population was, indeed, exploding, and massive corruption was beginning to take place, because of the situation. Many were starting to get violent, trying to steal each other's limited resources. Doesn't that sound a lot a lot of the areas we live in, or areas we know about, today?

One interesting thing to note, here: most of the reasons for producing a number of offspring are *not* the same, today, as they were in ancient times. Almost all of us are not concerned with the Genesis 3:15 Prophecy, today - the savior has already been born. Many of us do not need to have more and more children to work in the fields. Most no longer live as nomads, or have fields that have to be cared for, or domesticated animals that need tending. So often, children, today, are not needed to go to work, and to help keep the family afloat (financially).[70] Yet, there are *still* some reasons to have children - utilized back then - that remain, today.

Back then, as with *today*, many people want a *purpose* in life, or a *reason-to-be* - so, we create a child, with hopes that they would be able to fill some kind of "void" in our lives. And, also, if "everyone's doing it" around us, we'll may, deep down inside, desire to feel *honor* from others, when we do the same (or, "do our part"). Some people around us will give us *honor* and *respect*, if we show them what good parents we are. So, we see that: in some ways, *some* of the same, inner reasons to have a child still exist! As with before, so many of us might believe our offspring can "complete" us - giving us our "salvation," our reason to be. Many may, also, believe that we could inscribe all of what *we* thought we should become in life, or receive in life, onto *our children*.

Only terrestrial beings need to find immortality in their children.
             ("Enoch & the Nephilim: Liber VII", n. d., p. 53)[71]

On the other hand, we are not perfect human beings. We've all felt needs such as these, over time. It's human nature, and totally understandable. Although we are not to point the finger of blame at anyone for having these thoughts, at one time or another, we just need to have them think *reason*, about their situation - before they actually decide take the physical and emotional "plunge" into a child. People just have to look at the deeper reasons to *why* they desire children, and make the best decision, based on that. It shouldn't be for a selfish reason, assuredly. And, it shouldn't be done if one cannot even *afford* to have a child, or if their society surrounding them cannot afford to bear the grunt of their choices, as well.

Apparently, all of this rationalism was thrown out the window, in ancient times. The land was filled to overflow. Things were *not* getting better, with each new child born - quite the opposite. No savior. No resources. No immortality.

In the past (as with today), many people, now, became stuck - stuck with mouths to feed and not enough resources to fill them. Many had to take the "low road," to survive:

> *...And many who had **engaged for Paradise**
> Had gone the way of **earth***
> (Phifer, 1890, p. 86)[72]

To Be "Fruitful & Multiply" - or "Blessed"?

Wait. A variety of Christian beliefs, today, discourage birth-control? Isn't that correct? They actually *promote* a lot of children! Children are a blessing, right? And, isn't it stated, a few times in the Bible, that God desired us *all* to "be fruitful & multiply," and "fill all the earth?" If that's what the Bible says, then *that's* the way we should go, right? Now, the question remains: how could the world end up in these negative ways if the Bible *even* stated this? Yes, that's a great point. But, what we may, now, *really* need to understand is: did the Bible say that, *exactly*?

Beyond the opinions of many religious leaders, today, beyond the interpretations of many "movers and shakers" out there, in our Christian denominations, the best source to look at for answers is, of course, the Bible itself - in its original Hebrew and Greek texts! Some compelling interpretations of the Bible may have launched many of the faithful into breeding excessively. They may have even been bombarded with quotes, such as: "we should not have sex for the sake of pleasure, but only for procreation," or "we should never try to interrupt the procreation process, but allow God to give us as many children as *He* dictates." Is that *really* how it should go, and what all of us should do?

A few verses that may shed light on where a number these thoughts could have originated are:

<u>Gen. 8:17 (KJV)</u>
*Bring forth with thee every living thing that is with thee, of all flesh, both of fowl, and of cattle, and of every creeping thing that creepeth upon the earth; that they may **breed abundantly** in the earth, and be **fruitful**, and **multiply** upon the earth.*

<u>Gen. 9:1 (KJV)</u>
*And God blessed Noah and his sons, and said unto them, Be **fruitful**, and **multiply**, and **replenish** the earth.*

<u>Gen. 9:7 (KJV)</u>
*And you, be ye **fruitful**, and **multiply**; **bring forth abundantly** in the earth, and **multiply** therein.*

Sounds like an "open and shut case" - for the validation of having children... that is, until we look at the *original* Hebrew of the Bible. The English versions are what they are. The above *King James Version*, as in other versions, represents one *interpretation* of the Bible's original Hebrew. Specific English words may have been inserted by these early translators to collaborate preconceived notions they may have had. Our modern translations, as well, lean towards this way of thinking - even *more*:

<u>Gen. 8:17 (the New International Version)</u>
*...so they can **multiply** on the earth and be **fruitful** and **increase in number** on it.*

Again, this all looks "open and shut"... until we look at the corresponding *Strong's* numbers for each word, here. With these, we can actually discover the number of meanings for each Hebrew word, here. And, if we really look at it, we'll probably find that these verses mean something very different than those time-honored assumptions so many have held true.

Let's look at our first example:

<u>Gen. 8:17 (KJV)</u>
*...that they may **breed abundantly** in the earth, **and be fruitful**, and **multiply** upon the earth.*

Does the original Hebrew *really* imply that people should "breed abundantly," here? Also, the verse seems to state this once, and then repeats *almost the same* statement right after it, only in different words. Why the repetition? Why does it say to "breed abundantly," and then, soon after, say to "be fruitful, and multiply?" It really don't make sense, as it stands. Maybe the reason is because this *wasn't* the original meaning of the Hebrew, here!

Let's look at the Hebrew words used here (with their corresponding *Strong's* numbers). The phrase, "that they may breed abundantly" comes from the Hebrew *sharats* (H8317). Among others, this word could also mean to "move," "swarm" or "teem" - but *nothing* about "breeding abundantly." The phrase, "and be fruitful" comes from the

Hebrew *parah* (H6509). Among others, this word could also mean "to show fruitfulness." The phrase, "and multiply" comes from the Hebrew *rabah* (H7235). Among others, this word could also mean to "be or grow great," to "do much in respect of" or "increase greatly." Put all of these *other* possible meanings together, and an entirely different meaning for the entire verse seems to emerge:

<u>Gen. 8:17 (in retranslation)</u>
*...that they may **"swarm"** or **"teem"** about the earth; to **"show their fruitfulness"** and be **"great"** upon the earth!*

This represents something different entirely - rather than God commanding a group of people to breed like there was no tomorrow! God encourages each individual to "do their part" for their society around them, as well as, individually, work to make themselves the *best* individual they could be! Wow. That is different!

Instead of commanding people to breed abundantly, and, seemingly, *non-stop*, God may have been trying to *bless* the people coming off of the ark: petitioning them to be the *best* they could be (in this new world); to get *along* with each other, and show the world what a wonderful place they could make! This entire statement by God was supposed to be a blessing for the people. Telling them to just *breed* doesn't sound much like a blessing - *especially* when He left it so open. A person could actually believe, then, that they are honoring God by having children nonstop, then! The more the merrier.

But, looking at this other way the verse could be laid out, and we see His statement, now, sounds much more like one would think a *blessing* should.

Next,

<u>Gen. 9:1 (KJV)</u>
*...**Be fruitful, and multiply, and replenish** the earth.*

Again, we have the same "Be fruitful, and multiply" phase, as in Gen. 8:17. Again, we'll use the original Hebrew translation of to **"show their fruitfulness,"** and be **"great"** at it.

The second half of this verse states: "and replenish the earth." The phrase "and replenish" comes from the Hebrew *male'* (H4390). Among others, this word could also mean to "accomplish," to "fulfill" or "mass themselves against." What could this all *really* mean? What would people need to "fulfill" or "mass themselves against?"

Well, if we look at the *next* verse (Gen. 9:2), we have:

<u>Gen. 9:2 (KJV)</u>
And the fear of you and the dread of you shall be upon every beast of the earth, and upon every fowl of the air, upon all that moveth upon the earth, and upon all the fishes of the sea; into your hand are they delivered.

The above "replenish," quite probably, relates to the context of Gen. 9:2 - *not* for people to "replenish the earth," *per se'*, but to "accomplish" or "fulfill" their destiny on earth. And, their destiny corresponds to the next verse, Gen. 9:2 (above). God wanted the human race to be able to "fulfill" their destiny with, or, even be able to "mass themselves against" whatever may come their way. Again, this was, most probably, another *blessing* by God - to rule this world:

<u>Gen. 9:1 (in retranslation)</u>
*...to "**show your fruitfulness**" and be "**great**" at it; as well as "**fulfill**" your destiny on earth (to rule over the world).*

In our third verse, there is much of the same:

<u>Gen. 9:7 (KJV)</u>
*And you, be ye **fruitful**, and **multiply**; **bring forth abundantly** in the earth, and **multiply therein**.*

Looking at the above verse and, again, we see that it seems to be fairly repetitive. We have the same phrase "Be fruitful, and multiply" again, as well as the phrases "bring forth abundantly" and "multiply therein." Putting them all together, using our *alternate* Hebrew meanings, and we have:

<u>Gen. 9:7 (in retranslation)</u>
And you, "**show your fruitfulness**" *and be* "**great**" *at it; and* "**swarm**" *(or* "**teem**"*) about the earth, and be* "**great**" *at doing that, too!*

These really sound more like blessing should - the blessings God would *want* to give to people; rather than just "breed," "breed," and *still* "breed!"

So, that leads us to another important question: *why* might these early religious leaders, as well as the later translators of the Bible (and, even religious leaders of *today*), be so adamant about making *sure* the population increases like this - breed, breed and *still* breed? Why promote so much procreation, without promoting any rational thoughts on what might result because of too much population? Also, why isn't the thought of *birth-control* even thrown into play, here? We've had effective birth-control devices for over 100 years. There's no excuse.

Sadly enough, there is an answer - and it may not sound too good. It may not sound very good to say that all of this, most probably, lies in the desires for *control* and *wealth*. These religious leaders, or dignitaries, know what's really at stake, here. Praise for them, and hymns to God aren't going to put food on their tables! They need money. They need pews filled, to keep it all going. If all God asked for was to have each individual be strong within themselves, and be the best they could be, how would that impact these religious authorities and local preachers? They profit when people *need* them. They profit when more and more people fill their pews. It's sad to say, but realistic.

God, of course, wants us to be *blessed*, and not the other way around - and, surely, not preachers and religious dignitaries to be blessed *at our expense*.

Of course, many of these "movers and shakers" in the religious world, often, think they hold the "keys" to our current spiritual *order*, and the more they can keep people under their umbrella of dominion, the more *they* will stay *relevant*, and powerful.

Sad to say, it's better for a number of *them* if we breed, breed and fill the pews. Of course, all preachers and religious dignitaries aren't out there to use and abuse - not even close. But, since we are all human beings, we all need to keep food on the table and clothes on our back. And, this has truly led some individuals, and institutions, to stray.

If we look at the Pharisees of Jesus' day, for example, we understand that their knowledge of scripture should clearly have spoken to them. They should have understood that Jesus was fulfilling prophecies left and right, and should have welcomed him with open arms. Instead, the opposite happened. Why? For one thing: they were enjoying the benefits of being a dignitary. The steady stream of power and riches were flowing. Now, they were beginning to view Jesus as a threat to their current order, their "umbrella of control" - and we know what happened to him. Jesus was contrary to the protocol they presided over. Back then, it was about control, power and money. It hasn't changed that much (for a number of these dignitaries) today… it's just, for the most part, a lot more *subtle*.

Along with power and control, there is another mind-set that may generate from within: a number of these dignitaries might even being to think (although, for the most part, they will not want to admit it) that the "common folk" may not have the foresight, nor the capacity, to truly understand these deeper, spiritual elements of our world. The commoner really cannot figure out "what is" or "what is not" the right way to live their lives - that is, without *their help*. Again, they need people to *need* them.

Ordinary folks cannot really make an accurate decision on whether sex *is* or *is not* lustful or excessive (for example), so, now, it's up to members of the clergy to interpret the Bible in a way so that *they'll* have to come in, and *regulate* it properly. We know, now, that there are other meanings of the word *fornication*, beyond the usual "sex before marriage." And, we also know that God isn't really against the act of sex, *itself*, He's just against the excessive use, or indecent use, of it (i.e. the sin of "wrong use"). If it was up to an individual to decide these things, then the clergy wouldn't be as necessary as they currently are, in this situation! Now, no one should have sex - at all - until the couple comes to *them*, and exchanges wedding vows! Talk about control. Now, we can't have sex, or even *think* about sex, until we come to the clergy for them to sign off on - and pay them, in the process!

This works the same with couples *having children.* According to many religious leaders, the lay-people may not have "enough" of an understanding of God's way for their lives. They may not be able to decide, *for themselves*, when to have, or when not to have, children. It's just easier for the clergy to "carpet-bomb" a rule - that *no* birth-control is to be had, and let the "chips fall where they may." If *God* decides a couple is going to have a child, every time they have sex, then so be it. Who cares if the person is up to their ears with crying babies, and down to the last penny! It's obvious, in these examples, that there are *advantages* for religious leaders to have the general populous to keep *growing* and *growing*. See how it all works?

Yet, does the Bible really say that we should not participate in something as *natural* as sex, or only do it under strict circumstances, set up by some church? The patriarchs of the Old Testament had concubines, and God didn't seem to condemn them for that! Funny, we hardly ever hear about that one, however. Does the Bible really say that we shouldn't enjoy sex, at all, or use it *only* for the sake of procreation? Does the Bible really condemn people for wanting to control the rate that they have children? Or, should a couple have as many children as they physically can - even if it results in situational, financial or emotional hardships? It doesn't take much to start to see the forest through the trees, here.

Not surprisingly, even some of the ancient writers of the *Talmud* interpreted the "be fruitful and multiply" phrase as a *commandment*, and not a blessing![73] Wow. Now, it's even required! But, if we *really* think about it, it doesn't make too much sense to believe that God *really* wanted us to be miserable in our situation, to end up poor, or "behind the eight ball," *just* to "prove" our devotion to Him. God doesn't work like that. Pagan "gods" might, but, not the God of the Bible.

God also commanded to Adam to use a rational, conscious mind. Wouldn't *reason* and *logic* be there to help us decide whether we are doing something *right* or *wrong*, or choose something that *may*, or *may not*, be beneficial to us, in the end?

These above verses of the Bible were to be a *blessing*. God wanted us to be able to *teem* together, as a successful group of individuals. He wanted each of us to be the *best* we could be, and show the world our productivity! *That's* what a blessing truly is!

Now, why was this above discussion so important? Because *human beings* are important. And, every time we produce another child we are producing another living being - an individual who needs to be fed, sheltered and clothed. And, our earth has only *so many* resources. Why do we allow people to talk us into breeding *more* and *more*, when we see hunger and starvation already out there, in masse'? The world's resources are dwindling, and they still preach this! Again, we really need to understand the mindsets of a number of "movers and shakers" out there, and know how they may have helped to devastate the world of our past (through these policies), and are doing it, again, today! As we see, again: it's not the Bible with the problem, it's the interpretations of *very* human individuals. Many took some of the good ideas in the Bible and *twisted* them, to their own benefit.

So, as "good" (or as "blessed") a thing as having children might, traditionally, sound to us, we, now, realized that there may be some twisted rationales behind it all! And, as we notice, these rationales *did* help to push a number of people into lives of poverty, theft, and even violence - because of the decadence lifestyles these habits helped to facilitate.

Many of us are doing a lot of the same things, today, as they were doing, before the Flood. And, God had no other choice than to destroy most all of them. Doesn't that speak to what's *really* right and wrong, here?

Of course, we all need to make a living, and find meanings in life. Shouldn't we be able to make our *own* decision, about certain things? If we use a mind-set like Adam's - one of rationality, reason and foresight - we could make a decision on the *best* time to have children. We, also, could use *common sense* to decide if, and when, having a child would end up being a *blessing* for us, or not. These are really important decisions to us, not something for some religious dignitary to "carpet-bomb" with their own, self-centered interpretation.

We recall a statement of God, to Adam, early on:

> *"My intention in bringing you into the world... was that you should live your life **without pain or toil**, difficulty or sweat, and that you should be in a state of enjoyment and prosperity, and not be subject to the needs of the body but be **free** from all such and have the good fortune to experience **complete freedom**."*
> - *St. Chrysostom, Homilies on Genesis* Homily 17[74]

We are not free, when we continually listen to certain "powers that be," that have their own interests at hand, rather than what the Bible *truly* may be saying, here! This is another mystery in our world, being brought to light. Understanding some of *God's* true intentions could go a long way towards bringing ourselves, and everyone around us, *higher* up, not dragging us, slowly *down*. It's so important, in so many ways, to understand what God may, ultimately, want for the human race. It's important for us to blow beyond all of the "smoke and mirrors" currently placed in our way, as well.

Time For the Flood

Beyond overpopulation; beyond the warped desires for these ancient people to bring forth "the promised one;" there seemed to be another problem: there was an extremely *unbalanced* ratio of people out there. So many adopted the ways of Cain, and of the Serpent - compared to the very, very small number of people who followed the ways of God. So, their world was, soon, about to hit the proverbial "brick wall." God could not allow those of "the other side" to take over everything, and everybody - so, His Flood would, soon, be in order.

God, being the compassionate God He is, tried to be patient, and hoped many would leave their former ways of life.[75] As any disciplinarian would, He threatened many of them:

...for when your iniquity is full, the Lord will bring in a flood upon the earth which shall cover every abomination and wash the earth from all iniquity.
- The Book of the Generations of Adam *Chap. 8.6*[76]

Of course, they did not care.

*...Depart from us; for we desire not the knowledge of **thy** ways.*
- The Babylonian Talmud *Sanhedrin 108a*[77]

Now, God could not refrain from taking vengeance any longer.[78] The up-and-coming Flood could have easily been referred to as the "flood *of lust*."[79] It was time to put the *balance* back into that extremely-lopsided ratio.

To Bring Aboard

Another interesting topic, here: just *who* were saved aboard the ark, and how could it relate to the world we see around us, today? Were there only eight members of one family who were saved? And, if there were, how could they eventually branch out into all of the different peoples we see around us? All of these topics have, for many years, been a bit controversial. How could eight people, of *one* family, do this all? The most logical response to that question is: they probably *didn't*.

Let's look at a different, but very viable, approach to some of these hard questions, as well as on the Flood, itself.

Adam's "Spirit of Life"

*"(God speaking)... behold I am bringing the flood, water upon the earth, to destroy all flesh in which there is the **spirit of life**..."*
- *Rashi* Bereishit (Genesis) 6:17[80]

Just what is this "spirit of life" (or, as some have described it: the "breath of life")? Words such as these float around the Bible, and, quite often, seem to be routinely "passed over." We rarely seem to strive for the meaning of certain phrases such as this, and why it's even in there. We, so often, would just rather look for the parts of the verse that are easily understandable, and move on. But, *why*, indeed, is this particular phrase in there, in the first place?

Usually, the kind of flesh we're talking about is *alive*. Most of us can figure out that living things possess that "spirit" of life - they move; they breathe; they are animated. Noah, assuredly, wouldn't want to bring (or need to bring) dead things aboard the ark, so, why add on the phrase… for clarification? If the Bible, truly, is a perfect document, then there *had* to have been some divine reason why every word was inserted! Instead of skipping over it, let's assume that there is something to it - possibly, to help us understand the antediluvian world, a little further.

Really, what kind of animal, or human, has this particular "spirit of life?" Do we all? If human beings are, in certain ways, *above* the rest of the animal kingdom, if human beings have a soul - an unique way of thinking and understanding - then, could this "spirit (or breath) of life" related to his unique *soul*? We recall that God *breathed* a soul into Adam! Maybe, then, that's what this "spirit of life" could have meant. And, if it *is* our soul, then we see that the Bible, for the most part, was talking about *people*, here!

> *"…behold I am bringing the flood, water upon the earth, to destroy **all flesh** in **which** there is the **spirit of life**…"*
> - *Rashi* Bereishit (Genesis) 6:17

In other words, He destroyed all the living, breathing *human* beings, with a soul!

We've also gathered that there may not have been just eight immediate family members aboard the ark, but more - possibly a lot more. We've also gathered that these "eight souls" were all not just immediate members of Noah's family, but eight specific Adamic souls, destined to go aboard. We recall, in the Genesis 3:15 Prophecy, that a direct descendant of Adam and Eve, was to, eventually, bring forth the Messiah, or savior of the world. And, that's what made these eight particular *souls* "specific" (or "special"), in a way – and, that's why a few *had* to go aboard Noah's ark.

Could this "spirit of life," then, refer just to these *eight* individuals, or the rest of the human individuals around them, or *both*? Let's see.

Interestingly enough, we do seem to have *at least* two different kinds of "spirits," as mentioned in the Book of Genesis. Let's look at them both, and some Biblical examples of each:

The Neshamah (Strong's #H5397) - "the Spirit of God imparting **life** and wisdom;" "the spirit of man;" "once used for the mind" (Genesius' Hebrew-Chaldee Lexicon)

> *And the LORD God formed man of the dust of the ground, and breathed into his nostrils the breath (i.e. the **Neshamah**) of life; and man (i.e. Adam) became a living soul.   - Gen. 2:7 (KJV)*

This type of soul could, more or less, stand for the "general" soul, or spirit, given to every man and woman, by God (even Adam). And, now, we see (via the verse, below) that *all* the living, human beings died, who were not aboard the ark:

> ***All** in whose nostrils was the breath (i.e. the **Neshamah**) of life, of **all** that was in the dry land, died.   - Gen. 7:22 (KJV)*

All of these living beings - those *uniquely* identified as human beings (with this particular soul) - died.

Yet, there seemed to be *another* type of "soul," back in those days:

The Ruwach (Strong's #H7307) - "…as to the mode of thinking and acting, in which sense there is attributed to any one **a steadfast mind**… It is sometimes used of a spirit or disposition common to many… and such a disposition (such a spirit) is said to be divinely given to men, and to be poured upon them from heaven…"; "… the *rational* mind, or spirit…"; "endowment of mind"; "the *intellect*"; "the Spirit of God… by which men are led to live both *wisely* (Job 32:8) and *honestly*" (Genesius' Hebrew-Chaldee Lexicon)

> *And, behold, I, even I, do bring a flood of waters upon the earth, to destroy all flesh, wherein is the breath (i.e. the **Ruwach**) of life, from under heaven; and everything that is in the earth shall die.   - Gen. 6:17 (KJV)*

This spirit (or "soul") could, quite probably, refer to every human soul who may consistently *think* a certain way - in the way God wanted Adam and his followers to *think*. From what we already understand about Adam, and how he was supposed to think, it only makes sense to assume that anyone possessing this *soul*, as well, could be individuals who either are **of** Adam's direct seed, or may **think** as though they were (or both). Simple. All of this may not mean too much to us, today, but, probably, the way a person thought, in those days, meant a lot to God.

So, understanding things in this way could give us a bit more clarity, in regards to some of these Biblical verses, and what they are trying to say:

*And they went in unto Noah into the ark, two <u>and</u> two of all flesh, wherein is the breath (i.e. the **Ruwach**) of life.*   - *Gen.* 7:15 (KJV)

In other words, we see that there, quite possibly, could have been *two* distinct groups, or "classifications," of people going aboard the ark, at this time. We also discover that the original Hebrew, here, may not really be saying that there were just people - two at a time, and walking side by side - going aboard the ark in this manner, but two *distinct* classifications of people went aboard - *two* (of everyone else) <u>and</u> *two* of that particular flesh - those of the *Ruwach* (i.e. who thought in the same particular ways as Adam). Again, utilizing this knowledge, we see how things could read a little different than what so many of us may have assumed, over time.

The following verse seems to elaborate on things, a little further:

*All in whose nostrils was the **breath** (the **Neshamah** <u>and</u> the **Ruwach**) of life, of all that was in the dry land, died.*
     - *Gen.* 7:22 (KJV)

This is a very intriguing verse, here. *Both* of the Hebrew "spirits" (or souls) were mentioned in the same verse - yet the King James Translators utilized them as only one word: *breath*! Why didn't they differentiate the two? Why didn't they mention the two, either? Maybe, they felt that they *couldn't*! But, yet, they are clearly *two* different types of *spirits* (or souls) in this verse, and really should have been noted as such.

But, how could a person have *two* souls? As we begin to dig deeper, we discover that Gen. 7:22 (above) probably says that there were certain individuals out there who, quite possibly, had a "compounded" or "conjoined" soul. We know how important a person's individual *thoughts* or *moral code* was, in the ancients. People were often "branded" by this! Back then, someone who utilized this "second" soul was, probably, a little different *spiritually* than the average person. Those imbedded with (or utilizing this) second, conjoined soul - the *Ruwach* - thought, most probably a lot like Adam, or was in the same "spirit" of Adam.

We recall that Adam was considered "the thinker," because of how he thought a bit differently. We recall, he used a great deal of *logic*, *rationality* and *reason* (or, at least, tried to, most of the time)! It's not to say that other individuals never think in this *spirit*, or utilized their *Ruwach* (or, even *had* it). There just seemed to be individuals out there who could (and would) utilize this, most all of the time (and were *known* for it)! And, as we already stated, this particular *mindset* seemed very important, at least to God! He wanted Adam to be *His* example of how man should *think* on this earth, and *behave*.

Now, we see that: by using the *Ruwach*, one should be able to rely on it (as well as their conscience) to be their internal "regulator;" to utilize it for control over his or her *emotions*; and use it to be the "*seat* especially of moral character."[81] Ultimately, utilizing this *Ruwach* means that we are striving to be in the *same spirit* of God.

Animals, Creatures and Beasts - the Redux

We've just discovered the importance of how one's *spirit* could be utilized (back in the ancients), and the way one *thinks* could have a lot to do with how "akin" or "close" they are to the ways of God! Along these same lines, Noah may have, once, made a proclamation:

> "...*some of all flesh will come to be saved with me in the ark."*
> - *St. Ephrem the Syrian* Selected Prose Works, 139[82]

As we've already seen, this term - *flesh* - involves, not only a relationship akin to a certain genetic (or blood) line, but the way one *thinks*, or *their moral character*. This is important, because it helps to establish that there may have been more than just a bunch of *animals* going aboard the ark, and eight people - with *the Bible* even backing this up!

To continue further in this, we may need to take a second look at a number of preconceived notions society may have thrown at us: for one, the notion that *flesh*, primarily, stands for, "all different kinds of *animals*." When Noah brought *flesh* aboard the ark, were these *only* animals? Or, could they be what's truly important: *people*? And, if so, could they represent the different types of *human* individuals that may have gone aboard?

That leads us to:

*And all **flesh** died that moved upon the earth, both of fowl, and of cattle, and of beast, and of every creeping thing that creepeth upon the earth, and every man...*
- Gen. 7:21 (KJV)

Over the years, translators of the Bible, for whatever reason (agenda, preserving tradition, etc.), most probably, have assumed that these above groups were animals, and translated them as such. Again, if the Bible wanted to say that (only) *eight* human beings, and a few of each animal, went aboard the ark, then *just say so*. Why are these ancient references (almost) continually written in the same, elaborate fashion? Why are the same *groups* of individuals mentioned, in almost the exact, same way? There are even a number of ancient *pagan* works that lists *these* same groups in, practically, the same way! It's so much easier to just say "all animals" or "all of the people." Why take the time, and writing space, to mention these specific group names - over and over? The best answer is: maybe each above group *was* unique, and different. Maybe they *weren't* only animals! Maybe they were groups of people, stemming all the way back to the Garden of Eden!

> *Now **the beasts** and **the animals** were in the lower story...*
> - *The Armenian Apocryphal Adam Literature* Concerning the
>   Good Tidings of Seth 41[83]

Again, what's the difference between the two? Why differentiate them, if they're *all animals*? Wouldn't it be much easier, overall, for the Bible to say, "two of every non-human animal went aboard?"

We, really, must try to understand the people of the day, and their "common talk." Of course, their works of old also equated to how they many have thought about things. We must also recall how the King James translators, in the late middle ages, probably believed that all of these groups were *animals*, right from the start, and made sure their translations revolve around this assumption. These misunderstandings, over time, probably helped to cement *our* misunderstandings, today! But, as we begin to unwrap all of what was done, way back then, we may be able to conclude that these verses could, really, stand for something different.

We are *all* animals, in a way: we breathe air; we live in communities; we fight; we eat; we drink water. We do many of the same things as any other living member of the animal kingdom does - with just some extraordinary physical, mental and ***spiritual*** characteristics about us!

And, we've already seen a number of examples of how words, such as "creature," "beast" or "cattle," could easily have been used describe people, as well (in Volume 1). We see it, as well, in another example, here:

*And surely your blood of your lives will I require; at the **hand of every beast** will I require it, and at the hand of man...*   - *Gen.* 9:5 (KJV)

What kind of beast has *hands*, here, other than a human being?

We, also, recall how important a person's *moral* code was, back then - and, they were, most probably, labeled as reflecting one type of moral code or another. Even in our not-so-distant past, people may say things to other people, such as: "You are a most interesting *creature*, Sir." Often (as with the former example), these terms weren't exactly meant to be an insult. Could the use of these terms have been *much more commonplace* a thousand years ago? Most probably!

Even though they were still, quite often, used, up to the beginning of our last century, many people, now-a-days, have assumed these words were meant to be some kind of "insult." But, that doesn't mean that, in the ancient of days, it wasn't commonly used as just another way to describe someone!

The Clean & Unclean

We've also discovered how the word "flesh" doesn't always mean a person's skin, or bodily composition, but, also, whether they possess the blood of *a different kind* of being (i.e. a fallen, terrestrial angel), or whether they have adopted the ways of Cain, and these fallen, terrestrial beings, as well![84] So, with this in hand, we discover that: during the time Noah was to bring people on board his ark, God instructed him to bring a certain number of "clean" and "unclean" individuals aboard (again, most probably referring to *people*, here, and not animals). Some interpretations made it clear that there were "pairs" of clean and unclean individuals to go aboard, both male and female. Some believe there were "seven" individuals - *either* male or female (or both) to go aboard.[85] What could really be meant by "clean" and "unclean" individuals, here, and why bring a certain number of *each* aboard the ark?

As one may guess, a lot of people may also have guess - in our past and today - that these "clean" and "unclean" individuals were, of course, animals. There *are* animals that are considered *clean* and *unclean*, at least in a "religious" sense. A pig is one example of an *unclean* animal. But, if we view things in terms of what we've already been interpreting, there are more Bible verses that may just take on a whole new meaning.

> *These spirits are both morally and spiritually **unclean**, and the same applies **to their progeny on Earth**.* ("Enoch & the Nephilim: Liber VII", n. d., p. 38)[86]

Yes, this sense of "uncleanness" could, indeed, apply to whether or not a certain person brought aboard had *mixed blood,* or no! There, definitely, could have been a *genetic* side to this all. And, there even could have been - and, as equally important - a *moral* element to this state of "uncleanness." People could be (or live) in a state of moral "uncleanness," as well.

Here, we have an ancient interpretation of cleanness and uncleanness, and how it related to the way one *thought*, and *behaved*:

> *...he (Noah) called the gentle animals **clean**, the vicious ones **unclean**...*
> *- St. Ephrem the Syrian Selected Prose Works, p. 139*[87]

We also know how the Bible said that Noah was considered "perfect" in his generations. He was "clean," not only in bloodline - he also tried to live a "clean" life, "pure of vice."[88]

So, if this all was the case, wouldn't God only want *clean* individuals to board Noah's ark? As one might, easily, assume, God would only want *good* people to go aboard the ark - moral people, as well as anyone free of this mixed, angelic blood… right? Maybe not.

If not, why would God want *unclean* people to board the ark, anyhow? Wasn't the world supposed to be "purified" by a tremendous flood? What good would it for God to keep people alive who didn't really want to follow His ways? doesn't makes much sense… until we dig deeper. We'll soon see that God, in actuality, wanted a representative amount of *each* group of people back then - some of the "clean" and (even) the "unclean." But, *why*? We soon shall see.

According to Genesis, there was to be a ratio of 7 "clean" to 2 "unclean" individuals aboard the ark - at least for a particular group or two. But, again – *what's the reason*? By having a certain number of "unclean" individuals aboard the ark, God could have even desired to give certain people, who may not have originally wanted to follow Him, a *chance* to see good people around them, at work. Then, He hoped they could, possibly, begin to see the error of their ways - and repent! That's a truly merciful God. Let's see how this all could have gone down.

It was, also, God's hope that having 7 "clean" individuals *continually surrounding* the 2 "unclean" individuals, and living their lives, would help to "balance out" the minds of anyone who may, eventually, have *questionable* motives, or may be thinking about sinning in the future. The seven would be there to provide enough peer-pressure to "keep them in check," if you will.[89] We, actually, see examples of this in nature. In the human stomach, for example (a healthy human stomach, that is), there is both "good" and "bad" bacteria inside of it. In almost this same 7 to 2 ratio, "good" bacteria outnumbers the "bad" - believe it or not. When He created us, God did not dictate that our stomach would have absolutely *no* "bad" bacteria in there. We, naturally, have some! Interesting - but, for a purpose (and, a lesson learned). This ratio "balances" all of the bad bacteria out, and keeps them from getting out of control. Simple. Sometimes, this way works better, over all. The same thing applied here, in regards to the placing of people inside Noah's ark.[90] One ancient author implied that: "they might be **tamed** and **civilized** by having an intimate association… (with those who are "clean," obviously)."[91]

This also shows us that God didn't necessarily want *everyone* from any particular group to drown, even if most did not want to follow Him! He was just sick of their prideful dogma, and lewd behaviors, overall. *That* is true compassion. We will soon see how God may have had *all sorts* of individuals aboard the ark, from very different backgrounds. This also shows us how God wanted to give individuals from *each* group a chance at life - regardless of the circumstances of their past, as well as their genetics!

All of this leads us to one solid conclusion: no matter of one's bloodlines, and no matter what ideology that comes *out of* a person, *anyone* can make the right decision, and change their ways - if they really wanted to! Maybe, a lot of people may have this *Ruwach* spirit, as well, somewhere inside them - they just have to *opt* to utilize it:

> *…those…* which have **changed** the nature of wild beasts into that of **domestic creatures**.
> - *Works of Philo Judaeus* Questions and Answers on Genesis II, 27[92]

Towards the Obvious?

On top of this, there may be another thing to ponder: let us recall those 5 groups of Adamites and pre-Adamites (with their corresponding *Strong's* numbers, here):[93]

- The ***Adam*** (or Adamite)   (*Strong's* #H120)

- The ***Chay*** (Beasts) *of the Field*   (*Strong's* #H2416)

- The ***Behemah*** (Beasts)   (*Strong's* #H929)

- The **Remes** (Creeping Thing) *that Creepeth*   (*Strong's* #H7431)

- The **Owph** (Fowl) *of the Air*   (*Strong's* #H5775)

    Hebrew words, as in English words, could *easily* have more than one meaning. In some references, they, assuredly, stand for animals… but, in *every one*? If they weren't *always* animals, then, can we make an attempt to pin-point just where they weren't, and just who or what each individual group might represent?

    One thing the Bible never really seems to go into detail on is how the *races* of our world had developed, both before, and after, the Flood. We are left in the dark, with religious dignitaries scrambling to provide some (often) outlandish theories. If we all came from one man, and one woman (before the Flood), and came from *one* man's immediate family after the Flood, then **how** could all of these racial differences develop so quickly, or in such a short period of time?

    The Bible and other ancient traditions point to Noah as coming directly from Adam's blood line (i.e. his being "perfect" in his generations - implying a pure blood line, here). So, better yet: how did all of the racial differences come about, if Adam and Noah were *both* of one family, and, of one blood line? Where did they come from, if, supposedly, only *one* family (and blood line) was aboard Noah's ark?

    This has almost always been a grey area to most of us. It also makes it very hard to understand - and believe - Biblical stories, sometimes. As well, many of the explanations that "movers and shakers" in our faith give were not, in actuality, the most savory. In fact, a lot of them seem down-right insulting. But, now, we have another way to explain things. All of it, of course, may not sound too "politically correct," but, when it comes to topics such as this: what *is*? It evolution the only way we could go - without, possibly, "offending" anybody? That may be what *some* people out there might want us to think. Yet, if the Bible is to be believed, then there *has* to be some kind of answer, here! And, let's try to examine *one*.

    In all honesty, most ancient texts rarely gives us a hint about *race* and any groups of Adamites or pre-Adamites - no real "smoking guns," here. Possibly, there may not have been much of a need to state certain things, back then! It was just, more or less, common-knowledge. It would be like writing about flying in a plane, or owning a computer. We don't really *need* to *describe* what a plane is, or what a computer is. It's common knowledge. But, who knows, for sure?

Ancient writers, also, may not have felt the need to explain *all* of what the "cattle," "beasts" and "fowl" could *also* have been - most people just knew it. They may have known that these could have been groups of *human* individuals, as well! This ancient knowledge could, easily, lead to modern-day confusion, however. A person, today, may need to inform the general populous about how the ancients separated the wheat from the chaff, for example. It's just a way to "bridge the gap," to understand how life was lived back then, and how they saw things.

Today - and, most probably, back then - an easy way to identify someone is by looking at them: by their skin color, their different facial characteristics, their gender, etc. Hopefully, for now, we could put aside any quick-to-conclude, "politically incorrect" thoughts that might be floating around us, trying to influence us - at least, until we fully try to explain it all. Let's see if we could find another way for it to make sense.

Although the number of *actual* races in our world may vary, somewhat (according to so many "experts," today), we may be able to assume that there are a few major ones:

- *Caucasoid* (Caucasian, white, etc.)

- *Negroid* (Congoid, Capoid, Khoisanid, Black, etc.)

- *Australoid* (Australian aborigines, etc.)

- *Mongoloid* (Asian, oriental, etc.)

Let's go back to the Adamite and pre-Adamite groups (using their *original Hebrew* words, as well as the words used to translate them into English):

- The *Adam* (or Adamite)

- The *Chay* (or Beasts) *of the Field*

- The *Behemah* (or Beasts)

- The *Remes* (or Creeping Thing) *that Creepeth*

How about these four groups: could they, possibly, correspond to those four major *races* in our modern world (in some way)? It sure may shed some light on the many perplexing questions we've always had on this topic, over the years. Sure, those politically correct clichés - about referring to any member of a race as a "beast" or "creeping thing" - may, on the surface, sound offensive... until we research further, and understand what it's all about.

Also, we must remember the probably reasons *why* the original Hebrew words (such as *Chay*) may have been translated into English this way! The translators, for the most part, probably assumed that these groups of individuals were *animals* - so, obviously, it wasn't intentionally meant to be offensive. Many of the same type of individuals - past and present - also believe that eight close family members of Noah came off of the ark, and sired all of the races we have around us.

Well, just what if these groups were more than animals? Utilizing all the scriptural anomalies we have, as well as some extra-Biblical (and even pagan) "hints," we may have an idea why certain groups of people were continually referred to in certain ways - their "titles" may have reflected the roles that they, way back in the Garden of Eden, have been given!

Chay of the Field - Named for their Occupation?

Could the *Chay* (i.e. Beasts) *of the Field*, for example, be so-named because of their occupation, or associations they had with "the field?" Maybe this group specialized in tilling the ground, plant husbandry, or some other farming activity.

Interestingly enough, some *other* Hebrew meanings for the word *Chay* (i.e. *Strong's* #H2416) are "relatives" and "community."[94] Could this *Chay* group be just that: a "community" of people; a closely-knit family of people (or "relatives"), sharing a similar occupation? Of course, it could very-well be.

Also, what about these *Behemah*? This was another Hebrew word often translated into the English as "beast" and "cattle." Maybe this community (or group) of people were a little different than the *Chay* - maybe they didn't, necessarily, work the fields, but were, more often, involved in *animal* husbandry, domesticating the animals in, and around, the Garden, etc.[95] Possibly, they could have become associated with *cattle* or *beasts* because they already had an intimate association to animals they cared for (and nothing more)! It's much like one of us calling a cowboy a "**cow**-boy," today. A cowboy was, traditionally, a "boy" (or young man), assigned to worked with the animals around them. What's so wrong about this concept? The same thing may apply, here, with the *Behemah*.

Interestingly enough, in almost any dictionary, today, we see another definition of the English word *cattle* - "*human beings* especially en masse."[96] Could the Behemah just be another group of individuals - *human* individuals - who had a specialized skill, back then, in the Garden? Maybe *that's* why the Bible put so much time into listing these as particular groups - and not just amassing them *all together*, as "animals."

Maybe there, also, was a reason why Genesis lists these same groups as going aboard the ark - so that it's understood *who* may have really went aboard, and for what purpose. Maybe, some of these groups were even given tasks aboard the ark, such as caring for any animals brought aboard. If Noah, indeed, brought some animals aboard, assuredly, there would have been people needed to care for all of them!

Besides, as we've already stressed: *human* individuals are the important creatures of the Bible, here - *not*, necessarily, the animals. Of course, God cares about all of His creatures (animals and human), but, the Bible, really, is a book about human beings, written for human beings. The individuals with a *Neshamah* and a *Ruwach* were considered the important ones, here!

A Definitive Conclusion on Just "Who's Who"?

Now, we, again, reach a point of trying to decide just "who" might be "who" - in regards to the possible *race* of each group. Again, this could become a fairly "sticky" talking point - because it opens up the possibility of so many thinking "bigotry" or "racism," what have you. Of course, that is not the purpose of this book. We are here to provide answers (or, at least try to) - *not* to shape public opinion, and not to discriminate. With that said and done, let's attempt to conclude that, maybe, there *were* certain human groups, with certain working roles, in the Garden of Eden - all, originally, dictated by God, of course. And, of course, it's not this way, anymore. We all know that people, today, aren't set to do a particular job. Yet, hopefully, there's still not anything wrong with stating the ways things *may* have on been - hopefully.

And, if all this might have been possible, then who are *we* to tell God just *who* to put where, or how He should have done things? Who are we to dictate any way God set up His own garden? We can only question things if we think humanism trumps God, and that we're, naturally, entitled to allow *our* perceptions to supersede any Creator.

Anyone without blinders on should be able to conclude that - in regards to our racial makeup - we seem to be *different*, in a number of ways. But, we *all*, still, are human beings, regardless. If God had a certain working order of the Garden, that all really doesn't matter, today. What truly matters is what people *did* with their lives, **since the post-Fall** society had begun. What matters are the *ways*, and after *whom*, the individuals belonging to each group began to follow!

In other words, if certain members of the Adamite and pre-Adamites groups began to be seduced by the *ways of Cain*, and went in that pagan direction, then *this* can become a problem, and, henceforth, a new personal moniker, or way to "label" them. As we stated, *back then*, the way a person lived mattered a great deal to God. And, again, *these* are personal choices, things that a person **can** change… *not* something that they can't (such as their race). It's important for us to know, and understand, all of this, as we progress, further.

We've already seen how the Bible could, not only, use words - such as *beast* and *cattle* - to describe human beings *based upon their former occupation* in the Garden, but, also on their chosen *moral* stance! This, of course, is what's really important, today.

Interestingly enough, the Bible even uses words - such as *beast* - to describe the angelic beings of God - so, they can't just be negative!

*And when he had opened the fourth seal, I heard the voice of the fourth **beast** say, Come and see.   - Rev. 6:7 (KJV)*

Nothing negative, here… that's for sure! If we also look in Gen. 3:1, we'll see that the Serpent was even considered more subtle than any *beast* of the field - which implies he was more *intelligent*, or *crafty*, than any other sentient creature around him. He wasn't being compared to lowly animals, here - not an extremely powerful, *Seraphim* angel! Angels, obviously, were considered vastly superior in knowledge and understanding. Maybe, the Serpent was even being compared to *other angelic beings* of his immediate area!

As we've just seen, *beasts* weren't necessarily animals, nor were they *always* immoral (angelic or human) beings! It all depends on the context by which the description was placed into.

Down These Wrong Paths?

Quite often, however, the terms *cattle* and *beasts* were, appropriately, used to describe those who began to transcend the moral codes of their day (but not *always*, of course). Some sources, for example, mention how a *beast* could actually refer to an individual who operates "through pride and rebelliousness."[97] *Cattle* could also be considered an individual "who operate through ignorance" ("ignorance," here, referring to a person who continues to look *downward*, or to *the things of this world,* for their enlightenment, or salvation).

> *But the **natural** man receiveth not the things of the Spirit of God: for they are foolishness unto him…*   *- 1 Cor. 2:14 (KJV)*

This individual, according to ancient sources, operates *in ignorance* - as cattle do. They don't really care about any higher - they would much rather look to *other* religions of this world (i.e. idolatry), or anything pagan, because it's easier than doing the right thing. These individuals could, also, be considered (morally) *unclean* (as we mentioned, in the above).

Even though we may begin to take into account these *other* **human** meanings of *beast* and *cattle* (for example), we'll still need to try and come up with some racial identities for each group. Yet, sorry to say, there just isn't enough ancient evidence to come up with anything definitive. But, if we apply some logic, and what we do have, one might find some interesting parallels. First, we see the *Chay of the Field* and *Behemah* do have some similarities: one helped to farm the fields; the other helped to work the fields (through shepherding, animal husbandry, etc.). And, interestingly enough, there does seems to be two racial groups with darker-skin tones (the Negroid/Congoids and the Australoids). Could the *Negroid/Congoid* group have, originally, been the *Chay of the Field* - those of farming or plant husbandry of the field? Could the *Australoids* have, originally, been the *Behemah* – those of shepherding or animal husbandry? Again, these are assumptions, because the two groups were considered similar, in ways, in the past… nothing definitive.

And, if we hold onto the assumption that the Adamite group were those Caucasians, we have, left, the *Remes that Creepeth*. A number of ancient writers may have, actually, associated the "creeping things" with those "close to the earth." They also could have been considered "serpent-like" because snakes, and other small, creeping reptiles, are good examples of those animals near to the ground - *close* to the earth. Now, what do we mean by "close to the earth," again? These individuals may have, for the most part, been known to possess a good amount of engineering, technical, or even architectural, knowledge - the knowledge of "how the world works." They could have been among those considered able to design things, to fix things, or solve problems around our lower earth. We recall, the *serpent* angels were very knowledgeable of the world we live in. Could all of this have a play in the conception of what the *Remes that Creepeth* may have done in the Garden, or, even, have looked like?

Doing the "politically incorrect" thing, here, we seem have a group to, possibly, associate the *Remes that Creepeth* with. Logic dictates that maybe the *Remes* did not work in the fields, or work with the animals, as the others did. And, they were not the Adamites. So, maybe their positions in the Garden were, somewhat, dynamic - they were not tied down to any particular field, or pasture. Maybe, they had roles oriented more towards construction, or maintenance, of the Garden - hence, the reason they were typecast as continually "creeping about." Maybe they served as the engineers of any, and all, Garden problems.

Also, could the ancients have used members of the *animal kingdom* (in some respects) to label this group as the *Remes* (or *Creeping things*)… because of how they may have looked? A serpent seems to have eyes that are oblique, or slant, somewhat. If we look into the eyes of people in the Mongoloid group, however, we also see, somewhat, of the same obliqueness. Again, it wasn't meant to be derogatory… just, possibly, how the ancients differentiated people. Obviously, many of these ancient, most probably, named things after what they *saw* (including animals)!

Of course, some of this could cause some to, immediately, be thinking "political incorrectness"… but, still, they do lead one to pause. In fact, ancient **pagan** texts even seem to state that there were *already* different racial groups, all the way back to the time of Sargon (i.e. Cain)![98] Some of these texts, actually, *bragged* about Cain, and how he was able to have his way over the "black heads" of old, or any of those "dark races." They even so far as to claim that it was *he* who, in actually, "created" them (or, most appropriately - *made them what they now were*)!

<u>The Seven Tablets of Creation</u>
32 *In the mouth of the **Black-headed** whom his **hands have made**.*[99]

<u>The Enuma Elish</u>
106 *Let his lordship be **superior** and himself without rival.*
107 *Let him shepherd the **black-heads**, **his creatures**,*
108 *Let them tell of his character to future days without forgetting.*
113 *Let **him appoint** the **black-heads** to **worship him**.*
114 *The subject humans should take note and call on their **gods**,*[100]

These pagan texts of old, obviously, tried to give *Cain* all of the credit for *bringing* everyone together - "creating" civilization, if you will (after the Fall). He was the "great unifier," here. What a guy. Regardless, we see that **pagan** texts *still* used the color of one's *hair* (or, even the color of their *face*) to identify a person.

Beyond all this, we now see that there, assuredly, were a good many **Adamites** who, also, turned their backs on God, during this time. And, we also know: God did not want to favor just Adam, and the Adamite group, because of who they were, but, because of the choices they made. And, according to ancient sources, we see that Cain, most probably, had pre-Adamites **and Adamites** under him, a number of each group - all falling for the Serpent's seductive ways. Cain even subtly forced a number of these people to live in the cities he had built - they were very multicultural, if you will.

And, after the Fall, the Adamites, the Chay of the Field, the Behemah and the Remes that Creepeth, quite often, began to mix together - creating descendants.[101] But, Cain, on top of this, probably helped to usher in his Cainite offspring, as well as the Amalekites (i.e. the other sons of the Serpent), to mix right in, and create descendants, as well. Again, the mixing of human races was not, necessarily, the problem - it was Cain, trying to indoctrinate people into also mixing in with those of terrestrial, angelic blood.

Those "Indifferent" Adamites?

Well, just *what about* Adam, and the group he was a member of: the *Adamites*? Even though Adam was one of these Adamites, that didn't mean that *every* Adamite was righteous, special, or, somehow, marked for any manner of "greatness!" If we believe (as the Bible stated) that a good number of Israelites were part of the family-tree of Adam, Noah, and their direct descendants, and that Jesus, also, came from the 77th generation of Adam - as a direct seed - then, we could, also, assume that Jesus would have had, for the most part, these same, physical characteristics.

Most of the ancient pictographs had Jesus as a Caucasian. As "politically incorrect" all of this might begin to sound, we must understand something: Jesus, Adam, and Noah had to be of *some* racial "classification" - they couldn't be just "neutral," or of "no race." Does this imply some kind of *superiority*, however? Does "white-privilege" apply, here, because these individuals may have, once, belonged to it? Hardly. We'll, soon, see how these Adamites, as a group, were, really, nothing special.

We, also, recall that Adam was created *last* - and not first - in the early hierarchy of creation. God fashioned angels; *then* the **rest of the pre-Adamite** people; *then* the Adamites; and, then - *lastly* - Adam. Why this particular order? If mankind was indeed created "a little lower than the angels," then logic would assume that God should have create His direct beings in some kind of ascending, or descending, order! If Adam and the

Adamites were of His special seed, then they *should* have followed the formation of the angels - **not** the pre-Adamites.

Also, the pre-Adamites and Adamites were **both** formed from the ground - the same composition of ground! Adam was *even* created from something "lower" than the others - *dust*. He wasn't created from diamonds and rubies. Again, this all doesn't seem to follow the protocol on what, hypothetically, should have been "superiority." It doesn't, until we understand what the *true* mysteries (or ways) of God are, here. We already know that He wants each individual to *shine out* of what they do have, and what they *are* - even if it's lowly *dust*! We shine in our *attitudes*. We *shine* in how we use our minds. **Humility** is the way of God, not *superiority*.

And, on top of this all, the *Adamites* were rarely mentioned in ancient works (besides Adam, of course)! Why? Logic tells us that, if they were all superior, they *all* should have been doing as well as Adam, over time. But, that's simply wasn't the case. Adam, also, had terrestrial angels to help him out the Garden - interestingly enough, **not** other *Adamites*. If Adamites were a superior group of individuals, then all of them should have done special things!

And lastly, we must also remember that Adam - an Adamite - was the one who disobeyed God, here - not the others! He fell, very quickly, throwing the former world into a new and detrimental existence. We're not saying that any other group member wouldn't have done the same thing, under the same circumstances, here, but it does suggest that, in our whole scheme of things, an Adamite really couldn't do it *better*.

Again… superiority? Hardly.

Does it Really Matter?

Of course, there always could be speculation on which racial group could have been "which," in Genesis. The truth is: no one knows for sure. There are some ideas, as we put forth, but, in the end, does *it really matter*? No group has had a Garden role since Adam's fall. This set-up has all dissolved. It's all irrelevant, now. What *really* matters is that there *could* have been living, breathing groups of *people*, with different distinguishing characteristics, living in this early time (besides Adam and Eve). And, some of each group found favor with God, and were brought aboard Noah's ark.

These groups could have been created, way back then, each with their own unique characteristics - and *not* the result of some "curse" levied out to a misguided patriarch. *Cain*, of course, was a perfect example of this. As we recall, a number have theorized that Cain's skin turned *black*, as the result of his misdeeds. Did it really? We'll soon see that, along with Cain, the patriarch *Ham*, and even his son *Canaan*, were thought to have had their skin turned **black**, as well - for whatever crime they were accused of. Should the color of one's skin be significant of some curse, or punishment? Hardly!

Again, in both of these situations, we recall that: it is much more understandable to take this "blackness" as one's newly-acquired "darkened" heart, "darkened" thoughts, or some "blackness" of their soul they now inherited.

Now, if so much of this "blackness" represents something that is, indeed, *internalized*, then, why would a number of these misguided ancient zealots, or scribes, attributed it to something *on the outside*? Why were many of these zealots, in the past, so adamant that we came from only *one* man? What gives? Again, it's quite possible that: if many of those in "spiritual authority" could claim that we *all* came from Adam, then **they** would be able to claim "eminent domain" over *all* the people of Adam - in this case, the entire human race! If we *all* came from Adam, then the dogmas that *they preside over* should, theoretically, be what *every human person* should follow! Simple - another instrument of *control* and manipulation, here!

If other groups of people are out there, then these zealots could not claim this "authority," as easily. If these people wanted, they could, quite easily, claim that they were not necessarily under the spiritual domain of the Bible - the "book of the generations of Adam (Gen. 5:1)." It's as simple as that. These spiritual dignitaries want to be able to say they *everyone* is under their "umbrella" of spiritual authority.

It's funny how some religious denominations work so hard - by holding fast to certain Bible traditions – to be able to claim so much divine authority over our lives… from the cradle to the grave. We may need them at the earliest ages of life (to provide an infant baptism, for example). We may need them to perform one's last rights. It's hilarious to think that one may not even be able to die *correctly*, unless members of the clergy put their own "stamp of approval" on it! Talk about control, here.

Once we begin to see who, exactly, has their "fingers in the cookie jar," here, we may be able to peel-away what might, in actuality, be some real truths. Hopefully, by taking a different look at some traditions, here, and previously-held interpretations (as we did, in the above), we may, soon, be able to "open up" the channels of communication, between the different races, dispelling a lot of the previously-held misunderstandings, here - whether they be *incidental or* **intentional**.

Now, let's continue on, with the rest of our discussion on the ark.

Semi-Spiritual Beings, also, on Board?

We return, now, to the *Fowl of the Air* - the most obscured, and (probably) the most difficult-to-comprehend group out of all these pre-Adamites. We mentioned the rest of the pre-Adamite groups already, and their possible racial connections. Where does this one come in? The *Fowl of the Air* could also, in ways, be known as a *race*... but, this time, they could represent a very different kind of race.

We see, in the classic Jewish work, *The Legends of the Jews*, a number of interesting thoughts about ever-changing time, our ever-changing world, and how human consciousness may have also changed, over time, as well.[102] The source stated that our *physical* earth is on a continual "trajectory" of change, the more time passes. We're talking many, many years. When the earth reaches a certain temporal point, our spiritual "consciousness" - or, the ways we are able to view the current world - begins to change, slightly. This continues on, down a detrimental slope. The longer we are on the earth - reaching each new "plateau" of **conscious** sight, sound and perception - the *less* and *less* we are able to perceive, understand, and relate to the **spiritual** world, around us all! It's interesting, but may need a bit more explanation: over time, we seem to march towards thoughts that are more and more *rational*, and more and more focused on what the *natural* world might have to offer... not as much on the way it used to be. The way it used to be was a way of spiritual entities and the spiritual realm: God, angels, demons, spirits of some kind, etc. Anything with a spiritual or supernatural "tone" was, slowly, being replaced, or slowly "fading" from our consciousness. The ancients, for example, truly believed in the supernatural because it was much more apparent to them! Later on, as time progressed, the world changed, and our thoughts, as well, have changed. We began to think of things with more logic, with more science involved - all *without keeping God in the picture*. Science and rationality - as we see, today - begins to "rule the roost" of our minds. The rest of it (slowly) becomes reserved to something just of "fairy-lore." This really seems to make sense, though… if we think about it. What we believed and accepted as possible, now, is totally different than what the ancients believe. We, probably, wonder how the ancients could even have thought of such things (as mentioned in these volumes). They, probably, would have wondered how we *couldn't have*.

Within the last few hundred years, especially, we've had exponential increases in the uses of science and industrialization; we've had vast increases in writing and literature. All of these, in turn, allows a person to focus more on what they might be able to *see*, as opposed to what might "appear" and "disappear" into some spiritual world. They allow us to focus on, mainly, the elements of our *natural* existence, or focus on whatever obeys the laws of *science*. Anything, once, a part of the supernatural or spiritual world *slowly* (but *surely*) falls by the wayside. And, of course, losing most all of our perceptions of this state of existence, we may also be *leaving behind* a certain **faction of individuals**, still out there - dwelling in this sphere, as well! And, just because *we* are thinking differently, doesn't mean this other world just "went away," or did not exist.

What could this mean, in regards to our discussion on the *Fowl of the Air*? Simply: we've already proposed (in Volume 1) how the *Fowl of the Air* may, in actuality, be a group of "semi-spiritual" beings - a humanoid (or human-like) group of individuals, with *some* spiritual (or angelic-like) qualities. These *Fowl* could be quite similar to a group of beings that most of us have *heard of*… but, most probably, never thought of, to *link*.

Bob Curran, in his insightful and compelling book, *Dark Fairies*, provides a good amount of evidence to how these Fowl of the Air may, actually, be the same as one ancient (and "imaginary") group of diminutive beings - *fairies*. Sound impossible? Let's read on.

*The word fairy has therefore often become interchangeable with the name of any form of spirit, ancestral being, or **race**, and has become an umbrella term for many of*

> *them without every being all that specific.* (Curran, 2010, p. 112)[103]

Could this also be a *race*, another ancient racial group - that even may have originated all the way back, in the Garden of Eden? What one might call a *fairy*, another may call an *elf*, a *dwarf* or a *troll*. There are a number of different names for this group - could another name for them, actually, be the **Fowl (or Owph) of the Air**? In his book, Curran gives us a number of interesting thoughts to ponder. First, during the 13th and 14th centuries, ideas began to emerge about the origin of these fairies: "…fairies were the last remnants of a prehistoric race…" and they probably existed "since the **world began**."[104]

Maybe, also:

> *They were the last vestiges of ancient gods, the remnants of a hostile aboriginal race… beings composed out of… things that make up Humankind…*
> (Curran, 2010, p. 21)[105]

So, what if they *had* originated, way back, in ancient times? This could, in ways, parallel our story of the *Fowl of the Air*. And, the Bible surely said that these *Fowl* are from way back - all the way to day "5" (of the "Six-Day Creation"). This would, as well, make them an *aboriginal* race.

We have another, possible, interpretation of these fairies, and the early days:

> *In the Christian world… (there) was a concomitant theory that fairies might indeed be fallen **angels**… There was a legend, prevalent in some parts of the Western Christian world, that when Lucifer and his minions had risen up in rebellion against God… a **number of angels had "sat on the fence,"** unwilling to take either side. When God triumphed… God came to judge these indifferent angels. They were judged as not being evil enough to be consigned… with Lucifer, but not righteous enough (either)… Therefore, **a middle ground** was found for them…* (Curran, 2010, p. 12)[106]

Wow. What insight, here. This interpretation, also, takes us *back* to ancient times – even back to the formation of *Adam*, himself! We recall that a good number of angels (Sammael, the Serpent, the Nephilim, etc.) disapproved of Adam new position as viceroy, and were punished for their rebellion. The *Fowl of the Air* may have had some angelic-like qualities *superior* to Adam, as well. So, there was room for them to complain, too, if they so desired. They could have, easily, harbored thoughts along the *same* lines as these angels. And, although most may have begun to have this same resentment, they didn't really speak out to God at the time, about it (for whatever reason). Regardless (as we see, in the above), because they didn't *actually speak* out at that time, they *still* had to be "demoted," at least a little bit. Why? Probably, it was because they *still* harbored some negative thoughts, and God knew it!

They weren't demoted *as far down* as they *could* have been, and, as far as their angelic counterparts had been. Regardless of what happened, most were, probably, *still* under Adam's ultimate dominion, and they didn't like it.

And, their "demotion," or their taking this "middle ground" stance, probably allowed these Fowl to, permanently, *want* to stay negative, about the whole situation of Adam, as well as people in general. We also see that:

> *...they still retained at least some of their **former angelic powers** (and also **hostility** toward humans with whom they shared the world). It was believed that some angels were **jealous** of humans, who were, after all, God's supreme and favored creation.*
> (Curran, 2010, p. 12)[107]

So many of us may have pictured these fairies as nothing more than little, imaginary creatures. Sometimes, they were considered to be good-natured, "quirky" humanoids. Other times, they were even thought of as rambunctious, or even fun-loving - *benign* towards humans.[108] We, of course, get these positive images from books and movies of the not-so-distant past - the *Tooth Fairy*, a *Fairy Godmother*, as well the innocent-looking *Tinkerbell*.[109] But, according to Curran, these fairies - and their perceptions as being jolly, flittering and fun-loving - "is probably not that accurate at all."[110]

> *...the idea of a kindly fairy helping out a distressed human is something of a **myth**. Indeed, in many cases, they were **feared and avoided** if possible.*
> (Curran, 2010, p. 176)[111]

If the above is true (and, if they were the *Fowl of the Air*), then we might be able to conclude that *both* fairy and Fowl were a little *less* than dainty, beneficial beings of folklore.

The word *fairy*, in actuality, may even have roots in the Latin word *fatui*.

> *...such interpretations gave rise to a believe in a **race** of almost invisible beings - the **Fatui** - that lived in such places. The Fatui were generally considered to be **malignant** and **hostile toward human beings**... muddling their minds so much that they did not know where they were or what they were doing...*   (Curran, 2010, p. 7)[112]

What we're saying is this: if the fairies of old, probably, had *negative* thoughts about human beings, could not these *Fowl of the Air* have, also, had negative thoughts, as well? Could this all be because of Adam, and how God, once, elevated mankind, in the Garden?

Beyond this, are there *further* ways to connect the two? We recall (in Volume 1), there were a few *other* words in the Bible that could be associated with these *Fowl of the Air*: *air*, *wings* and *flying*, to name a few. These words helped us to understand a little bit more about this ancient group. And, interestingly enough, we discover *this* about the *fairy* group:

> *The idea of swarming **fairies** through the skies may well have its origins in the notion of elemental air spirits. In classical Greek and Roman thought, **air**... was one of the most universal and basic elements in the world... (a.k.a.) the breath of the Infinite... It is no coincidence that many of the earlier representations of spirits and supernatural forces - whether good or bad - are shown with **wings** and as **flying creatures**.*
>   (Curran, 2010, p. 62)[113]

We see some of the same terms being used, above, as well! Interesting.

Also, if we understand how the Bible might utilize the word **air**, here, we'll discover how it could, also, be associated with a "show of pride," or "haughtiness."[114] As well, some of the deeper, esoteric meanings (in the Bible) for *fly* could be "to insult," "to resist" or even "to revolt." It could also stand for "defiance" and in "direct opposition" to![115] If we notice: all of them seem to have a *negative* tone, here. Could these terms serve to describe both the *Fowls* and the *fairies* - both, ultimately, showing an animosity towards Adam, and any other human, since?

We've also established (in Volume 1), somewhat of a correlation between the term *birds* and these *Fowl*. In the Bible, we discover that both *birds* and *Fowls* were (at certain times) portrayed fairly *negatively*:

> *And he cried mightily with a strong voice, saying, Babylon the great is fallen, is fallen, and **is become the habitation of devils**, and the hold of every foul **spirit**, and a cage of every unclean and hateful **bird**...*   - Rev. 18:2 (KJV)

As we see, *demons*, *foul spirits* and *birds* are all mentioned in the same verse, as being associated, in some way. Could not this *fairy* race, as well, be *close* to one of these groups, or be associated with them, in ways?[116] Could not the *birds*, *Fowl* and *fairies* have degraded themselves, in some way - and turned to the *dark* side... now, hating and trying to take advantage of mankind (whenever possible)? Could they have found themselves going farther and farther *down*, towards all that is *of this world*? Could they - with these negative tendencies - have degenerated into those "tricksters" or "malignant creatures" of times past... the ones we think only exist in legends, or *fairy lore*?

If we *do* start to accept these as possible connections, here, we may have to, again, ask ourselves: *why* have fairies, monsters and the like, been so popular - and much more accepted - in times past... and not now? So many ancient people knew of these negative beings, and accepted their reality. They knew what they were all about! Were the people of old just being *overly* superstitious? Were they, somehow, less knowledgeable of the world around them? A good answer to this all may be: it's *not* that these ancients of old were *less* knowledgeable of their world, it's just that their *world* - and human *thought*, in general - was not the same as it is, today! These spiritual elements were, probably, more and more visible, more and more understood, and more and more *applicable* to everyday life.

As years progressed, these "facts of life" fell by the wayside. We, as a human race, continue to maintain a *diminished* ability to foster this other elements of our existence. Again, that doesn't mean these elements never existed, or aren't *still* around. Maybe, they have a *new* role, in our post-Fall world - as *birds* of prey, now working to destroy any and all human beings they have any chance to influence… to devour their "living flesh," if you will.[117]

One things for sure: all of these correlations do seem to push us closer and closer to connecting the ancient *Fowl of the Air* with these fairies of old.[118] And, we recall that God *did* allow some of the *Fowl of the Air* to board the ark. Why? Did some of them repent, and God answered their call? Or, was there something else. Let's read further.

80 Total?

So, with all the above said and done, and all of these human or humanoid groups, at least, somewhat accounted for, we're now beginning to understand that there, very well, could have been a good number of people aboard the ark - a lot *more* than just eight human beings. There *had* to have been… if our human race was to be able maintain racial consistencies before, and after, the Flood! That answers how our human race would be able to look like it does, today. How might people - with all of the different racial characteristics we see today - exist, if those who went aboard the ark were only members of *one*, close-knit family? Makes no sense, as it stands, otherwise!

Now, we'll begin to see even *more* ancient evidence supporting the idea of there being *additional* people aboard the ark - a *lot* more. There seems to be a number which, so often, keeps coming up, again and again, in ancient literature:

> *Noah built a town consisting of **eighty** houses - a house apiece for all who had been saved with him.* (Baring-Gould, 1881, p. 105)[119]

If, after the flood, this *was* the case, and up to **eighty** people were, once, on board, then how could we account for the large number of people, here? Does it say this in the Bible? Who could they have been, exactly? Now, let's see just *who* may have been among these eighty individuals, if this was the case.

Let's, first, gather evidence on how many of that *Adamite* group (including Noah and any of those close to him) may have gone aboard. The Bible seems to state (in Gen 7:1, for example) that Noah was only one of a *few* (Adamites) that God was proud of! There wasn't really any mention of the members of this Adamite group as going aboard, however - anywhere! And, the Bible seems to clarify that all the rest of them were destroyed in the Flood (as we see, in Gen. 7:21 and Gen. 7:23).

We, also, discover that the Bible seems to say this *same* thing, after the Flood:

> *...Noah went forth, and his sons, and his wife, and his sons' wives with him: (and) Every beast, every creeping thing, and every fowl,* and *whatsoever creepeth upon the earth, after their kinds, went forth out of the ark.*   - *Gen.* 8:19 (KJV)

Again, no mention of any other Adamites coming off the ark, here (beyond Noah, and a few of those close to him). One, then, could easily come to the conclusion that Noah, and a select few, were the *only* Adamites to go aboard - the famous *eight* souls so often mentioned in the Bible and other pseudo-biblical literature. Now, because of this, we can, most probably, assign the total number of *Adamites* who actually went aboard as *8*... and *only* 8.

Next, we'll have to take a look at what we've already touched upon (above): the time when God instructed Noah to bring 7 "clean" and 2 "unclean" human beings aboard the ark. Interestingly enough, though: we see that this command only was directed at *one* group of individuals, here - and not all of them. We see, in the Bible, that:

> *Of every clean beast (i.e.* **Behemah***) thou shalt take to thee by* **sevens***, the male and his female: and of beasts (Behemah) that* are **not clean** *by two, the male and his female.*
>   - *Gen.* 7:2 (KJV)

In actuality, when we look deeper into the *original* Hebrew words of Gen. 7:2, and *retranslate* this verse accordingly, we see that *the following* could, better, show us what may have really gone on, here:

> *Of every* **clean** *beast (i.e. Behemah) you shall take sevens* **(and) by sevens***, the* **male and his female***, and of beasts (Behemah) that are* **not clean** *he (take) by two (or* **both***),*

> *the **male and his female**.*   - Gen. 7:2 (in retranslation)

In other words, by looking at things in this new way, one, easily, could diagnose the possibly of what, "sevens (and) **by sevens**" might mean - because, that's what the *original* Hebrew seems to say. Instead, God wanted seven males *and* seven females (all considered "clean," here) to go aboard - seven of *each*. The total of them, then, would be **14**. And, on top of this, we add the 2 "unclean" individuals that were to go aboard (**one** male and **one** female). Now, we have a total of **16 Behemah** going aboard Noah's ark (14 + 2)… the most out of any group.

Incidentally, *why* would God want so many of *this* group to go aboard, as compared to other groups? Maybe, the *Behemah* were singled out, in such a way, because God knew that they had animal-taming or shepherding skills - and there may have been a number of animals aboard the ark, as well, and their help was needed. Maybe, God wanted more of them aboard because they weren't *reproducing* as quickly as members of other groups were. So, God figured, this might give them a better start, after the Flood. We, simply, don't know for sure.

Next, we'll look at another group - the *Fowl of the Air*:

> *Of **fowls** also of the air by **sevens**, the male and the female; to **keep seed alive** upon the face of all the earth.*
>   - Gen. 7:3 (KJV)

Again, it's fairly obvious, in this verse: maybe the Owph (or *Fowl*) were in the same position as the *Behemah*, here - maybe, God decided that the Fowl had some problems reproducing, over time, as a group - and needed a little "help."

Looking, again, at the original Hebrew, and we can retranslate it as something else:

> *…of the birds of the air sevens **(and) by sevens**, the **male and the female**, to keep seed on the face of all the earth.*   - Gen. 7:3 (in reinterpretation)

So, as before, we have *seven* males and *seven* females to go aboard - a total of **14** Fowl. It doesn't seem that there was "clean" *Fowl*, here, to go aboard, however (for whatever reason). But, still, we have more - **14** *more* - individuals to add to the list.

Next, regarding the *rest* of those pre-Adamite groups, God, assuredly, wanted some from each group go on board, as well. Logic tells us that God could have, easily, allowed a number of each group to board, as well. We know that *seven* Adamite individuals were allowed aboard (Noah, and a few of those close to him). We also found the need to bring *seven* males and *seven* females - of the *Behemah* and *Owph* groups - aboard. Plus, those two additional "unclean" Behemah were brought aboard. So far, we have:

- **7** Adamites (along with their leader, *Noah*; as the eighth)
- **7** male *and* **7** female Behemah (as well as **2** "clean" Behemah).
- **7** male *and* **7** female Fowl (Owph)

That's a good number of people, already. What the rest of the groups? Looking at the Bible, we see:

<u>Gen. 7</u>:
7 And Noah went in, and his sons, and his wife, and his sons' wives with him, into the ark, because of the waters of the flood.
8 *Of clean beasts (Behemah), and of beasts (Behemah) that* are *not clean, and of fowls Owph),* **and of every thing (every other human group)** *that creepeth upon (teems about, moves about, etc.) the earth…*

It seems that other group members were asked to board the ark, as well. And, it also seems that it was, at least somewhat, in the *same* manner as those before. Maybe God commanded Noah to bring on board:

- **7** (probable) individuals from each, other group (both, male and female, together)

So, now, we may be able to guess that the other pre-Adamite groups were, now, able to board - possibly, **7** of each, as well! These remaining groups are:

- The *Chay* (or "Beasts") *of the Field*

- The *Remes* (or "Creeping Thing") *that Creepeth*

Here, we have **7** more of each. And, to top it all off, we also may need to add in the groups of *mixed* offspring, as well (those formed by sexual unions between terrestrial angel and mortal women). Why? We know that Cain had to have made it through the Flood, because of the Genesis 3:15 Prophecy. We, also, know that the Anakim and Refaim giants made it through the Flood, somehow. So, if the Bible says that every man and woman outside of the ark had perished, then, a representative amount of each group *had to have* been aboard the ark!

So, if we include the mixed multitude groups, here, we have:

- The *Cainites* (descendants of Cain)

- The *Amalekites* (other descendants of the Serpent, himself)

- The *Giants/Anakim* (descendants of the Nephilim and mortal women)

- The *Mighty Men / Refaim* (descendants of the Watchers and mortal women)

This gives us a total of **6** more groups. And, if we maintain consistency, and say that **7** of each group would go aboard, as well, then, we'll have a total of **42** more individuals aboard (**6** x **7**)! Wow, the total number is really starting to add up, here!

Wait… before we come to a sum-total, we really need to ponder another thought: many of us may not want to believe that *any* individuals contrary to God (such as the four groups, above) would be allowed to board Noah's ark. Why would they? Many in this group, often, turned their backs on God, and were a major part of this antediluvian problem. It makes no sense why *any* of them should even be allowed aboard… until, first, we recall the prophecy of Genesis 3:15! And, we know that this prophecy *had* to be fulfilled, at all cost. Of course, it *wouldn't have been*… if Noah and his family were the only 8 allowed aboard Noah's ark! So, at least some of the Cainites had to survive. The Bible also tells us that there were *mixed* offspring of human beings and angels (the

Anakim and Refaim) *after* the Flood. As well, the *Amalekites* were mentioned. How could this be, if all people were, supposedly, consumed by the Flood? Some of each *had* to have been brought on board.

Regardless of the speculation, could there have been a Bible verse that suggests these mixed groups could *also* have been brought on board? We do seem to have a hint, in Genesis, Chapter 7:

<u>Gen. 7</u>:
13 *In the selfsame day entered Noah, and Shem, and Ham, and Japheth, the sons of Noah, and Noah's wife, and the three wives of his sons with them (all Adamites), into the ark;*
14 *They, and every beast (Chay of the Field) after his kind, and all the cattle (Behemah) after their kind, and every creeping thing that creepeth (Remes that Creepeth) upon the earth after his kind, and every fowl (Fowl of the Air) after his kind, **every bird of every sort**.*

It's the last section of verse 14 that gives one pause, here. We've already discussed the possibility of some "birds" being related to the supernatural. And, of course, those who may want to claim that phrases, such as the above, only refer to *birds* might have a problem with the rest of the verse! Why would Genesis mention, "every fowl after his kind" - *and* then, right after this - say, "every bird of every sort?" If these were *both* birds, why mention them - twice? Makes no sense... unless, of course, we may be willing to accept that one (or both) groups were *not*, in actuality, birds at all.

What if *neither* group represented birds (or, any other animal) - but *human* or *humanoid* groups, or groups of mixed offspring. Let's take a deeper look into this above verse. First, we've already discovered how the ancients may have, in actuality, utilized the *bird* as a symbol of *angels*, or angelic-like beings (as with the *Fowl of the Air*, above). Now, we'll see that the above verse could, as well, be referring to a *human* group of individuals - the mixed-blooded offspring of angels (and humans).

Examining the Hebrew words that make up the above verse, and we might be able to discover how it refers to something *beyond* the a simple group of flying birds. If we open up the possibility that the Hebrew words, here, might mean something else, we can, now, reinterpret this phrase as:

*...(and) every (single) beast or creature amongst the **whole of those seraphim (or angelic) groups**!*

- Gen. 7:14 (in retranslation)

Yes, using the original Hebrew, we see that it could, absolutely, be referring to these above groups - those with *mixed*, angelic blood. So, they could have come aboard, too, according to the Bible.

And, we, also, could have further reasons to make this conclusion. Let's, finally, look at the last word of the English translation (in the above, "every bird of every **sort**"). Looking deeper, we see that the original Hebrew word for *sort* could **also** represent a *wing*, or an *extremity*.[120] And, these could, easily, be thought of as extremities of an *angelic being*, as well![121] So, if this is the case: could not an *extremity*, or *flank*, of a terrestrial angel be their **offspring**, here on earth - an "extremity" that they, themselves, helped to spawn? It's possible, and, in our case, almost *probable*.

So, totaling it all up, together, and we have: We have 8 direct "souls" of Adam's bloodline. We, also, have 16 *Behemah* going on board (see Gen. 7:2). We have 14 *Owph (or Fowl) of the Air* going aboard. We, most probably, have 7 members of the other 6 groups going aboard. Add them up, and we have:

$8 + 16 + 14 + 7 + 7 + 7 + 7 + 7 + 7 = \mathbf{80}$

Exactly 80! Wow - the **same** number they used, so many years ago. Maybe there *was* something to this particular number, after all! The Bible *does* seem to hint on all of the different groups, here - and, we come up with a total of *80*. Maybe there *were* a lot more people aboard the ark, than just the 8. Maybe there were, even, mixed offspring - those of fallen, terrestrial angels - aboard the ark. Maybe there were even direct descendants of Cain and the **Serpent** on board, as well! If so, this could really change the perspective on things that so many of us have, at one time, held as the *real* story.

One thing that's undeniable: for some reason, *all* of these groups seemed to have shown up *after* the Flood. And, the Bible also clearly stated that: all living, sentient beings *not* aboard the ark had died! *How* could they have continued on… if they were all destroyed, and not aboard the ark? Simple: it's because they, probably, were all destined to go through this flood, *together*, in some shape or form.

So, if they *all* were to come aboard, and survive the Flood, then, what may be in store for all of these groups *after the Flood* - when it was time for them all to come off, and go their own ways?

Chapter 7

Angels, the Flood, & Saturn (Part 2)

Noah & Ham - Two "Wise" Ones

If there were, indeed, different groups of people who went aboard the ark - possibly, up to 80 individuals in all - then, we could have had a representative sample of the entire human race, after the Flood. These people, assuredly, must have been a little unsure of their future. They just went through a harrowing experience. On top of it, most of them were, most probably, very afraid - they didn't know if a flood would happen to them, again, in their lifetimes. They lost almost everything they once had, and were used to. God was there, however, to help them on their way. He was going to assure that they had a number of tools, to make it.

Knowledge was important, as this time. And, there was some that God wanted mankind to take advantage of, after the Flood, and some He didn't. Much of the "good" knowledge came from what *Adam* was taught, all the way back in the Garden, by which he handed down, generation to generation - to Noah.

Ultimately, it was Noah's turn to do something with all that God wanted for mankind.

Tradition tells us that an angel of God made sure that a good deal of information was to go to Noah. He instructed Noah to inscribe it all, on tablets of either stone or metal, and bury it. It was not to go aboard the ark. Noah did just that - he inscribed it all as he was told, and hid it - hoping it would, one day, be available - whenever they stood on solid ground, again.[1] Why would God want it this way? Quite probably, God knew the hearts of everybody on board the ark, and did not want any of it to fall into the *wrong* hands, while they were aboard. That tells us so much, however: maybe there were those already aboard the ark who, if given the chance, would have **abused** the information, and worked to have brought their post-Flood world right back into the same condition it once was, before! Keeping it buried, outside of the ark, was to assure that Noah (and Noah only) would be the one able to access it, at a time *God* decided was to be right.

On the other hand, we, also, know that there was a whole lot of supernatural knowledge that the Serpent, and other terrestrial angels, had revealed to the populous. This was the "forbidden" knowledge - knowledge that God didn't necessarily want mankind to have. It seemed that, with everyone going on board, that information was, finally, about to be lost - unless someone did the same thing as Noah did. Apparently, this did happen, however. *Someone* was able to inscribe this additional information onto metal or stone, as well, and bury it! Someone *was*, also, able to dig it all back up, and use it after the Flood. This "someone" was, in fact, very close to *Noah*, himself, sad to say!

Ham, one of the few in Noah's direct "camp," found a good deal of merit to this knowledge, and wanted to keep it - regardless if God was dead-set against this knowledge ever being out there, again. Ham, then, set out to do the same thing that Noah did - and was successful.[2]

Why would he do this? Why would Ham preserve the information that God deemed worthy to abolish? From the last volume, we already understood a good deal about Ham, and what his nature was. Ham's questionable (and negative) character would, continually, rise within him. At first, he "was looked on as a good person, following the orders of his father."[3] He also tried, at first, to be a lot like his brothers were; but there seemed to be something inside him - from the "get-go" - that wasn't "quite "right." This "something" shadowed Ham, throughout his days. A number of times, Ham didn't want to take the "high road," in regards to his decision-making (unlike Abel, for example, who almost always *did*). Ham *slowly* began to lean in the opposite direction – following in the example of Abel's *brother*.

He, subtly, began to take an interest in what the *Serpent*, and other terrestrial angels, were bringing to civilization: magic, spells and other occult arts. To preserve these "arts," Ham, clearly, "began to inscribe these secrets on metal and stone plates that would survive the flood."[4] Soon after the Flood, there would be some major problems on the horizon.

Regional or Global?

The Flood was underway. It, truly, was a devastating event. This, then, brings us into another intriguing thought: was the Flood a *local*, regional event, or a truly *global* event?

> *The evidence from the early church… is fairly conclusive. It was the **unanimous** opinion of the Jewish and early Christian writers who wrote on the subject that Noah's Flood was a global event.*
> ("Chapter 6: Noah's Flood & the Tower of Babel", n. d., p. 2)[5]

Again, why did so many believe this (and *still* do)? The purpose of the Flood was to devastate all human life, existing outside of Noah's ark - of course, leaving only those on board. Why does there seem to be so much (*ingrained*) tradition, here - regarding some key elements of the Flood (such as the magnitude of the Flood)… and, often, with little or no room for speculation? It brings us back to the concept that *only* Adam and Eve were in the Garden, back in these early days, and, they, only, could have been parents of the entire human race. Many Jewish and Christian authorities accept this tradition as the only way. But, of course, we've already discussed *why* they may feel this way - power, control, and filling the pews.

Again, why does this tradition seem rock solid, in the minds of many? Why can't we speculate a little, here? There, once again, does seem to be some *force* out there, desperately trying to make sure that most of these age-old assumptions are kept intact! Why does it *have* to be global? Did there really need to be a *world-wide* flood to do the job? And, was that *truly* what the Bible said?

What's so wrong about creationists taking a cold, hard look at other theories, such as *the Gap Theory*? Why are they so adamant about the earth only being six to twelve thousand years old? What about this possibility of pre-Adamites; the Serpent being more than just a slithering, winding animal; terrestrial angelic beings being able to copulate with human women? The list goes on and on. And, once again, there seems to be another age-old assumption, related to Noah and this Flood, which, again, seems to have protected "bubble" around it. Why does it have to be a *world-wide* flood?

> *If one suggests anything but the apparent meaning is practically viewed as **heresy**. It is this type of **blind piety** that has **generated so many misconceptions and erroneous** doctrines regarding the Bible. Instead of employing independent study and thought they **blindly follow the party line**… a **universal flood** becomes accepted and defended as a fact.* (Weisman, 1992, p. 48)[6]

Beyond this drive for control, could there have been the need, by some, to defend the accuracy of our English translations, maybe? If a few translated words were not exactly translated right, the rest of the Bible - and what it's *currently* saying - might be questioned. And, more importantly (for them), the **authority** of those presiding over our present Bible may also begin to be in question. What if they were not teaching something concrete, here? Ultimately, there arises the possibility that some of these dignitaries might lose a little bit of their "divine power," here - and they can't have that. But, of course, that doesn't do any good for those searching for *real* truths, here!

Why couldn't the Flood have been a terrible, *localized* flood? Couldn't the area of where Noah lived have been continually dumped on, or saturated with water - enough to kill all of those around him, and keep the ark afloat for an extended period of time? It's quite possible.

Let's look at what the *Bible* had to say about it - in the *original* Hebrew words used to describe the Flood.

"Land" or "Earth"?

As we look into Genesis (via the English versions), we see that the words seem to provide *assurance* to any of those who might believe the flood was world-wide - the word add "fuel to their fire." As we begin to look *deeper* in these versions (such as the *King James Version*, for example), we may begin see something a little out of the ordinary (compared to the rest of the bible). The original Hebrew *'erets* is a key word - to help us diagnose whether the flood may have been local, or global. This word describes the *kind* of flood that Noah's Flood was, and the world could, clearly, be translated as either "earth" or "land."

When translated as "earth," it seems logical to assume that the flood waters actually covered the whole earth. When translated into English as "land," it seems logical to assume that the Flood wouldn't have been of such magnitude. A flood that covered the entire *land* of Egypt, for example, may have been devastating. It could have wiped out the entire country, and even a lot around it - but, *nothing*, in comparison, to a flood that covered the entire earth!

The Hebrew *'erets* is used a good number of times in the Old Testament. And, it was translated 1543 times as "land," and only 712 times as "earth" - translated over *twice* as many times as land. Yet, this ratio does not hold close to the usual in the first eight chapters of Genesis! The word *'erets* was translated into English 79 times during the first eight chapters. How many times would we think it should have been translated as "land" (if it was, customarily, translated about twice as many times as "land")? It only makes sense to believe it was in the neighborhood of 40 or 50 times. Actually, it was only *3*! Yes, this is worth repeating: the Hebrew *'erets* was only translated *3* times into the English word "land" - out of 79 times. And, funny - it *only* seems to have been used as "land' when it so blatantly *had* to have been (such as in *the land* of Havilah (in Gen. 2:11), *the land* of Ethiopia (in Gen. 2:13), and *the land* of Nod (in Gen. 4:16)). We couldn't call any of those "earths," for sure - so they *had* to use "land." Why such a *vast* reversal in the average, 2:1 ratio, here? Could these early translators have wanted to *make sure* that there was **no** misunderstanding in what they were trying to portray - that the Flood was, indeed, universal? And, to make sure, they may have felt the need to only insert the word "land" when it was absolutely unavoidable? They may have figured: if the English word "earth" was used, 76 out of 79 times, then any reader has to accept that Noah's Flood *must* have been a flood, throughout the *earth*! Maybe the translating of, practically, everything as "earth" would "remove any temptation" to think otherwise. But, just because things were *translated* a certain way, that doesn't make it so! It almost seems somewhat *political*, here, doesn't it? Maybe the word *'erets* was translated with an agenda: to *make sure* their commonly-held tradition remained intact!

We must realize that, no matter how "learned" some people might seem, they are also *human*, and *politics*, so often, dominates human thought! We all have our traditions, and want to promote things which may benefit us. It's part of our humanity, but not too good of a good practice for any of those looking for truth.

We'll soon see that there may be other "problems," regarding the translation of these words - either unintentionally or intentionally. In Gen. 19:31, for example, we see that *'erets* may have been translated a little unconventionally, here: Lot's daughters had to hide out in a cave, with their father, from a number of people who were chasing them. As time went on, they, eventually, felt the need to propagate their family. Their conversation was as follows:

> *And the firstborn said unto the younger, Our father is old, and there is not a man* **in the earth** *to come in unto us after the manner of* **all the earth**:
>   - *Gen.* 19:31 (KJV)

Interesting. Is this verse trying to say that there were no men in *the entire world*, or, no men *in the land* around them?[7] As we see:

*Thus saith the LORD; Behold, waters rise up out of the north, and shall be an overflowing flood, and shall overflow the **land**...*
- Jer. 47:1-2 (KJV)

Again, the Hebrew *'erets* is part of the above verse, as well. A number of verses (such as we see, above) could, easily, have had "land" or "earth" inserted, in here. Either insertion might have worked.[8]

So, what's so "heretical" about Noah's Flood being a local - but terrible - flood? What, besides "shaking up" a commonly-held tradition, here, would it really hurt to suggest that the entire are around Noah could have been utterly destroyed - and, not necessarily, the entire earth?

It, clearly, would not be "compromising" what the Bible might be saying, here - the water destroyed all of the people outside the ark.

Local or global, the flood served a purpose. A massive, *regional* flood could have done just as well - wiping out every civilized area around. It may not sound as "colorful," of course, or be as glamorous of a story. Why couldn't a local flood of great magnitude, with a great deal of treacherous, continually-flowing water, have battered the entire area where Noah's ark was - for long periods of time?[9] Could Noah, and everyone else alive during this ancient period, have lived in a part of our world that was a little *lower* than the other areas around it - a huge "depression," of sorts? Could enough water have plundered the area, submerging it for a very, very long time?[10] It's entirely possible that shifts in the earth, for whatever reason, may have allowed for such devastation.

Interestingly enough, there's another way of looking at this whole thing:

> *...all flesh had **not** died from the earth but **the face of** the earth.*
> (Bandy, 1967, p. 34)[11]

If we look at things this way, we see everyone and everything in Noah's *immediate area* could have perished - not everything **from the earth**.

Also, if we look at it, there's really not many places in the Bible where the word "earth" refers exclusively to the *entire* earth. In so many examples, it may refer to the *land* of Israel, or some other *land*, or region, in the Middle East!

> *...there shall be a great shaking **in the land of Israel**; So that the fishes of the sea, and the fowls of the heaven, and the beasts of the field, and all creeping things that creep upon the earth, and all the men that are upon the **face of the earth**, shall shake at my presence...*   - Eze. 38:18-20 (KJV)

Couldn't this, also, mean that, "all the men shook in the areas *around Israel*?" Did everyone shake who may have lived in Australia or North America, also - or, where there even people living there, at the time? There really would be no need for God to flood, or even threaten, areas in the four corners of the world because, for the most part, there really wouldn't be too many reasons for the ancients to move so far away from other people - if they even *could*. Human beings are social creatures, for the most part. Barely anyone would really want to move to a place that was inhabited unless they *had* to go there, or was *forced* there. Cain, assuredly, was not out to chase anyone away. He wanted people to come together, for his cities, as well as his *empire*. He, and a lot of the pagan dignitaries of the day, considered it much more profitable to *unify* the population - under *them*, of course.

Yet, many might still disagree, and say that the following verse is most damning to the "local flood" theory:

And the waters prevailed exceedingly upon the earth; and all the high hills, that were **under the whole heaven**, *were covered.*   - Gen. 7:19 (KJV)

The above phrase - "under the whole heaven" - has been used, by some, as *proof* that this flood was worldwide. Yet, this same phrase was used elsewhere in the Bible… as a *local* event. The following passage in Deuteronomy seems to describe the invasion of Canaan (and, *not* the whole world) by the children of Israel:

…behold, I have given into thine hand Sihon the Amorite, king of Heshbon, and his land: begin to possess it, *and contend with him in battle. This day will I begin to put the dread of thee and the fear of thee upon the nations that are* **under the whole heaven**, *who shall hear report of thee, and shall tremble, and be in anguish because of thee.*   - Deut. 2:24-25 (KJV)

It's not the entire *world under heaven*, here… just the area of Canaan. Again, they didn't conquer *the whole earth*, just the *whole of the land*.

Again, just because God needed to take out some sinful people in an area doesn't mean He wanted to punish *the entire world*! Maybe the flood *was* something large, in a certain part of the world - encompassing the huge area wholly domesticated by people. The human race, as stated, didn't really need to expand to the "ends of the earth," way back then. For the most part, it's, usually, a lot easier for the populous to stay, at least somewhat, closer together - for a number of social and logistic reasons (trade, safety, companionship, etc.).

Maybe the Flood was an extremely *violent*, local flood, devastating one huge area of the earth.[12] When this flood flowed through this area, and stayed (temporarily), it was without equal - *no* human could escape. And, if the whole world wasn't exactly flooded, here, then maybe this massive flood was *enough* to do the entire job, here - taking out the *entire* civilized world. Of course, this would sound a lot more logical, and so much less fantastic. And, for any newcomers to this ark story, it would be a lot more believable.

As we may need to recall, when it comes to the Bible: it's the *perfect* original, with, so often, *imperfect* translations (and translators)!

Sex Aboard the Ark

Local or global, the flood *still* devastated Cain's "civilized" world, and it all seemed to end up as, "measure for measure." In other words, God's massive flood of water was used to "wash clean" the previous world's impure "stains" - sexual impurity, moral decay, what have you. All of the decadence, indulgences and lustful activities around them would, now, merit one more important "law," aboard the ark - there would be absolutely no *sex*!

It really made sense, if we think about it, here. So much indecent sex took place. Now, to dedicate the ark into something different, it became a place of solace and reflection. While the world was steeped in pain, God made it known that there was to be no enjoyment of the act, as well no attempts to be made for the world's replenishment - at least, not at the time.[13]

> *The individual should participate in the suffering of the community.*
> (Ginzberg, 1909, p. 188)[14]

Those outside the ark had to pay the price (even though most of them were extremely sinful), and God *still* wanted those aboard the ark to reflect on all that was going on. And, this prohibition of sex may also have been set in place to allow for those aboard the ark to prove *their stand* on lust - to serve as a testimonial to their strength. God didn't want them to just sit around, and gloat. God wanted those aboard to continue to show their devotion to Him, and continue to focus on what negative pathways they need to avoid, in the future:

> "...while you are actually in the ark, to ascend up into the marriage bed with your wives would be a proof of your being devoted to lasciviousness."
> - *The Works of Philo Judaeus* Questions and Answers on Genesis II, 49[15]

Most of them were able show their strength, and devotion to God, here - *most* of them.

Ham's Predicament

Ham, as we know, was already beginning to go down a slow (but sure) march towards "the other side," and this prohibition of God led him into a real dilemma. A lot in the following story may begin to sound a little bit *honorable*, but, as we'll see, it was still disobedient to God. Tradition tells us that, before the flood, Ham was to bring aboard his wife, but, she already may have had two twin children, fathered by someone else. These twins may been the result of her activity with, either, a terrestrial angel, or son of a terrestrial angel. Ham, then, begged Noah to bring them all aboard. These were, as previously mentioned, the giants *Og* and *Sihon*.[16] Although other giants may have been aboard Noah's ark, this scenario, most probably, wasn't part of God's plan. Yet, Noah still (reluctantly) agreed.[17]

To make things worse, his wife was pregnant *again*, possibly by one of the same fathers, just before they went aboard the ark. No one really knew it - no one, of course, except *Ham*. Pregnancies just don't go away, and God's rules were already set in place. God only wanted *a certain number* of individuals on board - specific individuals from specific groups. Ham, obviously, loved his wife; and wanted her to board at all costs, even though she would have soon brought an *additional* member aboard. So, he snuck her in, regardless.

Throughout their time on the water, nobody knew she was with child. The men were supposed to stay on one side of the ark, and the women, the other. No one, even if they were married, was to spend *one* single night with their mate.

Ham was truly in a true predicament, here.

> *...had he not lain with her himself, Shem and Japheth would have **known** she was already bearing a child...* (Graves and Patai, 1964, p. 114)[18]

The clock was ticking. She would be showing soon. Ham could, no longer, hide the fact that she was bringing aboard an individual who was not allowed. Ham figured that, if everyone knew about this, it would probably bring a lot of shame to her, her child, and, especially, to *him*. He had to make a decision: for his wife's sake, he set out to disobey God's commandment - *again*. He already wrote down the knowledge of those fallen, terrestrial angels, and hid them for later. Now this.

There is an interesting story regarding what may have happened next: To prove how honorable they all were, Noah had strewn ashes all over the floor, between the men and the women. If one went across the way, to the other side, everyone could observe their footprints in the ashes. Everyone else remained consistent with their father's wishes. Ham, however, could not.

To "help" him along, he may have even utilized some of the dark, occult secrets he had tucked away, hidden, before the Flood. Apparently, by calling up some "demon magic," Ham was able to, somehow, levitate over the ashes. He, then, crossed over to where the women were sleeping, and "rendered himself to his wife's embraces." Noah prayed for *all* of his sons to remain penitent; and, apparently, there was great power in Noah's prayers. Because of Noah, the demon was able to transport him over there, but *unable* to bring Ham back, without walking all over the ashes. It was getting close to daylight, and Ham gave up - he just walked over to where he was supposed to be, and, because of his footprints, could no longer hide his guilt![19]

Ham made the decision to do this. *Again*, he used man's rationality, and feelings of compassion, to override the commandments of God. Again, he went down the wrong pathway. It may sound noble - but this is *human* rationality. He wanted to protect his wife. He may have even been "in the mood." All of these might sound like something worth pursuing, but, again, God still has His rules - and that's what needs to be followed.

Who has the better insight, here: the **creature** or the *Creator*? No man should feel so haughty as to try and "top" God's rationality, here - with his *own*. This was the kind of man-centered rationale that plagued ancient people back then - with "every man doing what was right in his *own* eyes." Sadly enough, these rationales happen a great deal, *today*.

Regardless of his intent, Ham did a disrespectful thing to God, Noah and everyone aboard the ark! Within his self-centered rationale, he may have never understood *why* - it's just that his emotions were telling him this was right, and he went with it! Again, just because something sounds like the *humanitarian* thing to do, doesn't mean that it's the *right* thing to do!

The True "Blackness" of Ham

Now, how could Ham begin to go after these other ways, right out of the starting gate, and flat-out, disobey God and Noah - so easily? According to numerous Christian and Jewish traditions, it was around *this* time that Ham, also, was said to have been turned *black* - in his skin, after trying to return from that forbidden visit with his wife.[20]

> *These inmates of the ark... were **blackened** and dishonored...*
> (Ginzberg, 1909, p. 167)[21]

Was this "blackening" of Ham the same as what happened to Cain? As we recall:

> *...the Serpent... seduced Chavah (i.e. Eve) and brought curses on the world, and who was cursed himself and **darkened the faces** of the creatures by bringing death upon them.* - *Zohar* Noach 36[22]

Does this mean that all of those who stray from God, or follow the ways of Cain, will have their physical features darkened *on the outside*? Was this, actually, a "darkening" of their *skin*, for example - or something different, something *deeper*?

We recall (from Chapter 4), that there were a few traditions out there, trying to say that something outside of Cain, such as his *skin*, was darkened, right after his sacrifice to God was rejected. And, we've already discussed the strong probability that Cain's *blackness* was, indeed, *internal* - a *darkened* state of mind.

> *...so are the wicked: their erectness shall be bent and their faces blackened [with* **shame***]...*   - The Midrash Rabbah 12:10[23]

The same scenario may have played out with Ham: it was at *this* time that he may have totally *soured* on God, allowing some *darkened*, inner emotions to take hold, inside of him![24] As we see, in the above verse, Ham's heart became "black" - he felt totally *shamed*, *darkened* and *dishonored*. Maybe this was a tipping point, or a turning point, for Ham - in his irrevocable march towards "the other side!"

Ham became extremely despondent with Noah, because he was caught; and he knew Noah felt extremely *negative* about him, as a result. Whether things happened exactly the same as the above story, of course, under conjecture; but, many traditions assuredly point to this time as the beginning of Ham's "blackened soul!"

Explaining Away the Races

We've already discussed the probability of Adamites and pre-Adamites coming aboard the ark, even though so many out there would, of course, try to dismiss this. Understanding the origins of the different races may have proved a conundrum for many religious leaders, today. Yet, if race *was* a factor in differentiating the Adamites and pre-Adamite groups, then we may have found a way to explain how each may have already been aboard the ark - no need to "explain away" how these races could have, somehow, "originated" after the flood. And, as we've also stated, there's no need to try to explain any of the racial differences as being the result of some kind of *sin* or *divine darkening* by some ancient patriarch. They've been there, all along!

Yet, to hold onto tradition, they will say that *this* was, most probably, how some of the races came about. Some were "cursed" or "sentenced" to have dark skin, for example, and, now destined to be worthy of shame and ridicule, even *slavery* - and, all because of their patriarch's actions. Beyond Cain, even beyond Ham, we'll also see that Ham's son, *Canaan*, would be often thought of as "divinely darkened" in his skin.

These five Adamite and pre-Adamite groups already had their place aboard the ark. The sins of these patriarchs might have, indeed, been *entirely* internal. Why, then, would ancient religious leaders, and other "movers and shakers" of the day, continue to claim that the "blackness" of these patriarchs were on the outside? Good question. One of the most logical arguments, as we've seen, could have been, for them, to still be able to show "divine" authority over every person who walked the earth… regardless if pre-Adamite, or no. If everyone descended from Adam, then, they, in theory, should have the whole world under their sphere of theological influence, or "divine" authority. The same applies if we were all, ultimately, from Noah - after the Flood. Works the same.

The Bible *does* claim itself to be, "the book of the *generations of Adam*" (Gen 5:1). Again, it's not to say that anyone outside of this one generation is not important, or not a part of God's plan. Of course, we know that the Bible has shown us - countless times - that God's way of salvation is open for the entire human race… one just has to want it. But, why do religious dignitaries want their tradition unchallenged, in this case? Simple: if some races, indeed, did **not** come from Adam (and, now, did not come from *Noah*, as well), then, certain individuals (if they so desired) could easily choose to "opt out" of any supposed "divine jurisdiction" levied against them, by these religious leaders. If they are not "of this generation," then how could anyone touting the Bible tell them what to do! It's an argument that these elites would rather avoid.

A lot of ancient Jewish and Christian tradition (again) said that Ham was, somehow, *divinely* affected by his action. Could it have been a way for them to continue to hold on to their power? Could this have been a (horribly insensitive) way for them to try to explain away some more difficult questions that might arise, as result of this tradition?

The Ramifications of Ham's Act

Either way, we'll concentrate on his *inner* issue. This event, now, seemed to solidify the beginning of Ham's *blackness* (of mind). Shame was creeping into his family, as a result of it:

*Noah may have been very sad and dismayed when he found out his son had violated this commandment of God on the ark. Maybe, also, it was because he knew that retribution would come to Ham, and, possibly, the **rest** of the family.*
(Mullins, 1987, p. 6)[25]

*From then on, Noah began to hate Ham for his disobedience. This may have sparked the same **insubordination** hatred of Ham back to his father…*
(Haynes, 2002, p. 31)[26]

Thus began a revolving door of hatred, between the two, back and forth:

*(Ham also)… hated his father, because he thought himself **least loved** by him.*
- An Historical Treatise of the Travels of Noah Into Europe[27]

All of this grieved Noah, and even allowed him to be a little fearful of the future. He "continued to be haunted by his fears."[28] He may have even ended up with a desire to *drink*, continually trying to escape the events of his past - as well as the Flood, still going on around him.

Ham, assuredly, held on to the negative elements of these experiences - mainly, because he was "called out" on his deception. Thoughts of resentment and revenge may have been brewing towards Noah, from then on. As time passed, while still in the ark, things were, probably, becoming a little bit awkward between Noah and Ham. Noah was attempting to stay within the pathways of God's "light." Ham was marching towards a "darkened" soul.

Noah's Roaring Complication

After a period of time, the Flood was over. It was time for them to disembark. To further complicate matters, Jewish tradition says that Noah could no longer continue his duties as high priest - for a very good reason.[29] Either inside the ark itself, or, on the way out, Noah suffered a great injustice:[30]

*The **lion**, also, was said to have maimed him because he did not give him food at the right time.*   *- The Midrash Rabbah* 30:6[31]

The lion's paw mutilated Noah, right at his genitals, which gave him copulation problems, from then on.[32] He, no longer, could perform his wife very well, and, as a priest of God. Apparently, one with this kind of condition was not usually allowed to be high priest over the people - that's just the way it was. Noah's son *Shem*, then, took over all of the priestly duties, at this time.[33]

Getting Back the Books

The people of the post-Flood world *still* gave Noah a lot of respect, regardless of what happened with the lion. He was what so many of them looked up to (at least, at *first*). As we recall, he was the one who buried a great deal of knowledge that God wanted for mankind, after the Flood… and, now, it was time to retrieve it.

After things settled down a bit, he went back to the same spot where he buried it all, and, once again, mankind had another chance to utilize the knowledge that God wanted them to. With all of this information, Noah hoped to have *something* positive to give to the people, to help them all lead productive lives. In fact,

> *Noah was given **dominion** over the whole Earth after the Flood.*
> (Knight and Lomas, 1999, p. 86)[34]

In a way, Noah was considered a "giant" amongst all of his peers. We already know (from Volume 1) about the giant offspring of terrestrial angels and mortal women - called the *Anakim* and *Refaim*. And, no, Noah *wasn't* one of them. He was a normal-sized individual, but, still, was considered a *giant*, because he was a "giant" of character, a "giant" of knowledge.[35]

Beyond those who were truly tall, a number of people (pagan or God-following) would begin to call a few of their famous patriarchs *giants*, as well![36] Coming from *either* side, Noah was, now, considered their "giant" - their own celebrity.[37]

The "2nd Incarnation"

We, now, see how the term "giant" could have been used in a number of ways. The terms "black" and "blackness," as we've also seen, could have stood for the "darkness" of a person's soul. With all of these metaphors, is it ever a wonder why ancient mythology, so often, ends up a mystery? So many different names for the same individual. So many confusing, yet inter-related, gods and goddesses! Why, when so many of these "gods" were, so often, equated with each other, would it be so difficult to put all of the pieces together, and figure out just "who was whom?" Most of the time, as we know, the "powers that be" do not want the Bible to be correct, and give us valid history.

And, beyond the possible "smoke screens," erected by certain individuals (ancient and modern), trying to divert the truth, understand mythology may be a lot simpler, here, if we accept a few likely scenarios. First: so many of these ancient pagan gods and goddesses were, most probably, "reincarnations" of earlier gods; and, these being "reincarnations" of, still earlier, gods! Second: most of these ancient gods and goddesses had one source - a common origin. There were, as we've discovered, "original" gods and goddesses out there - the same individuals in the Garden of Eden.

In the case of Noah, people thought so highly of him, and his position over everyone else, that they actually turned *him* into a god - a "reincarnation" of, yet, another, earlier patriarch. Yes, Noah was now considered a "second Adam." And, we know how the ancients already made gods and goddesses out of *Adam*, *Eve*, the *Serpent*, *Cain* and even *Abel*. Adam and the Serpent, as we recall, were considered the "fathers" of ancient paganism. Now, after the flood, Noah was turned into another "father" - over everyone who carried on these pagan thoughts. He, then, became the second "incarnation" of all the gods once equated to the "father" god - Adam (and/or, the Serpent). This is what is meant by a "secondary incarnation." Understanding this makes the identification of so many of ancient pagan gods and goddesses so much easier.

And, as so many of us may already know, people would, eventually, travel to many different locations, after the Flood, to live. Many "gods" and "goddesses" would become specific to many different people, different empires, and different areas - but they still, most probably, came from these same "incarnations" - those that trace all the way back to the Garden!

> *...(the) angel said to Noah... "you will become **a new Adam**."*
> - *The Armenian Apocryphal Adam Literature* Concerning the
>   Good Tidings of Seth 27[38]

Biblical tradition also places Noah, in ways, as a second "Adam" - another "father" over the entire post-Flood population, as well! Because of his notoriety, Noah was also considered "father" of what direction human lifestyles, and existences, should have been progressing, after the Flood.[39] Let's see how long that will last.

Long Lives

On top of this all, Noah's long life (and, the long life of his wife, *Naamah*) would help to solidify any decision to turn them into "gods."[40] Noah was already 600 years old. After the Flood ravished the earth, the average life-span of people began to go down, on a steady decline. Noah, and those born before the flood, seemed to still be able to finish out their long lives.

Noah, actually, lived to be 950 years old - older than Adam ever was. But, Noah's son

Shem, for example, was only able to live to *a total* of about 500 years! Abraham, born approximately 200 years after the flood, lived only to 175 years. What a quick decline! But, pagans would, still, attest that this very long life of Noah was another reason he needed to be considered a "god," or, one who was "god-like."[41]

Not Only Noah

Just as Noah became the "new" Adam, in regards to these "reincarnations," we could expect that *other* characters of Noah's time would, quite probably, be put into the same boat - and, that's exactly what happened. Throughout ancient times, there would be those individuals who would, pompously, claim *themselves* as "reincarnations" of these same gods. At other times, people would commandeer them into "gods" (as was done with Noah). Some were made into "gods" or "goddesses," posthumously.

Once we discover how many of these ancient gods and goddesses were probably second or third "incarnations" of the same "Eden" individuals, pagan mythology becomes pretty clear.

Those with political and religious agendas, of course, would probably want to try to hide this. Why? Again, how many of them would want to, openly, let the world know that they were worshipping, or they even revere, *the Serpent* of the Garden of Eden? There are a few who wouldn't mind, but a great many more might stop to think a little, about proceeding further. This wouldn't sit too well with many who might be thinking about following the Christian faith, assuredly. Also, it seems like, even more and more today, any information that actually points *to the Bible* as a reliable source of history needs to be "dumbed down," or "discredited" in a way. That's just the "politically correct," corrupted world we live in, today.

We'll, soon, see *more* of these ancient individuals, claiming deity status for **themselves**, and, we'll also see the ways these "incarnates" began to spread the Serpent-seed doctrine to many of those around them, and into many parts of the world.

The 4th Son

First, however, we'll need to look a little more into this new "Adam," and what happened to diminish everyone's devotion to *his* "divine" authority (at least, in the *pagan* mind). Noah, in reality, seemed fairly passive, and humble - not one who strove at a chance of stardom, and be known as a "god." In fact, the opposite was more of his speed. He just wanted to pass on the wisdom that God gave him, and try to help *anyone* out, whenever he could.

Time had passed, since the flood. Noah, then, began to be involved with the cultivation of plants and vines. He was already well over 600 years old by this time. He, obviously, was getting old, and he was starting to feel it, as well. He had, at least, three sons already, but they were all grown. They had children and responsibilities of their own. Noah began to rationalize to himself: if he could have just *one* more son, in his old age, he may be able to get some of the help he may needed at this late time. He needed assistance for daily tasks, gardening, etc.[42]

Ham's mind was getting darker and darker. Both envy and bitterness (towards Noah) were beginning to get the better of him. He, also, knew that Noah desired a forth son, and the thought of his having to share *more*, in his up-and-coming inheritance, would begin to seethe in his mind.[43] Sounding disgusted by the whole concept, he went to his brothers, and said his piece:

> "...Adam had but two sons... and this man [Noah] has three sons and yet he wants four!" - *The Midrash Rabbah* 36:5[44]

The possibility of having to share any more "insulted" Ham's intelligence. Greed began to fester - and, eventually, bubble over. At first chance, he told himself he was going to do something to *stop* this.

Of Heavy Heart

In his husbandry, Noah began to grow grapes. He, then, turn these grapes into wine. "Noah continued to be distressed by Ham's transgression. So vexed was he that he **drank** too much wine…"[45] Long story short, Noah became so despondent about happened in the past - with Ham in the ark, what his son was turning into, and, of course, the massive loss of life during the Flood - that he began to drink a little too much wine.

> *…Give strong drink unto him that is ready to perish [i.e., the wicked], and wine unto those that be of **heavy hearts**.* - The Babylonian Talmud Sanhedrin 70a[46]

Obviously, the potency of his wine may have even caught him by surprise. It crept up on him. And, within in his drunken state, he may have thought about his desire to have a forth son, and remembered his wife was ovulating. He staggered over to his tent, and thought this may have been his chance to have a fourth child. Yet, as a result of that lion attack, and (most probably) because of his drunken state, Noah couldn't deliver on his intent. He failed miserably, spilling his semen all over the ground![47] Extremely despondent, Noah, then, probably fell asleep, in a naked, drunken stupor - his private parts still exposed, for all to see.

It was truly embarrassing, especially for this "grand" patriarch. While it was Noah's choice to drink, he, also, may have underestimated what he was actually consuming, and the true destructiveness of such a drunken state. Again, it wasn't the *wine* that was at fault, here, but Noah's lack of discretion. He was human, just like the rest of us. He, as with many, would succumb to the sin *of wrong use*, and had to pay a price (with his shame).

He Laughed at Him

> *(Ham) must have been of a wicked, perverse and crooked disposition.*
> (Haynes, 2002, p. 33)[48]

What did Ham do, when he came across Noah, lying in this drunken state? Did he do the respectful thing, to a man he called "father" - or did he take advantage of the situation?

When Ham saw Noah, lying like he was, he actually *laughed* at him, and mocked him. He even despised him for "the drunk he thought he was."[49] He, then, went, and fetched his brothers, inviting them over to mock him, as well.[50] Ham may have even went out into the streets, walking up and down, looking everywhere for his brothers - just to bring them over, to see what happened![51] It was that important to him. And, all of what he did, of course, was intentional - nothing accidental about it! Once he found them, he could have said something, such as:

> *"Come, come brothers... run and see this **controller** who **censured us wrongly**, and so often, see how he messes up his bed... governed by wine, and the **brute** - leaving his genitals uncovered for all to see!"*
> (Haynes, 2002, p. 37)[52]

What happened to Ham? How could he get this unsavory, with little, or no, pity? Maybe it was because he was "called out" in the ark.[53] Assuredly, Ham no longer had any honor for Noah, anymore.[54] Ham even:

> *...rejoiced in his father's fall, "as the ungodly rejoice at the fall of the godly."*
> (Haynes, 2002, p. 34)[55]

Japheth Cursed, Too

Japheth may have even seen a little humor to it. Apparently, for having smiled - even a little bit - at his father's shame, Japheth might have lost some "rank and file," in Noah's mind! Apparently, respect for one's elders was very important in those days. In Japheth's case, the "gift of prophecy" was said to be lost for him, and his family, for this incident.[56] Noah was not happy, as well, with Japheth.

This, interestingly enough, left Shem as sole "prophet" of Noah's family line.[57]

What Also Might Have Been Done to Noah

In the meantime, before Ham set out to get his brothers, he may have done something else, a lot worse than disrespecting the drunken Noah - something horrible. There are two different traditions about what might have happened: he could have either been castrated, or, even, sodomized![58]

There seems to be more ancient evidence pointing towards castration, however, so, we'll concentrate more on this possibility. Whatever happened, though, Noah must have felt truly *beguiled* by Ham.

Castration

Interestingly enough, we've talked about how Noah would have been considered the "second incarnation" of Adam, in ways. A number of ancient pagan gods, actually, were associated with this act of castration, or mutilation of the genitals - and many of them, not surprisingly, were associated with Noah, or his son, as well! The gods *Jupiter*, *Uranus* and *Kronos* were either castrated themselves, or castrated their own father.[59]

Jewish traditions also point towards the same:

*By his magic he bewitched his father in the "places of **generation**," so that he disabled him forever to have the use of women, or to get more children. For these and his other detestable impieties, he incurred the wrath and displeasure of God, in a most grievous manner, and was afterwards banished from his father.*
    - An Historical Treatise of the Travels of Noah Into Europe [60]

Noah, after this point, was no longer able to have children. At least for Ham, that helped to keep his inheritance intact!

To "Uncover His Father's Nakedness"

To add insult to injury, Naamah (Noah's wife, and mother of Ham) was, as we already know, most probably ovulating at this time, waiting for Noah to impregnate her. How could Ham stop Noah from succeeding - even further - from making good on this desire? Of course... by impregnating his own mother! This was, according to many, exactly what had happened![61]

Naamah may have been impregnated that night, but, not by Noah. A son *was* born to her, but, quite possibly, by her *own* son Ham - and this son's name was Canaan! Noah, in fact, cursed Canaan, as it says in the Bible. He did it, not just to be mean, but for the manner of how he was born. Canaan was supposed to be *Noah's* son, not Ham's!

Interestingly enough, Noah also says that Canaan was destined to be "a servant of servants shall he be unto his brethren" (Gen. 9:25) - the "brethren," most probably, Shem and Japheth. Now, if Ham *did* have sex with his own mother, then Canaan *could* have, technically, been considered a "brethren" to Shem and Japheth. A wife of Noah conceived *again* - even though it was without Noah. Both Shem and Japheth would have, technically, looked to Noah's current wife as a "mother figure." So, Canaan, in ways, could have been considered a *brother* to these two - at least, a "half-brother!" Why would Noah, then, call Canaan their "brethren" - if there was nothing to it?

After the Dastardly Deed

Because Ham had made such a mockery of Noah, he would be called "vile (or lascivious) all the days of his life…"[62] While working to understand all of the things that were going on with him, internally, the shift of our focus needs to migrate to him, almost *exclusively*, at least till the end of this section. The reason is: *Ham*, in many ways, would be one of those responsible for initiating the *Mystery* systems of *Mystery Babylon* after the flood, as we shall soon see.

Bringing Back Knowledge After the Flood

After this, Noah wanted Ham to leave his presence. He was very upset, and rightfully so. Now, it was time for Ham to leave, to go somewhere - anywhere. Now, he had to go and do something with the remainder of his existence. Where was he to go? What was he to do? He may have, then, remembered that he buried something before the flood, as Noah, himself, did - those tablets of forbidden, occult knowledge.

> *…Ham, **unhappily** discovered the magical art…*
> ("Looking for Jonitus", n. d., p. 13)[63]

Ham may have still been a little *torn*, about what he did, overall, and about utilizing this forbidden knowledge, once again. Even though his mind was going dark, he still had somewhat of a conscience, at some times. And, he knew this knowledge was a major part of why God destroyed our previous world, in the first place! Bringing back this same knowledge could affect the world, again, in the same ways; but, Ham felt the need to gain *some* advantage, here, in order to help him out. He was in a situation.

Now, Ham was starting to live up to his name. From the very definition of the word *Ham*, we recall that it meant "warm," "hot," "heat" and even "passion."[64]

> *(The name Ham)… pointed out the very disposition of his mind. The word doubles, and has more meanings than we are now acquainted with, two of which… we find are heat or **violence of temper**, exceedingly prone to **acts of ferocity and cruelty**… including beastly lusts and lasciviousness in its worst feature…*
> (Haynes, 2002, p. 101)[65]

Unlike Cain, Ham would often dance on the precipice of "crossing the line," or showing his "wild side."[66] Cain, apparently, didn't care what the ramifications were, regarding the things he did. With all that he did to Noah, however, Ham - awkwardly - was making huge strides towards "the other side." As the ancient author Augustine suggested:

> *(Ham's kind are)… The tribe of heretics, not with the spirit, not of patience, but of impatience, with which the breast of heretics are wont to blaze… which they disturb the peace of the saints.* (Haynes, 2002, p. 28)[67]

We, now, see how his darkened thoughts eventually manifested themselves into *action*.

As the waters abated, and areas became easier to navigate, Ham went back, to find the forbidden knowledge of these fallen, terrestrial angels - to do *something* with it all.[68] Of course, this made things worse for Ham. He, steadfastly, kept feeling "inferior in worth," and continued to give himself to uncivil and rude behaviors - "following the abominations and vices of **those horrible giants** before the flood…"[69]

> *When the Flood was over he sought them out with the same curiosity for sacrilegious things with which he had hidden them, and **transmitted the seeds of perpetual wickedness to later generations**.* (Orchard, 2003, p. 68)[70]

Not only did Ham bring this forbidden wisdom through the flood, he began to, openly, teach it to others![71] Ham *still*, most probably, did not want to jump with "both feet" into paganism, and the ways of the Serpent. He *did* spend a good number of years growing up inside the family of Noah, and he retained *some* sense of morality and decency from the experience. Ultimately, it seemed that Ham, "functioned as an **enabler** for the development of religion, but did not fully embrace it himself."[72] Noah's upbringing was bring conflicts to his soul.

Even though his eventual adoption of this Serpent-knowledge was "half-hearted," the pagan populous at large still believed he "turned his back" on Noah, and his God, and, for this, he was beginning to be brought into high esteem, by a number of these ancient people.[73]

Cain and Cham

So high, in fact, that:

*...he (Ham) is the **heir of Cain** after the Flood...*
(Orchard, 2003, p. 70)[74]

Yes, these "reincarnations" would continue… now, with *Ham* (and *Cain*).

*...for from all we gather about him from the Bible and ancient records, he "went in the way of **Cain**."* (Bristowe, 1927, p. 166)[75]

Soon, the ways of Cain and the Serpent would be on the rise, *again*! Many would adopt the same knowledge that was utilized, before the Flood. Ham would receive a great "honor," as well: he was considered "the second incarnation" of *Cain*!

Yes, just as Adam, and the Serpent, were considered the first "fathers" of old, with *Noah the second*, Cain was now considered the first "son" of old… and **Ham** *the second*! It only seemed natural - especially when *he* was the one who helped revive the ways of Cain![76]

> *There was, of course, considerable confusion between Cain and Ham, not only because of the similarity of the names (Cain and Cham, or Cainus and Chamus) but also because Ham... was traditionally regarded as **Cain's successor** in the figurative sense. Ham and Canaan and all the members of their line were thought to have **continued** the evil of Cain...*   - Anglo Saxon England, p. 194[77]

As we're beginning to see, a number of new "gods" were being established, in the post-Flood world. Interestingly enough: the first "father" (Adam) and the second "father" (Noah) were both *shamed* in some way; and the first "son" (Cain) and the second "son" (Ham) were both *blackened* in some way - very interesting.

Yes, this was how the world would eventually turn *dark* again - first, because of Cain, and, now, through his successor. Ham would pass on this same mental "blackness" to his current generation, as well. Many were, again, about to head into the same "perdition," as before the flood.[78] Are we not starting to see a *pattern*, here?

> *Ham... the notorious world-darkener...*
>   (Haynes, 2002, p. 27)[79]

Naamah - Now, the Second "Mother"

Along with Ham's newly-established "honor," *Naamah*, Noah's wife (and, probably, mother of **both** Ham and Canaan) may have been elevated to some honorable state, as well! Pagans ended up elevating her, in this same, "incarnated" pattern of ancestor worship. Now, Naamah was the new "mother" of all the earth, after the Flood - the new "Eve!" And, naturally, she should have to become a deity, as well. After all, she was the mother of *Ham*; Eve was the mother of *Cain*. We already know that there are "divine" parallels, here, between Ham and Cain - who better to give *this* honor to?

As the "second incarnation" of Eve, Naamah welcomed it all - a lot more than Noah ever wanted to. And, like Ham, Naamah was thought to have started out wholesome, while under Noah's roof - at least at first. By today's standards, Naamah would have been thought of as an "old fashioned" wife - at least, at first. Thoughts of her "ancestry, education, occupation, or life-philosophy were of no concern for her."[80] At first, she put her efforts into being a great help-meet for Noah, backing him in many ways, including his desire to "replenish the species."[81] She seemed to have changed, over time, into one who began to favor the ways of Cain and the Serpent - as well as her son, Ham.

As the popularity of paganism took off, so did her worship. Among the pagan descendants of Canaan, for example, their "mother" goddess was named *Nammu* - a name often equated to *Naamah*.[82] This deity was, also, considered an "earth-mother" or "goddess of the primordial waters."[83] Where might we get the association to *water* and *earth*, in the above? Quite probably, there was a *mountain*, by which the survivors of the ark had descended from - a tall pillar of *earth* - and everybody knew about that. So, she could have been associated with *water* and the *earth*, here - as the "mother" goddess, who left the "primordial waters" and ended up on dry land, on this big pillar of "earth."

Naamah - as this second incarnation of Eve - could have absorbed many of the characteristics given to the "goddess" Eve, as well; and, could have been worshipped under many names in the post-Flood world, such as *Athena*, *Astarte*, *Anat* and *Atagatis* (to name a few). She, most probably, was even worshipped under the goddess *Ashtaroth* (or *Asherah*) in the Bible (in Judg. 2:3, I Sam. 7:3-4, 12:10, etc.)![84]

That Child of Ham and Naamah

We move on to *another* offspring, bound to follow in the ways of Cain. The (probable) child of Naamah and Ham - *Canaan* - would seem to turn out in much the same as his mother and father.[85] One meaning of the name *Canaan* is "low," probably because of how he acted - so *low* in morality.[86]

His descendants weren't that much better. They may, for example, have pulled a stunt which caused a huge rift in the ancient civilized world (and still does, today)! When Noah, the grand "father," decided to divide up the people of the world, and give certain lands to certain families, the people of Canaan didn't exactly play ball. *Ham* was supposed to take his families and move to the southern portions of the world, including the southern part of Arabia, northern Africa, Egypt, etc. Shem was to have his descendants spread out into the entire Middle East. And Japheth would move his families to the lands in the north. As we see, *Shem* and his descendants would have also been assigned to the area we know as *Israel,* today.

As a member of Ham's family, Canaan's descendants were expected to re-locate to the north-western tip of Africa, near the Atlantic Ocean; but a number of Canaan's descendants (or *Canaanites*, as they were called) would not listen to Noah. In fact, they thought they didn't have to do anything of the kind. They decided to live wherever they felt like. And, guess where they ended up?

> *...again, after the Flood, the Devil... stirred up Canaan, the son of Ham, and he became the violent tyrant (or usurper) who rent the kingdom from the children of Shem.*
> - Book of the Glory of Kings (Kerba Nagast) 9. Concerning the Covenant of Noah[87]

> *...he (Canaan) seized* **seven of the great cities of Shem***... and he doubled the size of his own portion.*
> - Book of the Cave of Treasures p. 125 (notes)[88]

We recall, that "father" Noah should have been the one to dictate where the descendants of Shem were going to settle, and they did - but the Canaanites took most of it over. That's why it came to be known as the "Land of Canaan," for such a long time. That's also why the land of Israel was said to be "the Promised Land" - it was, at first, *promised* to the descendants of Shem. And, later on, God *promised* it to these same descendants! This was, probably, why God told Abraham (a son of Shem) that he and his descendants would re-take the land - because it was promised to them, in the first place!

Towards the "Other Side"

The Canaanites who already lived there, of course, would not see it this way. They, already, were in the land, and weren't going to give it up for anything. Again, it was "all about them" - they felt "entitled" to it, because their forefather, Canaan, already migrated there. Many of these ancients were beginning to adopt the same, self-centered ways of Cain, as before. They, as well, were not about to heed to *Shem*, or any new "high priest" of God. In fact, to many of these ancient peoples, the *opposite* extremes of paganism were becoming the law of the land. Not surprisingly:

> *There is definitely a Babylonian history of the Flood, which* **corresponds to the Biblical history**, *but with a different* **emphasis**:
> - *The Biblical post-flood history begins with Noah… It then continues, in much more detail, with the family of* **Shem**, *until the coming of Yeshua (Jesus) the Messiah.*
> - *The Babylonian post-flood history also begins with Noah, but places more emphasis on the families of* **Cham (Ham)** *and* **Japheth**.
> - *An Historical Treatise of the Travels of Noah Into Europe*[89]

As we see, the *opposite* views, again. Pagans seemed to want to spend much *more* of an effort on the other *sons* of Noah - *especially* Ham. Makes sense. The two, and their descendants, were now to be put into a "good light;" and Shem - not so much.

Indeed, their world was changing… *again*.

Ham, now deified as the second "incarnation" of Cain (by others around him), would slowly accept his "honor," and began to think of himself as the very one they were beginning to deifying him as, even holier, and more pious, than that grand "father" out there - Noah (at least, in his *own* mind).[90]

Kronos - The "Crowned One"

There is another name for this new, "deified" Ham (in Greek mythology, at least): *Kronos*. Kronos was known as "The Horned One," or one who "wore the horns."[91] In ancient times, a man wearing *horns* on his head (or wearing a crown) signified his position of personal power.

> *...he (Ham) proclaimed himself **king** and placed a crown on his head. It was from this... act that the Greeks called him Cronos... from Kroone, which signifies Crowned.*
> (DeLoach, 1995, p. 116)[92]

Magic & Idolatry

With the knowledge he brought back, Ham would, also, go on to be considered the "preserver" or "inventor" of pagan magic.[93] The ability to perform these feats gave him even more popularity. And, as a result, he, also, began to think more highly of himself!

> *...Ham developed magic in order "to be esteemed a god" among his contemporaries...* (Haynes, 2002, p. 29)[94]

Introducing these "black arts" back in the world allowed him to establish quite a name for himself (actually, a *number* of names).[95]

Cham, Chem or Khem

The name *Ham*, in ancient times, would, at times, read a little different. Sometimes, it would read *Cham*, sometimes *Chem*, or even *Khem*. Through these slight variations, we may be able to see just how much influence he actually had on the developing world. These were all *him*.

Ancient **chem**istry and al**chem**y could have, very well, contained his name, because they were probably "invented," or "preserved," by him, through the Flood.[96]

Ham, as well, could have become connected to some up-and-coming areas of influence (in our ancient world), such as:

*...(chemistry was) ultimately derived from the name khem, **Egypt**.*
("Chemistry", n. d., p. 1)[97]

Khem, another variant of this name *Ham*, was said to have played a major role in the development of a great, post-flood empire, one of *many*, actually:[98]

*...Ham... discovered the magical act, and handed down the instruction of it to one of his sons, who was called **Mesraim**, from whom the race of the **Egyptians** and Babylonians and Persians are descended.*
("Looking for Jonitus", n. d., p. 13)[99]

Through his use of magic, and his over-all "clout" as the "new Cain," Ham may have become instrumental in winning these early lands over to the ways of Cain.[100] It only makes sense. *Ham* even seems to be connected with the land of *Egypt*, in the Bible:

*- And smote all the firstborn in Egypt; the chief of their strength in the tabernacles of **Ham**.*   *- Psa. 78:51 (KJV)*

*- Israel also came into Egypt; and Jacob sojourned in the land of **Ham**.*
- Psa. 105:23 (KJV)

*- They forgot God their savior, which had done great things in Egypt; Wondrous works in the land of **Ham**...*   *- Psa. 106:21-22 (KJV)*

He Went "Too Far"

Ham began to go to "extremes," in this exploitation of occult magic. He continued to conjure up demonic spirits, in order to assist him (as he may have also done, aboard the ark).[101] This, eventually, might have even cost him his life:

*...the first sorcerer was Ham, who was later called **Zoroaster** (equal "living star", in Greek) by his worshippers. He was called so because by magical manipulation of a demon he tried to draw sparks from a star, and was **burned**. The foolish crowd, instead of discerning God's punishment in Ham's death, believed to have perceived a particular significance in his death by fire, and began to worship him as a living star... Zoroaster was worshipped by the Persians as the celestial **fire**.*
(Ginzberg, 1909, p. 200)[102]

...he was consumed by a fire of his own creation...
(Haynes, 2002, p. 29)[103]

The "Hidden One"

Before his untimely death, Ham, apparently, did a lot of traveling (to many lands around the Mediterranean Sea). He, also, deposited a great deal of influence to these areas - contributing towards the *Mystery* systems of *Mystery Babylon*!

Let's take a look at another "god" Ham was "deified" into, and what this "god" was said to have contributed to his post-Flood world. We already know how *Ham* was deified into the pagan god *Kronos*. In another ancient empire, the population began to call Kronos by another name:

*...the Romans continued to called him **Saturn**.*
(DeLoach, 1995, p. 116)[104]

Saturn, most probably, was - and still is - one of the most important figures behind the *Mystery* systems of *Mystery Babylon*. He was said to be a "god of hidden counsels," a "concealer of secrets" or a "god of 'mysteries.'"[105] One descriptive subtitle of this god was "The Hidden One." Now, what was so *mysterious* about this god, and why did he have to be *hidden* away?

We'll, eventually, see how the *God* of the Bible was, actually, the prototype for this pagan god. *He* was the original "God of mysteries" and "concealer of secrets." He knew it all (and still does)! And, it was up to Him to decide if a secret would be given to the general populous, or be hid away.

Next, as we begin to see how paganism established this god (for Cain's new religion), we'll begin by discovering that *Noah* was the first human individual they elevated to this status. Yes, Noah - the "Hidden One." Why? It's fairly simple: Noah was "hidden" away, in the ark, for an extended period of time![106] Because of this, he was called the *first* Saturn - "the first of the Hidden Ones"… but (as we'll see), not the last!

This *same* title would, either be transferred over to, or be adopted by, another man: *Ham*, of course.[107] We already understand that he and the original Saturn (i.e. Noah) were not getting along very well, and *Ham's* new ways were on the "upswing." People, then, were looking for someone to be more "attuned" to the ways they were falling for. Things were definitely be twisted - in Ham's favor. Time for him to assume the title:

*The exiled Saturn (i.e. Ham) is received most gladly by Janus (a.k.a. Noah) for his wisdom and **made co-ruler**...* ("Looking for Jonitus", n. d., p. 8)[108]

Obviously, public perception of Ham, as this new "Saturn," was being adopted all over. Ham was, actually, a "father" of a number of nations, already, so, it only makes sense for him to take over this "divine" authority from Noah.

Saturn now became sole master of all his father's dominions.
(DeLoach, 1995, p. 116)[109]

The ways of Cain and the Serpent were becoming much more viable in the post-Flood world, here. And, we're, also, beginning to see some parallels between *Sammael / the Serpent* and this "hidden" god, Saturn:

*...he (Sammael) was at once the Devil, the father of all sin and idolatry, who **hid himself** under the disguise of the serpent... and Noah, who lay hid for a whole year in the ark...* (Hislop, 1916, p. 23)[110]

We already recall that the angel *Sammael* (a.k.a. *Satan*) was allowed to possess the Serpent, and speak through him. He did this to help the Serpent seduce Eve. Now, the Serpent and Ham have something else in common: they *both* revealed information - *hidden* knowledge - to any, and all, of those interested. So, Sammael / the Serpent could, also, have been affiliated with *Saturn*, in a number of ways.

Now, where does the *Mystery* portion of *Mystery Babylon* come in?

*The name of the system is "Mystery" (Rev 17:5). Here, then, we have the key that at once unlocks the enigma. We have now only to inquire what was the name... (of) the god of the Chaldean Mysteries. That name... was Saturn... **Saturn** and **Mystery** are both Chaldean words, and they are correlative terms. As **Mystery signifies the***

> ***Hidden system***, *so Saturn signifies **the Hidden god***.
> (Hislop, 1916, p. 250)[111]

> *To those who were **initiated** the god was revealed; to all else **he was hidden***.
> (Hislop, 1916, p. 250)[112]

It makes perfect sense, and this is very important: the *hidden* knowledge (of Sammael, the Serpent, and the terrestrial angels) that Ham brought back from the tablets, as well as the ways of Cain and the Serpent in general, were all part of this *system*. *That's* the hidden element to this all! All of it may, on the surface, begin to sound somewhat *appealing*, somewhat *legitimate* or even *humanitarian*, but, on the inside, it comes straight from the *Darkness*, the "other side."

After while, there wouldn't be very many who actually knew, for sure, where it all *really* came from, or, eventually, they wouldn't care - nor would they, eventually, care where it would really lead them. They just wanted the short-term benefits of these earthly ways they were choosing!

Often, the true *nature* of what's really behind this knowledge, or these ways of life, will not be revealed to the initiate *up front*. If it ever would be, it wouldn't be until the participant is too far in to get out. That's how it works. That's how these ways of Cain are successful. People are taking part in this *Mystery* system of *Babylon* and not even know it!

Hence, we have a big link to *Mystery Babylon*: this god *Saturn* - the "god of hidden counsels," "concealer of secrets" or "god of 'mysteries.'" Now, we, also, know where it all *truly* comes from.

Interestingly enough, many of us have already heard of the "Beast," in the Book of Revelation, and how, in the end times, he would be released from the *Darkness* (his prison), to, again, plague the world. Without going too deep into things, there is a Jewish discipline, called *Gematria*, which states that each man's name could correspond to a specific "number," if you will. How does this happen? Each letter of their name could have a corresponding *number*, assigned to it. Add up all of the numbers and we get a total, which "describes" the individual, in ways.

Many of us understand that the number of the "Beast" is "666." This is the *number* corresponding to the individual Beast, himself! Could the *system* that backs him up, or is related to this whole antichrist workshop, be associated with the number "666," as well? Apparently, yes. Interestingly enough, we also see that:

> *...the name **Saturn** in Chaldee is pronounced Satur; but, as every Chaldee scholar knows, consists only of four letters, thus--**Stur**. This name contains exactly the Apocalyptic number **666**:--*
> $$\underline{S} = 060 \ \underline{T} = 400 \ \underline{U} = 006 \ \underline{R} = 200$$
> (Hislop, 1916, p. 250)[113]

Are we on to something, here, with *Ham* and *Sammael / the Serpent*? There, also, seems to have been an ancient similarity between the names *Cain* and *Kewan*. And, the name *Kewan*, also, had similarities to this "Saturn" of the past.[114]

So, these hidden (pagan) *mysteries*, from the "hidden one" (i.e. *Sammael* or the Serpent), would, again, rise in our post-Flood world! Now, from *Ham*, this resurgence would be put into high gear. It was all the same, as before the Flood. Now, it was all wrapped up, in a "new package," to the people of Ham's day. It was a new *system* (based upon the old), and a new database of knowledge (just regurgitated, again) - releasing venom, once again, onto society, just one more time.

And, interestingly enough, where might have Ham hid this knowledge, in the first place?

> *The voice told them to return to **Babylon**; they were destined to dig up the writings which had been **hidden**… and distribute them amongst men.*
> - *Eusebius* Chronicle 7(211)[115]

It all fits perfectly, here! The Babylonian *knowledge*, once hidden, had now formed into these *Mysteries of Babylon* - returning, with a vengeance.

Next, we'll look at a couple more of these pagan "incarnations" - of the earlier "gods" in Eden…beginning with an individual who was, already, close to Saturn (i.e. *Ham*), himself! This individual was the one who took what "The Hidden One," Ham, *subtly* brought back into our world, and launched it - "full blown" - into a political and religious powerhouse!

Chapter 8

Old Religion of Cush & Nimrod

We must, first, recall that there was a major event which took place aboard the ark. It involved Ham and his wife, as they were waiting for the Flood to end. This event may have passed right by us, somewhat, in the last section. It now, however, comes back to us, once again - in a major way.

We recall that Ham's wife was already pregnant, before she boarded the ark. This child was sired by an individual who was, either a fallen, terrestrial angel, or of Cainite blood, or *both*. The problem, before the Flood (as we know), was that a number of those top, terrestrial angels realized that their end was near, and tried desperately to sneak some of their seed aboard the ark. We also know that God only wanted *certain* individuals to board the ark, not the direct descendants of these top, terrestrial angels!

We also recall that this child made it in, by being inside of her mother's womb! And, that Ham had to "cross the line," while aboard the ark, to be able to have sex with his wife (and hide any possible shame that might have come with this reality). So, just who was this child? What was his name? And, why would he become so important to us, *now*?

Yes, it seems that there was a child born aboard the ark - this child. And yes, he does become extremely *significant* in this post-Flood world - for *pagans*, anyway. And, if we also think about it: this child was also "hidden" in the ark - hidden from almost every person aboard. In a way, it sounds like he also could have been a good candidate to be looked upon as another *Saturn* - "the Hidden One."

It shouldn't come as much of a surprise, however, to see that this baby would, eventually, have taken over Ham's position of authority (as well as his title: *Saturn*)! Ham, apparently, claimed him as his own. Who better, then? Yes, this child was none other than a not-so-famous patriarch in the Bible: *Cush*. And, yes, it would be this *Cush* who would, eventually, go on to reestablish the ways of Cain - on a scale *never* observed by his peers before![1]

Greek Views of the Post-Flood World

Some of the most detailed, and perhaps *best*, contributions we have, to help us understand the times just after the Flood, arrive from the ancient *Greeks*. The way the Greeks recorded their history (and *mythologies*), as well as how they decorated their pottery and artwork, helped to provide us a number of intimate details on just what may have occurred, after Noah came off of the ark.

To understand how this all might helps to build upon this expose' of *Mystery Babylon*, let's, first, understand that the ancient Greeks were, for the most part, *pagan*. Most of their interpretations would have, naturally, taken the side of Cain, and the Serpent.

Hence, most of the information they may provide us would definitely be skewed - not pointing positively towards Noah, Shem or anyone following God, that's for sure:

> *The Greek mythologies don't say anything about* **Shem** *because he… never got involved with their paganism… The Greek mythologies mention Ham and Japheth…*
> (Gascoigne, 2002, p. 64)[2]

The ancient Greeks, as we now see, would, rather, put anyone who *didn't* follow Noah in a positive light. They, also, seemed to heave almost all the blame for the flood onto the pre-Flood Sethites (i.e. the descendants of *Seth*), rather than on the fallen, terrestrial angels, or the Cainites - those who actually sinned![3] As we recall, the *Sethites* were those of the direct seed of Adam himself, who tried to follow the ways of God.

Now, a good number of Hamites (the sons of Ham) and Japhethites (the sons of Japheth) would begin to accept much of this pagan ideology. That's why they were mentioned a lot more, in Greek accounts. Those who followed the ways of God - led by Noah and Shem - were, quite often, considered "uncivilized," or even "brutal" (with those who followed the ways of Cain as being the "noble" ones - even, those who were "victimized").[4]

They even had these *opposing* interpretations all the way back to their interpretation of what happened in the Garden of Eden! When Adam and Eve ate the forbidden fruit, for example, the ancient Greeks didn't necessarily interpret this act as *wrong*, or *sinful*. It may have even been considered a *triumphant* act, of sorts! Their "brave" decision to go after this knowledge brought Adam and Eve into a state of "enlightenment," not despair. As we see, everything's turned upside down.

Their decision, according to the Greeks, gave humanity the power to "escape the slavery" that this God of Adam (and Noah) was trying to "subject" them to. The Serpent, through all of this **knowledge**, was the one who "freed" mankind from this bondage of an oppressive God. He (the *Serpent*) was the *real* "illuminator" to all who wanted follow the ways Cain (and Ham) were introducing to the world.[5] It's incredible how much these opposing viewpoints were twisted around - so much that, eventually, over time, they may have even been able to sound a bit *legitimized*… at least, to an unwary mind!

Let's begin by looking at some of the ancient information they gave to us. By piecing some of it together, we can fill in *even more* gaps - and decipher more of *Mystery Babylon*.

The Curse Is Over

As we begin, we need to realize, first off, that the early Greeks probably had a half-way decent understanding of the Genesis 3:15 Prophecy!

*And I will put enmity between thee and the woman, and between thy seed and her seed; it shall **bruise thy head**, and thou shalt bruise his heel.*
- Gen. 3:15 (KJV)

They may have realized that, early on, their theological positions - even their bloodlines - were on the side of Eve and the Serpent! They may have even been endowed with the blood of *Cain*, somewhere, in their bloodlines. Regardless, they surely leaned towards the side of those who followed the ways of Cain. And, as we know, those who go this contrary to God would probably take the story of the Bible - and twist it, a few degrees. Sometimes, it's twisted 180 degrees, sometimes not. To the Greeks, their spin was a little different: they may have already understood that whoever was of the bloodline of Cain, or followed the ways of Cain (as they did), were destined to have their **head** "bruised" (as in the above). The Greeks must have assumed that the prophecy was true, to an extent. They accepted it, at first, as it *read*: the seed line of Adam and Eve would eventually triumph over the seed line of Cain, and bruise (or crush) his head. Yet, they went off the rails, at this time, and interpreted *the Flood* as the actual fulfillment of the prophecy! There was, really, no savior. The Flood did God's "dirty work," here. And, now, the curse of Cain was *over*!

Greek mythology and artwork depicted the people of Cain (i.e. the pre-flood *Cainites*, and those who followed alongside them) as being *pounded*, or *crushed*, into the earth - by those "evil" Sethites of God. When the Flood came, it took everything that was "cursed" and swept it, far away. All of the "evil" elements of these ways of Cain were, then, washed away, as well - according to them. All the negativity was *dead* and *gone*, reduced to a pile of "nothingness."[6]

Then, the Greeks went on to say that this state of worthlessness (for the Cainite line) wouldn't last *forever*! This seed line, as well as the ways of Cain, were, in actuality, "invulnerable!"[7] They would not be crushed forever. This *pounding* down of everything Cain marked the end of the line for this prophecy, and their curse![8] But, it did not end the rebellious people, themselves, or their ways.[9] And, since the curse that Noah and his God inflicted upon them was now gone, their ways should be able to thrive again, *unabated*! They should be able to practice whatever they want, without fear. If we really think about it, they, in actuality, believed that their ways - the ways of Cain and the Serpent - were "victorious," in the long run! They were able to withstand the judgment of those "oppressive" Sethites, and the God who was behind it all![10]

Their politics they believed in, and the religious dogma that they followed, *must* have been the superior pathways - because of this "come back." The ways that Noah preached, and the God that he represented, really had to be "on their way out."

And, these perceptions didn't just happen in ancient Greece. They were happening all over. The authority of Cain, as it was before the Flood, was on the rise, again - with individuals such as **Cush** acting as the new spokesperson.[11] Although he was given much of the credit for this "comeback," he wasn't able to do it alone. We know that *Ham* helped to launch his career. He was also assisted by another relative - one we've already heard of.

Naamah - "Mother Earth"

*(She)... signified **end** the rule of the Old Man of the Sea (or Noah).*
                                                        (Johnson, 2004, p. 35)[12]

Interestingly enough, Greek mythology also seems to point towards *Naamah* as part of Cain's resurgence. She may have even worked to stifle Noah's dominion over the post-Flood world, and all that he preached.

Why, then, would she even do this to her husband? She used to be all for him! Why would she, seemingly, dump all of the morals she once held, before the Flood?

A *Cainite* in her own right, Naamah may have worked hard to be a satisfactory wife to Noah, at least for a good number of years. As most of us know, there is one situation, in married life, that could easily turn a wife against her husband: an *insult* to her children. That's what might have happened here.

As we may recall, two out of the three famous sons of Noah may have been sired by someone other than Naamah. *Shem* and *Japheth*, quite possibly, could have been the sons of Noah's earlier wife. Naamah, very well, could have wed Noah at a later period, and became the mother of *Ham*.

And, as we'll discover in the next section, certain descendants of Ham may have started participating in things, around the world, that Noah didn't particularly approve of. In fact, he condemned a couple of these groups! As any mother may, Naamah could have begun to harbor some anger over Noah's choice to condemn *her* offspring, and not his first wife's (which, most probably, was what happened)![13]

As we've, also, discovered in the last section, Naamah, most probably, was beginning to be hailed a "goddess" by pagans, all over the world, after the Flood. Now, we're beginning to see the probable reason *why*! She would, eventually, champion the ways of Cain, by trying to stifle Noah, and put him down. Greek mythology and artwork also seems to point to this woman as the new pagan "goddess" - the one who helped Cush turn the world around. Angered at Noah, she decided to popularize these "other" ways that were beginning to gain popularity. After all, if the wife of Noah was even beginning to go in these ways, then there must be something to them - the people thought.

We may also recall, from a previous section, that this "goddess," Naamah, was thought to be a goddess *of the earth*, or "Mother Earth," probably because she came down from the *mountain* of earth that the ark once rested on. It could, also, be because she was turned into a "mother figure," by pagans around her - a "mother" over everyone on our post-Flood earth (hence, "Mother Earth"). We, also, know that Eve was given the same honor.

While we're on the subject, let's take a deeper look at another important "symbol," here, of ancient times: the *earth*.

Earth

We recall that, in the ancients, a "wing" was often used to picture an individual with "swiftness," or some kind of "spiritual authority." A "serpent" may have symbolized an individual who was "very wise." The color "black" may have symbolized the "Darkness," or some "blight" in one's inner soul. The "earth," likewise, could have some ancient symbolism, here, as well.

We recall that the *earth* could, easily, have been associated with some *mountain*, or *high place* - a place (supernaturally) considered closer to the *Divine*, or towards *heaven*! God was said to have His own *high place*, or *mountain*, near the Garden of Eden! He had His own *high place* on top of Mount Sinai, etc. In like manner, the "goddess" Naamah may have been elevated to a "goddess of the earth" because she came down from her *own* high place, and, possibly, even because she began to follow the (Cainite) ways of the *earth*.[14]

All of this seems to pan out, as we further look into Greek mythology. We'll, now, see that one of Cush's titles was, most probably, *Erichthonius*: the "**Earth**-Born One." Now, why would he be called that? As we recall, Naamah, the "goddess" who came down from the ark-topped mountain (of earth), was not the ***only*** one who came down in this way.

Cush, *also*, came down from this same mountain of earth.

He was, as well, accredited for doing something *monumental* in the post-Flood world (according to the Greeks): since the ways of Cain, and Cain's bloodline, were *crushed*, or *pounded* down into the **earth**, Cush was celebrated as the one who brought it all back![15] Into the earth these "ways" were pounded, and **out of this same earth** would they return! Hence, another reason why Cush was associated with the *earth*.

There is *another* possible reason why he had this association with the *earth*, as we'll soon see. But, for now, we'll take more of a look into how Cush labored to bring back the ways of Cain - with a vengeance![16]

Departing from Noah's Ways

First, we know that God assigned *Noah* to be the "father" figure over every person after the Flood. His career, now, would be to establish homelands for the many groups of people coming down the mountain. It was an extremely monumental task, indeed, a task that merited a lot of traveling. But, Noah was only one man. It wasn't very easy for him to go around, and monitor every human settlement that he helped establish. He was, at least, able to bring some of them to a new land, give them a few pointers, and, then, move on. There, also, wasn't a lot of time to "drive home" all of the moral things God wanted him to supply them with. The rest of the responsibilities were up to the individual – and, Cain's paganism was ever looming. As a result, the sanctity of the known world didn't end up as *concrete* as Noah was hoping. The possibility for many of these fledgling civilizations to loosen from Noah's authority was very real - if the opportunity ever arose.

And arise it *did*, for *many*, because of people, such as Ham and Cush.

Certain ancient (Greek) artwork actually pictured Cush (and his own son) "fleeing" from the authority of Noah, even fleeing from *Ham*. This, of course, was symbolic of Cush, and how he *ran away* from Noah's authority - bringing back the older ways of the pre-Flood world.[17] Now, why would Cush flee from *Ham*, as well? Didn't Ham, quite often, go down these same moral pathways?

Ham Only "Gave a Hand"

As we've already mentioned, Ham was among the first to bring this forbidden knowledge (of the antediluvian Nephilim) *back* into the post-Flood world. Strangely enough, however, he didn't seem as *outspoken* about them as Cush was. He wasn't shouting from the rooftops. And, as stated, it's fairly easy to assume that, even though Ham *could* have gone down this wrong moral forever, he still grew up under Noah's teachings. His upbringing, probably, stood in the way of his desire to see these ways corrupt the entire world, and himself.[18] He just seemed to be more interested in embracing this knowledge for his *own*, selfish reasons, advancing his own *personal* agenda(s).

> *(Ham)… wanted his father's authority for himself as a member of the line of Seth, and **not** to establish a contrary belief system.* (Johnson, 2004, p. 114)[19]

So, according to the ancient Greeks, Ham served only as a *transitional* figure - giving "a *hand*" to its development.[20] Greek mythology even seemed to have equated Ham with the god *Chiron* - a god with one open, out stretched *hand*. Ham stretched out his hand, here, *in his support* of change (but that's all).

> *Ham functioned as an enabler for the development of religion but did not fully embrace it himself.* (Johnson, 2002, p. 26)[21]

It does seem that the way one was nurtured may, indeed, have something to do with the way they turn out, later on, in life!

Ham was, as well, beginning to feel some remorse, over time, about what he had done to Noah, and to the world. It's similar to a person who desired to see what was inside of Pandora's Box, and then feels remorse that the box was unleashed - more negatively than he ever anticipated.

This mindset was not the same for Cush, however. Cush seemed destined to use this knowledge to *its fullest potential*:

*...that's exactly what... Cush wants to do. He flees with his son... Nimrod, from the authority of **Ham** - from the authority of the line of Seth - and he's headed strait for **Babylon**...* (Johnson, 2004, p. 114)[22]

The Third "Adam"

Because he was instrumental in arranging for this "splendor" to come back, Cush would, of course, be deified for this "brave" act, as well! We recall that Noah was considered, by many pagans, the "second incarnation" of Adam, and Naamah, the "second incarnation" of Eve, and Ham, the "second incarnation" of Cain. Now, we are beginning to see the cycle repeat, *one more time*! We'll, once again, begin to see the "third incarnation" of this "father" god - Adam/the Serpent. This, of course, would begin with Cush - another new "father" of the faith!

One of the major Greek gods - *Hermes* - could easily have been equated to Cush, here, for example.[23] The name, itself, actually comes from a compounded world: the "**Her**" and "**mes**" equates to "**Ham**" and "**the son of**," respectively. Hence, we have "the son of Ham." And, who was this famous "son of Ham?" Of course, Cush.

Interestingly enough, Cush (as *Hermes*), was also known as *Hermes Trismagistus* - the "Thrice Great" or "Three Times Great" Hermes![24] Again, as far as pagan theology was concerned, this "thrice great" title could, easily, signify him as the *utmost*, or a *highest*, deity. And, in his day, he *was* one of the most influential "gods" of his day. Maybe, because Cush was elevated into this *"father"* position for *the third time*, he could have been also thought of as "thrice great!" It's possible.

The circular "resurgence" of ancient pagan gods and goddesses forms the essence of ancestor worship, as we already know. Their ancestors - as gods - never seemed to die… they just keep being "reincarnated" into the most **powerful people of their day**. What a scam - for control over the people! And, now, we see it's Cush's turn!

While we're on the subject, we'll soon see how there could have, also, been a *third* "Eve," and a *third* "Cain," coming onto the scene - both "reincarnating" into some famous mortal of Cush's day!

Time To Tell Noah "Who's Boss"

Greek mythology also made it known that, in no uncertain terms, *Cush* (a.k.a. Hermes) would soon let Noah know (and all of those who followed him) that their ways were no longer "politically correct." They were "on their way out." The ways of Cush, and all that he was establishing, were taking over![25]

The Greeks also made it known that Noah never really resisted this challenge.[26] He remained somewhat passive, throughout much of this religious transformation.[27] Noah was, as we know, was humble, and, probably, more soft spoken - attempting to settle new areas, and give people a new way to live (according to the ways of God).[28] He was probably getting a little *old* for any conflict, here, or confrontations.

With this, the *new* counter-culture movement, under Cush's authority, was beginning to empower itself, by leaps and bounds. Seeing that the moral authority of Noah could be toppled amongst a number of the colonies that he established, Ham may have begun to feel a little more wary about all that was going on, with Cush feeling more emboldened.

Greek mythology also stated that Ham (as the god *Chiron*), "ultimately regretted abetting the development" of Cush's new ways of culture, religion and politics.[29] When more and more members of Ham's family began to join in Cush's cause, Ham - interestingly enough - began to feel "in such continuous pain" that "he no longer wished to be immortal...[30] Ham still retained somewhat of a *conscience* about what was going on. Inner turmoil, here. Sometimes, it got so bad for him that he really didn't care whether or not he lived, or died.[31]

And, we already *know* what happened to him, before his time!

Cain's "Ways" Reborn

Regardless of all that might have been going on within him, Ham *still* allowed a few things to happen, which augmented these negative trends. Apparently, during the of an *unapologetic* act, Ham transferred a lot of his angelic knowledge to Cush![32] Cush took the knowledge and dedicated himself as the new *priest* (or prophet) of their time.[33]

> *(Hermes)... is a deification of Cush, the original postdiluvian prophet (of the serpent's wisdom from Babylon).* (Johnson, 2002, p. 46)[34]

But, one may ask: how could Cush become so popular, so *quickly* - when so many of the people knew why God destroyed the previous world? It was simply: human nature. This knowledge would, once again, allow the typical individual *power* - power to take control of their own destiny (at least in their minds), and power to get away from God, if they felt the need! The ancients were, once again, being conned into looking to something else, or something *of this earth*, to "save" their own souls, and not God. Cush, not only reestablished these same ways of Cain and the Serpent, but, also, the same "man-centered" ideologies that were popular before the Flood.[35]

This, also, parallels modern-day *Humanism* to a tee: *man* or *mankind* becomes the important element of our existence, here. No need to utilize faith in any so-called "Creator,"[36] What they had with Cush worked. All of what they had, down here on earth, could, eventually, provide them the answers they need.

Humanism - the "Re-Beginnings"

<u>Humanism</u> - *the denial of any power or moral value superior to **that of humanity**; the rejection of religion in favour of a belief in the **advancement of humanity** by **its own efforts*** ("Humanism", n. d., p. 1)[37]

Those who follow movements such as this, today, may claim that Humanism is *not* a religion, per se', but it actually *does* seem to fit the definition. It might not involve the worship of a particular god, but there *is* worship - *self*-worship. It could, then, be considered a "religion" - a *secular*, man-idolizing religion, if one really thinks about it.

And, with this, we could, easily, conclude that human *pride* represents a large element of what's behind this humanistic movement - interestingly enough, the same emotion which prompted the *Serpent* to take action, against man, way back in the Garden. Man, with this *same* pride, could, eventually, find a means to *any* of his own ends.[38] It's all about us. We hear so much of this kind of talk *today*, as well. We, now, can confirm how it, actually, has very ancient roots:

*Babylon… the post-diluvian type of the **city of men**…*
(Bandy, 1967, p. 161)[39]

Because this concept also had roots with Cain and the Serpent, Cush would go on to include *this* into his post-Flood, pagan dogma, as well. They're both related!

But, as we already know, anyone who tries to use things *of this world*, or do things *on their own*, will fall short, eventually - it's because *they*, and *their world*, are not perfect.

This was discussed by the ancient historian, Philo:

*…Chus was the elder son of evil… (as one) being the dissolved and loose nature of the earth… for the earth, when dense and fertile, and moist, is full of herbs, and hills, and trees, and is well arranged for the production of different fruits; but when dissolved and reduced to dust and dry, it is **unfruitful and barren**…*
- *Works of Philo Judaeus* Questions and Answers on Genesis II, 81[40]

It just won't work, in the end! Following this allegory: when a person tries, on their own, to be spiritually "filled," with fruit of their own, it usually ends up rotting - it won't be there for long. Following this protocol may even begin to have detrimental effects on the practitioner:

*...this is... the **cause** of barrenness to the soul and to all its parts.*
  - Works of Philo Judaeus Questions and Answers on Genesis II, 81[41]

It's obvious that: any short-term benefits gained by following these will, eventually, be reduced to "dust." Not only would they become unfruitful over time, but, also, open up one one's soul (i.e. mind) to be *blackened*! We've already seen this. The same happened to Cain, the same happened to Ham, and also to Canaan... they were all associated with the word "blackness."[42]

Cush's attempt at ideological dominion - over the post-Flood - could not have been complete without the help of his *son*, however. Cush, ended up, as more of the "mastermind," or "brains," behind this entire operation. He needed "muscle" to carry it to its fullest potential. His son would, soon, be there to answer the call, and become the main force behind its implementations.

So, in order to proceed further, lets travel back, a little bit into the past, and look at this de-evolution of Cush's son, and how he began to head *down* - towards the *darkness* of soul, once again.[43]

Nimrod

*"Nimrod... the greatest story **never** told."*
  - The Author

It was, approximately, one hundred and twenty years after the Flood, sometime in the neighborhood of 2254 B.C. This next Biblical patriarch was one of the most influential people of his time, but the story of his rise and fall isn't very well, today. It still remains obscure. Why? The answer is fairly simple: understanding just *who* he was, and *what* he did to the post-Flood world, tends to expose more and more of *Mystery Babylon*. So, let's go.

Many who know of this Biblical character may still hold the *opposite* perception of how he really was. When one thinks of a *Nimrod*, they may quickly picture an "awkward dunce," an "ogre" or, even, an "oaf." The reason many of us may have been conditioned to think in this way is because those responsible for passing on ancient, Jewish tradition, here, could have, continually, tried to make this character look *silly*, or *foolish*.[44] It's totally understandable, however - character-attacks such as this are widely practiced, even today. We'll soon see more of what he was *really* all about, and why the cover up.

Nimrod, in reality, wasn't an "oaf" at all - quite the contrary. He was a very strong, and intimidating, military figure. A powerful figure in his own right, he was able to commanded respect - even fear - from a good number of people around him. This individual would, also, begin to go down a familiar pathway - *away* from the true God of Adam, Noah and his son, Shem.

Strangely enough, Nimrod **didn't** start out this way, however. He was, probably, on the same side Noah was! Yet, peer pressure from his contemporaries and his *pride* both had a hand in getting the better of him.

> *And Cush the son of Ham, the son of Noah, took a wife in those days in his old age, and she bare a son, and they called his name Nimrod, saying,* **At that time** *the sons of men again began to rebel and transgress against God...*
> - *Book of Jasher* 7:23[45]

Something was already "in the air," thanks to Ham and Cush. Things were beginning to change, for sure. Cush was in the process of bringing these antediluvian ways back out, into the open. He just needed to be someone with enough charisma to *launch it*, like a rocket. Cush had the knowledge, he had the authority, but he really didn't have much of a way to connect with the people… like *some* people could.

At his young age, Nimrod was considered the "special favorite" of his father, Cush. Cush "loved him exceedingly, because he was the son of his old age."[46] Nimrod would, eventually, be considered *so* close to Cush, in a number of ways, that Cush would, in actuality, be thought of as the "old" Cush, and Nimrod, the "young" (or "new") Cush. The people really like Nimrod, however, and he was connecting with them. Cush definitely had plans for this son. But, there was a problem.

Interestingly enough, it was in his youth that *God*, actually, called Nimrod into *His* service, and Nimrod answered the call! Yes, *God* had great plans for this young Nimrod, as well, wanting to fashion him into one of His viceroys (like Noah and Shem)! Nimrod began to do what God wanted - passing on the ways of his great-grandfather Noah to everyone around him.

Nimrod grew up with a lot of strength and fortitude, and was really in a position to make a difference, here. If only *Cush* could convince him to follow another way! Yes, the proverbial "tug of war" was underway - for Nimrod's *soul*.

There is another interesting element to Nimrod, and his early life - an important element that traces all the way back to Adam, himself!

Wearing the "Clothes of Adam"

<u>Book of Jasher 7</u>:
24 *And the garments of skin which God made for Adam and his wife, when they went out of the garden, were given to Cush.*
25 *For after the death of Adam and his wife, the garments were given to Enoch, the son of Jared, and when Enoch was taken up to God, he gave them to Methuselah, his son.*
26 *And at the death of Methuselah, Noah took them and brought them to the ark, and they were with him until he went out of the ark.*
27 *And in their going out, Ham **stole those garments from Noah his father**, and he took them and hid them from his brothers.*
28 *And when Ham begat his first born Cush, he gave him the garments in secret, and they were with Cush many days.*
29 *And Cush also concealed them from his sons and brothers, and when Cush had begotten Nimrod, **he gave him** those garments through his love for him, and Nimrod grew up, and when he was twenty years old he put on those garments.*[47]

The garments of Adam were said to have had a special (and, obviously, supernatural) quality to them: when Adam wore them, the animals around him (and, probably, other *humans*, as well) felt compelled to *stoop*, or *bow down* to him! Adam could have used these clothes to tame any wild animals around the Garden, anything or *anyone* who may have gotten "out of hand." The clothes even seemed to work, years after Adam had passed them down, to his descendants.

They probably had another important significance: whomever owned these clothes could easily be attested to having some "divine authority," if you will. It was believed that Noah even wore these clothes, up to the time he fell asleep, drunken, outside of his tent. This was the point where Ham laughed at him. And, to add insult to injury, Ham could have used this as an opportunity to demean Noah even *further*, by stealing the garments, as well!

Eventually, as we've seen (above), Nimrod would, eventually, end up in possession of them. Tradition tells us that, around the age of 20, Cush gave them to him.[48] The battle for Nimrod's soul was intensifying, with this. Cush wanted him to follow his ways so badly; and, by giving him the garments, he was hoped he could win himself a little favor, here.

With the addition of these garments, Nimrod, one way or another, was on the pathway to stardom.

Using the Clothes "For Good"

*When Nimrod wore the skins of Adam his outward appears was that of Adam... creatures (were) **humbled**... thinking he was their king.*
(Schwartz, 2004, p. 437)[49]

Nimrod's ownership of the clothes may have worked out in God's favor, at least at first. God could have allowed Nimrod to use them for His ultimate will and purpose. After all, Nimrod wasn't wicked in his youth.[50] Nimrod was a man of virtue, for, at least, a good number of his young years - he really wanted to accept whatever God had laid out before him![51]

*And Nimrod became strong when put on the garments, and God gave him might and strength, and he was a mighty hunter in the earth... and he hunted the animals and he built altars, and he offered upon them the animals **before the Lord**.*
- Book of Jasher 7:30[52]

After this, Nimrod became very well-known for this ability to hunt, and kill large animals. Lions and bears were no obstacle. And, when the people around him saw that these animals crouched down, right in front of him, they were amazed. Many began to attribute this to the power Nimrod *alone*, and not the God who imbued power into these clothes![53] After while, it, quite often, began to seem that:

...none knew the source of his strength, and all ascribed it to his own mighty personality.   (Glenn, 1929, p. 30)[54]

The garments must have been incredible to see in action. Many were, obviously, somewhat confused on how they worked.[55] Nimrod was, seemingly, doing everything right. People were flocking to him, because of what he was, and could give. Contained within the strength of Adam's supernatural apparel, Nimrod seemed to have had all the wild beasts of the area "in check."[56] Many were glad they had someone on *their* side, who protected them from the many negative by-products of their post-Flood world, and gave them a sense of peace and security.[57]

Once, a "Warrior for God"

God, then, assigned Nimrod (and his garment) a larger task:

He was the first who carried on **war** *against his neighbours.*
                                       (Hislop, 1916, p. 23)[58]

Yes, there was strife already brewing, amongst the descendants of Noah. The offspring of Noah's three sons began to get on each other's nerves, probably because they lived so close to each other (and wanted resources). God gave Nimrod a brand new role: to use his power to "clean up" problems within the *human* animal, as well.

The First "Mighty One"

<u>Book of Jasher 7</u>:
31 *And Nimrod strengthened himself, and he rose up from amongst his brethren, and he fought the battles of his brethren against all their enemies round about.*
32 *And the Lord delivered all the enemies of his brethren in his hands, and God prospered him from time to time in his battles, and he reigned upon earth.*[59]

It was around this time that war began to break out between different groups of Noah's descendants.[60] Apparently, the Japhethites (the sons of Japheth) were becoming confrontational to other groups of people of the area. God gave Nimrod, his Hamitic brethren, as well as some Semites (the sons of Shem) the power to contain their unruliness. It's interesting, here, to see how God took the side of *Nimrod* and his brethren the *Hamites*, and not the Japhethites! We recall that Ham, the patriarch of the Hamites, laughed at Noah, and belittled him, while the patriarch Japheth rushed to try to cover his nakedness. Regardless, we see - time and time, again - that God clearly acted merciful and just… no matter *where* these people were from! If the Japhethites acted inappropriately, then they needed to be called out, pure and simple. God, apparently, didn't forget about these descendants of *Ham*, regardless if their patriarch went "off the deep end," and forgot about his loyalty to God!

<u>Book of Jasher 7</u>:
34 *…there was a war between his brethren and the children of Japheth, so that they (Nimrod and his clan) were in the power of their enemies.*
35 *And Nimrod went forth at that time, and he assembled all the sons of Cush and their families… and he hired also from some of his friends and acquaintances… and he went with them to battle, and when he was on the road, Nimrod strengthened* **the hearts of the people** *that went with him.*
36 *And he said to them, Do not fear, neither be alarmed, for all our enemies will be delivered into* **our hands**, *and you may do with them as you please.*
37 *…and they destroyed them, and subdued them…*[61]

Nimrod, once a mighty "hunter" of savage animals, now became victorious in the *human* arena, as well - "hunting" all of those opposed to God, and His will, and winning all of those "battles of the Lord."[62]

The "Shaking" of His Enemies

Now, that he was beginning to get the people of these areas under control, Nimrod decided he was going to build - or *rebuild* - the entire infrastructure. We may have already mentioned how the area Babylon was located in the land of *Shinar*; which, in actuality, seems to equate to the word "shaking." Could this "shaking" have, once, stood for the uncontrolled *shaking* that Cain had (as a punishment for disobeying God's will)? And, how about now? Nimrod, apparently, went back to this same land, named Shinar. Could the name, now, have taken on a whole new meaning? Could this "shaking," associated with the land of Shinar, now, stand for something entirely different?

<u>Book of Jasher 7</u>:
42 *And whilst he was reigning according to his heart's desire, after having conquered all his enemies around, he advised with his counselors to build a city for his palace, and they did so.*
43 *And they found a large valley opposite to the east, and they built him a large and extensive city, and Nimrod called the name of the city that he built Shinar, for the* **Lord had vehemently shaken his enemies** *and destroyed them.*
44 *And Nimrod dwelt in Shinar, and he reigned securely, and he fought with his enemies and he subdued them, and he prospered in all his battles, and his kingdom became very great.*[63]

Making the People Separate

As previously stated, the time was approximately 100 years after the flood, and Noah (under God's command) was trying to help people spread out, and occupy their own lands.[64] They were to expand to the continents of Africa, Asia and Europe. God wanted them to go to their own separate lands and, more or less, stop bickering with each other.

Many people, however, may not have wanted to follow this protocol. So, it was *Nimrod* who, at first, had to force them to go abroad, and stay within their appointed lands.[65] Noah was working on one end of the spectrum (by trying to establish the settlements), and Nimrod was working on the other (by making sure that the people stayed within them). Because of this, Nimrod became known as the great "civilizer" of mankind. While following God's direction, it seems that he was even able to raise the standards of living for all of those under his influence.[66] But, how long could this last? How long before Cush was able to twist his mind, into going another direction?

Nimrod, also, tried to continue where Noah may left off, *ideologically*. He worked to make sure that people understood what God expected from them, and wanted for them. Because of this, Nimrod was also considered the "messenger of light or truth," because he pushed the one, true God.[67] As the moon shone bright in the midnight sky, Nimrod was said to have "reflected the light" of God's reasoning over all the earth - everything he did, it seemed, was for the sake of God.[68]

Then, It All "Went to His Head"

> *And when Nimrod had joyfully returned from battle, after having conquered his enemies, all his brethren, together with those who knew him before, assembled to make him king over them, and they placed the regal* **crown** *upon his head.*
> — Book of Jasher 7:39[69]

Nimrod seemed to be doing everything right! And, those under him soon began to think of him as their king.[70] As with any young man, this could have really done a lot to raise Nimrod's feelings of self-esteem. With this, he could have, also, have been tempted to be "full of himself," or allow any inflated thoughts of *ego* to overshadow his purpose and judgment.[71] Assuredly, Cush may have also been whispering in his ear, quite a lot - trying to convince him to follow *other* ways.

Eventually, Nimrod became so "proud and self-opinionated" that he began to think that *he* and *his clothes alone* were the origin of all his mightiness. It seemed that God was given less and less credit.

More Passed on to Nimrod

To elevate his esteem even more, Nimrod began to discover that there was *other* knowledge out there - knowledge that might give him even *more* power, if he decided to use it. This, of course, was the *same* occult knowledge that his father was continually trying to turn him on to:

> *...the arts of **divination** began with Cham (Ham), the son of Noah, who was both of most subtle genius and trained in the schools of **demons**... **Nemroth (Nimrod)** revived the art of astronomy... and, was... deemed a god by many because of his great lore.*
> ("Looking for Jonitus", n. d., p. 14)[72]

It was around this time that Nimrod - "elated by so much glory" - began to change his behavior, for the *worse*... with his mind becoming so much *darker*.[73]

Into the Darkness - Again!

Most people of Nimrod's day were well-aware of the flood. A good number could still see the results of it, even in their day. A lot of the populous, then, respected God a great deal, because of it, and were more prone to follow Noah, and his teaching, without question. That would be, until *now*. Times were beginning to change. Nimrod's pride was now coming to the forefront, with his father bringing up the rear - both beginning to push *other* ideas onto the people. They say that absolute power corrupts - *absolutely*:

> *Before Nimrod, people walked in fear of God... everyone walked with great... fear of sinning... Nimrod's ambition... **soon** became to free the people from their fear of God.*
> ("Nimrod: King of the World", n. d., p. 4)[74]

God was, at first, able to put this "fear of God" into people - through Nimrod. But, now, Nimrod had forgotten about the "golden goose" that elevated him to such a position. He, as a number before him, had a *dark* side. The grand manipulation of the post-Flood populous was about to begin.

Nimrod, first, decided to "free" himself of anything he felt was of God's "rule!"[75] Creation, again, began to *rebel* against the Creator. With Cush's help, Nimrod was willing to go and describe to the populous, "how they might enjoy the pleasures of sin, without any fear of the wrath of a holy God."[76] This seemed to be how the manipulation of the post-Flood public began, on a large scale, and, also, how Nimrod ended up so "black in heart." Let's see how it all was so twisted.

Invisible God... To Visible Idol

At first, as we know, Nimrod tried to help people establish a personal relationship with God. People could see the results of God's wrath, but could not see *Him*, per se'. This might have come to be a little confusing, to some. Many knew how the antediluvian generation used *idols* for their religious practices, and what their purpose was, here - but, it wasn't the same, in regards to worshipping God.

> *The... people taught by Nimrod, however, could not grasp the abstract concept of an invisible God... they were accustomed to worshiping gods of wood and stone, which represented the material things in their lives.*
> ("Babylonian Paganism Becomes Trinitarian Christianity", n. d., p. 1)[77]

It, then, became a little hard for many of the post-Flood world to shake this religious tradition. God wanted people to worship *Him* and *Him alone*, and not any type of idol. He also wanted them to trust in certain men - with Nimrod being one of them. If Nimrod's mind was becoming corrupt, this might be a way for him to seduce others to follow him, and these new ways.

Before, in his attempt to show how God *was* really out there, Nimrod tried to explain to the people how God was, actually, an intangible essence, and out of their reach. He said that the *sky* and *heavens* were the abodes of God, and the people just had to use *faith*, and accept that He was up there.[78] Many, still, had a hard time accepting this. They were just "too deep" into those old ways of the pre-Flood world. So, to begin to "compromise" things a bit:

> *The people subsequently erected statues to depict Nimrod's **godly** attributes so that they could **touch these images**...*
> ("Babylonian Paganism Becomes Trinitarian Christianity", n. d., p. 1)[79]

Wow, doesn't that sound a lot like certain "Christian" religions, today? People were supposed to accept that God is invisible, and intangible; yet, some churches still set up icons, to allow the people something to *touch*. The same thing, here. It was as though Nimrod was trying to fuse one's pagan past with their modern belief in God. Obviously, as we'll see, the two cannot be successfully mixed. One will bring down the other. Maybe that's what Nimrod may have even started to want, here. We can only guess. But, after Nimrod set up these images, they, eventually, ended up taking "center stage," and the concept of a truly invisible God fell by the wayside. Eventually,

People of the flood began to say God did not exist.
- Book of Jasher 6:19[80]

Which "God"?

*...in the kingdom of Nimrod, each worshiped of his own make... each after the imagination of his **own heart**.* - Writings of Abraham 23:3[81]

It was Nimrod's opportunity to further utilize his *pride*, and make the most out of the situation. The ancient Rabbi *Rashi*, for example, said that Nimrod, now, began to use this occasion to manipulate, or ensnare, people into the false worship of paganism, once again. This manipulation was, in great part, enhanced by the use of Adam's clothing:

*Nimrod used to entice people into idolatrous worship by means of those garments, which enabled him to conquer the world and proclaim himself its ruler, so that mankind offered **him** worship.*
("Nimrod: Man, Maniac or Myth", n. d., p. 13)[82]

Ultimately, people **only** began to look to these images - and these images, over time, were changed into images of *other* gods, of even Nimrod, *himself*. Ancestor worship, as we now see, was on the upswing, once again. Also, since the people could *see* Nimrod, and *see* what he was doing, that began to make him more viable, and more "god-like."

Throughout the known world, people worshiped images of Nimrod rather than the one true invisible God.
                ("Babylonian Paganism Becomes Trinitarian Christianity", n. d., p. 1)[83]

He, of course, began to agree with their choices, and accepted *himself* as a "god" they could worship![84] First, he allowed other gods, as well as him, to be introduced into their religious spectrum. Second, he made up his mind to *stamp out* the existence of anyone or anything who may end up being a competitor - a.k.a. the *God of Noah*. Pride will, indeed, do this to people!

These self-centered, pagan, as well as humanistic, ways of looking at our world took hold of his soul. *Self-worship* and self-adoration were, also, on the rise - and, not only in Nimrod's mind:

For in our world we have no God; but we all are gods; **we all are** *of the light, heavenly, powerful, strong and glorious…*
  - *Second Book of Adam and Eve (The Conflict of Adam and Eve with Satan)* 5:11[85]

Nimrod's "new" views of politics and religion were nothing but these "old" ways of pagan thinking.

Desertion = Babylon

…as translated in the Bible it only says "He was a mighty hunter before the Lord"… and the name Nimrod, being interpreted, means, **desertion**… *Moses calls the seat of Nimrod's kingdom Babylon, and the interpretation of the word Babylon is* **"change;"** *a thing* **nearly akin to desertion**, *the name, too, being akin to the name, and the one action to the other; for the first step of every deserter* **is a change and alteration of mind**…
        - *Works of Philo Judaeus* On the Giants 15(66)[86]

Some very powerful words from Philo, himself! We hear many people talking about "hope and change," today. The same went on, back then. This "change" - then, as well as today - really stood for a desertion of God's ways! That's the reality of it all.

Eventually, many people became heavily dependent on what Nimrod said and did - and welcomed these new ways of thinking! As this desertion of God occurs, the changes of one's cultural, political and religious ideology also occurs - and we *know* what direction it, almost always, goes to! That's why the sin *of wrong use* is, so often, mentioned in the Bible! There are things of our world that may not be, necessarily, wrong to admire, or to enjoy, but when they become elevated *higher* than God, then it becomes a problem. This, also, include people! The ancients began to worship things in their *own ways*, or direct their worship towards whatever, or whomever, they pleased - and Nimrod was *right there*, ready to support these ideologies! Why not?

…(the people)… becoming deserters so as to fly to the lifeless and immovable nature of the flesh… (and) Nimrod being the first to set the example of this desertion…
  - *Works of Philo Judaeus* On the Giants 15(65)[87]

According to the system which Nimrod was the grand instrument in introducing, men were led to believe that **a real spiritual change of heart** *was unnecessary, and that so far as change was needful, they could be regenerated by mere* **external means**.
  ("Nimrod - Babylonian - Musical Worship Teams", n. d., p. 21)[88]

Wow, this also sounds like some "Christian" churches we see, today! To reach God's salvation, some churches claim that one needs to follow a number of religious *rituals*, and, more or less, "go through the motions" of their faith, and they might make it! But, that's not how God originally wanted it - He wanted (and wants) a true *change of heart*, not rituals, not "going through the motions" of just attending church every Sunday, and just obeying the sacraments laid out before them.

But, once again, a "compromise" religion was being established. And, thanks to Cush and Nimrod, the populous was beginning to go after *the flesh* again, and beginning to go after *earthly* things again, just as they did before the Flood. They were looking to things of *the earth* (such as idols) for their "redemption" and "salvation." Now, instead of Nimrod acting as a mighty hunter *in front of*, or *before*, the Lord, he was becoming the hunter *against*, or *in defiance of*, the Lord![89] He, now, began to go - full-blown - down the pathway of Cush's darkened ideologies:

> *...he (Nimrod) was a giant against God... (and) unmitigated wickedness has no participation in light, but imitates night and darkness: and the practice of the huntsman is as much as possible at variance with rational nature, for he who lives among wild beasts wishes to live the life of a beast, and to be equal to the brutes in the vices of wickedness...*
>   - *Works of Philo Judaeus* Questions and Answers on Genesis II, 82[90]

He was even starting to act in savage, "beast-like" ways! Nimrod was now a *rebel* in God's eyes - and a hero, or *giant*, in everyone else's![91]

New Meanings for the "Tower"

A symbol of his new rebellion was about to be constructed. Most of those who know the Bible have probably heard of the "Tower of Babel." The concept of building something as "high and mighty" as a *tower* may have already been on Nimrod's mind - back when he was on the side of God. This brainchild may have brewed inside of Nimrod's mind, at least at first, as a noble undertaking:

> *If others were impacted by the flood and now were in fear of God, Nimrod can show that he too is God-fearing. If we take this logic one step further, we can posit that his **original** stated **intention** of the Tower was to build a shrine for the service of God.*
> ("Nimrod: Man, Maniac or Myth", n. d., p. 13)[92]

> *Nimrod said to people "Let us build four pillars on all four corners of the earth to **support the heavens**!"* (Glenn, 1929, p. 30)[93]

To, either, show glory to God, or even show his support for his God, up in the heavens, the erection of a huge tower could have, already, been undertaken. As Nimrod was becoming more and more corrupt, however, "the original pretext was forgotten, and the rebellious work had begun."[94] Instead of honoring God, the whole purpose of the Tower became misdirected. Now, it was considered *Nimrod's* mountain - something made for *his* own throne, and to be *his* sanctuary.[95] It seemed that Nimrod, also, wanted somewhere to be worshipped - somewhere way up in the *sky* (in the *heavens*), as well. The tower was to have a temple placed on top of it - devoted to Nimrod, his new way of religion and whatever other "gods" he deemed worthy of devotion.

Any tradition that may have claimed the people wanted his tower to "reach up to the heavens" may not, entirely, be referring to *height*, but, also, towards their attainment of this *heavenly* understanding. These people wanted to reach - and possess - a "god-like" status, the same as their new "gods" had already reached. The pagan ways of Cain and the Serpent were coming back - in full-force. Changes to the original purpose of the Tower were now taking place. All of it began to be a bit detrimental to the society, at large. Things were, assuredly, changing:

*The atmosphere of the tower causes **forgetfulness**.*
  - The Babylonian Talmud Sanhedrin 109a[96]

And as a result of this there arose forgetfulness, error, sinful undisciplined passions, and evil promiscuity among humankind within the world. And thus the world turned back again to its original state of disorderliness and became filled with evils as it had been in the beginning before the flood.   (Layton, 1995, p. 189)[97]

Also, To Rebuild a Famous City

Instead of making sure that the people followed God, and relocate to their appointed lands, the *opposite* was about to occur! Of course, that only seems **natural** - in those who take on these pagan ways! Nimrod took this noble effort of "father" Noah and turned it all "on its ear." Instead of encouraging people to settle in the areas God said that they should go, Nimrod began to "bring them all together" - to unify the whole world.[98] Nimrod, now, was having plans to travel abroad, and go to the lands Noah had already established, and bring them all back under his "umbrella" of influence. Through this, he was about to establish a massive political empire, and all under *him*.[99]

Beyond these altered plans for the tower, and before he could establish any empire, he had it in the works to rebuild a very famous *city*, as well - a city that existed well before the Flood. And, the original inhabitants of this city once *celebrated* the ways of Cain.

There was a reason why Cain, and people like him, seemed to *cleave* to this city, and all it symbolized:

*What is said of Nimrod?... For he drew power from **Bavel (Babylon)** that helped him to cling on to **the dominion of the Other Side**. It also reads, "they found a plain in the land of Shinar," meaning they filled their hearts with desire derived from Shinar, to leave the upper dominion and join a different power... the land of Shinar, which is Bavel, is **the head and root of severance** from the Holy One, Blessed by He (God).*
- *Zohar* Noach 42[100]

Nimrod was heading all the way to the top, and, now, strived to reestablish a *centralized* earth, not an earth all spread out. The location chosen as the center of all this corruption? Of course, it's the *exact* same place it was - *before* the Flood![101] We all know this city as none other than <u>Babylon</u> - "the head and root of severance from the Holy One."

Apparently, there were at least *seven* cities of Cain in the area, destroyed by the flood. And, all of these Nimrod felt he wanted to bring "back to life," in one degree or another.[102] The survivors of the Flood, once again, began to centralized themselves (and their false religion) in these lands, rebuilding on the same old foundations that were once there, before.[103]

Encouraged further by his father Cush, Nimrod urged the people to, not only construct the Tower of Babel, but rebuild this corrupt city - turning it all into an abode where people "could remain forever," and, where man could "rule the world" (without the power of God to dictate anything over them).[104] This is another element of *Mystery Babylon* revealed.

> *Therefore Nymbrotus (Nimrod)… marked out the city and laid the foundations of a very great tower… and built up the tower to the height and size of mountains, as a sign and monument to the fact that the Babylonian people **is first in the world** and it should be called the kingdom of kingdoms.*   - *Annius*[105]

The people were turning just as self-absorbed as their leader already did. The tower and city of Babylon, *once again*, became the "flagship" of human pomp and pride, as well as blasphemy against God!

The Third "Cain"

Nimrod and Cush would, then, begin to stand "on the shoulders" of their antediluvian ancestors. This, ultimately, allowed Nimrod to become the "third incarnation" of that "son" figure - originating back to the Garden of Eden. Of course, we know that was *Cain*! Along with Cush, as the third "father" figure of the post-Flood world, the people now had their "third incarnation" the "son." This seemed natural since Cush was his father.

And, since Cain established Babylon before the Flood, it was, now, turned into an integral part of *Nimrod's* agenda: to restore this ancient city to its original pagan splendor.[106] Nimrod was beginning to act like his famous ancestor in, oh, so many ways:

> *The later… (people) under Nimrod reinhabited the cites of Cain and adopted his language, his religion and his civilization… (They) built upon the ruins of a civilization that existed in Shinar before the Flood… (and) **glorified** their ancient cities by ascribing to them a foundation in the ages before the Flood…*
> (Tannehill, 1916, p. 86-87)[107]

The Opposite

Next, Cush and Nimrod were beginning to stir up the emotional passions of people, by convincing them that everything was all about *themselves*. They didn't need any God of Noah. It was all about *man*, and the feats of *mankind*. It was about their own self-actualization. They, then, began to convince the populous to be *upset* with God - that God of Noah - for one important reason: *He* was the one keeps trying to *keep them down*. *He* was the one who, really, wants to *enslaving* them. Humanity wants to be "free," to do whatever they want! *He* was also the one who wiped out their glorious, divine ancestors - the ones they, now, were beginning to worship, once again!

Their original *fear* of God was turning into thoughts of contempt, hate and *revenge*.

Hate and Revenge

The Tower of Babel, now, was going to be used for, yet, another purpose: not just to *unite* the people, but to enact *revenge* upon the God who wiped out so many of their ancestors.[108] This was humanism at its worst. Nothing was going to stop their own pathways to achieving deity-status!

The people, then, postulated: if this God ever had an idea to send down another Flood again, humanity, with their new tower, was ready for Him! The tower was now designed to be as tall as a mountain, and, quite probably, there were to be prophets and priests on top (inside the temple), to cast spells or perform feats magic - stopping this from ever happening to them, again. All of this was to bring them beyond the reach of any punishment that this "hateful" God could ever bring![109] Talk about insubordination. Talk about corrupted, "politically correct" ideals of the day.

Own Bricks

The rebellious people took on this huge task, and started to work hand over foot. They wanted to make sure their tower fulfilled their unity against God. In the process, they may have even wanted to have their own participation in the tower-building process for all to see - by having their *own* name inserted into the building itself!

> *And they said everyone to his neighbour: Let us take **bricks** (lit. stones), and let us, each one, **write our names** upon the bricks and burn them with fire: and that which is thoroughly burned shall be for mortar and brick.*   - Pseudo-Philo 6:2[110]

Talk about hatred. This way, their names, *forever*, could be inscribed into these bricks, and onto their hearts! It was their way of "cementing" their counter-beliefs against the one, true God. It was as if they were putting their full *faith* in the tower, and all that these ways of Nimrod could, seemingly, bring them! They wanted to show the entire world what they - as a *united* people - could do. Humanity could "touch the stars," if they put their *devotion* to it![111] Again, we see how individuals - by putting everything they have towards something *of the earth* - are doing just the opposite of what God wants for us, in our daily lives!

> *(Cush) in this case, having a nature truly dissolute, does not at all keep fast the spiritual bond of the soul - but like a giant born of the earth, prefers **earthly** to heavenly things...*   (Cates, 1998, p. 52)[112]

We may, again, have another association between Cush and the *earth*! As one who was considered "**earth**-born," he may have, assuredly, felt a "divine" connection to all that was of, or "sprung up" out of, the physical earth... including this massive tower of mud and brick.[113] *Worldly* achievements, such as this, were the real source of Cush's pride (and Nimrod's, as well).

Tales of Determination

Their work to achieve this newly-dedicated Tower would become, from then on, a drive of "mad folly."[114] There were a few humorous legends regarding the insatiable drive of these maddened people. Whether or not their stories had a grain of truth is questionable, but it does show the ruthless, almost unbelievable, determination of the tower-building people.

For one, the continual pressure of laying brick by brick became so overwhelmingly fanatical, many individuals ended up paying little regards to their own health and wellness. They considered each brick laid as one brick less - towards the achievement of their hateful goals against God![115] These bricks, and all of what they stood for, became symbolic of their end-result - very valuable:

*And behold these ascended and others descended the whole day; and if a brick should fall from their hands and get broken, they would all **weep** over it, and if a man **fell** and **died**, **none of them would look at him**.*   - *Book of Jasher* 9:28[116]

Another tradition tells us that: if a woman was *pregnant* while laying these bricks, she was barely granted any leave - even if she had to deliver a baby! If she began to be in labor, she was moved aside, coaxed into giving birth very quickly, and expected to go right back, into her brick-laying role![117]

Even to "Kill" God Himself!

Tradition also tells us that these determined individuals may have branched out into three groups, based upon their individual intent:

They split up into three parties.
- One said, 'Let us ascend and dwell there'...
- the second, 'Let us ascend and serve idols'...
- and the third said, 'Let us ascend and wage war [with God].'
       - *Babylonian Talmud* Sanhedrin 109a[118]

Their animosity towards God seemed so filled with hate, here, that it looked like some were wanting to reach up, into the sky (where God was), and overthrow Him! Others wanted to, not only be able to set their *own* idols up there, but also bring up *swords* - to symbolize their own vengeance. Still others felt this desire to fight the oppressive God, one on one.[119]

It got worse:

Nimrod (wanted)… to get into heaven and destroy God himself.
                                        (Emerson, 1916, p. 929)[120]

Yes, even Nimrod wanted to "kill" God, Himself. Talk about brainwashing. The harder they worked towards finishing this Tower, the more obsessed they became.[121] With a corrupted leader like Nimrod at the helm, the atmosphere, below, exploded into a downward spiral of moral decay and decadence. It boggles the mind how flagrant these people really were! One question that may come to mind at this time may be: how *could* these ancients become *so* arrogant towards God, now - in such a short period of time? It was only 100 years or so since the Flood. Many of them knew - or even *remembered* - that God was strong enough to destroy their entire former world - and *did* it! But, they didn't care. They still thought: *this time*, they would be victorious. Little, squeaky human beings against the Creator of the universe! Such is the power of the human mind.

We see that:

Nimrod… is definitely the first in the world of the pattern of the Anti-Christ and of the New World Order… he was supreme authority in all matters of spiritual and religious understanding, as well as maintaining his empire. He was going to rule the world; also going against the spoken Word of God, spoken by Noah…
                                        ("Nimrod: King of the World", n. d., p. 4)[122]

These "new" political and religious ideologies were, as we stated, nothing but the "old" politics and religious ideologies of Cain and the Serpent - revived again, after the Flood. So intense were these mind-sets that *the Bible* even gives us a frightening perception about what was going on:

*And the LORD said, Behold, the people is one, and they have all one language; and this they begin to do: and now **nothing** will be restrained from them, which they have imagined to do.*   - Gen. 11:6 (KJV)

The people, falling for all of what Cain, the Serpent and the pre-flood Nephilim could give them, now believed that there was nothing - practically *nothing* - on this earth that could have stopped them, and their quests! A scary thought, indeed. It, also, seems that a lot of this hidden, pagan knowledge (of the Nephilim) helped their construction of such a tower. We see more of the *Mystery* side of *Mystery Babylon* coming into play, once again!

God already promised those of the post-Flood world that He wouldn't destroy the earth again… with a flood. He, also, already blessed them, and hoped that their new society would work for the better (under Noah, Shem, and even Nimrod). But, now, the people under Cush, and now *Nimrod*, were dead-set on finishing the Tower, and on achieving their "vengeance" against the God who "wronged" them.

What was God to do?

Chapter 9

New Religion of the Madonna

He did it again! God did it again. The God of the pre-Flood Sethites, the God of Noah and his son Shem, would disrupt, yet, another attempt of humanity to "better themselves!" This was this same God who threw their worthy ancestors out of the Garden of Eden; the same God who destroyed most all of their ancestors, with a devastating flood. And now, as we'll see, He'll do it to them, once again!

As facetious as all of the above may sound, God *did* stop humanity from making another horrible mistake - from their going down *another* erroneous moral pathway (even though the people, at the time, may not have thought so)! Let's see how God accomplished His *latest* disruption of those with evil intentions.

As we've seen, in the last chapter, the people fanatically attempted to build a tower - a tower large enough to achieve their pride-filled, opposition goals. The ancient and well-respected historian *Josephus* did a good job in summarizing what might have happened next. He tells us that God took it upon Himself to, now, "set the stage" for the vast majority of people He wanted to disperse to *actually* disperse!

God... commanded them to send colonies abroad, for the thorough peopling of the earth, that they might not raise seditions among themselves, but might cultivate a great part of the earth, and enjoy its fruits after a plentiful manner...
- *Flavius Josephus* Antiquities of the Jews 1.4.1[1]

Interestingly, it seemed that God wanted them to do this for *their own good*. He wanted them to be *blessed* by what their post-Flood world might have to offer, and not just fight amongst themselves. All it would take, from them, would be a little bit of effort.

God didn't want them to *unite*, either, in this case, because He already knew human nature: it's easy for groups to dispute over territory and resources. Interestingly enough, this seemed to echo the very *reason* why God asked Noah to spread the people abroad, in the first place.

That "Dirty Little Secret"

Apparently, to "jump-start" the post-Flood reproductive process, and make sure the fragile human population would not succumb to any large famine or catastrophe since, a majority of early people sired *twins* (again), when it was time to give birth. Much of the same, as we know, occurred soon after Adam and Eve had left the Garden.[2] Again, it seems that God wanted to make sure His Genesis 3:15 Prophecy was fulfilled, and did not want anything to disrupt the reproduction process during these critical times. He also wanted people to be *blessed*, not stressed, to be bountiful, not over-burdened. Assuredly, the increased frequency of twin births, here, was only to be temporary (for the most part), because the majority of children, today, do not seem part of a twin.

The people of the past really seemed to answer the call, and did their part in the reproductive process - *and then some*! For whatever reason, the population was increasing - rapidly - probably at a much higher rate than God ever strived for. Possibly, due to their close proximity to one another, it was easier for them to begin to plant roots, and have families. Possibly, this was another reason God wanted them to spread out, some. There was plenty of earth to go around (at least for the time being). Yet, with people like Cush and Nimrod slowly fading to the "dark side," there may have begun to be a shift in overall perception - away from what Noah kept recommending to the people.

Also, there is a "dirty little secret" behind a lot of the poverty, sickness and war we are seeing, back then - and, not surprisingly, are *still* seeing, today! It is something we don't hear a lot of people talking about… at least in any ways that may help to slow it down, or reverse the trend, because it's not "politically correct." And, also, there are a number of individuals out there who may even want this trend to continue, because it's good for them, in some way. Yes, this "dirty little secret" is a *huge* problem within our society, a problem that occurs, again and again - with no resolution in sigh. This problem, of course, is *overpopulation*.

Regardless of how some people may try to *spin* this issue, today, overpopulation **was**, and **still is**, a major concern for our human race. We do hear about all of the hungry and starving people around us, but nothing about slowing down the birth rate. It's obvious, if anyone's hungry, that there's too many people *being born*. Why don't we hear such an outcry, today, about such issue? It seems that so many "tippy-toe" around this one.

Back then, the population of Babylonia (a.k.a. Shinar) and Egypt also exploded. Since people were, fairly, close together, the resources were being used up, fast. A few (as with today) might have even been hungry. God, again, wanted to make sure that human numbers would increase - but they **also** needed to spread out, into nations. He, obviously, didn't want the people to succumb to these negative side-effects, which makes it the major reason why people *needed* to redistribute, throughout the world, and get out of their "comfort zones."

But, thanks to Nimrod, the *opposite* was beginning to pan out:

> *…they were so ill instructed that they did not obey God; for which reason they fell into calamities, and were made sensible, by experience, of what sin they had been guilty: for when they flourished with a numerous youth, God admonished them again to send out colonies; but they,* **imagining the prosperity they enjoyed** *was not derived from the favor of God, but supposing that their own power was the proper cause of the plentiful condition they were in, did not obey him.*

- Flavius Josephus Antiquities of the Jews 1.4.3[3]

Again, this represents self-centered, human *pride* at its worst!

At least until the population became too overwhelming, everyone, for a time, lived, somewhat, comfortably. It helped them, living so close, one to another. They felt pretty safe, where they were. They didn't even care if these satisfactions were only temporary. It was easier to stay, and ignore **what's coming**. God was, no longer, messing around - people had to take action. They had to go. It has been said that Noah, also, threatened to curse any ancient patriarchs who took their clan to portions of the world "not assigned to him by lot!"[4] This dispersion was serious business.

Humanism, again, seemed to overtake this mandate, and come into the forefront of one's decision making process. Nimrod, now, had the people believing that God was actually a tyrant - trying to make them separate for reasons that just weren't true:

> *Nay, they added to this their disobedience to the Divine will, the* **suspicion** *that they were therefore ordered to send out separate colonies, that,* **being divided asunder***, they might the more* **easily be oppressed***.*
> *- Flavius Josephus* Antiquities of the Jews 1.4.3[5]

Wow, just the opposite! Nimrod was, actually, convincing the people that God only wanted to separate the people to *control* them, to destroy the strength they had through their "unity," and destroy their "freedom" - ultimately, destroying their "humanity." Wow, what a twist **on the truth**, this mind set of humanism provided!

> *Now the multitude were very ready to follow the determination of Nimrod, and to esteem it a* **piece of cowardice** *to submit to God...*
> *- Flavius Josephus* Antiquities of the Jews 1.4.3[6]

Again, *self-worship, self-adoration* and *humanism* were (now) the norm. The *pride* of the individual, and (especially) their leaders, were esteemed, and considered more important. Through this, however, Nimrod did achieve something:

> *He also gradually changed the **government into tyranny**, seeing **no other way** of turning men from the fear of God, but to bring them into **a constant dependence** on his power.*
>
> — *Flavius Josephus* Antiquities of the Jews 1.4.3[7]

Now, this quote is from Flavius Josephus - a very famous historian of the ancients! We are not just pulling things out of any old "hat," here. Nimrod was, now, beginning to stand in, here, as their governmental authority. Sound a little like what's beginning to go on, today? The modern-day parallels of these ancient Genesis accounts abound! It's also humorous to see how Nimrod went around, accusing God of being a tyrant, and saying that He was trying to control people, when it was, in fact, *he* who was turning into the controlling and domineering tyrant! So much of the same is going on, today.

It's, also, obvious that a collective form of "lethargy" may have had something to do with the lack of desire to spread out. Many could have been afraid that, if they had to separate from each other (and, from Nimrod's government), they would have to rely on *their own*, individual efforts. They would have to be self-reliant - and this, assuredly, would not have been what Nimrod wanted. He wanted the people part of some *socialized*, working order - all under *him*, of course. That's how human tyrants act. They need people to have the opposite feelings as one who's self-reliant, and need them without the desire to follow God. Nimrod wasn't God (although, he may have strived to be, here)!

Of course, Nimrod's "unity" concept sounds good on paper. It seemed easier for people to sit back, and put their trust in *Nimrod* (and what he could give them), rather than trust in an invisible God. After all, it was Nimrod who was visible. He promised everyone "hope and change," "peace and order" as well as "security and prosperity." Interesting… doesn't this sound a lot like what many political leaders (in government) tell us, today? "Just rely on *us*, and you'll do alright in life. It's, probably, too much for you to handle all the stresses in your life, on your own, so, allow *us* to control and regulate your existence. You'll be much happier." Didn't it sound like Nimrod was devising an early form of "socialism?" And, yes, the people were falling for it - hook, line and sinker!

Their Confusion Might Have Been Necessary

Their ancient society seemed to have become a *socialized*, collective effort - in what Nimrod's government told them, as well as in their *hatred of God*! With all of this disobedience, God could have, easily, made it a lot worse for these individuals. But, of course, He had compassion.

> *When God saw that they acted with so madly, he did not resolve to destroy them utterly, since they were not grown wiser by the destruction of the former sinners; but he caused a tumult among them, by producing in them diverse languages, and causing that, through the multitude of those languages, they should not be able to understand one another.* - *Flavius Josephus* Antiquities of the Jews 1.4.3[8]

As many of us know, God had to do something. And, the Tower, first and foremost, was considered their "pride and joy." So, God decided to do something to this Tower, in order to make His point. He, then, changed the languages of all the tower-builders, in order to halt the progress. Everything went awry, because no one could understand each other!

The place wherein they built the tower is now called Babylon, because of the confusion of that language which they readily understood before…
          - *Flavius Josephus* Antiquities of the Jews 1.4.3[9]

Interestingly enough, these new ways of life, under Nimrod, assuredly confused the people on what was truly right or wrong. Yet, they "knew" that they were **right** about one thing: how they should be building the tower. And, of course, it's so ironic that: when God came down, and *confused* their languages, it was **at** the very thing these people "understood" the most, and were the most *clear* about! Now, they had none of it.

It also seems that: their willful ignorance about right and wrong, now, was going to be addressed by God - if they liked being in that particular state of mind (confused about what's right), then they *really* are going to be confused! God, again, merits the perfect punishments! Now, nobody could understand each other. And, many of them felt they had to leave Shinar, and go somewhere, with those of their same tongues (just to make sense of their lives, now)! Funny, their decisions, now, seemed a lot like what God wanted for them, in the first place. Their bliss of willful ignorance was, at least, temporarily halted, their "unity" project was over - at least, for the time being.

Things were about to change for Cush and Nimrod, as well.

After the Tower

After this time of separation, Nimrod was not about to fall very far from *his* pinnacle of power. He still maintained a great deal of popularity. After all, he was the "fan-favorite," here. It didn't turn out as well for Cush, however. People were, naturally, quite angry at God, for what He did. And, the populous was not only mad at *Him*, but were also disheartened with Cush - the one who helped facilitate all this rebellion, in the first place! It's a lot like, today, a whole number of people being laid off of work, and blaming the union leader for "not doing more." The attitude of the entire populous, towards him, had changed… for the worse.

Cush and Nimrod were becoming very unpopular to a famous patriarchs of God, and His ways - namely, the son of Noah, *Shem*.

Shem, a father of many descendants, and a major patriarch in his own right (of the *Semites*), tried to stay clear of all this atrocity going on - at least, at first. He tried to coexist, somewhat. We recall, the Semites maintained, somewhat, of a "joint venture" over this kingship of Shinar. And, during the time that Nimrod was on the side of God, Nimrod, the *Hamites* and *Semites* all stifled the uprising of those troublesome Japhethites. Shem and the Sethites lived alongside Nimrod, and possibly, integrated with the people Nimrod was starting to have sway over. After Nimrod went off the theological "deep end," however, Shem could, no longer, have any part of it. A canyon of indifference developed between the two, and this "joint-venture" would, no longer, last.

Their polarized views - with Shem teaching the ways of God and Nimrod teaching was that were the exact opposite - would, eventually, prove devastating. Things would degenerate into downright hostility between Nimrod and Shem, especially.

All of the top patriarchs were extremely well-respected by people of their day, much the same way that *Noah* was. Whomever was "on top" commanded so much authority and respect from the people - that's just the way it was (and still is). Because of this, Shem took it upon *himself* to do something about Nimrod's atrocities, and try to reverse the whole wayward ship.

"Cat and Mouse"

What would occur, soon after the Tower's fall, would be a tremendous game of "cat and mouse," between the top Patriarchs: Shem and his son on one side, Cush and Nimrod on the other. Shem's drive was more than just a struggle for some throne - it was for the ways of God! This pagan upswing was so massive, thanks to Cush and Nimrod, that Shem felt the only way to topple this unstoppable force was to have both of them… dead.

Even though Cush and (mainly) Nimrod would retain total authority over the lands they were currently living in (at the time), their domination - thanks to Shem - was, at best, sporadic. Shem began to chase them, all over the civilized world, continually "knocking them out" as the top spot of authority, whenever he arrived. Cush and Nimrod would stay in Babylon, and, then, Shem would arrive. At least Nimrod would flee to Egypt, and rule there, for a bit. Shem, eventually, would go to Egypt, and they'd flee again, with Shem taking over there, next! It was "cat and mouse," and extremely deadly for all of those involved. Shem was playing for keeps.

All of these upheavals, in the ancients, assuredly, made it a very confusing time for anyone, today, trying to understand what history was all about, back then.

Saturn, Jupiter & Hercules

To complicate things even more, there seemed to be a number of ancient historians out there, writing about they saw at the time. They, often, reported their story in different languages, coming from different empires, and, each, from a different point of view. All of this could add to our confusion, all the more! There were no real rules of writing back then, no manuals of style, no ISBN numbers on their books. Sometimes, the line between absolute history and exaggerated mythology could have easily become blurred, making the task of wading through all of this historical muck all-the-more monumental.

On top of it, there wasn't really any kind of *protocol* to name these ancient patriarchs! Nowadays, we have a leader, a president, a king, etc. One would rule, and another would come to take his place. It seems a lot simpler today than back then. Back in Noah's day, for example, there wasn't a leader "A," who solely ruled, and then retired, only to pass everything on to leader "B." It was, quite often, top patriarchs battling amongst each other, trying to claim power! Sometimes, there was more than one leader attempting to lead at the same time. Succession was never easy. And, it would, often, involve some type of intimidation, bloodshed or death.

To make things worse, there could have been many different *titles* given out to these early dignitaries. *Edward VII*, for example, was probably the **prince** of England at one time. And, then, he became **king**. One author may have written about Edward VII when he was still a prince, and another after he became king! Still another may have written about Edward VII, not even giving him a title. They were all the same person, however - only written from different perspectives. This becomes another reason why our attempt to understanding this crucial era of history can be so confusing - so many different names, so many different cross-referenced titles that could, in actuality, have been referring to one particular individual!

Eventually, over time, a few ancient titles became, somewhat, of a standard (instead of "president," "king," etc.). These seem to pop up, all over these ancient legends and mythologies:

Saturn   - once considered the "father," leader, or "first" of some particular line (usually because he *was* a father, or leader, of a certain people, a nation, or an empire).

Jupiter   - usually considered a "son" of the (above) Saturn patriarch, or god (usually, again, because he actually *was* a son of the above Saturn).

Hercules   - usually considered a "grandson" of the above Saturn patriarch/god (usually, again, because he actually *was* a son of the above Jupiter patriarch/god, and grandson of the above Saturn patriarch/god).

A lot like today, power usually passed down through bloodlines - from father to son, from son to grandson, etc. So, as a consequence, many individuals were given titles such *these*. And, it also depended on how a historian portrayed a particular individual. We already know, for example, that Ham was considered "Saturn," the "hidden god," because he was *hidden* aboard the ark. But, *Noah* was considered "hidden" aboard the ark, as well. So, theoretically, they both could have been thought of as the "Saturn" god (which, in fact, they *were*)!

And, we'll soon see that, due to the circumstances, *Cush*, also, could have been considered a "Saturn," because he was the "first" to initiate this Tower-building project, and was a "father" of many people, in a whole number of ways. *Nimrod*, then, could have been considered "Jupiter," because he was the son of this Saturn (i.e. Cush). He could have even been considered "Hercules," because he was grandson of another Saturn (i.e. Ham), as well. And, he could have even been thought of as another "Saturn," as well, because he was "father," or founder, of the Babylonian empire. The possibilities seem endless, and so does the confusion! The one thing to remember, though, is this: although so many of these patriarchs could take on so many different titles, or names, they are, quite often, the same character - or are "incarnated" as these same characters of the Garden of Eden. Again, this was another reason why the deciphering just "who's who," here, has always been a little difficult.

On top of these above titles, there seemed to be even *more* titles handed down (such as "Belus" and "Ninus"), that followed along this same "father" and "son" pattern! Some historians even used a number of these titles, interchangeably. How confusing would it be to decipher just "who's who," when an ancient historian called an individual "Jupiter *Belus*?"

Again, all of it might sound a little difficult to understand, but it's not impossible to figure out. Along with these volumes, it took a few brave (contemporary) authors (such as Herman Hoeh, Mike Gascoigne, Ken Johnson, etc.) to do more research, as well, and bring everything into some level of understanding.

So, to simplify things (as much as possible), we'll take most of these ancient, mythological titles *out*, and insert their probable, Biblical equivalents *in*. This, assuredly, will help us unleash what's, most probably, the true story - a story not taught in most modern history books, that's for sure. It will also help us understand how the story of *Nimrod*, for example, is "the greatest story *never* told."

Another reason this post-Flood history is so garbled, and rarely explored, is that it tends to expose *Mystery Babylon* a great deal, which may end up *unappealing* to vast a number of individuals - those who, in actuality, *want* it that way. So, let's continue to unravel this all - a tightly-wound *web* of clouded, and often misinterpreted, historical information!

From Armenia - To the Limelight

Whatever was about to happen next will include the person of whom things *really* should have been about, for so much of this, already - *Noah*.

Noah's original "world tour," as we recall it, took place about 100 years after the Flood. It, eventually, ended, when he returned back, to the general area of where he first set out, and came down from the ark - *Armenia*.[10] Noah, then, began to dedicated more groups of colonists to other parts of the world, and go on a second tour.[11] It all came from the pre-ordained and organized manner inspired to him, by God:

And (God) hath made… all nations of men… to dwell on all the face of the earth… and hath determined… the bounds of their habitation.
 - *Acts* 17:26 (KJV)

The lands around ancient Armenia, while located close to the Black and Caspian Seas (in Asia), also bordered, somewhat, the land of Shinar (where Babylon was). These areas, now, were near to, or within, the countries now know as Turkey, Russia, Iraq, Iran, etc.

Noah began this second tour from his Armenian "home base," and, then, headed northward, up to the Caucasus Mountains (between these Black and Caspian Seas). After leaving a few colonists there, Noah went southbound, spreading into Shinar and Arabia (depositing colonists). From there, he and his clan headed into Africa. Eventually, father Noah left Africa, and moved northward, into what would be modern-day Spain. Ultimately, at the end of his migration, Noah ended up in what would, now, be the nation of *Italy*.[12] Noah finished this lengthy, sophomore tour around 2001 B.C., almost 260 years after he started![13]

Noah's stopping point was most important, here, in regards to our study of *Mystery Babylon*. Why here? What's so important about this land? Much more will be discussed on this topic, soon enough.

The Tower's Fall - the Untold Story

And, it would be less than a decade after Noah's initial "world-tour" that construction of the Tower of Babel had begun. This anti-God, "unity" movement of Nimrod and Cush was just coming out, in full force.[14] After the Tower's fall, however, there was a struggle, for authority over most of these people that Noah, initially, deposited into certain areas. This time frame for the Tower's dispersion was in the neighborhood of 2254 B.C.[15]

The first patriarch affected by the Tower's fall would, of course, be *Cush* (as we've mentioned). Although he was still considered a top figure in most everyone's mind, he was also disgraced - called "Chaos," or the father of "confusion." Interestingly enough, the word *chaos* could have even come from the name "Cush." Although he maintained *some* control over the people in Shinar and Babylon, it was loosely-held control, at best.

His weak influence and authority over Babylonia lasted, after the Tower's fall, for about 30 more years. Then, for some reason, he had to leave. Apparently, there was a power struggle going on, in this area, for quite some time.[16] We, also, recall that Shem and the Semites were after Cush and (especially) Nimrod, for their insolence.

Shem's son *Asshur* was, also, considered a "father" of many people, and was on the rise, politically. Legend has it that this Asshur could have driven Cush out of the area, around 2222 B.C.[17] Cush, then, may have ended up in Egypt (another stronghold area of this pagan, anti-God theology), where he could have, quickly, joined up with another person, very familiar to him: *Ham*. *Ham*, as we know, may have lived, predominately, in Egypt, during this whole time. Soon after Cush arrived, however, he usurped most of the authority that Ham may have already had over the people, and ruled Egypt. He was said to have ruled it for about 30 years, on his own.[18]

Asshur was beginning to stir things up in Shinar, however. His father Shem wasn't just sitting around, idle, either. Shem was taking action, in a different part of the world. While Asshur was attempting to dominate the area of Babylon, Shem, with some backing, began to migrate to another area of the world: *Europe*.

*The date of this migration into Europe from Mesopotamia and the Near East is placed at 2214 B.C. by German history... Shem or **Tuitsch** came into Europe with members of his family, as well as with certain of the sons of Japheth and two of the sons of Ham...*

(Hoeh, 1969, p. 12-13)[19]

In Europe, there began to be "an extensive settlement of farmers;" or loosely-organized farming communities throughout![20]

Nimrod, Again

Everything seemed to change, around the end of Cush's 60 year stint in Babel and Egypt. After the initial separation of tongues, Nimrod still maintained some control over Babylon, along with Cush. But, Nimrod and Cush both would, eventually, have to leave. We already know that Cush was chased out of there, and where he went. Something happened in approximately 2194 B.C., and *Nimrod* had to leave, as well. Apparently, the ancient *Medes* - the descendants of Noah's son *Japheth* - also had a part in driving

Nimrod out of the area.[21] For quite some time, there seemed to have been a struggle for this area, involving numerous participants.

Around 2192 B.C., Nimrod went to Egypt, as well, and, once again, began to overshadow his father's authority.[22] He ruled Egypt for about 30 years, "along with" his father, but, subtly, ousting Cush, slowly, in the process.[23] Cush, then, may have fled to the vicinity of Armenia. We're not quite sure.

Around 2167 B.C., things began to change, again! It, now, seemed that Nimrod was forced to leave Egypt, as well![24] Shem, the great Shem, was on the warpath; his scope - poised directly at catching up to him, and taking him out! Although Shem was in Europe for a little while, he may have felt the need to "clean up" the areas of Babylon and Egypt, once and for all - forcing them to change the corrupted ways they had turned to. Most notably, Shem's major goal would be to wipe out these corrupted leaders, once and for all. Shem traveled far and wide, to put down this authority of Cush and Nimrod.

When Shem finally arrived in Egypt, not only did he drive out Nimrod, he also drove out Cush's wife (whose name was Semiramis). There's a reason for this, of course. This woman would, soon, become another dominating *force* in these ancient of times, as well. So, let's take a quick look at the woman who would, in actuality, become Cush's wife, and mother of Nimrod - *Semiramis*!

The Rise of Semiramis

> *...tradition states that she was an inn/brothel keeper...*
> ("Semiramis, Queen of Babylon", n. d., p. 2)[25]

Who was this woman, and why would she become so important to our story of Babylon? She did seemed to have a "history," in ways (such as her beginnings, as a prostitute), but, the rest of her story was, for the most part, *obscured*! This gorgeous, golden-haired and blue-eyed wife of Cush probably began as one of Cush's harlot - one he decided, one day, to keep for his own.[26] Before the Tower's fall, she lived in the shadows of Cush's monarchy; but, eventually - after all of this *chaos* began, and Cush and Nimrod were moving from place to place - she ended up moving up the ladder of success. Eventually, she reached the *forefront* of ancient pagan power and fame. How could she have accomplished this?

> *Very little has come down to us through the millennia concerning Semiramis' rise to power, but it is safe to assume that initially upon Nimrod's coattails that she rode, although later in life as well as throughout history her influence overwhelmingly obscured that of her husband.* ("Semiramis, Queen of Babylon", n. d., p. 2)[27]

As Cush's power was diminishing, she did not want to go *down*, alongside of him. Nimrod was her son, and his popularity continually seemed to be on an upswing, regardless of the circumstances. What was she to do? The only thing that would *really* cement her place in stardom, amongst these leaders, was to do what so many of us would consider the unthinkable: she married *her own son*![28]

Yes, back then, this was one technique the ancients could have used, in order to maintain their control and popularity. She really "got around" in all of this, and in other ways, as well! For all practical purposes, she, soon, would totally abandon Cush. Her devotion, and passion, now lied solely with her new husband - Nimrod.

And, when Nimrod was, eventually, driven out of Egypt, she was forced to leave, as well.

One Catching Up to the Other

After Shem arrived in Egypt (in approximately 2167 B.C.), the mother-son duo of Semiramis and Nimrod could not *continually* rule the land – they, often, had to leave, when Shem was back in town..[29] For the next 30 years, one (or both) retained at least some degree of authority over the land, be that what it was And, the people of Egypt and Babylon still respected the two, a great deal. But, somewhere near the end of their 30-year "reign-from-*afar*," a monumental event occurred.

Change was in the air. Shem and his clan finally caught up with Nimrod, one day, and changed the world, forever. After all of those years, chasing him over hill and dale, Shem finally caught up with him, and *killed* him![30]

Yes, Shem killed him. God was definitely on Shem's side, here. Time for their sacrilege to take a downward turn.

When word got out about Nimrod's execution, many of those who followed Cush and Nimrod were completely devastated. Their "god-like" leader was dead. Was he even a "god," then… if he could be killed like this? What a blow to their ideology, and ancestor-based worship!

Because of this, certain people (in pagan lore) now gave Shem - righteous *Shem*, the son of Noah - a new (pagan) "title." Instead of Cush, they began to refer to *Shem* as a second "Belus" - a second "father" of Babylon.[31] He took over the land. This time, the new "father and son" duo would not be pagan Cush and Nimrod, but *God-fearing* Shem and his son *Asshur*. For a while, Shem felt a need to maintain a sense of responsibility over both lands (Babylon and Egypt) - trying to push everyone *back*, towards a God-centered way of life.

Semiramis' Zodiacal Plot

> *…in the height of his power, Nimrod died. It was a violent death, shrouded in mystery. Semiramis, pregnant from an adulterous relationship and **desperate** to keep her position, **devised a scheme**.*
> ("Nimrod and Babylon: The Birth of Idolatry", n. d., p. 2)[32]

Semiramis, while on the run, was looking for any way to take full advantage of this situation. And, she had an idea. A little background on what she was about to do, here: tradition tells us that, in actuality, the stars above (the *Zodiac*, the *Constellations*, etc.) contain the entire story of the Genesis 3:15 Prophecy! Believe it or not. We have the "virgin;" we have a "crushing of the Serpent's head." We have an "Eve" character. We have an "Adam" character. It all seems to be there - divinely "written in the stars."

Beyond Shem, there were a few other men out there, over time, trying to teach the ways of God to the people. Among the most famous ones, we have: *Enoch* (before the Flood) and *Noah* (after the Flood). They may have even taught the use of the stars, here. Yet, this knowledge was corrupted, over time, by these antediluvian angels - probably because they were teaching everyone *more* than God wanted anyone to, here! As a result, the stars became "adulterated," the Zodiac was now impractical - in God's eyes. It was now considered "damaged goods," and ruined… with God outlawing its understanding, and use, by His people. But, pagans, however, still found this forbidden knowledge appealing and important, and *Semiramis* was about to use it all - to her own advantage!

We already know how much the stars were related to the Genesis 3:15 Prophecy. The people could see evidence of this future, "in the stars." Semiramis, now, jumped on the bandwagon - and provided her *own*, twisted interpretation to it all! A lot of pagans took the bait.

She, then, began to use *Nimrod's* death as a way to "reinterpret" it all … and inserted *herself* as another important element to the entire situation, as well!

> *Taking **advantage of the prophecy written in the sky** with which the remaining inhabitants of Babylon were familiar, Semiramis **covered up the details** of Nimrod's death and publicly proclaimed that:*
> - *Nimrod's death was **voluntary** and **self-sacrificial** for the benefit of the world.*
> - *She was a **virgin**.*
> - *Nimrod would **rise again**…*
> - *Nimrod "visited her in a flash of light and the **baby was the reincarnated Nimrod**".*
> - *Nimrod's rising in the form of her son was the **fulfillment of the ancient prophecy** (Gen. 3:15).*
>   ("Nimrod and Babylon: The Birth of Idolatry", n. d., p. 2)[33]

In other words, Semiramis took Noah's words, and *twisted* them all around - to her *own* benefit! She began to claim that she was with "no man" - just as a *virgin* - when the spirit of *Nimrod* came into her, and *impregnated* her! This allowed him to be "born again" - into another human body!

Doesn't this all sound familiar... maybe, 2000 years early?

As we already know, the former religion of Cush and Nimrod pushed idolatry, as well as a humanistic form of self-worship, the worship of the *sun*, the worship of the *Serpent*, the worship of ancestors, etc. Some of their practices may have even involved human (i.e. infant) sacrifice, among other atrocious deeds! So much of it began to look harsh and cruel, especially to those who actually wanted to follow God. Because Shem, and others, kept overpowering them, Semiramis felt that she had to do something - to change the momentum. She decided to "sanitize" their faith of old, a bit. Maybe the momentum of persecution might slow down a little bit, if people began to perceive their faith a little differently, here! She, eventually, began to accomplished this - by *combining* the two belief systems (in some ways) This *twisting* of Zodiac, and the Genesis 3:15 Prophecy, was only the beginning.

Semiramis needed to make her pagan beliefs seem less and less distasteful to Shem, and all of those on his side. "You shouldn't persecute those who are, basically, on a similar side as you are, *overall*." This manipulation began to work - slowly but *surely*.

> *Semiramis was the instigator in forming the **false religion** aimed at supporting their rule, and of course her suggestion fell upon open ears. The religion she **invented** was based primarily upon a **corruption of the primeval astronomy formulated by Noah's** righteous ancestors before the flood... the promise of **One to come who would suffer** and **die to relieve man from the curse of sin**...*
> ("Semiramis, Queen of Babylon", n. d., p. 2)[34]

We recall, a number of pagans, before the Flood, were actually starting to believe that *Cain*, and his seed line, was the fulfillment of the Genesis 3:15 Prophecy. The ancient post-Flood Greeks, as we also recall, thought the prophecy was fulfilled at the time of the Flood. We, now, have another pagan "reinterpretation," here. This would help to usher in another, "softer" version of their former pagan powerhouse. It would, now, even contain some *hybrid* elements - elements, of which almost everyone (on both sides) could utilize! Maybe Shem, and those alongside him, would "soften up" a little bit, if it didn't appear as pagan! Maybe, if it looked a little more Godly…

It worked. That's exactly was what happened!

Eventually, this allowed her to be elevated, once again, to fulfill the "top spot" (on her pagan stage). What if she was right? It *was* written in the stars. What if she was, actually, the *mother* (or "Madonna") of this "savior in the stars." If she actually was, and her baby was this "reincarnated" Nimrod, she, surely, was destined to become a huge part of this newly-twisted, compromised pagan religion. The end-result of her "redefining" her old pagan ways would, still, not head one back, towards God, again.

> *…a **child**… one day born of a divine mother… would **supplant God**, become a god himself, and return rulership of the Earth to the serpent.*
> ("Semiramis, Queen of Babylon", n. d., p. 2)[35]

This child - their "savior" - would, now, become their main object of worship… not the God who set this all up! Of course, it's that typical pagan twist. Now, Nimrod's embarrassing death could even been considered "justified" - into one of *martyrdom*. It was, now, all for a good *purpose*:

> *In life [Nimrod] had been honored as a hero; in death she will have him worshiped as a god...* ("Mystery of Civilization", n. d., p. 10)[36]

Nimrod as the "savior," here? Semiramis, as the "Madonna?" This "Madonna," as a *virgin* - bore a child "by the spirit"? Doesn't this all sound familiar? Yes, Semiramis hijacked the **absolute** end-result of the Genesis 3:15 Prophecy… 2000 years early! She claimed her "miracle child" was the "paganized" version of what would be <u>Jesus Christ</u>!

After this, images of her - and her "miracle" child - began to pop up everywhere:

Again, doesn't this look familiar? The Virgin Mary and baby Jesus? A number of Christian images, today, look a lot like this ancient woodcut carving. The question that might come into one's mind, now, is: what percentage of Christianity, today, may have some elemental *roots* in this early "reinterpretation" of paganism?

As we'll see, this would only be the *beginning* of pagan infusions into, what were then, the true *ways of God*! A major problem, indeed!

"Thrice-Great" Semiramis

And, of course, if Cush and Nimrod were considered the "reconstituted" pagan gods of before, it only made sense for everyone to elevate *Semiramis* to the third "incarnation" of *Eve*. And, that's exactly what she was elevated to! She was given "thrice great" status, or, the "thrice-born" incarnation of the goddess!

It all seemed to fit: Semiramis, naturally, seemed the perfect candidate for any "mother" figure (or Madonna), here - because she was the *wife* of Cush, and mother of Nimrod. And, now, she became the mother of this "miracle" child (by the so-called "virgin" birth), the mother of the "savior" (who fulfilled the Genesis 3:15 Prophecy), and the mother of another Nimrod - Nimrod, once again… "reborn!"

All of the other deities who were considered the "incarnation" Eve, such as the goddess *Ishtar* and *Athena*, for example, also were equated to Semiramis.[37] And, through this, Semiramis was able to turn the religion of Cush and Nimrod into somewhat of a "smoke and mirror" religion: *some* elements "on the surface" appeared good and worthy (maybe even *Godly*), while other elements, a little "deeper in," began to look like their original paganism, again. Often, the unsavory elements of their religion were hidden to the population. One, now, had to be wade through the "smoke and mirrors," and go deeper into it all, to find the real truth! And, *that's* why (and how) we see so many religions, today, sounding somewhat similar to one another! The pagan religion of Cain and the Serpent is still there - just "clouded" a bit, to slow people from being able to point out the true differences, between the two. You can't persecute what you can't find!

This, also, began to complicate matters for any (and all) of those wanting to follow what Noah and Shem preached… to the letter. Semiramis had done it! She, at least, confused enough people to stop the train of persecution! Many began to see her "new" take on the religion as something "close enough" (to their own), ultimately wearing down their convictions! The tides were, surely, beginning to change – Semiramis' favor.

The "Beginning of Civilization"

This one tarnished woman then, had such a lasting impact upon world history that… we call by her name the land from which civilization flowed…
           ("Semiramis, Queen of Babylon", n. d., 2)[38]

Something else may have *really* been going on, "behind the scenes," around this same time, however - something extraordinary. Semiramis, through her deception, was able to escape Shem's onslaught, and return to Egypt. As we could assume, Semiramis, probably, wasn't as "virgin-like" as she made herself out to be.[39] The *opposite* was more likely the truth. One tradition stated that she may have even gotten pregnant, at this time, by Shem's own son... *Asshur*! Wait. How could this happen?

Of course, as beautiful she was, it was easy for practically anyone to fall for her. And, we also know that Asshur and Nimrod may have battled for the throne of Babylon and Egypt. Asshur, most likely, may have encountered Semiramis, while coming to these lands. Now, with Nimrod gone, it's likely that Semiramis could have done whatever she had to, in order to stay in power! If this means "sleeping with the enemy," then so *be it*. Maybe Asshur caught up with her, and threatened her. Maybe, that was her way of "buying him off." We're not sure. We do understand that things like this may have happened, in those days (just like today)!

Regardless of who she may have *actually* slept with (even if it was the "enemy"), Semiramis, still, claimed that her *miracle child* had no father. She, assuredly, wouldn't want her pagan constituents to know that *Asshur* was the father - that's for sure. So, why not claim that she was a "virgin," here, regarding this birth?

And, soon after, in approximately 2137 B.C., Semiramis reestablished her rule, once again, in Egypt, bringing her little son with her. She ruled the area, until the child was old enough to rule on his own.[40] For a total of 42 years, Semiramis held some control over both lands.[41] And, around the year 2125 B.C., Semiramis first began to allow her "miracle" child, *Horus*, to begin his quest for power. Their rule, together, lasted in Egypt for over 31 years.

Shem, in the meanwhile, may not have known what happened between her and Asshur (if anything), and charged him with retaining the lands of Babylon (for their cause) - while he, himself, would return to Europe. Asshur (also known as *Ninus II*) did, in a little over 17 years, go on to conquer the entire the Middle East.

But, there would be, yet, *another* event, occurring in the neighborhood of 2094 B.C. (a couple of years after Asshur conquered the Middle East), which would affect the entire area of Babylon. As one author put it, the whole area just "died." Was it a drought? Was it famine? No one knows for sure. For whatever reason, here, Asshur and a number of people began to leave the area. Whatever happened here, Asshur felt the need to go to the area where his father was - Europe. A lot of Asshur's people headed north-westward, as well, towards this same continent.

To top it all off, around the same time, another ruler was about to take action. *Horus*, that so-called "miracle child," decided to leave Egypt (leaving Semiramis in charge), and head over to Babylonia, reclaiming Babylon as his own. Horus must have felt the desire to do a little *chasing* of his own. And, after regaining what was left of Babylon, he took after Shem and Asshur, up into Europe! He ended up taking over much of the known European continent, as well. No more would Europe be the place of simple, God-fearing people, living in simple farming communities. Now, a hoard of individuals were moving into the lands, setting up *civilizations* inside the European continent!

Some authors actually place this drive by Horus as an actual "starting point" of, what many call, *Western civilization*.

> *Why does the history of Western Europe begin with the Romans? Eastern Asia's history begins with the Chinese over 22 centuries before the birth of Christ. Africa's history commenced along the Nile equally early… Irish history reaches into the dim past to within three centuries after the Flood. Why should the history of continental Western Europe be so different? Was Europe **really uninhabited all this time**?*
> (Hoeh, 1967, p. 211)[42]

"Passing the Gavel"

Time had passed, with all of the "back and forth" - the fighting between the two religious power-houses - still going on. And, around the year 2037 B.C., Shem found himself needing to head back into Egypt, and "clean it up," once again. This time, he really did a number on the empire, actually remaining in the land, and *ruling* for a decade, or so.

Around the year 2019 B.C., it was becoming apparent that *Noah*, in his Italian abode, was becoming a little ill. Shem had to leave Egypt, once again, and take over the responsibilities his father had, here, in this land. Noah would die a year later, surviving a full 350 years after the flood.

What was so special about this Italian peninsula - the one that Noah retired on, and the area Shem felt he needed to go back, and protect, still? *Italy* just seemed to have been a power-house of the day - in a *spiritual* way. But, why? Both Shem and Noah must have, also, felt strongly about keeping law and order, here, a lot more than all the other areas. There must have been something to it all.

Let's go back, and take a little look at the history of the Italian peninsula, and discover *why*.

God of Noah vs. Gods of Paganism

Gomer, a son of Japheth, was originally given dominion over this land, from the earliest of times, to the year 2120 B.C. It seemed that, in this year, Gomer passed away, and he left authority over it all to his son. At this *same* crucial juncture, however, *Ham* left his current outpost in Egypt, and began to settle in same, general area, as well!

Ham quickly began to usurp a lot of the authority that Gomer's son inherited. Many colonists began to have a change of heart - for the worse. Gomer's son did not seem to be powerful enough to maintain authority, here. *Ham*, on the other hand, continued to have a *huge* impact on Italy, corrupting the people on so many levels. Even Noah noticed the change. They were turning away from Noah's teaching, left and right. A *new* war was going on in Italy - not a physical war, but a "war" of religious dogma.

> *There is a very special reason why* **Italy** *originally became the home of* **religious apostasy** *in the West... The pagan mystery religions had a very special problem confronting them in Italy - they had to counter the* **teachings of Noah!**
> (Hoeh, 1969, p. 97)[43]

Once the spiritual stronghold of God's teachings, Italy was, now, heading in the direction of paganism, as well. Shem felt the need to stop this. Shem probably figured: if they lost Italy, they lost their *foundation*. The rest of the world, then, would probably begin, in some way, to follow along this same pathway. The "old" pagan religion, and the "new" pagan religion (of Semiramis), in combination, were beginning to work.

Italy - The "Capital" of Conflicting Ideologies

Before he died, Noah made the decision to "step up," and confront Ham. Eventually, Noah was able to oust him to the southern island of Sicily. Noah still continued to have a loose network of religious dominance over the mainland, but he was getting old. His power was waning. The respect and authority he once commanded was slowly being compromised, here - brick by brick, and stone by stone. Ham, and all of those who began to follow him, were patiently waiting. They knew Noah wasn't going to live forever.

Upon Noah's death, their plight had become so much easier! All they had to do, next, was to make a *god* out of Noah - something they did with many *other* Biblical patriarchs before them. Their goal was, again, to get everyone to worship *Noah*, and *other* gods of their own design - and *not* God!

> *Nearly everyone has heard of the ancient pagan Greek and Roman gods and goddesses. But almost no one knows that they were originally great* **rulers of Italy***... It was the vogue of the last century to ridicule the myths of Rome and of Greece. The*

> *gods and goddesses were regarded as mere human inventions - regiments of the superstitious madness of the ancients. To admit that they were originally flesh-and-blood human beings would have been tantamount to admitting the **reality of the Bible**. For several of the heroes-made-god of ancient Italy are characters of the **Bible**.*
> (Hoeh, 1969, p. 97)[44]

Of course, the ancients may have known where these gods *really* came from. But, for the sake of obscurity, prominent pagans, many years ago, decided that this all had to change. The funny part is: they had to *assure* that the obscurity of these gods continued for a reason - to defeat the up-and-coming rise in **Christianity**! Yes, almost two thousand years ago, Christianity, as most of us know, was on a *huge* upswing. So many things about our past, once considered "common knowledge," had to be brushed under the carpet… this, they figured, would help to slow the upswing, over time. It's also funny that: the rise of Christianity, itself, was - of course - due to Jesus Christ… the *actual* savior, and true fulfillment of the Genesis 3:15 Prophecy! It's so interesting how this actually interrelates.

Also, in these early times of Noah, we know that the true ways of God were being diluted (due to Semiramis) Now, *mixing* the ways of God, somewhat, with their ancient, pagan dogma was beginning to take place. The more they were successful at combining and corrupting the two, here, the *darker* things seemed to have become. This whole process can be compared to one combining a pure cup of water with a very-dark cup of *ink*. When you add the two together, we notice that the water doesn't stay pure, or even head in that direction - it becomes *darker* and *darker*. The same for the two ideologies.

Noah and Shem both knew this - and that's, probably, why they tried to do everything they could to, at least, keep **one** area of our world clean and pure! When Shem eventually entered the area, he tried to keep Noah's theological dominance in the region; but *he* was getting old, as well. Giving the trend, here, the true ways of God were being overshadowed - it was only a matter of time, present course.

But, God has a plan. It was around this same time that the patriarch ***Abraham*** walked the earth. God was getting ready to take His fight to another area, and another descendant of Noah. Although most of the rest of the world was beginning to go dark, God was about to bring forth a new nation - a nation of *light* - from Abraham's seed. This nation would become a nation He could call his own: *Israel*. Of course, those on the "other side" would know of God's plan, and, once again, would try to introduce their *own*, corrupt version of Israel into the mix - once again, to dilute and thwart *this* process (as we'll see).

But, until then, the current struggle for the soul of Italy was still waging - seemingly, the *last* stronghold of God's ways, here. What would happen next, and what would this all have to do with our expose' of *Mystery Babylon*?

Coming up, we'll see how *another* Biblical character had to make his debut. This famous *hunter* was, in fact, extremely close to the patriarch *Jacob* - father of those twelve tribes of Israel! Do we sense a little bit of corruption **brewing**? But, *why* bring this particular human being into our Babylonian puzzle, and what might this patriarch have to do with this ongoing struggle we have, here, in *Italy*?

We'll soon see, in Part 2.

"Myth"... or No?

These "cat and mouse" games would *still* continue on, between famous patriarchs and their descendants, far beyond the scope of this volume. The world is pretty big, with many stories, or "myths," rising to the surface of antiquity, as a result: from the god *Osiris* being cut into 14 pieces, to the god *Hercules* having to travel all around the world (killing as many giants as he could), to *Abraham* finding himself being tossed into a fiery furnace - by a ruler of Babylon, calling himself "Nimrod." They, all, seem to be "offshoots" of our main story, here. And, if we spent enough time to research it all, we could probably find many correlations.

A question remains: were these stories just "myths;" or could many of them have, at least, *some* grain of ("glamorized") truth to them? Could so many of them ride on the coattails of our main account, here? And, could there have been *reasons* why certain individuals ("in the know") have twisted these stories into sounding a little more obscured, or turning them into what they are, now, called today: *myths*?

> *...the only reason for ever inventing **myth** is to **hide, obscure or pervert** some evidence or truth.* (Hoeh, 1967, p. 210)[45]

Maybe, there *was* a lot more to these ancient "myths" than what this contemporary designation now labels them. Maybe, a lot of the "smoke and mirrors" - seemingly surrounding a lot of this, making it harder for one to understand - wasn't placed there by **accident**:

> *One of Satan's clever artifices is manifest in the form of **corrupted history**! This diabolical plot to make God and His Word appear **untrue** has <u>deceived the whole world</u>.* (Hoeh, 1967, p. 177)[46]

They have worked very hard, to take out these ways of God, over time.

And, if we *really* believe that there could be something beyond our world - as well as forces out there, working *against* our discovering the truths of this world - then it's possible, quite possible, that there could be much more of a *rhyme* to this all than we may have ever *reasoned*… which adds more and more to the *mystery* of what would be *Mystery Babylon*.

- End of Part 1 -

Endnotes

Preface
1. *The Chronography of George Synkellos* (Oxford, England: Oxford University Press, 2002), 12.

Chapter 1
1. Eusebius: *Chronicle*, 2, http://www.attalus.org/translate/eusebius.html (accessed May 5, 2011); Alexander Hislop, *The Two Babylons or the Papal Worship: Proved to be the Worship of Nimrod and His Wife* (Neptune, New Jersey: Loizeaux Brothers, 1916), 12; Mrs. Sydney Bristowe, *Sargon the Magnificent* (London: The Covenant Publishing Co., 1927), 103; Mrs. Sydney Bristowe, *Sargon the Magnificent* (London: The Covenant Publishing Co., 1927), 39.
2. Donald Mackenzie, *Myths of Babylonia and Assyria* (1915), 1.
3. *Nimrod: King of the World*, 1, http://www.iwc.net/~levi/nimrod.htm (accessed June 2, 2000).
4. *Ancient Near East (Babylonia) Glossary and Texts*, 4, http://www.piney.com/BabGloss.html (accessed June 21, 2013).
5. American Scientific Affiliation: Creation/Evolution Page, *In Search of the Historical Adam: Part 2*, 8, http://www.asa3.org/ASA/PSCF/1994/PSCF3-94Fischer.html (accessed April 12, 2005); Mrs. Sydney Bristowe, *Sargon the Magnificent* (London: The Covenant Publishing Co., 1927), 19.
6. Mrs. Sydney Bristowe, *Sargon the Magnificent* (London: The Covenant Publishing Co., 1927), 19.
7. A. H. Sayce, *The Races of the Old Testament* (London: The Religious Tract Society, 1891), 141; *Ancient Near East (Babylonia) Glossary and Texts*, 5, http://www.piney.com/BabGloss.html (accessed June 21, 2013).
8. Theophilus G. Pinches, *The Old Testament: In The Light of The Historical Records and Legends of Assyria and Babylonia* (Brighton: Society For Promoting Christian Knowledge, 1903), 125; Donald Mackenzie, *Myths of Babylonia and Assyria* (1915), 12; Donald Mackenzie, *Myths of Babylonia and Assyria* (1915), 13; A. H. Sayce, *The Races of the Old Testament* (London: The Religious Tract Society, 1891), 141; *Nimrod: King of the World*, 1, http://www.iwc.net/~levi/nimrod.htm (accessed June 2, 2000).
9. *Adam, the Flood & The Tower of Babel*, 1, http://www.biblehistory.net/newsletter/tower_of_babel.htm (accessed May 10, 2011).
10. Donald Mackenzie, *Myths of Babylonia and Assyria*, (1915), 2.
11. *Ancient Near East (Babylonia) Glossary and Texts*, 20, http://www.piney.com/BabGloss.html (accessed June 21, 2013); Drusilla Dunjee Houston, *Wonderful Ethiopians of the Ancient Cushite Empire* (1926), 160; *Ancient Near East (Babylonia) Glossary and Texts*, 49, http://www.piney.com/BabGloss.html (accessed June 21, 2013); Theophilus G. Pinches, *The Old Testament: In The Light of The Historical Records and Legends of Assyria and Babylonia* (Brighton: Society For Promoting Christian Knowledge, 1903), 124; *Ancient Near East (Babylonia) Glossary and Texts*, 9, http://www.piney.com/BabGloss.html (accessed June 21, 2013).
12. American Scientific Affiliation: Creation/Evolution Page, *In Search of the Historical Adam: Part 2*, 1, http://www.asa3.org/ASA/PSCF/1994/PSCF3-94Fischer.html (accessed April 12, 2005); E. S. G. Bristowe, *Cain - An Argument* (Leicester: Edgar Backus, 1950), 14, 24.
13. American Scientific Affiliation: Creation/Evolution Page, *In Search of the Historical Adam: Part 2*, 1, http://www.asa3.org/ASA/PSCF/1994/PSCF3-94Fischer.html (accessed April 12, 2005).
14. American Scientific Affiliation: Creation/Evolution Page, *In Search of the Historical Adam: Part 2*, 1, http://www.asa3.org/ASA/PSCF/1994/PSCF3-94Fischer.html (accessed April 12, 2005).
15. Drusilla Dunjee Houston, *Wonderful Ethiopians of the Ancient Cushite Empire* (1926), 80.
16. Robert Bowie Johnson, Jr., *The Parthenon Code: Mankind's History in Marble* (Annapolis, Maryland: Solving Light Books, 2004), 26.
17. Mrs. Sydney Bristowe, *Sargon the Magnificent* (London: The Covenant Publishing Co., 1927), 20.
18. Mrs. Sydney Bristowe, *Sargon the Magnificent* (London: The Covenant Publishing Co., 1927), 49.
19. Mrs. Sydney Bristowe, *Sargon the Magnificent* (London: The Covenant Publishing Co., 1927), 14.
20. Robert Bowie Johnson, Jr., *The Parthenon Code: Mankind's History in Marble* (Annapolis, Maryland: Solving Light Books, 2004), 7.
21. Philip Gardiner, *Secrets of the Serpent: in Search of the Secret Past* (Foresthill Ca.: Reality press, 2006), 10.
22. *The Babylonian Legends of the Creation and the Fight Between Bel and the Dragon As Told by Assyrian Tablets from Nineveh* (London: Harrison & Sons, 1931), 31.
23. Bertrand L. Comparet, *What Happened to Cain*, 24, http://www.posse-comitatus.org/Bible_Studies/what_happened_to_cain.htm (accessed Aug. 21, 2000).
24. Bertrand L. Comparet, *What Happened to Cain*, 24, http://www.posse-comitatus.org/Bible_Studies/what_happened_to_cain.htm (accessed Aug. 21, 2000).
25. Robert Bowie Johnson, Jr., *The Parthenon Code: Mankind's History in Marble* (Annapolis, Maryland: Solving Light Books, 2004), 9.

[26] Robert Bowie Johnson, Jr., *The Parthenon Code: Mankind's History in Marble* (Annapolis, Maryland: Solving Light Books, 2004), 26.
[27] Robert Bowie Johnson, Jr., *The Parthenon Code: Mankind's History in Marble* (Annapolis, Maryland: Solving Light Books, 2004), 258.
[28] *Ancient Near East (Babylonia) Glossary and Texts*, 35, http://www.piney.com/BabGloss.html (accessed June 21, 2013).
[29] George Smith, *The Chaldean Account of the Deluge* (Transactions of the Society of Biblical Archaeology 2 [1873]), 213-234.
[30] Donald Mackenzie, *Myths of Babylonia and Assyria* (1915), 28.
[31] G. H. Pember, M. A., *Earth's Earliest Ages and their Connection With Modern Spiritualism, Theosophy, and Buddhism* (Grand Rapids, Michigan: Kregel Publications, 1975), 27.
[32] Albert T. Clay, *The Origin of Biblical Traditions: Hebrew Legends in Babylonia and Israel* (New Haven: Yale University Press), 91-92.
[33] G. H. Pember, M. A., *Earth's Earliest Ages and their Connection With Modern Spiritualism, Theosophy, and Buddhism* (Grand Rapids, Michigan: Kregel Publications, 1975), 27; Albert T. Clay, *The Origin of Biblical Traditions: Hebrew Legends in Babylonia and Israel* (New Haven: Yale University Press,), 70, 216; Alfred Jeremias, *The Old Testament in the Light of the Ancient East Vol. I* (New York: G. P. Putnam's Sons, 1911), 5.
[34] *Ancient Near East (Babylonia) Glossary and Texts*, 2, http://www.piney.com/BabGloss.html (accessed June 21, 2013).
[35] *The difference between Hades, Shoel, TarTarum, Hell?*, 1, http://answers.yahoo.com/question/index?qid=20081125101656AAL4zku (accessed Aug. 12, 2013).
[36] Stephen Charles Bandy, *Caines Cynn: A Study of Beuwolf and the Legends of Cain* (Stephen Charles Bandy, 1967), 47.
[37] Stephen Charles Bandy, *Caines Cynn: A Study of Beuwolf and the Legends of Cain* (Stephen Charles Bandy, 1967), 44.
[38] *The difference between Hades, Shoel, TarTarum, Hell?*, 1, http://answers.yahoo.com/question/index?qid=20081125101656AAL4zku (accessed Aug. 12, 2013).
[39] Stephen Charles Bandy, *Caines Cynn: A Study of Beuwolf and the Legends of Cain* (Stephen Charles Bandy, 1967), 45.
[40] Anonymous, *New Interpretation of a Portion of the Third Chapter of Genesis, Viewed in Connection With Other Parts of the Bible; Including an Inquiry Into the Introduction, Nature, and Extent of Satanic Influence in the World* (London, J. Hatchard and Son, 1834), 73.
[41] Stephen Charles Bandy, *Caines Cynn: A Study of Beuwolf and the Legends of Cain* (Stephen Charles Bandy, 1967), 127.
[42] Robert William Rogers, *Cuneiform Parallels to the Old Testament* (New York: Jennings & Graham, 1912), 48.
[43] Robert Bowie Johnson, Jr., *The Parthenon Code: Mankind's History in Marble* (Annapolis, Maryland: Solving Light Books, 2004), 202.
[44] E. S. G. Bristowe, *Cain - An Argument* (Leicester: Edgar Backus, 1950), 41.
[45] Howard B. Rand, *Study in Daniel* (Merrimac, Massachusetts: Destiny Publishers, 1948), 396.
[46] Drusilla Dunjee Houston, *Wonderful Ethiopians of the Ancient Cushite Empire* (1926), 195.
[47] Robert William Rogers, *Cuneiform Parallels to the Old Testament* (New York: Jennings & Graham, 1912), 32.
[48] Robert Bowie Johnson, Jr., *The Parthenon Code: Mankind's History in Marble* (Annapolis, Maryland: Solving Light Books, 2004), 10.
[49] Mrs. Sydney Bristowe, Sargon the Magnificent (London: The Covenant Publishing Co., 1927), 126.
[50] Robert Bowie Johnson, Jr., *The Parthenon Code: Mankind's History in Marble* (Annapolis, Maryland: Solving Light Books, 2004), 11.
[51] Robert Bowie Johnson, Jr., *The Parthenon Code: Mankind's History in Marble* (Annapolis, Maryland: Solving Light Books, 2004), 11.
[52] E. S. G. Bristowe, *Cain - An Argument* (Leicester: Edgar Backus, 1950), 62.
[53] Zecharia Sitchin, *There Were Giants Upon the Earth, Gods, Demigods, and Human Ancestry: The Evidence of Alien DNA* (Rochester, Vermont: Bear & Company, Inc., 2010), 127.
[54] Alexander Heidel, *The Babylonian Genesis* (Chicago: The University of Chicago Press, 1942), 150.
[55] E. S. G. Bristowe, *Cain - An Argument* (Leicester: Edgar Backus, 1950), 62.
[56] American Scientific Affiliation: Creation/Evolution Page, *In Search of the Historical Adam: Part 2*, 1, http://www.asa3.org/ASA/PSCF/1994/PSCF3-94Fischer.html (accessed April 12, 2005); Theophilus G. Pinches, *The Religion of Babylonia and Assyria* (London: Archibald Constable & Co. LTD., 1906), 50; Theophilus G. Pinches, *The Old Testament: In The Light of The Historical Records and Legends of Assyria and Babylonia* (Brighton: Society For Promoting Christian Knowledge, 1903), 103; Mrs. Sydney Bristowe, *Sargon the Magnificent* (London: The Covenant Publishing Co., 1927), 97; *The Babylonian Legends of the Creation and the Fight Between Bel and the Dragon As Told by Assyrian Tablets from Nineveh* (London: Harrison & Sons, 1931), 60; Alfred Jeremias, *The Old Testament in the Light of the Ancient East Vol. I* (New York: G. P. Putnam's Sons, 1911), 102-103; E. S. G. Bristowe,

Cain - An Argument (Leicester: Edgar Backus, 1950), 62.

57 Christian and Barbara Joy O'Brien, *The Shining Ones* (Cirencester, England: Dianthus Publishing Limited, 1988), 68.

58 Christian and Barbara Joy O'Brien, *The Shining Ones* (Cirencester, England: Dianthus Publishing Limited, 1988), 68; *Ancient Near East (Babylonia) Glossary and Texts*, 44, http://www.piney.com/BabGloss.html (accessed June 21, 2013); Zecharia Sitchin, *There Were Giants Upon the Earth, Gods, Demigods, and Human Ancestry: The Evidence of Alien DNA* (Rochester, Vermont: Bear & Company, Inc., 2010), 258; Theophilus G. Pinches, *The Old Testament: In The Light of The Historical Records and Legends of Assyria and Babylonia* (Brighton: Society For Promoting Christian Knowledge, 1903), 115; Alfred Jeremias, *The Old Testament in the Light of the Ancient East Vol. I* (New York: G. P. Putnam's Sons, 1911), 115.

59 Alfred Jeremias, *The Old Testament in the Light of the Ancient East Vol. I* (New York: G. P. Putnam's Sons, 1911), 115.

60 American Scientific Affiliation: Creation/Evolution Page, *In Search of the Historical Adam: Part 2*, http://www.asa3.org/ASA/PSCF/1994/PSCF3-94Fischer.html (accessed April 12, 2005).

61 Zecharia Sitchin, *There Were Giants Upon the Earth, Gods, Demigods, and Human Ancestry: The Evidence of Alien DNA* (Rochester, Vermont: Bear & Company, Inc., 2010), 193; *Ancient Near East (Babylonia) Glossary and Texts*, 2, http://www.piney.com/BabGloss.html (accessed June 21, 2013).

62 Zecharia Sitchin, *There Were Giants Upon the Earth, Gods, Demigods, and Human Ancestry: The Evidence of Alien DNA* (Rochester, Vermont: Bear & Company, Inc., 2010), 193; American Scientific Affiliation: Creation/Evolution Page, *In Search of the Historical Adam: Part 2*, http://www.asa3.org/ASA/PSCF/1994/PSCF3-94Fischer.html (accessed April 12, 2005).

63 American Scientific Affiliation: Creation/Evolution Page, *In Search of the Historical Adam: Part 2*, http://www.asa3.org/ASA/PSCF/1994/PSCF3-94Fischer.html (accessed April 12, 2005).

64 Robert William Rogers, *Cuneiform Parallels to the Old Testament* (New York: Jennings & Graham, 1912), 76.

65 American Scientific Affiliation: Creation/Evolution Page, *In Search of the Historical Adam: Part 2*, http://www.asa3.org/ASA/PSCF/1994/PSCF3-94Fischer.html (accessed April 12, 2005).

66 American Scientific Affiliation: Creation/Evolution Page, *In Search of the Historical Adam: Part 2*, http://www.asa3.org/ASA/PSCF/1994/PSCF3-94Fischer.html (accessed April 12, 2005).

67 American Scientific Affiliation: Creation/Evolution Page, *In Search of the Historical Adam: Part 2*, 4, http://www.asa3.org/ASA/PSCF/1994/PSCF3-94Fischer.html (accessed April 12, 2005).

68 American Scientific Affiliation: Creation/Evolution Page, *In Search of the Historical Adam: Part 2*, 4, http://www.asa3.org/ASA/PSCF/1994/PSCF3-94Fischer.html (accessed April 12, 2005).

69 American Scientific Affiliation: Creation/Evolution Page, *In Search of the Historical Adam: Part 2*, 4, http://www.asa3.org/ASA/PSCF/1994/PSCF3-94Fischer.html (accessed April 12, 2005).

70 Theophilus G. Pinches, *The Old Testament: In The Light of The Historical Records and Legends of Assyria and Babylonia* (Brighton: Society For Promoting Christian Knowledge, 1903), 83.

71 American Scientific Affiliation: Creation/Evolution Page, *In Search of the Historical Adam: Part 2*, 9, http://www.asa3.org/ASA/PSCF/1994/PSCF3-94Fischer.html (accessed April 12, 2005).

72 American Scientific Affiliation: Creation/Evolution Page, *In Search of the Historical Adam: Part 2*, 9, http://www.asa3.org/ASA/PSCF/1994/PSCF3-94Fischer.html (accessed April 12, 2005); Theophilus G. Pinches, *The Religion of Babylonia and Assyria* (London: Archibald Constable & Co. LTD., 1906), 72.

73 Joseph Campbell, *The Masks of God: Occidental Mythology* (New York: The Viking Press), 14.

74 *Ancient Near East (Babylonia) Glossary and Texts*, 46, http://www.piney.com/BabGloss.html (accessed June 21, 2013).

75 Theophilus G. Pinches, *The Religion of Babylonia and Assyria* (London: Archibald Constable & Co. LTD., 1906), 80.

76 Theophilus G. Pinches, *The Religion of Babylonia and Assyria* (London: Archibald Constable & Co. LTD., 1906), 80.

77 Robert Bowie Johnson, Jr., *Athena and Kain: The True Meaning of Greek Myth* (Annapolis, Maryland: Solving Light Books, 2003), 60.

78 Robert Bowie Johnson, Jr., *Athena and Kain: The True Meaning of Greek Myth* (Annapolis, Maryland: Solving Light Books, 2003), 62.

79 Stephen Quayle, *Genesis 6 Giants: The Master Builders of Prehistoric and Ancient Civilizations* (Bozeman, Montana: End Time Thunder Publishers, 2005), 64.

80 The Free Dictionary, *bane*, 1, http://www.thefreedictionary.com/bane (accessed Aug. 12, 2013); The Free Dictionary, *renegade*, 1, http://www.thefreedictionary.com/renegade (accessed Aug. 12, 2013).

81 Alfred Jeremias, *The Old Testament in the Light of the Ancient East Vol. I* (New York: G. P. Putnam's Sons, 1911), 105.

82 *Ancient Near East (Babylonia) Glossary and Texts*, 19, http://www.piney.com/BabGloss.html (accessed June 21, 2013); Alfred Jeremias, *The Old Testament in the Light of the Ancient East Vol. I* (New York: G. P. Putnam's Sons, 1911), 103; Donald Mackenzie, *Myths of Babylonia and Assyria* (1915), 35.

[83] *Ancient Near East (Babylonia) Glossary and Texts*, 10, http://www.piney.com/BabGloss.html (accessed June 21, 2013).
[84] Zecharia Sitchin, *There Were Giants Upon the Earth, Gods, Demigods, and Human Ancestry: The Evidence of Alien DNA* (Rochester, Vermont: Bear & Company, Inc., 2010), 68.
[85] Christian and Barbara Joy O'Brien, *The Shining Ones* (Cirencester, England: Dianthus Publishing Limited, 1988), 68.
[86] Andrew Collins, *From the Ashes of Angels* (Rochester, Vermont: Bear & Company, 1996), 207.
[87] *Ancient Near East (Babylonia) Glossary and Texts*, 45, http://www.piney.com/BabGloss.html (accessed June 21, 2013).
[88] Christian and Barbara Joy O'Brien, *The Shining Ones* (Cirencester, England: Dianthus Publishing Limited, 1988), 68.
[89] *Ancient Near East (Babylonia) Glossary and Texts*, 40, http://www.piney.com/BabGloss.html (accessed June 21, 2013).
[90] Theophilus G. Pinches, *The Religion of Babylonia and Assyria* (London: Archibald Constable & Co. LTD., 1906), 81; Christian and Barbara Joy O'Brien, *The Shining Ones* (Cirencester, England: Dianthus Publishing Limited, 1988), 68.
[91] Ancient Near East (Babylonia) Glossary and Texts, 45, http://www.piney.com/BabGloss.html (accessed June 21, 2013).
[92] Philip Gardiner, *Secrets of the Serpent: in Search of the Secret Past* (Foresthill Ca.: Reality press, 2006), 9; Theophilus G. Pinches, *The Religion of Babylonia and Assyria* (London: Archibald Constable & Co. LTD., 1906), 53; *Ancient Near East (Babylonia) Glossary and Texts*, 10, http://www.piney.com/BabGloss.html (accessed June 21, 2013).
[93] Alfred Jeremias, *The Old Testament in the Light of the Ancient East Vol. I* (New York: G. P. Putnam's Sons, 1911), 105; Theophilus G. Pinches, *The Old Testament: In The Light of The Historical Records and Legends of Assyria and Babylonia* (Brighton: Society For Promoting Christian Knowledge, 1903), 104; *Ancient Near East (Babylonia) Glossary and Texts*, 10, http://www.piney.com/BabGloss.html (accessed June 21, 2013).
[94] Theophilus G. Pinches, *The Religion of Babylonia and Assyria* (London: Archibald Constable & Co. LTD., 1906), 54.
[95] *Ancient Near East (Babylonia) Glossary and Texts*, 10, http://www.piney.com/BabGloss.html (accessed June 21, 2013); Theophilus G. Pinches, *The Religion of Babylonia and Assyria* (London: Archibald Constable & Co. LTD., 1906), 53; Bertrand L. Comparet, *What Happened to Cain*, 24, http://www.posse-comitatus.org/Bible_Studies/what_happened_to_cain.htm (accessed Aug. 21, 2000 334).
[96] Philip Gardiner, *Secrets of the Serpent: in Search of the Secret Past* (Foresthill Ca.: Reality press, 2006), 9.
[97] Mrs. Sydney Bristowe, *Sargon the Magnificent* (London: The Covenant Publishing Co., 1927), 100.
[98] *Ancient Near East (Babylonia) Glossary and Texts*, 42, http://www.piney.com/BabGloss.html (accessed June 21, 2013).
[99] *Ancient Near East (Babylonia) Glossary and Texts*, 17, http://www.piney.com/BabGloss.html (accessed June 21, 2013).
[100] *Ancient Near East (Babylonia) Glossary and Texts*, 41, http://www.piney.com/BabGloss.html (accessed June 21, 2013).
[101] Theophilus G. Pinches, *The Religion of Babylonia and Assyria* (London: Archibald Constable & Co. LTD., 1906), 51; *Ancient Near East (Babylonia) Glossary and Texts*, 41, http://www.piney.com/BabGloss.html (accessed June 21, 2013).
[102] *Ancient Near East (Babylonia) Glossary and Texts*, 17, http://www.piney.com/BabGloss.html (accessed June 21, 2013).
[103] Zecharia Sitchin, *There Were Giants Upon the Earth, Gods, Demigods, and Human Ancestry: The Evidence of Alien DNA* (Rochester, Vermont: Bear & Company, Inc., 2010), 94; Donald Mackenzie, *Myths of Babylonia and Assyria* (1915), 36.
[104] *Ancient Near East (Babylonia) Glossary and Texts*, 17, http://www.piney.com/BabGloss.html (accessed June 21, 2013); E. S. G. Bristowe, *Cain - An Argument* (Leicester: Edgar Backus, 1950), 42.
[105] *Ancient Near East (Babylonia) Glossary and Texts*, 41, http://www.piney.com/BabGloss.html (accessed June 21, 2013).
[106] Bertrand L. Comparet, *What Happened to Cain*, 24, http://www.posse-comitatus.org/Bible_Studies/what_happened_to_cain.htm (accessed Aug. 21, 2000).
[107] *Ancient Near East (Babylonia) Glossary and Texts*, 5, http://www.piney.com/BabGloss.html (accessed June 21, 2013).
[108] *Ancient Near East (Babylonia) Glossary and Texts*, 27, http://www.piney.com/BabGloss.html (accessed June 21, 2013).
[109] *Ancient Near East (Babylonia) Glossary and Texts*, 27, http://www.piney.com/BabGloss.html (accessed June 21, 2013).
[110] *Ancient Near East (Babylonia) Glossary and Texts*, 27, http://www.piney.com/BabGloss.html (accessed June 21,

2013).

[111] *Ancient Near East (Babylonia) Glossary and Texts*, 18, http://www.piney.com/BabGloss.html (accessed June 21, 2013).

[112] *Ancient Near East (Babylonia) Glossary and Texts*, 17, http://www.piney.com/BabGloss.html (accessed June 21, 2013).

[113] American Scientific Affiliation: Creation/Evolution Page, *In Search of the Historical Adam: Part 2*, 11, http://www.asa3.org/ASA/PSCF/1994/PSCF3-94Fischer.html (accessed April 12, 2005 320); Zecharia Sitchin, *The Lost Book of Enki* (Rochester, Vermont: Bear & Company, Inc., 2002), 6; Zecharia Sitchin, *There Were Giants Upon the Earth, Gods, Demigods, and Human Ancestry: The Evidence of Alien DNA* (Rochester, Vermont: Bear & Company, Inc., 2010), 78.

[114] S. G. F. Brandon, *Creation Legends of the Ancient Near East* (London: Hodder and Stoughton, 1963), 79.

[115] S. G. F. Brandon, *Creation Legends of the Ancient Near East* (London: Hodder and Stoughton, 1963), 79.

[116] Christian and Barbara Joy O'Brien, *The Shining Ones* (Cirencester, England: Dianthus Publishing Limited, 1988), 68.

[117] Christian and Barbara Joy O'Brien, *The Shining Ones* (Cirencester, England: Dianthus Publishing Limited, 1988), 68.

[118] Zecharia Sitchin, *There Were Giants Upon the Earth, Gods, Demigods, and Human Ancestry: The Evidence of Alien DNA* (Rochester, Vermont: Bear & Company, Inc., 2010), 68.

[119] Donald Mackenzie, *Myths of Babylonia and Assyria* (1915), 31; Theophilus G. Pinches, *The Old Testament: In The Light of The Historical Records and Legends of Assyria and Babylonia* (Brighton: Society For Promoting Christian Knowledge, 1903), 104.

[120] Zecharia Sitchin, *There Were Giants Upon the Earth, Gods, Demigods, and Human Ancestry: The Evidence of Alien DNA* (Rochester, Vermont: Bear & Company, Inc., 2010), 94; *Ancient Near East (Babylonia) Glossary and Texts*, 18, http://www.piney.com/BabGloss.html (accessed June 21, 2013).

[121] *Ancient Near East (Babylonia) Glossary and Texts*, 25, http://www.piney.com/BabGloss.html (accessed June 21, 2013).

[122] E. S. G. Bristowe, *Cain - An Argument* (Leicester: Edgar Backus, 1950), 41.

[123] E. S. G. Bristowe, *Cain - An Argument* (Leicester: Edgar Backus, 1950), 41.

[124] *Ancient Near East (Babylonia) Glossary and Texts*, 26, http://www.piney.com/BabGloss.html (accessed June 21, 2013).

[125] *Ancient Near East (Babylonia) Glossary and Texts*, 5, http://www.piney.com/BabGloss.html (accessed June 21, 2013).

[126] Bertrand L. Comparet, *What Happened to Cain*, 24, http://www.posse-comitatus.org/Bible_Studies/what_happened_to_cain.htm (accessed Aug. 21, 2000); E. S. G. Bristowe, *Cain - An Argument* (Leicester: Edgar Backus, 1950), 41.

[127] *Ancient Near East (Babylonia) Glossary and Texts*, 27, http://www.piney.com/BabGloss.html (accessed June 21, 2013).

[128] *Ancient Near East (Babylonia) Glossary and Texts*, 25, http://www.piney.com/BabGloss.html (accessed June 21, 2013).

[129] Bertrand L. Comparet, *What Happened to Cain*, 24, http://www.posse-comitatus.org/Bible_Studies/what_happened_to_cain.htm (accessed Aug. 21, 2000).

[130] *Ibn Ezra, Commentary on the Pentateuch: Genesis (Bereshit)* (New York: Menorah Publishing Company, Inc., 1988), 63; E. S. G. Bristowe, *Cain - An Argument* (Leicester: Edgar Backus, 1950), 40.

[131] *Ancient Near East (Babylonia) Glossary and Texts*, 2, http://www.piney.com/BabGloss.html (accessed June 21, 2013); Wikipedia, the free encyclopedia, *Adapa*, 1, http://en.wikipedia.org/wiki/Oannes#As_Oannes (accessed Aug. 12, 2013).

[132] Robert William Rogers, *Cuneiform Parallels to the Old Testament* (New York: Jennings & Graham, 1912), 69.

[133] American Scientific Affiliation: Creation/Evolution Page, *In Search of the Historical Adam: Part 2*, 2, http://www.asa3.org/ASA/PSCF/1994/PSCF3-94Fischer.html (accessed April 12, 2005).

[134] *Ancient Near East (Babylonia) Glossary and Texts*, 10, http://www.piney.com/BabGloss.html (accessed June 21, 2013).

[135] *Ancient Near East (Babylonia) Glossary and Texts*, 10, http://www.piney.com/BabGloss.html (accessed June 21, 2013).

[136] *Ancient Near East (Babylonia) Glossary and Texts*, 44, http://www.piney.com/BabGloss.html (accessed June 21, 2013).

[137] *Ancient Near East (Babylonia) Glossary and Texts*, 39, http://www.piney.com/BabGloss.html (accessed June 21, 2013).

[138] *Ancient Near East (Babylonia) Glossary and Texts*, 3, http://www.piney.com/BabGloss.html (accessed June 21, 2013).

[139] Mrs. Sydney Bristowe, *Sargon the Magnificent* (London: The Covenant Publishing Co., 1927), 4.

[140] Mrs. Sydney Bristowe, *Sargon the Magnificent* (London: The Covenant Publishing Co., 1927), 93.

[141] Bertrand L. Comparet, *What Happened to Cain*, 28, http://www.posse-comitatus.org/Bible_Studies/what_happened_to_cain.htm (accessed Aug. 21, 2000).
[142] Bertrand L. Comparet, *What Happened to Cain*, 28, http://www.posse-comitatus.org/Bible_Studies/what_happened_to_cain.htm (accessed Aug. 21, 2000).
[143] Victor H. Matthews and Don C. Benjamin, *Old Testament Parallels: Laws and Stories from the Ancient Near East* (New York: Paulist Press, 1991), 55.
[144] Drusilla Dunjee Houston, *Wonderful Ethiopians of the Ancient Cushite Empire* (1926), 172.
[145] E. S. G. Bristowe, *Cain - An Argument* (Leicester: Edgar Backus, 1950), 5.
[146] Mrs. Sydney Bristowe, *Sargon the Magnificent* (London: The Covenant Publishing Co., 1927), 27.
[147] Drusilla Dunjee Houston, *Wonderful Ethiopians of the Ancient Cushite Empire* (1926), 172.
[148] Theophilus G. Pinches, *The Old Testament: In The Light of The Historical Records and Legends of Assyria and Babylonia* (Brighton: Society For Promoting Christian Knowledge, 1903), 1.
[149] *Ancient Near East (Babylonia) Glossary and Texts*, 43, http://www.piney.com/BabGloss.html (accessed June 21, 2013).
[150] Bertrand L. Comparet, *What Happened to Cain*, 24, http://www.posse-comitatus.org/Bible_Studies/what_happened_to_cain.htm (accessed Aug. 21, 2000).
[151] Mrs. Sydney Bristowe, *Sargon the Magnificent* (London: The Covenant Publishing Co., 1927), 97; E. S. G. Bristowe, *Cain - An Argument* (Leicester: Edgar Backus, 1950), 8.
[152] Bertrand L. Comparet, *What Happened to Cain*, 19, http://www.posse-comitatus.org/Bible_Studies/what_happened_to_cain.htm (accessed Aug. 21, 2000).
[153] E. S. G. Bristowe, *Cain - An Argument* (Leicester: Edgar Backus, 1950), 1.
[154] Bertrand L. Comparet, *What Happened to Cain*, 19, http://www.posse-comitatus.org/Bible_Studies/what_happened_to_cain.htm (accessed Aug. 21, 2000).
[155] Bertrand L. Comparet, What Happened to Cain, 27, http://www.posse-comitatus.org/Bible_Studies/what_happened_to_cain.htm (accessed Aug. 21, 2000).
[156] Mrs. Sydney Bristowe, *Sargon the Magnificent* (London: The Covenant Publishing Co., 1927), 93; Bertrand L. Comparet, *What Happened to Cain*, 28, http://www.posse-comitatus.org/Bible_Studies/what_happened_to_cain.htm (accessed Aug. 21, 2000 334); Strong's H5175 - *Nachash*, 1, http://www.blueletterbible.org/lang/lexicon/lexicon.cfm?strongs=H5175 (accessed Aug. 12, 2013).
[157] Mrs. Sydney Bristowe, *Sargon the Magnificent* (London: The Covenant Publishing Co., 1927), 26; E. S. G. Bristowe, *Cain - An Argument* (Leicester: Edgar Backus, 1950), 5.
[158] Robert William Rogers, *Cuneiform Parallels to the Old Testament* (New York: Jennings & Graham, 1912), 135-137.
[159] Theophilus G. Pinches, *The Religion of Babylonia and Assyria* (London: Archibald Constable & Co. LTD., 1906), 59.
[160] Zecharia Sitchin, *There Were Giants Upon the Earth, Gods, Demigods, and Human Ancestry: The Evidence of Alien DNA* (Rochester, Vermont: Bear & Company, Inc., 2010), 19; E. S. G. Bristowe, *Cain - An Argument* (Leicester: Edgar Backus, 1950), 43.
[161] *The Babylonian Legends of the Creation and the Fight Between Bel and the Dragon As Told by Assyrian Tablets from Nineveh* (London: Harrison & Sons, 1931), 65.
[162] Victor H. Matthews and Don C. Benjamin, *Old Testament Parallels: Laws and Stories from the Ancient Near East* (New York: Paulist Press, 1991), 9.
[163] Theophilus G. Pinches, *The Religion of Babylonia and Assyria* (London: Archibald Constable & Co. LTD., 1906), 53.
[164] Theophilus G. Pinches, *The Religion of Babylonia and Assyria* (London: Archibald Constable & Co. LTD., 1906), 58.
[165] E. S. G. Bristowe, *Cain - An Argument* (Leicester: Edgar Backus, 1950), 44.
[166] Bertrand L. Comparet, *What Happened to Cain*, 25, http://www.posse-comitatus.org/Bible_Studies/what_happened_to_cain.htm (accessed Aug. 21, 2000).
[167] S. G. F. Brandon, *Creation Legends of the Ancient Near East* (London: Hodder and Stoughton, 1963), 87.
[168] *Ancient Near East (Babylonia) Glossary and Texts*, 31, http://www.piney.com/BabGloss.html (accessed June 21, 2013); Theophilus G. Pinches, *The Religion of Babylonia and Assyria* (London: Archibald Constable & Co. LTD., 1906), 47; Robert William Rogers, *Cuneiform Parallels to the Old Testament* (New York: Jennings & Graham, 1912), 47.
[169] *Ancient Near East (Babylonia) Glossary and Texts*, 31, http://www.piney.com/BabGloss.html (accessed June 21, 2013).
[170] *The Babylonian Legends of the Creation and the Fight Between Bel and the Dragon As Told by Assyrian Tablets from Nineveh* (London: Harrison & Sons, 1931), 65.
[171] *Ancient Near East (Babylonia) Glossary and Texts*, 27, http://www.piney.com/BabGloss.html (accessed June 21, 2013); *The Babylonian Legends of the Creation and the Fight Between Bel and the Dragon As Told by Assyrian Tablets from Nineveh* (London: Harrison & Sons, 1931), 20.

[172] *The Babylonian Legends of the Creation and the Fight Between Bel and the Dragon As Told by Assyrian Tablets from Nineveh* (London: Harrison & Sons, 1931), 20.
[173] Albert T. Clay, *The Origin of Biblical Traditions: Hebrew Legends in Babylonia and Israel* (New Haven: Yale University Press, 1923), 79.
[174] Albert T. Clay, *The Origin of Biblical Traditions: Hebrew Legends in Babylonia and Israel* (New Haven: Yale University Press, 1923), 79; *The Babylonian Legends of the Creation and the Fight Between Bel and the Dragon As Told by Assyrian Tablets from Nineveh* (London: Harrison & Sons, 1931), 17.
[175] *Ancient Near East (Babylonia) Glossary and Texts*, 17, http://www.piney.com/BabGloss.html (accessed June 21, 2013); Theophilus G. Pinches, *The Old Testament: In The Light of The Historical Records and Legends of Assyria and Babylonia* (Brighton: Society For Promoting Christian Knowledge, 1903), 104.
[176] Donald Mackenzie, *Myths of Babylonia and Assyria* (1915), 29.
[177] *Ancient Near East (Babylonia) Glossary and Texts*, 7, http://www.piney.com/BabGloss.html (accessed June 21, 2013); *The Babylonian Legends of the Creation and the Fight Between Bel and the Dragon As Told by Assyrian Tablets from Nineveh* (London: Harrison & Sons, 1931), 14; Howard Schwartz, *Tree of Souls: The Mythology of Judaism* (Oxford: University Press, 2004), 76; Robert William Rogers, *Cuneiform Parallels to the Old Testament* (New York: Jennings & Graham, 1912), 10; James E. Thorold Rogers, *Bible Folk-Lore; a Study in Comparative Mythology* (London: Kegan Paul, Trench and Co., 1884), 5.
[178] *The Babylonian Legends of the Creation and the Fight Between Bel and the Dragon As Told by Assyrian Tablets from Nineveh* (London: Harrison & Sons, 1931), 16.
[179] *Ancient Near East (Babylonia) Glossary and Texts*, 47, http://www.piney.com/BabGloss.html (accessed June 21, 2013).
[180] *The Babylonian Legends of the Creation and the Fight Between Bel and the Dragon As Told by Assyrian Tablets from Nineveh* (London: Harrison & Sons, 1931), 20.
[181] Donald Mackenzie, *Myths of Babylonia and Assyria* (1915), 38.
[182] Robert William Rogers, *Cuneiform Parallels to the Old Testament* (New York: Jennings & Graham, 1912), 20.
[183] *Ancient Near East (Babylonia) Glossary and Texts*, 47, http://www.piney.com/BabGloss.html (accessed June 21, 2013).
[184] I. P. Cory, *Ancient Fragments* (1832), http://www.masseiana.org/cory_fragments.htm (accessed Nov. 2, 2011).
[185] *Ancient Near East (Babylonia) Glossary and Texts*, 19, http://www.piney.com/BabGloss.html (accessed June 21, 2013).
[186] Christian and Barbara Joy O'Brien, The Shining Ones (Cirencester, England: Dianthus Publishing Limited, 1988), 87.
[187] Howard Schwartz, *Tree of Souls: The Mythology of Judaism* (Oxford: University Press, 2004), 112.
[188] Robert William Rogers, *Cuneiform Parallels to the Old Testament* (New York: Jennings & Graham, 1912), 67.
[189] Robert William Rogers, *Cuneiform Parallels to the Old Testament* (New York: Jennings & Graham, 1912), 65.
[190] Robert William Rogers, *Cuneiform Parallels to the Old Testament* (New York: Jennings & Graham, 1912), 67.
[191] Robert William Rogers, *Cuneiform Parallels to the Old Testament* (New York: Jennings & Graham, 1912), 67.
[192] Drusilla Dunjee Houston, Wonderful Ethiopians of the Ancient Cushite Empire (1926), 170.
[193] Robert William Rogers, *Cuneiform Parallels to the Old Testament* (New York: Jennings & Graham, 1912), 33.
[194] *The Babylonian Legends of the Creation and the Fight Between Bel and the Dragon As Told by Assyrian Tablets from Nineveh* (London: Harrison & Sons, 1931), 62.
[195] Theophilus G. Pinches, *The Old Testament: In The Light of The Historical Records and Legends of Assyria and Babylonia* (Brighton: Society For Promoting Christian Knowledge, 1903), 103.
[196] *Ancient Near East (Babylonia) Glossary and Texts*, 17, http://www.piney.com/BabGloss.html (accessed June 21, 2013).
[197] *Ancient Near East (Babylonia) Glossary and Texts*, 47, http://www.piney.com/BabGloss.html (accessed June 21, 2013).
[198] Theophilus G. Pinches, *The Religion of Babylonia and Assyria* (London: Archibald Constable & Co. LTD., 1906), 55-56.
[199] Theophilus G. Pinches, *The Religion of Babylonia and Assyria* (London: Archibald Constable & Co. LTD., 1906), 53.
[200] Donald Mackenzie, *Myths of Babylonia and Assyria*, (1915), 35.
[201] *The Babylonian Legends of the Creation and the Fight Between Bel and the Dragon As Told by Assyrian Tablets from Nineveh* (London: Harrison & Sons, 1931), 21.
[202] Albert T. Clay, *The Origin of Biblical Traditions: Hebrew Legends in Babylonia and Israel* (New Haven: Yale University Press), 66.
[203] Andrew Collins, *Gods of Eden: Egypt's Lost Legacy and the Genesis of Civilization* (London: Headline Book Publishing, 1998), 281.
[204] S. G. F. Brandon, *Creation Legends of the Ancient Near East* (London: Hodder and Stoughton, 1963), 79.
[205] *The Babylonian Legends of the Creation and the Fight Between Bel and the Dragon As Told by Assyrian Tablets from Nineveh* (London: Harrison & Sons, 1931), 55.

[206] *The Babylonian Legends of the Creation and the Fight Between Bel and the Dragon As Told by Assyrian Tablets from Nineveh* (London: Harrison & Sons, 1931), 70.
[207] Theophilus G. Pinches, *The Religion of Babylonia and Assyria* (London: Archibald Constable & Co. LTD., 1906), 58.
[208] *The Babylonian Legends of the Creation and the Fight Between Bel and the Dragon As Told by Assyrian Tablets from Nineveh* (London: Harrison & Sons, 1931), 55.
[209] Andrew Collins, *Gods of Eden: Egypt's Lost Legacy and the Genesis of Civilization* (London: Headline Book Publishing, 1998), 281.
[210] Bertrand L. Comparet, *What Happened to Cain*, 21, http://www.posse-comitatus.org/Bible_Studies/what_happened_to_cain.htm (accessed Aug. 21, 2000).
[211] *The Babylonian Legends of the Creation and the Fight Between Bel and the Dragon As Told by Assyrian Tablets from Nineveh* (London: Harrison & Sons, 1931), 65.
[212] Zecharia Sitchin, *The Lost Book of Enki* (Rochester, Vermont: Bear & Company, Inc., 2002), introduction 1; James B. Pritchard, *Ancient Near Eastern Texts Relating to the Old Testament* (Princeton, New Jersey: Princeton University Press, 1955), 52, 55.
[213] *The Babylonian Legends of the Creation and the Fight Between Bel and the Dragon As Told by Assyrian Tablets from Nineveh* (London: Harrison & Sons, 1931), 22.
[214] Christian and Barbara Joy O'Brien, *The Shining Ones* (Cirencester, England: Dianthus Publishing Limited, 1988), 87.
[215] Victor H. Matthews and Don C. Benjamin, *Old Testament Parallels: Laws and Stories from the Ancient Near East* (New York: Paulist Press, 1991), 8.
[216] *Ancient Near East (Babylonia) Glossary and Texts*, 6, http://www.piney.com/BabGloss.html (accessed June 21, 2013).
[217] Zecharia Sitchin, *There Were Giants Upon the Earth, Gods, Demigods, and Human Ancestry: The Evidence of Alien DNA* (Rochester, Vermont: Bear & Company, Inc., 2010), 125.
[218] Zecharia Sitchin, *The 12th Planet* (New York: Avon Books, 1976), 328-332.
[219] *The Babylonian Legends of the Creation and the Fight Between Bel and the Dragon As Told by Assyrian Tablets from Nineveh* (London: Harrison & Sons, 1931), 22; Christian and Barbara Joy O'Brien, *The Shining Ones* (Cirencester, England: Dianthus Publishing Limited, 1988), 144; *Ancient Near East (Babylonia) Glossary and Texts*, 25, http://www.piney.com/BabGloss.html (accessed June 21, 2013); Christian and Barbara Joy O'Brien, *The Shining Ones* (Cirencester, England: Dianthus Publishing Limited, 1988), 147.
[220] Victor H. Matthews and Don C. Benjamin, *Old Testament Parallels: Laws and Stories from the Ancient Near East* (New York: Paulist Press, 1991), 8.
[221] Christian and Barbara Joy O'Brien, *The Shining Ones* (Cirencester, England: Dianthus Publishing Limited, 1988), 144; *Ancient Near East (Babylonia) Glossary and Texts*, 25, http://www.piney.com/BabGloss.html (accessed June 21, 2013).
[222] Christian and Barbara Joy O'Brien, *The Shining Ones* (Cirencester, England: Dianthus Publishing Limited, 1988), 144.
[223] Christian and Barbara Joy O'Brien, *The Shining Ones* (Cirencester, England: Dianthus Publishing Limited, 1988), 144.
[224] *The Epic of Atrahasis*, http://www.piney.com/Atrahasis.html (accessed July 6, 2013).
[225] Robert William Rogers, *Cuneiform Parallels to the Old Testament* (New York: Jennings & Graham, 1912), 57; Albert T. Clay, *The Origin of Biblical Traditions: Hebrew Legends in Babylonia and Israel* (New Haven: Yale University Press, 1923), 66.
[226] S. G. F. Brandon, *Creation Legends of the Ancient Near East* (London: Hodder and Stoughton, 1963), 110.
[227] Victor H. Matthews and Don C. Benjamin, *Old Testament Parallels: Laws and Stories from the Ancient Near East* (New York: Paulist Press, 1991), 15.
[228] *Ancient Near East (Babylonia) Glossary and Texts*, 17, http://www.piney.com/BabGloss.html (accessed June 21, 2013).
[229] *The Babylonian Legends of the Creation and the Fight Between Bel and the Dragon As Told by Assyrian Tablets from Nineveh* (London: Harrison & Sons, 1931), 73.
[230] Victor H. Matthews and Don C. Benjamin, *Old Testament Parallels: Laws and Stories from the Ancient Near East* (New York: Paulist Press, 1991), 9.
[231] Victor H. Matthews and Don C. Benjamin, *Old Testament Parallels: Laws and Stories from the Ancient Near East* (New York: Paulist Press, 1991), 15.
[232] Robert William Rogers, *Cuneiform Parallels to the Old Testament* (New York: Jennings & Graham, 1912), 57.
[233] *The Babylonian Legends of the Creation and the Fight Between Bel and the Dragon As Told by Assyrian Tablets from Nineveh* (London: Harrison & Sons, 1931), 68-69.
[234] S. G. F. Brandon, *Creation Legends of the Ancient Near East* (London: Hodder and Stoughton, 1963), 70.
[235] James B. Pritchard, *Ancient Near Eastern Texts Relating to the Old Testament* (Princeton, New Jersey: Princeton

University Press, 1955), 43; S. G. F. Brandon, *Creation Legends of the Ancient Near East* (London: Hodder and Stoughton, 1963), 81; Robert William Rogers, *Cuneiform Parallels to the Old Testament* (New York: Jennings & Graham, 1912), 50.

[236] Albert T. Clay, *The Origin of Biblical Traditions: Hebrew Legends in Babylonia and Israel* (New Haven: Yale University Press), 83.

[237] Theophilus G. Pinches, *The Old Testament: In The Light of The Historical Records and Legends of Assyria and Babylonia* (Brighton: Society For Promoting Christian Knowledge, 1903), 1; *The Babylonian Legends of the Creation and the Fight Between Bel and the Dragon As Told by Assyrian Tablets from Nineveh* (London: Harrison & Sons, 1931), 65.

[238] *The Babylonian Legends of the Creation and the Fight Between Bel and the Dragon As Told by Assyrian Tablets from Nineveh* (London: Harrison & Sons, 1931), 65.

[239] *The Babylonian Legends of the Creation and the Fight Between Bel and the Dragon As Told by Assyrian Tablets from Nineveh* (London: Harrison & Sons, 1931), 30.

[240] *The Babylonian Legends of the Creation and the Fight Between Bel and the Dragon As Told by Assyrian Tablets from Nineveh* (London: Harrison & Sons, 1931), 66.

[241] Victor H. Matthews and Don C. Benjamin, *Old Testament Parallels: Laws and Stories from the Ancient Near East* (New York: Paulist Press, 1991), 15.

[242] *The Babylonian Legends of the Creation and the Fight Between Bel and the Dragon As Told by Assyrian Tablets from Nineveh* (London: Harrison & Sons, 1931), 66.

[243] Robert William Rogers, *Cuneiform Parallels to the Old Testament* (New York: Jennings & Graham, 1912), 48.

[244] *The Babylonian Legends of the Creation and the Fight Between Bel and the Dragon As Told by Assyrian Tablets from Nineveh* (London: Harrison & Sons, 1931), 31.

[245] *The Babylonian Legends of the Creation and the Fight Between Bel and the Dragon As Told by Assyrian Tablets from Nineveh* (London: Harrison & Sons, 1931), 30.

[246] Zecharia Sitchin, *There Were Giants Upon the Earth, Gods, Demigods, and Human Ancestry: The Evidence of Alien DNA* (Rochester, Vermont: Bear & Company, Inc., 2010), 125-126.

Chapter 2

[1] Dan Gayman, *The Two Seeds of Genesis 3:15* (Daniel Lee Gayman, 1977), 15.

[2] Michael E. Stone, *Adamgirk: The Adam Book of Arak'el of Siwnik* (Oxford: University Press, 2007), 218.

[3] *3 Enoch (The Hebrew Book of Enoch)*, Chapter 44(6), trans. Hugo Odeberg (New York: KTAV Publishing House, Inc., 1973).

[4] Abdul-Sahib Al-Hasani Al-amili, *The Prophets, Their Lives and Their Stories*, 2, http://www.sacred-texts.com/isl/pro/index.htm (accessed Oct. 11, 2004).

[5] Herbert W. Armstrong, *Mystery of the Ages*, Part 8 (1985).

[6] Herbert W. Armstrong, *Mystery of the Ages*, Part 10 (1985).

[7] E. S. G. Bristowe, *Cain - An Argument* (Leicester: Edgar Backus, 1950), 8.

[8] *Enthronement of the Archangel Michael*, http://www2.iath.virginia.edu/anderson/vita/pericopes/Apocrypha/Cop.Enth.Mich.html; Alan Unterman, *Dictionary of Jewish Lore and Legend* (London: Thames and Hudson Ltd., 1991), 173.

[9] Robert Graves and Raphael Patai, *Hebrew Myths: The Book of Genesis* (Garden City, New York: Doubleday & Company, 1964), 57; Ibn Kathir, *Stories of the Prophets* (London: Darussalam, 2003), 27, 31; *Enthronement of the Archangel Michael*, http://www2.iath.virginia.edu/anderson/vita/pericopes/Apocrypha/Cop.Enth.Mich.html (accessed Aug. 19, 2013).

[10] Wikipedia, the free encyclopedia, *Samael*, http://en.wikipedia.org/wiki/Samael (accessed Aug. 19, 2013); *Enthronement of the Archangel Michael*, http://www2.iath.virginia.edu/anderson/vita/pericopes/Apocrypha/Cop.Enth.Mich.html (accessed Aug. 19, 2013).

[11] *Enthronement of the Archangel Michael*, 3, http://www2.iath.virginia.edu/anderson/vita/pericopes/Apocrypha/Cop.Enth.Mich.html (accessed Aug. 19, 2013).

[12] Robert Graves and Raphael Patai, *Hebrew Myths: The Book of Genesis* (Garden City, New York: Doubleday & Company, 1964), 85.

[13] *Enthronement of the Archangel Michael*, 3, http://www2.iath.virginia.edu/anderson/vita/pericopes/Apocrypha/Cop.Enth.Mich.html (accessed Aug. 19, 2013).

[14] Anonymous, *New Interpretation of a Portion of the Third Chapter of Genesis, Viewed in Connection With Other Parts of the Bible; Including an Inquiry Into the Introduction, Nature, and Extent of Satanic Influence in the World* (London, J. Hatchard and Son, 1834), 53.

[15] Ibn Kathir, *The Story of Creation* (Karachi, Pakistan: Darul Ishaat, 2006), 91, 102.

[16] *The History of al-Tabari - Volume I: General Introduction and From the Creation to the Flood*, The Story of Iblis, 83, trans. Franz Rosenthal (Albany: New York Press, 1989), 254.

[17] Christian and Barbara Joy O'Brien, *The Shining Ones* (Cirencester, England: Dianthus Publishing Limited, 1988), 65.

[18] Andrew Collins, *From the Ashes of Angels* (Rochester, Vermont: Bear & Company, 1996), 261.
[19] Anonymous, *New Interpretation of a Portion of the Third Chapter of Genesis, Viewed in Connection With Other Parts of the Bible; Including an Inquiry Into the Introduction, Nature, and Extent of Satanic Influence in the World* (London, J. Hatchard and Son, 1834), 53.
[20] Christian and Barbara Joy O'Brien, *The Shining Ones* (Cirencester, England: Dianthus Publishing Limited, 1988), 139, 142.
[21] *The History of al-Tabari - Volume I: General Introduction and From the Creation to the Flood*, The Story of Iblis, 82, trans. Franz Rosenthal (Albany: New York Press, 1989), 253.
[22] Ibn Kathir, *The Story of Creation* (Karachi, Pakistan: Darul Ishaat, 2006), 102; *The History of al-Tabari - Volume I: General Introduction and From the Creation to the Flood*, The Story of Iblis, 83, trans. Franz Rosenthal (Albany: New York Press, 1989), 254.
[23] *The History of al-Tabari - Volume I: General Introduction and From the Creation to the Flood*, The Story of Iblis, 82, 83, trans. Franz Rosenthal (Albany: New York Press, 1989), 253, 254.
[24] *The History of al-Tabari - Volume I: General Introduction and From the Creation to the Flood*, The Story of Iblis, 83, trans. Franz Rosenthal (Albany: New York Press, 1989), 254.
[25] *The History of al-Tabari - Volume I: General Introduction and From the Creation to the Flood*, The Story of Iblis, 82, trans. Franz Rosenthal (Albany: New York Press, 1989), 253.
[26] *The History of al-Tabari - Volume I: General Introduction and From the Creation to the Flood*, The Story of Iblis, 82, trans. Franz Rosenthal (Albany: New York Press, 1989), 253-254.
[27] *The History of al-Tabari - Volume I: General Introduction and From the Creation to the Flood*, The Story of Iblis, 83, trans. Franz Rosenthal (Albany: New York Press, 1989), 254; Ibn Kathir, *The Story of Creation* (Karachi, Pakistan: Darul Ishaat, 2006), 110.
[28] Ibn Kathir, *The Story of Creation* (Karachi, Pakistan: Darul Ishaat, 2006), 110.
[29] Church Blog, *The Power of Choice*, 1, http://www.plymouthchristiancentre.org/news/church-blog/posts/45/The-Power-of-Choice (accessed June 26, 2017).
[30] S. Baring-Gould, *Legends of the Patriarchs and Prophets and Other Old Testament Characters* (New York: American Book Exchange, 1881), 15.
[31] Brian S. Wright, *Blood & Seed: What Really Happened in Eden* (The American Biblical Institute of Holy Land Studies, 2010), 81.
[32] *The Chronicles of Jerahmeel (The Hebrew Bible Historiale)*, 22(1), trans. M. Gaster, Ph. D. (London: The Royal Asiatic Society, 1899).
[33] St. Ambrose, *On Paradise*, http://www2.iath.virginia.edu/anderson/commentaries/Amb.html (accessed Jan. 12, 2011), 332-333; John Skinner, *A Critical and Exegetical Commentary on Genesis* (Edinburgh: T. & T. Clark, 1956), 73, 88; *St. Chrysostom*, Homilies on Genesis, Homily 16, http://www2.iath.virginia.edu/anderson/commentaries/ChrGen.html (accessed Jan. 12, 2011), 215; *Wisdom of Ben Sira (Ecclesiasticus)*, 2:24, http://www.usccb.org/bible/wisdom/2 (accessed June 21, 2017); Ibn Kathir, *The Story of Creation* (Karachi, Pakistan: Darul Ishaat, 2006), 113; *Sammael*, 1, http://www.adamqadmon.com/watchers/sammael.html (accessed Feb. 6, 2001).
[34] C. A. Phifer, *Annals of the Earth* (Chicago, Illinois: American Publishers Association, 1890), 88.
[35] *Disdain*, dictionary.reference.com/browse/disdain (accessed Oct. 11, 2014).
[36] *The Gospel of Barnabas*, 40, trans. Lonsdale and Laura Ragg (London, 1907), http://www.sacred-texts.com/isl/gbar/index.htm (accessed Oct. 27, 2011).
[37] Abdul-Sahib Al-Hasani Al-amili, *The Prophets, Their Lives and Their Stories*, 1, http://www.sacred-texts.com/isl/pro/index.htm (accessed Oct. 11, 2004).
[38] Wikipedia, the free encyclopedia, *Viceroy*, en.wikipedia.org/wiki/Viceroy (accessed Jan. 12, 2011).
[39] Abdul-Sahib Al-Hasani Al-amili, *The Prophets, Their Lives and Their Stories*, 1, http://www.sacred-texts.com/isl/pro/index.htm (accessed Oct. 11, 2004).
[40] *Enthronement of the Archangel Michael*, http://www2.iath.virginia.edu/anderson/vita/pericopes/Apocrypha/Cop.Enth.Mich.html (accessed Aug. 19, 2013).
[41] Robert Graves and Raphael Patai, *Hebrew Myths: The Book of Genesis* (Garden City, New York: Doubleday & Company, 1964), 82.
[42] Robert Graves and Raphael Patai, *Hebrew Myths: The Book of Genesis* (Garden City, New York: Doubleday & Company, 1964), 82.
[43] Abdul-Sahib Al-Hasani Al-amili, *The Prophets, Their Lives and Their Stories*, 3, http://www.sacred-texts.com/isl/pro/index.htm (accessed Oct. 11, 2004); Ibn Kathir, *Stories of the Prophets* (London: Darussalam, 2003), 17-18, 25; David Max Eichhorn, *Cain: Son of the Serpent* (New York: Whittier Books, Inc., 1957), 11; St. Ambrose, *On Paradise*, http://www2.iath.virginia.edu/anderson/commentaries/Amb.html (accessed Jan. 12, 2011), 325, 333; Howard Schwartz, *Tree of Souls: The Mythology of Judaism* (Oxford: University Press, 2004), 133.
[44] *St. Chrysostom*, Homilies on Genesis, Homily 12, http://www2.iath.virginia.edu/anderson/commentaries/ChrGen.html (accessed Jan. 12, 2011) 164.
[45] *Barhebraeus' Scholia on the Old Testament Part I: Genesis - II Samuel*, Translation and Collation 6b 7, trans.

Martin Sprengling and William Creighton Graham (Chicago, Illinois: University of Chicago Press, 1931), 19.
[46] Michael E. Stone, *Adamgirk: The Adam Book of Arak'el of Siwnik* (Oxford: University Press, 2007), 197.
[47] Michael E. Stone, *Adamgirk: The Adam Book of Arak'el of Siwnik* (Oxford: University Press, 2007), 196.
[48] E. Basil Redlich, *The Early Traditions of Genesis* (London: Gerald Duckworth & Co. Ltd., 1950), 79.
[49] *St. Chrysostom*, Homilies on Genesis, Homily 12, http://www2.iath.virginia.edu/anderson/commentaries/ChrGen.html (accessed Jan. 12, 2011), 165.
[50] Robert Graves and Raphael Patai, *Hebrew Myths: The Book of Genesis* (Garden City, New York: Doubleday & Company, 1964), 82.
[51] St. Ambrose, *On Paradise*, http://www2.iath.virginia.edu/anderson/commentaries/Amb.html (accessed Jan. 12, 2011), 293, 332-333.
[52] St. Ambrose, *On Paradise*, http://www2.iath.virginia.edu/anderson/commentaries/Amb.html (accessed Jan. 12, 2011), 333.
[53] St. Ambrose, *On Paradise*, http://www2.iath.virginia.edu/anderson/commentaries/Amb.html (accessed Jan. 12, 2011), 333.
[54] Howard Schwartz, *Tree of Souls: The Mythology of Judaism* (Oxford: University Press, 2004), 85.
[55] Howard Schwartz, *Tree of Souls: The Mythology of Judaism* (Oxford: University Press, 2004), 437-438.
[56] David Max Eichhorn, *Cain: Son of the Serpent* (New York: Whittier Books, Inc., 1957), 85.
[57] Christian and Barbara Joy O'Brien, *The Shining Ones* (Cirencester, England: Dianthus Publishing Limited, 1988), 138.
[58] Louis Ginzberg, *The Legends of the Jews Volume I: From the Creation to Jacob*, trans. Henrietta Szold (Baltimore, Maryland: The Johns Hopkins University Press, 1909), 28.
[59] Ronald H. Isaacs, *Legends of Biblical Heroes: A Sourcebook* (Northvale, N. J.: Jason Aronson, Inc., 2002), 3; *Peskita de Rav Kahana*, 101.
[60] Quran Search Section, *The Qur'an*, 015:026-027, http://www.answering-christianity.com/cgi-bin/quran/quran_search.cgi?search_text=smokeless&search_type=Exact+String&mohsin_khan=1&B1=Search (accessed June 19, 2017); Ibn Kathir, *The Story of Creation* (Karachi, Pakistan: Darul Ishaat, 2006), 99, 104; Billie Brinkley, *The Lost Books of the Bible: The Supernatural* (Berkeley, California: Oracle Research Publishing, 2005), 121-122; Johann Andreas Eisenmenger, *The Traditions of the Jews, Contained in the Talmud and Other Mystical Writings* (London: J. Robinson, 1748), Preface, 22; Ibn Kathir, *Stories of the Prophets* (Karachi, Pakistan: Darul Ishaat, 2009), 32.
[61] Ibn Kathir, *Stories of the Prophets* (Karachi, Pakistan: Darul Ishaat, 2009), 32.
[62] Ronald H. Isaacs, *Legends of Biblical Heroes: A Sourcebook* (Northvale, N. J.: Jason Aronson, Inc., 2002), 3.
[63] Ibn Kathir, *Stories of the Prophets* (London: Darussalam, 2003), 24.
[64] Merriam Webster Dictionary, *Perseverance*, www.merriam-webster.com/dictionary/perseverance (accessed Oct. 17, 2013).
[65] Ibn Kathir, *Stories of the Prophets* (London: Darussalam, 2003), 25.
[66] Ibn Kathir, *The Story of Creation* (Karachi, Pakistan: Darul Ishaat, 2006), 2, 34.
[67] *The History of al-Tabari - Volume I: General Introduction and From the Creation to the Flood*, The Story of Adam, 87, trans. Franz Rosenthal (Albany: New York Press, 1989), 258.
[68] *The Works of Philo Judaeus*, Questions and Answers I, 5, trans. C. D. Yonge (London: H. G. Bohn, 1854-1855).
[69] Howard Schwartz, *Tree of Souls: The Mythology of Judaism* (Oxford: University Press, 2004), 136.
[70] S. G. F. Brandon, *Creation Legends of the Ancient Near East* (London: Hodder and Stoughton, 1963), 124.
[71] E. S. G. Bristowe, *Cain - An Argument* (Leicester: Edgar Backus, 1950), 92.
[72] Howard Schwartz, *Tree of Souls: The Mythology of Judaism* (Oxford: University Press, 2004), 135.
[73] E. S. G. Bristowe, *Cain - An Argument* (Leicester: Edgar Backus, 1950), 91.
[74] E. S. G. Bristowe, *Cain - An Argument* (Leicester: Edgar Backus, 1950), 6.
[75] Merriam Webster Dictionary, *Intelligence*, http://www.merriam-webster.com/dictionary/intelligence (accessed Oct. 17, 2013).
[76] Merriam Webster Dictionary, *Prudence*, www.merriam-webster.com/dictionary/prudence (accessed Oct. 17, 2013).
[77] Merriam Webster Dictionary, *Intelligence*, http://www.merriam-webster.com/dictionary/intelligence (accessed Oct. 17, 2013).
[78] *Barhebraeus' Scholia on the Old Testament Part I: Genesis - II Samuel*, Translation and Collation, Folio 6b 7, trans. Martin Sprengling and William Creighton Graham (Chicago, Illinois: University of Chicago Press, 1931), 19.
[79] James L. Kugel, *Traditions of the Bible* (Cambridge, Massachusetts: Harvard University Press, 1998), 113; *The Book of Jubilees*, 3:3-4, trans. R. H. Charles, The Apocrypha and Pseudepigrapha of the Old Testament (Oxford: Clarendon Press, 1913).
[80] Johann Andreas Eisenmenger, *The Traditions of the Jews, Contained in the Talmud and Other Mystical Writings* (London: J. Robinson, 1748), 22.
[81] St. Chrysostom, *Homilies on Genesis*, Homily 15, http://www2.iath.virginia.edu/anderson/commentaries/ChrGen.html (accessed Jan. 12, 2011) 201.
[82] St. Chrysostom, *Homilies on Genesis*, Homily 15,

http://www2.iath.virginia.edu/anderson/commentaries/ChrGen.html (accessed Jan. 12, 2011) 200.

[83] Jayim Nahman Bialik and Yehoshua Hana Ravnitzky, *The Book of Legends (Sefer Ha-Aggadah): Legends of the Talmud and Midrash*, 76 (New York: Shocken Books, 1992), 19.

[84] Shira Halevi, *The Life Story of Adam and Havah*, Genesis (Northvale, New Jersey: Jason Aronson, Inc., 1997), 243.

[85] *The Chronicles of Jerahmeel (The Hebrew Bible Historiale)*, 6(16), trans. M. Gaster, Ph. D. (London: The Royal Asiatic Society, 1899).

[86] *Ah, Those -ah words in English*, 2-3, http://www.dailywritingtips.com/ah-those-ah-words-in-english/ (accessed Aug. 19, 2013); *What does ah mean in Hebrew*, 1, http://wiki.answers.com/Q/What_does_ah_mean_in_hebrew (accessed Aug. 19, 2013).

[87] David Max Eichhorn, *Cain: Son of the Serpent* (New York: Whittier Books, Inc., 1957), 21.

[88] *Barhebraeus' Scholia on the Old Testament Part I: Genesis - II Samuel*, Translation and Collation, Folio 6a 28, trans. Martin Sprengling and William Creighton Graham (Chicago, Illinois: University of Chicago Press, 1931), 17.

[89] Andrew Collins, *From the Ashes of Angels* (Rochester, Vermont: Bear & Company, 1996), 151.

[90] John Skinner, *A Critical and Exegetical Commentary on Genesis* (Edinburgh: T. & T. Clark, 1956), 66.

[91] *The Book of the Bee*, Chap. 13: On the Formation of Adam 2 02 10 (notes), trans. Earnest A. Wallis Budge, M. A., http://www.sacred-texts.com/chr/bb/bb.htm (accessed Oct. 10, 2004); St. Chrysostom, *Homilies on Genesis*, Homily 14, http://www2.iath.virginia.edu/anderson/commentaries/ChrGen.html (accessed Jan. 12, 2011), 184.

[92] St. Chrysostom, *Homilies on Genesis*, Homily 14, http://www2.iath.virginia.edu/anderson/commentaries/ChrGen.html (accessed Jan. 12, 2011) 184-185.

[93] E. S. G. Bristowe, *Cain - An Argument* (Leicester: Edgar Backus, 1950), 94.

[94] St. Ephrem the Syrian, *Selected Prose Works*, Section 2, 22(2), trans. Edward G. Mathews, Jr. and Joseph P. Amar (Washington, D. C.: The Catholic University of America Press, 1994), 114.

[95] *The History of al-Tabari - Volume I: General Introduction and From the Creation to the Flood*, The Story of Iblis, 82-83, trans. Franz Rosenthal (Albany: New York Press, 1989), 253-254.

[96] *Saltair na Rann*, 1193-1196, trans. David Greene.

[97] David Max Eichhorn, *Cain: Son of the Serpent* (New York: Whittier Books, Inc., 1957), 15.

[98] Ibn Kathir, *The Story of Creation* (Karachi, Pakistan: Darul Ishaat, 2006), 109.

[99] St. Ephrem the Syrian, *Selected Prose Works*, Section 2, 18, trans. Edward G. Mathews, Jr. and Joseph P. Amar (Washington, D. C.: The Catholic University of America Press, 1994), 109.

[100] *Saltair na Rann*, 1781-1784, trans. David Greene.

[101] *Rabbi Abraham Ibn Ezra's Commentary on the Creation*, 77, trans. Michael Linetsky (Northvale, New Jersey: Jason Aronson Inc., 1998).

[102] Padraic Colum, *Orpheus, Myths of the World* (1930).

[103] St. Ambrose, *On Paradise*, http://www2.iath.virginia.edu/anderson/commentaries/Amb.html (accessed Jan. 12, 2011), 333.

[104] David Max Eichhorn, *Cain: Son of the Serpent* (New York: Whittier Books, Inc., 1957), 13-14.

[105] David Max Eichhorn, Cain: *Son of the Serpent* (New York: Whittier Books, Inc., 1957), 14.

[106] St. Ambrose, *On Paradise*, http://www2.iath.virginia.edu/anderson/commentaries/Amb.html (accessed Jan. 12, 2011), 336.

[107] David Max Eichhorn, *Cain: Son of the Serpent* (New York: Whittier Books, Inc., 1957), 17.

[108] St. Ambrose, *On Paradise*, http://www2.iath.virginia.edu/anderson/commentaries/Amb.html (accessed Jan. 12, 2011), 334.

[109] *Pirke De Rabbi Eliezer*, Chapter 13: The Serpent in Paradise, Pro. 9:13 [A. i.], trans. Gerald Friedlander (New York: Sepher-Hermon Press, 1981).

[110] *The Works of Philo Judaeus*, Questions and Answers on Genesis I, 33, trans. C. D. Yonge (London: H. G. Bohn, 1854-1855).

[111] St. Ambrose, *On Paradise*, http://www2.iath.virginia.edu/anderson/commentaries/Amb.html (accessed Jan. 12, 2011), 335-336.

[112] St. Ambrose, *On Paradise*, http://www2.iath.virginia.edu/anderson/commentaries/Amb.html (accessed Jan. 12, 2011), 334.

[113] *The Apocalypse of Moses / Apocalypsis Mosis*, 16:3, trans. R. H. Charles, http://www.pseudepigrapha.com/pseudepigrapha/aprmose.htm (accessed June 27, 2005).

[114] *Saltair na Rann*, 1234-1252, trans. David Greene.

[115] *Rabbi Abraham Ibn Ezra's Commentary on the Creation*, 79, trans. Michael Linetsky (Northvale, New Jersey: Jason Aronson Inc., 1998).

[116] S. G. F. Brandon, *Creation Legends of the Ancient Near East* (London: Hodder and Stoughton, 1963), 134.

[117] C. A. Phifer, *Annals of the Earth* (Chicago, Illinois: American Publishers Association, 1890), 61.

[118] *The Gospel of Barnabas*, 40, trans. Lonsdale and Laura Ragg (London, 1907), http://www.sacred-texts.com/isl/gbar/index.htm (accessed Oct. 27, 2011).

[119] *The Gospel of Barnabas*, 40, trans. Lonsdale and Laura Ragg (London, 1907), http://www.sacred-texts.com/isl/gbar/index.htm (accessed Oct. 27, 2011).

[120] *The Works of Philo Judaeus*, Questions and Answers on Genesis I, 33, trans. C. D. Yonge (London: H. G. Bohn, 1854-1855).
[121] Shira Halevi, *The Life Story of Adam and Havah*, Genesis (Northvale, New Jersey: Jason Aronson, Inc., 1997), 168.
[122] Dan Gayman, *The Two Seeds of Genesis 3:15* (Daniel Lee Gayman, 1977), 102.
[123] St. Ephrem the Syrian, *Selected Prose Works*, Section 2, 20(3), trans. Edward G. Mathews, Jr. and Joseph P. Amar (Washington, D. C.: The Catholic University of America Press, 1994), 113.
[124] *Esau/Edom, and the Trail of the Serpent - IV*, 1, http://www.biblebelievers.org.au/bb980930.htm (accessed July 8, 2000).
[125] David Max Eichhorn, *Cain: Son of the Serpent* (New York: Whittier Books, Inc., 1957), 20.
[126] St. Ambrose, *On Paradise*, http://www2.iath.virginia.edu/anderson/commentaries/Amb.html (accessed Jan. 12, 2011), 336.
[127] *The Chronicles of Jerahmeel (The Hebrew Bible Historiale)*, 22(4), trans. M. Gaster, Ph. D. (London: The Royal Asiatic Society, 1899).
[128] David Max Eichhorn, *Cain: Son of the Serpent* (New York: Whittier Books, Inc., 1957), 20.
[129] David Max Eichhorn, *Cain: Son of the Serpent* (New York: Whittier Books, Inc., 1957), 20.
[130] David Max Eichhorn, *Cain: Son of the Serpent* (New York: Whittier Books, Inc., 1957), 23.
[131] Michael E. Stone, *Adamgirk: The Adam Book of Arak'el of Siwnik* (Oxford: University Press, 2007), 102.
[132] David Max Eichhorn, *Cain: Son of the Serpent* (New York: Whittier Books, Inc., 1957), 20.
[133] Johann Andreas Eisenmenger, *The Traditions of the Jews, Contained in the Talmud and Other Mystical Writings* (London: J. Robinson, 1748), 21.
[134] Michael E. Stone, *Adamgirk: The Adam Book of Arak'el of Siwnik* (Oxford: University Press, 2007), 101.
[135] Dan Gayman, *The Two Seeds of Genesis 3:15* (Daniel Lee Gayman, 1977), 77; The Serpent Seed, *The Original Sin*, http://www.propheticrevelation.net/original_sin/the_serpent_seed_index.htm (accessed May 25, 2017).
[136] Dan Gayman, *The Two Seeds of Genesis 3:15* (Daniel Lee Gayman, 1977), 78.
[137] Andrew Collins, *From the Ashes of Angels* (Rochester, Vermont: Bear & Company, 1996), 40.
[138] *The Zohar*, Chayei Sara 3, http://www.zohar.com/chayei-sarah/he-who-tills-field-king%C2%9D (accessed Feb. 25, 2010).
[139] *The Babylonian Talmud*, Shabbath 145b-146a, http://halakhah.com/pdf/moed/Shabbath.pdf (accessed April 14, 2011).
[140] Louis Ginzberg, *The Legends of the Jews Volume V: Notes for Volume One and Two*, II Adam 85, trans. Henrietta Szold (Baltimore, Maryland: The Johns Hopkins University Press, 1909), 101.
[141] *The History of al-Tabari - Volume I: General Introduction and From the Creation to the Flood*, God's Testing of Adam, 107, trans. Franz Rosenthal (Albany: New York Press, 1989), 278.
[142] *The Zohar*, Bersheet A:47; David Max Eichhorn, *Cain: Son of the Serpent* (New York: Whittier Books, Inc., 1957), 27-28.
[143] Alan Unterman, *Dictionary of Jewish Lore and Legend* (London: Thames and Hudson Ltd., 1991), 74.
[144] David Max Eichhorn, *Cain: Son of the Serpent* (New York: Whittier Books, Inc., 1957), 15; *The Zohar*, Naso 5, http://www.zohar.com/naso/wife-suspected-adultery-sota (accessed Feb. 25, 2010).
[145] Daniel Parker, *Treatise on the Two Seeds*, 9-10, http://74.6.117.48/search/srpcache?ei=UTF-8&p=Daniel+parker+views+two+seeds&fr=yfp-t-701-1&u=http://cc.bingj.com/cache.aspx?q=Daniel+parker+views+two+seeds&d=4739874550581774&mkt=en-US&setlang=en-US&w=436227cc,3f1eddc9&icp=1&.intl=us&sig=gImURE75iMtbnov6bdTbKg-- (accessed April 1, 2011).
[146] Ibn Ezra, *Commentary on the Pentateuch: Genesis (Bereshit)* (New York: Menorah Publishing Company, Inc., 1988), 78.
[147] Howard Schwartz, *Tree of Souls: The Mythology of Judaism* (Oxford: University Press, 2004), 447.
[148] *The Apocalypse of Moses / Apocalypsis Mosis*, 19:3, trans. R. H. Charles, http://www.pseudepigrapha.com/pseudepigrapha/apcmose.htm (accessed June 27, 2005).
[149] David Max Eichhorn, *Cain: Son of the Serpent* (New York: Whittier Books, Inc., 1957), 22.
[150] *The Second Book of Adam and Eve (The Conflict of Adam and Eve with Satan)*, Book II 5, 10, trans. S. C. Malan (London: Williams and Norgate, 1882), 64.
[151] *The Babylonian Talmud*, Mas. Yevamoth 103b, Shabbath 145b-146a.
[152] *Mystery of Civilization*, 1, http://www.servantsofyahweh.mcmail.com/Armstrong/Armstrong07.htm (accessed April 24, 2001).
[153] *Mystery of Civilization*, 1, http://www.servantsofyahweh.mcmail.com/Armstrong/Armstrong07.htm (accessed April 24, 2001).
[154] *The Works of Philo Judaeus*, On Husbandry 24, 108, trans. C. D. Yonge (London: H. G. Bohn, 1854-1855).
[155] *The Armenian Apocryphal Adam Literature*, The History of the Creation and Transgression of Adam 31, trans. William Lowndes Lipscomb (Ann Arbor, Michigan: University Microfilms International, 1983), 123.
[156] *The Apocalypse of Moses / Apocalypsis Mosis*, 19:3, trans. R. H. Charles, http://www.pseudepigrapha.com/pseudepigrapha/aprmose.htm (accessed June 27, 2005).

[157] Johann Andreas Eisenmenger, *The Traditions of the Jews, Contained in the Talmud and Other Mystical Writings* (London: J. Robinson, 1748), 21.
[158] St. Ephrem the Syrian, *Selected Prose Works*, trans. Edward G. Mathews, Jr. and Joseph P. Amar (Washington, D. C.: The Catholic University of America Press, 1994), 108.
[159] Howard Schwartz, *Tree of Souls: The Mythology of Judaism* (Oxford: University Press, 2004), 435; *The Chronicles of Jerahmeel (The Hebrew Bible Historiale)*, 22(4), trans. M. Gaster, Ph. D. (London: The Royal Asiatic Society, 1899).
[160] David Max Eichhorn, *Cain: Son of the Serpent* (New York: Whittier Books, Inc., 1957), 26.
[161] Michael E. Stone, *Adamgirk: The Adam Book of Arak'el of Siwnik* (Oxford: University Press, 2007), 108.
[162] Michael E. Stone, *Adamgirk: The Adam Book of Arak'el of Siwnik* (Oxford: University Press, 2007), 104.
[163] Michael E. Stone, *Adamgirk: The Adam Book of Arak'el of Siwnik* (Oxford: University Press, 2007), 104.
[164] *The Armenian Apocryphal Adam Literature*, History and Sermon: Concerning the Creation of Adam and the Incarnation of Christ our God 22, trans. William Lowndes Lipscomb (Ann Arbor, Michigan: University Microfilms International, 1983), 263.
[165] Jayim Nahman Bialik and Yehoshua Hana Ravnitzky, *The Book of Legends (Sefer Ha-Aggadah): Legends of the Talmud and Midrash*, 85 (New York: Shocken Books, 1992), 20.
[166] Michael E. Stone, *Adamgirk: The Adam Book of Arak'el of Siwnik* (Oxford: University Press, 2007), 107.
[167] *The Armenian Apocryphal Adam Literature*, History and Sermon: Concerning the Creation of Adam and the Incarnation of Christ our God 26, trans. William Lowndes Lipscomb (Ann Arbor, Michigan: University Microfilms International, 1983), 263; David Max Eichhorn, *Cain: Son of the Serpent* (New York: Whittier Books, Inc., 1957), 26.
[168] *The Chronicles of Jerahmeel (The Hebrew Bible Historiale)*, 22(5), trans. M. Gaster, Ph. D. (London: The Royal Asiatic Society, 1899).
[169] Michael E. Stone, *Adamgirk: The Adam Book of Arak'el of Siwnik* (Oxford: University Press, 2007), 104.
[170] Michael E. Stone, *Adamgirk: The Adam Book of Arak'el of Siwnik* (Oxford: University Press, 2007), 104.
[171] *The Armenian Apocryphal Adam Literature*, History and Sermon: Concerning the Creation of Adam and the Incarnation of Christ our God 26, trans. William Lowndes Lipscomb (Ann Arbor, Michigan: University Microfilms International, 1983), 263.
[172] Michael E. Stone, *Adamgirk: The Adam Book of Arak'el of Siwnik* (Oxford: University Press, 2007), 107.
[173] *The Armenian Apocryphal Adam Literature*, History and Sermon: Concerning the Creation of Adam and the Incarnation of Christ our God 28, trans. William Lowndes Lipscomb (Ann Arbor, Michigan: University Microfilms International, 1983), 263.
[174] *The Armenian Apocryphal Adam Literature*, History and Sermon: Concerning the Creation of Adam and the Incarnation of Christ our God 29, trans. William Lowndes Lipscomb (Ann Arbor, Michigan: University Microfilms International, 1983), 263.
[175] *The Armenian Apocryphal Adam Literature*, History and Sermon: Concerning the Creation of Adam and the Incarnation of Christ our God 31, trans. William Lowndes Lipscomb (Ann Arbor, Michigan: University Microfilms International, 1983), 263-64.
[176] Ibn Ezra, *Commentary on the Pentateuch: Genesis (Bereshit)* (New York: Menorah Publishing Company, Inc., 1988), 78.
[177] Robert Graves and Raphael Patai, *Hebrew Myths: The Book of Genesis* (Garden City, New York: Doubleday & Company, 1964), 76.
[178] Robert Graves and Raphael Patai, *Hebrew Myths: The Book of Genesis* (Garden City, New York: Doubleday & Company, 1964), 76.
[179] *The Original Sin 2/3*, 5, http://www.biblebelievers.org.au/bb930113.htm (accessed March 24, 2011 312).

Chapter 3

[1] Michael E. Stone, *Adamgirk: The Adam Book of Arak'el of Siwnik*, 1.3.20 (Oxford: University Press, 2007), 107.
[2] S. G. F. Brandon, *Creation Legends of the Ancient Near East* (London: Hodder and Stoughton, 1963), 131.
[3] David Max Eichhorn, *Cain: Son of the Serpent* (New York: Whittier Books, Inc., 1957), 22; *The Armenian Apocryphal Adam Literature*, The History of the Creation and Transgression of Adam 31, trans. William Lowndes Lipscomb (Ann Arbor, Michigan: University Microfilms International, 1983), 123.
[4] St. Chrysostom, *Homilies on Genesis*, Homily 16, http://www2.iath.virginia.edu/anderson/commentaries/ChrGen.html (accessed Jan. 12, 2011).
[5] C. A. Phifer, *Annals of the Earth* (Chicago, Illinois: American Publishers Association, 1890), 44.
[6] T. W. Doane, *Bible Myths and Their Parallels in Other Religions: Being a Comparison of the Old And New Testament Myths and Miracles With Those of Heathen Natioins of Antiquity Considering Also Their Origin and Meaning* (New York: University Books, 1882), 15.
[7] T. W. Doane, *Bible Myths and Their Parallels in Other Religions: Being a Comparison of the Old And New Testament Myths and Miracles With Those of Heathen Natioins of Antiquity Considering Also Their Origin and Meaning* (New York: University Books, 1882), 15.
[8] *The Babylonian Talmud*, Sanhedrin 70b, http://halakhah.com/sanhedrin/sanhedrin_70.html (accessed April 14, 2011).

[9] Dan Gayman, *The Two Seeds of Genesis 3:15* (Daniel Lee Gayman, 1977), 79.
[10] *The Golden Legend or Lives of the Saints: Volume I*, trans. William Caxton (1483), http://www.fordham.edu/halsall/basis/goldenlegend/GoldenLegend-Volume1.htm (accessed Jan. 13, 2011), 61.
[11] *The Chronicles of Jerahmeel (The Hebrew Bible Historiale)*, 22(4), trans. M. Gaster, Ph. D. (London: The Royal Asiatic Society, 1899).
[12] Dan Gayman, *The Two Seeds of Genesis 3:15* (Daniel Lee Gayman, 1977), 89.
[13] St. Ambrose, *On Paradise*, http://www2.iath.virginia.edu/anderson/commentaries/Amb.html (accessed Jan. 12, 2011), 349.
[14] *The Second Book of Adam and Eve (The Conflict of Adam and Eve with Satan)*, Book II 5 10, trans. S. C. Malan (London: Williams and Norgate, 1882), 64.
[15] *The Armenian Apocryphal Adam Literature*, History and Sermon: Concerning the Creation of Adam and the Incarnation of Christ our God 37, trans. William Lowndes Lipscomb (Ann Arbor, Michigan: University Microfilms International, 1983), 264.
[16] Hyman E. Goldin, *The Book of Legends: Tales From the Talmud and Midrash* (New York: The Jordan Publishing Co., 1929), 23.
[17] St. Chrysostom, *Homilies on Genesis*, Homily 17, http://www2.iath.virginia.edu/anderson/commentaries/ChrGen.html (accessed Jan. 12, 2011).
[18] David Max Eichhorn, *Cain: Son of the Serpent* (New York: Whittier Books, Inc., 1957), 21.
[19] *Literature on Adam and Eve: Collected Essays*, 99, trans. Gary Anderson, Michael Stone and Johannes Tromp (Leiden: Brill, 2000), 198.
[20] St. Chrysostom, *Homilies on Genesis*, Homily 17, http://www2.iath.virginia.edu/anderson/commentaries/ChrGen.html (accessed Jan. 12, 2011).
[21] *The Gospel of Barnabas*, 41, trans. Lonsdale and Laura Ragg (London, 1907), http://www.sacred-texts.com/isl/gbar/index.htm (accessed Oct. 27, 2011).
[22] *The Book of the Cave of Treasures*, Adam's Expulsion From Paradise (notes), trans. Sir E. A. Wallis Budge (London: The Religious Tract Society, 1927), 68.
[23] *Rashi*, (Bereishit) Genesis 3:17, http://www.chabad.org/library/bible_cdo/aid/8168/showrashi/true (accessed Oct. 27, 2010).
[24] Perry Stone, *Urgent Warning to America (Part 10 of 12)*, https://www.dailymotion.com/video/x4lhchx_part-10-of-12-perry-stone-urgent-warning-to-america_music (accessed Oct. 13, 2014).
[25] *The Armenian Apocryphal Adam Literature*, The Words of Adam to Seth 20, trans. William Lowndes Lipscomb (Ann Arbor, Michigan: University Microfilms International, 1983), 224.
[26] E. Basil Redlich, *The Early Traditions of Genesis* (London: Gerald Duckworth & Co. Ltd., 1950), 82.
[27] Johann Andreas Eisenmenger, *The Traditions of the Jews, Contained in the Talmud and Other Mystical Writings* (London: J. Robinson, 1748), 24.
[28] Hyman E. Goldin, *The Book of Legends: Tales From the Talmud and Midrash* (New York: The Jordan Publishing Co., 1929), 25.
[29] *Saltair na Rann*, 1449-1452, trans. David Greene.
[30] *The Golden Legend or Lives of the Saints: Volume I*, trans. William Caxton (1483), http://www.fordham.edu/halsall/basis/goldenlegend/GoldenLegend-Volume1.htm (accessed Jan. 13, 2011), 61.
[31] *The Armenian Apocryphal Adam Literature*, The History of the Creation and Transgression of Adam 41, trans. William Lowndes Lipscomb (Ann Arbor, Michigan: University Microfilms International, 1983), 125.
[32] Johann Andreas Eisenmenger, *The Traditions of the Jews, Contained in the Talmud and Other Mystical Writings* (London: J. Robinson, 1748), 24.
[33] St. Chrysostom, *Homilies on Genesis*, Homily 17, http://www2.iath.virginia.edu/anderson/commentaries/ChrGen.html (accessed Jan. 12, 2011).
[34] St. Chrysostom, *Homilies on Genesis*, Homily 17, http://www2.iath.virginia.edu/anderson/commentaries/ChrGen.html (accessed Jan. 12, 2011).
[35] *The Book of Adam*, (44)24.3, trans. J. P. Mahe, http://www.pseudepigrapha.com/pseudepigrapha/TheBookOfAdam.htm (accessed June 27, 2005).
[36] *The Apocalypse of Moses / Apocalypsis Mosis*, 24:3, trans. R. H. Charles, http://www.pseudepigrapha.com/pseudepigrapha/apcmose.htm (accessed June 27, 2005).
[37] St. Ephrem the Syrian, *Selected Prose Works*, trans. Edward G. Mathews, Jr. and Joseph P. Amar (Washington, D. C.: The Catholic University of America Press, 1994), 120.
[38] Howard Schwartz, *Tree of Souls: The Mythology of Judaism* (Oxford: University Press, 2004), 128.
[39] *The History of al-Tabari – Volume I: General Introduction and From the Creation to the Flood*, The First House on Earth, 130, trans. Franz Rosenthal (Albany: New York Press, 1989), 301; *Saltair na Rann*, 1493-1496, trans. David Greene; *The First Book of Adam and Eve* 4 8.
[40] Michael E. Stone, *Adamgirk: The Adam Book of Arak'el of Siwnik* (Oxford: University Press, 2007), 108.
[41] St. Chrysostom, *Homilies on Genesis*, Homily 18, http://www2.iath.virginia.edu/anderson/commentaries/ChrGen.html (accessed Jan. 12, 2011); St. Ephrem the Syrian,

Selected Prose Works, trans. Edward G. Mathews, Jr. and Joseph P. Amar
(Washington, D. C.: The Catholic University of America Press, 1994), 121-122.

[42] C. A. Phifer, *Annals of the Earth* (Chicago, Illinois: American Publishers Association, 1890), 47.

[43] *The Golden Legend or Lives of the Saints: Volume I*, trans. William Caxton (1483), http://www.fordham.edu/halsall/basis/goldenlegend/GoldenLegend-Volume1.htm (accessed Jan. 13, 2011), 61.

[44] St. Ephrem the Syrian, *Selected Prose Works*, trans. Edward G. Mathews, Jr. and Joseph P. Amar (Washington, D. C.: The Catholic University of America Press, 1994), 121.

[45] Richard Gan, *The Doctrine of the Serpent Seed: Section II - Doctrinal Presentation*, 15, http://www.propheticrevelation.net/original_sin/the_serpent_seed_3.htm (accessed Feb. 22, 2011).

[46] *Blood*, Bible History Online, 1-2, http://www.bible-history.com/faussets/B/Blood/ (accessed Oct. 4, 2012).

[47] Shira Halevi, *The Life Story of Adam and Havah*, Genesis (Northvale, New Jersey: Jason Aronson, Inc., 1997), 208.

[48] Brian S. Wright, *Blood & Seed: What Really Happened in Eden* (The American Biblical Institute of Holy Land Studies, 2010), 194.

[49] Brian S. Wright, *Blood & Seed: What Really Happened in Eden* (The American Biblical Institute of Holy Land Studies, 2010), 131.

[50] *The Works of Philo Judaeus*, Questions and Answers on Genesis I, 65, trans. C. D. Yonge (London: H. G. Bohn, 1854-1855).

[51] Johann Andreas Eisenmenger, *The Traditions of the Jews, Contained in the Talmud and Other Mystical Writings* (London: J. Robinson, 1748), 23.

[52] *The Zohar*, Beresheet a46, 2, http://www.zohar.com/beresheet/and-hashem-elohim-commanded-adam%C2%9D (accessed May 14, 2011).

[53] *The Original Sin 1/3*, 1, http://www.biblebelievers.org.au/bb930112.htm (accessed March 24, 2011).

[54] *The Zohar*, Beresheet a46, 2, http://www.zohar.com/beresheet/and-hashem-elohim-commanded-adam%C2%9D (accessed May 14, 2011).

[55] *The Zohar*, Vol. 15 Tazria 8., Verse 33, Circumcision and the Foreskin, https://www2.kabbalah.com/k/index.php/p=zohar/zohar&vol=30&sec=1076#11273 ().

[56] St. Chrysostom, *Homilies on Genesis*, Homily 17, http://www2.iath.virginia.edu/anderson/commentaries/ChrGen.html (accessed Jan. 12, 2011).

[57] St. Chrysostom, *Homilies on Genesis*, Homily 17, http://www2.iath.virginia.edu/anderson/commentaries/ChrGen.html (accessed Jan. 12, 2011).

[58] *The Golden Legend or Lives of the Saints: Volume I*, trans. William Caxton (1483), http://www.fordham.edu/halsall/basis/goldenlegend/GoldenLegend-Volume1.htm (accessed Jan. 13, 2011), 61.

[59] *The Golden Legend or Lives of the Saints: Volume I*, trans. William Caxton (1483), http://www.fordham.edu/halsall/basis/goldenlegend/GoldenLegend-Volume1.htm (accessed Jan. 13, 2011), 61.

[60] Dan Gayman, *The Two Seeds of Genesis 3:15* (Daniel Lee Gayman, 1977), 106.

[61] Howard Schwartz, *Tree of Souls: The Mythology of Judaism* (Oxford: University Press, 2004), 435.

[62] John Skinner, *A Critical and Exegetical Commentary on Genesis* (Edinburgh: T. & T. Clark, 1956), 83.

[63] *Gates of Jewish Heritage, Nor Forcing Woman, the Punishment of Eve, and Learning From Animals*, 3, http://www.jewishgates.org/taland/talmud/gender/force.html (accessed Dec. 25, 2000 340).

[64] Dan Gayman, *The Two Seeds of Genesis 3:15* (Daniel Lee Gayman, 1977), 94.

[65] Dan Gayman, The Two Seeds of Genesis 3:15 (Daniel Lee Gayman, 1977), 94.

[66] Richard Gan, *The Doctrine of the Serpent Seed: Section II - Doctrinal Presentation*, 18, http://www.propheticrevelation.net/original_sin/the_serpent_seed_3.htm (accessed Feb. 22, 2011); Dan Gayman, *The Two Seeds of Genesis 3:15* (Daniel Lee Gayman, 1977), 52-53.

[67] St. Chrysostom, *Homilies on Genesis*, Homily 17, http://www2.iath.virginia.edu/anderson/commentaries/ChrGen.html (accessed Jan. 12, 2011).

[68] Michael E. Stone, *Adamgirk: The Adam Book of Arak'el of Siwnik* (Oxford: University Press, 2007), 147.

[69] David Max Eichhorn, *Cain: Son of the Serpent* (New York: Whittier Books, Inc., 1957), 31.

[70] Flavius Josephus, *Jewish Antiquities, Book 1*, 45-50, trans. H. ST. J. Thackeray (London: William Heinemann Ltd., 1961), 23.

[71] St. Ambrose, *On Paradise*, http://www2.iath.virginia.edu/anderson/commentaries/Amb.html (accessed Jan. 12, 2011), 350.

[72] St. Ambrose, *On Paradise*, http://www2.iath.virginia.edu/anderson/commentaries/Amb.html (accessed Jan. 12, 2011), 351.

[73] St. Chrysostom, *Homilies on Genesis*, Homily 17, http://www2.iath.virginia.edu/anderson/commentaries/ChrGen.html (accessed Jan. 12, 2011).

[74] Dan Gayman, *The Two Seeds of Genesis 3:15* (Daniel Lee Gayman, 1977), 90.

[75] Michael E. Stone, *Adamgirk: The Adam Book of Arak'el of Siwnik* (Oxford: University Press, 2007), 103.

[76] *The Armenian Apocryphal Adam Literature*, The History of the Creation and Transgression of Adam 42, trans. William Lowndes Lipscomb (Ann Arbor, Michigan: University Microfilms International, 1983), 125.

[77] Hyman E. Goldin, *The Book of Legends: Tales From the Talmud and Midrash* (New York: The Jordan Publishing

Co., 1929), 24.

[78] Ibn Kathir, *Stories of the Prophets* (London: Darussalam, 2003), 28-29.

[79] Louis Ginzberg, *The Legends of the Jews Volume V: Notes for Volume One and Two*, trans. Henrietta Szold (Baltimore, Maryland: The Johns Hopkins University Press, 1909), 101.

[80] *The Book of Adam*, (44)25.1, trans. J. P. Mahe, http://www.pseudepigrapha.com/pseudepigrapha/TheBookOfAdam.htm (accessed June 27, 2005).

[81] *Gates of Jewish Heritage, Nor Forcing Woman, the Punishment of Eve, and Learning From Animals*, 2-3, http://www.jewishgates.org/taland/talmud/gender/force.html (accessed Dec. 25, 2000 340).

[82] Richard Gan, *The Doctrine of the Serpent Seed: Section II - Doctrinal Presentation*, 18, http://www.propheticrevelation.net/original_sin/the_serpent_seed_3.htm (accessed Feb. 22, 2011).

[83] *The Book of Adam*, (44)25.2, trans. J. P. Mahe, http://www.pseudepigrapha.com/pseudepigrapha/TheBookOfAdam.htm (accessed June 27, 2005).

[84] *The Original Sin 1/3*, 1, http://www.biblebelievers.org.au/bb930112.htm (accessed March 24, 2011 311).

[85] Shira Halevi, *The Life Story of Adam and Havah*, Genesis (Northvale, New Jersey: Jason Aronson, Inc., 1997), 204.

[86] Shira Halevi, *The Life Story of Adam and Havah*, Genesis (Northvale, New Jersey: Jason Aronson, Inc., 1997), 246.

[87] *The Apocalypse of Moses / Apocalypsis Mosis*, 25:3-4, trans. R. H. Charles, http://www.pseudepigrapha.com/pseudepigrapha/aprmose.htm (accessed June 27, 2005).

[88] *The Original Sin 1/3*, 1, http://www.biblebelievers.org.au/bb930112.htm (accessed March 24, 2011 311).

[89] Dan Gayman, *The Two Seeds of Genesis 3:15* (Daniel Lee Gayman, 1977), 93.

[90] *The Golden Legend or Lives of the Saints: Volume I*, trans. William Caxton (1483), http://www.fordham.edu/halsall/basis/goldenlegend/GoldenLegend-Volume1.htm (accessed Jan. 13, 2011), 61.

[91] David Kevin Delaney, *The Sevenfold Vengeance of Cain: Genesis 4 in Early Jewish and Christian Interpretation* (University of Virginia, 1996), 12.

[92] Gospel of Barnabas, 41, (accessed, 2011 315).

[93] *The Golden Legend or Lives of the Saints: Volume I*, trans. William Caxton (1483), http://www.fordham.edu/halsall/basis/goldenlegend/GoldenLegend-Volume1.htm (accessed Jan. 13, 2011), 61.

[94] *The Golden Legend or Lives of the Saints: Volume I*, trans. William Caxton (1483), http://www.fordham.edu/halsall/basis/goldenlegend/GoldenLegend-Volume1.htm (accessed Jan. 13, 2011), 61.

[95] St. Ambrose, *On Paradise*, http://www2.iath.virginia.edu/anderson/commentaries/Amb.html (accessed Jan. 12, 2011), 353.

[96] *The Works of Philo Judaeus*, Questions and Answers I, 48, number, trans. C. D. Yonge (London: H. G. Bohn, 1854-1855).

[97] *The Babylonian Talmud*, Yoma 75a, http://halakhah.com/pdf/moed/Yoma.pdf (accessed April 14, 2011).

[98] St. Ambrose, *On Paradise*, http://www2.iath.virginia.edu/anderson/commentaries/Amb.html (accessed Jan. 12, 2011), 351-352.

[99] St. Ambrose, *On Paradise*, http://www2.iath.virginia.edu/anderson/commentaries/Amb.html (accessed Jan. 12, 2011), 353-354.

[100] *The Golden Legend or Lives of the Saints: Volume I*, trans. William Caxton (1483), http://www.fordham.edu/halsall/basis/goldenlegend/GoldenLegend-Volume1.htm (accessed Jan. 13, 2011), 61.

[101] *The Apocalypse of Moses / Apocalypsis Mosis*, 26:2, trans. R. H. Charles, http://www.pseudepigrapha.com/pseudepigrapha/aprmose.htm (accessed June 27, 2005).

[102] John Skinner, *A Critical and Exegetical Commentary on Genesis* (Edinburgh: T. & T. Clark, 1956), 79; Bentley Layton, The Gnostic Scriptures (New York, New York: Doubleday, 1995), 297.

[103] Louis Ginzberg, *The Legends of the Jews Volume I: From the Creation to Jacob*, trans. Henrietta Szold (Baltimore, Maryland: The Johns Hopkins University Press, 1909), 105.

[104] Ellen Frankel, *The Classic Tales: 4000 Years of Jewish Lore* (Northvale, New Jersey: Jason Aronson Inc., 1989), 30.

[105] Shira Halevi, *The Life Story of Adam and Havah* (Northvale, New Jersey: Jason Aronson, Inc., 1997), 203.

[106] *The Companion Bible*, Gen. 3:14 (notes) (Grand Rapids, Michigan: Kregel Publications, 1990).

[107] Andrew Collins, *From the Ashes of Angels* (Rochester, Vermont: Bear & Company, 1996), 70.

[108] *The Gospel of Barnabas*, 41, trans. Lonsdale and Laura Ragg (London, 1907), http://www.sacred-texts.com/isl/gbar/index.htm (accessed Oct. 27, 2011).

[109] Ellen Frankel, *The Classic Tales: 4000 Years of Jewish Lore* (Northvale, New Jersey: Jason Aronson Inc., 1989), 30.

[110] Alan Unterman, *Dictionary of Jewish Lore and Legend* (London: Thames and Hudson Ltd., 1991), 170.

[111] *The Armenian Apocryphal Adam Literature*, The Words of Adam to Seth 14, trans. William Lowndes Lipscomb (Ann Arbor, Michigan: University Microfilms International, 1983), 222.

[112] Rabbi Leo Jung, Ph. D., *Fallen Angels in Jewish, Christian and Mohammedan Literature* (New York: KTAV Publishing House, 1974), 155.

[113] *The Golden Legend or Lives of the Saints: Volume I*, trans. William Caxton (1483), http://www.fordham.edu/halsall/basis/goldenlegend/GoldenLegend-Volume1.htm (accessed Jan. 13, 2011), 61.

[114] *The Companion Bible*, Gen. 3:15 (notes) (Grand Rapids, Michigan: Kregel Publications, 1990).
[115] David Max Eichhorn, *Cain: Son of the Serpent* (New York: Whittier Books, Inc., 1957), 19.
[116] James L. Kugel, *Traditions of the Bible* (Cambridge, Massachusetts: Harvard University Press, 1998), 133.
[117] *The Book of the Apocalypse of Baruch (2 Baruch)*, 56:6, trans. R. H. Charles, http://www.pseudepigrapha.com/pseudepigrapha/2Baruch.html (accessed Oct. 31, 2006).
[118] *The Original Sin 1/3*, 1, http://www.biblebelievers.org.au/bb930112.htm (accessed March 24, 2011 311).
[119] Shira Halevi, *The Life Story of Adam and Havah* (Northvale, New Jersey: Jason Aronson, Inc., 1997), 208.
[120] David Max Eichhorn, *Cain: Son of the Serpent* (New York: Whittier Books, Inc., 1957), 19.

Chapter 4

[1] T. W. Doane, *Bible Myths and Their Parallels in Other Religions: Being a Comparison of the Old And New Testament Myths and Miracles With Those of Heathen Nations of Antiquity Considering Also Their Origin and Meaning* (New York: University Books, 1882), 10.
[2] T. W. Doane, *Bible Myths and Their Parallels in Other Religions: Being a Comparison of the Old And New Testament Myths and Miracles With Those of Heathen Nations of Antiquity Considering Also Their Origin and Meaning* (New York: University Books, 1882), 11.
[3] David Max Eichhorn, *Cain: Son of the Serpent* (New York: Whittier Books, Inc., 1957), 40.
[4] *The Book of the Bee*, 18 (notes), trans. Earnest A. Wallis Budge, M. A., http://www.sacred-texts.com/chr/bb/bb18.htm (accessed Oct. 10, 2004).
[5] David Max Eichhorn, *Cain: Son of the Serpent* (New York: Whittier Books, Inc., 1957), 40.
[6] Ralph Edward Woodrow, *Babylon Mystery Religion: Ancient and Modern* (Riverside, California: Ralph Woodrow Evangelistic Association, Inc., 1966), 90; Dan Gayman, *The Two Seeds of Genesis 3:15* (Daniel Lee Gayman, 1977), 69-70.
[7] C. A. Phifer, *Annals of the Earth* (Chicago, Illinois: American Publishers Association, 1890), 154.71 1.
[8] *Rabbi Abraham Ibn Ezra's Commentary on the Creation*, trans. Michael Linetsky (Northvale, New Jersey: Jason Aronson Inc., 1998), 75 (notes).
[9] Dan Gayman, *The Two Seeds of Genesis 3:15* (Daniel Lee Gayman, 1977), 416.
[10] *The Midrash Rabbah*, trans. Rabbi Dr. H. Freedman and Maurice Simon (London: The Soncino Press, 1961), 180.
[11] *Saltair na Rann*, 1961-1964, trans. David Greene.
[12] *The Zohar*, Beresheet a50, http://www.zohar.com/beresheet/aza-and-azael (accessed Feb. 25, 2010); Oliver Farrar Emerson, *Legends of Cain, Especially in Old and Middle English* (Philadelphia, Pennsylvania: American Sunday-School Union, 1916), 839, 878 (notes), 896; *The Zohar*, Acharei Mot 59, http://www.zohar.com/acharei-mot/two-female-spirits (accessed Feb. 25, 2010); *The Zohar*, Safra Det'zniuta 3, http://www.zohar.com/safra-detzniuta/third-chapter (accessed Feb. 25, 2010); Louis Ginzberg, *The Legends of the Jews Volume I: From the Creation to Jacob*, trans. Henrietta Szold (Baltimore, Maryland: The Johns Hopkins University Press, 1909), 105; *The Zohar*, Beresheet a47, http://www.zohar.com/beresheet/now-serpent-was-craftier (accessed Feb. 25, 2010).
[13] C. A. Phifer, *Annals of the Earth* (Chicago, Illinois: American Publishers Association, 1890), 146.
[14] C. A. Phifer, *Annals of the Earth* (Chicago, Illinois: American Publishers Association, 1890), 54.126.
[15] Dan Gayman, *The Two Seeds of Genesis 3:15* (Daniel Lee Gayman, 1977), 33.
[16] *The History of al-Tabari - Volume I: General Introduction and From the Creation to the Flood*, Iblis and Adam's Children, 150, trans. Franz Rosenthal (Albany: New York Press, 1989), 321.
[17] *The History of al-Tabari - Volume I: General Introduction and From the Creation to the Flood*, Iblis and Adam's Children, 150, trans. Franz Rosenthal (Albany: New York Press, 1989), 321.
[18] *The History of al-Tabari - Volume I: General Introduction and From the Creation to the Flood*, Iblis and Adam's Children, 149, trans. Franz Rosenthal (Albany: New York Press, 1989), 320.
[19] David Max Eichhorn, *Cain: Son of the Serpent* (New York: Whittier Books, Inc., 1957), 29.
[20] Howard Schwartz, *Tree of Souls: The Mythology of Judaism* (Oxford: University Press, 2004), 449.
[21] *Vita Adae Et Evae (The Life of Adam and Eve)*, 31 (notes), trans. R. H. Charles, The Apocrypha and Pseudepigrapha of the Old Testament (Oxford: Clarendon Press, 1913).
[22] *Saltair na Rann*, 1909-1912, trans. David Greene.
[23] Johann Andreas Eisenmenger, *The Traditions of the Jews, Contained in the Talmud and Other Mystical Writings* (London: J. Robinson, 1748), 197.
[24] Bentley Layton, *The Gnostic Scriptures*, "Other" Gnostic Teachings According to St. Irenaeus 1.30.7 (New York: Doubleday, 1995), 176; Louis Ginzberg, *The Legends of the Jews Volume V: Notes for Volume One and Two*, III The Ten Generations 6, trans. Henrietta Szold (Baltimore, Maryland: The Johns Hopkins University Press, 1909), 135; *Saltair na Rann*, 1901-1904, trans. David Greene; Howard Schwartz, *Tree of Souls: The Mythology of Judaism* (Oxford: University Press, 2004), 443; Dan Gayman, *The Two Seeds of Genesis 3:15* (Daniel Lee Gayman, 1977), 416.
[25] Brian S. Wright, *Blood & Seed: What Really Happened in Eden* (The American Biblical Institute of Holy Land Studies, 2010), 114; Oliver Farrar Emerson, *Legends of Cain, Especially in Old and Middle English* (Philadelphia, Pennsylvania: American Sunday-School Union, 1916), 896; Anonymous, *New Interpretation of a Portion of the Third Chapter of Genesis, Viewed in Connection With Other Parts*

of the Bible; Including an Inquiry Into the Introduction, Nature, and Extent of Satanic Influence in the World (London, J. Hatchard and Son, 1834), 103; *St. Chrysostom, Homilies on Genesis*, Homily 18.9, http://www2.iath.virginia.edu/anderson/commentaries/ChrGen.html (accessed Jan. 12, 2011); St. Ephrem the Syrian, *Selected Prose Works*, trans. Edward G. Mathews, Jr. and Joseph P. Amar (Washington, D. C.: The Catholic University of America Press, 1994), 124.

[26] Dan Gayman, *The Two Seeds of Genesis 3:15* (Daniel Lee Gayman, 1977), 369; *The Zohar*, Beresheet b62, http://www.zohar.com/beresheet-b/cain-killed-abel (accessed Feb. 25, 2010); Andrew Collins, *From the Ashes of Angels* (Rochester, Vermont: Bear & Company, 1996), 55.

[27] Dan Gayman, *The Two Seeds of Genesis 3:15* (Daniel Lee Gayman, 1977), 33.

[28] *Mystery of Civilization*, 1, http://www.servantsofyahweh.mcmail.com/Armstrong/Armstrong07.htm (accessed April 24, 2001).

[29] *The Original Sin*, 1, http://www.biblebelievers.org.htm (accessed June 4, 2010); C. A. Phifer, *Annals of the Earth* (Chicago, Illinois: American Publishers Association, 1890), 146.

[30] C. A. Phifer, *Annals of the Earth* (Chicago, Illinois: American Publishers Association, 1890), 147.

[31] Louis Ginzberg, *The Legends of the Jews Volume I: From the Creation to Jacob*, trans. Henrietta Szold (Baltimore, Maryland: The Johns Hopkins University Press, 1909), 105.

[32] Richard Gan, *The Original Sin*, 2, http://www.propheticrevelation.net/original_sin/the_serpent_seed_1.htm (accessed March 24, 2011).

[33] *The Gospel of Philip*, trans. Wesley W. Isenberg, http://www.gnosis.org/naghamm/gop.html (accessed Feb. 4, 2010).

[34] *The Zohar*, Beresheet b60, http://www.zohar.com/beresheet-b/and-man-knew (accessed Feb. 25, 2010).

[35] Louis Ginzberg, *The Legends of the Jews Volume I: From the Creation to Jacob*, trans. Henrietta Szold (Baltimore, Maryland: The Johns Hopkins University Press, 1909), 106.

[36] *Saltair na Rann*, 1897-1900, trans. David Greene.

[37] Howard Schwartz, *Tree of Souls: The Mythology of Judaism* (Oxford: University Press, 2004), 449.

[38] *Literature on Adam and Eve: Collected Essays*, 116, trans. Gary Anderson, Michael Stone and Johannes Tromp (Leiden: Brill, 2000), 203.

[39] *Saltair na Rann*, 1957-1960, trans. David Greene.

[40] *The Zohar*, Idra Raba 47, http://www.zohar.com/idra-raba/cain-and-abel (accessed Feb. 25, 2010).

[41] the *"Garden of Eden" Bible Study*, 17, http://www.frank.germano.com/gardenofeden.htm (accessed Nov. 15, 2006).

[42] the *"Garden of Eden" Bible Study*, 16, http://www.frank.germano.com/gardenofeden.htm (accessed Nov. 15, 2006); Bentley Layton, *The Gnostic Scriptures* (New York, New York: Doubleday, 1995), 25, 35-38, 197; Robert Graves and Raphael Patai, *Hebrew Myths: The Book of Genesis* (Garden City, New York: Doubleday & Company, 1964), 99; John Skinner, *A Critical and Exegetical Commentary on Genesis* (Edinburgh: T. & T. Clark, 1956), 103.

[43] *The Zohar*, Beresheet b62, http://www.zohar.com/beresheet-b/cain-killed-abel (accessed Feb. 25, 2010).

[44] the *"Garden of Eden" Bible Study*, 16, http://www.frank.germano.com/gardenofeden.htm (accessed Nov. 15, 2006).

[45] Louis Ginzberg, *The Legends of the Jews Volume I: From the Creation to Jacob*, trans. Henrietta Szold (Baltimore, Maryland: The Johns Hopkins University Press, 1909), 108.

[46] Robert Graves and Raphael Patai, *Hebrew Myths: The Book of Genesis* (Garden City, New York: Doubleday & Company, 1964), 99.

[47] *Saltair na Rann*, 2493-2496, trans. David Greene.

[48] *Book of the Glory of Kings (Kerba Nagast)*, 3. Concerning the Kingdom of Adam, trans. Sir. E. A. Wallis Budge (London: Humphrey Milford, 1932).

[49] *The Zohar*, Beresheet a47, http://www.zohar.com/beresheet/now-serpent-was-craftier (accessed Feb. 25, 2010).

[50] *The Zohar*, Beresheet a47, http://www.zohar.com/beresheet/now-serpent-was-craftier (accessed Feb. 25, 2010).

[51] *Vita Adae Et Evae (The Life of Adam and Eve)*, i.3, trans. R. H. Charles, The Apocrypha and Pseudepigrapha of the Old Testament (Oxford: Clarendon Press, 1913).

[52] *Saltair na Rann*, 1901-1904, trans. David Greene.

[53] Louis Ginzberg, *The Legends of the Jews Volume V: Notes for Volume One and Two*, III The Ten Generations 12, trans. Henrietta Szold (Baltimore, Maryland: The Johns Hopkins University Press, 1909), 136.

[54] *The Book of the Generations of Adam*, Ch. 5.1, http://www.earth-history.com/Pseudepigrapha/generations-adam.htm (accessed May 5, 2007).

[55] Flavius Josephus, *Jewish Antiquities, Book 1*, I 50-54, trans. H. ST. J. Thackeray (London: William Heinemann Ltd., 1961), 25.

[56] *Pirke De Rabbi Eliezer*, Chapter 22: The Fall of the Angels [26a. i.] (and notes) [A. i.], trans. Gerald Friedlander (New York: Sepher-Hermon Press, 1981), 158.

[57] David Max Eichhorn, *Cain: Son of the Serpent* (New York: Whittier Books, Inc., 1957), 37.

[58] Bentley Layton, *The Gnostic Scriptures*, 1.30.9 Cain and Abel (New York: Doubleday, 1995), 177.

[59] Samuel A. Berman, *Midrash Tanhuma-Yelammedenu: An English Translation of Genesis and Exodus from the Printed Version of Tanhuma-Yelammedenu with an Introduction, Notes, and Indexes* (Hoboken, New Jersey: KTAV Publishing House, 1996), 28; David Max Eichhorn, *Cain: Son of the Serpent* (New York: Whittier Books, Inc., 1957), 64.

⁶⁰ *Saltair na Rann*, 1977-1980, trans. David Greene.
⁶¹ E. S. G. Bristowe, *Cain - An Argument* (Leicester: Edgar Backus, 1950), 95.
⁶² *The Book of the Generations of Adam*, Ch. 5.3, http://www.earth-history.com/Pseudepigrapha/generations-adam.htm (accessed May 5, 2007).
⁶³ *The Works of Philo Judaeus*, Questions and Answers on Genesis 59, trans. C. D. Yonge (London: H. G. Bohn, 1854-1855).
⁶⁴ David Max Eichhorn, *Cain: Son of the Serpent* (New York: Whittier Books, Inc., 1957), 36.
⁶⁵ *The Works of Philo Judaeus*, Questions and Answers on Genesis 59, trans. C. D. Yonge (London: H. G. Bohn, 1854-1855).
⁶⁶ David Max Eichhorn, *Cain: Son of the Serpent* (New York: Whittier Books, Inc., 1957), 36.
⁶⁷ David Max Eichhorn, *Cain: Son of the Serpent* (New York: Whittier Books, Inc., 1957), 37; Shira Halevi, *The Life Story of Adam and Havah* (Northvale, New Jersey: Jason Aronson, Inc., 1997), 246.
⁶⁸ Shira Halevi, *The Life Story of Adam and Havah* (Northvale, New Jersey: Jason Aronson, Inc., 1997), 246.
⁶⁹ David Max Eichhorn, *Cain: Son of the Serpent* (New York: Whittier Books, Inc., 1957), 38.
⁷⁰ *The Works of Philo Judaeus*, The Cherubim 22.65, trans. C. D. Yonge (London: H. G. Bohn, 1854-1855); David Max Eichhorn, *Cain: Son of the Serpent* (New York: Whittier Books, Inc., 1957), 35.
⁷¹ David Max Eichhorn, *Cain: Son of the Serpent* (New York: Whittier Books, Inc., 1957), 36.
⁷² David Max Eichhorn, *Cain: Son of the Serpent* (New York: Whittier Books, Inc., 1957), 36.
⁷³ *Rashi*, (Bereishit) Genesis 4:1, http://www.chabad.org/library/bible_cdo/aid/8168/showrashi/true (accessed Oct. 27, 2010).
⁷⁴ Robert Graves and Raphael Patai, *Hebrew Myths: The Book of Genesis* (Garden City, New York: Doubleday & Company, 1964), 92; *The Book of the Bee*, Chap. 18, Of Adam's Knowing Eve, trans. Earnest A. Wallis Budge, M. A., http://www.sacred-texts.com/chr/bb/bb18.htm (accessed Oct. 10, 2004) 1 (notes); *The History of al-Tabari - Volume I: General Introduction and From the Creation to the Flood*, Cain and Abel, 137, trans. Franz Rosenthal (Albany: New York Press, 1989), 308.
⁷⁵ *The Book of the Bee*, Chap. 18, Of Adam's Knowing Eve. Trans. Earnest A. Wallis Budge, M. A., http://www.sacred-texts.com/chr/bb/b18.htm (accessed Oct. 10, 2004).
⁷⁶ Glen W. Chapman, *Life and Times Before the Flood: Taken From Ancient Documents*, "Livre d'Adam," in Migne, Dictionnaire 1:56, 5, http://bookofthenephilim.blogspot.com/2009/02/life-and-times-before-flood-taken.html (accessed Dec. 3, 2000).
⁷⁷ *The Book of the Bee*, Chap. 18, Of Adam's Knowing Eve. Trans. Earnest A. Wallis Budge, M. A., http://www.sacred-texts.com/chr/bb/b18.htm (accessed Oct. 10, 2004); *The Book of the Rolls (Kitab Al-Magall)*, trans. Margaret Dunlop Gibson, Apocrypha Arabica (London: C. J. Clay and Sons, 1901), 17.
⁷⁸ *The Armenian Apocryphal Adam Literature*, This is the History of Abel and Cain the Sons of Adam 15, trans. William Lowndes Lipscomb (Ann Arbor, Michigan: University Microfilms International, 1983), 161.
⁷⁹ *The Golden Legend or Lives of the Saints: Volume I*, trans. William Caxton (1483), http://www.fordham.edu/halsall/basis/goldenlegend/GoldenLegend-Volume1.htm (accessed Jan. 13, 2011), 62.
⁸⁰ St. Ephrem the Syrian, *Selected Prose Works*, Section III 3(3), trans. Edward G. Mathews, Jr. and Joseph P. Amar (Washington, D. C.: The Catholic University of America Press, 1994), 125.
⁸¹ Oliver Farrar Emerson, *Legends of Cain, Especially in Old and Middle English* (Philadelphia, Pennsylvania: American Sunday-School Union, 1916), 847.
⁸² Hyman E. Goldin, *The Book of Legends: Tales From the Talmud and Midrash* (New York: The Jordan Publishing Co., 1929), 31.
⁸³ *Rashi*, (Bereishit) Genesis 4:3, http://www.chabad.org/library/bible_cdo/aid/8168/showrashi/true (accessed Oct. 27, 2010); St. Ephrem the Syrian, *Selected Prose Works*, Section III 2, trans. Edward G. Mathews, Jr. and Joseph P. Amar (Washington, D. C.: The Catholic University of America Press, 1994), 124; Samuel A. Berman, *Midrash Tanhuma-Yelammedenu: An English Translation of Genesis and Exodus from the Printed Version of Tanhuma-Yelammedenu with an Introduction, Notes, and Indexes* (Hoboken, New Jersey: KTAV Publishing House, 1996), 28; *The Book of the Generations of Adam*, Ch. 5.5, http://www.earth-history.com/Pseudepigrapha/generations-adam.htm (accessed May 5, 2007).
⁸⁴ James L. Kugel, *The Bible As It Was* (Cambridge, Massachusetts: Harvard University Press, 1997), 89.
⁸⁵ *The Zohar*, Tetzaveh 4, http://www.zohar.com/tetzaveh/and-it-came-pass-end-days (accessed Feb. 25, 2010); *The Zohar*, Bo 2, http://www.zohar.com/bo/now-there-was-day¦and-adversary-came-also-among-them (accessed Feb. 25, 2010).
⁸⁶ Oliver Farrar Emerson, *Legends of Cain, Especially in Old and Middle English* (Philadelphia, Pennsylvania: American Sunday-School Union, 1916), 849-850; *The Golden Legend or Lives of the Saints: Volume I*, trans. William Caxton (1483), http://www.fordham.edu/halsall/basis/goldenlegend/GoldenLegend-Volume1.htm (accessed Jan. 13, 2011), 62.
⁸⁷ *The Book of the Bee*, Chap. 18, Of Adam's Knowing Eve 1 (notes). Trans. Earnest A. Wallis Budge, M. A., http://www.sacred-texts.com/chr/bb/b18.htm (accessed Oct. 10, 2004).
⁸⁸ *The Armenian Apocryphal Adam Literature*, This is the History of Abel and Cain the Sons of Adam 7 (notes), trans.

William Lowndes Lipscomb (Ann Arbor, Michigan: University Microfilms International, 1983), 158.
[89] *The Book of the Bee*, Chap. 18, Of Adam's Knowing Eve 1 (notes). Trans. Earnest A. Wallis Budge, M. A., http://www.sacred-texts.com/chr/bb/b18.htm (accessed Oct. 10, 2004).
[90] David Goldstein, *Jewish Legends (Library of the World's Myths and Legends)* (New York: Peter Bedrick Books, 1933), 43.
[91] *The Armenian Apocryphal Adam Literature*, This is the History of Abel and Cain the Sons of Adam 9, trans. William Lowndes Lipscomb (Ann Arbor, Michigan: University Microfilms International, 1983), 159.
[92] Rev. G. Oliver, *The Antiquities of Free-Masonry; Comprising Illustrations of the Five Grand Periods of Masonry, From the Creation of the World to the Dedication of King Solomon's Temple* (London: Richard Spencer, 314, High Holborn, 1843), 43.
[93] *St. Ephrem the Syrian: Selected Prose Works*, Section III 4, trans. Edward G. Mathews, Jr. and Joseph P. Amar (Washington, D. C.: The Catholic University of America Press, 1994), 126.
[94] *St. Ephrem the Syrian: Selected Prose Works*, Section III 3(2), trans. Edward G. Mathews, Jr. and Joseph P. Amar (Washington, D. C.: The Catholic University of America Press, 1994), 125.
[95] *St. Ephrem the Syrian: Selected Prose Works*, Section III 3(3), trans. Edward G. Mathews, Jr. and Joseph P. Amar (Washington, D. C.: The Catholic University of America Press, 1994), 125.
[96] *St. Ephrem the Syrian: Selected Prose Works*, Section III 2(2), trans. Edward G. Mathews, Jr. and Joseph P. Amar (Washington, D. C.: The Catholic University of America Press, 1994), 125.
[97] David Kevin Delaney, *The Sevenfold Vengeance of Cain: Genesis 4 in Early Jewish and Christian Interpretation* (University of Virginia, 1996), 179.
[98] S. Baring-Gould, *Legends of the Patriarchs and Prophets and Other Old Testament Characters* (New York: American Book Exchange, 1881), 73.
[99] S. Baring-Gould, *Legends of the Patriarchs and Prophets and Other Old Testament Characters* (New York: American Book Exchange, 1881), 75.
[100] James L. Kugel, *The Bible As It Was* (Cambridge, Massachusetts: Harvard University Press, 1997), 89.
[101] *The Works of Philo Judaeus*, Questions and Answers on Genesis 76, trans. C. D. Yonge (London: H. G. Bohn, 1854-1855).
[102] *The Zohar*, Beresheet b60, http://www.zohar.com/beresheet-b/and-man-knew (accessed Feb. 25, 2010).
[103] *The Zohar*, Beresheet b60, http://www.zohar.com/beresheet-b/and-man-knew (accessed Feb. 25, 2010).
[104] St. Ephrem the Syrian, *Selected Prose Works*, Section III 2-3, trans. Edward G. Mathews, Jr. and Joseph P. Amar (Washington, D. C.: The Catholic University of America Press, 1994), 124-125.
[105] *The Book of the Bee*, Chap. 18, Of Adam's Knowing Eve 1 (notes). Trans. Earnest A. Wallis Budge, M. A., http://www.sacred-texts.com/chr/bb/b18.htm (accessed Oct. 10, 2004); *The Works of Philo Judaeus*, Questions and Answers on Genesis I, 60, trans. C. D. Yonge (London: H. G. Bohn, 1854-1855); http://www.propheticrevelation.net/original_sin/the_serpent_seed_index.htm.
[106] David Kevin Delaney, *The Sevenfold Vengeance of Cain: Genesis 4 in Early Jewish and Christian Interpretation* (University of Virginia, 1996), 13.
[107] *The Book of the Bee*, Chap. 18, Of Adam's Knowing Eve 1 (notes). Trans. Earnest A. Wallis Budge, M. A., http://www.sacred-texts.com/chr/bb/b18.htm (accessed Oct. 10, 2004).
[108] *The Golden Legend or Lives of the Saints: Volume I*, trans. William Caxton (1483), http://www.fordham.edu/halsall/basis/goldenlegend/GoldenLegend-Volume1.htm (accessed Jan. 13, 2011), 62.
[109] James L. Kugel, *Traditions of the Bible* (Cambridge, Massachusetts: Harvard University Press, 1998), 159; *The History of al-Tabari - Volume I: General Introduction and From the Creation to the Flood*, Cain and Abel, 159, trans. Franz Rosenthal (Albany: New York Press, 1989), 311.
[110] St. Ephrem the Syrian, *Selected Prose Works*, Section III 3(3), trans. Edward G. Mathews, Jr. and Joseph P. Amar (Washington, D. C.: The Catholic University of America Press, 1994), 125.
[111] *The Golden Legend or Lives of the Saints: Volume I*, trans. William Caxton (1483), http://www.fordham.edu/halsall/basis/goldenlegend/GoldenLegend-Volume1.htm (accessed Jan. 13, 2011), 62.
[112] *The Armenian Apocryphal Adam Literature*, History of Cain and Abel 10, trans. William Lowndes Lipscomb (Ann Arbor, Michigan: University Microfilms International, 1983), 271.
[113] Louis Ginzberg, *The Legends of the Jews Volume I: From the Creation to Jacob*, trans. Henrietta Szold (Baltimore, Maryland: The Johns Hopkins University Press, 1909), 108.
[114] *The Armenian Apocryphal Adam Literature*, This is the History of Abel and Cain the Sons of Adam 12, trans. William Lowndes Lipscomb (Ann Arbor, Michigan: University Microfilms International, 1983), 160; David Max Eichhorn, *Cain: Son of the Serpent* (New York: Whittier Books, Inc., 1957), 42.
[115] *The Armenian Apocryphal Adam Literature*, This is the History of Abel and Cain the Sons of Adam 10, trans. William Lowndes Lipscomb (Ann Arbor, Michigan: University Microfilms International, 1983), 160; Louis Ginzberg, *The Legends of the Jews Volume I: From the Creation to Jacob*, trans. Henrietta Szold (Baltimore, Maryland: The Johns Hopkins University Press, 1909), 108; *The Second Book of Adam and Eve (The Conflict of Adam and Eve with Satan)* Chap. 1:9, 2:1; *Saltair na Rann*, 2717-2720, trans. David Greene; *The Armenian Apocryphal Adam Literature*, History of Cain and Abel 10, trans. William Lowndes Lipscomb (Ann Arbor, Michigan: University Microfilms

International, 1983), 271; *The Midrash Rabbah*, Bereshith (Genesis), trans. Rabbi Dr. H. Freedman and Maurice Simon (London: The Soncino Press, 1961) 22 6 (notes).

[116] Dan Rogers, *Evidence of Blacks in the Bible*, 1, http://www.christianodyssey.com/bible/africans.html (accessed March 24, 2006).

[117] E. S. G. Bristowe, *Cain - An Argument* (Leicester: Edgar Backus, 1950), 35.

[118] Shakespeare, *The Merry Wives of Windsor*, 1.41, www.loop.com/~bramble/mark.html (accessed March 22, 2016).

[119] Stephen Quayle, *Genesis 6 Giants: The Master Builders of Prehistoric and Ancient Civilizations* (Bozeman, Montana: End Time Thunder Publishers, 2005), 93, 205, 216; *The Book of Enoch*, http://www.yahwehsword.org/book-of-enoch/hanoch_enoch_106.htm (accessed Feb. 5, 2014); Andrew Collins, *From the Ashes of Angels* (Rochester, Vermont: Bear & Company, 1996), 54.

[120] Stephen Quayle, *Genesis 6 Giants: The Master Builders of Prehistoric and Ancient Civilizations* (Bozeman, Montana: End Time Thunder Publishers, 2005), 214, 217; Stephen Quayle, *Aliens and Fallen Angels: The Sexual Corruption of the Human Race* (Bozeman, Montana: End Time Thunder Publishers, 2008), 34; Andrew Collins, *From the Ashes of Angels* (Rochester, Vermont: Bear & Company, 1996), 54.

[121] Shira Halevi, *The Life Story of Adam and Havah* (Northvale, New Jersey: Jason Aronson, Inc., 1997), 248.

[122] Robert Graves and Raphael Patai, *Hebrew Myths: The Book of Genesis* (Garden City, New York: Doubleday & Company, 1964), 91.

[123] *Saltair na Rann*, 1957-1960, trans. David Greene.

[124] *Rashi*, (Bereishit) Genesis 4:5, http://www.chabad.org/library/bible_cdo/aid/8168/showrashi/true (accessed Oct. 27, 2010).

[125] David Max Eichhorn, *Cain: Son of the Serpent* (New York: Whittier Books, Inc., 1957), 42.

[126] St. Ephrem the Syrian, *Selected Prose Works*, Section III 3(3), trans. Edward G. Mathews, Jr. and Joseph P. Amar (Washington, D. C.: The Catholic University of America Press, 1994), 125.

[127] St. Ephrem the Syrian, *Selected Prose Works*, Section III 3, trans. Edward G. Mathews, Jr. and Joseph P. Amar (Washington, D. C.: The Catholic University of America Press, 1994), 125.

[128] St. Ephrem the Syrian, *Selected Prose Works*, Section III 3(3), trans. Edward G. Mathews, Jr. and Joseph P. Amar (Washington, D. C.: The Catholic University of America Press, 1994), 125.

[129] St. Ephrem the Syrian, *Selected Prose Works*, Section III 2(2), trans. Edward G. Mathews, Jr. and Joseph P. Amar (Washington, D. C.: The Catholic University of America Press, 1994), 125.

[130] *Genizah Manuscripts of Palestinian Targum to the Pentateuch Volume One*, Genesis 4:8, trans. Michael L. Klein (Cincinnati: Hebrew Union College Press, 1986).

[131] *St. Ephrem the Syrian: Selected Prose Works*, Section III 3(3), trans. Edward G. Mathews, Jr. and Joseph P. Amar (Washington, D. C.: The Catholic University of America Press, 1994), 125.

[132] *Literature on Adam and Eve: Collected Essays*, 122, trans. Gary Anderson, Michael Stone and Johannes Tromp (Leiden: Brill, 2000), 204.

[133] *Triumph Prophetic Ministries (Church of God)*, The Mark of the Beast and the Mark of Cain, 9, http://www.triumphpro.com/the_mark_of_cain.html (accessed June 5, 2000).

[134] *Book of the Glory of Kings (Kerba Nagast)*, 4 Concerning Envy, trans. Sir. E. A. Wallis Budge (London: Humphrey Milford, 1932).

[135] Merriam-Webster Dictionary, *Envy*, www.merriam-webster.com/dictionary/envy (accessed Feb. 19, 2014).

[136] *The Golden Legend or Lives of the Saints: Volume I*, trans. William Caxton (1483), http://www.fordham.edu/halsall/basis/goldenlegend/GoldenLegend-Volume1.htm (accessed Jan. 13, 2011), 62; David Kevin Delaney, *The Sevenfold Vengeance of Cain: Genesis 4 in Early Jewish and Christian Interpretation* (University of Virginia, 1996), 104; *Literature on Adam and Eve: Collected Essays*, 123, trans. Gary Anderson, Michael Stone and Johannes Tromp (Leiden: Brill, 2000) 204; Hyman E. Goldin, *The Book of Legends: Tales From the Talmud and Midrash* (New York: The Jordan Publishing Co., 1929), 32; *The Book of the Bee*, Chap. 18, Of Adam's Knowing Eve 3 (notes). Trans. Earnest A. Wallis Budge, M. A., http://www.sacred-texts.com/chr/bb/b18.htm (accessed Oct. 10, 2004).

[137] Hyman E. Goldin, *The Book of Legends: Tales From the Talmud and Midrash* (New York: The Jordan Publishing Co., 1929), 32.

[138] David Kevin Delaney, *The Sevenfold Vengeance of Cain: Genesis 4 in Early Jewish and Christian Interpretation* (University of Virginia, 1996), 178.

[139] *Book of the Glory of Kings (Kerba Nagast)*, 4. Concerning Envy, trans. Sir. E. A. Wallis Budge (London: Humphrey Milford, 1932).

[140] Stephen Charles Bandy, *Caines Cynn: A Study of Beuwolf and the Legends of Cain* (Stephen Charles Bandy, 1967), 33.

[141] Stephen Charles Bandy, *Caines Cynn: A Study of Beuwolf and the Legends of Cain* (Stephen Charles Bandy, 1967), 33.

[142] Wikipedia, the free encyclopedia, *John Reeve*, 2, http://en.wikipedia.org/wiki/John_Reeve_(religious_leader) (accessed Oct. 8, 2012).

[143] *The History of al-Tabari - Volume I: General Introduction and From the Creation to the Flood*, Cain and Abel,

138, trans. Franz Rosenthal (Albany: New York Press, 1989), 308.

[144] *Rashi*, (Bereishit) Genesis 4:8, http://www.chabad.org/library/bible_cdo/aid/8168/showrashi/true (accessed Oct. 27, 2010).

[145] David Max Eichhorn, *Cain: Son of the Serpent* (New York: Whittier Books, Inc., 1957), 87.

[146] *Targum Neofiti 1: Genesis/Translated, With Apparatus and Notes*, Apparatus, Genesis Chap. 4, trans. Martin McNamara (Collegeville, Minnesota: Liturgical Press, 1992) 65-66 (notes).

[147] David Max Eichhorn, *Cain: Son of the Serpent* (New York: Whittier Books, Inc., 1957), 66.

[148] Johann Andreas Eisenmenger, *The Traditions of the Jews, Contained in the Talmud and Other Mystical Writings* (London: J. Robinson, 1748), 31.

[149] Johann Andreas Eisenmenger, *The Traditions of the Jews, Contained in the Talmud and Other Mystical Writings* (London: J. Robinson, 1748), 30.

[150] C. A. Phifer, *Annals of the Earth* (Chicago, Illinois: American Publishers Association, 1890), 141.

[151] David Max Eichhorn, *Cain: Son of the Serpent* (New York: Whittier Books, Inc., 1957), 63.

[152] David Max Eichhorn, *Cain: Son of the Serpent* (New York: Whittier Books, Inc., 1957), 63.

[153] David Max Eichhorn, *Cain: Son of the Serpent* (New York: Whittier Books, Inc., 1957), 41.

[154] Ireneus David Kevin Delaney, *The Sevenfold Vengeance of Cain: Genesis 4 in Early Jewish and Christian Interpretation* (University of Virginia, 1996), 102.

[155] C. A. Phifer, *Annals of the Earth* (Chicago, Illinois: American Publishers Association, 1890), 142.

[156] *Saltair na Rann*, 1909-1912, trans. David Greene.

[157] Samuel A. Berman, *Midrash Tanhuma-Yelammedenu: An English Translation of Genesis and Exodus from the Printed Version of Tanhuma-Yelammedenu with an Introduction, Notes, and Indexes* (Hoboken, New Jersey: KTAV Publishing House, 1996), 29-30.

[158] *The Armenian Apocryphal Adam Literature*, History of Cain and Abel 17-18, trans. William Lowndes Lipscomb (Ann Arbor, Michigan: University Microfilms International, 1983), 272; *The Armenian Apocryphal Adam Literature*, This is the History of Abel and Cain the Sons of Adam 17, trans. William Lowndes Lipscomb (Ann Arbor, Michigan: University Microfilms International, 1983), 161-162.

[159] Samuel A. Berman, *Midrash Tanhuma-Yelammedenu: An English Translation of Genesis and Exodus from the Printed Version of Tanhuma-Yelammedenu with an Introduction, Notes, and Indexes* (Hoboken, New Jersey: KTAV Publishing House, 1996), 29-30.

[160] *The Zohar*, Idra Raba 47, http://www.zohar.com/idra-raba/cain-and-abel (accessed Feb. 25, 2010).

[161] Ibn Kathir, *Stories of the Prophets* (London: Darussalam, 2003), 46; David Max Eichhorn, *Cain: Son of the Serpent* (New York: Whittier Books, Inc., 1957), 67.

[162] *The Armenian Apocryphal Adam Literature*, This is the History of Abel and Cain the Sons of Adam 17, trans. William Lowndes Lipscomb (Ann Arbor, Michigan: University Microfilms International, 1983), 161-162.

[163] Ibn Kathir, *Stories of the Prophets* (London: Darussalam, 2003), 47.

[164] Dictionary.com, *Piety*, 1, http://www.dictionary.com/browse/piety (accessed Dec. 15, 2011).

[165] Robert Graves and Raphael Patai, *Hebrew Myths: The Book of Genesis* (Garden City, New York: Doubleday & Company, 1964), 92.

[166] *The Book of the Bee*, Chap. 18, Of Adam's Knowing Eve 3 (notes). Trans. Earnest A. Wallis Budge, M. A., http://www.sacred-texts.com/chr/bb/b18.htm (accessed Oct. 10, 2004); David Max Eichhorn, *Cain: Son of the Serpent* (New York: Whittier Books, Inc., 1957), 67.

[167] *The Armenian Apocryphal Adam Literature*, History of Cain and Abel 22, trans. William Lowndes Lipscomb (Ann Arbor, Michigan: University Microfilms International, 1983), 272.

[168] *The Armenian Apocryphal Adam Literature*, The Words of Adam to Seth 36, trans. William Lowndes Lipscomb (Ann Arbor, Michigan: University Microfilms International, 1983), 227.

[169] *The Armenian Apocryphal Adam Literature*, History of Cain and Abel 24, trans. William Lowndes Lipscomb (Ann Arbor, Michigan: University Microfilms International, 1983), 272.

[170] *The Armenian Apocryphal Adam Literature*, History of Cain and Abel 25, trans. William Lowndes Lipscomb (Ann Arbor, Michigan: University Microfilms International, 1983), 272.

[171] *The Armenian Apocryphal Adam Literature*, History of Cain and Abel 29, trans. William Lowndes Lipscomb (Ann Arbor, Michigan: University Microfilms International, 1983), 273.

[172] *The Armenian Apocryphal Adam Literature*, History of Cain and Abel 30, trans. William Lowndes Lipscomb (Ann Arbor, Michigan: University Microfilms International, 1983), 273.

[173] *The Armenian Apocryphal Adam Literature*, History of Cain and Abel 31, trans. William Lowndes Lipscomb (Ann Arbor, Michigan: University Microfilms International, 1983), 273.

[174] *The Armenian Apocryphal Adam Literature*, History of Cain and Abel 32, trans. William Lowndes Lipscomb (Ann Arbor, Michigan: University Microfilms International, 1983), 273.

[175] *The Armenian Apocryphal Adam Literature*, History of Cain and Abel 26, trans. William Lowndes Lipscomb (Ann Arbor, Michigan: University Microfilms International, 1983), 272-273.

[176] *The Armenian Apocryphal Adam Literature*, This is the History of Abel and Cain the Sons of Adam 32, trans. William Lowndes Lipscomb (Ann Arbor, Michigan: University Microfilms International, 1983), 165; *The Armenian*

Apocryphal Adam Literature, This is the History of Abel and Cain the Sons of Adam 7, trans. William Lowndes Lipscomb (Ann Arbor, Michigan: University Microfilms International, 1983), 158.

[177] Robert Graves and Raphael Patai, *Hebrew Myths: The Book of Genesis* (Garden City, New York: Doubleday & Company, 1964), 92; *Rabbi Abraham Ibn Ezra's Commentary on the Creation*, (notes), trans. Michael Linetsky (Northvale, New Jersey: Jason Aronson Inc., 1998), 104.

[178] *Pirke De Rabbi Eliezer*, Chapter 14: Cain and Abel [25A. i.] (notes), trans. Gerald Friedlander (New York: Sepher-Hermon Press, 1981), 155; David Max Eichhorn, *Cain: Son of the Serpent* (New York: Whittier Books, Inc., 1957), 67; Robert Graves and Raphael Patai, *Hebrew Myths: The Book of Genesis* (Garden City, New York: Doubleday & Company, 1964), 92.

[179] Oliver Farrar Emerson, *Legends of Cain, Especially in Old and Middle English* (Philadelphia, Pennsylvania: American Sunday-School Union, 1916), 855.

[180] Louis Ginzberg, *The Legends of the Jews Volume I: From the Creation to Jacob*, trans. Henrietta Szold (Baltimore, Maryland: The Johns Hopkins University Press, 1909), 109.

[181] David Max Eichhorn, *Cain: Son of the Serpent* (New York: Whittier Books, Inc., 1957), 74.

[182] Robert Graves and Raphael Patai, *Hebrew Myths: The Book of Genesis* (Garden City, New York: Doubleday & Company, 1964), 93.

[183] Stephen Charles Bandy, *Caines Cynn: A Study of Beuwolf and the Legends of Cain* (Stephen Charles Bandy, 1967), 29.

[184] Stephen Charles Bandy, *Caines Cynn: A Study of Beuwolf and the Legends of Cain* (Stephen Charles Bandy, 1967), 30.

[185] David Kevin Delaney, *The Sevenfold Vengeance of Cain: Genesis 4 in Early Jewish and Christian Interpretation* (University of Virginia, 1996), 159.

[186] St. Ephrem the Syrian, *Selected Prose Works*, Section III 3, trans. Edward G. Mathews, Jr. and Joseph P. Amar (Washington, D. C.: The Catholic University of America Press, 1994), 125.

[187] Jayim Nahman Bialik and Yehoshua Hana Ravnitzky, *The Book of Legends (Sefer Ha-Aggadah): Legends of the Talmud and Midrash*, 105 (New York: Shocken Books, 1992), 24.

[188] St. Ephrem the Syrian, *Selected Prose Works*, Section III 5(2), trans. Edward G. Mathews, Jr. and Joseph P. Amar (Washington, D. C.: The Catholic University of America Press, 1994), 127.

[189] Jayim Nahman Bialik and Yehoshua Hana Ravnitzky, *The Book of Legends (Sefer Ha-Aggadah): Legends of the Talmud and Midrash*, 101 (New York: Shocken Books, 1992), 24; *Gen.* 4:3 (KJV).

[190] Samuel A. Berman, *Midrash Tanhuma-Yelammedenu: An English Translation of Genesis and Exodus from the Printed Version of Tanhuma-Yelammedenu with an Introduction, Notes, and Indexes* (Hoboken, New Jersey: KTAV Publishing House, 1996), 30; Hyman E. Goldin, *The Book of Legends: Tales From the Talmud and Midrash* (New York: The Jordan Publishing Co., 1929), 34.

[191] *Gen.* 4:3 (KJV); Samuel A. Berman, *Midrash Tanhuma-Yelammedenu: An English Translation of Genesis and Exodus from the Printed Version of Tanhuma-Yelammedenu with an Introduction, Notes, and Indexes* (Hoboken, New Jersey: KTAV Publishing House, 1996), 30.

[192] David Max Eichhorn, *Cain: Son of the Serpent* (New York: Whittier Books, Inc., 1957), 73.

[193] St. Ephrem the Syrian, *Selected Prose Works*, Section III 2(2), trans. Edward G. Mathews, Jr. and Joseph P. Amar (Washington, D. C.: The Catholic University of America Press, 1994), 125.

[194] James L. Kugel, *The Bible As It Was* (Cambridge, Massachusetts: Harvard University Press, 1997), 96.

[195] David Max Eichhorn, *Cain: Son of the Serpent* (New York: Whittier Books, Inc., 1957), 72.

[196] David Kevin Delaney, *The Sevenfold Vengeance of Cain: Genesis 4 in Early Jewish and Christian Interpretation* (University of Virginia, 1996), 211.

[197] *The Armenian Apocryphal Adam Literature*, History of Cain and Abel 37, trans. William Lowndes Lipscomb (Ann Arbor, Michigan: University Microfilms International, 1983), 273.

[198] *The Armenian Apocryphal Adam Literature*, This is the History of Abel and Cain the Sons of Adam 36, trans. William Lowndes Lipscomb (Ann Arbor, Michigan: University Microfilms International, 1983), 165.

[199] David Kevin Delaney, *The Sevenfold Vengeance of Cain: Genesis 4 in Early Jewish and Christian Interpretation* (University of Virginia, 1996), 141.

[200] *Targum Neofiti 1: Genesis/Translated, With Apparatus and Notes*, Genesis 4:7, trans. Martin McNamara (Collegeville, Minnesota: Liturgical Press, 1992).

[201] *The First Book of Adam and Eve (The Conflict of Adam and Eve with Satan)*, 78:28, trans. S. C. Malan (London: Williams and Norgate, 1882), 59.

[202] John Skinner, *A Critical and Exegetical Commentary on Genesis*, 4 12 (Edinburgh: T. & T. Clark, 1956), 108.

[203] David Kevin Delaney, *The Sevenfold Vengeance of Cain: Genesis 4 in Early Jewish and Christian Interpretation* (University of Virginia, 1996), 210.

[204] *Targum Neofiti 1: Genesis/Translated, With Apparatus and Notes*, Genesis 4:7, trans. Martin McNamara (Collegeville, Minnesota: Liturgical Press, 1992); *Genizah Manuscripts of Palestinian Targum to the Pentateuch Volume One*, Genesis 4:7, trans. Michael L. Klein (Cincinnati: Hebrew Union College Press, 1986).

²⁰⁵ *Targum Neofiti 1: Genesis/Translated, With Apparatus and Notes*, Genesis 4:7, trans. Martin McNamara (Collegeville, Minnesota: Liturgical Press, 1992); *Ibn Ezra, Commentary on the Pentateuch: Genesis (Bereshit)* (New York: Menorah Publishing Company, Inc., 1988), 83; David Kevin Delaney, *The Sevenfold Vengeance of Cain: Genesis 4 in Early Jewish and Christian Interpretation* (University of Virginia, 1996), 210; *Genizah Manuscripts of Palestinian Targum to the Pentateuch Volume One*, Genesis 4:7, trans. Michael L. Klein (Cincinnati: Hebrew Union College Press, 1986).

²⁰⁶ *Rashi*, (Bereishit) Genesis 4:7, http://www.chabad.org/library/bible_cdo/aid/8168/showrashi/true (accessed Oct. 27, 2010).

²⁰⁷ Flavius Josephus, *Jewish Antiquities, Book 1*, I 54-59, trans. H. ST. J. Thackeray (London: William Heinemann Ltd., 1961), 27; *Literature on Adam and Eve: Collected Essays*, 125, trans. Gary Anderson, Michael Stone and Johannes Tromp (Leiden: Brill, 2000), 205; *The Armenian Apocryphal Adam Literature*, This is the History of Abel and Cain the Sons of Adam 35, trans. William Lowndes Lipscomb (Ann Arbor, Michigan: University Microfilms International, 1983), 165.

²⁰⁸ *The Armenian Apocryphal Adam Literature*, The Words of Adam to Seth 49, trans. William Lowndes Lipscomb (Ann Arbor, Michigan: University Microfilms International, 1983), 228.

²⁰⁹ *Pirke De Rabbi Eliezer*, Chapter 14: Cain and Abel [25A. i.], trans. Gerald Friedlander (New York: Sepher-Hermon Press, 1981), 155.

²¹⁰ Mikal Bin Gorion, *Mimekor Yisrael - Volume I*, 7 (Bloomington, Indiana: University Press, 1976).

²¹¹ David Kevin Delaney, *The Sevenfold Vengeance of Cain: Genesis 4 in Early Jewish and Christian Interpretation* (University of Virginia, 1996), 106.

²¹² David Kevin Delaney, *The Sevenfold Vengeance of Cain: Genesis 4 in Early Jewish and Christian Interpretation* (University of Virginia, 1996), 10; Flavius Josephus, Jewish Antiquities, Book 1, I 54-59, trans. H. ST. J. Thackeray (London: William Heinemann Ltd., 1961), 27.

²¹³ David Max Eichhorn, *Cain: Son of the Serpent* (New York: Whittier Books, Inc., 1957), 43.

²¹⁴ David Max Eichhorn, *Cain: Son of the Serpent* (New York: Whittier Books, Inc., 1957), 43.

²¹⁵ David Max Eichhorn, *Cain: Son of the Serpent* (New York: Whittier Books, Inc., 1957), 42-43.

²¹⁶ David Kevin Delaney, *The Sevenfold Vengeance of Cain: Genesis 4 in Early Jewish and Christian Interpretation* (University of Virginia, 1996), 101.

²¹⁷ *Rashi*, Bereshit - Genesis - Chapter 4, 9, http://www.chabad.org/library/bible_cdo/aid/8168/showrashi/true (accessed Oct. 27, 2010).

²¹⁸ David Max Eichhorn, *Cain: Son of the Serpent* (New York: Whittier Books, Inc., 1957), 74.

²¹⁹ Louis Ginzberg, *The Legends of the Jews Volume I: From the Creation to Jacob*, trans. Henrietta Szold (Baltimore, Maryland: The Johns Hopkins University Press, 1909), 110.

²²⁰ Louis Ginzberg, *The Legends of the Jews Volume I: From the Creation to Jacob*, trans. Henrietta Szold (Baltimore, Maryland: The Johns Hopkins University Press, 1909), 110; Samuel A. Berman, *Midrash Tanhuma-Yelammedenu: An English Translation of Genesis and Exodus from the Printed Version of Tanhuma-Yelammedenu with an Introduction, Notes, and Indexes* (Hoboken, New Jersey: KTAV Publishing House, 1996), 29-30.

²²¹ David Max Eichhorn, *Cain: Son of the Serpent* (New York: Whittier Books, Inc., 1957), 75.

²²² Samuel A. Berman, *Midrash Tanhuma-Yelammedenu: An English Translation of Genesis and Exodus from the Printed Version of Tanhuma-Yelammedenu with an Introduction, Notes, and Indexes* (Hoboken, New Jersey: KTAV Publishing House, 1996), 29-30.

²²³ David Max Eichhorn, *Cain: Son of the Serpent* (New York: Whittier Books, Inc., 1957), 74.

²²⁴ David Max Eichhorn, *Cain: Son of the Serpent* (New York: Whittier Books, Inc., 1957), 75.

²²⁵ David Max Eichhorn, *Cain: Son of the Serpent* (New York: Whittier Books, Inc., 1957), 75.

²²⁶ *Gen. 4:3* (KJV); Samuel A. Berman, *Midrash Tanhuma-Yelammedenu: An English Translation of Genesis and Exodus from the Printed Version of Tanhuma-Yelammedenu with an Introduction, Notes, and Indexes* (Hoboken, New Jersey: KTAV Publishing House, 1996), 30.

²²⁷ David Max Eichhorn, *Cain: Son of the Serpent* (New York: Whittier Books, Inc., 1957), 71; Hyman E. Goldin, *The Book of Legends: Tales From the Talmud and Midrash* (New York: The Jordan Publishing Co., 1929), 33.

²²⁸ David Max Eichhorn, *Cain: Son of the Serpent* (New York: Whittier Books, Inc., 1957), 71.

²²⁹ David Max Eichhorn, *Cain: Son of the Serpent* (New York: Whittier Books, Inc., 1957), 71.

²³⁰ Jayim Nahman Bialik and Yehoshua Hana Ravnitzky, *The Book of Legends (Sefer Ha-Aggadah): Legends of the Talmud and Midrash*, 101 (New York: Shocken Books,.1992), 23.

²³¹ Robert Graves and Raphael Patai, *Hebrew Myths: The Book of Genesis* (Garden City, New York: Doubleday & Company, 1964), 92.

²³² Louis Ginzberg, *The Legends of the Jews Volume I: From the Creation to Jacob*, trans. Henrietta Szold (Baltimore, Maryland: The Johns Hopkins University Press, 1909), 110.

²³³ David Max Eichhorn, *Cain: Son of the Serpent* (New York: Whittier Books, Inc., 1957), 74.

²³⁴ David Kevin Delaney, *The Sevenfold Vengeance of Cain: Genesis 4 in Early Jewish and Christian Interpretation* (University of Virginia, 1996), 111.

235 C. A. Phifer, *Annals of the Earth* (Chicago, Illinois: American Publishers Association, 1890), 143.
236 David Max Eichhorn, *Cain: Son of the Serpent* (New York: Whittier Books, Inc., 1957), 74.
237 David Max Eichhorn, *Cain: Son of the Serpent* (New York: Whittier Books, Inc., 1957), 93.
238 S. Baring-Gould, *Legends of the Patriarchs and Prophets and Other Old Testament Characters* (New York: American Book Exchange, 1881), 76.
239 *Rashi*, Bereshit - Genesis - Chapter 4, 13 http://www.chabad.org/library/bible_cdo/aid/8168/showrashi/true (accessed Oct. 27, 2010).
240 David Kevin Delaney, *The Sevenfold Vengeance of Cain: Genesis 4 in Early Jewish and Christian Interpretation* (University of Virginia, 1996), 21.
241 Robert Graves and Raphael Patai, *Hebrew Myths: The Book of Genesis* (Garden City, New York: Doubleday & Company, 1964), 92.
242 *Rashi*, http://www.chabad.org/library/bible_cdo/aid/8168/showrashi/true (accessed Oct. 27, 2010); *Gen.* 4:3 (KJV); Samuel A. Berman, *Midrash Tanhuma-Yelammedenu: An English Translation of Genesis and Exodus from the Printed Version of Tanhuma-Yelammedenu with an Introduction, Notes, and Indexes* (Hoboken, New Jersey: KTAV Publishing House, 1996), 30.
243 *Targum Neofiti 1: Genesis/Translated, With Apparatus and Notes*, Genesis 4:13, trans. Martin McNamara (Collegeville, Minnesota: Liturgical Press, 1992).
244 Ibn Ezra, *Commentary on the Pentateuch: Genesis (Bereshit)* (New York: Menorah Publishing Company, Inc., 1988), 90.
245 St. Ephrem the Syrian, *Selected Prose Works*, Section III 8(2), trans. Edward G. Mathews, Jr. and Joseph P. Amar (Washington, D. C.: The Catholic University of America Press, 1994), 128.
246 Stephen Charles Bandy, *Caines Cynn: A Study of Beuwolf and the Legends of Cain* (Stephen Charles Bandy, 1967), 31.
247 David Kevin Delaney, *The Sevenfold Vengeance of Cain: Genesis 4 in Early Jewish and Christian Interpretation* (University of Virginia, 1996), 156.
248 St. Ephrem the Syrian, *Selected Prose Works*, Section III 2, trans. Edward G. Mathews, Jr. and Joseph P. Amar (Washington, D. C.: The Catholic University of America Press, 1994), 124.
249 David Max Eichhorn, *Cain: Son of the Serpent* (New York: Whittier Books, Inc., 1957), 85.
250 David Max Eichhorn, *Cain: Son of the Serpent* (New York: Whittier Books, Inc., 1957), 77.
251 Samuel A. Berman, *Midrash Tanhuma-Yelammedenu: An English Translation of Genesis and Exodus from the Printed Version of Tanhuma-Yelammedenu with an Introduction, Notes, and Indexes* (Hoboken, New Jersey: KTAV Publishing House, 1996), 29-30.
252 David Max Eichhorn, *Cain: Son of the Serpent* (New York: Whittier Books, Inc., 1957), 92.
253 Stephen Charles Bandy, *Caines Cynn: A Study of Beuwolf and the Legends of Cain* (Stephen Charles Bandy, 1967), 108.
254 David Max Eichhorn, *Cain: Son of the Serpent* (New York: Whittier Books, Inc., 1957), 72.
255 Stephen Charles Bandy, *Caines Cynn: A Study of Beuwolf and the Legends of Cain* (Stephen Charles Bandy, 1967), 31.
256 Stephen Charles Bandy, *Caines Cynn: A Study of Beuwolf and the Legends of Cain* (Stephen Charles Bandy, 1967), 31.
257 St. Ephrem the Syrian, *Selected Prose Works*, Section III 6(2), trans. Edward G. Mathews, Jr. and Joseph P. Amar (Washington, D. C.: The Catholic University of America Press, 1994), 127.
258 *The Book of the Generations of Adam*, Ch. 5.8, http://www.earth-history.com/Pseudepigrapha/generations-adam.htm (accessed May 5, 2007).
259 *The Book of the Generations of Adam*, Ch. 5.5, http://www.earth-history.com/Pseudepigrapha/generations-adam.htm (accessed May 5, 2007).

Chapter 5

1 Michael E. Stone, *Adamgirk: The Adam Book of Arak'el of Siwnik*, 1.21.19 (Oxford: University Press, 2007), 207.
2 Oliver Farrar Emerson, *Legends of Cain, Especially in Old and Middle English* (Philadelphia, Pennsylvania: American Sunday-School Union, 1916), 855.
3 *The Zohar*, Beresheet b60, http://www.zohar.com/beresheet-b/and-man-knew (accessed Feb. 25, 2010).
4 David Max Eichhorn, *Cain: Son of the Serpent* (New York: Whittier Books, Inc., 1957), 86.
5 *The Book of the Generations of Adam*, Ch. 5.5, http://www.earth-history.com/Pseudepigrapha/generations-adam.htm (accessed May 5, 2007).
6 David Kevin Delaney, *The Sevenfold Vengeance of Cain: Genesis 4 in Early Jewish and Christian Interpretation* (University of Virginia, 1996), 104 (notes).
7 St. Ephrem the Syrian, *Selected Prose Works*, Section III 7, trans. Edward G. Mathews, Jr. and Joseph P. Amar (Washington, D. C.: The Catholic University of America Press, 1994), 128.
8 Stephen Charles Bandy, *Caines Cynn: A Study of Beuwolf and the Legends of Cain* (Stephen Charles Bandy, 1967), 31.

[9] David Kevin Delaney, *The Sevenfold Vengeance of Cain: Genesis 4 in Early Jewish and Christian Interpretation* (University of Virginia, 1996), 103; *The Armenian Apocryphal Adam Literature*, The Words of Adam to Seth 51, trans. William Lowndes Lipscomb (Ann Arbor, Michigan: University Microfilms International, 1983), 228.

[10] Howard Schwartz, *Tree of Souls: The Mythology of Judaism* (Oxford: University Press, 2004), 446.

[11] David Kevin Delaney, *The Sevenfold Vengeance of Cain: Genesis 4 in Early Jewish and Christian Interpretation* (University of Virginia, 1996), 11; Moses Aberbach and Bernard Grossfield, *Targum Onkelos to Genesis: A Critical Analysis Together with an English Translation of the Text*, Genesis 3:11 (notes) (New York: KTAV Publishing House, Inc., 1995), .

[12] David Kevin Delaney, *The Sevenfold Vengeance of Cain: Genesis 4 in Early Jewish and Christian Interpretation* (University of Virginia, 1996), 131; Stephen Charles Bandy, *Caines Cynn: A Study of Beuwolf and the Legends of Cain* (Stephen Charles Bandy, 1967), 72; Howard Schwartz, *Tree of Souls: The Mythology of Judaism* (Oxford: University Press, 2004), 446.

[13] *The Zohar*, Beresheet a47, http://www.zohar.com/beresheet/now-serpent-was-craftier%C2%9D (accessed Feb. 25, 2010).

[14] *Barhebraeus' Scholia on the Old Testament Part I: Genesis - II Samuel*, Translation and Collation, 10a 4 16, trans. Martin Sprengling and William Creighton Graham (Chicago, Illinois: University of Chicago Press, 1931), 33.

[15] Herman L. Hoeh, *Compendium of World History*, Vol. 2, Ch. 18, The Sin of Cain and Geology 10, http://www.earth-history.com/Various/Compendium (accessed Dec. 19, 2007).

[16] Stephen Charles Bandy, *Caines Cynn: A Study of Beuwolf and the Legends of Cain* (Stephen Charles Bandy, 1967), 72.

[17] David Max Eichhorn, *Cain: Son of the Serpent* (New York: Whittier Books, Inc., 1957), 89-90.

[18] Shira Halevi, *The Life Story of Adam and Havah* (Northvale, New Jersey: Jason Aronson, Inc., 1997), 204.

[19] Stephen Charles Bandy, *Caines Cynn: A Study of Beuwolf and the Legends of Cain* (Stephen Charles Bandy, 1967), 53.

[20] David Max Eichhorn, *Cain: Son of the Serpent* (New York: Whittier Books, Inc., 1957), 87.

[21] St. Ephrem the Syrian, *Selected Prose Works*, Section III 7, trans. Edward G. Mathews, Jr. and Joseph P. Amar (Washington, D. C.: The Catholic University of America Press, 1994), 128.

[22] St. Ephrem the Syrian, *Selected Prose Works*, Section III 8, trans. Edward G. Mathews, Jr. and Joseph P. Amar (Washington, D. C.: The Catholic University of America Press, 1994), 128.

[23] David Kevin Delaney, *The Sevenfold Vengeance of Cain: Genesis 4 in Early Jewish and Christian Interpretation* (University of Virginia, 1996), 168.

[24] James L. Kugel, *Traditions of the Bible* (Cambridge, Massachusetts: Harvard University Press, 1998), 163.

[25] David Kevin Delaney, *The Sevenfold Vengeance of Cain: Genesis 4 in Early Jewish and Christian Interpretation* (University of Virginia, 1996), 131.

[26] *Barhebraeus' Scholia on the Old Testament Part I: Genesis - II Samuel*, Translation and Collation, 10a 4 16, trans. Martin Sprengling and William Creighton Graham (Chicago, Illinois: University of Chicago Press, 1931), 33; *The First Book of Adam and Eve (The Conflict of Adam and Eve with Satan)*, 79:24, trans. S. C. Malan (London: Williams and Norgate, 1882); *Barhebraeus' Scholia on the Old Testament Part I: Genesis - II Samuel*, Translation and Collation, 9b 4 12, trans. Martin Sprengling and William Creighton Graham (Chicago, Illinois: University of Chicago Press, 1931), 31; James L. Kugel, *Traditions of the Bible* (Cambridge, Massachusetts: Harvard University Press, 1998), 163; David Kevin Delaney, *The Sevenfold Vengeance of Cain: Genesis 4 in Early Jewish and Christian Interpretation* (University of Virginia, 1996), 168; Stephen Charles Bandy, *Caines Cynn: A Study of Beuwolf and the Legends of Cain* (Stephen Charles Bandy, 1967), 51.

[27] *Literature on Adam and Eve: Collected Essays*, 126, trans. Gary Anderson, Michael Stone and Johannes Tromp (Leiden: Brill, 2000), 206.

[28] Stephen Charles Bandy, *Caines Cynn: A Study of Beuwolf and the Legends of Cain* (Stephen Charles Bandy, 1967), 40-41, 84.

[29] James L. Kugel, *Traditions of the Bible* (Cambridge, Massachusetts: Harvard University Press, 1998), 164.

[30] *The First Book of Adam and Eve (The Conflict of Adam and Eve with Satan)*, 79:24, trans. S. C. Malan (London: Williams and Norgate, 1882), 59; James L. Kugel, *Traditions of the Bible* (Cambridge, Massachusetts: Harvard University Press, 1998), 164.

[31] James L. Kugel, *Traditions of the Bible* (Cambridge, Massachusetts: Harvard University Press, 1998), 163; David Kevin Delaney, *The Sevenfold Vengeance of Cain: Genesis 4 in Early Jewish and Christian Interpretation* (University of Virginia, 1996), 22, 168; Rev. G. Oliver, *The Antiquities of Free-Masonry; Comprising Illustrations of the Five Grand Periods of Masonry, From the Creation of the World to the Dedication of King Solomon's Temple* (London: Richard Spencer, 314, High Holborn, 1843), 45.

[32] *Barhebraeus' Scholia on the Old Testament Part I: Genesis - II Samuel*, Translation and Collation 9b 4 12, trans. Martin Sprengling and William Creighton Graham (Chicago, Illinois: University of Chicago Press, 1931), 31.

[33] *The Armenian Apocryphal Adam Literature*, This is the History of Abel and Cain the Sons of Adam 41, trans. William Lowndes Lipscomb (Ann Arbor, Michigan: University Microfilms International, 1983), 167.

[34] David Kevin Delaney, *The Sevenfold Vengeance of Cain: Genesis 4 in Early Jewish and Christian Interpretation*

(University of Virginia, 1996), 131.

[35] David Max Eichhorn, *Cain: Son of the Serpent* (New York: Whittier Books, Inc., 1957), 88.

[36] *The First Book of Adam and Eve (The Conflict of Adam and Eve with Satan)*, 79:25, trans. S. C. Malan (London: Williams and Norgate, 1882), 59.

[37] David Max Eichhorn, *Cain: Son of the Serpent* (New York: Whittier Books, Inc., 1957), 93.

[38] Shira Halevi, *The Life Story of Adam and Havah* (Northvale, New Jersey: Jason Aronson, Inc., 1997), 251.

[39] Flavius Josephus, *Jewish Antiquities*, Book I, 59-64, trans. H. ST. J. Thackeray (London: William Heinemann Ltd., 1961),29.

[40] *The Book of the Generations of Adam*, Ch. 5.8, http://www.earth-history.com/Pseudepigrapha/generations-adam.htm (accessed May 5, 2007).

[41] David Kevin Delaney, *The Sevenfold Vengeance of Cain: Genesis 4 in Early Jewish and Christian Interpretation* (University of Virginia, 1996), 17 (notes); Stephen Charles Bandy, *Caines Cynn: A Study of Beuwolf and the Legends of Cain* (Stephen Charles Bandy, 1967), 76.

[42] Merriam-Webster Dictionary, *Anthema*, www.merriam-webster.com/dictionary/anathema (accessed Oct. 27, 2010).

[43] David Max Eichhorn, *Cain: Son of the Serpent* (New York: Whittier Books, Inc., 1957), 106.

[44] *Rashi*, (Bereishit) Genesis 4:16, http://www.chabad.org/library/bible_cdo/aid/8168/showrashi/true (accessed Oct. 27, 2010).

[45] Stephen Charles Bandy, *Caines Cynn: A Study of Beuwolf and the Legends of Cain* (Stephen Charles Bandy, 1967), 81.

[46] Oliver Farrar Emerson, *Legends of Cain, Especially in Old and Middle English* (Philadelphia, Pennsylvania: American Sunday-School Union, 1916), 863.

[47] David Kevin Delaney, *The Sevenfold Vengeance of Cain: Genesis 4 in Early Jewish and Christian Interpretation* (University of Virginia, 1996), 11; David Max Eichhorn, *Cain: Son of the Serpent* (New York: Whittier Books, Inc., 1957), 107; *Rashi*, (Bereishit) Genesis 4:12, http://www.chabad.org/library/bible_cdo/aid/8168/showrashi/true (accessed Oct. 27, 2010).

[48] Robert Graves and Raphael Patai, *Hebrew Myths: The Book of Genesis* (Garden City, New York: Doubleday & Company, 1964), 93.

[49] Oliver Farrar Emerson, *Legends of Cain, Especially in Old and Middle English* (Philadelphia, Pennsylvania: American Sunday-School Union, 1916), 865.

[50] Stephen Charles Bandy, *Caines Cynn: A Study of Beuwolf and the Legends of Cain* (Stephen Charles Bandy, 1967), 39.

[51] Stephen Charles Bandy, *Caines Cynn: A Study of Beuwolf and the Legends of Cain* (Stephen Charles Bandy, 1967), 40.

[52] Stephen Charles Bandy, Caines Cynn: *A Study of Beuwolf and the Legends of Cain* (Stephen Charles Bandy, 1967), 21.

[53] Shira Halevi, *The Life Story of Adam and Havah* (Northvale, New Jersey: Jason Aronson, Inc., 1997), 251.

[54] Stephen Charles Bandy, *Caines Cynn: A Study of Beuwolf and the Legends of Cain* (Stephen Charles Bandy, 1967), 51.

[55] David Kevin Delaney, *The Sevenfold Vengeance of Cain: Genesis 4 in Early Jewish and Christian Interpretation* (University of Virginia, 1996), 132.

[56] *The Book of the Generations of Adam*, Ch. 5.11, http://www.earth-history.com/Pseudepigrapha/generations-adam.htm (accessed May 5, 2007).

[57] David Max Eichhorn, *Cain: Son of the Serpent* (New York: Whittier Books, Inc., 1957), 11; Robert Graves and Raphael Patai, *Hebrew Myths: The Book of Genesis* (Garden City, New York: Doubleday & Company, 1964), 93; *The Book of the Cave of Treasures*, trans. Sir E. A. Wallis Budge (London: The Religious Tract Society, 1927), 70.

[58] Stephen Charles Bandy, *Caines Cynn: A Study of Beuwolf and the Legends of Cain* (Stephen Charles Bandy, 1967), 51.

[59] Richard Gan, *The Mark of the Wicked Ones*, 10-11, http://www.propheticrevelation.new/w-ones.htm (accessed Aug. 22, 2007).

[60] Stephen Charles Bandy, *Caines Cynn: A Study of Beuwolf and the Legends of Cain* (Stephen Charles Bandy, 1967), 52.

[61] David Max Eichhorn, *Cain: Son of the Serpent* (New York: Whittier Books, Inc., 1957), 98.

[62] David Kevin Delaney, *The Sevenfold Vengeance of Cain: Genesis 4 in Early Jewish and Christian Interpretation* (University of Virginia, 1996), 144.

[63] David Kevin Delaney, *The Sevenfold Vengeance of Cain: Genesis 4 in Early Jewish and Christian Interpretation* (University of Virginia, 1996), 102.

[64] David Kevin Delaney, *The Sevenfold Vengeance of Cain: Genesis 4 in Early Jewish and Christian Interpretation* (University of Virginia, 1996), 180.

[65] Robert Graves and Raphael Patai, *Hebrew Myths: The Book of Genesis* (Garden City, New York: Doubleday & Company, 1964), 94.

[66] John Reeve and T. L. Underwood, *Acts of the Witnesses*, 2,

http://en.wikipedia.org/wiki/John_Reeve_(religious_leader) (accessed Oct. 8, 2013), 151.
[67] Christian and Barbara Joy O'Brien, *The Shining Ones* (Cirencester, England: Dianthus Publishing Limited, 1988), 162; Samuel A. Berman, *Midrash Tanhuma-Yelammedenu: An English Translation of Genesis and Exodus from the Printed Version of Tanhuma-Yelammedenu with an Introduction, Notes, and Indexes* (Hoboken, New Jersey: KTAV Publishing House, 1996), 35; *The Book of the Giants*, trans. W. B. Henning, http://www.sacred-texts.com/chr/giants/giants.htm (accessed July 13, 2005).
[68] Howard Schwartz, *Tree of Souls: The Mythology of Judaism* (Oxford: University Press, 2004), 458.
[69] *The Second Book of Adam and Eve (The Conflict of Adam and Eve with Satan)*, 12:16, trans. S. C. Malan (London: Williams and Norgate, 1882), 69.
[70] Herman L. Hoeh, *Compendium of World History*, Vol. 2, Chap. 18, The Sin of Cain and Geology 10, http://www.earth-history.com/Various/Compendium (accessed Dec. 19, 2007).
[71] Tertullian, *Against All Heresies*, Chapter 2. Ophites, Cainites, Sethites, http://www.newadvent.org/fathers/0319.htm (accessed Dec. 9, 2007).
[72] *Book of the Glory of Kings (Kerba Nagast)*, 7. Concerning Noah, trans. Sir. E. A. Wallis Budge (London: Humphrey Milford, 1932).
[73] *The Book of the Generations of Adam*, Ch. 6.4, http://www.earth-history.com/Pseudepigrapha/generations-adam.htm (accessed May 5, 2007).
[74] David Max Eichhorn, *Cain: Son of the Serpent* (New York: Whittier Books, Inc., 1957), 36.
[75] David Max Eichhorn, *Cain: Son of the Serpent* (New York: Whittier Books, Inc., 1957), 142.
[76] C. A. Phifer, *Annals of the Earth* (Chicago, Illinois: American Publishers Association, 1890), 67.
[77] *The Book of the Rolls (Kitab Al-Magall)*, trans. Margaret Dunlop Gibson, Apocrypha Arabica (London: C. J. Clay and Sons, 1901), 21.
[78] Louis Ginzberg, *The Legends of the Jews Volume I: From the Creation to Jacob*, trans. Henrietta Szold (Baltimore, Maryland: The Johns Hopkins University Press, 1909), 117.
[79] Andy Orchard, *Pride and Prodigies: Studies in the Monsters of the Beowulf-Manuscript* (Toronto: University of Toronto Press Incorporated, 2003), 82.
[80] *The Midrash Rabbah*, Bereshith (Genesis) 31:3, trans. Rabbi Dr. H. Freedman and Maurice Simon (London: The Soncino Press, 1961); Moses Aberbach and Bernard Grossfield, *Targum Onkelos to Genesis: A Critical Analysis Together with an English Translation of the Text*, Gen. 6:11 (New York: KTAV Publishing House, Inc., 1995); *The Second Book of Adam and Eve (The Conflict of Adam and Eve with Satan)*, 13:2, trans. S. C. Malan (London: Williams and Norgate, 1882), 70; Ibn Ezra, *Commentary on the Pentateuch: Genesis (Bereshit)* (New York: Menorah Publishing Company, Inc., 1988), 99; *Rashi*, (Bereishit) Genesis 6:11, http://www.chabad.org/library/bible_cdo/aid/8168/showrashi/true (accessed Oct. 27, 2010).
[81] Mysterious World, *Giants in the Earth Part I: Giants of the Ancient Near East*, 12, http://mysteriousworld.com/Journal/2003/Spring/Giants/#16 (accessed June 38, 2017); *The Midrash Rabbah*, trans. Rabbi Dr. H. Freedman and Maurice Simon (London: The Soncino Press, 1961), 239; Ibn Ezra, *Commentary on the Pentateuch: Genesis (Bereshit)* (New York: Menorah Publishing Company, Inc., 1988), 99.
[82] Robert Graves and Raphael Patai, *Hebrew Myths: The Book of Genesis* (Garden City, New York: Doubleday & Company, 1964), 112.
[83] Stephen Charles Bandy, *Caines Cynn: A Study of Beuwolf and the Legends of Cain* (Stephen Charles Bandy, 1967), 67.
[84] Glen W. Chapman, *Life and Times Before the Flood: Taken From Ancient Documents*, 5, http://bookofthenephilim.blogspot.com/2009/02/life-and-times-before-flood-taken.html (accessed Dec. 3, 2000).
[85] W. J. Perry, *The Children of the Sun: A Study in the Early History of Civilization* (London: Methuen & Co. LTD., 1923), 141, 167; E. S. G. Bristowe, *Cain - An Argument* (Leicester: Edgar Backus, 1950), 53; Mrs. Sydney Bristowe, *Sargon the Magnificent* (London: The Covenant Publishing Co., 1927), 88, 127-129, 163.
[86] *The Second Book of Adam and Eve (The Conflict of Adam and Eve with Satan)*, 20:27, trans. S. C. Malan (London: Williams and Norgate, 1882), 78; Bertrand L. Comparet, *What Happened to Cain*, 3, http://www.posse-comitatus.org/Bible_Studies/what_happened_to_cain.htm (accessed Aug. 21, 2000).
[87] Stephen Charles Bandy, *Caines Cynn: A Study of Beuwolf and the Legends of Cain* (Stephen Charles Bandy, 1967), 191.
[88] Stephen Charles Bandy, *Caines Cynn: A Study of Beuwolf and the Legends of Cain* (Stephen Charles Bandy, 1967), 27.
[89] Rev. G. Oliver, *The Antiquities of Free-Masonry; Comprising Illustrations of the Five Grand Periods of Masonry, From the Creation of the World to the Dedication of King Solomon's Temple* (London: Richard Spencer, 314, High Holborn, 1843), 48.
[90] S. Baring-Gould, *Legends of the Patriarchs and Prophets and Other Old Testament Characters* (New York: American Book Exchange, 1881), 75; E. S. G. Bristowe, Cain - An Argument (Leicester: Edgar Backus, 1950), 95.
[91] *The Chronicles of Jerahmeel (The Hebrew Bible Historiale)*, 24(2), trans. M. Gaster, Ph. D. (London: The Royal Asiatic Society, 1899).
[92] *The Golden Legend or Lives of the Saints: Volume I*, trans. William Caxton (1483),

http://www.fordham.edu/halsall/basis/goldenlegend/GoldenLegend-Volume1.htm (accessed Jan. 13, 2011), 62.

[93] James L. Kugel, *Traditions of the Bible* (Cambridge, Massachusetts: Harvard University Press, 1998), 169.

[94] Robert Graves and Raphael Patai, *Hebrew Myths: The Book of Genesis* (Garden City, New York: Doubleday & Company, 1964), 94.

[95] Stephen Charles Bandy, *Caines Cynn: A Study of Beuwolf and the Legends of Cain* (Stephen Charles Bandy, 1967), 203.

[96] Dan Gayman, *The Two Seeds of Genesis 3:15* (Daniel Lee Gayman, 1977), 215.

[97] Robert Bowie Johnson, Jr., *Athena and Kain: The True Meaning of Greek Myth* (Annapolis, Maryland: Solving Light Books, 2003), 54.

[98] Stephen Charles Bandy, *Caines Cynn: A Study of Beuwolf and the Legends of Cain* (Stephen Charles Bandy, 1967), 26.

[99] Stephen Charles Bandy, *Caines Cynn: A Study of Beuwolf and the Legends of Cain* (Stephen Charles Bandy, 1967), 14.

[100] Jonah House, *Cain and the Meaning of the City*, 1, http://www.jonahhouse.org/McAlisterKirkridgeB05.htm (accessed April 13, 2011).

[101] Jonah House, *Cain and the Meaning of the City*, 2-3, http://www.jonahhouse.org/McAlisterKirkridgeB05.htm (accessed April 13, 2011).

[102] Jonah House, *Cain and the Meaning of the City*, 3, http://www.jonahhouse.org/McAlisterKirkridgeB05.htm (accessed April 13, 2011).

[103] Stephen Charles Bandy, *Caines Cynn: A Study of Beuwolf and the Legends of Cain* (Stephen Charles Bandy, 1967), 209.

[104] Alfred Jeremias, *The Old Testament in the Light of the Ancient East Vol. I* (New York: G. P. Putnam's Sons, 1911), 1.

[105] Stephen Charles Bandy, *Caines Cynn: A Study of Beuwolf and the Legends of Cain* (Stephen Charles Bandy, 1967), 11.

[106] *The Works of Philo Judaeus*, On the Posterity of Cain and His Exile, 15(52), trans. C. D. Yonge (London: H. G. Bohn, 1854-1855).

[107] Bertrand L. Comparet, *What Happened to Cain*, 21, http://www.posse-comitatus.org/Bible_Studies/what_happened_to_cain.htm (accessed Aug. 21, 2000).

[108] E. Basil Redlich, *The Early Traditions of Genesis* (London: Gerald Duckworth & Co. Ltd., 1950), 80.

[109] Stephen Charles Bandy, *Caines Cynn: A Study of Beuwolf and the Legends of Cain* (Stephen Charles Bandy, 1967), 160.

[110] Stephen Charles Bandy, *Caines Cynn: A Study of Beuwolf and the Legends of Cain* (Stephen Charles Bandy, 1967), 245.

[111] *Jubal - Genun Musical Worship - #2*, 14, http://www.adamqadmon.com/nephilim/mugenun.html (accessed Dec. 11, 2000).

[112] *Jubal - Genun Musical Worship - #2*, 14, http://www.adamqadmon.com/nephilim/mugenun.html (accessed Dec. 11, 2000).

[113] *Rev. 17* (KJV); Zen Garcia, *Lucifer - Father of Cain* (Zen Garcia, 2010), 274.

[114] Stephen Charles Bandy, *Caines Cynn: A Study of Beuwolf and the Legends of Cain* (Stephen Charles Bandy, 1967), 153.

[115] Stephen Charles Bandy, *Caines Cynn: A Study of Beuwolf and the Legends of Cain* (Stephen Charles Bandy, 1967), 228.

[116] David Max Eichhorn, *Cain: Son of the Serpent* (New York: Whittier Books, Inc., 1957), 107.

[117] David Kevin Delaney, *The Sevenfold Vengeance of Cain: Genesis 4 in Early Jewish and Christian Interpretation* (University of Virginia, 1996), 104 (notes).

[118] David Max Eichhorn, *Cain: Son of the Serpent* (New York: Whittier Books, Inc., 1957), 144.

[119] *Pseudo-Philo (The Biblical Antiquities of Philo)*, II 9, trans. M. R. James (1917), http://www.sacred-texts.com/bib/bap/bap19.htm (accessed July 13, 2006).

[120] Richard Gan, *The Mark of the Wicked Ones*, 12, http://www.propheticrevelation.new/w-ones.htm (accessed Aug. 22, 2007).

[121] Triumph Prophetic Ministries (Church of God), *The Mark of Cain*, 5, http://www.triumphpro.com/the_mark_of_cain.htm (accessed Aug. 22, 2007).

[122] *Nimrod - Babylonian - Musical Worship Teams*, 13, http://www.piney.com/MuBabylo.html (accessed March 13, 2008).

[123] Stephen Charles Bandy, *Caines Cynn: A Study of Beuwolf and the Legends of Cain* (Stephen Charles Bandy, 1967), 148.

[124] Strong's H1320 - *Basar*, 1, http://www.blueletterbible.org/lang/lexicon/lexicon.cfm?Strongs=H1320&t=KJV (accessed Oct. 4, 2012).

[125] *Rabbi Abraham Ibn Ezra's Commentary on the Creation*, trans. Michael Linetsky (Northvale, New Jersey: Jason Aronson Inc., 1998), 126.

[126] Strong's H1320 - *Basar*, 1, http://www.blueletterbible.org/lang/lexicon/lexicon.cfm?Strongs=H1320&t=KJV, (accessed Oct. 4, 2012).
[127] *The Companion Bible*, Gen. 6:3 (notes) (Grand Rapids, Michigan: Kregel Publications, 1990); Johann Andreas Eisenmenger, *The Traditions of the Jews, Contained in the Talmud and Other Mystical Writings* (London: J. Robinson, 1748), 105.
[128] *The Works of Philo Judaeus*, That the Worse is Wont to Attack the Better 23(83), trans. C. D. Yonge (London: H. G. Bohn, 1854-1855).
[129] Ibn Ezra, *Commentary on the Pentateuch: Genesis (Bereshit)* (New York: Menorah Publishing Company, Inc., 1988), 94 (notes).
[130] David Max Eichhorn, *Cain: Son of the Serpent* (New York: Whittier Books, Inc., 1957), 43.
[131] David Max Eichhorn, *Cain: Son of the Serpent* (New York: Whittier Books, Inc., 1957), 43.

Chapter 6

[1] Louis Ginzberg, *The Legends of the Jews Volume I: From the Creation to Jacob*, trans. Henrietta Szold (Baltimore, Maryland: The Johns Hopkins University Press, 1909), 145.
[2] *The Qur'an*, Surah 11:43, http://www.quran.mu/surah-hud.html (accessed May 29, 2017).
[3] James L. Kugel, *Traditions of the Bible* (Cambridge, Massachusetts: Harvard University Press, 1998), 166.
[4] Howard Schwartz, *Tree of Souls: The Mythology of Judaism* (Oxford: University Press, 2004), 456.
[5] David Max Eichhorn, *Cain: Son of the Serpent* (New York: Whittier Books, Inc., 1957), 69.
[6] David Max Eichhorn, *Cain: Son of the Serpent* (New York: Whittier Books, Inc., 1957), 70.
[7] *Genizah Manuscripts of Palestinian Targum to the Pentateuch Volume One*, Gen. 4:23, trans. Michael L. Klein (Cincinnati: Hebrew Union College Press, 1986); *The Armenian Apocryphal Adam Literature*, This is the History of Abel and Cain the Sons of Adam 58, trans. William Lowndes Lipscomb (Ann Arbor, Michigan: University Microfilms International, 1983), 170-171; *The Chronicles of Jerahmeel* (*The Hebrew Bible Historiale*), 23(1), trans. M. Gaster, Ph. D. (London: The Royal Asiatic Society, 1899).
[8] Mrs. Sydney Bristowe, *Sargon the Magnificent* (London: The Covenant Publishing Co., 1927), 89.
[9] E. Basil Redlich, *The Early Traditions of Genesis* (London: Gerald Duckworth & Co. Ltd., 1950), 78.
[10] E. Basil Redlich, *The Early Traditions of Genesis* (London: Gerald Duckworth & Co. Ltd., 1950), 77.
[11] Mrs. Sydney Bristowe, *Sargon the Magnificent* (London: The Covenant Publishing Co., 1927), 87.
[12] Mrs. Sydney Bristowe, *Sargon the Magnificent* (London: The Covenant Publishing Co., 1927), 95.
[13] Christian and Barbara Joy O'Brien, *The Shining Ones* (Cirencester, England: Dianthus Publishing Limited, 1988), 68.
[14] Christian and Barbara Joy O'Brien, *The Shining Ones* (Cirencester, England: Dianthus Publishing Limited, 1988), 100.
[15] Christian and Barbara Joy O'Brien, *The Shining Ones* (Cirencester, England: Dianthus Publishing Limited, 1988), 90.
[16] Christian and Barbara Joy O'Brien, *The Shining Ones* (Cirencester, England: Dianthus Publishing Limited, 1988), 89-90.
[17] Christian and Barbara Joy O'Brien, *The Shining Ones* (Cirencester, England: Dianthus Publishing Limited, 1988), 149.
[18] Christian and Barbara Joy O'Brien, *The Shining Ones* (Cirencester, England: Dianthus Publishing Limited, 1988), 71.
[19] Christian and Barbara Joy O'Brien, *The Shining Ones* (Cirencester, England: Dianthus Publishing Limited, 1988), 82.
[20] Christian and Barbara Joy O'Brien, *The Shining Ones* (Cirencester, England: Dianthus Publishing Limited, 1988), 149.
[21] Christian and Barbara Joy O'Brien, *The Shining Ones* (Cirencester, England: Dianthus Publishing Limited, 1988), 149.
[22] Bertrand L. Comparet, *What Happened to Cain*, 16-17, http://www.posse-comitatus.org/Bible_Studies/what_happened_to_cain.htm (accessed Aug. 21, 2000).
[23] Christian and Barbara Joy O'Brien, *The Shining Ones* (Cirencester, England: Dianthus Publishing Limited, 1988), 94.
[24] Christian and Barbara Joy O'Brien, *The Shining Ones* (Cirencester, England: Dianthus Publishing Limited, 1988), 91; Theophilus G. Pinches, *The Religion of Babylonia and Assyria* (London: Archibald Constable & Co. LTD., 1906), 96.
[25] Christian and Barbara Joy O'Brien, *The Shining Ones* (Cirencester, England: Dianthus Publishing Limited, 1988), 91.
[26] Christian and Barbara Joy O'Brien, *The Shining Ones* (Cirencester, England: Dianthus Publishing Limited, 1988), 87, 91.
[27] Christian and Barbara Joy O'Brien, *The Shining Ones* (Cirencester, England: Dianthus Publishing Limited, 1988), 71.

[28] Christian and Barbara Joy O'Brien, *The Shining Ones* (Cirencester, England: Dianthus Publishing Limited, 1988), 84.
[29] Christian and Barbara Joy O'Brien, *The Shining Ones* (Cirencester, England: Dianthus Publishing Limited, 1988), 149.
[30] Christian and Barbara Joy O'Brien, *The Shining Ones* (Cirencester, England: Dianthus Publishing Limited, 1988), 75.
[31] Christian and Barbara Joy O'Brien, *The Shining Ones* (Cirencester, England: Dianthus Publishing Limited, 1988), 74.
[32] Christian and Barbara Joy O'Brien, *The Shining Ones* (Cirencester, England: Dianthus Publishing Limited, 1988), 74.
[33] Christian and Barbara Joy O'Brien, The Shining Ones (Cirencester, England: Dianthus Publishing Limited, 1988), 100.
[34] Christian and Barbara Joy O'Brien, *The Shining Ones* (Cirencester, England: Dianthus Publishing Limited, 1988), 101.
[35] Christian and Barbara Joy O'Brien, *The Shining Ones* (Cirencester, England: Dianthus Publishing Limited, 1988), 99.
[36] Christian and Barbara Joy O'Brien, *The Shining Ones* (Cirencester, England: Dianthus Publishing Limited, 1988), 100.
[37] Christian and Barbara Joy O'Brien, *The Shining Ones* (Cirencester, England: Dianthus Publishing Limited, 1988), 186.
[38] Christian and Barbara Joy O'Brien, *The Shining Ones* (Cirencester, England: Dianthus Publishing Limited, 1988), 76.
[39] Christian and Barbara Joy O'Brien, *The Shining Ones* (Cirencester, England: Dianthus Publishing Limited, 1988), 77.
[40] Christian and Barbara Joy O'Brien, *The Shining Ones* (Cirencester, England: Dianthus Publishing Limited, 1988), 76.
[41] Christian and Barbara Joy O'Brien, *The Shining Ones* (Cirencester, England: Dianthus Publishing Limited, 1988), 77.
[42] Christian and Barbara Joy O'Brien, *The Shining Ones* (Cirencester, England: Dianthus Publishing Limited, 1988), 77.
[43] Christian and Barbara Joy O'Brien, The Shining Ones (Cirencester, England: Dianthus Publishing Limited, 1988), 77.
[44] Bertrand L. Comparet, What Happened to Cain, 17, http://www.posse-comitatus.org/Bible_Studies/what_happened_to_cain.htm (accessed Aug. 21, 2000).
[45] *The B.B.C. - Going after strange flesh*, 1, http://www.adamqadmon.com/nephilim/bbcstrange.html (accessed Feb. 25, 2001).
[46] Christian and Barbara Joy O'Brien, *The Shining Ones* (Cirencester, England: Dianthus Publishing Limited, 1988), 184, 186.
[47] Dan Gayman, *The Two Seeds of Genesis 3:15* (Daniel Lee Gayman, 1977), 23.
[48] Alan Unterman, *Dictionary of Jewish Lore and Legend* (London: Thames and Hudson Ltd., 1991), 138.
[49] James L. Kugel, *Traditions of the Bible* (Cambridge, Massachusetts: Harvard University Press, 1998), 216; *The B.B.C. - Going after strange flesh*, 1, http://www.adamqadmon.com/nephilim/bbcstrange.html (accessed Feb. 25, 2001).
[50] *The Chronography of George Synkellos* (Oxford, England: Oxford University Press, 2002), 18-19.
[51] *The Book of the Cave of Treasures*, trans. Sir E. A. Wallis Budge (London: The Religious Tract Society, 1927), 99.
[52] *The Book of the Generations of Adam*, Chap. 8.6, http://www.earth-history.com/Pseudepigrapha/generations-adam.htm (accessed May 5, 2007).
[53] *The Golden Legend or Lives of the Saints: Volume I*, 64, trans. William Caxton (1483), http://www.fordham.edu/halsall/basis/goldenlegend/GoldenLegend-Volume1.htm (accessed Jan. 13, 2011).
[54] Samuel A. Berman, *Midrash Tanhuma-Yelammedenu: An English Translation of Genesis and Exodus from the Printed Version of Tanhuma-Yelammedenu with an Introduction, Notes, and Indexes* (Hoboken, New Jersey: KTAV Publishing House, 1996), 34.
[55] *Lechery*, http://dictionary.reference.com/browse/lechery (accessed Jan. 20, 2012).
[56] Robert William Rogers, *Cuneiform Parallels to the Old Testament* (New York: Jennings & Graham, 1912), 96.
[57] Victor H. Matthews and Don C. Benjamin, *Old Testament Parallels: Laws and Stories from the Ancient Near East* (New York: Paulist Press, 1991), 16, 21.
[58] Victor H. Matthews and Don C. Benjamin, *Old Testament Parallels: Laws and Stories from the Ancient Near East* (New York: Paulist Press, 1991), 23.
[59] *Ancient Near East (Babylonia) Glossary and Texts*, 23, http://www.piney.com/BabGloss.html (accessed May 10, 2012).
[60] *Adam, the Flood & The Tower of Babel*, 8, http://www.biblehistory.net/newsletter/tower_of_babel.htm (accessed

May 10, 2011).

[61] *Adam, the Flood & The Tower of Babel*, 8, http://www.biblehistory.net/newsletter/tower_of_babel.htm (accessed May 10, 2011).

[62] Victor H. Matthews and Don C. Benjamin, *Old Testament Parallels: Laws and Stories from the Ancient Near East* (New York: Paulist Press, 1991), 22; Robert William Rogers, *Cuneiform Parallels to the Old Testament* (New York: Jennings & Graham, 1912), 114.

[63] Victor H. Matthews and Don C. Benjamin, *Old Testament Parallels: Laws and Stories from the Ancient Near East* (New York: Paulist Press, 1991), 22.

[64] Victor H. Matthews and Don C. Benjamin, *Old Testament Parallels: Laws and Stories from the Ancient Near East* (New York: Paulist Press, 1991), 23.

[65] C. A. Phifer, *Annals of the Earth* (Chicago, Illinois: American Publishers Association, 1890), 117.

[66] C. A. Phifer, *Annals of the Earth* (Chicago, Illinois: American Publishers Association, 1890), 83, 86.

[67] C. A. Phifer, *Annals of the Earth* (Chicago, Illinois: American Publishers Association, 1890), 270.

[68] C. A. Phifer, *Annals of the Earth* (Chicago, Illinois: American Publishers Association, 1890), 84.

[69] C. A. Phifer, *Annals of the Earth* (Chicago, Illinois: American Publishers Association, 1890), 83-84.

[70] C. A. Phifer, *Annals of the Earth* (Chicago, Illinois: American Publishers Association, 1890), 84-85.

[71] *Enoch & the Nephilim: Liber VII*, 53, http://www.adamqadmon.com/nephilim/bbcwatchers.html (accessed Feb. 6, 2001).

[72] C. A. Phifer, *Annals of the Earth* (Chicago, Illinois: American Publishers Association, 1890), 86.

[73] Kiddushin 35a Ibn Ezra, *Commentary on the Pentateuch: Genesis (Bereshit)* (New York: Menorah Publishing Company, Inc., 1988), 46-47 (notes).

[74] St. Chrysostom, *Homilies on Genesis*, Homily 17, http://www2.iath.virginia.edu/anderson/commentaries/ChrGen.html (accessed Jan. 12, 2011) 243-244.

[75] Mendel G. Glenn, *Jewish Tales and Legends* (New York: Star Hebrew Book Co., 1929), 26.

[76] *The Book of the Generations of Adam*, Chap. 8.6, http://www.earth-history.com/Pseudepigrapha/generations-adam.htm (accessed May 5, 2007).

[77] *The Babylonian Talmud*, Sanhedrin 108a.

[78] *The Book of the Mysteries of the Heavens and the Earth and Other Works of Bakhayla Mikael (Zosimas)*, trans. E. A. Wallis Budge (London: Oxford University Press, 1935), 29 (and notes).

[79] *The Armenian Apocryphal Adam Literature*, Concerning the Good Tiding of Seth Which God Gave to Adam on Account of Abel, Whom Cain Killed, in Order to Console Adam and Eve 59, trans. William Lowndes Lipscomb (Ann Arbor, Michigan: University Microfilms International, 1983), 282.

[80] *Rashi*, (Bereishit) Genesis 6:17, http://www.chabad.org/library/bible_cdo/aid/8168/showrashi/true (accessed Oct. 27, 2010).

[81] Strong's H7307 - *ruwach*, 1, https://www.blueletterbible.org/lang/lexicon/lexicon.cfm?Strongs=H7307&t=KJV (accessed Feb. 6, 2001).

[82] St. Ephrem the Syrian, *Selected Prose Works*, trans. Edward G. Mathews, Jr. and Joseph P. Amar (Washington, D. C.: The Catholic University of America Press, 1994), 139.

[83] *The Armenian Apocryphal Adam Literature*, Concerning the Good Tidings of Seth Which God Gave to Adam on Account of Abel, Whom Cain Killed, in Order to Console Adam and Eve 41, trans. William Lowndes Lipscomb (Ann Arbor, Michigan: University Microfilms International, 1983), 281.

[84] *The Babylonian Talmud*, Sanhedrin 108b, http://halakhah.com/sanhedrin/sanhedrin_108.html (accessed April 14, 2011).

[85] *The Babylonian Talmud*, Sanhedrin 108b, http://halakhah.com/sanhedrin/sanhedrin_108.html (accessed April 14, 2011).

[86] *Enoch & the Nephilim: Liber VII*, 38, http://www.adamqadmon.com/nephilim/bbcwatchers.html (accessed Feb. 6, 2001).

[87] St. Ephrem the Syrian, *Selected Prose Works*, trans. Edward G. Mathews, Jr. and Joseph P. Amar (Washington, D. C.: The Catholic University of America Press, 1994), 139.

[88] James L. Kugel, *Traditions of the Bible* (Cambridge, Massachusetts: Harvard University Press, 1998), 216; Jack P. Lewis, *Noah*, 63.

[89] *Pirke De Rabbi Eliezer*, Chapter 23: The Ark and the flood [26B. ii.], trans. Gerald Friedlander (New York: Sepher-Hermon Press, 1981), 166.

[90] St. Ephrem the Syrian, *Selected Prose Works*, trans. Edward G. Mathews, Jr. and Joseph P. Amar (Washington, D. C.: The Catholic University of America Press, 1994), 142.

[91] *The Works of Philo Judaeus*, Questions and Answers on Genesis II, 27, trans. C. D. Yonge (London: H. G. Bohn, 1854-1855).

[92] *The Works of Philo Judaeus*, Questions and Answers on Genesis II, 27, trans. C. D. Yonge (London: H. G. Bohn, 1854-1855).

[93] Wikipedia, the free encyclopedia, *Carleton S. Coon*, 2, https://en.wikipedia.org/wiki/Carleton_S._Coon (accessed May 15, 2014).

[94] Strong's H2416 - *chay*, 1, http://www.blueletterbible.org/lang/lexicon/lexicon.cfm?Strongs=H2416&t=KJV (accessed Feb. 6, 2001).
[95] Alexander Heidel, *The Gilgamesh Epic and Old Testament Parallels* (Chicago: The University of Chicago Press, 1946), 237.
[96] Merriam-Webster Dictionary, *Cattle*, http://www.merriam-webster.com/dictionary/cattle (accessed May 15, 2014).
[97] House of Israel... Journey in YHWH, *Beasts in the Bible*, 3, https://tribeharvest.com/2013/05/13/beasts-cattle/ (accessed May 29, 2017).
[98] George Smith, *The Chaldean Account of Genesis* (New York, New York: Scribner, Armstrong & Co., 1876), 82; Mrs. Sydney Bristowe, *Sargon the Magnificent* (London: The Covenant Publishing Co., 1927), 15-18, 22, 94-95, 145.
[99] *The Babylonian Legends of the Creation and the Fight Between Bel and the Dragon As Told by Assyrian Tablets from Nineveh*, Tablet 7, 32, trans. by Sir E. A. Wallis Budge (London: Harrison & Sons, 1931),
[100] *The Enuma Elish*, Tablet 6, 107, http://www.ancient.eu/article/225/ (accessed May 29, 2017).
[101] *The Chronicles of Jerahmeel* (*The Hebrew Bible Historiale*), (), trans. M. Gaster, Ph. D. (London: The Royal Asiatic Society, 1899).
[102] Louis Ginzberg, *The Legends of the Jews Volume I: From the Creation to Jacob*, trans. Henrietta Szold (Baltimore, Maryland: The Johns Hopkins University Press, 1909), 113-115.
[103] Bob Curran, *Dark Fairies* (Pompton Plaines, New Jersey: The Career Press, Inc., 2010), 112.
[104] Bob Curran, *Dark Fairies* (Pompton Plaines, New Jersey: The Career Press, Inc., 2010), 7, 12.
[105] Bob Curran, *Dark Fairies* (Pompton Plaines, New Jersey: The Career Press, Inc., 2010), 21.
[106] Bob Curran, *Dark Fairies* (Pompton Plaines, New Jersey: The Career Press, Inc., 2010), 12.
[107] Bob Curran, *Dark Fairies* (Pompton Plaines, New Jersey: The Career Press, Inc., 2010), 12.
[108] Bob Curran, *Dark Fairies* (Pompton Plaines, New Jersey: The Career Press, Inc., 2010), 6.
[109] Bob Curran, *Dark Fairies* (Pompton Plaines, New Jersey: The Career Press, Inc., 2010), 6.
[110] Bob Curran, *Dark Fairies* (Pompton Plaines, New Jersey: The Career Press, Inc., 2010), 7.
[111] Bob Curran, *Dark Fairies* (Pompton Plaines, New Jersey: The Career Press, Inc., 2010), 176.
[112] Bob Curran, *Dark Fairies* (Pompton Plaines, New Jersey: The Career Press, Inc., 2010), 7.
[113] Bob Curran, *Dark Fairies* (Pompton Plaines, New Jersey: The Career Press, Inc., 2010), 62.
[114] The King James Bible Page, *KJV Dictionary Definition: air*, 1, http://av1611.com/kjbp/kjv-dictionary/air.html (accessed May 29, 2017).
[115] The King James Bible Page, *KJV Dictionary Definition: fly*, 1, http://av1611.com/kjbp/kjv-dictionary/fly.html http://biblehub.com/revelation/18-2.htm (accessed March 22, 2017).
[116] Bob Curran, *Dark Fairies* (Pompton Plaines, New Jersey: The Career Press, Inc., 2010), 12, 176.
[117] Bob Curran, *Dark Fairies* (Pompton Plaines, New Jersey: The Career Press, Inc., 2010), 20.
[118] Bob Curran, *Dark Fairies* (Pompton Plaines, New Jersey: The Career Press, Inc., 2010), 12.
[119] S. Baring-Gould, *Legends of the Patriarchs and Prophets and Other Old Testament Characters* (New York: American Book Exchange, 1881), 105.
[120] Blue Letter Bible, *Strong's H3671 - kanaph*, 1, https://www.blueletterbible.org/lang/lexicon/lexicon.cfm?Strongs=H3671&t=KJV (accessed March 22, 2017).
[121] Bible Hub, *3671. kanaph*, 1-2, http://biblehub.com/hebrew/3671.htm (accessed March 22, 2017).

Chapter 7

[1] Alexander Heidel, *The Gilgamesh Epic and Old Testament Parallels* (Chicago: The University of Chicago Press, 1946), 237; *An Historical Treatise of the Travels of Noah Into Europe: Containing the First Inhabitation and Peopling Thereof*, trans. Richard Lynche (1601), http://www.annomundi.com/history/travels_of_noah.htm (accessed Dec. 7, 2007); Louis Ginzberg, *The Legends of the Jews Volume I: From the Creation to Jacob*, trans. Henrietta Szold (Baltimore, Maryland: The Johns Hopkins University Press, 1909), 145.
[2] Stephen R. Haynes, *Noah's Curse: The Biblical Justification of American Slavery* (Oxford: University Press, 2002), 38.
[3] Louis Ginzberg, *The Legends of the Jews Volume V: Notes for Volume One and Two*, trans. Henrietta Szold (Baltimore, Maryland: The Johns Hopkins University Press, 1909), 179.
[4] Stephen R. Haynes, *Noah's Curse: The Biblical Justification of American Slavery* (Oxford: University Press, 2002), 30; Andy Orchard, *Pride and Prodigies: Studies in the Monsters of the Beowulf-Manuscript* (Toronto: University of Toronto Press Incorporated, 2003), 67-68, 73.
[5] Creationism & the Early Church, *Chapter 6: Noah's Flood & the Tower of Babel*, 2, http://www.robibrad.demon.co.uk/Chapter6.htm (accessed June 3, 2000).
[6] Charles A. Weisman, *Facts and Fictions Regarding Noah's Flood* (Apple Valley, Minnesota: Weisman Publications, 1992), 48.
[7] Charles A. Weisman, *Facts and Fictions Regarding Noah's Flood* (Apple Valley, Minnesota: Weisman Publications, 1992), 6.
[8] Charles A. Weisman, *Facts and Fictions Regarding Noah's Flood* (Apple Valley, Minnesota: Weisman Publications, 1992), 9.

[9] Andy Orchard, *Pride and Prodigies: Studies in the Monsters of the Beowulf-Manuscript* (Toronto: University of Toronto Press Incorporated, 2003), 67.
[10] Charles A. Weisman, *Facts and Fictions Regarding Noah's Flood* (Apple Valley, Minnesota: Weisman Publications, 1992), 5.
[11] Stephen Charles Bandy, *Caines Cynn: A Study of Beuwolf and the Legends of Cain* (Stephen Charles Bandy, 1967), 34.
[12] Blue Letter Bible, *Strong's H2986 - yabal*, 1-2, https://www.blueletterbible.org/lang/lexicon/lexicon.cfm?strongs=H2986&t=KJV (accessed March 22, 2017).
[13] Robert Graves and Raphael Patai, *Hebrew Myths: The Book of Genesis* (Garden City, New York: Doubleday & Company, 1964), 114; *Rashi*, (Bereishit) Genesis 7:7, http://www.chabad.org/library/bible_cdo/aid/8168/showrashi/true (accessed Oct. 27, 2010).
[14] Louis Ginzberg, *The Legends of the Jews Volume V: Notes for Volume One and Two*, IV Noah, 54, trans. Henrietta Szold (Baltimore, Maryland: The Johns Hopkins University Press, 1909), 188.
[15] *The Works of Philo Judaeus*, Questions and Answers II, 49, trans. C. D. Yonge (London: H. G. Bohn, 1854-1855).
[16] Robert Graves and Raphael Patai, *Hebrew Myths: The Book of Genesis* (Garden City, New York: Doubleday & Company, 1964), 112.
[17] Louis Ginzberg, *The Legends of the Jews Volume V: Notes for Volume One and Two*, IV Noah, 54, trans. Henrietta Szold (Baltimore, Maryland: The Johns Hopkins University Press, 1909), 188.
[18] Robert Graves and Raphael Patai, *Hebrew Myths: The Book of Genesis* (Garden City, New York: Doubleday & Company, 1964), 114.
[19] Stephen R. Haynes, *Noah's Curse: The Biblical Justification of American Slavery* (Oxford: University Press, 2002), 31.
[20] S. Baring-Gould, *Legends of the Patriarchs and Prophets and Other Old Testament Characters* (New York: American Book Exchange, 1881), 124; Louis Ginzberg, *The Legends of the Jews Volume V: Notes for Volume One and Two*, trans. Henrietta Szold (Baltimore, Maryland: The Johns Hopkins University Press, 1909), 156.
[21] Louis Ginzberg, *The Legends of the Jews Volume I: From the Creation to Jacob*, trans. Henrietta Szold (Baltimore, Maryland: The Johns Hopkins University Press, 1909), 167.
[22] *The Zohar*, Noach 36, http://www.zohar.com/noach/and-sons-noah-went-forth-ark%C2%9D (accessed Feb. 25, 2010).
[23] *The Midrash Rabbah*, 12:10, trans. Rabbi Dr. H. Freedman and Maurice Simon (London: The Soncino Press, 1961).
[24] David Padfield, *Interracial Marriage*, 3, http://padfield.com/1996/racial.html (accessed April 22, 2001).
[25] Eustace Mullins, *The Curse of Canaan* (Staunton, Virginia: Revelation Books, 1987), 6.
[26] Stephen R. Haynes, *Noah's Curse: The Biblical Justification of American Slavery* (Oxford: University Press, 2002), 31.
[27] *An Historical Treatise of the Travels of Noah Into Europe: Containing the First Inhabitation and Peopling Thereof*, trans. Richard Lynche (1601), http://www.annomundi.com/history/travels_of_noah.htm (accessed Dec. 7, 2007).
[28] Eustace Mullins, *The Curse of Canaan* (Staunton, Virginia: Revelation Books, 1987), 6.
[29] David Allen Deal, *Noah's Ark: The Evidence* (Muskogee, Oklahoma: Artisan Publishers, 2007), 126.
[30] Noah's Flood: Ancient Stories of Natural Cataclysm, *Lions and Noah and Groans, Oh My!: Dangerous Beasts Aboard the Ark*, http://www.floodofnoah.com/post-lion-rabbinics-beasts-on-ark (accessed June 15, 2017).
[31] *The Midrash Rabbah*, 30:6, trans. Rabbi Dr. H. Freedman and Maurice Simon (London: The Soncino Press, 1961).
[32] Louis Ginzberg, *The Legends of The Jews: Volume I* (Baltimore, Maryland: Johns Hopkins University Press, 1998), 165-166; Louis Ginzberg, *The Legends of The Jews: Volume V: Notes for Volume One and Two* (Baltimore, Maryland: Johns Hopkins University Press, 1998), 187.
[33] Louis Ginzberg, *The Legends of the Jews Volume I: From the Creation to Jacob*, trans. Henrietta Szold (Baltimore, Maryland: The Johns Hopkins University Press, 1909), 165.
[34] Christopher Knight and Robert Lomas, *Uriel's Machine* (Boston, Massachusetts: Element Books, 1999), 86.
[35] *An Historical Treatise of the Travels of Noah Into Europe: Containing the First Inhabitation and Peopling Thereof*, trans. Richard Lynche (1601), http://www.annomundi.com/history/travels_of_noah.htm (accessed Dec. 7, 2007).
[36] *The Second Book of Adam and Eve (The Conflict of Adam and Eve with Satan)*, 11:4, trans. S. C. Malan (London: Williams and Norgate, 1882), 68.
[37] Charles DeLoach, *Giants: A Reference Guide from History, the Bible, and Recorded Legend* (Metuchen, N. J.: The Scarecrow Press, Inc., 1995), 287.
[38] *The Armenian Apocryphal Adam Literature*, Concerning the Good Tidings of Seth, to Which We Ought to Give Ear 27, trans. William Lowndes Lipscomb (Ann Arbor, Michigan: University Microfilms International, 1983), 196.
[39] *Gen. 6:9-10* (KJV); Rev. Alexander Hislop, *The Two Babylons or the Papal Worship: Proved to be the Worship of Nimrod and His Wife*, (Neptune, New Jersey: Loizeaux Brothers, 1916), 244; Mrs. Sydney Bristowe, *Sargon the Magnificent* (London: The Covenant Publishing Co., 1927), 17; Colin Kidd, *The Forging of Races: Race and Scripture in the Protestant Atlantic World, 1600-2000* (Cambridge: Cambridge University Press, 2006), 116.
[40] Robert William Rogers, *Cuneiform Parallels to the Old Testament* (New York: Jennings & Graham, 1912), 100.
[41] The New York Times, *Babylon Gave Bible Story to the Jews (June 24, 1914)*, 1,

http://query.nytimes.com/mem/archive-free/pdf?res=9507E0DA1F39E633A25757C2A9609C946596D6CF (accessed July 3, 2017).

[42] Louis Ginzberg, *The Legends of The Jews: Volume I: From the Creation to Jacob*, trans. Henrietta Szold (Baltimore: Johns Hopkins University Press, 1998), 168-169; Louis Ginzberg, *The Legends of The Jews: Volume V Notes for Volume One and Two* (Baltimore: Johns Hopkins University Press, 1998), 191.

[43] Louis Ginzberg, *The Legends of the Jews Volume I: From the Creation to Jacob*, trans. Henrietta Szold (Baltimore, Maryland: The Johns Hopkins University Press, 1909), 168.

[44] *The Midrash Rabbah*, 36:5, trans. Rabbi Dr. H. Freedman and Maurice Simon (London: The Soncino Press, 1961).

[45] Eustace Mullins, *The Curse of Canaan* (Staunton, Virginia: Revelation Books, 1987), 7.

[46] *The Babylonian Talmud*, Sanhedrin 70a.

[47] Gen. 9:21 (KJV).

[48] Stephen R. Haynes, *Noah's Curse: The Biblical Justification of American Slavery* (Oxford: University Press, 2002), 33.

[49] *The Book of the Bee*, Chapter 20, trans. Earnest A. Wallis Budge, M. A., http://www.sacred-texts.com/chr/bb/bb20.htm (accessed Oct. 10, 2004); *The Book of the Rolls (Kitab Al-Magall)*, trans. Margaret Dunlop Gibson, Apocrypha Arabica (London: C. J. Clay and Sons, 1901), 31; *The Works of Philo Judaeus*, On the Prayers and Curses Uttered by Noah When He Became Sober, 7(32), trans. C. D. Yonge (London: H. G. Bohn, 1854-1855).

[50] *The Book of the Rolls (Kitab Al-Magall)*, trans. Margaret Dunlop Gibson, Apocrypha Arabica (London: C. J. Clay and Sons, 1901), 31; *The Book of the Cave of Treasures*, trans. Sir E. A. Wallis Budge (London: The Religious Tract Society, 1927), 118.

[51] St. Ephrem the Syrian, *Selected Prose Works*, Section VII 2, trans. Edward G. Mathews, Jr. and Joseph P. Amar (Washington, D. C.: The Catholic University of America Press, 1994), 144.

[52] Stephen R. Haynes, *Noah's Curse: The Biblical Justification of American Slavery* (Oxford: University Press, 2002), 37.

[53] Stephen R. Haynes, *Noah's Curse: The Biblical Justification of American Slavery* (Oxford: University Press, 2002), 31.

[54] *Pirke De Rabbi Eliezer*, Chapter 23: The Ark and the Flood [26B. ii.], trans. Gerald Friedlander (New York: Sepher-Hermon Press, 1981), 170.

[55] Stephen R. Haynes, *Noah's Curse: The Biblical Justification of American Slavery* (Oxford: University Press, 2002), 34.

[56] S. Baring-Gould, *Legends of the Patriarchs and Prophets and Other Old Testament Characters* (New York: American Book Exchange, 1881), 124.

[57] *The History of al-Tabari - Volume II: Prophets and Patriarchs*, trans. William M. Brinner (Albany: New York Press, 1987), 14; *The Bible, The Koran, and the Talmud (Biblical Legends of the Mussulmans)*, Noah, Hud and Salih, trans. Dr. G. Weil (New York, 1863), 55.

[58] Louis Ginzberg, *The Legends of the Jews Volume I: From the Creation to Jacob*, trans. Henrietta Szold (Baltimore, Maryland: The Johns Hopkins University Press, 1909), 168.

[59] Colin Kidd, *The Forging of Races: Race and Scripture in the Protestant Atlantic World, 1600-2000* (Cambridge: Cambridge University Press, 2006), 74; Mrs. Sydney Bristowe, *Sargon the Magnificent* (London: The Covenant Publishing Co., 1927), 83; Stephen Quayle, *Genesis 6 Giants: The Master Builders of Prehistoric and Ancient Civilizations* (Bozeman, Montana: End Time Thunder Publishers, 2005), 65; Robert Graves and Raphael Patai, *Hebrew Myths: The Book of Genesis* (Garden City, New York: Doubleday & Company, 1964), 122; Stephen R. Haynes, *Noah's Curse: The Biblical Justification of American Slavery* (Oxford: University Press, 2002), 38.

[60] *An Historical Treatise of the Travels of Noah Into Europe: Containing the First Inhabitation and Peopling Thereof*, trans. Richard Lynche (1601), http://www.annomundi.com/history/travels_of_noah.htm (accessed Dec. 7, 2007).

[61] E. S. G. Bristowe, *Cain - An Argument* (Leicester: Edgar Backus, 1950), 36.

[62] *The Book of the Cave of Treasures*, Vineyard, The Third 1000 Years, trans. Sir E. A. Wallis Budge (London: The Religious Tract Society, 1927), 120.

[63] C. J. Verduin, *Looking for Jonitus*, 13, http://leidenuniv.nl/fsw/verduin/jonitus/jonitus.htm (accessed Aug. 1, 2005).

[64] Abarim Publications, *Ham Meaning*, 1-4, http://www.abarim-publications.com/Meaning/Ham.html#.WULio7mpU2z (accessed June 15, 2017).

[65] Stephen R. Haynes, *Noah's Curse: The Biblical Justification of American Slavery* (Oxford: University Press, 2002), 101.

[66] David Allen Deal, *Noah's Ark: The Evidence* (Muskogee, Oklahoma: Artisan Publishers, 2007), 186.

[67] Stephen R. Haynes, *Noah's Curse: The Biblical Justification of American Slavery* (Oxford: University Press, 2002), 28.

[68] S. Baring-Gould, *Legends of the Patriarchs and Prophets and Other Old Testament Characters* (New York: American Book Exchange, 1881), 110.

[69] *An Historical Treatise of the Travels of Noah Into Europe: Containing the First Inhabitation and Peopling Thereof*, trans. Richard Lynche (1601), http://www.annomundi.com/history/travels_of_noah.htm (accessed Dec. 7, 2007).

[70] Andy Orchard, *Pride and Prodigies: Studies in the Monsters of the Beowulf-Manuscript* (Toronto: University of

Toronto Press Incorporated, 2003), 68.

[71] Andy Orchard, *Pride and Prodigies: Studies in the Monsters of the Beowulf-Manuscript* (Toronto: University of Toronto Press Incorporated, 2003), 69, 73.

[72] Robert Bowie Johnson, Jr., *Athena and Eden: The Hidden Meaning of the Parthenon's East Facade* (Annapolis, Maryland: Solving Light Books, 2002), 26.

[73] Robert Bowie Johnson, Jr., *Athena and Eden: The Hidden Meaning of he Parthenon's East Facade* (Annapolis, Maryland: Solving Light Books, 2002), 58.

[74] Andy Orchard, *Pride and Prodigies: Studies in the Monsters of the Beowulf-Manuscript* (Toronto: University of Toronto Press Incorporated, 2003), 70.

[75] Mrs. Sydney Bristowe, *Sargon the Magnificent* (London: The Covenant Publishing Co., 1927), 166.

[76] Andy Orchard, *Pride and Prodigies: Studies in the Monsters of the Beowulf-Manuscript* (Toronto: University of Toronto Press Incorporated, 2003), 69-70, 73, 79.

[77] *Anglo Saxon England* (Cambridge University Press), 194.

[78] *The Book of the Cave of Treasures*, trans. Sir E. A. Wallis Budge (London: The Religious Tract Society, 1927), 99 (notes).

[79] Stephen R. Haynes, *Noah's Curse: The Biblical Justification of American Slavery* (Oxford: University Press, 2002), 27.

[80] David Max Eichhorn, *Cain: Son of the Serpent* (New York: Whittier Books, Inc., 1957), 133.

[81] David Max Eichhorn, *Cain: Son of the Serpent* (New York: Whittier Books, Inc., 1957), 133.

[82] Robert Bowie Johnson, Jr., *Athena and Eden: The Hidden Meaning of he Parthenon's East Facade* (Annapolis, Maryland: Solving Light Books, 2002), 20.

[83] David Allen Deal, *Noah's Ark: The Evidence* (Muskogee, Oklahoma: Artisan Publishers, 2007), 62, 128.

[84] Robert Bowie Johnson, Jr., *Athena and Eden: The Hidden Meaning of he Parthenon's East Facade* (Annapolis, Maryland: Solving Light Books, 2002), 29; David Allen Deal, *Noah's Ark: The Evidence* (Muskogee, Oklahoma: Artisan Publishers, 2007), 62; *Definitions /God_Messiah_and_Angels, Who was Baal, who was Asherah?*, 1, http://www.jewish.com/askarabbi/askarabbi/askr2417.htm (accessed May 25, 2000); Wikipedia, the free encyclopedia, *Atargatis*, http://en.wikipedia.org/wiki/Atargatis (accessed April 11, 2012); *The World According to Abufares of Tartous*, 2, http://www.abufares.net/2010/02/atargatis.html (accessed April 11, 2012).

[85] *The Midrash Rabbah*, 36:2, trans. Rabbi Dr. H. Freedman and Maurice Simon (London: The Soncino Press, 1961).

[86] *The Midrash Rabbah*, 36:2 (notes), trans. Rabbi Dr. H. Freedman and Maurice Simon (London: The Soncino Press, 1961).

[87] *Book of the Glory of Kings (Kerba Nagast)*, 9. Concerning the Covenant of Noah, trans. Sir. E. A. Wallis Budge (London: Humphrey Milford, 1932).

[88] *The Book of the Cave of Treasures*, trans. Sir E. A. Wallis Budge (London: The Religious Tract Society, 1927), 125 (notes).

[89] *An Historical Treatise of the Travels of Noah Into Europe: Containing the First Inhabitation and Peopling Thereof*, trans. Richard Lynche (1601), http://www.annomundi.com/history/travels_of_noah.htm (accessed Dec. 7, 2007).

[90] Stephen R. Haynes, *Noah's Curse: The Biblical Justification of American Slavery* (Oxford: University Press, 2002), 32.

[91] Alexander Hislop, *The Two Babylons or the Papal Worship: Proved to be the Worship of Nimrod and His Wife* (Neptune, New Jersey: Loizeaux Brothers, 1916), 35.

[92] Charles DeLoach, *Giants: A Reference Guide from History, the Bible, and Recorded Legend* (Metuchen, N. J.: The Scarecrow Press, Inc., 1995), 116.

[93] S. Baring-Gould, *Legends of the Patriarchs and Prophets and Other Old Testament Characters* (New York: American Book Exchange, 1881), 124.

[94] Stephen R. Haynes, Noah's Curse: The Biblical Justification of American Slavery (Oxford: University Press, 2002), 29.

[95] Colin Kidd, *The Forging of Races: Race and Scripture in the Protestant Atlantic World, 1600-2000* (Cambridge: Cambridge University Press, 2006), 75; Stephen R. Haynes, *Noah's Curse: The Biblical Justification of American Slavery* (Oxford: University Press, 2002), 33.

[96] Montague Rhodes James, *The Lost Apocrypha of the Old Testament: Their Titles and Fragments Collected, Translated and Discussed* (London: Society For Promoting Christian Knowledge, 1920), 16; S. Baring-Gould, *Legends of the Patriarchs and Prophets and Other Old Testament Characters* (New York: American Book Exchange, 1881), 124.

[97] Wikipedia, the free encyclopedia, *Chemistry*, 1, en.wikipedia.org/wiki/Chemistry (accessed Aug. 21, 2010).

[98] Stephen R. Haynes, *Noah's Curse: The Biblical Justification of American Slavery* (Oxford: University Press, 2002), 38.

[99] C. J. Verduin, *Looking for Jonitus*, 13, http://leidenuniv.nl/fsw/verduin/jonitus/jonitus.htm (accessed Aug. 1, 2005).

[100] Mrs. Sydney Bristowe, *Sargon the Magnificent* (London: The Covenant Publishing Co., 1927), 166.

[101] S. Baring-Gould, *Legends of the Patriarchs and Prophets and Other Old Testament Characters* (New York: American Book Exchange, 1881), 124.

[102] Louis Ginzberg, *The Legends of the Jews Volume V: Notes for Volume One and Two*, trans. Henrietta Szold (Baltimore, Maryland: The Johns Hopkins University Press, 1909), 200.
[103] Stephen R. Haynes, *Noah's Curse: The Biblical Justification of American Slavery* (Oxford: University Press, 2002), 29.
[104] Charles DeLoach, *Giants: A Reference Guide from History, the Bible, and Recorded Legend* (Metuchen, N. J.: The Scarecrow Press, Inc., 1995), 116.
[105] Alexander Hislop, *The Two Babylons or the Papal Worship: Proved to be the Worship of Nimrod and His Wife* (Neptune, New Jersey: Loizeaux Brothers, 1916), 40.
[106] Alexander Hislop, *The Two Babylons or the Papal Worship: Proved to be the Worship of Nimrod and His Wife* (Neptune, New Jersey: Loizeaux Brothers, 1916), 134.
[107] Alexander Hislop, *The Two Babylons or the Papal Worship: Proved to be the Worship of Nimrod and His Wife* (Neptune, New Jersey: Loizeaux Brothers, 1916), 124.
[108] C. J. Verduin, *Looking for Jonitus*, 8, http://leidenuniv.nl/fsw/verduin/jonitus/jonitus.htm (accessed Aug. 1, 2005).
[109] Charles DeLoach, *Giants: A Reference Guide from History, the Bible, and Recorded Legend* (Metuchen, N. J.: The Scarecrow Press, Inc., 1995), 116.
[110] Alexander Hislop, *The Two Babylons or the Papal Worship: Proved to be the Worship of Nimrod and His Wife* (Neptune, New Jersey: Loizeaux Brothers, 1916), 23.
[111] Alexander Hislop, *The Two Babylons or the Papal Worship: Proved to be the Worship of Nimrod and His Wife* (Neptune, New Jersey: Loizeaux Brothers, 1916), 250.
[112] Alexander Hislop, *The Two Babylons or the Papal Worship: Proved to be the Worship of Nimrod and His Wife* (Neptune, New Jersey: Loizeaux Brothers, 1916), 250.
[113] Alexander Hislop, *The Two Babylons or the Papal Worship: Proved to be the Worship of Nimrod and His Wife* (Neptune, New Jersey: Loizeaux Brothers, 1916), 250.
[114] Louis Ginzberg, *The Legends of the Jews Volume V: Notes for Volume One and Two*, trans. Henrietta Szold (Baltimore, Maryland: The Johns Hopkins University Press, 1909), 135.
[115] Eusebius, *Chronicle*, 7, http://www.attalus.org/translate/eusebius.html (accessed May 5, 2011).

Chapter 8

[1] Robert Bowie Johnson, Jr., *Athena and Kain: The True Meaning of Greek Myth* (Annapolis, Maryland: Solving Light Books, 2003), 114, 187.
[2] Mike Gascoigne, *Forgotten History of the Western People* (Camberley, England: Anno Mundi Books, 2002), 64.
[3] Robert Bowie Johnson, Jr., *The Parthenon Code: Mankind's History in Marble* (Annapolis, Maryland: Solving Light Books, 2004), 19.
[4] Robert Bowie Johnson, Jr., *The Parthenon Code: Mankind's History in Marble* (Annapolis, Maryland: Solving Light Books, 2004), 60.
[5] Robert Bowie Johnson, Jr., *The Parthenon Code: Mankind's History in Marble* (Annapolis, Maryland: Solving Light Books, 2004), 12.
[6] Robert Bowie Johnson, Jr., *The Parthenon Code: Mankind's History in Marble* (Annapolis, Maryland: Solving Light Books, 2004), 74.
[7] Robert Bowie Johnson, Jr., *Athena and Kain: The True Meaning of Greek Myth* (Annapolis, Maryland: Solving Light Books, 2003), 15.
[8] Robert Bowie Johnson, Jr., *The Parthenon Code: Mankind's History in Marble* (Annapolis, Maryland: Solving Light Books, 2004), 72.
[9] Robert Bowie Johnson, Jr., *The Parthenon Code: Mankind's History in Marble* (Annapolis, Maryland: Solving Light Books, 2004), 72.
[10] Robert Bowie Johnson, Jr., *The Parthenon Code: Mankind's History in Marble* (Annapolis, Maryland: Solving Light Books, 2004), 72, 176.
[11] Robert Bowie Johnson, Jr., *The Parthenon Code: Mankind's History in Marble* (Annapolis, Maryland: Solving Light Books, 2004), 111.
[12] Robert Bowie Johnson, Jr., *The Parthenon Code: Mankind's History in Marble* (Annapolis, Maryland: Solving Light Books, 2004), 35.
[13] Mike Gascoigne, *Forgotten History of the Western People* (Camberley, England: Anno Mundi Books, 2002), 38, 49, 59.
[14] Mike Gascoigne, *Forgotten History of the Western People* (Camberley, England: Anno Mundi Books, 2002), 49.
[15] Robert Bowie Johnson, Jr., *Athena and Kain: The True Meaning of Greek Myth* (Annapolis, Maryland: Solving Light Books, 2003), 82.
[16] Robert Bowie Johnson, Jr., *The Parthenon Code: Mankind's History in Marble* (Annapolis, Maryland: Solving Light Books, 2004), 74.
[17] Robert Bowie Johnson, Jr., *The Parthenon Code: Mankind's History in Marble* (Annapolis, Maryland: Solving Light Books, 2004), 114; Robert Bowie Johnson, Jr., *Athena and Eden: The Hidden Meaning of the Parthenon's East Facade* (Annapolis, Maryland: Solving Light Books, 2002), 26.

[18] Robert Bowie Johnson, Jr., *Athena and Kain: The True Meaning of Greek Myth* (Annapolis, Maryland: Solving Light Books, 2003), 124.
[19] Robert Bowie Johnson, Jr., *The Parthenon Code: Mankind's History in Marble* (Annapolis, Maryland: Solving Light Books, 2004), 114.
[20] Robert Bowie Johnson, Jr., *The Parthenon Code: Mankind's History in Marble* (Annapolis, Maryland: Solving Light Books, 2004), 110, 112.
[21] Robert Bowie Johnson, Jr., *Athena and Eden: The Hidden Meaning of the Parthenon's East Facade* (Annapolis, Maryland: Solving Light Books, 2002), 26.
[22] Robert Bowie Johnson, Jr., *The Parthenon Code: Mankind's History in Marble* (Annapolis, Maryland: Solving Light Books, 2004), 114.
[23] Robert Bowie Johnson, Jr., *The Parthenon Code: Mankind's History in Marble* (Annapolis, Maryland: Solving Light Books, 2004), 55; Robert Bowie Johnson, Jr., *Athena and Kain: The True Meaning of Greek Myth* (Annapolis, Maryland: Solving Light Books, 2003), 122; Robert Bowie Johnson, Jr., *Athena and Eden: The Hidden Meaning of the Parthenon's East Facade* (Annapolis, Maryland: Solving Light Books, 2002), 46.
[24] *Inigo Jones Manuscript*, 5, http://www.freemasonry.com/masonic_manuscripts_jones.html (accessed May 24, 2011); Margi B., *Al-Uzza and 'Uzza - Historical Origins and Theory*, 3, http://www.geocities.com/mabcosmic/essays/utheory.html?200719 (accessed April 19, 2007).
[25] Robert Bowie Johnson, Jr., *Athena and Eden: The Hidden Meaning of the Parthenon's East Facade* (Annapolis, Maryland: Solving Light Books, 2002), 61.
[26] Robert Bowie Johnson, Jr., *The Parthenon Code: Mankind's History in Marble* (Annapolis, Maryland: Solving Light Books, 2004), 40.
[27] Robert Bowie Johnson, Jr., *The Parthenon Code: Mankind's History in Marble* (Annapolis, Maryland: Solving Light Books, 2004), 40.
[28] 12 Tribe History, *What Really Happened After the Flood?*, 1, http://12tribehistory.com/what-really-happened-after-the-flood-2/ (accessed May 12, 2014).
[29] Robert Bowie Johnson, Jr., *Athena and Eden: The Hidden Meaning of the Parthenon's East Facade* (Annapolis, Maryland: Solving Light Books, 2002), 60.
[30] Robert Bowie Johnson, Jr., *Athena and Eden: The Hidden Meaning of the Parthenon's East Facade* (Annapolis, Maryland: Solving Light Books, 2002), 60.
[31] Robert Bowie Johnson, Jr., *Athena and Eden: The Hidden Meaning of the Parthenon's East Facade* (Annapolis, Maryland: Solving Light Books, 2002), 60.
[32] *The Writings of Abraham*, Chapter 18, http://www.earth-history.com/Pseudepigrapha/Mormonism/writings-abraham-1.htm (accessed May 10, 2007).
[33] Robert Bowie Johnson, Jr., *The Parthenon Code: Mankind's History in Marble* (Annapolis, Maryland: Solving Light Books, 2004), 55, 110; *Inigo Jones Manuscript*, 5, http://www.freemasonry.com/masonic_manuscripts_jones.html (accessed May 24, 2011).
[34] Robert Bowie Johnson, Jr., *Athena and Eden: The Hidden Meaning of the Parthenon's East Facade* (Annapolis, Maryland: Solving Light Books, 2002), 46.
[35] Robert Bowie Johnson, Jr., *The Parthenon Code: Mankind's History in Marble* (Annapolis, Maryland: Solving Light Books, 2004), 114.
[36] Robert Bowie Johnson, Jr., *The Parthenon Code: Mankind's History in Marble* (Annapolis, Maryland: Solving Light Books, 2004), 191.
[37] World English Dictionary, *Humanism*, http://dictionary.reference.com/browse/humanism (accessed July 21, 2014).
[38] Robert Bowie Johnson, Jr., *The Parthenon Code: Mankind's History in Marble* (Annapolis, Maryland: Solving Light Books, 2004), 118.
[39] Stephen Charles Bandy, *Caines Cynn: A Study of Beuwolf and the Legends of Cain* (Stephen Charles Bandy, 1967), 161.
[40] *The Works of Philo Judaeus*, Questions and Answers on Genesis II, 81, trans. C. D. Yonge (London: H. G. Bohn, 1854-1855).
[41] *The Works of Philo Judaeus*, Questions and Answers on Genesis II, 81, trans. C. D. Yonge (London: H. G. Bohn, 1854-1855).
[42] *Hitchcock's Bible Names Dictionary*, 14, http://www.adamqadmon.com/nephilim/definitions/biblenames.html (accessed March 8, 2001).
[43] Robert Bowie Johnson, Jr., *The Parthenon Code: Mankind's History in Marble* (Annapolis, Maryland: Solving Light Books, 2004), 220.
[44] *Nimrod: Man, Maniac or Myth?*, 2, http://essaysbyekowa.com/Nimrod.htm (accessed March 22, 2011).
[45] *The Book of Jasher*, 7:23, trans. Albinus Alcuin (Pomeroy, Washington: Health Research, 1966).
[46] *The Book of Jasher*, 7:23, trans. Albinus Alcuin (Pomeroy, Washington: Health Research, 1966).
[47] *The Book of Jasher*, 7:24-29, trans. Albinus Alcuin (Pomeroy, Washington: Health Research, 1966).
[48] Mendel G. Glenn, *Jewish Tales and Legends* (New York: Star Hebrew Book Co., 1929), 29.
[49] Howard Schwartz, *Tree of Souls: The Mythology of Judaism* (Oxford: University Press, 2004), 437.

[50] Mysterious World, *Autumn 2003: Ah, Osiria! Part III: Nimrod Hunting*, 10, http://www.mysteriousworld.com/Journal/2003/Autumn/Osiria/ (accessed July 12, 2007).
[51] *Saltair na Rann*, 2693-2696, trans. David Greene,.
[52] *The Book of Jasher*, 7:30, trans. Albinus Alcuin (Pomeroy, Washington: Health Research, 1966).
[53] Jewish Encyclopedia.com, *Nimrod*, 2, http://www.jewishencyclopedia.com/view.jsp?artid=295&letter=N&search=nimrod (accessed July 12, 2007).
[54] Mendel G. Glenn, *Jewish Tales and Legends* (New York: Star Hebrew Book Co., 1929), 30.
[55] *Nimrod: Man, Maniac or Myth?*, 13, http://essaysbyekowa.com/Nimrod.htm (accessed March 22, 2011).
[56] *Nimrod: King of the World*, 3, http://www.iwc.net/~levi/nimrod.htm (accessed June 2, 2000).
[57] *Nimrod: King of the World*, 3, http://www.iwc.net/~levi/nimrod.htm (accessed June 2, 2000).
[58] Alexander Hislop, *The Two Babylons or the Papal Worship: Proved to be the Worship of Nimrod and His Wife* (Neptune, New Jersey: Loizeaux Brothers, 1916), 23.
[59] *The Book of Jasher*, 7:31-32, trans. Albinus Alcuin (Pomeroy, Washington: Health Research, 1966).
[60] Louis Ginzberg, *The Legends of the Jews Volume I: From the Creation to Jacob*, trans. Henrietta Szold (Baltimore, Maryland: The Johns Hopkins University Press, 1909), 177; Jewish Encyclopedia.com, *Nimrod*, 2, http://www.jewishencyclopedia.com/view.jsp?artid=295&letter=N&search=nimrod (accessed July 12, 2007); *The Book of Jasher*, 7:34-44, trans. Albinus Alcuin (Pomeroy, Washington: Health Research, 1966).
[61] *The Book of Jasher*, 7:34-37, trans. Albinus Alcuin (Pomeroy, Washington: Health Research, 1966).
[62] St. Ephrem the Syrian, *Selected Prose Works*, Section VIII 1(2), trans. Edward G. Mathews, Jr. and Joseph P. Amar (Washington, D. C.: The Catholic University of America Press, 1994), 146-147.
[63] *The Book of Jasher*, 7:42-44, trans. Albinus Alcuin (Pomeroy, Washington: Health Research, 1966).
[64] Ken Johnson, *Ancient Post-Flood History* (Ken Johnson, 2010), 135.
[65] St. Ephrem the Syrian, *Selected Prose Works*, Section VIII 1(2), trans. Edward G. Mathews, Jr. and Joseph P. Amar (Washington, D. C.: The Catholic University of America Press, 1994), 146.
[66] Mysterious World, *Autumn 2003: Ah, Osiria! Part III: Nimrod Hunting*, 2, http://www.mysteriousworld.com/Journal/2003/Autumn/Osiria/ (accessed July 12, 2007).
[67] *Babylonian Paganism Becomes Trinitarian Christianity*, 1, http://www.montana.com/bupc/whores/babypag.html (accessed May 7, 2000).
[68] Louis Ginzberg, *The Legends of the Jews Volume V: Notes for Volume One and Two*, trans. Henrietta Szold (Baltimore, Maryland: The Johns Hopkins University Press, 1909), 198.
[69] *The Book of Jasher*, 7:39, trans. Albinus Alcuin (Pomeroy, Washington: Health Research, 1966).
[70] Mendel G. Glenn, *Jewish Tales and Legends* (New York: Star Hebrew Book Co., 1929), 30; Jewish Encyclopedia.com, *Nimrod*, 2, http://www.jewishencyclopedia.com/view.jsp?artid=295&letter=N&search=nimrod (accessed July 12, 2007); *The Book of Jasher*, 7:39, trans. Albinus Alcuin (Pomeroy, Washington: Health Research, 1966).
[71] *Pseudo-Philo (The Biblical Antiquities of Philo)*, 4:7, trans. M. R. James, http://www.sacred-texts.com/bib/bap/bap19.htm (accessed July 13, 2006).
[72] C. J. Verduin, *Looking for Jonitus*, 14, http://leidenuniv.nl/fsw/verduin/jonitus/jonitus.htm (accessed Aug. 1, 2005).
[73] Mysterious World, *Autumn 2003: Ah, Osiria! Part III: Nimrod Hunting*, 2, http://www.mysteriousworld.com/Journal/2003/Autumn/Osiria/ (accessed July 12, 2007); Alexander Hislop, *The Two Babylons or the Papal Worship: Proved to be the Worship of Nimrod and His Wife* (Neptune, New Jersey: Loizeaux Brothers, 1916), 11-12; Jewish Encyclopedia.com, *Nimrod*, 1, http://www.jewishencyclopedia.com/view.jsp?artid=295&letter=N&search=nimrod (accessed July 12, 2007).
[74] *Nimrod: King of the World*, 4, http://www.iwc.net/~levi/nimrod.htm (accessed June 2, 2000).
[75] Mysterious World, *Autumn 2003: Ah, Osiria! Part III: Nimrod Hunting*, 2, http://www.mysteriousworld.com/Journal/2003/Autumn/Osiria/ (accessed July 12, 2007).
[76] *Nimrod - Babylonian - Musical Worship Teams*, 3, http://www.piney.com/MuBabylo.html (accessed Dec. 21, 2001).
[77] *Babylonian Paganism Becomes Trinitarian Christianity*, 1, http://www.montana.com/bupc/whores/babypag.html (accessed May 7, 2000).
[78] *Babylonian Paganism Becomes Trinitarian Christianity*, 1, http://www.montana.com/bupc/whores/babypag.html (accessed May 7, 2000).
[79] *Babylonian Paganism Becomes Trinitarian Christianity*, 1, http://www.montana.com/bupc/whores/babypag.html (accessed May 7, 2000).
[80] *The Book of Jasher*, 6:19, trans. Albinus Alcuin (Pomeroy, Washington: Health Research, 1966).
[81] *The Writings of Abraham*, Chapter 23:3, http://www.earth-history.com/Pseudepigrapha/Mormonism/writings-abraham-1.htm (accessed May 10, 2007).
[82] *Nimrod: Man, Maniac or Myth?*, 13, http://essaysbyekowa.com/Nimrod.htm (accessed March 22, 2011).
[83] *Babylonian Paganism Becomes Trinitarian Christianity*, 1, http://www.montana.com/bupc/whores/babypag.html (accessed May 7, 2000).
[84] Mendel G. Glenn, *Jewish Tales and Legends* (New York: Star Hebrew Book Co., 1929), 30.
[85] *The Second Book of Adam and Eve (The Conflict of Adam and Eve with Satan)*, Book II, 5:11, trans. S. C. Malan

(London: Williams and Norgate, 1882), 64.
[86] *The Works of Philo Judaeus*, On the Giants 15(66-67), trans. C. D. Yonge (London: H. G. Bohn, 1854-1855).
[87] *The Works of Philo Judaeus*, On the Giants 15(65-66), trans. C. D. Yonge (London: H. G. Bohn, 1854-1855).
[88] Nimrod - Babylonian - Musical Worship Teams, 21, http://www.piney.com/MuBabylo.html (accessed Dec. 21, 2001).
[89] *The Companion Bible*, Gen. 10:9 (notes) (Grand Rapids, Michigan: Kregel Publications, 1990); Dr. David Livingston, *Who Was Nimrod*, 4, http://www.davelivingston.com/nimrod.htm (accessed July 5, 2017).
[90] *The Works of Philo Judaeus*, Questions and Answers on Genesis II, 82, trans. C. D. Yonge (London: H. G. Bohn, 1854-1855).
[91] *Nimrod: Man, Maniac or Myth?*, 12-13, http://essaysbyekowa.com/Nimrod.htm (accessed March 22, 2011); *The Companion Bible*, Gen. 10:8 (notes) (Grand Rapids, Michigan: Kregel Publications, 1990); *The Zohar*, Noach 40, http://www.zohar.com/noach/he-was-mighty-hunter%C2%9D (accessed Feb. 25, 2010); *Babel, Nimrod, Architect of the Tower of Babel*, 1, http://www.cwd.co.uk/babel.htm (accessed May 11, 2000); Ralph Edward Woodrow, *Babylon Mystery Religion: Ancient and Modern* (Riverside, California: Ralph Woodrow Evangelistic Association, Inc., 1966), 3.
[92] *Nimrod: Man, Maniac or Myth?*, 13, http://essaysbyekowa.com/Nimrod.htm (accessed March 22, 2011).
[93] Mendel G. Glenn, *Jewish Tales and Legends* (New York: Star Hebrew Book Co., 1929), 30.
[94] Mendel G. Glenn, *Jewish Tales and Legends* (New York: Star Hebrew Book Co., 1929), 30.
[95] *Nimrod: King of the World*, 5, http://www.iwc.net/~levi/nimrod.htm (accessed June 2, 2000).
[96] *The Babylonian Talmud*, Sanhedrin 109a, http://www.halakhah.com/sanhedrin/sanhedrin_109.html (accessed Feb. 9, 2009).
[97] Bentley Layton, *The Gnostic Scriptures*, 39.3.3 (New York: Doubleday, 1995), 189.
[98] Mysterious World, *Autumn 2003: Ah, Osiria! Part III: Nimrod Hunting*, 3, http://www.mysteriousworld.com/Journal/2003/Autumn/Osiria/ (accessed July 12, 2007).
[99] Bryce Self, *Semiramis, Queen of Babylon*, 1, http://www.ldolphin.org/semir.html (accessed June 20, 2000).
[100] *The Zohar*, Noach 42, http://www.zohar.com/noach/city-and-tower%C2%9D (accessed Feb. 25, 2010).
[101] Mysterious World, *Autumn 2003: Ah, Osiria! Part III: Nimrod Hunting*, 4-5, http://www.mysteriousworld.com/Journal/2003/Autumn/Osiria/ (accessed July 12, 2007).
[102] Drusilla Dunjee Houston, *Wonderful Ethiopians of the Ancient Cushite Empire (1926)*, 166.
[103] Drusilla Dunjee Houston, *Wonderful Ethiopians of the Ancient Cushite Empire (1926)*, 166.
[104] *Nimrod: King of the World*, 4, http://www.iwc.net/~levi/nimrod.htm (accessed June 2, 2000).
[105] R. E. Asher, *National Myths in Renaissance France* (Edinburgh: Edinburgh University Press Ltd., 1993), 203.
[106] Drusilla Dunjee Houston, *Wonderful Ethiopians of the Ancient Cushite Empire (1926)*, 161-162.
[107] J. B. Tannehill, *Naamah and Nimrod: A Defense of the Faith of Our Fathers* (Columbus, Ohio: The New Franklin Printing Co., 1916), 86-87.
[108] Biblical Information of Giants (8,850 B.C. to 1,300 B.C.), *Giants before the Flood*, 2, http://www.mazzaroth.com/ChapterThree/BiblicalInfoOfGiants.htm (accessed June 28, 2000).
[109] *Nimrod: King of the World*, 5, http://www.iwc.net/~levi/nimrod.htm (accessed June 2, 2000).
[110] *Pseudo-Philo (The Biblical Antiquities of Philo)*, 6:2, trans. M. R. James, http://www.sacred-texts.com/bib/bap/bap19.htm (accessed July 13, 2006).
[111] James L. Kugel, *Traditions of the Bible* (Cambridge, Massachusetts: Harvard University Press, 1998), 240.
[112] Dudley F. Cates, *The Rise and Fall of King Nimrod* (Raleigh, North Carolina: Pentland Press, Inc., 1998), 52.
[113] WordReference.com, *earthborn*, 1, http://www.wordreference.com/definition/earthborn (accessed June 2, 2007).
[114] *St. Ephrem the Syrian: Selected Prose Works*, Section VIII 3, trans. Edward G. Mathews, Jr. and Joseph P. Amar (Washington, D. C.: The Catholic University of America Press, 1994), 147.
[115] James L. Kugel, *Traditions of the Bible* (Cambridge, Massachusetts: Harvard University Press, 1998), 241.
[116] *The Book of Jasher*, 9:28, trans. Albinus Alcuin (Pomeroy, Washington: Health Research, 1966).
[117] James L. Kugel, *Traditions of the Bible* (Cambridge, Massachusetts: Harvard University Press, 1998), 241.
[118] *The Babylonian Talmud*, Sanhedrin 109a, http://www.halakhah.com/sanhedrin/sanhedrin_109.html (accessed Feb. 9, 2009).
[119] Jayim Nahman Bialik and Yehoshua Hana Ravnitzky, *The Book of Legends (Sefer Ha-Aggadah): Legends of the Talmud and Midrash*, 136, (New York: Shocken Books,.1992), 29; David W. Daniels, *Babylon Religion: How a Babylonian Goddess became the Virgin Mary* (Ontario, California: Chick Publications, 2006), 29.
[120] Oliver Farrar Emerson, *Legends of Cain, Especially in Old and Middle English* (Philadelphia, Pennsylvania: American Sunday-School Union, 1916), 929.
[121] *Nimrod: King of the World*, 5, http://www.iwc.net/~levi/nimrod.htm (accessed June 2, 2000).
[122] *Nimrod: King of the World*, 4, http://www.iwc.net/~levi/nimrod.htm (accessed June 2, 2000).

Chapter 9

[1] Flavius Josephus, *The Antiquities of the Jews*, Book 1.4.1, trans. William Whiston (1737), http://www.ccel.org/j/josephus/works/war-2.htm (accessed Aug. 16, 2010).

[2] 12 Tribe History, *What Really Happened After the Flood?*, 3, http://12tribehistory.com/what-really-happened-after-the-flood/ (accessed May 12, 2014).

[3] Flavius Josephus, *The Antiquities of the Jews*, Book 1.4.3, trans. William Whiston (1737), http://www.ccel.org/j/josephus/works/war-2.htm (accessed Aug. 16, 2010).

[4] Louis Ginzberg, *The Legends of the Jews Volume I: From the Creation to Jacob*, trans. Henrietta Szold (Baltimore, Maryland: The Johns Hopkins University Press, 1909), 172.

[5] Flavius Josephus, *The Antiquities of the Jews*, Book 1.4.3, trans. William Whiston (1737), http://www.ccel.org/j/josephus/works/war-2.htm (accessed Aug. 16, 2010).

[6] Flavius Josephus, *The Antiquities of the Jews*, Book 1.4.3, trans. William Whiston (1737), http://www.ccel.org/j/josephus/works/war-2.htm (accessed Aug. 16, 2010).

[7] Flavius Josephus, *The Antiquities of the Jews*, Book 1.4.3, trans. William Whiston (1737), http://www.ccel.org/j/josephus/works/war-2.htm (accessed Aug. 16, 2010).

[8] Flavius Josephus, *The Antiquities of the Jews*, Book 1.4.3, trans. William Whiston (1737), http://www.ccel.org/j/josephus/works/war-2.htm (accessed Aug. 16, 2010).

[9] Flavius Josephus, *The Antiquities of the Jews*, Book 1.4.3, trans. William Whiston (1737), http://www.ccel.org/j/josephus/works/war-2.htm (accessed Aug. 16, 2010).

[10] Herman L. Hoeh, *Compendium of World History: Volume 2* (Herman L. Hoeh, 1969), 16; 12 Tribe History, *What Really Happened After the Flood?*, 2, http://12tribehistory.com/episode-57-2-10-14-noah-was-written-in-history/ (accessed May 12, 2014).

[11] 12 Tribe History, *What Really Happened After the Flood?*, 4, http://12tribehistory.com/what-really-happened-after-the-flood/ (accessed May 12, 2014).

[12] 12 Tribe History, *What Really Happened After the Flood?*, 5, http://12tribehistory.com/what-really-happened-after-the-flood/ (accessed May 12, 2014).

[13] 12 Tribe History, *What Really Happened After the Flood?*, 5, http://12tribehistory.com/what-really-happened-after-the-flood/ (accessed May 12, 2014).

[14] Herman L. Hoeh, *Compendium of World History: Volume 2* (Herman L. Hoeh, 1969), 117, 163; Herman L. Hoeh, *Compendium of World History: Volume 1* (Herman L. Hoeh, 1967), 21.

[15] Herman L. Hoeh, *Compendium of World History: Volume 1* (Herman L. Hoeh, 1967), 21, Herman L. Hoeh, *Compendium of World History: Volume 2* (Herman L. Hoeh, 1969), 233.

[16] Herman L. Hoeh, *Compendium of World History: Volume 1* (Herman L. Hoeh, 1967), 23-24, 109-110.

[17] Herman L. Hoeh, *Compendium of World History: Volume 1* (Herman L. Hoeh, 1967), 24.

[18] Herman L. Hoeh, *Compendium of World History: Volume 1* (Herman L. Hoeh, 1967), 111.

[19] Herman L. Hoeh, *Compendium of World History: Volume 2* (Herman L. Hoeh, 1969), 12-13.

[20] Herman L. Hoeh, *Compendium of World History: Volume 2* (Herman L. Hoeh, 1969), 12.

[21] Herman L. Hoeh, *Compendium of World History: Volume 1* (Herman L. Hoeh, 1967), 114.

[22] Herman L. Hoeh, *Compendium of World History: Volume 1* (Herman L. Hoeh, 1967), 114.

[23] Herman L. Hoeh, *Compendium of World History: Volume 1* (Herman L. Hoeh, 1967), 21, 24, 93, 114.

[24] Herman L. Hoeh, *Compendium of World History: Volume 1* (Herman L. Hoeh, 1967), 24.

[25] Bryce Self, *Semiramis, Queen of Babylon*, 2, http://www.ldolphin.org/semir.html (accessed June 20, 2000).

[26] Alexander Hislop, *The Two Babylons or the Papal Worship: Proved to be the Worship of Nimrod and His Wife* (Neptune, New Jersey: Loizeaux Brothers, 1916), 86.

[27] Bryce Self, *Semiramis, Queen of Babylon*, 2, http://www.ldolphin.org/semir.html (accessed June 20, 2000).

[28] Herman L. Hoeh, *Compendium of World History: Volume 1* (Herman L. Hoeh, 1967), 23.

[29] Herman L. Hoeh, *Compendium of World History: Volume 2* (Herman L. Hoeh, 1969), 11; Herman L. Hoeh, *Compendium of World History: Volume 1* (Herman L. Hoeh, 1967), 25.

[30] Alexander Hislop, *The Two Babylons or the Papal Worship: Proved to be the Worship of Nimrod and His Wife* (Neptune, New Jersey: Loizeaux Brothers, 1916), 61-62.

[31] Herman L. Hoeh, *Compendium of World History: Volume 2* (Herman L. Hoeh, 1969), 13.

[32] *4. Nimrod and Babylon, Lesson Four: Nimrod and Babylon: The Birth of Idolatry*, 2, http://www.ctelcom.net/koinoia/bible/nimrod.htm (accessed May 25, 2000).

[33] *4. Nimrod and Babylon, Lesson Four: Nimrod and Babylon: The Birth of Idolatry*, 2, http://www.ctelcom.net/koinoia/bible/nimrod.htm (accessed May 25, 2000).

[34] Bryce Self, *Semiramis, Queen of Babylon*, 2, http://www.ldolphin.org/semir.html (accessed June 20, 2000).

[35] Bryce Self, *Semiramis, Queen of Babylon*, 2, http://www.ldolphin.org/semir.html (accessed June 20, 2000).

[36] *Mystery of Civilization*, 10, http://www.valleylife.net/tcg/armstrong/MOA/CHAP4.HTM (accessed July 2, 2000).

[37] Richard M. Rives, *Too Long in the Sun* (Charlotte, North Carolina: Partakers Publications, 1998), 68.

[38] Bryce Self, *Semiramis, Queen of Babylon*, 2, http://www.ldolphin.org/semir.html (accessed June 20, 2000).

[39] Moses Kohrenats'i, *History of the Armenians* (London: Harvard University Press, 1978), 96.

[40] Herman L. Hoeh, *Compendium of World History: Volume 1* (Herman L. Hoeh, 1967), 25.

[41] Herman L. Hoeh, *Compendium of World History: Volume 1* (Herman L. Hoeh, 1967), 24-25.

[42] Herman L. Hoeh, *Compendium of World History: Volume 1* (Herman L. Hoeh, 1967), 211.

[43] Herman L. Hoeh, *Compendium of World History: Volume 2* (Herman L. Hoeh, 1969), 97.
[44] Herman L. Hoeh, *Compendium of World History: Volume 2* (Herman L. Hoeh, 1969), 97.
[45] Herman L. Hoeh, *Compendium of World History: Volume 1* (Herman L. Hoeh, 1967), 210.
[46] Herman L. Hoeh, *Compendium of World History: Volume 1* (Herman L. Hoeh, 1967), 177.

www.ingramcontent.com/pod-product-compliance
Lightning Source LLC
Chambersburg PA
CBHW081124170426
43197CB00017B/2735